ALSO BY THE EDITORS AT AMERICA'S TEST KITCHEN

The America's Test Kitchen Family Cookbook

The Best of America's Test Kitchen 2007

THE BEST RECIPE SERIES:
The Best Make-Ahead Recipe
The Best 30-Minute Recipe
The Best Light Recipe
The Cook's Illustrated Guide to Grilling & Barbecue
Best American Side Dishes
The New Best Recipe
Cover & Bake
Steaks, Chops, Roasts, & Ribs
Baking Illustrated
Restaurant Favorites at Home
The Best Vegetable Recipes
The Best American Classics
The Best Soups & Stews

THE TV COMPANION SERIES:
Test Kitchen Favorites
Cooking at Home with America's Test Kitchen
America's Test Kitchen Live!
Inside America's Test Kitchen
Here in America's Test Kitchen
The America's Test Kitchen Cookbook

834 Kitchen Quick Tips

To order any of our books, visit us at
http://www.cooksillustrated.com
http://www.americastestkitchen.com
or call 800-611-0759

THE BEST ITALIAN CLASSICS

A BEST RECIPE CLASSIC

THE
BEST
ITALIAN
CLASSICS

A BEST RECIPE CLASSIC

BY THE EDITORS OF

COOK'S ILLUSTRATED

PHOTOGRAPHY

CARL TREMBLAY AND DANIEL J. VAN ACKERE

ILLUSTRATIONS

JOHN BURGOYNE

AMERICA'S TEST KITCHEN

BROOKLINE, MASSACHUSETTS

America's Test Kitchen
17 Station Street
Brookline, Massachusetts 02445

ISBN-13: 978-1-933615-15-8
ISBN-10: 1-933615-15-X
Library of Congress Cataloging-in-Publication Data
The Editors of Cook's Illustrated

The Best Italian Classics
Would you cook 35 vegetable lasagne recipes to find the best version? We did.
Here are more than 300 exhaustively tested recipes for our favorite Italian dishes.
1st Paperback Edition

ISBN-13: 978-1-933615-15-8
ISBN-10: 1-933615-15-X
(paperback): $19.95 US/$23.50 CAN
I. Cooking. I. Title
2007

10 9 8 7 6 5 4 3 2

Manufactured in the United States of America

Distributed by America's Test Kitchen, 17 Station Street, Brookline, MA 02445

Series Design by Amy Klee
Cover Design by Carolynn DeCillo
Edited by Jack Bishop

Pictured on front cover: Spinach and Mushroom Lasagne (page 183)
Pictured on back cover: Chicken Parmesan (page 230), Fettuccine Alfredo (page 189),
Minestrone (page 108), Spaghetti and Meatballs (page 155)

CONTENTS

PREFACE

I AM FAMOUS AROUND THE TEST KITCHEN for being suspicious of "foreign" recipes. That does not mean that I do not have cravings for curried goat, almost any type of pho soup, or smoked eel. I am, instead, deeply skeptical about translating recipes from one culture to another. What makes sense to a family of four in Saigon may seem absurd to a farming family in Iowa.

Of course, because we are a nation of immigrants, all American cooking is foreign. We have borrowed, stolen, and adapted recipes from just about every nation on Earth to cobble together our own national cuisine. Until recently, however, American food had been based mostly on Northern European cuisines. The one major exception to this rule is Italian cooking.

The reason is clear. Italian cuisine is simple, familiar, and home-oriented. Even Italian restaurant cooking tends to be uncomplicated and direct. These characteristics lend themselves admirably to the needs of the American home cook. But two problems exist. First, many of these recipes have been Americanized—put through the melting pot of common kitchen experience and convenience foods to produce lackluster results. Second, the ingredients and techniques that are traditional in Venice or Rome sometimes make little sense in the suburbs of New York. Our task was to adapt recipes without losing sight of their fundamental nature.

Two of my neighbors in Vermont are characters in the best sense of the word. Both are close to 80 years old; one is Polish, and the other is Italian. Both drive big equipment, working outside all day in logging or construction. John is famous for his home-made kielbasa and pear wine. He is also well known for his 20-year-old brown VW Rabbit, which starts occasionally and has a unique jury-rigged defroster: a votive candle stuck on the dashboard. (He claims that it works pretty good as a heater, too.) Danny, the Italian, was a Navy cook in World War II and was able to roast 25 turkeys in three ovens for a crew of 250. Last year, he got stuck under his backhoe for the better part of an hour while the back wheel slowly turned on his leg, crushing it. He miraculously walked away in one piece but complained of a slight limp for a couple of months. Of course he never bothered to see a doctor. Both John and Danny are true originals, yet they are as familiar to townsfolk as the sight of Charlie Bentley riding down Main Street on his red 1949 Farmall.

That's the trick with neighbors and recipes. You love what makes them special, but it is also handy to be able to speak their language. I hope this book of Italian classics delivers on both counts, becoming, over the years, a good friend to both you and your family.

Christopher Kimball
Founder and Editor
Cook's Illustrated and *Cook's Country*
Host, *America's Test Kitchen*

ACKNOWLEDGMENTS

ALL OF THE PROJECTS UNDERTAKEN AT *Cook's Illustrated* are collective efforts, the combined experience and work of editors, test cooks, and writers all joining in the search for the best cooking methods. This book is no exception.

Editor Jack Bishop spearheaded this project. Julia Collin and Matthew Card were the main researchers, recipe developers, and writers for the book. Shannon Blaisdell, Eva Katz, Bridget Lancaster, Raquel Pelzel, Adam Ried, Sally Sampson, Meg Suzuki, and Dawn Yanagihara also developed recipes and wrote portions of the text. Madeline Gutin Perri copyedited the manuscript.

Art director Amy Klee and graphic designer Nina Madjid transformed computer files and digital images into a book. Julia Sedykh designed the cover, and Christopher Hirsheimer photographed the front cover image. Carl Tremblay captured the images that appear throughout the book as well as on the back cover. Daniel van Ackere took photographs of the equipment and ingredients, and John Burgoyne drew all the illustrations. Erin McMurrer ran all the photography shoots in the *Cook's Illustrated* test kitchen.

The following individuals on the editorial, production, circulation, customer service, and office staffs also worked on the book: Ron Bilodeau, Barbara Bourassa, Jana Branch, Rich Cassidy, Sharyn Chabot, Mary Connelly, Cathy Dorsey, Larisa Greiner, Mike Haggerty, Rebecca Hays, India Koopman, Sarah Lorimer, Jim McCormack, Jennifer McCreary, Nicole Morris, Henrietta Murray, Juliet Nusbaum, Jessica Quirk, Sumantha Selvakumar, and Mandy Shito. And without help from members of the sales, marketing, and publicity staff, readers might never find our books. Special thanks to Deborah Broide, Steven Browall, Shekinah Cohn, Connie Forbes, Jason Geller, Robert Lee, David Mack, Steven Sussman, Jacqui Valerio, and Jonathan Venier, all of whom contributed to our marketing and distribution efforts.

WELCOME TO AMERICA'S TEST KITCHEN

THIS BOOK HAS BEEN TESTED, WRITTEN, AND edited by the folks at America's Test Kitchen, a very real 2,500-square-foot kitchen located just outside of Boston. It is the home of *Cook's Illustrated* magazine and *Cook's Country* magazine and is the Monday through Friday destination for more than two dozen test cooks, editors, food scientists, tasters, and cookware specialists. Our mission is to test recipes over and over again until we understand how and why they work and until we arrive at the "best" version.

We start the process of testing a recipe with a complete lack of conviction, which means that we accept no claim, no theory, no technique, and no recipe at face value. We simply assemble as many variations as possible, test a half dozen of the most promising, and taste the results blind. We then construct our own hybrid recipe and continue to test it, varying ingredients, techniques, and cooking times until we reach a consensus. The result, we hope, is the best version of a particular recipe, but we realize that only you can be the final judge of our success

(or failure). As we like to say in the test kitchen, "We make the mistakes, so you don't have to."

All of this would not be possible without a belief that good cooking, much like good music, is indeed based on a foundation of objective technique. Some people like spicy foods and others don't, but there is a right way to sauté, there is a best way to cook a pot roast, and there are measurable scientific principles involved in producing perfectly beaten, stable egg whites. This is our ultimate goal: to investigate the fundamental principles of cooking so that you become a better cook. It is as simple as that.

You can watch us work (in our actual test kitchen) by tuning in to *America's Test Kitchen* (www.americastestkitchen.com) on public television or by subscribing to *Cook's Illustrated* magazine (www.cooksillustrated.com) or *Cook's Country* magazine (www.cookscountry.com), which are each published every other month. We welcome you into our kitchen, where you can stand by our side as we test our way to the "best" recipes in America.

Using the Recipes in This Book

A TRADITIONAL ITALIAN MENU, EVEN FOR a simple family supper, contains more courses than its American counterpart. The conventional structure for an Italian meal is *antipasto* (appetizer), *primo* (a first course that can be soup, pasta, rice, or polenta), *secondo* (a second course that can be poultry, meat, or seafood) accompanied by the *contorno* (a vegetable side dish or two), and *dolce* (dessert). If salad is part of the menu, it is served as a palate cleanser between the second course and dessert.

As you might imagine, this structure means that Italian meals last a long time. Italians will regularly spend an hour or two (or even more) at the table. In addition, portions are generally quite small. While most Americans consider a pound of pasta to be adequate for four main-course servings, Italians will eat half as much when pasta is served as a first course that will be followed by meat, poultry, or seafood. And while Americans often estimate a half pound of meat per person, Italians eat far less in a meal that might also contain a small bowl of risotto and two vegetable side dishes.

Although the structure of the traditional Italian meal has many elements that we find appealing, the reality is that most Americans don't have the time to prepare and eat so many courses on a regular basis. For this reason, we have adopted American notions of serving sizes for the recipes in this book. Unless otherwise indicated, we assume that pasta, rice, meat, chicken, and seafood dishes will stand alone as main courses, and portions are quite generous. If you decide to follow the Italian menu structure and serve both pasta and meat courses at the same meal, our recipes will yield more servings than indicated.

One final note about serving savory dishes. At mealtime, many Italians place a bottle of fine olive oil on the table, much as Americans generally keep a saltshaker and pepper mill within arm's reach. Extra-virgin olive oil gets drizzled over bowls of soup, pasta, beans, vegetables, seafood, and more. As the cook, you may choose to drizzle the oil over these dishes before serving them (recommendations appear in many recipes throughout the book) or to bring the oil to the table and let each diner add oil to taste. Either way, make sure to use only the best olive oil for this purpose.

1

ANTIPASTI

THE WORD ANTIPASTO LITERALLY MEANS "before the meal." It is the Italian equivalent to the American appetizer (which the dictionary defines as "a food or drink that stimulates the appetite") and the French hors d'oeuvre (which translates as "apart from the work"). All of these terms refer to the fact that these little finger foods are eaten before the main meal, often away from the dining table, and often on the hoof.

The question we hear most often about antipasti concerns quantity. How many types of antipasti and how many pieces are required? The answer depends on how long you plan to be serving the appetizers and what follows. Some examples:

If you plan a short cocktail hour (let's say 45 minutes, while you wait for all of your guests to arrive) followed by a multicourse meal, you want to serve just one or two antipasti. (If you are expecting a large crowd, you might consider making three antipasti.) Plan on three or four pieces per person if you plan on one hour or less for cocktails. For more than one hour, make at least two antipasti and plan on four to six pieces per person.

Take into account how heavy and filling the antipasti that you have chosen are. Guests are likely to be satisfied by two or three stuffed clams but might want a half dozen marinated olives.

The other area that perplexes many cooks is choosing particular antipasti. There are no hard and fast rules, but these guidelines should help.

- Keep the season in mind, serving lighter foods in summer and heavier fare in winter.
- Figure out where you plan to serve antipasti. If guests will be seated on sofas and can hold forks, knives, and plates, then almost anything will work. If guests will be gathering on foot or outside, limit your selection to true finger foods and dips.
- Plan the meal first and then, for the appetizers, use foods not already represented. For example, if your menu calls for beef, mushrooms, and asparagus as the main course, you would not want to want to serve any of these foods as appetizers.
- If serving more than one or two antipasti, choose dishes that go well together. It's fine to have one rich antipasto with cheese, but don't serve three cheese antipasti.
- For a shorter cocktail hour before dinner, you many want to stick with cold appetizers,

INGREDIENTS: Olives

There are literally hundreds of varieties of olives, but all can be categorized by two factors: their ripeness when picked and the manner in which they are cured. Green olives, picked before they are fully ripe, tend to have fruitier and somewhat lighter flavors, while ripe olives—which range in color from dark brown to purple or deep black—have deeper, more fully developed flavors. Most olives are brine-cured by a process that involves fermenting them in a strong salt solution. Others are oil-cured by a process that gives them a wrinkled appearance and sharper flavor.

As for particular names, olives may be named after their type of cure, their place of origin, or their actual varietal name. The most important thing to remember about these little fruits (yes, olives are technically a fruit) is that they vary wildly from batch to batch and year to year. Tasting is the only way to judge the quality of any particular batch. Finally, it almost goes without saying that canned pitted olives are to be avoided. We find they are devoid of flavor.

which don't require any last-minute preparation. If you want to serve a hot appetizer, consider gathering guests in the kitchen so you don't have to slave away in solitude.

MARINATED OLIVES

IF YOU START WITH GOOD OLIVES (and that can be a big if) and good olive oil, it's pretty hard to make bad marinated olives. That said, some olive mixes are better than others, with more complex flavors. We wanted to make a mixture of marinated olives that would be easy to put together and worth the wait.

Good olives are the right place to begin, and that means olives with their pits and packed in brine. (Oil-cured olives can be added in small quantities, but in large quantities we find their flavors too potent for this dish.) Pitted olives generally have little flavor, and you can't expect marinating to make them taste better. Our tasters liked a mix of black and green olives. We tested a half dozen varieties of each color and didn't find a bad olive.

In addition to the olive oil, the marinade typically includes garlic (to release the flavor of the whole cloves, we found it best to crush them), herbs (our tasters liked thyme best), and hot red pepper flakes (we found that more heat was better than less and opted for a full teaspoon). We liked thinly sliced shallots as well; they softened in the marinade and added their gentle allium flavor to the mix. Grated orange zest (rather than the more traditional lemon zest) won the day in the test kitchen for its fresh, lively citrus kick.

The real surprise of the day was the addition of sambuca, an Italian after-dinner liqueur that tastes like licorice. The boozy anise flavor worked wonders on the olives and made the mix much more interesting.

The final issue was timing—how long should the olives marinate in their flavorful bath? Tasters found that the olives required 12 hours to pick up sufficient flavor and were better after a day or two. In fact, we held marinated olives in the refrigerator for several weeks and felt that they improved with time.

Marinated Black and Green Olives

MAKES ABOUT 3 CUPS

These olives will keep in the refrigerator for at least a month and are perfect for impromptu entertaining. Sambuca is a sweet, licorice-flavored Italian spirit. You can substitute ouzo.

8	ounces large, brine-cured green olives with pits
8	ounces large, brine-cured black olives with pits
5	large cloves garlic, crushed
3	large shallots, sliced thin
I	teaspoon grated orange zest
I	teaspoon minced fresh thyme leaves
I	teaspoon hot red pepper flakes
½	cup sambuca
¼	cup extra-virgin olive oil
¾	teaspoon salt
	Pinch cayenne pepper

1. Drain the olives in a colander and rinse them well under cold running water. Drain the olives well.

2. Combine the remaining ingredients in a glass or plastic bowl. Add the olives and toss to combine. Cover and refrigerate for at least 12 hours. Remove from the refrigerator at least 30 minutes before serving.

Marinated Sun-Dried Tomatoes

MARINATED SUN-DRIED TOMATOES are a simple addition to almost any antipasto spread. They also can dress up a plain salad, pizza, piece of fish, or stray crust of bread. Best of all, these tomatoes are easy to make and keep in the refrigerator for a week.

After trying a few basic recipes, we realized that the trick to making good marinated sun-dried tomatoes wasn't in the dressing but rather the degree to which the tomatoes were rehydrated. Overhydrated tomatoes simply fell apart and turned to mush, while tomatoes that weren't hydrated enough tasted chewy and tough.

We tested several rehydrating methods; in the end, we liked the ease and simplicity of the microwave. We combined dry tomatoes and water in a microwave-safe container and microwaved them on high for 2 minutes. At this point, the tomatoes were a tad chewy, so we let them finish softening on the counter to just the right consistency. Simmering them on the stove worked too; however, the microwave was faster. Dousing the tomatoes with boiling water or hot tap water and letting them sit on the counter (a method recommended by several recipes) simply took too long, and the water seemed to cool before the tomatoes were fully soft.

After the tomatoes are properly rehydrated, the only preparation they require is the removal of the hard, bitter-tasting core with a paring knife or scissors. We found that a simple dressing made of extra-virgin olive oil, parsley, hot red pepper flakes, and garlic complemented the sweet, toothsome tomatoes best. Set off by this elegant, clean, slightly spicy vinaigrette, the real flavor of the tomatoes shines through, making this an easy and versatile condiment for the refrigerator door.

Marinated Sun-Dried Tomatoes

MAKES ABOUT 2 CUPS

These tomatoes will keep in the refrigerator for up to 1 week.

3 ounces whole sun-dried tomatoes
½ cup extra-virgin olive oil
1 tablespoon lemon juice
1 tablespoon minced fresh parsley leaves
¼ teaspoon salt
   Pinch hot red pepper flakes
   Pinch ground black pepper
1 small clove garlic, minced or pressed through a garlic press

1. Mix the tomatoes with 2 cups hot tap water in a medium microwave-safe bowl. Cover with plastic wrap, cut several steam vents in the plastic wrap with a paring knife, and microwave on high power for 2 minutes. Let stand, covered, until the tomatoes soften, about 5 minutes. Lift the tomatoes from the liquid with a fork and pat dry on paper towels.

2. Trim the tough core from the end of each tomato and place the tomatoes in a bowl. Add the other ingredients and toss gently. Serve immediately or cover and refrigerate until needed.

Marinated Mushrooms

MARINATED MUSHROOMS ARE SUPPOSED to be easy and flavorful. Although most recipes are easy, we find that few deliver enough flavor. According to the few authentic recipes we found, button mushrooms are simply doused with vinaigrette and allowed to marinate. As if by magic, they are supposed to emerge from the marinade tender and full of flavor.

But none of these recipes turned out as we had hoped. After several hours of marinating, the mushrooms turned somewhat slimy on the outside while the inside remained raw, having taken on none of the vinaigrette flavor. Wanting the mushrooms to be tender and full of flavor without letting them marinate for days, we set out to find a technique that would yield great-tasting marinated mushrooms in about the same time it takes to get ready for a party.

To start, we tried several ways of preparing the mushrooms to help speed the marinating process. Blanching (a quick dip in boiling salted water) and steaming both produced tender mushrooms; however, the extra moisture soaked up by the mushrooms was released later into the dressing. Although these techniques didn't quite work, they sparked a thought. What if the mushrooms were steamed in the vinaigrette?

It took just one batch of mushrooms quickly steamed in vinaigrette to know we were onto something. As the mushrooms cooked, they soaked up and then released the flavorful dressing, emerging tender and seasoned. Nevertheless, although these mushrooms tasted better, they were still too bland. In a final effort to reinforce the mushroom flavor, we added a small amount of dried porcini to the vinaigrette and found it made a big difference.

With an eye toward keeping the rest of the dressing simple, we liked the flavors of garlic, parsley, lemon, red onion, and red bell pepper, along with a small kick from hot red pepper flakes. One final problem remained. Although the steaming process was good for the mushrooms, it deadened the fresh, bright flavors of the vinaigrette. We removed many of the delicate ingredients from the steaming liquid (such as the red bell pepper, lemon juice, and parsley)

REHYDRATING DRIED PORCINI MUSHROOMS

We find that the microwave cuts the soaking time from 20 minutes at room temperature to just 5 minutes. Place the dried porcini in a microwave-safe bowl, cover with plastic wrap, cut several steam vents in the plastic wrap, and microwave on high power for 30 seconds. Remove the bowl from the microwave and let stand, covered, until the mushrooms soften, about 5 minutes. Here's how to remove the softened mushrooms from the liquid and leave the sand behind.

1. When soaking dried porcini mushrooms, most of the sand and dirt will fall to the bottom of the bowl. Use a fork to lift the rehydrated mushrooms from the liquid without stirring up the sand. If the mushrooms still feel gritty, rinse them briefly under cool running water.

2. The soaking liquid is quite flavorful and can be reserved. To remove the grit, pour the liquid through a small strainer lined with a single sheet of paper towel and placed over a measuring cup.

and found the mushrooms still emerged well seasoned. We then allowed the steamed mushrooms to cool fully before combining them with the remaining fresh ingredients. This method produced perfect, fully flavored marinated mushrooms in merely 30 minutes.

Marinated Mushrooms

MAKES ABOUT 4 CUPS

See the illustrations on page 5 for tips on rehydrating dried mushrooms. The soaking liquid can be discarded once the mushrooms have softened.

¼	ounce dried porcini mushrooms
⅔	cup extra-virgin olive oil
	Pinch hot red pepper flakes
	Salt
1	pound small white button mushrooms, halved (quartered if large)
2	tablespoons lemon juice
1	medium clove garlic, slivered
1	tablespoon minced fresh parsley leaves
½	small red onion, minced (about ¼ cup)
½	small red bell pepper, stemmed, seeded, and minced (about ¼ cup)
	Ground black pepper

1. Mix the dried porcini mushrooms with ½ cup hot tap water in a small microwave-safe bowl. Cover with plastic wrap, cut several steam vents in the plastic wrap with a paring knife, and microwave on high power for 30 seconds. Let stand until the mushrooms soften, about 5 minutes. Lift the mushrooms from the liquid with a fork and mince. Discard the soaking liquid.

2. Bring the minced porcini mushrooms, olive oil, hot red pepper flakes, and ¼ teaspoon salt to a simmer in a medium saucepan over medium heat. Simmer until the flavors blend, about 2 minutes. Add the button mushrooms and cook until a paring knife can be inserted into the mushrooms with little resistance, about 10 minutes. Remove the pan from the heat and transfer the mushrooms and the liquid to a medium bowl. Cool to room temperature, about 20 minutes.

3. When the mushrooms are cool, add the remaining ingredients and season with salt and ground black pepper to taste. Allow the flavors to meld for about 5 minutes before serving. (The mushrooms and marinade can be refrigerated in an airtight container for up to 2 days.)

STUFFED MUSHROOMS

HUNTED, SOLD, AND COOKED WITH reverence, mushrooms are an important ingredient in Italian cuisine. Stuffed mushrooms, although small enough to eat in one bite, are thoughtfully prepared and potently flavored with the earthy, robust flavors of the forest. The trick, however, is teasing this flavor out of the mushrooms found at the local grocery store. Sure, a great wild mushroom will taste woodsy when stuffed, but what about the common white button mushroom?

We began by trying a few recipes and immediately noted two main issues: the lack of any true mushroom flavor and the mushy, wet texture of the fillings. As the stuffed mushrooms cooked in the oven, they released their moisture, becoming watery and turning the filling wet. We realized that the mushrooms had to be cooked before they were stuffed and knew that roasting was the answer. The dry heat would allow the released moisture to evaporate while the roasting would intensify the mushroom flavor. By roasting the mushrooms upside down, we were able to drain much of the mushrooms' natural moisture before flipping them over and roasting the other side.

Although this technique produced better flavor, the mushrooms still tasted too bland. In an effort to introduce flavor to the mushrooms as they cooked, we tossed them with olive oil, garlic, lemon juice, salt, and pepper before roasting. This last-minute boost worked wonders, and the mushroom caps emerged dry, full of flavor, and ready for the filling.

Wanting to pack the stuffing with even more mushroom flavor, we thought it would be great to use the mushroom stems as the main ingredient, but after several trials we noted that they were simply too bland and watery, even with a quick marinade and a roast. Instead, we used dried porcini mushrooms and quickly found the potent mushroom flavor we were looking for. Pancetta (Italian-style bacon), Parmesan, and fresh parsley rounded out the filling in terms of flavor, yet we were still having trouble with its texture, having gone from wet and mushy to dry and crumbly. To correct this, we used bread soaked in milk, a combination often used in meatballs to help hold the mixture together without making it sodden or greasy.

Once stuffed and topped with a pinch of grated Parmesan, the mushrooms took only 10 minutes to heat through and emerged from the oven with the unmistakable, earthy aroma of mushrooms cooked to perfection.

Stuffed Mushrooms

MAKES 24 MUSHROOMS,
ENOUGH TO SERVE 8

Roasting the mushrooms drives off excess moisture and concentrates the mushroom flavor. The roasted mushrooms are then stuffed and quickly heated through. We found that mushroom caps that measure between 1½ and 2 inches in diameter (before roasting) are ideal for this recipe. See the illustrations on page 5 for tips on rehydrating dried porcini mushrooms.

ROASTED MUSHROOMS

24	medium mushroom caps
¼	cup extra-virgin olive oil
3	large cloves garlic, minced or pressed through a garlic press
½	teaspoon lemon juice
¼	teaspoon salt
	Pinch ground black pepper

STUFFING

¾	ounce dried porcini mushrooms
2	slices high-quality sandwich bread
2	tablespoons milk
3	ounces pancetta, minced
2	large cloves garlic, minced or pressed through a garlic press
¼	cup plus 2 tablespoons grated Parmesan cheese
1	tablespoon minced fresh parsley leaves
	Salt and ground black pepper

1. FOR THE MUSHROOMS: Adjust the oven rack to the middle position and heat the oven to 450 degrees. Toss the mushrooms with the oil, garlic, lemon juice, salt, and pepper in a medium bowl. Place the mushrooms, gill side down, on a large rimmed baking sheet and roast until the brown juices are released, about 20 minutes. Turn the caps over and roast until the liquid has evaporated completely and the mushrooms are brown all over, about 10 minutes. Remove the baking sheet from the oven and turn the mushrooms gill side down to drain any excess moisture. (Do not turn off the oven.)

2. FOR THE STUFFING: Meanwhile, mix the dried porcini mushrooms with ½ cup hot tap water in a small microwave-safe bowl. Cover with plastic wrap, cut several steam vents in the plastic wrap with a paring knife, and microwave on high power for 30 seconds. Let stand until the mushrooms soften, about

5 minutes. Lift the mushrooms from the liquid with a fork and mince. Pour the liquid through a small strainer lined with a single sheet of paper towel and placed over a measuring cup.

3. Process the sandwich bread in a food processor fitted with a metal blade until the bread has a coarse texture resembling Grape-Nuts cereal, about eight 1-second pulses. Transfer the crumbs to a small bowl and toss with the milk.

4. Cook the pancetta in a small nonstick pan over medium heat until lightly browned, about 5 minutes. Add the minced porcini and cook for 1 minute. Add the porcini soaking liquid and simmer until the liquid evaporates, about 2 minutes. Add the garlic and sauté until aromatic, about 30 seconds. Remove the pan from the heat and scrape the mixture into a medium bowl. Add the soaked bread crumbs, ¼ cup Parmesan, parsley, and salt and pepper to taste.

5. To stuff the mushrooms: Flip the cooked mushroom caps gill side up and stuff each with about 1 teaspoon stuffing. Top each mushroom with a pinch of the remaining 2 tablespoons cheese. Bake at 450 degrees until the cheese has melted and is browning in spots and the filling is heated through, about 10 minutes. Serve immediately.

Stuffed Clams

STUFFED CLAMS ARE CLASSICALLY SERVED with a crisp white wine to awaken the appetite just before dinner. We wanted to discover a simple, elegant stuffed clam that was easy to make and highlighted the flavor of the clam itself.

To begin, we knew it would be easiest to steam the clams open before attempting to remove their meat. Shucking raw clams is simply too difficult for most home cooks. Using a small amount of white wine spiked with shallots and hot red pepper flakes, it only took a few minutes to steam the clams in a small covered pan. To ensure that none of the clams would overcook, we removed the lid after a few minutes of steaming and, with a pair of tongs, removed the clams as soon as they opened. (We discarded any clams that refused to pop after 7 to 8 minutes—they shouldn't be eaten.) When the clams were cool enough to handle, the shells were easy to remove, and the meat was perfectly cooked.

Thinking the rest of this recipe would be a breeze to develop, we were surprised when trouble arose. The delicate flavor of the clam, as it turned out, was easily overpowered by other ingredients. Prosciutto and pancetta, although commonly found in stuffed clam recipes, masked the clam flavor. In the end, we found ourselves removing these classic ingredients from the list of possibilities.

In an effort to boost the clam flavor, we decided to make use of the steaming broth, into which much of the clams' natural flavor was deposited. Reducing the wine-based clam broth to a syrup, we mixed it with a little butter and some herbs.

When we topped the clams with this potent, buttery mixture and some fresh bread crumbs, their flavor was finally pushed into the limelight. Served with wedges of lemon and cool white wine, these clams are elegant, simple, and, above all, genuinely flavorful.

Stuffed Clams

MAKES ABOUT 24, ENOUGH TO SERVE 8
We had the best luck with clams about the size of a half dollar coin.

4	tablespoons unsalted butter, cut into 4 pieces
½	medium red bell pepper, roasted and peeled (see page 10), then minced
2	medium scallions, minced

1   tablespoon minced fresh parsley leaves
1   tablespoon minced fresh oregano leaves
    Pinch ground black pepper
1   large shallot, minced
    Pinch hot red pepper flakes
½   cup white wine
2   pounds littleneck or small cherrystone
    clams, well scrubbed (about 24 clams)
¼   cup fresh bread crumbs (about 1 slice
    high-quality sandwich bread ground in a
    food processor to coarse crumbs)
1   lemon, cut into wedges

1. Adjust the oven rack so it is about 6 inches from the broiler element and heat the broiler. Place 3 tablespoons butter and the bell pepper, scallions, parsley, oregano, and black pepper in a small bowl. Set aside.

2. Melt the remaining tablespoon butter in a medium sauté pan over medium-high heat until the foaming subsides, about 1 minute. Add the shallot and hot red pepper flakes and sauté until the shallot is softened, about 2 minutes. Add the wine and clams, cover, and steam until the clams begin to open, about 3 minutes. Remove the lid and, using a pair of tongs, transfer the clams to a clean bowl as they open, allowing the steaming juice to fall back into the pan. (Once the lid has been removed, let the clams cook for about 5 minutes longer. Discard any clams that haven't opened by this point.)

3. Once all the clams have been removed from the pan, simmer the steaming juices until they reduce to 3 tablespoons, about 5 minutes. Pour the reduced steaming juices into the bowl with the butter and herbs, mix to form a loose paste, and set aside.

4. When the clams are cool enough to handle, remove the meat from the shells using a paring knife or clean hands. Separate the joined clamshells, discard half of the halves, and nestle the clam meat neatly into each remaining shell half. Arrange the clamshells on a rimmed baking sheet. Place 1 teaspoon butter mixture on top of each shell and top with ½ teaspoon fresh bread crumbs.

5. Broil until the crumbs are toasted and the clams are heated through, 4 to 5 minutes. Serve immediately with lemon wedges.

ROASTED PEPPERS

ROASTED PEPPERS ARE A COMMON addition to antipasto spreads. When roasted, sweet red bell peppers assume a new layer of complex, smoky flavor. In testing the many methods of roasting peppers, we sought the most efficient way to achieve a tender but not mushy flesh, smoky flavor, and skin that peeled off easily.

After flaming (over a gas burner), broiling, baking, and steaming dozens of peppers, we found that oven broiling is clearly the superior method. It's neat and fast, and the peppers are delicious.

To reach this conclusion, we roasted dozens of peppers. We found that you must take care not to overroast the peppers. When the skin of the pepper just puffs up and turns black, you have reached the point at which flavor is maximized and the texture of the pepper flesh is soft but not mushy. After this point, continued exposure to heat will result in darkened flesh that is thin, flabby, and slightly bitter.

Broiling peppers does present some challenges. The broiler element in most ovens is approximately 3 inches away from the upper rack, which means that whole peppers usually touch the element. A lower rack level means the broiling takes too long and cooks the flesh too much. The answer, then, is to cut the peppers.

Unless you have asbestos fingers, you need to allow roasted peppers time to cool before handling them, and steaming during this time does make the charred skin a bit easier to peel off; however, the skin will still come off if you decide to omit this step. The ideal steaming time is 15 minutes—any less and the peppers are still too hot to work with comfortably. The best approach is to use a heat-resistant bowl (glass, ceramic, or metal) with a piece of plastic wrap secured over the top to trap the steam.

Seeding the peppers before roasting makes it possible to peel them without having to rinse them to wash away the seeds. If you are still tempted to rinse, notice the rich oils that accumulate on your fingers as you work. It seems silly to rinse away those oils rather than savoring them later with your meal.

The way peppers are treated after they are peeled determines how long they keep. Unadorned and wrapped in plastic wrap, peppers will keep their full, meaty texture only about 2 days in the refrigerator. Drizzled with a generous amount of olive oil and kept in an airtight container, peppers will keep

ROASTING PEPPERS

1. Slice ¼ inch from the top and bottom of the pepper, then gently remove the stem from the top lobe.

2. Pull the core out of the pepper.

3. Make a slit down one side of the pepper, then lay it flat, skin side down, in one long strip. Slide a sharp knife along the inside of the pepper and remove all ribs and seeds.

4. Arrange the strips of peppers and the top and bottom lobes on a foil-lined rimmed baking sheet, skin side up. Flatten the strips with the palm of your hand.

5. Adjust the oven rack to its top position. If the rack is more than 3½ inches from the heating element, set a rimmed baking sheet, bottom up, on the rack under the baking sheet.

6. Roast until the skin of the peppers is charred and puffed like a balloon but the flesh is still firm. You may steam the peppers at this point or not, as you wish. Start peeling where the skin has charred and bubbled the most. The skin will come off in large strips.

about 1 week without losing texture or flavor. Completely covered with olive oil, peppers will last in the refrigerator 3 to 4 weeks.

~~~

Roasted Red Bell Peppers

MAKES 4 ROASTED PEPPERS, ENOUGH TO SERVE 8

Cooking times vary, depending on the broiler, so watch the peppers carefully as they roast. You will need to increase the cooking time slightly if your peppers are just out of the refrigerator instead of at room temperature. Yellow and orange peppers roast faster than red ones, so decrease their cooking time by 2 to 4 minutes. Do not roast green or purple peppers—their flavor is bitter and not worth the effort.

4   red medium to large bell peppers (6 to 9 ounces each), prepared according to illustrations 1 through 4 on page 10
    Extra-virgin olive oil
    Salt

1. Adjust the oven rack to the top position. The oven rack should be 2½ to 3½ inches from the heating element. If it is not, set a rimmed baking sheet, turned upside down, on the oven rack to elevate the pan (see illustration 5 on page 10). Turn the broiler on and heat for 5 minutes. Broil the peppers until spotty brown, about 5 minutes. Reverse the pan in the oven and roast until the skin is charred and puffed but the flesh is still firm, 3 to 5 minutes longer.

2. Remove the pan from oven; let the peppers sit until cool enough to handle. Peel and discard the skin from each piece (see illustration 6 on page 10). To facilitate peeling, transfer the peppers right out of oven to a large heat-resistant bowl, cover it with plastic wrap, and steam for 15 minutes before peeling.

3. To serve, slice the peppers and arrange them on a platter. Drizzle with oil just until lightly moistened and sprinkle with salt to taste.

CAPONATA

CAPONATA IS A CLASSIC SICILIAN relish featuring sautéed eggplant, onions, celery, and bell peppers spiked with vinegar and garnished with capers and olives. Although many caponata recipes promote the eggplant to center stage, we wanted our version to highlight the flavors and textures of all caponata vegetables equally.

To start, we focused on finding a method that would cook each ingredient to the correct degree of doneness before combining them. Most recipes accomplish this by cooking the vegetables separately in several pans, but we wanted to streamline the technique and use just one pan. After several tries, we found that a nonstick skillet worked best because its slippery surface was able to sauté multiple batches of vegetables without letting any browned bits stick and burn. The nonstick surface also allowed us to use just enough oil to lightly coat the celery, eggplant, onions, and peppers as we sautéed them, preventing the caponata from becoming too greasy, a common problem with most recipes.

When all the vegetables were sautéed, it was easy to combine them with a can of chopped tomatoes and allow the mixture to simmer briefly until the flavors melded. This method ensured that each vegetable retained its integrity. The result was a beautiful caponata with varying textures and nuances of flavor.

With the method figured out, we focused next on the preparation of the vegetables and the remaining ingredients. Turning our attention to the eggplant, we were surprised to discover it did not need to be salted. Salting, which usually helps draw some of the bitter juices out, just wasn't necessary, as the combination of sautéing and simmering mellowed any residual bitterness. Some tasters preferred the eggplant peeled; however, most didn't mind the purple-colored skin, which softened and mellowed as it cooked, adding a nice contrast to the other vegetables.

We noted the traditional additions of anchovies, fresh oregano, fresh basil, olives, capers, and raisins to caponata, and tasters approved of each. Caponata is usually finished with a small splash of red wine vinegar. Our tasters also liked a little sugar to balance the acidity of the vinegar.

Caponata

MAKES 6 CUPS, ENOUGH TO SERVE AT LEAST 12

As an antipasto, caponata can be served as is and eaten on plates with forks or spooned over plain bruschetta (see page 19) that was rubbed with garlic and brushed with oil. Caponata can also be served as a relish alongside a pork roast or fish.

7	tablespoons extra-virgin olive oil
3	stalks celery, cut into ¹/₂-inch pieces
1	medium eggplant (about 1 pound), cut into ¹/₂-inch cubes
1	medium onion, minced
1	medium red bell pepper, stemmed, seeded, and cut into ¹/₂-inch pieces
2	anchovy fillets
1	tablespoon minced fresh oregano leaves
¹/₄	cup raisins
1	can (14.5 ounces) diced tomatoes
2	tablespoons roughly chopped fresh basil leaves
2	tablespoons capers, rinsed
2	tablespoons pitted and minced black olives
¹/₄	cup red wine vinegar
1	tablespoon sugar

1. Heat 1 tablespoon oil in a large nonstick skillet over medium–high heat until shimmering, about 1½ minutes. Add the celery and cook until softened, with slightly browned edges, about 6 minutes. Transfer the celery to a large bowl and reserve. Return the pan to medium heat and add 4 tablespoons oil. Heat the oil until shimmering, about 30 seconds. Add the eggplant and stir to coat (do not add any more oil to pan). Cook until the eggplant is soft, with slightly browned edges, about 6 minutes. Transfer the eggplant to the bowl with the celery.

2. Return the pan to medium heat, add the remaining 2 tablespoons oil, and heat until shimmering, about 10 seconds. Add the onion and sauté until softened, about 3 minutes. Stir in the red bell pepper, cover, and cook until softened, about 6 minutes. Remove the cover, stir in the anchovies, oregano, and raisins, and cook until aromatic, about 30 seconds.

3. Add the tomatoes and their juices as well as the reserved celery and eggplant and reduce the heat to medium-low. Cover and cook until the flavors blend, 15 to 20 minutes. Remove the pan from the heat and stir in the basil, capers, olives, vinegar, and sugar. Transfer the caponata to a clean bowl, cover, and refrigerate until chilled, at least 1 hour or up to 2 days.

PEELING MELON

Trim a ¹/₄-inch slice from the top and bottom of the melon so that it will sit flat on a work surface. Using a chef's knife and working from top to bottom, carefully cut away the rind in long strips. Repeat until all the rind is removed.

MELON AND PROSCIUTTO

THE CLASSIC PAIRING OF SWEET, JUICY melon and salty, toothsome prosciutto is a favorite both in Italy and the United States. Although prosciutto is now produced in various parts of the world, the best comes from two regions of Italy: Parma and San Daniele. The term *prosciutto* refers to a ham that has been salted and air-dried in the Italian fashion. Unlike many other hams produced elsewhere, prosciutto is not smoked, and it is usually not cooked. As an antipasto, it is served raw (or *crudo,* in Italian) in paper-thin slices. Although prosciutto can be served on its own, the addition of melon (or figs) is customary and delicious.

A signature product for more than two thousand years, Italian prosciutto is legally protected and tightly monitored by Italian law. All aspects of production, from the pigpen to the aging house, are strictly regulated and quality-controlled to ensure that only the highest-quality prosciutto receives the stamp of approval. Italian prosciutto has been available in the United States for more than a decade, and our testers found it is the best choice for this recipe. You are most likely to see prosciutto di Parma. Our tasters were wowed by the gentle flavors in this buttery, tender ham.

There are no secrets in the making of this dish, but, due to its simplicity, each ingredient must be in its prime. The prosciutto should be supple and perfumed, and the melon must be as sweet and ripe as can be. It is best not to let the melon and prosciutto sit around together for too long, or the salt from the meat will draw moisture out of the melon, turning the fruit wet and the meat soggy. This dish is best eaten immediately after it is assembled.

Melon and Prosciutto

MAKES 16 PIECES,
ENOUGH TO SERVE 6 TO 8

Cantaloupe is the classic choice, but any ripe melon, including honeydew, can be used in this recipe.

1	medium cantaloupe
½	pound thinly sliced Italian prosciutto

1. Trim the rind from the melon (see the illustration on page 12), cut the melon in half, and scoop out the seeds with a spoon; discard the seeds. Cut each half into eight ½-inch-wide crescents.

2. If the prosciutto slices are long (over 6 inches in length), wrap one piece of prosciutto around the middle of each melon slice. If the prosciutto slices are short (under 6 inches in length), wrap two around the middle of each melon slice. Serve immediately.

ASPARAGUS WRAPPED WITH PROSCIUTTO

ALTHOUGH MOST AMERICANS ARE familiar with prosciutto wrapped around melon slices, they are less familiar with prosciutto as a wrapping for cooked asparagus. This savory antipasto starts with cooked asparagus. Most recipes suggest roasting the asparagus. Although we found this worked fine, we had even quicker results under the broiler. This delicate dish is best made with thin asparagus spears (no thicker than your pinkie), which brown nicely after just 5 minutes under the broiler.

Although plain broiled asparagus, oiled lightly (to prevent sticking) and salted (for flavor), can be wrapped with prosciutto, we saw several recipes that added other classic Italian flavors—balsamic vinegar and cheese. We tried sprinkling a little vinegar and Parmesan cheese over the asparagus as soon as it came out of the oven, and tasters approved. The vinegar and cheese added sharp, sweet, and buttery notes that contrasted nicely with the asparagus and salty ham.

It's easiest to let the asparagus cool slightly before trying to wrap them in prosciutto. However, don't let the asparagus cool completely. Part of the charm of this dish comes from the contrasting temperatures (and textures) of the main ingredients.

Asparagus Wrapped with Prosciutto

MAKES ABOUT 20 PIECES, ENOUGH TO SERVE 4 TO 6

Make sure you have the same number of asparagus spears and pieces of prosciutto (count them once they have been cut into 3-inch lengths). You should have around 20 of each. If you like, serve the asparagus on a warm platter to keep them from cooling too quickly.

1	pound thin asparagus spears, tough ends snapped off (see illustration on page 59)
1	teaspoon extra-virgin olive oil
	Salt and ground black pepper
1	teaspoon balsamic vinegar
3	tablespoons grated Parmesan cheese
3	ounces thinly sliced prosciutto, cut crosswise into 3-inch pieces

1. Adjust the oven rack to the highest position and heat the broiler. Toss the asparagus with the oil on a rimmed baking sheet. Sprinkle with salt and pepper to taste. Broil, shaking the pan halfway through to turn the asparagus, until lightly browned, about 5 minutes.

2. Sprinkle the asparagus with the vinegar and Parmesan cheese. Cool slightly. Wrap a piece of prosciutto around the bottom half of each asparagus spear, making sure to leave the tip of the asparagus exposed. Arrange the asparagus on a platter and serve immediately.

FRITTO MISTO

SERVED THROUGHOUT ITALY AT TRATTORIAS and *enotecas* (wine bars), *fritto misto* is Italy's answer to french fries. Broadly translated, fritto misto means "mixed fry"—more specifically, a combination of deep-fried vegetables and, sometimes, seafood. Depending on what is in season, everything from cauliflower, fennel, carrots, bell peppers, zucchini, and zucchini blossoms to onions, snap peas, and herbs is battered and fried. As long as it is fresh and flavorful, any vegetable is fair game. After trying a variety of fritto misto recipes, we realized that the biggest problem was the batter; it is often saturated with oil or gummy and bland. We therefore set out to create a batter that would fry to a crisp, oil-free coating.

Fritto misto batters come in a variety of forms, from simple flour and water mixtures to more complicated batters leavened with baking powder, seltzer water, and beer. We tried several kinds and were most impressed by the batters that employed whipped egg whites for leavening, because the batter was airy and clean-tasting. Both baking powder and beer imparted bitterness to the batter, and the beer's carbonation made for a grease-laden coating. Seltzer water inflated the batter nicely but cooked to a greasy coating.

To keep the coating light, we employed a mixture of cornstarch and flour (which we discovered approximates the low-protein, finely ground flour commonly used for fritto misto in Italy). Regular, all-purpose flour alone in the batter made for a gummy, thick coating, and cornstarch alone lacked structure. For seasoning, tasters favored a little cayenne and black pepper; no salt was necessary because the fritto misto is sprinkled with salt before serving. For the most volume, the egg whites are folded in just before frying.

For the crispest texture and most appealing browning, we found that a fairly high oil temperature was the secret. We experimented with temperatures from 325 to 400 degrees and found that 375 degrees yielded the best results; the vegetables were golden and airy. Lower oil temperatures yielded greasy and wan vegetables. To keep the oil clean-tasting, it was essential to skim the fat for impurities between batches. During recipe development, bits of the batter quickly charred and imparted a bitter, burnt flavor to the oil unless removed with a mesh skimmer.

Most vegetables can be successfully batter-fried. The trick is to identify which vegetables must be salted and drained to remove excess moisture and which must be precooked. If fried without salting, eggplant soaks up the frying oil like a sponge. Salting draws out the vegetable's moisture and collapses the spongy cell walls so that it does not become saturated with the cooking oil.

For dense vegetables like carrots, cauliflower, and fennel, parcooking is a must. Because the vegetables are fried so quickly—just a couple of minutes—they barely cook in the oil. For the best texture, we blanched the vegetables in rapidly boiling salted water until al dente, or just shy of fully cooked, and shocked them in ice water to stop the cooking instantly. The vegetables finished cooking through in the oil. You must thoroughly dry the blanched vegetables before frying them; otherwise, the batter slides off.

With respect to garnish or sauce, restraint is

Preparing Vegetables for Frying

We like a mix of colors, flavors, and textures when preparing fritto misto. A total of six vegetables is especially nice, but use any combination of the vegetables below to yield 8 cups prepared vegetables. Fried sage leaves are a traditional part of fritto misto and can be included, if you like.

VEGETABLE	PREPARATION
Carrot	Peel and cut into 3- to 4-inch lengths. Cut each length into sticks ½ inch thick. Blanch in boiling salted water for 3½ minutes. Drain, shock in a bowl of ice water, drain again, and pat dry.
Cauliflower	Cut into small florets. Blanch in boiling salted water for 3½ minutes. Drain, shock in a bowl of ice water, drain again, and pat dry.
Eggplant	Cut in half lengthwise and then crosswise into slices ½ inch thick. Toss the eggplant slices with salt (use 2 teaspoons per 1 pound eggplant) in a colander. Let drain 30 minutes. Place the eggplant slices between layers of paper towels and press firmly to squeeze out as much moisture as possible.
Fennel	Remove and discard the stalks and fronds. Cut the bulb in half lengthwise and remove the triangular core from each half. Cut into slices ½ inch thick. Blanch in boiling salted water for 3 minutes. Drain, shock in a bowl of ice water, drain again, and pat dry.
Red Onion	Cut crosswise into rounds ½ inch thick and separate into individual rings. Soak onions in ice water for 30 minutes. Drain and pat dry.
Red Pepper	Stem, seed, and cut into strips ½ inch wide.
Sage	Wash and dry.
Zucchini	Cut crosswise into rounds ½ inch thick.
Zucchini Blossoms	Inspect for bugs and shake clean if necessary.

best. While Americans douse their fried foods in a variety of sauces, Italians understand that a simple spritz of lemon juice cuts the oily richness of fried food and brightens its flavor.

Fritto Misto

SERVES 4 TO 6

When assembling a mixture of vegetables to fry, think of contrasting flavors, shapes, and textures. For example, the velvety softness of eggplant is nicely countered by a bell pepper's crispness. Choose only the freshest vegetables; the crisp batter and sprinkle of lemon juice serve to highlight the vegetable's natural flavor.

To keep the process relatively clean, keep one pair of tongs in the bowl of batter and another pair clean for removing the vegetables from the hot oil. Fritto misto is best eaten immediately (have everyone in the kitchen to eat the vegetables as soon as they come out of the oil), but the fried vegetables can be held for up to ½ hour in a 200-degree oven on a paper towel–lined baking sheet or ovensafe plate.

BATTER

1	cup (5 ounces) unbleached all-purpose flour
¾	cup (3.5 ounces) cornstarch
½	teaspoon ground black pepper
½	teaspoon cayenne pepper
1½	cups water
2	tablespoons extra-virgin olive oil
3	large egg whites
8	cups prepared vegetables (see chart on page 15)
6	cups vegetable or canola oil
	Salt and ground black pepper
1	lemon, cut into 8 wedges and seeds removed

1. FOR THE BATTER: Combine the flour, cornstarch, black pepper, and cayenne in a medium bowl. In a measuring cup, mix together the water and olive oil. While whisking the flour mixture, pour in the water and oil mixture in a steady stream until the mixture is just combined. It should resemble heavy cream in texture. Cover with plastic wrap and set aside for at least 1 hour. Just before frying, use an electric mixer to beat the egg whites to stiff peaks. With a large rubber spatula, fold the beaten egg whites completely into the batter.

2. Meanwhile, prepare the vegetables.

3. Heat the oil in a heavy-bottomed 6-quart Dutch oven over medium-high heat until it reaches 375 degrees. (Use an instant-read thermometer that registers high temperatures or clip a candy/deep-fry thermometer onto the side of the pot before turning on the heat.) To coat the vegetables, submerge them in the batter and, using tongs, remove them from the batter, allowing the excess to drip back into the bowl. Making sure not to overcrowd the pan, fry the vegetables in batches until light golden brown, 2 to 3 minutes per batch, depending on the vegetable. Adjust the temperature as necessary to maintain an oil temperature of 375 degrees. Remove the vegetables with a second pair of tongs, allowing the excess oil to run off the vegetables and back into the pot, then drain the vegetables on an oven-safe plate layered with paper towels. Use a mesh skimmer to remove any burned bits of batter from the oil and repeat with another batch of vegetables. Lightly salt and pepper the vegetables while still hot. Serve immediately with lemon wedges.

BAGNA CAUDA

BAGNA CAUDA CAN BE EITHER ONE OF the most glorious or most disgusting culinary experiences you'll ever have. Originating in the Piedmont region of northern Italy, bagna cauda is a warm anchovy and garlic sauce that is served alongside vegetables and bread, fondue-style. When made badly, the sauce tastes bitter and fishy and has a greasy mouth-feel. But when the sauce is made well, the rich, perfumed flavors of anchovy and garlic are balanced and tempered within a base of warm olive oil or cream, tasting just this side of heaven.

As we began to research the history of bagna cauda we discovered, as with most things Italian, that every chef has an opinion about how to cook it. While most recipes use olive oil or heavy cream, some claim that milk is the key, while others use a hearty red wine. After we gave a few of these recipes a whirl, it became obvious which bagna cauda our test kitchen preferred. The sauce made with cream turned out smooth and rich, easily coating the vegetables and pieces of bread without being

CRUDITÉS

You need something to dip into bagna cauda, and vegetables are a must, accompanied by either cubes of rustic bread or breadsticks. In our testing, we found the preparation of vegetables for crudités essential. There are two key elements: how the vegetable is sliced and whether or not it should be blanched (cooked briefly in salted boiling water) to make the texture more palatable and to improve its flavor.

The information that follows details the findings of our testing. When deciding which vegetables to use together for crudités, consider these factors: First and foremost, use what's in season and looks good at the market. Second, choose a variety of colors. A platter consisting entirely of green vegetables is not as attractive as a platter of green, white, yellow, orange, and red vegetables. Last, consider the texture of the vegetables. Crunchy, hard carrots work well with crisp, juicy bell peppers and soft cherry tomatoes.

Each of the preparations listed below yields about 3 cups vegetables. Choose at least four vegetables for serving with bagna cauda.

ASPARAGUS Snap tough ends from 12 ounces asparagus. Blanch in boiling salted water until bright green, 30 to 60 seconds. Drain, shock in ice water, drain again, and pat dry.

BROCCOLI Cut florets from 1 small bunch (about 1 pound) into bite-sized pieces. Blanch in boiling salted water until bright green, about 1 minute. Drain, shock in ice water, drain again, and pat dry.

CARROTS Blanch ¾ pound baby carrots in boiling salted water until bright orange, about 15 seconds. Drain, shock in ice water, drain again, and pat dry.

CAULIFLOWER Cut florets from ½ medium head (about 1 pound) into bite-sized pieces. Blanch in boiling salted water until slightly tender, 1 to 1½ minutes. Drain, shock in ice water, drain again, and pat dry.

CELERY Trim ends from 4 medium stalks (about ½ pound). Cut stalks in half lengthwise, then crosswise into 3-inch lengths.

FENNEL Remove and discard the stalks and fronds from 1 medium fennel bulb (about 1 pound). Cut the bulb in half lengthwise and remove the triangular core from each half. Cut into slices ½ inch thick. Blanch in boiling salted water until crisp-tender, about 1 minute. Drain, shock in ice water, drain again, and pat dry.

GREEN BEANS Trim ends from 8 ounces thin green beans. Blanch in boiling salted water until bright green, about 1 minute. Drain, shock in ice water, drain again, and pat dry.

BELL PEPPERS Stem and seed 3 small red, yellow, or orange bell peppers. Cut into strips about 3 inches long and ¾ inch wide.

SUGAR SNAP PEAS Remove ends and strings from 8 ounces sugar snap peas. Blanch in boiling salted water until bright green, about 15 seconds. Drain, shock in ice water, drain again, and pat dry.

TOMATOES Stem 1 pound cherry tomatoes.

greasy. As the anchovy, garlic, and heavy cream cooked, their flavors melded and mellowed, transforming these simple ingredients into a beautiful, aromatic sauce. By comparison, the olive oil sauce tasted harsh, and it separated as it sat. As the oil collected at the surface, it provided a greasy barrier to the flavorful anchovy and garlic that had sunk to the bottom. Milk produced a sauce that was thin and watery, while the tannic, overpowering flavor of red wine was just plain wrong. Out of curiosity, we tried using half-and-half, but we found the result lacked the texture and heft that we found so appealing in the sauce made with heavy cream.

Using 1 cup heavy cream, we tested various amounts of anchovy and garlic to get the balance just right. Anchovies are usually packed in 2-ounce tins, but we found that a single tin didn't offer enough flavor while two tins was too much. One and a half tins (3 ounces) yielded the pungency we were looking for, neither too potent nor too weak. Next, we tested various amounts of garlic ranging from one clove to an entire head and found five large cloves offered the perfect balance. Bagna cauda is often finished with a pinch of cayenne or sliced white truffle; seeing as white truffle is one of the most expensive ingredients in the world, we opted for a small spike of cayenne to round out the sauce.

With the ingredients figured out, we moved on to perfecting the method. Focusing first on the anchovies, we tried several methods of incorporating them into the sauce. Most recipes call for them to be mashed into the sauce as it cooks, while others recommend a more thorough blending. We found that the sauce tasted best when the cream and anchovies spent a few seconds in the blender. Not only did the anchovy fillets quickly break apart but the cream was also immediately infused with anchovy.

The garlic, on the other hand, tasted best when allowed to sauté with the cayenne for a few minutes. Last, we noted that the sauce needed a good 15 to 20 minutes over medium-low heat, allowing the flavors to combine and the sauce to thicken. Lightly seasoned with salt and black pepper, this sophisticated sauce has an alluring aroma and angelic flavor that beautifully coats anything from a vegetable or piece of bread to a stray finger.

Bagna Cauda

SERVES 8 TO 12

This sauce should be served warm, so use a fondue pot or double boiler for serving. Serve with crudités-style vegetables and either rustic pieces of bread or fresh breadsticks.

1	cup heavy cream
3	ounces anchovy fillets, drained (about 35 fillets)
1	tablespoon extra-virgin olive oil
5	large cloves garlic, minced or pressed through a garlic press
	Pinch cayenne pepper
	Salt and ground black pepper
12	cups prepared vegetables (see page 17)
	Several cups cubed rustic bread or 12 to 24 fresh breadsticks

1. Place the heavy cream and anchovy fillets in a blender and blend until smooth, about 5 seconds. Set aside.

2. Heat the oil, garlic, and cayenne in a small saucepan over medium heat until the garlic is translucent, about 2 minutes. Reduce the heat to medium-low and add the anchovy-cream mixture. Cook, stirring occasionally, until the mixture is slightly thickened, 15 to 20 minutes. Season to taste with salt and pepper. Serve warm with the vegetables and bread.

BRUSCHETTA

AUTHENTIC ITALIAN GARLIC BREAD, called *bruschetta*, is never squishy or soft. Crisp, toasted slices of country bread are rubbed with raw garlic, brushed with extra-virgin olive oil (never butter), then topped with various ingredients. Toppings can be as simple as salt and pepper or fresh herbs. Ripe tomatoes, grilled mushrooms, and sautéed onions make more substantial toppings.

We found that narrow loaves of Italian bread are not suitable for bruschetta. Crusty country loaves that yield larger slices are preferable. Oblong loaves that measure about 5 inches across are best, but round loaves will work. As for thickness, we found that about 1 inch provides enough heft to support weighty toppings and gives a good chew.

Toasting the bread, which can be done over a grill fire or under the broiler, creates little jagged edges that pull off tiny bits of garlic when the raw clove is rubbed over the bread. For more garlic flavor, rub vigorously.

Oil can be drizzled over the garlicky toast or brushed on for more even coverage. One large piece of toast is enough for a single antipasto serving. Two or three slices makes a good lunch when accompanied by a salad.

Bruschetta with Tomatoes and Basil

SERVES 8

This is the classic bruschetta, although you can substitute other herbs. Decrease the quantity of stronger herbs, such as thyme and oregano.

- 4 medium ripe tomatoes (about 1⅔ pounds), cored and cut into ½-inch dice
- ⅓ cup shredded fresh basil leaves
  Salt and ground black pepper
- 1 12 by 5-inch loaf country bread, sliced crosswise into 1-inch-thick pieces, ends removed
- 1 large clove garlic, peeled
- 3 tablespoons extra-virgin olive oil

1. Heat the broiler or light a grill fire.
2. Mix the tomatoes, basil, and salt and pepper to taste in a medium bowl. Set aside.
3. Broil or grill the bread until golden brown on both sides. Place the toast slices on a large platter, rub the garlic over the tops, then brush with the oil.
4. Use a slotted spoon to divide the tomato mixture among the toast slices. Serve immediately.

Bruschetta with Fresh Herbs

SERVES 8

This simple recipe is ideal as an accompaniment to meals as well as an antipasto.

- 5 tablespoons extra-virgin olive oil
- 1½ tablespoons minced fresh parsley leaves
- 1 tablespoon minced fresh oregano or fresh thyme leaves
- 1 tablespoon minced fresh sage leaves
  Salt and ground black pepper
- 1 12 by 5-inch loaf country bread, sliced crosswise into 1-inch-thick pieces, ends removed
- 1 large clove garlic, peeled

1. Heat the broiler or light a grill fire.
2. Mix the oil, herbs, and salt and pepper to taste in a small bowl. Set aside.
3. Broil or grill the bread until golden brown on both sides. Place the toast slices on a large platter, rub the garlic over the tops, brush with the herb oil, and serve immediately.

Bruschetta with Red Onions, Herbs, and Parmesan

SERVES 8

The sautéed onions may be prepared an hour or two in advance and the toasts assembled at the last minute. Because this bruschetta contains cheese, we like to use the broiler rather than the grill. The heat from above (rather than below) melts the cheese more effectively.

6	tablespoons extra-virgin olive oil
4	medium red onions (about 1½ pounds), halved lengthwise and sliced thin
4	teaspoons sugar
1½	tablespoons minced fresh mint leaves
2	tablespoons balsamic vinegar
	Salt and ground black pepper
1	12 by 5-inch loaf country bread, sliced crosswise into 1-inch-thick pieces, ends reserved
1	large clove garlic, peeled
3	tablespoons grated Parmesan cheese

1. Heat 3½ tablespoons oil in a large skillet set over medium-high heat. Add the onions and sugar; sauté, stirring often, until softened, 7 to 8 minutes. Reduce the heat to medium-low. Continue to cook, stirring often, until the onions are sweet and tender, 7 to 8 minutes longer. Stir in the mint and vinegar and season to taste with salt and pepper. Set the onion mixture aside.

2. Heat the broiler. Place the bread on a large baking sheet. Broil the bread until golden brown on both sides.

3. Remove the baking sheet from the oven. Rub the garlic over the toast tops. Brush the remaining 2½ tablespoons oil over the bread. Divide the onion mixture among the slices, then sprinkle with the Parmesan cheese.

4. Broil until the cheese just melts. Transfer the bruschetta to a large platter and serve immediately.

Bruschetta with Grilled Portobello Mushrooms

SERVES 8

Grill the mushrooms with the gills facing up to prevent loss of juices. For serving, flip the mushrooms onto the bread so their juices seep down into the toast.

4	large portobello mushrooms (about 1⅓ pounds), stemmed
6	tablespoons extra-virgin olive oil
1	tablespoon minced fresh rosemary leaves
	Salt and ground black pepper
1	12 by 5-inch loaf country bread, sliced crosswise into 1-inch-thick pieces, ends removed
1	large clove garlic, peeled

1. Light the grill. Place the mushroom caps on a large baking sheet. Mix 3½ tablespoons oil, the rosemary, and salt and pepper to taste in a small bowl. Brush the oil mixture over both sides of the mushrooms.

2. Grill the mushrooms, gill side up, over a medium-hot fire until the caps are cooked through and grill-marked, 8 to 10 minutes.

3. Meanwhile, grill the bread until golden brown on both sides. Place the toast slices on a large platter. Rub the garlic over the tops, then brush with the remaining 2½ tablespoons oil.

4. Halve the grilled mushrooms. Place one mushroom half, gill side down, over each slice of toast. Serve immediately.

CROSTINI WITH CHICKEN LIVERS

UNLIKE FRENCH PÂTÉS, WHICH ARE smooth, creamy, and time-consuming to prepare, Italian liver spreads have a rustic, chunky texture and are easy to make at the last minute. Seasoned with white wine and sage, they are often served on crostini (small pieces of toast that have been rubbed with a clove of garlic) alongside a glass of wine before dinner. When made well, the liver mixture has a smooth, mellow flavor and a chopped texture that melts to a creamy consistency as you eat it. Bad liver puree, as we learned after trying out a few recipes, is dry and chalky with a potent, offal flavor that permeates throughout the puree.

To start, we found it necessary to buy the freshest chicken livers we could find and to trim them well. Old, untrimmed livers produced a spread that was overbearingly metallic-tasting, with stringy, fibrous bits. Although most recipes we researched employed similar cooking techniques, we found a few small tricks that made all the difference between good and bad liver puree. First, most recipes cook the livers through until they are no longer pink in the middle (about 15 to 20 minutes). We found, however, that they actually cook much faster (in about 6 minutes) and produce a better spread when left with a rosy interior. When liver is overcooked, the texture turns chalky and mealy and the delicate nuances of flavor are lost. But when cooked quickly, the liver retains its soft, creamy texture and a clean, mellow flavor that blends easily with other ingredients.

To round out the flavor of the liver mixture, tasters liked the customary additions of white wine, sage, onion, and capers, but not olive oil, anchovy, tomato paste, or parsley. The olive oil and anchovy, for lack of better words, tasted too oily and fishy. The tomato paste turned the pâté sweet, and the parsley added nothing but specks of color.

The remaining problem was that we needed a technique that would cook all the spread ingredients properly, yet accommodate the livers' small cooking window. We started by sautéing the aromatics, then added the livers for a quick sear. We then added the wine and allowed the livers to finish cooking at a gentle simmer as the wine reduced to a light syrup. Transferring the mixture straight from the sauté pan to a food processor fitted with a steel blade, we quickly pulsed it to the correct texture. The resulting spread tasted clean and balanced, with an authentically rustic texture that melts in the mouth. It takes merely a few minutes to make.

Crostini with Chicken Liver Spread

MAKES 24 TOASTS,
ENOUGH TO SERVE 8 TO 10

This spread is fairly potent and best spread on tiny toasts, called crostini. Like bruschetta, these pieces of bread are toasted and rubbed with garlic. Their diminutive size means you can eat one in just a few bites. We think it's best to spread the warm liver mixture on the toasts and serve immediately, but the warm (or room-temperature spread) can be served in a bowl alongside the garlic-rubbed toasts for guests to take themselves. The spread will keep in the refrigerator for up to 1 day.

12	slices high-quality Italian bread, cut in half
1	large clove garlic, peeled
8	tablespoons (1 stick) unsalted butter
1	small onion, diced small
8	small fresh sage leaves, chopped
	Salt
1	pound chicken livers, rinsed and patted dry, fat and connective tissue removed
1/2	cup dry white wine
2	tablespoons capers, rinsed
	Ground black pepper

1. Adjust an oven rack to the middle position and heat the oven to 400 degrees. Arrange the bread slices in a single layer on a baking sheet and bake until the bread is dry and crisp, 8 to 10 minutes, turning the slices over halfway through baking. While still hot, rub each slice of bread with the raw garlic clove. Set the crostini aside.

2. Heat the butter in a large skillet over medium-high heat until the foaming subsides, about 2 minutes. Add the onion, sage, and ¼ teaspoon salt and cook until the onion softens, about 5 minutes. Add the chicken livers and toss, cooking briefly, about 1 minute. Add the wine and simmer until the liquid is slightly syrupy and the livers have a rosy interior, 4 to 5 minutes.

3. Transfer all pan contents to a food processor fitted with a steel blade and process until coarsely chopped, about seven 1-second pulses. Transfer the liver spread to a clean bowl, stir in the capers, and adjust the seasonings with salt and pepper to taste. Spread about 1 tablespoon warm liver mixture on each piece of toast and serve immediately.

CROSTINI WITH OLIVADA

A PUREE OF BLACK OLIVES, CALLED *olivada* in Italy and *tapenade* in southern France, often appears spread on little toasts as an antipasto. The paste is similar to pesto, but black olives take the place of the basil. Olivada is rich and potent, so it is best used sparingly. Tiny crostini are the perfect way to enjoy these flavors.

As with pesto, we find that the food processor is the best tool for preparing this paste. Rich, meaty kalamata olives are the most common choice, and we found they work perfectly in this recipe. Although you could use any high-quality black olive in brine, the kalamata has a high meat-to-pit ratio, and the pit is fairly easy to remove—two factors that make it the most logical choice for this recipe.

Most recipes include capers and anchovies in the puree, and our tasters liked both additions. Olive oil helps bring the ingredients together, but we preferred a slightly rough texture and found it best to use oil sparingly. Too much oil will make the puree perfectly smooth. Herbs are another component of most recipes, and we liked the fresh anise flavor of basil coupled with woodsy rosemary. That said, tasters felt that thyme or oregano could easily replace the rosemary and that parsley could stand in for the basil, with slightly different but still delicious results.

Crostini with Olivada
MAKES 24 TOASTS,
ENOUGH TO SERVE 8 TO 10

If you have any leftover olivada, toss it with linguine or spaghetti, the same way you might use pesto.

1 ½	cups pitted kalamata olives
3	tablespoons extra-virgin olive oil
1	tablespoon capers, rinsed
4	anchovy fillets
2	tablespoons shredded fresh basil leaves
2	teaspoons fresh rosemary leaves
12	slices high-quality Italian bread, cut in half
1	large garlic clove, peeled

1. Place the olives, oil, capers, anchovies, basil, and rosemary in the workbowl of a food processor fitted with a metal blade. Process, scraping down the sides of the bowl, until the mixture is finely minced and forms a chunky paste, about 1 minute. Transfer the olivada to a small bowl. (The paste can be refrigerated for a day or two, or longer if covered with a film of oil.)

2. Adjust an oven rack to the middle position and heat the oven to 400 degrees. Arrange the bread slices in a single layer on a baking

sheet and bake until the bread is dry and crisp, 8 to 10 minutes, turning the slices over halfway through baking. While still hot, rub each slice of bread with the raw garlic clove.

3. Spread about 2 teaspoons olivada over each piece of toast and serve immediately.

CHEESE ANTIPASTO

YOU CAN ALWAYS ASSEMBLE A VARIETY of Italian cheeses and crackers or breads and serve them as an antipasto. When serving several cheeses together, select a variety based on texture (soft, hard, crumbly), flavor (mild, sharp, pungent), and milk types (cow, sheep, goat). It's hard to imagine an Italian cheese selection without Parmigiano-Reggiano. Serve this crumbly cheese with a small, blunt knife and let guests break off small shards themselves.

The following cheeses are used most frequently in Italian cooking. For long-term storage in the refrigerator, we find that cheeses are best wrapped in parchment paper and then in aluminum foil. The paper allows the cheese to breathe a bit, while the foil keeps out off flavors from the refrigerator and prevents the cheese from drying out. Simply placing the cheese in a plastic bag, pressing out all the air, and then sealing the bag tight is our second choice. We find that pressing plastic wrap directly against the surface of most cheeses will cause a slight sour flavor to develop over time, and we do not recommend this method.

ASIAGO This cow's-milk cheese comes from the Veneto and is sold at various ages. Fresh Asiago is firm like cheddar or Havarti, and the flavor is fairly mild. Aged Asiago is drier, almost like Parmesan, and has a much sharper, saltier flavor.

FONTINA Real Italian fontina comes from the Val d'Aosta area in the far northern reaches of the country. It has a creamy, semisoft texture and a nutty, buttery flavor. Fontina is also made in Denmark, Sweden, and the United States. These cheeses tend to be much firmer (almost like cheddar) and sometimes rubbery. We find that these versions also lack the full flavor of the Italian cheese and are often quite bland.

GORGONZOLA Italy's most famous blue cheese, Gorgonzola can be aged and quite crumbly or rather young and creamy. Aged Gorgonzola has a much more potent blue cheese flavor, similar to Roquefort. In general, we like young Gorgonzola; its flavor is less overwhelming, and the cheese yields a luxurious, creamy sauce when melted. When shopping, look for Gorgonzola dolce (sweet Gorgonzola), or simply shop by texture. If the cheese looks creamy enough to spread on bread, it should have a pleasant but not overpowering blue cheese flavor.

MASCARPONE This creamy Italian cheese is now made on both sides of the Atlantic. It is generally sold in tubs and has a consistency similar to cream cheese beaten with a little heavy cream. Unlike American cream cheese, mascarpone is not tangy and, in fact, it has a buttery, creamy flavor. Although there is no substitute for mascarpone, we find that American versions of this cheese are admirable and work as well as Italian mascarpone in recipes.

MOZZARELLA The two types of mozzarella do not taste alike, and they perform quite differently in the kitchen. Shrink-wrapped mozzarella is fine for pizzas. It melts beautifully, and no one notices how bland this cheese is when covered with pepperoni and tomato sauce. However, in simple salads, we prefer fresh mozzarella packed in water. This cheese has a milky, sometimes floral flavor and moist, appealing texture. For more information about mozzarella, see page 373.

PARMESAN When shopping, look for the words Parmigiano-Reggiano stenciled on the rind. Expect to pay at least $10 a pound for this cheese. If the price is less, you are not buying the real thing. For more information about Parmesan, see page 25.

PECORINO ROMANO This bone-white cheese has an intense peppery flavor and a strong sheepy quality. Pecorino is best in dishes with assertive ingredients like capers, olives, or hot red pepper flakes. It is traditionally made from sheep's milk, although some manufacturers add some cow's milk to reduce the pungency and/or save money. In Italy, Pecorino is often sold fresh or lightly aged and served as an eating cheese. (These young Pecorinos are not widely known elsewhere.) Most of the Pecorino that is exported has been aged much longer. Like Parmesan, it is designed for grating, but it has a much saltier and more pungent flavor.

Most of the exported Pecorino is from the Rome area, hence the name Pecorino Romano. (Pecorino cheeses are also made in Sardinia, Sicily, and Tuscany.) As is the case with Parmigiano-Reggiano, the words Pecorino Romano are stenciled on the rind to make shopping for the authentic product easy. Many American-made Pecorinos taste of salt and nothing else and should be avoided.

RICOTTA Good ricotta is creamy and thick, not watery and curdish like so many supermarket brands sold in plastic containers. In Italy, local cheesemakers produce fresh ricotta with a dry, firm consistency (akin to goat cheese). The flavor is sweet and milky. This cheese is so perishable that it is rarely exported. In the United States, however, locally made fresh ricotta is available in and near urban centers with large Italian-American populations. This cheese shares many qualities with the Italian version. You can use supermarket ricotta cheese, but it tastes bland by comparison.

RICOTTA SALATA Fresh ricotta cheese is salted and pressed to make this firm but crumbly cheese with a texture that is similar to feta but a flavor that is milder and far less salty. Ricotta salata is pleasingly piquant, although it is milder than Pecorino. This cheese is generally shredded and used like mozzarella in baked pasta dishes or tossed with hot pasta when a sharper, saltier cheese flavor is desired.

The following recipes highlight some of our favorite cheeses in basic antipasti.

Warm Figs with Goat Cheese and Honey

MAKES 16 PIECES,
ENOUGH TO SERVE 4 TO 6

The figs should be baked briefly—just long enough to soften the cheese and warm the figs.

16	walnut halves (about ½ cup)
1	tablespoon brown sugar
⅛	teaspoon salt
⅛	teaspoon ground cinnamon
1½	ounces goat cheese (about 3 tablespoons)
8	fresh figs, halved lengthwise
2	tablespoons honey

1. Combine the walnuts, brown sugar, salt, and cinnamon in a small, heavy-bottomed skillet. Cook over medium-high heat until the sugar melts and coats the nuts evenly, about 3 minutes. Remove the nuts from the pan, separating them from each other. Cool.

2. Adjust the oven rack to the middle position and heat the oven to 500 degrees. Spoon a heaping ½ teaspoon goat cheese onto each fig half and place on a parchment-lined rimmed baking sheet. Bake the figs for 4 minutes. Transfer the warm figs to a serving platter.

3. Place a candied walnut half on each fig half and drizzle the honey over the figs. Serve immediately.

INGREDIENTS: Parmesan Cheese

When it comes to grated Parmesan cheese, there's a wide range of options—everything from the whitish powder in green jars to imported cheese that costs $14 a pound. You can buy cheese that has been grated, or you can pick out a whole hunk and grate it yourself. We wondered if "authentic" Parmigiano-Reggiano would be that much better when tasted side by side with a domestic Parmesan at half the price.

The samples in a tasting conducted in our test kitchen included five pregrated Parmesan cheeses (domestic and imported), three wedges of domestic Parmesan, a wedge of Grana Padano (from Italy), one of Reggianito (from Argentina), and two of Parmigiano-Reggiano. To see if differences in store handling could affect the quality of the latter two, one was purchased at a specialty cheese store that cuts from the wheel per order and has controlled humidity; the other was purchased precut and wrapped in plastic at a large supermarket. All of the cheeses were tasted grated, at room temperature.

To get an idea of what the tasters should look for when tasting the different cheeses, we spoke to a number of cheese experts. All recommended that the tasters rate cheeses on the basics: aroma, flavor (particularly depth of flavor and saltiness versus sweetness), and overall texture. The Parmesans should also be left to sit on the tasters' tongues to see if they melt smoothly into creaminess in the mouth. All of the experts we spoke to expressed confidence that Parmigiano-Reggiano would be the hands-down winner.

This time the experts were correct. Parmigiano-Reggiano had a depth and complexity of flavor and a smooth, melting texture that none of the others could match. Parmigiano-Reggiano owes much of its flavor to the unpasteurized milk used to produce it. It is a controlled-district cheese, which means not only that it must be made within the boundaries of a defined geographic zone but also that the milk used to make it and even the grass, hay, and grain fed to the cows that make the milk must come from the district. Consequently, just like good wine, a lot of character comes from the soil and climate where it was made. We found that none of the other cheeses had the sweet, nutty, creamy flavor of Parmigiano-Reggiano.

We found almost all of the cheeses in the tasting—except the Parmigiano-Reggiano—to be extremely salty. In fact, Parmigiano-Reggiano contains about two-thirds less sodium than the other Parmesans. This is because wheels of Parmigiano-Reggiano are so large that they do not become as saturated with salt during the brining process that is one of the final steps in making the cheese. (The average wheel weighs 75 to 90 pounds; domestic Parmesan wheels average 24 pounds.)

The lower salt content of Parmigiano-Reggiano makes it more perishable, once cut from the wheel, than the other cheeses. Once cut, the cheese also begins to dry out. This was evident in the Parmigiano-Reggiano sample purchased at the grocery store. Tasters rated this a few tenths of a point lower than the sample purchased at the specialty cheese store because of a chalky finish. The drying effect was even more glaring with the chalky pregrated products, which received consistently poor ratings.

Another benefit of the larger wheel is that Parmigiano-Reggiano can age longer. Parmigiano-Reggiano ages for about 24 months, while domestic Parmesan ages for about 10 months. The longer aging allows more complex flavors and aromas to develop. The aging also makes a difference in texture, creating a distinctive component that tasters described as "crystal crunch." The crunch stems from proteins breaking down into free amino acid crystals during the latter half of the aging process. The crystals are visible, appearing as white dots in the cheese. No other Parmesan had this effect.

Other textural differences are the result of the curds for Parmigiano-Reggiano being cut into fragments the size of wheat grains, much finer than the fragments created in the manufacture of domestic Parmesan. The benefit of smaller curds is that they drain more effectively. Domestic Parmesans have to be mechanically pressed to get rid of excess moisture. The consequence, as our tasting panel discovered with the domestic Parmesans that were not pregrated, is a cheese that is much more dense. Tasters characterized it as "rubbery," "tough," and "squeaky."

Dates Stuffed with Parmesan

MAKES 16 PIECES,
ENOUGH TO SERVE 4 TO 6

Use high-quality dates (such as Medjools) and only the finest Parmigiano-Reggiano in this antipasto. See page 25 for tips on buying Parmesan.

16	large pitted dates
1	piece (3 ounces) Parmesan cheese
16	walnut halves, toasted

1. Slit the dates lengthwise with a paring knife.

2. Following the illustrations below, cut the cheese into thin shards about 1 inch long. Place a piece of cheese and one walnut half in each date and close the date around the cheese to seal. Place the dates on a platter

CUTTING PARMESAN INTO SHARDS

1. Use a chef's knife to remove the rind from a square block of Parmesan cheese. Cut the trimmed block in half on the diagonal.

2. Lay each half on its cut side and slice the cheese into thin triangles, about 1/16 inch wide. These thin shards should be about the size of a date.

and serve. (The stuffed dates can be wrapped in plastic and kept at room temperature for several hours.)

Marinated Goat Cheese

SERVES 4

The garlic should be broken down into a fine puree for this recipe. After you mince it, sprinkle the garlic with salt, mash the garlic-salt mixture with the side of a chef's knife, and then continue to mince until the garlic forms a smooth puree (see illustration on page 137). Serve with bread or crackers.

1	log (8 ounces) goat cheese
1/4	cup extra-virgin olive oil
3/4	teaspoon chopped fresh thyme leaves
3/4	teaspoon minced fresh chives
1/4	teaspoon minced fresh rosemary leaves
1	small clove garlic, minced and then worked into a puree with 1/8 teaspoon salt
	Ground black pepper

1. Use a piece of dental floss to cut the cheese crosswise into slices 1/3 inch thick. Place the goat cheese slices on a small platter.

2. Whisk together the oil, thyme, chives, rosemary, garlic-salt puree, and pepper to taste in a small bowl. Pour the oil mixture over the cheese. Serve immediately or cover and refrigerate for up to 1 day.

Broiled Mozzarella and Sun-Dried Tomato Skewers

MAKES 24 SKEWERS

Use dried, loose tomatoes, not those packed in oil, for this recipe.

| 48 | large sun-dried tomatoes (about 3 ounces) |
| 1 | pound fresh mozzarella, cut into 1-inch cubes (about 48 pieces) |

3   tablespoons extra-virgin olive oil

1 ½   teaspoons salt

     Ground black pepper

48   small fresh basil leaves

1. Adjust the oven rack so it is about 6 inches from the broiler. Heat the broiler.

2. Mix the tomatoes with 2 cups hot tap water in a medium microwave-safe bowl. Cover with plastic wrap, cut several steam vents in the plastic wrap with a paring knife, and microwave on high power for 2 minutes. Let stand, covered, until the tomatoes soften, about 5 minutes. Lift the tomatoes from the liquid with a fork and pat dry on paper towels.

3. Meanwhile, toss the mozzarella with the oil, salt, and pepper to taste in a medium bowl. Using 24 short bamboo or wooden skewers, thread a piece of mozzarella, a basil leaf, and a tomato (in that order) onto each skewer; repeat with a second piece of mozzarella, basil leaf, and tomato. Brush the skewers with any oil remaining in the bowl.

4. Line the bottom of a broiler pan with foil and coat the broiler pan rack with

MAKING BROILED MOZZARELLA SKEWERS

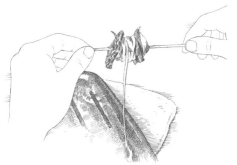

The cheese melts slightly under the broiler. Once the skewers have cooled for about 30 seconds, pick up one at a time and spin it gently in your fingers to wrap any strings of melted cheese back around the skewer.

cooking spray. Place 12 skewers on the broiler pan rack. Broil the skewers, turning once, until the cheese begins to melt, about 2 minutes. Remove from the oven and let rest for 30 seconds. Pick up each skewer, twirl any melted cheese around it (see the illustration below), and serve immediately. Repeat with the remaining skewers.

FRICO

FRICO IS PROBABLY THE SIMPLEST AND most addictive snack you'll ever eat. It is a thin, golden, flavorful cheese crisp. Classically made from a cheese called Montasio, this snack hails from the region of Fruili in northern Italy. It is nothing more than grated cheese sprinkled into a pan, melted, and then browned to form a crisp wafer. When made well, frico is light and airy, with a heavenly and intense cheese flavor. More often than not, however, it turns out chewy, bitter, and overly salty. Wondering what the key to this one-ingredient wonder was, we set out to make the perfect frico.

Although most of the recipes we researched were similar, we did encounter minor differences in technique. Some recipes call for a regular skillet and butter, while others call for olive oil and a well-seasoned cast-iron pan. After making a few rounds in the test kitchen, we found it easiest to use a 10-inch nonstick skillet. The nonstick surface repels any fat released from the melting cheese, which ensures a smooth and effortless release without the use of butter or olive oil.

After making and eating a few rounds of frico, we picked up a few more tips for success. First, we discovered an easy way to flip the frico over midway through its cooking process to brown the second side. After the first side browned, we simply removed the pan from the heat for several seconds to cool. As the cheese wafer began to cool and set up, it was easy to flip without tearing or stretching. We then quickly returned the pan to the heat and continued to brown the frico on the second side.

Using the right level of heat is also essential. If the pan is too hot, the cheese cooks too fast and turns bitter. But when cooked slowly over low heat, the cheese dries out, becomes crunchy and doesn't turn a beautiful, golden color. We

MAKING FRICO

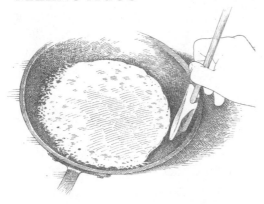

1. After sprinkling the cheese into the skillet, use a heat-resistant spatula or wooden spoon to gently push the scattered shreds of cheese around the edges inward to form a tidy rim.

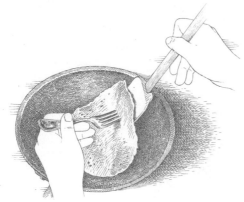

2. Once the first side is browned, remove the pan from the heat and let cool for 30 seconds so the frico firms slightly. Using a fork and a heatproof spatula, carefully flip the cheese wafer over and return the pan to medium heat to cook the second side.

found it necessary to adjust the heat between medium-high and medium between flips.

Last, we tried using a variety of cheeses other than Montasio, which can be difficult to find in the United States. Many recipes we found called for Parmesan; however, we found aged Asiago a more appropriate substitution. When tasted side by side, the frico made with Parmesan was salty and harsh while the frico made with aged Asiago was smooth and clean. But for the ultimate frico, with a deep, complex flavor that is neither too bitter nor too salty, a good hunk of Montasio is worth tracking down.

Frico

MAKES 8 LARGE WAFERS

Serve frico with drinks and a bowl of marinated olives or marinated sun-dried tomatoes.

I   **pound Montasio or aged Asiago cheese, finely grated**

Sprinkle 2 ounces (about ½ cup) shredded cheese over the bottom of an 10-inch non-stick skillet set over medium-high heat. Use a heat-resistant rubber spatula or wooden spoon to tidy the lacy outer edges of the cheese (see illustration 1, left). Cook, shaking the pan occasionally to ensure an even distribution of the cheese over the pan bottom, until the edges are lacy and toasted, about 4 minutes. Remove the pan from heat and allow the cheese to set for about 30 seconds. Using a fork and a heatproof spatula (see illustration 2, left), carefully flip the cheese wafer over and return the pan to medium heat. Cook until the second side is golden brown, about 2 minutes. Slide the cheese wafer out of the pan and transfer to a plate. Repeat with the remaining cheese. Serve the frico within 1 hour.

2

SALADS

MANY ITALIAN SALADS COME TO THE table at room temperature, moistened and flavored with a little olive oil and vinegar. These salads range from the conventional leafy greens to more exotic and unusual mixtures made with fennel, oranges, and olives, or perhaps tuna and white beans.

Depending on their heft, Italian salads show at various times during the meal. Leafy salads are generally served after the main course as a palate cleanser. That said, Americans will probably want to eat these salads before the main course, as is our custom, and that's perfectly fine.

Heartier salads made from rice, bread, or pasta often are part of a light summer meal or can be a meal on their own. For instance, a small portion of pasta salad can be served alongside grilled chicken or fish, or it can be served on a bed of greens for lunch.

SALAD DRESSING

WHAT DO SALADS MADE WITH LEAFY greens have in common with pasta salad and seafood? The answer is dressing. When it comes to Italian cooking, dressing means olive oil, vinegar, salt, and pepper. In Italy, most cooks simply drizzle the vinegar and oil over the food to be dressed (including salad greens), add salt and pepper, toss, and taste.

In the United States, we are more likely to turn these ingredients into a vinaigrette, a relatively thin emulsion made of oil, vinegar, and seasonings. An emulsion is a mixture of two things that don't ordinarily mix, such as oil and water or oil and vinegar. The only way to mix them is to stir or whisk so strenuously that the two ingredients break down into tiny droplets. Many of these droplets will continue to find each other and recoalesce into pure fluid. (This is what happens when the emulsion breaks.) Eventually, one of the fluids (usually the less plentiful one) will break entirely into droplets so tiny that they remain separated by the opposite fluid, at least temporarily.

The liquid in the droplet form is called the dispersed phase (vinegar in a vinaigrette) because the droplets are dispersed throughout the emulsion. The liquid that surrounds the droplets is the continuous phase (oil in a vinaigrette). Because the continuous phase forms the surface of the emulsion, that's what the mouth and tongue feel and taste first.

Italians commonly dress a salad with vinegar and then oil, but the results are quite different when these ingredients are combined before being poured over greens. To demonstrate this difference, try this test. Dress a simple green salad first with oil, then a mixture of vinegar, salt, and pepper. The result will be harsh, with an extremely prominent vinegar bite. If you are using a particularly good vinegar, you may like this approach.

Next, take another batch of greens and the same dressing ingredients. Mix the salt and pepper into the vinegar and then whisk in the oil until the dressing is translucent. When this emulsified dressing is poured over greens, the flavor will be smoother, with a greater emphasis on the oil. We find that most Americans prefer the smoother flavors of this method and have adopted this non-Italian custom in many recipes. You can opt to follow the Italian method and simply drizzle salad ingredients with oil and vinegar, season with salt and pepper, and toss.

The science of emulsions explains why the same ingredients can taste so different. In the first-oil-then-vinegar salad, the oil and vinegar don't mix, so both race up the tongue. The less viscous vinegar wins, hence this salad tastes more acidic. In the emulsion, the oil is whipped into tiny molecules that surround dispersed droplets of vinegar. The oil is the continuous phase and is tasted first. Your tongue is coated with fat droplets that cushion the impact of the acid.

The correct ratio of oil to vinegar is open to much discussion and can depend on the acidity of the vinegar as well as the flavor of the oil. In general, we prefer a ratio of 4 parts oil to 1 part acid, but this can vary, especially when using citrus juices, which are much less acidic than common vinegars.

To form a vinaigrette, use either a fork or small whisk to generate the whipping action necessary to disperse the oil and vinegar in small droplets. (You can also shake all the ingredients together in a sealed jar.) With either tool, the emulsion will break rather quickly, so rewhisk the dressing just before pouring it over salad greens. We found that adding the salt and pepper to the vinegar is best, because the vinegar mutes these flavors a bit and prevents them from overpowering the salad. On the other hand, we prefer to add herbs and some other seasonings to the finished dressing to maximize their impact.

INGREDIENTS: Common Oils and Vinegars

The following oils and vinegars are used in recipes throughout this book. To keep oils from becoming rancid, store bottles in a cool, dark pantry and buy small quantities that will be used within a few months. Storing oils in the refrigerator will prolong their freshness.

EXTRA-VIRGIN OLIVE OIL This is the gold standard for most Italian salads. In blind tastings, we could not tell the difference between extra-virgin oils that cost $10 per liter and that cost $80 per liter. However, cheaper pure and "light" oils are characterless and decidedly inferior in salads, although they may be fine for some cooking. For more information about supermarket extra-virgin olive oils, see page 33.

WALNUT OIL This oil has a warm, nutty flavor that works well in salads with fruits and/or toasted nuts. Like other nut oils, walnut oil tends to go rancid quickly and is best stored in the refrigerator.

CANOLA OIL This bland oil is best used to soften a particularly strong oil, especially walnut. Alone, its flavor is unremarkable, but in combination with a potent nut oil, canola can be part of a good dressing.

RED WINE VINEGAR Red wine vinegar is the most versatile choice in salads. Its flavor is sharp but clean. The acidity of domestic brands is usually around 5 percent, while that of imported brands is often as much as 7 percent. In our tasting of red wine vinegars, Heinz beat other domestic brands as well as imports, some of which cost 10 times as much.

WHITE WINE VINEGAR This vinegar is similar to red wine vinegar but is often not quite as complex. It is our choice when a pink vinaigrette made with red wine vinegar might seem odd.

BALSAMIC VINEGAR This rich, sweet, oaky vinegar is best used in combination with red wine vinegar in salads. Real balsamic vinegar is aged at least a dozen years and can cost $50 an ounce. Cheaper supermarket versions vary tremendously in quality. Some are nothing more than caramel-colored red wine vinegar. Others follow the traditional process (unfermented white grape juice, called must, is fermented in wood casks) but cut back on the aging time. Our advice is to avoid products with artificial colors and flavors; they were deemed harsh and unpleasant in our tasting of leading brands. It's usually a good sign if the word "must" appears on the label. For more information on balsamic vinegar, see page 36.

CITRUS JUICES Orange and lemon juices can be used in salad dressing. They add acidity (although not as much as most vinegars) as well as flavor. Lemon juice is more acidic and can stand on its own. Orange juice is usually combined with vinegar. To add more citrus flavor without disturbing the ratio of acid to oil, stir in some grated zest.

Master Recipe for Vinaigrette

MAKES ABOUT ½ CUP, ENOUGH TO DRESS 4 QUARTS (8 SERVINGS) SALAD GREENS

Salt and pepper are mixed first with the vinegar for subtlety. If you like, you can adjust the seasonings after the salad has been dressed by sprinkling additional salt and/or pepper directly onto the greens. Extra dressing can be refrigerated for several days. Variations that contain fresh herbs should be used within several hours for maximum freshness.

1½	tablespoons red wine vinegar
¼	teaspoon salt
⅛	teaspoon ground black pepper
6	tablespoons extra-virgin olive oil

Combine the vinegar, salt, and pepper in a bowl with a fork. Add the oil, then whisk or mix with a fork until smooth, about 30 seconds. The dressing will separate after 5 to 10 minutes, so use it immediately or cover and refrigerate for several days and mix again before tossing with greens.

➤ VARIATIONS

Mediterranean Vinaigrette

Follow the recipe for Vinaigrette, replacing the vinegar with 2¼ teaspoons lemon juice, increasing the pepper to ¼ teaspoon, and decreasing the oil to 4 tablespoons. Whisk 1 tablespoon drained and minced capers, 1 tablespoon minced fresh parsley leaves, 1 teaspoon minced fresh thyme leaves, and 1 medium garlic clove, minced fine, into the finished dressing.

Balsamic Vinaigrette

Follow the recipe for Vinaigrette, reducing the red wine vinegar to 1½ teaspoons and combining it with 1½ tablespoons balsamic vinegar.

Mixed Herb Vinaigrette

Follow the recipe for Vinaigrette, adding 1 tablespoon minced fresh basil leaves, 1½ teaspoons minced fresh parsley leaves, and 1 teaspoon minced fresh oregano leaves to the finished dressing. Use the dressing within several hours for optimal freshness.

LEAFY SALADS

LEAFY SALADS START WITH GREENS OF some sort. Most greens have a short shelf life, so it's especially important to buy specimens that look healthy at the market. Greens with stems and roots will stay fresher longer and should be purchased over cut greens when possible. Also, look for rot among bunches as you shop. Decay can spread quickly, so it's best to avoid greens on which this process has already begun. If you get greens home and notice a few slimy leaves, pick them out immediately rather than waiting until you make salad. If you wait, the rot may well spread throughout the bunch.

Because they are mostly water, greens should be stored in the crisper drawer of the refrigerator, where the humidity is the

USING A SALAD SPINNER

Place the salad spinner in the corner of your sink. This increases your leverage by lowering the height of the crank. The extra leverage also acts to push the spinner down to the sink floor and into the sink walls, thereby stabilizing it.

INGREDIENTS: Supermarket Extra-Virgin Olive Oils

When you purchase an artisanal oil in a high-end shop, certain informational perks are expected (and paid for). These typically include written explanations of the character and nuances of the particular oil as well as the assistance of knowledgeable staff. But in a supermarket, it's just you and a price tag. How do you know which supermarket extra-virgin oil best suits your needs? To provide some guidance, we decided to hold a blind tasting of the nine best-selling extra-virgin oils typically available in American supermarkets.

The label extra-virgin denotes the highest quality of olive oil, with the most delicate and prized flavor. (The three other grades are virgin, pure, and olive pomace. Pure oil, often labeled simply olive oil, is the most commonly available.) To be tagged as extra-virgin, an oil must meet three basic criteria. First, it must contain less than I percent oleic free fatty acids per 100 grams of oil. Second, the oil must not have been treated with any solvents or heat. (Heat is used to reduce strong acidity in some nonvirgin olive oils to make them palatable. This is where the term cold pressed comes into play, meaning that the olives are pressed into a paste using mechanical wheels or hammers and are then kneaded to separate the oil from the fruit.) Third, it must pass taste and aroma standards as defined by groups such as the International Olive Oil Council (IOOC), a Madrid-based intergovernmental olive oil regulatory committee that sets the bar for its member countries.

Tasting extra-virgin olive oil is much like tasting wine. The flavors of these oils range from citrusy to herbal, musty to floral, with every possibility in between. And what one taster finds particularly attractive—a slight briny flavor, for example—another might find unappealing. Also like wine, the flavor of a particular brand of olive oil can change from year to year, depending on the quality of the harvest and the olives' place of origin.

We chose to taste extra-virgin olive oil in its most pure and unadulterated state: raw. Tasters were given the option of sampling the oil from a spoon or on neutral-flavored French bread and were asked to eat a slice of green apple—for its acidity—to cleanse the palate between oils. The olive oils were evaluated for color, clarity, viscosity, bouquet, depth of flavor, and lingering of flavor.

Whereas in a typical tasting we are able to identify a clear winner and loser, in this case we could not. In fact, the panel seemed to quickly divide itself into those who liked a gutsy olive oil with bold flavor and those who preferred a milder, more mellow approach. Nonetheless, in both camps one oil clearly had more of a following than any other—the all-Italian-olive Davinci brand. Praised for its rounded and buttery flavor, it was the only olive oil we tasted that seemed to garner across-the-board approval with olive oil experts and in-house staff alike. Among tasters who preferred full-bodied, bold oils, Colavita and Filippo Berio also earned high marks. Tasters in the mild and delicate camp gave high scores to Pompeian and Whole Foods oils.

THE BEST ALL-PURPOSE OIL
Davinci Extra-Virgin Olive Oil was the favorite in our tasting of leading supermarket brands. It was described as "very ripe," "buttery," and "complex."

THE BEST MILD OIL
Pompeian Extra-Virgin Olive Oil was the favorite among tasters who preferred a milder, more delicate oil. It was described as "clean," "round," and "sunny."

THE BEST FULL-BODIED OIL
Colavita Extra-Virgin Olive Oil was the favorite among tasters who preferred a bolder oil. It was described as "heavy," "complex," and "briny."

highest. Moist air will help prolong their freshness, however excessive amounts of water won't.

Because they grow so close to the ground, salad greens are often quite sandy. Thorough washing in a deep bowl or sink filled with cold water is a must. Swish the greens in the water to loosen any sand. Once the bottom of the bowl is free of grit (you may need to drain the bowl and add clean water several times), dry the greens in a salad spinner and then use paper or kitchen towels to blot off any remaining moisture. It's imperative to remove all visible moisture. Dressing will slide off damp greens and pool at the bottom of the salad bowl. Washed and dried greens can be refrigerated in a dry zipper-lock bag for several days.

While whole leaves can be washed and dried in advance, do not tear lettuce until ready to dress the salad. Tearing the leaves leads to oxidation and browning. This process happens quite quickly in delicate greens, such as arugula, but can take several hours in tougher greens like romaine. Whatever you do, don't take a knife to salad greens. The more violently they are cut, the quicker they will brown. Gently tearing large leaves by hand is best.

Nothing is worse than a limp, soggy salad with too much dressing. Dressed greens should glisten. We find that ¼ cup vinaigrette is sufficient to dress 2 quarts salad greens, enough for four servings. We lightly pack a 4-cup plastic measure to portion out greens.

Once a leafy salad is dressed, the clock is ticking. Waiting even 15 minutes to eat the salad may cause some loss in freshness and crispness. The longer salad greens sit under a coating of dressing, the less appetizing they become, as the salt in the dressing draws moisture out of the greens and causes them to become limp.

ADDING MILD GARLIC FLAVOR TO SALADS

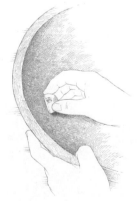

For salads where only the mildest hint of garlic is desired (and there's no garlic in the dressing), rubbing the bowl with a cut garlic clove does the trick. The oils released from the clove impart a subtle bite and aroma as the greens are tossed. Peel and cut a clove of garlic. With the cut side down, rub the interior of your salad bowl.

INSALATA MISTA

ITALIANS EAT SALAD AFTER THE MAIN course, just before dessert. Used as a palate cleanser and digestive aid, an *insalata mista* (Italian green salad) is usually spicy and robust, containing several varieties of greens dressed with a small amount of simple vinaigrette. To recreate this type of salad at home, we found it easiest to group lettuce types into three groups: mild, spicy, and bitter. Because of its even balance of mild greens and spicy and bitter greens, the salad is refreshingly vigorous without being overly harsh.

Far from the bottles of "Italian" dressing sold at the supermarket, an authentic dressing for an insalata mista should be simple and fresh. Most recipes contain only extra-virgin olive oil, red wine vinegar, and salt, but we liked the sweet, complex addition of balsamic vinegar as well. By using a 4 to 1 ratio of oil to vinegar, we were able to make a dressing with good balance and flavor.

Insalata Mista

SERVES 4 TO 6

This is your basic Italian leafy salad. Carrot, cucumber, and red onion add nice color and contrasting texture to the greens.

1 ½	teaspoons red wine vinegar
1 ½	teaspoons balsamic vinegar
⅛	teaspoon salt
4	tablespoons extra-virgin olive oil
4	cups mild greens (Bibb, green leaf, red oak, baby romaine), washed and dried
2	cups spicy greens (arugula or watercress), washed and dried
2	cups bitter greens (radicchio or endive), washed and dried
1	medium carrot, peeled and shredded on the large holes of a box grater
½	cucumber, peeled, halved, seeded, cut crosswise into ⅛-inch slices
¼	medium red onion, sliced very thin

1. Whisk the vinegars and salt together in small bowl. Whisk in the oil until the mixture is smooth.

2. Place the greens, carrot, cucumber, and red onion in a large bowl. Drizzle with the dressing and toss gently. Serve immediately.

BITTER GREEN SALAD WITH CITRUS

THE COMBINATION OF BITTER ENDIVE and spicy watercress is commonly used as a backdrop for pieces of fresh orange and grapefruit. This salad is especially refreshing and light, making it an excellent bridge between the main course and dessert.

Many recipes call for bits of minced red onion, which often seem harsh in salads with other strong flavors. Several sources we consulted suggested that soaking the minced onion in vinegar would tame its bite. Sure enough, after 30 minutes in the vinegar, the onion was sweeter and not as harsh.

Many leafy Italian salads are garnished with Parmesan shavings. The cheese works particularly well with the citrus in this recipe.

SECTIONING AN ORANGE OR GRAPEFRUIT

1. Start by slicing a ½-inch piece from the top and bottom of the fruit.

2. With the fruit resting flat against a work surface, use a sharp paring knife to slice off the rind, including all of the bitter white pith. Slide the knife edge from top to bottom of the fruit and try to follow the outline of the fruit as closely as possible.

3. Working over a bowl to catch the juice, slip the blade between a membrane and one section and slice to the center, separating one side of the section.

4. Turn the blade of the knife so that it is facing out and is lined up along the membrane on the opposite side of the section. Slide the blade from the center out along the membrane to completely free the section. Continue until all the sections are done.

INGREDIENTS: Balsamic Vinegar

You can buy a decent bottle of nonvintage French table wine for $8, or you can invest in a bottle of 1975 Château Lafite Rothschild Bordeaux for $300—but no one would ever compare the two. They are two different beasts. The same holds true for balsamic vinegars. There are balsamic vinegars you can buy for $2.50 and ones that nudge the $300 mark. The more expensive vinegars bear the title tradizionale or extra-vecchio tradizionale aceto balsamico (traditional or extra-old traditional). According to Italian law, these traditional vinegars must come from the northern Italian provinces of Modena or Reggio Emilia and be created and aged in the time-honored fashion.

Unfortunately, American consumers cannot really be sure that the industrial-style balsamic vinegar they purchase in their grocery or specialty foods store is a high-quality product. Unlike the makers of trademark-protected products of Italy, including tradizionale balsamico, Parmigiano-Reggiano, and Prosciutto di Parma (all from the Reggio Emilia region), Italian producers of commercial balsamic vinegars failed to unite before market demand for their products ballooned in the United States in the early 1980s. The result has been high consumer demand with little U.S. regulation—the perfect scenario for producers who take advantage of the system by misleading consumers about the integrity of their products.

For hundreds of years, tradizionale balsamico vinegar has been made from Trebbiano grapes grown in the Modena or Reggio Emilia regions of northern Italy. The grapes are crushed and slowly cooked into must over an open flame. The must begins mellowing in a large wooden barrel, where it ferments and turns to vinegar. The vinegar is then passed through a series of barrels made from a variety of woods. To be considered worthy of the tradizionale balsamico title, the vinegar must be moved from barrel to barrel for a minimum of 12 years. An extra-vecchio vinegar must be aged for at least 25 years.

Because of its complex flavor and high production cost, tradizionale balsamico is used by those in the know as a condiment rather than an ingredient. The longer the vinegar ages, the thicker and more intense it becomes, maturing from a thin liquid into a spoon-coating, syrupy one—perfect for topping strawberries or cantaloupe. This is the aristocrat of balsamic vinegars.

The more common varieties, those with a price tag under $30, are categorized as commercial or industrial balsamic vinegars. These vinegars are the kind with which most Americans are familiar and are often used to complete a vinaigrette or flavor a sauce. The flavor profile of commercial balsamic vinegars ranges widely from mild, woody, and herbaceous to artificial and sour, depending on the producer and the style in which the vinegar was made. Commercial balsamic vinegar may or may not be aged and may or may not contain artificial caramel color or flavor.

We wondered how bad—or good—inexpensive commercial balsamic vinegars would be when compared in a blind tasting. To level the playing field—and ease the burden on our budget—we limited the tasting to balsamic vinegars that cost $15 and under. We included some vinegars from supermarkets (we held a preliminary supermarket balsamic vinegar tasting and included the three most favored by our tasters in the final tasting) and some from mail-order sources and specialty foods stores. We also included samples of the many production styles, including some aged in the traditional fashion, some with added caramel color and flavor, and some made from a blend of aged red wine vinegar and grape must.

We found that a higher price tag did not correlate with a better vinegar. In addition, age seemed to play a less important role than we had expected. There were young vinegars among the winners as well as older vinegars among the losers.

Across the board, tasters found balsamic vinegars containing caramel color or flavor "sour" and "uninteresting." The top brands from our tasting contain no artificial colors or flavors whatsoever. Our findings led us to believe that much as fond (the browned bits left in a pan after food has been sautéed) is instrumental in creating a high-quality pan sauce, must is paramount to making a full-flavored balsamic vinegar. As the must ages, it becomes thick and sweet, contributing a character almost like sherry or port. Producers who substitute artificial color and flavor for must end up with a shallow product that was routinely derided by our tasters. Some connoisseurs might argue that the only balsamic vinegars worth buying are aged ones, but we found that age didn't make nearly as big a difference as did artificial additives.

So how can consumers figure out what type of balsamic vinegar to buy? The easy answer is to check the label. If it discloses that artificial ingredients have been added, don't buy it. Unfortunately, it's not only commonplace but legal for the ingredient label to skirt the issue and completely avoid publishing the contents of the vinegar. This is because Italian law dictates that "Balsamic Vinegar of Modena," which is how 9 out of 10 vinegars are labeled, is itself an ingredient and product, so no further description of the vinegar's contents is required. Label specifications from the U.S. Food and Drug Administration require only that the producer identify whether or not the vinegar

contains sulfites, a preservative that produces a severe allergic reaction in some people.

"Whatever you want to call a balsamic vinegar, you can call a balsamic vinegar," says John Jack, vice president of sales and marketing for Fiorucci Foods in Virginia. "It's become very much of a commodity-oriented business." Even if a vinegar is labeled "Balsamic Vinegar of Modena," a title that conveys the idea of quality to consumers, it may not have been produced in, or even near, Modena. In fact, several manufacturers bottle their vinegar right here in the United States. Young vinegars can bear the balsamic title, too. As a result of the less-than-stringent regulations, many producers and importers look forward to the passage of a new regulation in Italy that would make it illegal to label a vinegar younger than three years balsamic.

For now, check the label. If the vinegar contains artificial color or sweetener, keep looking.

THE BEST INEXPENSIVE BALSAMIC VINEGARS

365 Every Day Value Balsamic Vinegar of Modena is started from must and is a blend of older (up to five years) and younger balsamic vinegars. Tasters loved its vanilla, fruit, and caramel underpinnings as well as its "balanced acidity."

Masserie Di Sant'Eramo Balsamic Vinegar of Modena is started from must and aged a minimum of five years. Our tasters liked the fruit and honey notes as well as its "balanced spice and acidity." One taster called it "demure" and "floral."

Fiorucci Riserva Balsamic Vinegar of Modena is a mixture of aged wine vinegar and must that is aged an additional six years. Described as "mellow" and "tangy-sweet" in flavor, this vinegar reminded some tasters of plums and apples.

Bitter Green Salad with Citrus and Parmesan

SERVES 4

The term "sectioned" refers to the process by which individual pieces of citrus fruit are separated from the tough membranes that divide them. See the illustrations on page 35.

½	small red onion, minced
2	tablespoons red wine vinegar
⅓	cup extra-virgin olive oil
	Salt and ground black pepper
4	cups watercress, washed, stemmed, and dried
2	heads Belgian endive, leaves separated and cut into 2-inch pieces
1	large orange, peeled and sectioned, juices reserved
1	large grapefruit, peeled and sectioned, juices reserved
2	tablespoons chopped fresh parsley leaves
12	shavings Parmesan cheese (see illustration on page 41)

1. Mix the onion and vinegar in a small bowl and let stand for 30 minutes. Whisk in the oil and season with salt and pepper to taste.

2. Mix the watercress and endive in a medium bowl. Add the fruit and juices, onion mixture, and parsley and toss to coat. Divide the salad among four plates. Garnish each portion with 3 cheese shavings. Serve immediately.

ARUGULA SALAD WITH PEARS, WALNUTS, AND GORGONZOLA

SPICY ARUGULA IS PERHAPS ITALY'S best-known salad green. Because of its punch, arugula is commonly served with sweet elements (such as ripe pear) as well as toasted walnuts and mild Gorgonzola cheese. This rich salad works well as a first course (as long as the meal doesn't contain much cheese). It also can be served after the main course.

Although this salad is often dressed with olive and lemon juice, we wondered if walnut oil would add another layer of nut flavor. We tried replacing the olive oil with walnut oil, and the nut flavor was too intense. We then tried a blend of olive and walnut oils, but tasters felt that the olive oil flavor competed with the walnut oil. In the end, a blend of walnut oil and neutral-tasting canola oil worked well. The nut flavor was strong but not overpowering.

Arugula Salad with Pears, Walnuts, and Gorgonzola

SERVES 4

Watercress can stand in for the arugula. Use a mild Gorgonzola dolce if possible. Take the time to toast the nuts; it makes them more flavorful. To toast walnuts, heat them in a dry skillet over medium heat, shaking the pan occasionally, until fragrant, about 5 minutes.

2	large, ripe but firm red pears, each halved, cored, and cut into 12 wedges
3	tablespoons lemon juice
¼	teaspoon salt
	Ground black pepper
4	tablespoons canola oil
2	tablespoons walnut oil
6	cups arugula, stemmed, washed, and dried
3	ounces Gorgonzola cheese, crumbed
½	cup walnuts, toasted and chopped coarse

1. Toss the pear wedges and 1 tablespoon lemon juice in a medium bowl. Set aside.

2. Combine the remaining 2 tablespoons lemon juice, salt, and ⅛ teaspoon pepper in a bowl with a fork. Add the oils, then whisk or mix with a fork until smooth, about 30 seconds.

3. Toss the arugula and the dressing in a large bowl. Divide the dressed greens among four plates. Arrange the pears over the greens. Sprinkle with the Gorgonzola cheese, walnuts, and a generous grinding of pepper. Serve immediately.

INSALATA CAPRESE

ITALY IS FAMOUS FOR ITS END-OF-summer salad highlighting the flavors of fresh mozzarella, ripe tomatoes, and fragrant basil—*insalata caprese*. Although it seemed silly to research a recipe for such a simple dish, we wondered if there were any tricks in its preparation that might make a difference.

Obviously, this salad is meant to be made with only fully ripened tomatoes and a good-

EQUIPMENT: Salad Spinners

All salad spinners have the same basic design. A perforated basket is fitted into a larger outer bowl, and gears connected to a mechanism in the lid spin the basket rapidly, creating centrifugal force that pulls the greens to the sides of the basket and the water on the leaves through the perforations into the outer bowl. Beyond this, however, there are three important ways in which models can differ.

First is the lid. Some lids are solid, and some have a hole so water can be run directly into the basket while it spins. Second is the outer bowl. As with lids, some are solid and others are perforated so water can flow through. The third major difference is the mechanism that makes the baskets spin—pull cord, turning crank, lever crank, or pump knob.

To be fair, all of the eight spinners we tested did a reasonably good job of drying wet lettuce leaves and parsley, though none dried the greens so thoroughly that they wouldn't benefit from a quick blotting with paper towels before being dressed. Because the differences between models in terms of drying performance are not terribly dramatic, what you really want is a spinner that is well designed, easy to use, and sturdy.

We didn't like the spinners with flow-through lids. The greens we cleaned by running water into the basket tended to bruise from the rushing water and never got clean enough. We also didn't like models with bowls that had holes in the bottom so the water could flow right out. Again, we did not consider this a benefit, in part because it assumes you have an empty sink in which to place the spinner. Second, we like to use the outer bowl of the spinner to soak the leaves clean, something you can't do if it has holes.

As for the turning mechanism, the real standout in terms of design and ease of use was the spinner made by Oxo. You can use the Oxo with just one hand because of its clever nonskid base and the pump knob by which it operates. Pushing the pump down both makes the basket spin and pushes the whole unit down onto the counter.

Among the other models tested, the pull cord on the Zyliss was the easiest to grip, and the Zyliss did in fact get the greens a tad drier than other spinners, including the Oxo. The Zyliss and the Oxo were also the sturdiest of the bunch.

THE BEST SALAD SPINNERS

Salad spinners made by Zyliss (left) and Oxo Good Grips (right) won our test of leading models. They both excelled at drying greens, though they had minor trade-offs: The Zyliss finished the task nominally faster, but the Oxo had a more ergonomic handle and a nonskid bottom, a big bonus. The design enhancements lifted the Oxo's price to $25, five dollars more than the Zyliss.

quality fresh mozzarella packed in water. If either the tomatoes or mozzarella are unripe and bland, the flavor of the salad will suffer significantly. Tasters preferred the salad made with equal amounts of tomato and mozzarella.

Some recipes call for minced red onion and red wine vinegar; however, we liked the salad without them. Unadorned, the acidity of the tomatoes and the delicate flavor of the mozzarella can shine through. As for the basil, it was best when roughly chopped and sprinkled over the top instead of layering whole leaves among the slices of mozzarella and tomato. The leaves are simply too big and too chewy. Lastly, we noted the importance of using a high-quality extra-virgin olive oil and coarse salt. Both pure olive oil and table salt tasted too heavy and dense for this light, aromatic salad.

Although it is difficult not to eat the salad right away, allowing the platter to sit for a few minutes lets the flavors meld.

Tomato, Mozzarella, and Basil Salad
(Insalata Caprese)
SERVES 4 TO 6

Served as an appetizer, light lunch, or snack, this salad is best eaten with a crust of bread to help sop up the tasty tomato-flavored dressing that pools in the bottom of the platter. For best presentation, discard the first and last slice from each tomato.

4	medium, very ripe tomatoes (about 1½ pounds), cored and cut into slices ¼ inch thick
16	ounces fresh mozzarella, cut into slices ¼ inch thick
2	tablespoons roughly chopped fresh basil leaves
¼	teaspoon kosher salt or sea salt
⅛	teaspoon ground black pepper
¼	cup extra-virgin olive oil

Layer the tomatoes and mozzarella alternately and in concentric circles on a medium platter. Sprinkle the tomatoes and cheese with the basil, salt, and pepper. Drizzle the oil over the platter and allow the flavors to meld for 5 to 10 minutes. Serve immediately.

TOMATO SALAD

ITALY IS A LAND OF GOOD TOMATOES, and tomatoes are the basis for countless summer salads. A bonus of summer tomato salads is that the mildly acidic juices from the tomatoes themselves provide a delicious base for a dressing, so little additional acid is needed in the dressing. To make this work, you need to extract a little of the juice from the tomatoes before you make the salads. This is easily done. Simply cutting the tomatoes into wedges and letting them sit for about 15 minutes allows them to exude their juices. Salting the cut tomatoes helps this process and seasons the tomatoes and their juices at the same time.

Some cooks recommend peeling the tomatoes, but we find the skin on local vine-ripened tomatoes thin and unobtrusive. If home-grown or locally grown tomatoes are unavailable, substitute halved cherry tomatoes.

Tomato Salad with Canned Tuna, Capers, and Black Olives
SERVES 6

Oil-packed tuna is more consistent with the Mediterranean flavors in this salad, but you may use water-packed tuna if you prefer. See page 50 for information about buying oil-packed tuna.

4	medium ripe tomatoes (about 1½ pounds)
½	teaspoon salt

3   tablespoons extra-virgin olive oil
1   tablespoon lemon juice
3   tablespoons capers, chopped
12 large black olives, such as kalamata or
    other brine-cured variety, pitted and
    chopped
¼   cup finely chopped small red onion
2   tablespoons chopped fresh parsley leaves
    Ground black pepper
1   6-ounce can tuna, drained

1. Core and halve the tomatoes lengthwise, then cut each half into 4 or 5 wedges. Toss the wedges with the salt in a large bowl; let rest until a small pool of liquid accumulates, 15 to 20 minutes.

2. Meanwhile, whisk the oil, lemon juice, capers, olives, onion, parsley, and pepper to taste in a small bowl. Pour the mixture over the tomatoes and their accumulated liquid; toss to coat. Set aside to blend flavors, about 5 minutes.

3. Crumble the tuna over the tomatoes; toss to combine. Adjust the seasonings and serve immediately.

MAKING PARMESAN SHAVINGS

Thin shavings of Parmesan can be used to garnish almost any leafy Italian salad. Simply run a sharp vegetable peeler along the length of the piece of cheese to remove paper-thin curls.

Tomato Salad with Arugula and Shaved Parmesan

SERVES 6

Use a vegetable peeler to remove thin shavings from the hunk of cheese. See the illustration below.

4   medium ripe tomatoes (about
    1½ pounds)
½   teaspoon salt
2   tablespoons extra-virgin olive oil
1   tablespoon balsamic vinegar
1   small clove garlic, minced or pressed
    through a garlic press
    Ground black pepper
1   small bunch arugula, washed, dried, and
    chopped coarse (about 1 cup)
24 shavings Parmesan cheese

1. Core and halve the tomatoes lengthwise, then cut each half into 4 or 5 wedges. Toss the wedges with the salt in a large bowl; let rest until a small pool of liquid accumulates, 15 to 20 minutes.

2. Meanwhile, whisk the oil, vinegar, garlic, and pepper to taste in a small bowl. Pour the mixture over the tomatoes and their accumulated liquid; toss to coat. Set aside to blend flavors, about 5 minutes.

3. Add the arugula and Parmesan; toss to combine. Adjust the seasonings and serve immediately.

FENNEL, ORANGE, AND OLIVE SALAD

FENNEL, CALLED FINOCCHIO IN ITALY, is used throughout Italy in all manner of dishes from antipasti to dessert. It has a delicate, sweet, light anise flavor and delicious crunch that is similar to celery, only without the strings. In Sicily, fennel is often paired with oranges and olives to make a simple, fresh-tasting salad.

Although we found many recipes for this simple combination, we noted a few tricks in the preparation of both the fennel and oranges that made all the difference. First, we liked the fennel best when it was sliced as thin as possible. Making this task easier, we used the slicing blade in a food processor for even-sized pieces.

Second, we noted the importance of cutting the orange into bite-sized pieces; the trick is to avoid letting the orange segments fall apart as the salad is tossed. We achieved this by trimming the outer rind and bitter white pith from the orange with a sharp knife, then breaking the orange down into quarters. We trimmed the inner pith and seeds from inside each quarter, then cut crosswise through each quarter (across the segments). By cutting crosswise, the segment borders and connective tissue helped keep the orange from breaking down further as it was tossed in the salad.

To finish the salad off, we added a small amount of potent black olives, some fresh mint, good extra-virgin olive oil, salt, and black pepper. Because this dish is so simple, each ingredient, from the fennel to the salt, must be of the best quality.

Fennel, Orange, and Olive Salad
SERVES 4 TO 6

Blood oranges, whose skin is tinted with red and whose flesh is reddish-orange, are traditional in this dish; do use them if you can find them. See the illustrations below for tips on preparing the orange for this salad.

1	small fennel bulb (about 1 pound), stems and fronds removed
2	large oranges, preferably blood oranges
2	tablespoons mild black olives, such as gaeta or niçoise, pitted and slivered
2	tablespoons roughly chopped fresh mint leaves
½	teaspoon kosher salt or sea salt
⅛	teaspoon ground black pepper
3	tablespoons extra-virgin olive oil
2	teaspoons lemon juice

1. Slice the fennel in half and remove the hard core. Using the slicing disk of a food processor, thinly slice each fennel half. Transfer the sliced fennel to a large bowl.

2. Using a sharp paring knife, remove the skin from the oranges, then cut them into quarters and trim away the inside pith and any

CUTTING ORANGE SLICES

1. Once the peel and pith have been removed with a knife, cut the orange in quarters, making each cut through the top and bottom ends.

2. Trim away the inside pith and any seeds.

3. Cut each quarter crosswise into pieces ¼ inch thick.

seeds (see illustrations on page 42). Cut each quarter widthwise into pieces ¼ inch thick and add them to the bowl with the fennel. Add the remaining ingredients and toss. The salad can be served immediately or held at room temperature for up to 1 hour.

GRILLED VEGETABLE SALADS

IN ITALY, GRILLED VEGETABLE SALADS are served as warm-weather side dishes for chicken, fish, or meat. Most grilled vegetable salads taste best at room temperature, after the cooked vegetables and seasonings have had a chance to blend.

The problem for most cooks is figuring out how to use the same fire to grill-roast peppers or char onions for salad and to cook chicken parts or tuna steaks. On a gas grill, your strategy is simple: Grill the vegetables, let them cool, assemble the salad, and then fire up the grill again when you want to cook dinner.

Grilling on charcoal requires more planning. Vegetables should be cooked over a medium-hot fire (you should be able to hold your hand 5 inches above the grill rack for no more than 3 to 4 seconds). If you don't mind serving the main course at room temperature, you can cook it first (when the fire is hot) and then cook the vegetables as the fire begins to cool. If you work really quickly, this strategy can work.

An easier plan is to build the fire, let it die down a bit, then grill your vegetables. Once the vegetables come off the grill, add a handful of unlit coals. While waiting for the fire to become hot again, assemble the salad, which can then sit around while you grill the main course. This second strategy is a bit more work (adding coals is a bother), but it keeps you from having to work quickly on the vegetable salad while you worry about the main course cooling too much.

Another concern when preparing grilled vegetable salads is the dressing. Because the vegetables must be oiled generously before grilling to prevent sticking (use extra-virgin olive oil for the best flavor), the dressing must be light or the salad will taste greasy.

Grilled Pepper Salad with Green Olives and Capers

SERVES 4 TO 6

Use a mix of red and yellow peppers, if possible. This dish works especially well with grilled fish, pork, or chicken.

4	medium red and/or yellow bell peppers (about 1½ pounds)
1	tablespoon red wine vinegar
2	tablespoons extra-virgin olive oil
	Salt and ground black pepper
6	large green olives, pitted and chopped (about ¼ cup)
1	tablespoon drained capers
1	tablespoon minced fresh parsley leaves

1. Grill the peppers over medium-hot heat (you can hold your hand 5 inches above grill surface for 3 to 4 seconds), turning several times with tongs until the skins are blistered and charred on all sides, about 15 minutes. Transfer the peppers to a medium bowl and cover with plastic wrap; let steam to loosen the skins. Remove the skins; core and seed the peppers, then cut them into strips 1 inch wide. Return the pepper strips with their accumulated juices to a bowl.

2. Add the vinegar, oil, and salt and pepper to taste; toss gently. Add the olives, capers, and parsley and toss again. (The salad can be covered and set aside for up to 3 hours.)

Grilled Onion and Tomato Salad

SERVES 4

The sweetness of grilled onions is an excellent foil for the acidity of tomatoes. Use a high-quality aged balsamic vinegar. This salad is especially good with steaks.

- 3 medium-large red onions (about 1¼ pounds), cut into rounds ½ inch thick, rounds left intact
- 3 tablespoons extra-virgin olive oil
  Salt and ground black pepper
- 3 small ripe tomatoes (about 1 pound), cored and cut into wedges ¾ inch thick
- 10 large fresh basil leaves, chopped coarse
- 2 teaspoons balsamic vinegar

1. Skewer each onion round to keep the layers intact on the grill (see illustrations below). Lay the onion rounds on a large baking sheet and brush both sides with 2 tablespoons oil. Season generously with salt and pepper.

2. Grill the onions over medium-hot heat (you can hold your hand 5 inches above the grill surface for 3 to 4 seconds) until lightly charred, turning once, about 6 minutes per side. Transfer the onions to a cutting board and cool slightly. Remove the skewers. Cut the onion rounds in half and place in a serving bowl; toss gently to separate the layers.

3. Add the tomatoes, basil, and salt and pepper to taste; drizzle with the remaining 1 tablespoon oil and the vinegar. Toss gently and serve. (The salad can be covered and set aside for up to 1 hour.)

GRILLING ONIONS

Onions slices can be difficult to handle on the grill, with rings often slipping through the grate and onto the coals. Here's how to grill onions safely and easily.

1. Slide a skewer through the side of thick onion slices.

2. The skewered onion slices remain intact and can be easily flipped on the grill with tongs.

ITALIAN–STYLE TOMATO PASTA SALAD

PASTA SALAD IS A PURELY AMERICAN invention. Most Italians would never dream of eating chilled pasta. Of course, that Italians may scoff at the notion is no reason not to enjoy a good pasta salad, especially one dressed with a light vinaigrette rather than leaden mayonnaise.

While Italians may not understand the concept of pasta salad, they don't always eat pasta piping hot, either. In the summer, they often toss pasta with a raw tomato sauce and cool the dish to room temperature. This "salad" can be taken on picnics, served at barbecues, or eaten on a sultry night when the thought of hot food is unappetizing. We've eaten these salads dozens of times. They are usually quite good, but we have encountered a recurring problem—the raw tomatoes often make a rather watery sauce.

With this issue in mind, we formulated a list of questions to address in our testing. Do the tomatoes need to be peeled and/or seeded? Should they be salted? Is there a way to add garlic without overwhelming the other flavors? Should the ingredients be marinated? Working with a classic recipe of chopped tomatoes, olive oil, basil, a little raw garlic, salt, and pepper, we began to make observations.

When we use fresh tomatoes in a cooked sauce, we prefer to peel them. The tiny bits of skin separate from the tomato flesh and are not terribly appealing in terms of flavor or texture. But when preparing pasta salads by tossing raw tomato sauce with hot pasta, we noticed that while the heat did soften the tomatoes slightly, making their texture more appealing and bringing out their flavor, the skins were still firmly attached to each tomato cube. Therefore, we see no need to remove the skin.

The seeds are another matter. The tiny seeds are bitter (try tasting them alone), but within the context of a pasta salad their sharpness is hard to detect. The more pressing issue is the liquid that surrounds them. When we made two salads—one with seeded tomatoes, the other with unseeded—we were surprised that they were so different.

The unseeded tomatoes shed a lot of liquid that sat at the bottom of the bowl when the sauce was tossed with the hot pasta. The pasta salad tasted watery and bland. When we looked at the juices at the bottom of the bowl, we noticed that tiny droplets of oil were dispersed in this liquid. The sauce made with seeded tomatoes was meatier and more flavorful. Although each batch contained the same amount of seasonings, the salad made with seeded tomatoes tasted more like olive oil, garlic, basil, and salt because the oil, which

carries all these flavors, was clinging to the noodles, not lying in a watery mess underneath the pasta.

Next, we wondered if marinating the ingredients would affect the sauce. After half an hour, the tomatoes were giving off a lot of clear liquid, with a little oil dispersed in it. After an hour, we tossed the sauce with hot pasta, and we did not like the results. The tomatoes had given up a lot of their flavorful juices, which again sat at the bottom of the bowl. We also thought that the garlic flavor had intensified and become overpowering. For these reasons, it is best to assemble the raw tomato sauce while the pasta is cooking.

A last series of tests concerned timing. When should the sauce and pasta marry? Was it better to oil the drained pasta, let it cool, and then sauce it, as several cookbooks we looked at suggested? We tried this method but did not like the results. The oil formed a barrier that prevented the pasta from absorbing the flavors of the tomato sauce. The sauce also slipped off the noodles. We vastly preferred tossing the hot pasta with a raw sauce that included the oil. The pasta and the sauce elements were unified this way, and the heat of the pasta also cooked the tomatoes and garlic a bit.

Once the pasta and sauce are combined, you have several options. You can eat the pasta right away—it's warm but not piping hot at this point—or you can wait half an hour or so until the pasta salad is at room temperature, then eat it or cover the bowl tightly with plastic wrap and set it aside for up to 4 hours. After 4 hours, the pasta will start to soften. The refrigerator does nothing for this pasta salad; in fact, it irrevocably damages the flavor and texture of the ripe tomatoes.

Pasta Salad with Fresh Tomatoes and Basil

SERVES 6 TO 8 AS A SIDE DISH

Use only the ripest, most flavorful round tomatoes you can find. Avoid plum tomatoes because they are too firm and tend not to soften, even with the heat of the just-cooked pasta. The tomatoes can be diced a couple of hours in advance, but to prevent the garlic from becoming too pungent and the salt from drawing out the tomatoes' juices, wait until the pasta is cooking to add the seasonings to the tomatoes. Short, stubby pasta shapes such as orecchiette, fusilli, and farfalle (bow ties) are the best choices for catching juicy bits of sauce.

	Salt
1	pound pasta (see note above)
2	pounds ripe tomatoes, cored, seeded, and cut into ½-inch dice
¼	cup extra-virgin olive oil
1	medium clove garlic, minced or pressed through a garlic press
¼	cup shredded fresh basil leaves
	Ground black pepper

1. Bring 4 quarts water to a rolling boil in a large stockpot. Add 1 tablespoon salt and the pasta. Cook until the pasta is al dente. Drain well.

2. While the pasta is cooking, toss together the tomatoes, oil, garlic, basil, ¾ teaspoon salt, and pepper to taste in a large bowl. Add the drained pasta to the tomatoes and toss well. Serve immediately, or, if desired, cool to room temperature before serving, about 30 minutes. (The pasta salad can be covered with plastic wrap and kept at room temperature for up to 4 hours.)

➤ VARIATIONS

Pasta Salad with Tomatoes, Olives, and Capers

Follow the recipe for Pasta Salad with Fresh Tomatoes and Basil, adding ⅓ cup pitted and sliced black kalamata olives (or other brine-cured black olives) and 2 tablespoons drained capers to the tomatoes along with the oil and garlic and reducing the salt to ¼ teaspoon.

Pasta Salad with Tomatoes and Fresh Mozzarella

Follow the recipe for Pasta Salad with Fresh Tomatoes and Basil, adding 6 ounces fresh mozzarella cheese, cut into small dice, to the tomatoes along with the oil and garlic.

BREAD SALAD

TO THE ITALIANS, BREAD IS HOLY; IT is almost unthinkable to throw it away. It is not surprising, then, that there are so many uses for bread throughout Italy. One of the most delightful and perhaps surprising dishes that evolved in this part of the world is what amounts to a stale bread salad.

Such thrifty salads are superb dishes because they allow flavorful and fresh tomatoes to be fully experienced, along with fragrant mint, parsley, and oregano. Another crucial ingredient is high-quality extra-virgin olive oil. Because the dry bread so readily absorbs moisture, much of the flavor of the dish is derived from the dressing.

Last but not least, fundamental to the success of these salads is the quality of the bread. Sliced white bread or airy supermarket bread that is highly refined and becomes rock-hard within a few days simply won't do. Ideally, bread used in bread salads should not contain sugar or sweeteners of any kind, which would conflict with the savory nature of the other ingredients, nor should it include such ingredients as raisins or nuts. What the bread should have is a sturdy texture and a good wheaty flavor.

Depending on how stale the bread is, it may need to be dampened with a little water.

The extent of dampening is determined by the dryness of the bread; if the bread receives too much dampening, it will collapse into a soggy mess when the dressing is added. Therefore, assemble the salad, see how much the bread softens, and then adjust the texture by sprinkling lightly with water.

Because the bread becomes soggy fairly quickly, none of these salads should be made much in advance of serving (see individual recipes for suggested preparation ahead of time). The best approach is to assemble all of the salad ingredients, then combine them just before serving.

Bread Salad with Tomatoes, Herbs, and Red Onions

SERVES 4

Use coarse peasant bread or any sturdy Italian-style bread in this classic Italian recipe.

1	pound day-old coarse peasant bread or sturdy Italian-style bread, crusts removed, cut or torn into 1-inch cubes (about 6 cups)
1/2	cup extra-virgin olive oil
3	tablespoons red wine vinegar
2	large ripe round tomatoes or 4 ripe plum tomatoes (about 1 pound total), cored, seeded, and cut into medium dice
1/2	red onion, sliced very thin
2	tablespoons torn fresh basil or mint leaves
2	teaspoons whole fresh oregano leaves
1	tablespoon minced fresh parsley leaves
1/2	teaspoon salt
1/4	teaspoon ground black pepper

Place the bread cubes in a shallow bowl. Mix the oil, vinegar, tomatoes, onion, and half of the herbs in a medium bowl. Let stand to allow the flavors to develop, about 10 minutes, then add to the bread, along with remaining the herbs,

and toss well. Season with the salt and pepper or to taste. If the bread still seems dry, sprinkle with 1 or 2 tablespoons water to rehydrate it a bit. Serve. (If sturdy bread is used, the salad can be covered and set aside up to 2 hours.)

Bread Salad with Roasted Peppers and Olives

SERVES 4 TO 6

Sourdough or a sturdy peasant bread is needed for this salad. Airy, unsubstantial bread will become soggy quickly.

1	pound sturdy Italian bread, crusts removed, cut or torn into 1-inch cubes (about 6 cups)
2	bell peppers, 1 red and 1 yellow, roasted (page 11), stemmed, seeded, and cut into 1/2-inch strips
1/2	cup extra-virgin olive oil
1/4	cup cider vinegar
1	small red or white onion, quartered and sliced thin
1	medium scallion, sliced thin, including 2 inches of green part
3	tablespoons pitted and sliced green olives
1	tablespoon minced fresh oregano leaves
1/2	teaspoon salt
1/4	teaspoon ground black pepper

1. Mix the bread cubes and pepper strips in a large bowl; set aside.

2. Mix the oil, vinegar, onion, scallion, olives, oregano, salt, and pepper in a medium bowl; let stand to allow the flavors to develop, about 10 minutes. Add the dressing to the bread and peppers; toss to combine. If the bread still seems dry, sprinkle with 1 or 2 tablespoons water to rehydrate it a bit. Serve. (If sturdy bread is used, the salad can be covered and set aside up to 2 hours.)

RICE SALAD

IN THE SUMMER, ITALIANS TURN RICE into light, bright salads studded with vegetables and herbs. The concept of making rice salad seems quite simple, yet it presents two types of problems. For starters, this understated grain does not hold up to assertive flavors the way pasta can. It is readily bogged down by a vinaigrette that would be well suited to a green salad.

Even more troubling than the delicate dance of flavors is the texture of the rice. Long-grain rice normally just isn't good cold; it tends to turn hard, clumpy, and slightly crunchy. Short-grain rice holds up better as it cools, but it has a sticky heaviness that we didn't want in a rice salad. We needed to isolate a cooking method for long-grain rice that would preserve its fresh-from-the-pan characteristics once cooled.

We began with our favorite technique for cooking rice pilaf. This made for a nice pilaf dish, but its buttery flavor was ill suited to a rice salad and, as the rice cooled, it lost its appealing fluffiness. A similar master recipe for long-grain white rice produced similar results—great when hot from the pot but pasty, dense, and slightly crunchy once cooled.

Stymied, we started testing every method of cooking rice imaginable. While many methods cooked up great rice, inevitably the quality deteriorated upon cooling.

We finally realized that the source of these failures is the same component of long-grain rice that makes it cook up fluffy: amylose, one of the two primary starches contained in rice. As it turns out, when long-grain rice cools, the long amylose molecules form rigid crystals that squeeze liquid out and turn the rice rock-hard. Technically speaking, this is called retrogradation. We realized that if we were going to come up with a palatable rice salad, we would need to apply some kind of sorcery to the starch.

In a last-ditch effort, we tried cooking the long-grain rice with the abundant water technique, whereby rice is boiled in a large volume of water, just like pasta, until it is toothsome and cooked through but has not yet begun to fray. At this point, the water is simply strained out. The drawback of this technique is that it tends to turn out rice that tastes waterlogged. This is true, yet the light and separated texture of the rice held up so well after cooling that we did not dare disregard the method. Instead, we added a couple of steps to the process to cope with the waterlogging problem.

Taking a cue from the pilaf recipe, we toasted the rice before boiling to tease out its nutty essence. Actually, its aroma might be better likened to popcorn. We did this, however, without the oil, as we found that oil made the rice heavy and greasy in salad form. (A bonus is that all that's needed to clean the pan is a swipe with a dry towel.)

SCIENCE: The Starch Story

Learning how rice cooks helps explain why this unorthodox method of boiling rice works best for rice salad. Starch granules, which are the primary component of rice, tend not to absorb water. As you heat rice in water, however, the energy from the rapidly moving water molecules begins to loosen the bonds between the starch molecules so that water can seep in. This in turn causes the starch molecules to swell, softening the rice but also making it more sticky, or "starchy." If you use the abundant water method for cooking long-grain rice, some of this starch leaches into the water, which is ultimately drained off. The result is a pot of long-grain rice with less concentrated starch. This is what allows the grains to cook up so remarkably light and separate and to maintain that consistency as they cool to room temperature.

After the rice was boiled, we spread it across a baking sheet to cool. This creates a great deal of surface area, which allows the excess moisture to evaporate. Spreading the rice to cool also prevents it from clumping, as it would if left to rest in a bowl. In addition, because the rice cools to room temperature in about 10 minutes, the salad can be assembled quickly.

Rice salads are not meant to be doused in oil and vinegar—just a small amount does the trick. This also permits you to use a dark-colored vinegar, such as balsamic vinegar, without discoloring the rice.

Rice salad is particularly suited to flavors that are politely understated, not bold or loud. It is a side dish that should taste light, not at all filling, yet every forkful should have character. Rice salads pair particularly well with grilled fish or chicken and are best served at room temperature. Toss the rice with the dressing about 20 minutes before serving so that the subtle flavors have time to develop. If you dress it too far ahead, the rice absorbs the flavor and mutes it. The rice in this salad does stand up to refrigeration. Simply let it rest at room temperature for 30 minutes before serving.

Boiled Rice for Rice Salad

MAKES ABOUT 6 CUPS COOKED RICE

Taste the rice as it nears the end of its cooking time; it should be cooked through and toothsome but not crunchy. Be careful not to overcook the rice or the grains will blow out and fray.

1½ cups long-grain rice
1½ teaspoons salt

1. Bring 4 quarts water to a boil in a large stockpot. Meanwhile, heat a medium skillet over medium heat until hot, about 3 minutes. Add the rice and toast, stirring frequently, until faintly fragrant and some grains turn opaque, about 5 minutes.

2. Add the salt to the boiling water and stir in the toasted rice. Return to a boil and cook, uncovered, until the rice is tender but not soft, 8 to 10 minutes. Meanwhile, line a rimmed baking sheet with foil or parchment paper. Drain the rice in a large fine-mesh strainer or colander and then spread it on the prepared baking sheet. Let the rice cool while you prepare the salad ingredients in the following recipes.

Rice Salad with Oranges, Olives, and Almonds

SERVES 6 TO 8

This salad is inspired by southern Italian flavors. It is especially good with grilled fish.

2 tablespoons olive oil
1 small clove garlic, minced or pressed through a garlic press
¼ teaspoon grated zest plus 1 tablespoon juice from 1 small orange
2 teaspoons red wine vinegar
1 teaspoon salt
½ teaspoon ground black pepper
1 recipe Boiled Rice for Rice Salad (left)
⅓ cup coarsely chopped pitted green olives
2 medium oranges, peeled and cut into segments (see illustrations on page 35)
⅓ cup slivered almonds, toasted in small dry skillet over medium heat until fragrant and golden, about 2 minutes
2 teaspoons minced fresh oregano leaves

Stir together the oil, garlic, orange zest and juice, vinegar, salt, and pepper in a small bowl. Combine the rice, olives, oranges, almonds, and oregano in a large bowl. Drizzle the oil mixture over the rice mixture and toss thoroughly to combine. Let stand 20 minutes to blend flavors and serve.

Rice Salad with Cherry Tomatoes, Parmesan, Peas, and Prosciutto

SERVES 6 TO 8

Cherry tomatoes are less juicy and a better choice than round tomatoes for rice salad.

2	tablespoons extra-virgin olive oil
1	tablespoon balsamic vinegar
1	small clove garlic, minced or pressed through a garlic press
1	teaspoon salt
½	teaspoon ground black pepper
1	recipe Boiled Rice for Rice Salad

½	cup frozen peas, thawed
6	ounces cherry tomatoes, quartered and seeded (about 1 cup)
1	ounce thinly sliced prosciutto, chopped fine (about ¼ cup)
¼	cup grated Parmesan cheese
¼	cup shredded fresh basil leaves

Stir together the oil, vinegar, garlic, salt, and pepper in a small bowl. Combine the rice, peas, tomatoes, prosciutto, Parmesan cheese, and basil in a large bowl. Drizzle the oil mixture over the rice mixture and toss thoroughly to combine. Let stand 20 minutes to blend flavors and serve.

INGREDIENTS: Tuna Packed in Olive Oil

Given our tasters' preference for olive oil–packed tuna in a tuna and white bean salad, we wondered if all brands were created equal. The six we found in our local grocery and natural foods stores fell into three categories: white (made from albacore tuna), light (made from bluefin, yellowfin, or skipjack tuna, or a mixture thereof), and imported "white tuna" (made from bonito tuna).

Our panel of tasters did not care for the light tunas packed in olive oil. Our representative brands, Cento Solid Pack Light Tuna and Pastene Fancy Light Tuna, both had "potent" and "metallic" flavors with a "bitter finish," as well as "chewed" and "unpleasant" textures. Surprisingly, our albacore contender, Dave's Albacore Fillets, came in dead last. "It's like eating nothing" was the comment that summed it up.

The three best-tasting tunas were made by Ortiz, a small Spanish company. Ortiz cans only northern bonito white tuna fished off the coast of Spain—a tuna not used by American packers. Europeans consider this tuna to be of highest quality due to its extremely white meat, tender texture, and full, clean flavor. The superior flavor is attributed to the migratory nature of bonito tuna, which is considered a high-energy fish. High energy means a high oil content, which in turn means flavor, and lots of it. Though each of the three Ortiz tunas consists of the same ingredients—bonito del norte, olive oil, and salt— they have markedly different textures, and it was this that distinguished them and produced a winner.

FIRST PLACE

Ortiz Bonito del Norte Ventresca is $9.95 for a 3.88-ounce can. The word ventresca refers to the underside of the fish, where the fat, and therefore flavor, is more concentrated. These small fillets of tuna blew all other contenders out of the water with their "silky, gorgeous texture," "fresh and potent fish flavor," and "light olive oil presence."

SECOND PLACE

Ortiz Bonito del Norte (tinned) is $4.99 for a 3.95-ounce can. The "flaky," "tender," and "pleasant" texture of this "intense and delicious" tuna was perfect for salads such as Niçoise.

THIRD PLACE

Ortiz Bonito del Norte (jarred) is $7.99 for a 7.76-ounce jar. The large, dense chunks of tuna were somewhat "dry" and a tad "tough," but the flavor was great—"light," "clean," and "mild."

TUNA AND WHITE BEAN SALAD

THIS QUICK TUSCAN SALAD IS A standard in Florence, where hearty portions of round white beans and good canned tuna are lightly dressed with vinegar and olive oil. Wanting to duplicate this classic dish in the test kitchen, we focused on finding an easy recipe that wouldn't sacrifice flavor.

Although beans always taste better when cooked slowly for several hours, we found this was simply too much time to invest for such a simple salad. We were pleasantly surprised at the quality of canned cannellini beans, finding they needed only a good rinse after coming out of the can. Moving on to the tuna, we found that tuna packed in olive oil was far superior to any packed in spring water. With a luxurious texture and honest flavor, good olive oil–packed tuna made all the difference in this salad. Red onion and fresh parsley were the only flavoring garnishes the salad really needed for finishing.

Tuna and White Bean Salad

SERVES 4

See page 50 for information about buying tuna packed in olive oil.

2	4-ounce cans tuna packed in olive oil, drained
1	15½-ounce can cannellini beans, drained and thoroughly rinsed
2	tablespoons minced red onion
1	tablespoon minced fresh parsley leaves
½	teaspoon kosher salt or sea salt
⅛	teaspoon ground black pepper
3	tablespoons extra-virgin olive oil
2	teaspoons red wine vinegar
½	medium lemon, cut into 4 wedges

Gently mix all the ingredients except the lemon wedges together in a medium bowl and allow flavors to meld for 5 minutes. Serve with the lemon wedges.

SEAFOOD SALAD

WITH SUCH PROXIMITY TO THE SEA, IT is no wonder that shellfish is a staple ingredient for most of Italy. Seafood salad, made from an array of shellfish tossed in bright, lemony vinaigrette, is served in many regions.

Raw shrimp, small sea scallops, mussels, and even squid are widely available and sold by the pound, requiring only a quick rinse and, in the case of the squid, a quick check over for inedible parts. Squid often has a plasticlike spear running through the main part of its body; this must be removed before the squid is cut into bite-sized pieces.

The next question was how to cook the shellfish. While most recipes we researched steam or sauté the shellfish before tossing them with the vinaigrette, we found this didn't work. The shellfish not only cooked at different rates but also the dry heat of the sauté pan turned the squid rubbery, while steaming drew out much of the shellfish's delicate flavor. Instead, we looked for an easy technique that would work well for all the seafood.

Poaching turned out to be our answer. Using a simple broth made with the shrimp shells and a few aromatics, we were able to gently simmer (poach) the shellfish without ruining their textures or losing any flavor. In the case of the mussels, we found it easiest to steam them over the poaching broth. As they steamed, they added extra flavor to the broth, and the meat was easy to extract from the shells after they popped open. To prevent the poaching liquid from watering down the final salad, we drained the cooked shellfish in a colander for a few minutes.

Wanting the dressing to be bright, with a potent lemon flavor, we found it necessary to call for a 2-to-1 ratio of olive oil to fresh lemon juice. Rounding out the dish, we liked the additions of red onion, fresh parsley, capers, red bell pepper, and hot red pepper flakes, which together added flavor, texture, color, and a little kick. Letting the cooked shellfish and dressing sit for 20 minutes allowed the flavors to meld, producing an authentic Italian seafood salad.

Seafood Salad

SERVES 4 TO 6

This salad makes an excellent light lunch. It also can be served as an antipasto.

DRESSING

½ cup extra-virgin olive oil
¼ cup lemon juice
¼ cup capers, rinsed
1 tablespoon minced fresh parsley leaves
½ small red bell pepper, stemmed, seeded, and minced (about ¼ cup)
½ small red onion, minced (about ¼ cup)
   Pinch hot red pepper flakes

SEAFOOD

1 cup dry white wine
4 whole black peppercorns
1 small bay leaf
5 sprigs fresh parsley
   Salt
½ pound medium shrimp, peeled and deveined, shells reserved
2 pounds mussels, scrubbed clean
½ pound sea scallops, tendons removed and discarded
½ pound squid, rinsed, cut into rings ¼ inch wide, tentacles cut in half
   Ground black pepper

1. FOR THE DRESSING: Whisk all the ingredients together in a large bowl and set aside.

2. FOR THE SEAFOOD: Bring 3 cups water, the wine, peppercorns, bay leaf, parsley, 1 teaspoon salt, and reserved shrimp shells to a boil in a large saucepan over medium-high heat. Reduce the heat to medium and simmer until the broth is flavorful, about 15 minutes. Strain the broth through a fine-mesh sieve into a clean saucepan with a steamer insert. Bring the broth to a simmer over medium heat.

3. Place a colander over a medium bowl and set aside. Place the mussels in the steamer insert, cover, and cook until the mussels begin to pop open, about 4 minutes. Remove the lid and, using a pair of tongs, transfer the mussels to the colander as they open, discarding any that don't open after 4 to 5 minutes longer (they are not safe to eat). Remove the steamer insert and return the broth to a simmer.

4. Add the shrimp to the simmering broth and cook until they begin to curl, about 1½ minutes. Use a slotted spoon to transfer the shrimp to the colander. Add the scallops to the simmering broth and cook until firm on the outside yet tender inside, about 1 minute. Use a slotted spoon to transfer the scallops to the colander. Add the squid to the simmering broth and cook until slightly firm to the bite, 2 to 3 minutes. Use a slotted spoon to transfer the squid to the colander. Remove the broth from the heat and discard or save for another use. (It is an ideal base for seafood risotto or a seafood pasta sauce.)

5. Gently shake the colander to help remove any excess water, then add the shrimp, scallops, and squid to the bowl with the dressing. Remove the mussel meat from the open shells and add to the bowl. Gently toss the seafood with the dressing and season with salt and pepper to taste. Cover and refrigerate until the flavors meld, at least 20 minutes or up to 4 hours.

3

VEGETABLES

ITALIANS LOVE VEGETABLES, FROM artichokes to zucchini and everything in between. No Italian meal is complete without at least one vegetable dish, if not more. A few general points come to mind. Italians eat local vegetables and thus eat vegetables that are in season. Zucchini, tomatoes, and eggplant are summer fare, and few Italian cooks would consider preparing these vegetables in the winter. Because Italians rely on local growers, vegetables are generally fresh and flavorful. Most Italian vegetable recipes rely on simple seasonings that highlight rather than over-whelm the vegetable's delicate flavor. For the best results, we suggest shopping at farmers' markets. The recipes in this chapter are basic and don't have lots of cream and butter that would hide defects in less-than-fresh produce.

In Italy, the vegetable course, called the contorno, is served with the meat, poultry, or fish. However, a few of the recipes in this chapter, especially the stuffed artichokes, onions agrodolce, and stuffed tomatoes, are appropriate as an antipasto or first course.

UNDERSTANDING AN ARTICHOKE

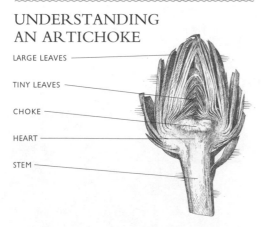

LARGE LEAVES

TINY LEAVES

CHOKE

HEART

STEM

Much of an artichoke is inedible, including the entire exterior as well as the fuzzy choke and tiny inner leaves in the center. Only the heart, stem, and bottom portions of the inner leaves become meaty and tender when cooked. The cooked heart can be eaten with a knife and fork. The edible portion at the bottom of the leaves is best scraped off with your teeth.

ROMAN-STYLE STUFFED BRAISED ARTICHOKES

ARTICHOKES' SPRINGTIME ARRIVAL IN Roman markets is cause for celebration, and dining tables overflow with an abundance of dishes highlighting the vegetable's subtle yet distinctive flavor. Nowhere else in Italy is the humble thistle as vaunted, starring in dozens of preparations. One of our favorite arti-choke dishes is so common to Rome that its Italian name, *carciofi alla Romana,* indelibly links it to the city. Whole artichokes are stuffed with an intensely flavored garlic, herb, and bread crumb mixture that perme-ates the whole artichoke as it braises. Except for cleaning the artichokes, this dish is sim-ple to prepare—certainly one reason for its popularity.

Ninety percent of preparing most arti-choke dishes is cleaning the artichokes. For this dish, the first step is ripping off the fibrous outer leaves, stopping when the bottoms of the leaves turn from dark green to pale yellow-green. Then, for ridding the stem of its coarse outer layer, use a sturdy, razor-sharp peeler (see page 60 for details on our testing), which cleanly strips the tough exterior to reveal its pale green edible interior. (In this respect, Italians prepare artichokes differently from the French and most Americans, who simply cut off the entire stem and forsake the delicate flesh.)

Removing the fuzzy inner choke poses a bigger problem, but after cleaning dozens of artichokes we devised a method. First, use your fingers to pull apart the leaves and open the artichoke. We discovered that, once the artichoke leaves are spread apart, a grapefruit spoon, with its sharp serrated edges, is the ideal tool for tearing at the stubborn leaves and fibers that comprise the choke. Once cleaned, the artichokes can be easily stuffed with the aid of a long teaspoon.

Classically, the stuffing is nothing more than herbs, garlic, and bread crumbs moistened with olive oil, but tasters found this combination flat and in need of refinement. Additional herbs, like oregano and marjoram, merely muddied the taste, and cheese added richness but turned gummy during steaming. Then it occurred to us that the filling had the same components—excluding the mint and bread crumbs—as gremolata, the assertive garnish used to lighten osso buco (see page 305 for more information about gremolata). With the addition of lemon zest, the artichokes were newly defined; the zest sharpened both the filling and the artichoke's flavors. Sometimes classics can be improved.

Cooking the artichokes took little more than half an hour in a large Dutch oven filled with just enough water to cover the stems three-quarters of the way. Any more liquid

PREPARING ARTICHOKES

1. Removing the pin-sharp thorns at the tips of the leaves makes for easier handling and a more attractive presentation. Grasp the artichoke by the stem and hold it horizontal to your body. Using kitchen shears, trim the tips of the leaves row by row, skipping the top two rows.

2. Rest the artichoke on a cutting board. Holding the stem in one hand, cut off the top quarter (the top two rows) of the artichoke with a sharp chef's knife.

3. With a sharp vegetable peeler, remove the tough outer skin that covers the stem.

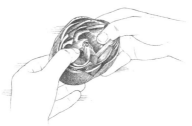

4. Using the tips of your fingers, gently spread apart the leaves to reveal the inner core.

5. Using a sharp-edged spoon, such as a grapefruit spoon, dig out the fuzzy choke. Rinse the artichoke well to remove any remaining bits of choke.

6. Onion rings keep the artichokes upright while they steam. Cut $\frac{1}{2}$-inch-thick slices from the onion and use your fingers to pop the outer three or four rings from the rest of the slice. Space the onion rings evenly across the bottom of a Dutch oven and set one artichoke at an angle in each ring.

made for sodden stems and a gummy filling. To boost the braising liquid's flavor, we added the parsley stems left over from making the filling. We set the ball of each artichoke into a thickly cut onion ring to prevent the filling from spilling out. For even cooking, rotate the artichokes at the midway point so that they lean one way and then the other. This ensures that the side closest to the steaming liquid doesn't overcook.

After removing the artichokes from the braising liquid, we were left with a surpris-ingly strong-flavored broth, with accents from the filling and the artichoke and a deep sweetness from the onions used to steady the artichokes. We simmered the broth until it reduced to a saucelike consistency, then brightened the sauce with a squirt of lemon juice. We passed this sauce at the table, using it as a dipping sauce for the leaves.

INGREDIENTS: Artichokes

Artichokes are a perennial belonging to the sunflower family, with the edible portion of the plant being an immature thistle. The plants grow quite large, reaching up to six feet in diameter and three to four feet in height. While artichokes are available sporadically throughout the year, the spring months are their high season, when they are widely available and their price is generally low.

Artichokes are commonly marketed in three sizes: small, medium, and large. Surprisingly, different sized artichokes simultaneously bud on the same plant; the artichokes that grow on the plant's center stalk are the largest, and the smallest grow at the juncture between the plant's leaves and the stem.

After preparing, cooking, and eating all three sizes, we found that we preferred medium artichokes (roughly 8 to 10 ounces each) for stuffing. Large artichokes can be tough and fibrous, and small artichokes are too hard to stuff.

There are a few rules of thumb for picking fresh arti-chokes at the market. They should be tight and compact, like a flower blossom (which they are), unblemished bright green, and they should squeak when you rub the leaves together—evidence that the artichoke still retains much of its moisture. If you tug at a leaf, it should cleanly snap off; if it bends, the artichoke is old. Also be on guard for leaves that look dried and feathery around the edges—sure signs of an over-the-hill artichoke.

Roman-Style Stuffed Braised Artichokes

SERVES 4

Although artichokes are available through much of the year in the United States, their high season is the spring. The bulk of the artichoke crop is grown in Monterey County, California, where the plants respond well to the Mediterranean-like climate. For this recipe, the artichokes are braised and removed from the pan, and the sauce is reduced. By the time the braising liquid is reduced to a saucelike consis-tency, the artichokes have cooled to a comfortable temperature. Serve each artichoke accompanied by a spoon so that diners can fish out the stuffing as they scrape the edible flesh from the bottom of each leaf with their teeth. Use a knife and fork to eat the tender heart once it is exposed. For information about buying artichokes, see left.

1	large lemon
4	medium artichokes (8 to 10 ounces each)
½	cup fresh bread crumbs (see page 57)
4	medium cloves garlic, minced or pressed through a garlic press
¼	cup minced fresh parsley leaves, stems reserved
¼	cup minced fresh mint leaves
½	cup extra-virgin olive oil
	Salt
1	medium onion, cut crosswise into ½-inch-thick slices and separated into rings (see illustration 6 on page 55)
	Ground black pepper

1. Grate the zest from the lemon and reserve. Squeeze 1 teaspoon juice from the lemon and reserve. Squeeze the remaining lemon juice into a large mixing bowl halfway filled with water and add the spent lemon halves. Working with one artichoke at a time, clean the artichokes (see illustrations 1 through 5 on page 55) and immediately add them to the bowl of water to prevent discoloration.

2. Once the artichokes are all clean, combine the lemon zest, bread crumbs, garlic, minced parsley leaves, mint, olive oil, ½ teaspoon salt, and pepper in a small bowl. Using a small spoon, divide the filling equally among the artichokes, placing it in the center of the artichoke where the choke was.

3. Spread the onion rings evenly over the bottom of a Dutch oven and sprinkle them with the reserved parsley stems and ¼ teaspoon salt. Position the artichokes evenly around the pan, with the stems facing downward at an angle and set into the onion rings

(see illustration 6 on page 55). Fill the pan with enough cold water so that the stems are three-quarters submerged. Cover the pot and bring the water to a boil over medium-high heat. Reduce the heat to medium-low and simmer for 15 minutes. Use tongs to rotate the artichokes so that the side pointing down toward the water faces away from the water. Continue cooking until a knife tip easily punctures and pulls cleanly from the heart, about 15 minutes longer.

4. Carefully remove the artichokes from the pot and transfer them to a large plate. Strain the braising liquid through a fine-mesh strainer and return the liquid to the pot. Over high heat, briskly cook the liquid until it reduces to ½ cup, about 20 minutes. Pour the thickened liquid into a serving dish and stir in the reserved 1 teaspoon lemon juice. Season with salt and pepper to taste. Pass the artichokes and the sauce separately at the table; use the sauce for dipping.

MAKING FRESH BREAD CRUMBS

Fresh bread crumbs are far superior to bland, overly fine commercial crumbs. Any stray hunk of good-quality bread (preferably made without sweetener, seeds, or other extraneous ingredients) can be turned into fresh crumbs. Country white bread, plain Italian bread, and baguettes are ideal. Slightly stale bread is easier to cut, but crumbs can be made from fresh bread. You can use the crumbs as is or toast them in a dry skillet over medium heat until golden brown.

1. Slice off and discard the bottom crust of the bread if it is tough and over-baked.

2. Slice the bread into ³⁄₈-inch-thick pieces. Cut these slices into ³⁄₈-inch strips, then cut these into cubes and chop until you have small pieces about the size of a lemon seed.

3. To make the crumbs in a food processor, cut the trimmed loaf into 1½-inch cubes, then pulse the cubes in a food processor to the desired crumb size.

BROILED ASPARAGUS WITH PARMESAN CHEESE

FROM THUMB-FAT TO PENCIL-THIN, deep purple to emerald green, asparagus of all shapes and sizes is hugely popular throughout Italy. Simply topped with a dusting of Parmesan cheese, asparagus is at its very best. The nuttiness of the cheese intensifies the vegetable's sweet, herbal flavor. And, as we found, this dish could not be any easier to make.

Most Italian asparagus preparations are simple, allowing the vegetable's assertive flavor to stand on its own. While blanching and grilling are both typical cooking methods, we liked this vegetable best grilled or broiled because the high heat evaporates its moisture, effectively concentrating the flavor. Further, the exterior is rendered crisp and browned and the interior succulent. While the grill lends a delicious smoky edge, we tend to broil asparagus because of the convenience.

After broiling asparagus of varying width, we decided that slim, pencil-thin asparagus are the best choice. They cook quickly and uniformly, and they are easy to prepare because they do not have to be peeled. Outside of snapping off the fibrous ends, they require nothing more than a quick rinse.

For the best results, we found, cook the asparagus quite close to the heating element— the highest setting for the oven rack, or about four inches away. Within minutes, the asparagus are cooked through and browned.

In an attempt to save on dishwashing, we tried coating the asparagus with olive oil, salt, and pepper on the baking sheet. The technique was successful; the asparagus could simply be rolled around on the sheet until thoroughly coated.

We tried both thin, shaved curls and finely grated Parmesan, and tasters unanimously preferred the grated cheese. While appealingly rustic, the curls did not flavor the asparagus as well as the grated cheese, which tenaciously clung to the individual spears as it melted.

Broiled Asparagus with Parmesan Cheese

SERVES 4

Thick spears will burn on the surface before they cook through, so use spears no thicker than ³⁄₈ inch for this recipe. To keep asparagus in their optimal shape, store them upright, covered with a damp towel and the bottoms submerged in an inch of water. For a quick and easy dinner, serve these asparagus with softly scrambled eggs (or tucked into an omelet) and some crusty bread to soak up the juices.

1¼	pounds thin asparagus, tough ends snapped off (see illustration on page 59)
2	tablespoons extra-virgin olive oil
	Salt and coarsely ground black pepper
1½	teaspoons lemon juice from 1 lemon
¼	cup finely grated Parmesan cheese

1. Adjust the oven rack to the highest position (about 4 inches below the heating element) and heat the broiler. Lay the asparagus in a single layer on a rimmed baking sheet. Drizzle them with the oil and sprinkle with ¼ teaspoon salt and ⅛ teaspoon pepper. Roll the asparagus back and forth to evenly coat.

2. Cook the asparagus until they are beginning to brown lightly and a knife easily punctures the stalk, 8 to 10 minutes. Remove the baking sheet from the oven, drizzle the asparagus with the lemon juice, and transfer to a warmed serving plate. Pour any juices from the baking sheet over the asparagus, sprinkle the Parmesan cheese evenly over the top, and season with salt and pepper to taste. Serve immediately.

➤ VARIATION
Grilled Asparagus with Parmesan Cheese

Although broiling makes sense as a year-round method for preparing asparagus, grilling gives the spears a nice smoky edge and is the best choice in the summer or whenever the grill is already lit.

Coat the asparagus with the oil, salt, and pepper on a rimmed baking sheet, as directed in step 1 of the recipe for Broiled Asparagus with Parmesan Cheese. Transfer the asparagus to a preheated grill and cook, turning once, until tender and streaked with light grill marks, 5 to 7 minutes. Transfer the grilled asparagus to a warmed serving plate, drizzle with the lemon juice, and sprinkle with the cheese.

SNAPPING OFF TOUGH ENDS FROM ASPARAGUS

In our tests, we found that the tough, woody part of the stem will break off in just the right place if you hold the spear the right way. Hold the asparagus about halfway down the stalk; with the other hand, hold the cut end between the thumb and index finger about an inch or so up from the bottom; bend the stalk until it snaps.

BROCCOLI WITH GARLIC

VEGETABLES SAUTÉED WITH OLIVE OIL, garlic, and hot red pepper flakes are standard fare throughout Italy. This is one of Italy's simplest vegetable preparations, and one of the most delicious. The fruity olive oil enriches the vegetable's natural flavor (without masking it, as butter can), and the garlic and spicy pepper flakes add zest and brightness to the dish. The secret to the technique, as for most Italian recipes, is using top-quality ingredients. The vegetables should be perfectly fresh; you cannot hide weary vegetables behind such simple flavors. Luckily for us, first-rate broccoli is available year-round in most American markets.

While we found nothing particularly tricky about this dish, both the broccoli and garlic must be cooked correctly for the best flavor. Before sautéing, the broccoli must be either steamed or blanched. The dry heat of a skillet is not enough to cook the thick broccoli florets. We prefer blanching to steaming broccoli because it both seasons the broccoli and sets the color. Also, because the blanching time is so short, the broccoli is not robbed of its nutritional value—one of the accusations routinely leveled at blanching. As little as 2½ minutes cooked the broccoli until it was al dente, or retaining a bit of crunch. Because the broccoli finishes cooking in the skillet, it's important that it doesn't overcook during the blanching phase.

Shocking blanched vegetables—dropping them into ice water as soon as they are drained—is crucial to prevent overcooking and to preserve the vegetables' color. We found it good practice to ready a bowl of ice water as the blanching water comes to a boil so that it's ready when needed. The vegetables can be scooped from the boiling water with a strainer or tongs and deposited directly into the ice bath. For the best color, we found the vegetables should sit in the bath until they are chilled thoroughly. They can then either be cooked immediately—as we did the broccoli—or held in the refrigerator until needed.

Traditionally, the amount of garlic and pepper flakes used to flavor the broccoli varies from region to region. Conventionally, southern Italians prefer more robust flavors and include a healthy amount of both. Northerners, on the other hand, use a lighter hand with such assertive seasonings.

Many recipes we found suggested that the garlic was only for flavoring the oil; once the garlic is lightly browned, it should be removed. The resulting oil is subtly flavored—too meekly for most of our tasters, who demanded that the garlic be left in. Lightly browning the garlic brings out its sweetness and adds a faint nuttiness that complements the broccoli. Toasting the hot red pepper flakes disperses their flavor through the oil and mellows any bitterness.

EQUIPMENT: Vegetable Peelers

You might imagine that all vegetable peelers are pretty much the same. Not so. In our research, we turned up 25 peelers, many with quite novel features. The major differences were the fixture of the blade (either stationary or swiveling), the material of the blade (carbon stainless steel, stainless steel, or ceramic), and the orientation of the blade to the handle (either straight in line with the body or perpendicular to it). The last arrangement, with the blade perpendicular to the handle, is called a harp or Y peeler because the frame looks like the body of a harp or the letter Y. This type of peeler, which is popular in Europe, works with a pulling motion rather than the shucking motion of most American peelers.

To test the peelers, we recruited several cooks and asked them to peel carrots, potatoes, lemons, butternut squash, and celery root. In most cases, testers preferred the Oxo Good Grips peeler with a sharp stainless steel blade that swivels. Peelers with stationary blades are fine for peeling carrots, but they have trouble hugging the curves on potatoes. As for blade material, we found both sharp and dull peelers made from each type of material. We concluded that sharpness is a factor of quality control during the manufacturing process and not of blade material.

The Y-shaped peelers tested well, although they removed more flesh along with the skin on potatoes, lemons, and carrots and therefore did not rate as well as the Oxo Good Grips. The one case where this liability turned into an asset was with butternut squash, where these peelers took off the skin as well as the greenish-tinged flesh right below the skin in one pass. With the Oxo Good Grips, it was necessary to go over the peeled flesh once the skin had been removed. Among Y-shaped peelers, testers preferred the Kuhn Rikon. Because both the Oxo Good Grips and Kuhn Rikon peelers can be had for less than $10, we recommend that you purchase both.

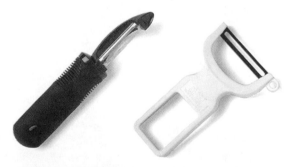

THE BEST PEELERS

The Oxo Good Grips (left) is our favorite all-purpose peeler. The blade is sharp and great on curves. However, testers in the kitchen with very small hands did complain about the bulky handle. The Kuhn Rikon (right) is our favorite Y-shaped peeler. Because this type of peeler removes more skin than a conventional peeler, it's an especially good choice for peeling items with a thick skin, such as butternut squash and celery root.

Broccoli with Garlic

SERVES 4 TO 6

Fresh broccoli is crisp and firm to the touch, and the stems cleanly snap off. If they bend, look for another bunch. The simplicity of this preparation demands freshness. While perfect as a side dish, the broccoli can also be served over pasta for a light main dish. After removing the broccoli from the blanching water, add the pasta. A short, tubular pasta, like penne, is traditional. While the pasta cooks, sauté the broccoli, then toss it with the drained pasta. Add a grating of Parmesan cheese and a drizzle of good-quality olive oil if you like. You may want to reserve some of the pasta cooking water to moisten this dish.

	Salt
1 ½	pounds broccoli, prepared according to illustrations at right
2	tablespoons extra-virgin olive oil
5	medium cloves garlic, sliced thin
¼	teaspoon hot red pepper flakes
2	teaspoons lemon juice from 1 lemon
	Ground black pepper

1. Bring 4 quarts water to a boil in a large Dutch oven or stockpot over high heat. Meanwhile, fill a large bowl with ice water. Once the water is boiling, add 1 tablespoon salt and the broccoli and cook until the broccoli is softened but a knife tip still meets with resistance, about 2½ minutes. With a slotted spoon, transfer the broccoli to the ice water; allow it to cool, then drain.

2. Combine the oil, garlic, and hot red pepper flakes in a large skillet over medium-high heat. As the oil begins to sizzle, shake the pan back and forth so that the garlic does not stick. Once the garlic begins to turn very light brown, about 2 minutes, add the broccoli and cook, stirring frequently, until the broccoli is hot, 1 to 2 minutes. Remove the pan from the heat and sprinkle with the lemon juice. Season with salt and pepper to taste and serve immediately.

BROCCOLI RABE

ITALIANS LOVE BROCCOLI RABE, ALSO known as *rapini, cime de rape, rape, raab,* and *broco-letti.* A perfect plate of broccoli rabe is intensely flavored but not intensely bitter, allowing the other ingredients and flavors in the dish to be tasted. So we set our sights on developing a dependable, quick method of cooking this aggressive vegetable that would deliver less bitterness and a round, balanced flavor.

PREPARING BROCCOLI

1. Place the broccoli upside down on a cutting board and cut off the florets very close to their heads with a large knife.

2. Once the florets are removed, stand each stalk on the cutting board and square it off with a large knife. This will remove the outer ⅛ inch from the stalk, which is quite tough. Now cut the stalk in half lengthwise and into bite-sized pieces.

Parcooking bitter greens helps to carry off some of the bitter flavor. We found that steaming produced little change in the broccoli rabe; the bitterness was still intense. When blanched in a small amount of salted boiling water (1 quart water for about 1 pound broccoli rabe), the rabe was much better, but the bitterness was still pronounced. When we increased the boiling salted water to 3 quarts, sure enough, the broccoli rabe was delicious; it was complex, mustardy, and peppery as well as slightly bitter, and the garlic and olive oil added later complemented rather than competed with its flavor. Depending on personal taste, you can reduce the amount of blanching water for stronger flavor or, to really tone down the bitterness, increase it.

After considerable testing, we found that the lower two inches or so of the stems were woody and tough, while the upper portions of the stems were tender enough to include in the recipes. When we used only the upper portions, there was no need to go through the laborious task of peeling the stems. Cutting the stems into pieces about one inch long made them easier to eat and allowed them to cook in the same amount of time as the florets and the leaves.

Once the broccoli rabe is blanched and dried, it can be sautéed in olive oil with any number of seasonings. We particularly liked assertive flavors, such as garlic and sun-dried tomatoes, which can stand up to the punch of this vegetable.

Blanched Broccoli Rabe
SERVES 4

Once the broccoli rabe is blanched, it should be seasoned and sautéed according to one of the variations that follow.

2	teaspoons salt
I	pound broccoli rabe, bottom 2 inches of stems trimmed and discarded, remainder cut into 1-inch pieces

Bring 3 quarts water to a boil in a large saucepan or Dutch oven. Meanwhile, fill a large bowl with ice water. Once the water is boiling, add the salt and broccoli rabe and cook until the broccoli rabe is wilted and tender, about 2½ minutes. With a slotted spoon, transfer the broccoli rabe to the ice

PREPARING BROCCOLI RABE

1. The thick stalk ends on broccoli rabe should be trimmed and discarded. Use a sharp knife to cut off the thickest part (usually the bottom 2 inches) of each stalk.

2. Cut the remaining stalks and florets into bite-sized pieces, about 1 inch long.

water; allow it to cool, then drain it. Squeeze it well to dry and proceed with one of the following variations.

➤ VARIATIONS

Broccoli Rabe with Sun-Dried Tomatoes and Pine Nuts

This variation can be turned into a main-course pasta dish. Increase the oil to 4 tablespoons and toss the broccoli rabe with 1 pound pasta, cooked al dente. Season to taste with salt and ground black pepper and serve with grated Parmesan cheese.

2	tablespoons extra-virgin olive oil
3	medium cloves garlic, minced or pressed through a garlic press
¼	teaspoon hot red pepper flakes
¼	cup drained oil-packed sun-dried tomatoes, cut into thin strips
1	recipe Blanched Broccoli Rabe
3	tablespoons pine nuts, toasted
	Salt

Broccoli rabe works best with assertive ingredients such as sun-dried tomatoes, pine nuts, garlic, and hot red pepper flakes.

Heat the oil, garlic, hot red pepper flakes, and sun-dried tomatoes in a medium skillet over medium heat until the garlic begins to sizzle, about 3 minutes. Increase the heat to medium-high, add the blanched broccoli rabe and pine nuts, and cook, stirring to coat with the oil, until the broccoli rabe is heated through, about 1 minute. Season to taste with salt. Serve immediately.

Broccoli Rabe with Garlic and Red Pepper Flakes

2	tablespoons extra-virgin olive oil
3	medium cloves garlic, minced or pressed through a garlic press
¼	teaspoon hot red pepper flakes
1	recipe Blanched Broccoli Rabe
	Salt

Heat the oil, garlic, and hot red pepper flakes in a medium skillet over medium heat until the garlic begins to sizzle, about 3 minutes. Increase the heat to medium-high, add the blanched broccoli rabe, and cook, stirring to coat with the oil, until heated through, about 1 minute. Season to taste with salt. Serve immediately.

SAVOY CABBAGE WITH PANCETTA

BRAISED—OR, AS THE VENETIANS CALL it, smothered—savoy cabbage with pancetta is a warming dish found from Venice northward through Friuli-Venezia. This comfort food combines the earthy, slightly pungent flavor of savoy cabbage with subtly spiced pancetta to great effect; we could not ask for more on a blustery winter day. As with many Italian vegetable dishes, braised cabbage is simple to prepare but, as we discovered, requires careful attention to detail.

Savoy cabbage is a mild cousin to green and red cabbage, identifiable by its trademark wrinkles and pale celery-green hue. Its texture is light and feathery, closer to Chinese or napa than green cabbage. Pancetta is the closest thing Italians have to American slab bacon. It employs the same cut of meat from the pig's fatty belly, but instead of smoking it, the Italians season it heavily with a combination of salt and spices that always includes coarsely ground black pepper and usually includes cloves. It's cured for two weeks, rolled up tightly like a jelly roll, and packed into a casing.

The recipe is pretty straightforward. The pancetta is cooked to render some of its fat. The cabbage is added, along with liquid (usually stock), and the pot is partially covered. The cabbage braises until it is tender and the liquid has evaporated. Although the cooking technique for this dish provided few challenges, we did find ourselves breaking with tradition.

Some authentic recipes added the stock along with the cabbage so that the cabbage never sees dry heat, but we found that this led to rubbery cabbage and an excessively long cooking time before it was cooked through and soft. Sautéing the cabbage until wilted remedied the situation; the cabbage softened quickly, and the end texture was significantly better. Most tasters also thought that the sautéed cabbage had a richer flavor.

Assigning a doneness level to the cabbage proved surprisingly tricky. Tasters fell into two camps: those who wanted it cooked to a melting softness just shy of baby food, and the rest, who requested a modicum of texture. The Italians lean toward the soft side; some recipes we researched cooked the cabbage for upwards of two hours. To please everyone, we braised it until soft but with the slightest hint of bite.

While several Italian recipes we found called for little beyond cabbage and pancetta, we felt the dish needed more depth. Sautéed onion bolstered the sweetness of the cabbage and added to the overall depth of the dish. Garlic, too, built depth and accented the cabbage's subtle earthiness. Minced parsley, stirred in at the end, added some much-needed lightness and visual appeal.

A final caveat: Like all cabbage dishes, this must be cooked only partially covered so that the sulfurous odors have a chance to escape. Otherwise, the cabbage's aroma can be less than enticing, to put it mildly.

SLICING SAVOY CABBAGE

1. Cut the cabbage into quarters. Cut away the hard piece of the core attached to each quarter.

2. Lay each quarter flat side down on a cutting board and cut crosswise to yield long, thin strips.

Smothered Savoy Cabbage with Pancetta

SERVES 4 TO 6

Not all pancetta is cut of the same cloth. During testing, we picked up pancetta from several stores, and it varied considerably. Some was thickly coated with peppercorns and other seasonings, while others were practically naked in comparison. If you succeed in finding heavily seasoned pancetta, which we prefer, use a light hand when adding salt and pepper. If you happen to have leftovers, the cabbage is delicious tucked into a grilled cheese sandwich made with fontina cheese.

2	tablespoons unsalted butter
4	ounces pancetta, diced fine
1	medium onion, sliced thin
4	medium cloves garlic, sliced thin
1½	pounds savoy cabbage, cored and sliced thin (see illustrations on page 64)
1	(14½-ounce) can low-sodium chicken broth
1	bay leaf
2	tablespoons minced fresh parsley leaves
	Salt and ground black pepper

1. Melt the butter in a large, heavy-bottomed saucepan over medium heat. Once the foaming subsides, add the pancetta and cook, stirring occasionally, until the fat is rendered and the meat is beginning to brown, 6 to 7 minutes. Increase the heat to medium-high, add the onion, and cook, continuing to stir, until the onion has softened and lightly browned around the edges, about 6 minutes.

2. Add ¼ cup water and deglaze the pan, scraping any browned bits off the bottom of the pan. Once the water has evaporated, add the garlic and the cabbage. Cook, stirring frequently, until the cabbage has wilted, 5 to 6 minutes.

3. Reduce the heat to low, add the broth and bay leaf, and partially cover the pot. Cook until the cabbage is soft and no stock remains in the pan, 40 to 45 minutes. Stir in the parsley and season with salt and pepper to taste. Serve immediately.

SAUTÉED CARROTS WITH MARSALA

EMINENTLY DRINKABLE AND USED frequently in the Italian kitchen to flavor dishes like chicken Marsala (see page 233), Marsala is a versatile wine. Its complex sweetness and mild smokiness pair well with many foods, including sautéed carrots. The wine's fruity, maplelike flavor brings out the natural sugars in the carrots and mellows the often metallic finish of this vegetable. After trying a variety of traditional recipes that produced mediocre results, we achieved success by staying true to the ingredients but altering the authentic technique.

Marsala is a fortified wine (that is, beefed up with extra alcohol) native to the town of Marsala in western Sicily. Its manufacture dates to the mid-eighteenth century, when an English wine merchant who found similarities between the region's wines and those of Spain

SLICING CARROTS

Position the peeled carrot parallel to the edge of the counter, hold the knife at a 45-degree angle, and cut the carrot into ¼-inch slices.

and Portugal—where sherry and port are made—began producing it. Like sherry, Marsala is produced via a solera system, or the blending of wines from different years to produce consistent, nonvintaged bottles (although unblended Marsala does exist). Like most wines, it is available in a range of prices, though we found inexpensive bottles to be fine for both drinking and cooking (we developed this recipe with a $12 bottle). Although price may not matter greatly, style does. For this dish, we found that a sweet Marsala, not a dry one, is essential.

To begin, we had to pick the type of carrots we were to cook. We hoped to use the peeled baby carrots because they make preparation so easy, but we found them dried out and, surprisingly, unevenly cut—some were large and lumpy, while others were whittled down to nubs. Worst of all, they had little taste. While baby bunched carrots looked pretty and tasted great raw, their delicate flavor faded when cooked and was completely buried under the Marsala. We had the best luck with basic bagged carrots. They were sweet, crisp, and deeply carroty.

To cut the carrots, we borrowed bias-cut slices (cut on the diagonal at 45 degrees) from Asian cookery. The method allows for uniform pieces regardless of the shape or size of the carrots. They were attractive, too.

While the high, dry heat of sautéing emphasizes carrots' sweetness, it does not efficiently cook them through; the exterior may be alluringly glossy and browned, but the interior is still crunchy and metallic-tasting. Unless they are baby carrots or sliced wafer thin, carrots must be cooked in liquid (they

---

EQUIPMENT: Cutting Boards

What separates good cutting boards from bad ones? Is it material? Size? Thickness? Weight? Whether the board warps or retains odors with use? And what about the issue of bacteria retention?

To sort all of this out, we gathered boards made from wood, polyethylene (plastic), acrylic, glass, and Corian (the hard countertop material) and used them daily in our test kitchen for eight weeks. We found the two most important factors to be size and material.

In terms of size, large boards provide ample space for both cutting and pushing aside cut foods and waste. The disadvantage of really large boards is that they may not fit in the dishwasher. We are willing to make that sacrifice for the extra work area. If you are not, buy the largest board that will fit in your dishwasher.

Material is important primarily in terms of the way the board interacts with the knife, but it is also relevant to odor retention and warping. We disliked cutting on hard acrylic, glass, and Corian boards because they don't absorb the shock of the knife strike. Plastic and wood boards are softer and therefore cushion the knife's blow, making for more controlled cutting. The pebbly surface texture of the acrylic and glass boards was another point against them. We found that a rough texture promotes knife slide.

There is one advantage to hard boards—they don't retain odors like plastic and wood can. A dishwasher will remove odors from plastic boards as well as specially treated dishwasher-safe wood boards.

If your boards are too large to fit in the dishwasher, use one for onions, garlic, and the like; another for raw poultry and meat; and a third for other foods. To remove most odors and bacteria, wash with hot soapy water after each use and then sanitize with a light bleach solution (1 tablespoon bleach to 1 gallon water).

Makers of wood boards advise consumers to season their boards with mineral oil to build up water resistance and, thereby, warp resistance. As none of the cooks we know will go this extra mile, plastic boards probably make the most sense for home cooks. Keep them away from the heating element in the dishwasher to prevent warping.

are a root vegetable, after all). Most of the traditional recipes for this dish we found cooked the carrots until they were browned and then added Marsala to finish the cooking, literally braising the carrots in the wine. The approach worked, but the carrots were occasionally cooked through long before the liquid evaporated, resulting in mushy, overcooked carrots.

We inverted the technique and cooked the carrots from the inside out. We started the carrots in Marsala, added a sprig of thyme, and simmered them until barely tender, then added butter and sautéed them until they were browned. We reduced the excess wine to a highly flavored, syrupy gloss that, with the addition of a pinch of sugar, tenaciously clung to the carrots.

To finish the dish, we added a splash of fresh Marsala. The cooked carrots were already deeply flavored with Marsala, and the uncooked wine reinforced the flavor. Parsley and lemon brightened the flavors and appearance of the finished dish.

Sautéed Carrots with Marsala

SERVES 4

When shopping for Marsala, make sure to pick up a sweet, not dry, type. Bagged carrots should be quite firm and bright orange. If they look dried out or are cracked, they have been sitting for too long. Also be on the guard for bags with water inside, as the carrots are most certainly slimy and may have begun to rot. If you do not have fresh thyme, substitute 2 bay leaves.

I	pound whole carrots, peeled and cut into ¼-inch slices on the bias (see illustration on page 65)
	Salt
I	sprig fresh thyme
½	cup plus I tablespoon sweet Marsala wine

I	tablespoon unsalted butter, cut into 4 pieces
I	tablespoon sugar
I	teaspoon juice from I lemon
2	teaspoons minced fresh parsley leaves
	Ground black pepper

1. Bring the carrots, ½ teaspoon salt, thyme, and ½ cup Marsala to a boil in a covered 12-inch skillet over medium-high heat. Reduce the heat to medium and simmer, stirring occasionally, until the carrots are just tender when poked with the tip of a paring knife, about 5 minutes.

2. Uncover, increase the heat to high, and simmer, stirring occasionally, until the liquid is reduced to about 2 tablespoons, 1 to 2 minutes. Add the butter and sugar, toss the carrots to coat, and cook, stirring occasionally, until the carrots are completely tender and the glaze is light golden, about 3 minutes.

3. Off the heat, add the remaining 1 tablespoon Marsala, the lemon juice, and the parsley; toss to coat. Transfer the carrots to a serving bowl with a heatproof rubber spatula, scraping any glaze from the pan. Discard the sprig of thyme, season with salt and pepper to taste, and serve immediately.

EGGPLANT

FEW VEGETABLES ARE MORE CLOSELY associated with Italian cooking than eggplant. Italians prepare eggplant in several ways, including sautéing, broiling, grilling, and frying. The biggest challenge that confronts the cook when preparing eggplant is excess moisture. While the grill will evaporate this liquid and allow the eggplant to brown nicely, this won't happen under the broiler or in a hot pan. The eggplant will steam in its own juices. The result is an insipid flavor and mushy texture. And if you don't remove the moisture when frying, the results can be dangerous and messy. (For more on frying eggplant, see the eggplant Parmesan recipe on page 70.)

Salting is the classic technique for drawing moisture out of the eggplant before cooking. We experimented with both regular table salt and kosher salt and preferred kosher salt because the crystals are large enough to wipe away after the salt has done its job. Finer table salt crystals dissolved into the eggplant flesh and had to be flushed out with water. The eggplant must then be thoroughly dried, which adds more prep time, especially if the eggplant has been diced for sautéing. (We prefer to dice eggplant that will be sautéed to increase the surface area that can brown and absorb flavorings.)

Eggplant destined for the broiler should be sliced very thin so that the salt can work quickly. The salt will take more time to penetrate thicker slices and will be less effective. However, when grilling, you want thicker slices that won't fall apart on the cooking grate. We found ¾-inch rounds perfect for grilling.

Sautéed Eggplant
SERVES 4

Very small eggplants (less than 6 ounces each) may be cooked without salting. However, we found that large eggplants generally have a lot of moisture, which is best removed before cooking.

1	large eggplant (about 1½ pounds), ends trimmed, cut into ¾-inch cubes
1	tablespoon kosher salt
2	tablespoons extra-virgin olive oil
	Ground black pepper
1	medium clove garlic, minced or pressed through a garlic press
2	tablespoons minced fresh parsley or finely shredded fresh basil leaves

1. Place the eggplant cubes in a large colander and sprinkle with the salt, tossing to coat evenly. Let stand 30 minutes. Using paper towels or a large kitchen towel, wipe the salt off and pat the excess moisture from the eggplant.

2. Heat the oil in a heavy-bottomed 12-inch skillet over medium-high heat until it shimmers. Add the eggplant cubes and sauté until they begin to brown, about 4 minutes. Reduce the heat to medium-low and cook, stirring occasionally, until the eggplant is fully tender and lightly browned, 10 to 15 minutes. Stir in pepper to taste and add the garlic. Cook to blend the flavors, about 2 minutes. Off the heat, stir in the parsley or basil and adjust the seasonings. Serve immediately.

➤ VARIATION
Sautéed Eggplant with Crisped Bread Crumbs

Melt 2 tablespoons unsalted butter in small skillet. Add ½ cup fresh bread crumbs (see page 57) and toast over medium-high heat until deep golden and crisp, stirring frequently, about 5 to 6 minutes. Follow the recipe for Sautéed Eggplant, adding the toasted bread crumbs with the parsley or basil.

Broiled Eggplant
SERVES 4

For broiling, it's best to slice the eggplant very thin.

1	large eggplant (about 1½ pounds), ends trimmed, sliced crosswise into ¼-inch-thick rounds
1	tablespoon kosher salt
3	tablespoons extra-virgin olive oil
2	tablespoons minced fresh parsley or finely shredded fresh basil leaves
	Ground black pepper

1. Place the eggplant in a large colander and sprinkle with the salt, tossing to coat evenly. Let stand 30 minutes. Using paper towels or a large kitchen towel, wipe the salt off and pat the excess moisture from the eggplant.

2. Adjust the oven rack to the highest position (about 4 inches below the heating element) and heat the broiler. Arrange the eggplant slices on a foil-lined baking sheet. Brush both sides with the oil. Broil the eggplant slices until the tops are mahogany brown, 3 to 4 minutes. Turn the slices over and broil until the other side browns, another 3 to 4 minutes.

3. Remove the eggplant from the oven and sprinkle with the parsley or basil. Season with pepper to taste and serve hot, warm, or at room temperature.

➤ VARIATION

Broiled Eggplant with Parmesan Cheese

This dish is delicious on its own and perfect as a vegetarian main course for two when served with a basic tomato sauce.

Follow the recipe for Broiled Eggplant through step 2. Sprinkle the cooked eggplant with ½ cup grated Parmesan cheese. Return the eggplant to the broiler until the cheese melts and becomes bubbly and browned, 2 to 3 minutes. Sprinkle with parsley or basil, sprinkle with pepper to taste, and serve immediately.

Grilled Eggplant

SERVES 4

There's no need to salt eggplant destined for the grill. The intense grill heat will vaporize excess moisture.

- 3 tablespoons extra-virgin olive oil
- 2 medium cloves garlic, minced or pressed through a garlic press
- 2 teaspoons minced fresh thyme or fresh oregano leaves
- Salt and ground black pepper
- 1 large eggplant (about 1 ½ pounds), ends trimmed, cut crosswise into ¾-inch rounds

1. Light the grill. Combine the oil, garlic, herb, and salt and pepper to taste in a small bowl. Place the eggplant on a platter and brush both sides with the oil mixture.

2. Grill the eggplant, turning once, until both sides are marked with dark stripes, 8 to 10 minutes. Serve hot, warm, or at room temperature.

EGGPLANT PARMESAN

FEW ITALIAN DISHES HAVE BEEN MORE distorted in the United States than eggplant Parmesan. The oil-sodden, dense mass sold by every street-corner pizza joint has little to do with the authentic version from Naples, which is infinitely lighter in texture and richer in flavor. Ideally, eggplant Parmesan features crisp slices of greaseless fried eggplant layered with a bright basil-laced tomato sauce and bound with a minimum of fresh mozzarella and Parmesan cheeses. We hoped we could create a recipe that captured the deep flavor and light texture of the original.

Addressing the dish's texture first, we set to work on the eggplant. Eggplant has the propensity to act like a sponge and soak up oil when fried. To avoid this problem, it is traditionally coated with salt and allowed to sit anywhere from 15 minutes to several hours. The salt draws out the eggplant's juices, effectively collapsing the cell walls so that it will not absorb oil quite so effectively. We tried different lengths of salting time and found that ½ hour was all that was necessary. The salt also serves another purpose: As the moisture is wicked from the eggplant, its bitterness is removed. Firmly blotting the slices with kitchen towels or paper towels after salting helped remove the salt and the remaining liquid. We found that firmly pressing the eggplant helped compress the slices so they would absorb less oil and fry up better.

While salting helped prevent the eggplant from absorbing oil, we found that a thick breading was also necessary. We tried dredging the eggplant in flour prior to frying, but this was not thick enough and resulted in gummy, oil-soaked eggplant. A thicker bread-crumb coating, made first by dusting the eggplant in seasoned flour, then dipping it in egg, provided a more substantial barrier that proved relatively impervious to oil. Toasted bread crumbs made for an exceptionally crisp, caramel-brown crust on the eggplant. We found that the crunchier the crust was after frying, the crisper it would stay when baked with the cheese and sauce.

Most Americans are familiar with excessive amounts of stringy mozzarella in eggplant Parmesan, but the dish's name tells the true story about this recipe. Parmesan cheese is the authentic cheese (the name of the dish literally means "in the style of Parma") that flavors the dish; mozzarella binds everything together. Mozzarella made from buffalo milk is traditional, but it can be hard to find and is generally quite expensive. We found that standard whole-milk mozzarella worked just fine, as its presence is more about texture than flavor. Good-quality Parmesan, however, is important to the dish.

To cut the richness of the eggplant and cheese, we made a slightly spicy tomato sauce. A quick-cooked sauce kept the tomato flavors bright, and lightly toasted garlic added depth and body. Basil brought freshness and an anise note that complemented both the eggplant and the tomato, and hot red pepper flakes sharpened the flavors. We kept the amount of

sauce in the casserole to a minimum so the eggplant would not be too soggy. A light coating of the flavorful sauce between layers proved plenty.

To maintain crispness, we assembled the casserole in a shallow baking dish and baked it at a high temperature just until the cheese browned and everything was heated through. We found that a deeper baking dish, lower temperature, and/or longer cooking time made the eggplant watery.

Eggplant Parmesan
SERVES 6 TO 8

While many types of eggplant are on the market these days, we found that conventional globe eggplants were best for this dish. Their large size means fewer slices to bread and fry—the most time-consuming step in the recipe. Look for eggplants whose skin is shiny and taut and that feel very firm to the touch. Wrinkled skin is a sure sign of age and should be avoided. This is a labor-intensive dish, so plan accordingly. Make the sauce first and, while it simmers, salt the eggplant and toast the crumbs.

TOMATO SAUCE

2	tablespoons extra-virgin olive oil
4	medium cloves garlic, sliced thin
½	teaspoon hot red pepper flakes
3	(14½-ounce) cans diced tomatoes, 2 cans briefly processed in a food processor or blender until smooth, 1 can left whole
¼	cup coarsely chopped fresh basil leaves
	Salt and ground black pepper

CASSEROLE

2	eggplants (about 1 pound each), cut crosswise into ½-inch-thick slices
1	tablespoon kosher salt
8	slices white sandwich bread (about 8 ounces)

~~~~~~

2   cups vegetable oil
1   cup unbleached all-purpose flour
1   teaspoon ground black pepper
3   large eggs, beaten
½   pound whole-milk mozzarella, shredded
1   cup finely grated Parmesan cheese
      Torn fresh basil leaves for garnish

1. FOR THE SAUCE: Combine the oil, garlic, and hot red pepper flakes in a large, heavy-bottomed saucepan over medium-high heat. As the oil begins to sizzle, shake the pan back and forth so that the garlic does not stick (stirring with a wooden spoon will cause the garlic to clump). Once the garlic turns light golden, about 2 to 3 minutes, immediately add the pureed and diced tomatoes. When the sauce begins to boil, reduce the heat to medium-low and simmer until the sauce is thick enough to coat the back of a spoon, about 15 minutes. You should have about 4 cups. Stir in the basil and season with salt and pepper to taste.

2. FOR THE CASSEROLE: While the sauce simmers, place the eggplant in a large colander and sprinkle with the salt, tossing to coat evenly. Let stand 30 minutes. Lay the eggplant slices on several layers of paper towels and set another layer of towels over top. Using the heel of your hand, forcefully press each slice to remove as much liquid as possible. Also wipe off excess salt crystals. Set the pressed eggplant slices on a paper towel–lined plate.

3. Adjust an oven rack to the middle position and heat the oven to 400 degrees. Crumble the bread with your hands into the workbowl of a food processor fitted with a steel blade, then pulse the bread repeatedly until it is reduced to coarse crumbs the size of Grape-Nuts cereal, about 12 one-second pulses. Spread the crumbs evenly on a rimmed baking sheet and toast, shaking the pan once or twice to redistribute them, until light golden, 8 to 10 minutes. Transfer the crumbs to a shallow bowl or pie plate and cool.

4. Pour the oil into a 12-inch skillet set over medium heat and heat to 375 degrees. Fill another shallow bowl or pie plate with the flour and pepper and stir to combine. Fill a third shallow bowl or pie plate with the eggs. Working with batches of 6 to 8 eggplant slices (just enough to fit into the skillet), flour each slice, dip it into the eggs, and coat it with bread crumbs, making certain to remove excess coating in each step. Fry the slices, turning once, until golden brown, 3 to 5 minutes. With tongs, remove the slices from the oil, allowing the excess oil to drain back into the pan, and set on a baking sheet covered with several layers of paper towels. Repeat the process until all of the eggplant is fried.

5. Meanwhile, heat the oven to 425 degrees. Once all of the eggplant is fried, assemble the casserole in a 9 by 13-inch baking dish. In the bottom of the baking dish, ladle 1½ cups tomato sauce and spread it out evenly. Top this with a layer of eggplant, half the mozzarella and Parmesan, and 1 cup sauce, then repeat with a second layer of eggplant and the remaining sauce. Sprinkle the rest of the cheeses across the top. Bake until the top is well browned and bubbling, 13 to 15 minutes. Allow to cool for 10 minutes and serve garnished with torn basil leaves.

~~~~~~

BRAISED FENNEL WITH WHITE WINE AND PARMESAN

UNLIKE MOST VEGETABLES, RAW FENNEL HAS a long history of use in salads and antipasti. Italians often put out strips of fennel with a bowl of fine olive oil and salt as a quick antipasto. The fennel is simply dipped in the oil, sprinkled with salt, and enjoyed with cocktails. Raw fennel can also be cut into thin strips or diced and used in salads. Add a handful of diced fennel to a leafy salad or use thin strips of fennel in a citrus salad.

When it comes to cooking, we find that fennel responds to a variety of methods. When fennel is sautéed, roasted, or grilled, the natural sugars caramelize and cause the fennel to brown. The anise flavor and sweetness are quite intense.

But there is something appealing about a braise, in which the fennel is cooked in liquid (usually wine or stock) and then dusted with Parmesan before serving. This dish is more subtle than roasted or grilled fennel, which makes braised fennel a better partner on the table with other foods.

The first choice we had to make when developing this recipe was about the fat—butter or olive oil. Tasters felt that the butter added richness to this dish and worked better with the cheese that is added later.

Next, we considered the braising liquid. Chicken stock, water, and white wine were the leading candidates. Water made the fennel bland and hollow-tasting. The chicken stock was rich and good but a bit overpowering.

We preferred the mild acidity of the white wine, which enlivened the fennel but did not mask its flavor.

Our attempts to hurry the fennel along did not succeed. The fennel must be cut into fairly thick ½-inch slices so it won't fall apart, but these thick slices need nearly 30 minutes of cooking to soften properly. For added flavor, we found it best to cook the fennel until all the liquid in the pan evaporates and the vegetable begins to brown.

Braised Fennel with White Wine and Parmesan

SERVES 4

In this recipe, the fennel cooks slowly in butter and white wine until tender, then receives a dusting of cheese just before serving. This rich side dish works well with beef or veal.

3   tablespoons butter
3   small fennel bulbs (about 2¼ pounds), stems and fronds discarded, blemished portions of bulb trimmed, and bulb cut vertically into ½-inch-thick slices (see illustrations below)

PREPARING FENNEL

1. Cut off the stems and feathery fronds. (The fronds can be minced and used for a garnish.)

2. Trim a very thin slice from the base and remove any tough or blemished outer layers.

3. Slice the bulb vertically through its base into ½-inch-thick pieces that resemble fans.

Salt and ground black pepper
⅓ cup dry white wine
¼ cup grated Parmesan cheese

1. Heat the butter in a large sauté pan over medium heat. Add the fennel and sprinkle with salt and pepper to taste. Add the wine and cover the pan. Simmer for 15 minutes. Turn the slices and continue to simmer, covered, until the fennel is quite tender, has absorbed most of the pan liquid, and starts to turn golden, about 10 minutes longer. Turn the fennel again and continue cooking until the fennel starts to color on the other side, about 4 minutes longer.

2. Sprinkle the fennel with the Parmesan. Transfer to a platter and serve immediately.

GREEN BEANS

ITALIANS HAVE TWO BASIC TREATMENTS for green beans. In the first, they are either boiled or steamed until crisp-tender, drained, and then drizzled with oil, seasoned, and served. In the second, they are braised in a covered pan, usually with tomatoes, until they are extremely tender (some would say overcooked).

For the first option, we find that green beans respond better to boiling than steaming. A pound of beans in a standard steamer basket will not cook evenly; the beans close to the steaming water cook more quickly than the beans at the top of the pile. Stirring the beans once or twice as they cook solves this problem, but it is somewhat dangerous to stick your hand into the hot pot. Boiling is simpler—just add the beans and cook until tender. Boiling also permits the addition of salt during cooking.

Unlike other vegetables, which can become soggy when boiled, the thick skin on green beans keeps their texture crisp and firm. Leave beans whole when boiling; cut beans will become waterlogged. Boiled beans can be flavored with extra-virgin olive oil, salt, and pepper, or more elaborately with toasted nuts, herbs, or brown butter.

The second cooking option is braising. We found that the thick skin on most beans means that they are fairly slow to absorb flavorful liquids like that from tomatoes. For this reason, we had the best success when we braised the beans for a full 20 minutes. Braised beans lose their bright green color. Older, tougher beans benefit from long cooking, but really fresh green beans are best boiled and then seasoned, which retains as much of their flavor and texture as possible.

Blanched Green Beans
SERVES 4

The freshness and thickness of the beans can greatly affect cooking time. Thin, farm-fresh beans not much thicker than a strand of cooked linguine may be done in just 2 minutes. Most supermarket beans are considerably thicker and have traveled some distance, hence the 5-minute cooking time recommended below. Dress the beans with a drizzle of extra-virgin olive oil as well as a generous sprinkling of salt and pepper, or make one of the variations on page 74.

Salt
1 pound green beans, ends snapped off
Extra-virgin olive oil
Ground black pepper

Bring 2½ quarts water to a boil in a large saucepan. Add 1 teaspoon salt and the beans and cook until tender, about 5 minutes. Drain well and transfer the beans to a serving bowl. Drizzle with oil and season with salt and pepper to taste.

Green Beans with Toasted Walnuts and Tarragon

This dish can also be made with toasted pine nuts and/or basil.

Follow the recipe for Blanched Green Beans, placing the drained beans in a large serving bowl. Add ¼ cup chopped and toasted walnuts and 1½ tablespoons minced fresh tarragon leaves. Drizzle with 1½ tablespoons extra-virgin olive oil and toss gently to coat. Sprinkle with salt and pepper to taste and serve warm or at room temperature.

Green Beans with Toasted Hazelnuts and Brown Butter

Chop fine ½ cup hazelnuts (about 2½ ounces) and toast them in a small, heavy-bottomed skillet over medium heat until just fragrant, 3 to 4 minutes. Transfer the toasted nuts to a small plate. Clean the skillet. Heat 4 tablespoons unsalted butter in the skillet over medium heat and cook, swirling frequently, until nut-brown and fragrant, 4 to 5 minutes. Add the hazelnuts and cook, stirring constantly, until fragrant, about 1 minute. Season with salt and pepper to taste. Follow the recipe for Blanched Green Beans, placing the drained beans in a large serving bowl. Add the butter mixture and toss to coat. Serve immediately.

Green Beans with Fresh Tomato, Basil, and Goat Cheese

Follow the recipe for Blanched Green Beans, placing the drained beans in a large serving bowl. Add ½ cup chopped fresh tomato, 2 tablespoons chopped fresh basil leaves, and 1 ounce crumbled goat cheese. Drizzle with 2 tablespoons extra-virgin olive oil and 1 teaspoon balsamic vinegar and toss gently to coat. Season with salt and pepper to taste and serve warm or at room temperature.

Braised Green Beans with Tomatoes and Garlic
SERVES 4

The beans lose their bright green color but gain flavor from cooking in a tomato sauce. This recipe is best suited to older, slightly tougher beans.

2	tablespoons extra-virgin olive oil
1	small onion, diced
2	medium cloves garlic, minced or pressed through a garlic press
1	cup canned diced tomatoes, undrained
1	pound green beans, ends snapped off
	Salt and ground black pepper
2	tablespoons minced fresh parsley leaves

1. Heat the oil in a large sauté pan over medium heat. Add the onion and cook until softened, about 5 minutes. Add the garlic and cook until fragrant, about 1 minute. Add the tomatoes and simmer until the juices thicken slightly, about 5 minutes.

2. Add the green beans, ¼ teaspoon salt, and a few grindings of pepper to the pan. Stir well, cover, and cook, stirring occasionally, until the beans are tender but still offer some resistance to the bite, about 20 minutes. Stir in the parsley and adjust the seasonings. Serve immediately.

MUSHROOMS

COOKS WHO OOH AND AAH OVER porcini, portobellos, and other exotic mushrooms widely available in Italy often find the white mushroom, also called the button, beneath their consideration. But button mushrooms are inexpensive and almost always available (they are the only choice in some markets), which gives them at least some appeal. We figured there must be a way of cooking them that would bring out the deep, rich, earthy flavors for which their tonier cousins are so highly prized.

The most common method of cooking mushrooms is sautéing. The sautéing time seemed crucial, so we cut a handful of mushrooms into uniform ⅜-inch slices and sautéed them in a bit of oil over medium-high heat for times ranging from three minutes to eight minutes, removing one slice from the pan every minute. We preferred those cooked for six minutes, because at this point the mushrooms were moist all the way through—a condition we had learned to recognize as indicating doneness—and slightly browned but not burned on the exterior. Much of the moisture had been cooked out and evaporated, but some still remained in the pan. These mushrooms also tasted pretty good,

with a fairly deep, somewhat complex, nutty flavor from the exterior browning. The texture, however, was not ideal; while tender, the mushrooms were also a bit rubbery.

We tried sautéing the mushrooms until they exuded no more liquid, as suggested in several cookbooks. This took about 12 minutes, though, and by that time the mushrooms had acquired a dark, almost burned taste and again were slightly rubbery. Not terrible, but not great either.

We decided to try roasting to see if we could improve on the flavor and texture delivered by sautéing. Roasted mushrooms were not only moist all the way through but had a deep, rich, pronounced flavor that seemed at once meaty and nutty. This was the real mushroom flavor that we had been trying to coax from this everyday mushroom.

SCIENCE: To Wash or Not to Wash Mushrooms

Common culinary wisdom dictates that mushrooms should never, ever be washed. Put these spongy fungi under the faucet or in a bowl, the dictum goes, and they will soak up water like a sponge.

Like most cooks, we had always blindly followed this precept. But when we learned that mushrooms were over 80 percent water, we began to question their ability to absorb yet more liquid. As we so often do in situations like this, we consulted the works of food scientist and author Harold McGee. Sure enough, in his book *The Curious Cook* (North Point Press, 1990) we found an experiment he had devised to test this very piece of accepted mushroom lore. We decided to duplicate McGee's work in our test kitchen.

We weighed out 6 ounces white mushrooms and put them in a bowl, then added water to cover and let them sit. After 5 minutes we shook off the surface water and weighed them again. Our results replicated McGee's—

the total weight gain for all the mushrooms together was ¼ ounce, which translates to about 1½ teaspoons water.

We suspected that even this gain represented mostly surface moisture rather than absorption, so we repeated the experiment with 6 ounces broccoli, which no one would claim is an absorbent vegetable. The weight gain after a 5-minute soak was almost identical—⅕ ounce—suggesting that most of the moisture was clinging to the surface of both vegetables rather than being absorbed by them.

So, as it turns out, mushrooms can be cleaned in the same way as other vegetables are—rinsed under cold water. However, it's best to rinse them just before cooking and to avoid rinsing altogether if you are using them uncooked, as the surfaces of wet mushrooms turn dark and slimy when they're exposed to air for more than four to five minutes.

Roasted Mushrooms

SERVES 4

This basic recipe can be served as is or flavored in numerous ways. See the variation for one idea.

1   pound white mushrooms, halved if small, quartered if medium, cut into sixths if large
2   tablespoons extra-virgin olive oil
     Salt and ground black pepper

1. Adjust the oven rack to the lowest position and heat the oven to 450 degrees.

2. Toss the mushrooms with the oil and salt and pepper to taste in a medium bowl. Arrange them in a single layer on a large low-sided roasting pan or rimmed baking sheet. Roast until the released juices have nearly evaporated and the mushroom surfaces facing the pan are browned, 12 to 15 minutes. Remove the pan from the oven and turn the mushrooms with a metal spatula. Continue to roast until the mushroom liquid has completely evaporated and the mushrooms are brown all over, 5 to 10 minutes longer. Serve immediately.

➤ VARIATION

Roasted Mushrooms with Garlic, Olives, and Thyme

1   small clove garlic, minced or pressed through a garlic press
1   tablespoon minced fresh thyme leaves
12   brine-cured black olives, pitted and chopped coarse
1   recipe Roasted Mushrooms
1   tablespoon balsamic vinegar

Mix the garlic, thyme, and olives in a medium bowl. Add the roasted mushrooms and vinegar; toss to coat. Serve immediately.

ONIONS AGRODOLCE

AGRODOLCE, ITALIAN FOR "SWEET and sour," is the term for a bracing sauce of vinegar and sugar usually flavored with bay leaves and spices. The sauce has roots in Italian cooking dating back to the Middle Ages and shows a strong connection to North African cooking (as much of Sicilian cooking does). While the original use of agrodolce was to preserve and mask the pungency of rotting fish and meat (before refrigeration was invented or widely available), its assertive flavor is a suitable complement to a variety of vegetables. Piquant onions may be the best choice. As part of an antipasto platter or as an accompaniment to roasted meat or rich cheese, onions agrodolce provide a vigorous counterpoint.

We were surprised by the diversity of recipes for such a simple dish. Ingredient lists were wildly different, and cooking technique followed one of two directions. Cipollini onions were the only standard ingredient, but they are virtually unavailable throughout most of the United States (although we have had good luck finding them at our local farmers' market during the spring and summer months). Pearl onions make a suitable, if not authentic, substitution. They are similar in both size and flavor, though they lack the characteristic squashed shape of cipollini, and are readily available fresh and frozen. We opted for the frozen because they are so much easier to prepare—peeling fresh ones can take a great deal of time—and their flavor is uncompromised by freezing.

With respect to technique, some recipes simply simmered the onions in the sauce, while others sautéed them prior to cooking in the sauce. Plain simmering was the easier approach, but the resulting flavor was bland and the texture squishy. Sautéing the onions added a depth of flavor as the sugars caramelized and the exterior browned enough to provide a modicum of resiliency. Relatively high heat prompted heavy caramelization of the onions (we found it helpful to add some sugar to coax things along), which added depth and a mild bitterness to this dish. After sautéing, we added the liquid ingredients and simmered the onions until they were soft and the syrupy sauce clung to them.

Red wine vinegar was our choice for its bright, fairly neutral acidity and the dark hue it lent the onions. Balsamic vinegar was too assertive for our tasters and muddied the flavors in the sauce. Butter beat out olive oil as the cooking medium because it encouraged browning and contributed a mild nuttiness. Pancetta is another traditional choice but, as with balsamic vinegar, tasters felt it muddied the otherwise clean flavors.

Balancing the amount of sugar and vinegar required several tests. We discovered it was easy to make the onions either saccharine sweet or lip-puckeringly sour. The ideal onions agrodolce should be sour on first bite, then sweet with a tart background. A ratio of slightly more than 2 parts vinegar to 1 part sugar provided ideal. For additional flavorings, we kept it simple. Bay leaves imparted a musky, herbal flavor, and black pepper added mild warmth. Everything else we tested was merely a distraction.

Onions Agrodolce
SERVES 6 AS A CONDIMENT

Surprisingly, the frozen onions can be sautéed straight from the freezer without defrosting. The pan's heat quickly evaporates any moisture that may leach out from them. If you choose to use fresh pearl onions, blanching them in boiling water for 30 seconds can help in removing the skins but, frankly, we don't think fresh onions are worth the bother in this recipe. Because of the high acidity of this dish, it keeps well in the refrigerator for at least a week.

1	tablespoon unsalted butter
1	pound frozen pearl onions
2	tablespoons sugar
	Salt
⅓	cup red wine vinegar
2	bay leaves
	Ground black pepper

1. Combine the butter, onions, 1 tablespoon sugar, and ¼ teaspoon salt in a medium skillet over medium-high heat. Cook the onions, stirring occasionally, until they are golden brown and the sugar has caramelized, 8 to 9 minutes (you may need to scrape down the caramelized sugars from the sides of the pan with a rubber spatula to prevent burning).

2. Remove the pan from the heat and add the vinegar, bay leaves, remaining 1 tablespoon sugar, and ⅓ cup water. Stir to remove any browned bits stuck to the pan. Cover and place the pan over low heat. Simmer until the onions are soft and the liquid is reduced to about 2 tablespoons, 15 to 17 minutes.

3. Uncover, increase the heat to medium-high, and cook until the onions are very glossy and the liquid is reduced to a thick syrup, 1 to 2 minutes. Season with salt and

pepper to taste and allow to cool at least 10 minutes or up to 1 hour before serving. Serve warm or at room temperature.

PEAS WITH PROSCIUTTO

PORK (IN SOME MANIFESTATION) AND peas is a classic combination, the flavors marrying perfectly. What would pea soup be without a ham bone? In Italy, fresh spring peas are paired with prosciutto. Generally ranked as one of the world's best hams, prosciutto has a nutty, sweet flavor and supple, silky texture all its own. While the peas and meat taste delicious together, the textural contrast of the two is what really steals the show; the subtle pop of the pea's shell and its starchy flesh are juxtaposed with the chewy strands of sautéed prosciutto.

Prosciutto is an uncooked, unsmoked ham that is salted and cured for anywhere from eight months to two years, depending on the manufacturer. One of the secrets of traditional prosciutto is that the pigs are fed on the leftover whey from the production of Parmesan cheese, which imparts its characteristic nuttiness to the animal's flesh. While prosciutto can be eaten raw, and generally is, it is briefly sautéed for this dish.

While we normally avoid frozen vegetables, peas are an exception. Peas are so delicate that their flavor is compromised as soon as they are picked; like corn, their sugars instantly begin converting to starch after harvesting. What the market calls fresh has most likely been out of the fields for days and lost most flavor. Frozen peas, on the other hand, are frozen within hours of being picked and are at their very best. They can be blanched directly from the freezer and require only a couple minutes of cooking.

Peas and prosciutto are such a felicitous combination that we found very few additional ingredients were necessary to improve the dish. After several tests, we switched from olive oil to butter, as the oil's bitterness and robust flavor were too strong. A little diced red onion added a note of piquancy that cut the sweetness of the peas and sharpened the meatiness of the ham. A little lemon juice brightened the flavor, but everything else we tried was superfluous.

Peas with Prosciutto
SERVES 4

While prosciutto is available presliced in many markets, we prefer to purchase it from the deli counter, sliced fresh to order. The meat begins to dry out and lose flavor as soon as it is sliced, so keep it wrapped tightly and use it shortly after purchasing it.

1½	teaspoons salt
1	pound frozen peas
1½	tablespoons unsalted butter
2	ounces thinly sliced prosciutto, rolled into logs and cut crosswise into thin ribbons
1	small red onion, diced small
1	teaspoon lemon juice from 1 small lemon
	Salt and ground black pepper

1. Bring 2 quarts water to a boil in a large saucepan over high heat. Add the salt and peas and cook until the peas are tender, about 3 minutes. Drain and set aside.

2. Heat the butter in a large nonstick skillet over medium-high heat. Once the foaming subsides, add the prosciutto and cook, stirring frequently, until it darkens slightly, about 2 minutes. Add the onion and

cook, stirring occasionally, until it softens and is lightly browned about the edges, about 5 minutes. Mix in the peas and cook until they are warmed through and the ingredients are uniformly mixed, 1 to 2 minutes. Sprinkle with the lemon juice and adjust the seasonings by adding salt and pepper to taste (some brands of prosciutto may be saltier than others). Serve immediately.

PEPERONATA

PEPERONATA IS A SIMPLE DISH OF long-cooked bell peppers that is consumed in a variety of ways. It can be used as a sauce for roasted or braised meats or as a topping for egg dishes or bruschetta. Its origins are hard to pinpoint, as it is eaten all over Italy, although such mutually distant locations as Emilia-Romagna and Naples claim it as their own. Both France and Spain have similar dishes, further complicating matters.

As the name points out, the most important element of peperonata is the peppers. They should be the predominant flavor and ingredient. In fact, some recipes we found included nothing but peppers, maybe a tomato or two, olive oil, and salt. While simple and delicious, these pared-down versions lacked a balanced flavor—they tasted of nothing but sweet peppers. We chose to pursue a richer (and still traditional) version that also included onions, garlic, and herbs.

Red and yellow peppers are the best choices for peperonata because of their natural sweetness. While green peppers may be visually appealing thrown into the mix, tasters found their harsh, bitter flavor off-putting. We decided a little parsley was a better choice for color. The peppers are traditionally cut into long slices that, depending on the recipe, vary from a skinny ¼-inch-thick julienne to a meaty 1-inch-thick slab. The thin julienne took a little more knifework but was well worth the effort. The thin slices cooked down to a soft, velvety consistency reminiscent of roasted peppers. The thicker slices maintained some crunch even after lengthy cooking. The fibrous skins of the thicker slices also slid off and marred the smooth texture of this sauce, whereas the skins of the julienne disappeared.

We wanted just enough onion to lend depth and additional sweetness to the peppers without distracting from them. An equal volume of onion to pepper overwhelmed the peppers, but about three times as much pepper as onion proved perfect. Red onions and yellow onions both worked well, but the yellow onions provided an eye-catching color contrast. A fairly substantial amount of slivered garlic virtually melted away, rendered soft and sweet by the pan's heat.

With respect to cooking technique, some recipes kept the peppers over a low flame for up to two hours, while others cooked them quite quickly. The long-cooked versions were too soft for our tasters—they were more like a confit or jam. Faster cooking meant the peppers retained some texture and vegetal flavor. After many batches with varying heat levels, we discovered that a combination of high and low heat provided the best results. Starting the peppers and onions at a relatively high heat prompted them to wilt quickly and brown around the edges, which increased their sweetness. Subsequently stewing them over low heat with the diced tomatoes produced a creamy, unctuous texture.

Filling out the rest of the flavors was easy. For herbs, a small sprig of rosemary cooked with the peppers and removed at the end added a faint resinous note, and parsley mixed in at the end of cooking brightened the entire dish. A splash of red wine vinegar sharpened the flavor of the peppers and cut the sweetness.

Peperonata

SERVES 4 TO 6

Feel free to use a single color of peppers, if that is all you can find. The mixture is more about visual appeal than flavor, as the different-colored peppers taste nearly identical. The volatile oil contained in rosemary leaves is extremely potent, so a little goes a long way. We like simmering small sprigs in sauces and then removing the sprig before serving. It is much easier than mincing the leaves, and there are no tough bits of rosemary to mar the dish's texture. Peperonata is fairly juicy, making it a good accompaniment to plain roasted meats that might otherwise need a sauce. Leftover peperonata is delicious in sandwiches, omelets, and eaten the Tuscan way, with roasted or boiled potatoes.

3	tablespoons extra-virgin olive oil
2	medium red bell peppers (about 1 pound), cored, seeded, and cut into ¼-inch-thick slices (see illustrations at right)
2	medium yellow or orange bell peppers (about 1 pound), cored, seeded, and cut into ¼-inch-thick slices (see illustrations at right)
1	medium onion, halved and cut into ¼-inch-thick slices
	Salt
4	medium cloves garlic, sliced thin
¼	teaspoon hot red pepper flakes
1	(14½-ounce) can diced tomatoes, drained, ¼ cup juices reserved
1	small sprig rosemary
2	teaspoons red wine vinegar
2	tablespoon minced fresh parsley leaves
	Ground black pepper

1. Place the oil, bell peppers, onion, and ½ teaspoon salt in a large skillet over medium-high heat and cook, stirring occasionally, until the vegetables have softened and browned a little around the edges, 6 to 8 minutes. Reduce the heat to medium, add the garlic and hot red pepper flakes, and continue cooking until the peppers lose most of their rigidity and the onion turns golden, 5 to 6 minutes.

2. Stir in the tomatoes, their juice, and the rosemary sprig, reduce the heat to low, and cover. Cook until the flavors have blended and any juices have evaporated, about 15 minutes. Remove and discard the rosemary sprig. Stir in the vinegar, parsley, and salt and pepper to taste. Allow to cool for at least 10 minutes or up to 1 hour before serving. Peperonata can be served warm or at room temperature.

SEEDING BELL PEPPERS

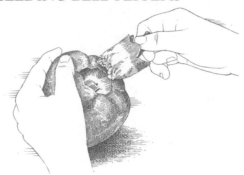

1. Cut around the stem with a small, sharp knife. Pull out the stem and the attached core, which should be filled with seeds.

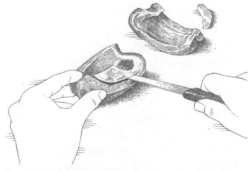

2. Cut the pepper lengthwise into quarters. Slide a knife under the white ribs to remove them as well as the remaining seeds. Slice the cleaned pepper as directed.

Parmesan Mashed Potatoes

WHILE NOT AS POPULAR IN ITALY AS in the rest of Europe, potatoes are eaten from Sicily in the south to Friuli-Venezia in the northeast. Butter-enriched mashed potatoes belong to northern Italy, where butter and cream supplant the olive oil of the south. With Parmesan cheese whipped in, mashed potatoes are taken to a new level—deeply rich and distinctly nutty.

We have exhaustively tested mashed potatoes for previous recipes and are confident that our method is faultless. For the driest, fluffiest potatoes, we simmer them whole in their jackets over a low flame so that the skins do not burst and open conduits for water to seep in. While it takes a little longer to cook them this way, the skins repel moisture so that the potatoes do not absorb water, as peeled and diced potatoes do. Water is the enemy of airy mashed potatoes because it floods the potatoes' starch granules, preventing the cream and butter from working their magic.

Peeling a hot potato may sound like a daunting task, but it's actually quite easy if you first skewer it on a fork, creating an easily maneuverable handle. With the gentle encouragement of a paring knife in the other hand, the peel will fall away in thick ribbons.

There may be a time and place for lumpy mashed potatoes, but tasters in our test kitchen unanimously favored a smooth and velvety texture. We tried a variety of standard methods for pureeing the potatoes and felt that our grandmothers did know best; old-fashioned but still dependable ricers and food mills yielded the best results. While somewhat rare in home kitchens, both are worth owning for mashed potatoes, if for nothing else. It is simple work to use either utensil. A ricer involves fewer parts and is easier to clean, but a food mill can handle more potatoes at once.

With the pureed potatoes light and bone-dry, the butter is added (melted to keep everything hot) and then the scalded half-and-half (cream is too rich, milk too lean). No short-cuts here; adding the butter first, independent of the half-and-half, made for significantly lighter potatoes. One final caveat: a light hand and minimal stirring were essential during mixing to keep the potatoes fluffy.

With a foolproof technique in hand, we fiddled with the flavors. To add depth, we infused the cream with bay leaves and nutmeg.

MAKING MASHED POTATOES

1. Hold the drained potato with a dinner fork and peel off the skin with a paring knife.

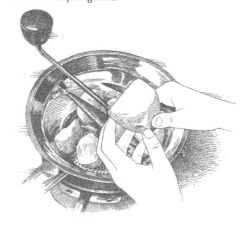

2. Cut the peeled potato into rough chunks, then drop the chunks into a food mill (shown here) or ricer.

Nutmeg is essential to virtually every creamy sauce in Italy—it adds character to the half-and-half, lending form to an otherwise bland flavor. Bay leaves, too, are a constant companion to dairy sauces in Italy, adding fragrance and an almost vanillalike mustiness. The Parmesan itself we added at the very end so that it saw as little heat as possible and retained its distinct sharpness and nutty aroma.

Parmesan Mashed Potatoes

SERVES 4 TO 6

Extensive testing has conclusively proven to us that any starchy potato, such russets and Idahos, will make delicious mashed potatoes. Slightly waxier in texture, Yukon Golds and Yellow Finns also work, but make for a denser consistency. (For more information on potato varieties, see page 85.) Do not use pregrated Parmesan for this dish. Because the cheese is the primary flavor, make sure it is fresh. Grate it just before you need it; it dries out quickly. Nutmeg, too, should be freshly grated for the best flavor. While a perfect accompaniment to any number of roasts or braises, Parmesan mashed potatoes is ideal with osso buco (page 306).

2	pounds potatoes, scrubbed
8	tablespoons unsalted butter
1¼	cups half-and-half
2	bay leaves
⅛	teaspoon freshly grated nutmeg
¾	teaspoon salt
1	cup finely grated Parmesan cheese
	Ground black pepper

1. Place the potatoes in a large saucepan and cover them with 1 inch water. Bring to a boil over high heat, then reduce the heat to medium-low and simmer until the potatoes are tender (a paring knife can be slipped into and out of the center of the potatoes with very little resistance), 20 to 30 minutes. Drain.

2. In a small saucepan, melt the butter and keep it warm over very low heat. In another small saucepan, combine the half-and-half, bay leaves, nutmeg, and salt and heat over low heat. Once bubbles appear around the circumference of the pan, remove from the heat and keep warm.

3. Set a food mill or ricer over the now empty but still warm saucepan. Spear a potato with a dinner fork, then peel back the skin with a paring knife, following illustration 1 on page 81. Working in batches, cut the peeled potatoes into rough chunks and process through the food mill or ricer (see illustration 2 on page 81). Stir in the butter with a wooden spoon until incorporated, then gently stir in the half-and-half (extracting the bay leaves first) and the Parmesan cheese. Season with pepper to taste and serve immediately in a warmed bowl.

ROASTED POTATOES

ROASTED POTATOES ARE AMONG THE most common vegetable side dishes served in Italy. They accompany countless roasts, chicken dishes, and eggs. The perfect roast potato is crisp and deep golden brown on the outside, with moist, velvety, dense interior flesh. The potato's slightly bitter skin is intact, providing a contrast to the sweet, caramelized flavor that the flesh develops during the roasting process. It is rich but never greasy, and it is accompanied by the heady taste of garlic and herbs.

To start, we roasted several kinds of potatoes. We liked high-starch/low-moisture potatoes (we used russets) the least. They did not brown well, their dry, fluffy texture was more like baked than roasted potatoes, and their flavor reminded us of raw potatoes. The medium-starch all-purpose potatoes (we used Yukon Golds) produced a beautiful golden crust, but the interior flesh was still rather dry. The best roasting potatoes came from the low-starch/high-moisture category (we used Red Bliss). These potatoes emerged from the oven with a light, delicate crust and a moist, dense interior that had a more complex, nutty flavor than the others, with hints of bitterness and tang.

After choosing the Red Bliss potatoes, we began to test oven temperatures. At 425 degrees, the result was an even-colored, golden-brown potato with a thin, crisp crust and an interior that was soft and dense, although still slightly dry.

In our research, we came across some recipes that called for parboiling the potatoes before roasting them. Hoping that this approach would produce a texturally superior potato that retained more of its moisture after cooking, we tried boiling the potatoes for seven minutes prior to roasting. This produced a potato closer to our ideal, but preparation required considerable attention owing to the additional step.

We then tried covering the potatoes for a portion of their roasting time. We were especially drawn to this technique because it provided a way to steam the potatoes in their own moisture that required little extra effort on the cook's part. The results were perfect. The crisp, deep golden-brown crust was perfectly balanced by a creamy, moist interior. These potatoes had a sweet and nutty caramelized flavor, with just a hint of tang from the skin. This simplest of methods produced the very best roasted potatoes.

The next step in the process was figuring out how to add garlic flavor, which makes a good variation on the standard roasted potatoes. If we added minced garlic during the last five minutes of cooking, it burned almost instantly; coating the potatoes with garlic-infused oil failed to produce the strong garlic flavor that we were after; and roasting whole, unpeeled garlic cloves alongside the potatoes and squeezing the pulp out afterwards to add

SCIENCE: Stress-Free Potato Storage

Because potatoes seem almost indestructible compared with other vegetables, little thought is generally given to their storage. But because various problems can result from inadequate storage conditions, we decided to find out how much difference storage really made. We stored all-purpose potatoes in five environments: in a cool (50–60 degrees), dark place; in the refrigerator; in a basket near a sunlit window; in a warm (70–80 degrees), dark place; and in a drawer with some onions at room temperature. We checked all the potatoes after four weeks.

As expected, the potatoes stored in the cool, dark place were firm, had not sprouted, and were crisp and moist when cut. There were no negative marks on the potatoes stored in the refrigerator, either. Although some experts say that the sugar level dramatically increases in some potato varieties under these conditions, we could not see or taste any difference between these potatoes and the ones stored in the cool, dark, but unrefrigerated environment.

Our last three storage tests produced unfavorable results. The potatoes stored in sunlight, in warm storage, and with onions ended up with a greenish tinge along the edges. When potatoes are stressed by improper storage, the level of naturally occurring toxin, called solanine, increases, causing the greenish tinge. Because solanine is not destroyed by cooking, any part of the potato with this greenish coloring should be completely cut away before cooking.

The skin of the potatoes stored in sunlight became gray and mottled, while the potatoes stored in a warm place and those stored with onions sprouted and became soft and wrinkled. Sprouts also contain solanine and should be cut away before cooking.

to the potatoes was too tedious. The best method turned out to be both simple and flavorful. Mash raw garlic into a paste, place it in a large stainless-steel bowl, put the hot roast potatoes in the bowl, and toss. This method yields potatoes with a strong garlic flavor yet without the raw spiciness of uncooked garlic.

Roasted Potatoes

SERVES 4

To roast more than two pounds of potatoes at once, use a second pan rather than crowding the first. If your potatoes are small, such as new potatoes, cut them in halves instead of wedges and turn them cut side up during the final 10 minutes of roasting. For information on potato varieties, see page 85.

> 2 pounds Red Bliss or other low-starch potatoes, scrubbed clean, dried, halved, and cut into ¾-inch wedges
> 3 tablespoons extra-virgin olive oil
>   Salt and ground black pepper

1. Adjust the oven rack to the middle position and heat the oven to 425 degrees. Toss the potatoes and oil in a medium bowl to coat; season generously with salt and pepper and toss again to blend.

2. Place the potatoes flesh side down in a single layer in a shallow roasting pan. Cover tightly with aluminum foil and bake about 20 minutes. Remove the foil and roast until the side of the potato touching the pan is crusty golden brown, about 15 minutes more. Remove the pan from the oven and, with a metal spatula, carefully turn over the potatoes. (Press the spatula against the pan as it slides under the potatoes to protect the crusts.) Return the pan to the oven and roast until the side of the potato now touching the pan is crusty golden brown and the skins have raisin-like wrinkles, 5 to 10 minutes more. Transfer the potatoes to a serving dish (again, using a metal spatula and extra care not to rip the crusts) and serve hot or warm.

> VARIATION

Roasted Potatoes with Garlic and Rosemary

Follow the recipe for Roasted Potatoes. While the potatoes roast, mince 2 medium garlic cloves. Sprinkle them with ⅛ teaspoon salt and mash with the flat side of a chef's knife blade until a paste forms. Transfer the garlic paste to a large bowl; set aside. In the last 3 minutes of roasting time, sprinkle 2 tablespoons chopped fresh rosemary evenly over the potatoes. Immediately transfer the finished potatoes to the bowl with the garlic, toss to distribute, and serve warm.

To prevent them from burning, garlic and rosemary are added to roasted potatoes at the end of the cooking time.

INGREDIENTS: Potatoes

Dozens of potato varieties are grown in the United States, and at any time you may see as many as five or six in your supermarket. Some potatoes are sold by varietal name (such as Yukon Gold), but others are sold by generic name (baking, all-purpose, etc.). To make sense of this confusion, we find it helpful to group potatoes into three major categories based on the ratio of solids (mostly starch) to water. The categories are high-starch/low-moisture potatoes, medium-starch potatoes, and low-starch/high-moisture potatoes.

The high-starch/low-moisture category includes baking, russet, and white creamer potatoes. (The formal name of the russet is russet Burbank potato, named after its developer, Luther Burbank of Idaho. This type of potato is also known as the Idaho. In all of our recipes, we call them russets.) These potatoes are best for baking and mashing. The medium-starch category includes all-purpose, Yukon Gold, Yellow Finn, and purple Peruvian potatoes. These potatoes can be mashed or baked, but are generally not as fluffy as the high-starch potatoes. The low-starch/high-moisture category includes Red Bliss, red creamer, new, white rose, and fingerling potatoes. These potatoes are best roasted or boiled and used in salad.

GRILLED RADICCHIO

RADICCHIO IS USUALLY THOUGHT OF as a salad ingredient, but it is commonly cooked and served as a side dish in Italy. When grilled, the purple leaves become lightly crisp and smoky-tasting. To keep the layers from falling apart, we found it necessary to cut the radicchio heads through the core into thick wedges. Brush the pieces with a fair amount of olive oil to keep them from burning. For maximum grill flavor, turn each wedge of radicchio twice so that each side spends time facing the fire. The technique is quite simple. Grilled radicchio makes an especially fine accompaniment to grilled steaks.

Grilled Radicchio
SERVES 4

This slightly bitter vegetable is delicious with any grilled meat or poultry. The heads of radicchio are cut into wedges and lightly grilled, bringing out the sweetness of the vegetable while retaining its pleasantly crisp texture.

- 3 medium heads radicchio, cut into quarters with core intact (see illustration on page 86)
- 4 tablespoons extra-virgin olive oil
  Salt and ground black pepper

1. Place the 12 radicchio wedges on a large baking sheet and brush all sides with the oil. Season with salt and pepper to taste.

2. Grill the radicchio over a medium–hot fire, turning every 1½ minutes, until the edges are browned and wilted but the center still remains slightly firm, about 4½ minutes total. Serve immediately.

VARIATION

Grilled Radicchio with Sweet Balsamic Vinaigrette

The small amount of sugar in the vinaigrette promotes browning and works well with the bitter flavor of the radicchio.

- 1½ tablespoons balsamic vinegar
- 1 teaspoon sugar
- 1 medium clove garlic, minced or pressed through a garlic press
- 4 tablespoons extra-virgin olive oil
- 3 medium heads radicchio, cut into quarters with core intact (see illustrations on page 86)
  Salt and ground black pepper

1. Mix the vinegar, sugar, garlic, and oil in a small bowl.

PREPARING RADICCHIO

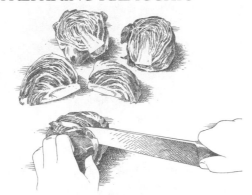

Remove any brown outer leaves. Cut the radicchio in half through the core. Cut each half again through the core so that you end up with four wedges.

2. Place the 12 radicchio wedges on a large baking sheet and brush all sides with the vinaigrette. Season with salt and pepper to taste.

3. Grill the radicchio over a medium-hot fire, turning every 1½ minutes, until the edges are browned and wilted but the center still remains slightly firm, about 4½ minutes total. Serve immediately.

SPINACH WITH GARLIC AND LEMON

SPINACH IS ONE OF THE MOST POPULAR greens in Italy, appearing in pasta stuffings, salads, soups, sauces, and side dishes. Sautéed in olive oil, garlic, and lemon juice, it is an example of Italian culinary simplicity at its finest. The lemon and garlic are perfect accents to the earthy, sweet spinach. While this dish can be rapidly whipped together, choosing and properly preparing the spinach is of utmost importance to the outcome.

For a quick sauté, we found that flat-leaf spinach is the best choice. Its flavor is more intense than curly-leaf spinach, which is far more suitable for stuffings and fillings, where a pronounced flavor is not as important. Baby spinach is delicious raw but does not have the structure or developed flavor necessary for cooking; it wilts to an unpleasant texture, almost like tissue paper. We also prefer bunched spinach with the stems still attached to cleaned and bagged leaves. While convenient, bagged spinach is sometimes past its prime and stringy or beginning to rot.

Cleaning the spinach is easily the most time-consuming step in preparing this dish. Bunched spinach is often extremely gritty and must be cleaned diligently in a deep bowl or sink filled with lots of cold water. The dirt sinks to the bottom and can be easily drained away. Most spinach requires at least two changes of water before it is really clean. A thorough drying in a salad spinner is the last step, which we discovered is quite important because wet spinach leads to a soggy, overcooked mess (unlike tougher chard, which needs additional moisture for more intensive cooking).

After experimenting with different cooking temperatures, we chose high heat because it wilted the spinach quickly and prevented it from exuding all of its moisture. The longer the spinach cooks, the more the leaves break down and release moisture.

To keep the lemon flavor sharp and bright, we added it to the spinach off the stove. Heat quickly mellowed the lemon's acidic bite, which we wanted to preserve to balance the nutty sweetness of the garlic.

Spinach with Garlic and Lemon

SERVES 4

An ideal side dish for a variety of meat and fish dishes, this also makes a delicious topping for soft polenta. Tossed with additional olive oil, it makes a quick sauce perfect for chunky pasta. Leftovers are delicious cold in sandwiches.

2   tablespoons extra-virgin olive oil, plus
     additional for drizzling
4   medium cloves garlic, sliced thin
     Pinch hot red pepper flakes
2   pounds flat-leaf bunch spinach, stems
     trimmed, leaves washed and dried
     Coarse kosher or sea salt
2   teaspoons lemon juice from 1 lemon

Place the oil, garlic, and red pepper flakes in a large skillet over medium-high heat. As the oil begins to sizzle, shake the pan back and forth so that the garlic does not stick to the pan. Once the garlic begins to turn very light brown, about 2 minutes, add the spinach by the handful, using tongs to coat it with the oil and garlic. Sprinkle ¼ teaspoon salt over the spinach. Once all of the spinach has wilted and is a uniform dark green, about 2 minutes, remove the pan from the heat, sprinkle the lemon juice over top, and serve immediately, topped with a drizzle of oil and a sprinkling of salt.

ROASTED SQUASH WITH BROWN BUTTER AND SAGE

WINTER SQUASH AND PUMPKIN ARE popular vegetables throughout northern Italy. They are used as a filling for stuffed pastas, pickled for antipasto, and pureed, boiled, baked, and roasted. The sweet, neutral flavor of the squash can be paired with any number of assertive ingredients, from anchovies and olives to garlic and tomatoes. Our favorite combination is one of the simplest—cubes of roasted squash tossed with browned butter and sage. The butter's toasted nuttiness and the sage's sweet sharpness are unbeatable companions to the squash. While this dish's ingredient list is short and its cooking method easy, we found that, for the best results, good timing is essential.

While many types of squash and pumpkin—collectively called *zucca*—are grown and eaten in Italy, butternut squash is one of the most popular. It is also widely available in the United States, unlike other Italian varieties. Compared to most winter squash, butternut is easy to peel, and its compact shape can be cut into uniform pieces.

Roasting brings out squash's natural sweetness and intensifies the flavor and color better than any other cooking method. Further, it requires little effort beyond the initial preparation. The trick to roasting vegetables is finding the perfect temperature whereby the vegetable is cooked through and caramelized but not burned. Too often, roasting seems to be an excuse for a charred exterior and bitter flavor. While the recipes we researched suggested anywhere from 350 to 500 degrees for cooking squash, we found 475 degrees to be perfect: the cubes were soft on the inside, lightly browned on the outside, and, most important, still firm. At 350 degrees, the squash cubes turned mushy and tasted bland; it would have been much easier simply to scrape the pulp from baked, unpeeled squash halves. At 500 degrees, the squash charred around the edges before the interior was cooked through.

Timing is important here; the squash will quickly turn squishy if overcooked. A paring knife will easily puncture and pull cleanly from properly cooked squash—remove the squash from the oven immediately when this is the case. Part of the allure of this dish is the individual chunks of squash.

Prior to roasting them, we tossed the squash cubes with salt, pepper, and melted butter. Although we initially used olive oil, the herbaceous bitterness of the oil muddied the flavor of the finished dish. Butter kept the flavor clean, and it browned better than the olive oil did.

Once the squash was roasted, it was time to add the brown butter and sage. Browning butter brings out a hazelnutlike flavor that complements the squash's sweetness quite well. The butter browns because the milk solids suspended in the butterfat cook and caramelize. Like a caramel sauce, the darker the butter is, the more complex the flavor— only to a point, though. Overcooked butter tastes charred and acrid. It is crucial to pay keen attention as the butter cooks and seize it (stop the browning) as soon as it reaches a chestnut-brown hue. We found that adding the squash to the pan accomplished this by lowering the pan's temperature.

The flavor of sage can be aggressive, but when it is fried the brashness is mellowed and the leaves take on an airy crispness. We initially tried cooking the sage in the butter as it browned, but it darkened and turned very bitter. Adding it with the squash proved perfect; quick cooking yielded the milder flavor and crisp texture we desired. We also switched from coarsely chopping the leaves to slivering them—while the sage is delicious, a little goes a long way.

Roasted Squash with Brown Butter and Sage

SERVES 4

Peeling butternut squash requires a sturdy, very sharp vegetable peeler (see page 60). If your model has a thin blade, you might have better luck with a very sharp knife. To cut the squash in half, place the bottom on a cutting board and cut toward the board. Be careful; it can be slippery work. While dried sage can be successfully used in some recipes, this is not one of them. Fresh leaves are critical for both flavor and texture; the crispy strips add a pleasing contrast to the creamy squash.

I	large butternut squash (3½ to 4 pounds), peeled, seeded, and cut into I-inch cubes
5	tablespoons unsalted butter, 2 tablespoons melted Salt and ground black pepper
2	tablespoons thinly sliced fresh sage leaves
I	teaspoon balsamic vinegar

1. Adjust an oven rack to the lower middle position and heat the oven to 475 degrees. In a large mixing bowl, combine the squash, melted butter, ½ teaspoon salt, and ¼ teaspoon pepper, and toss with a rubber spatula to uniformly coat the cubes of squash. Arrange the cubes on a rimmed baking sheet in a single layer. Roast until they are lightly browned and can be pierced easily with the tip of a knife, about 40 minutes. Remove the pan from the oven.

2. Melt the remaining butter in a large skillet over medium-high heat and cook until golden brown, about 2 minutes. Stir in the sage and squash and cook, stirring frequently, until the squash is evenly coated with the sage and glossy, about 1 minute more. Sprinkle with the vinegar, toss to coat, and season with salt and pepper to taste. Serve immediately.

SWISS CHARD WITH RAISINS AND PINE NUTS

SAUTÉED GREENS, USUALLY CHARD, but sometimes spinach with raisins and pine nuts, is a traditional combination found in Rome and throughout much of southern Italy. An identical dish is also found in the Balearic Islands of southern Spain, pointing to a northward migration of flavors from Africa. Dried fruits and nuts are common additions to savory dishes in Arabic cooking.

The dish is a classic because the simple ingredients perfectly complement each other: The raisins contribute a deep, musky sweetness that highlights the natural sugars in the greens, and the pine nuts add a resinous note and toothsomeness to an otherwise tender dish. While the dish is extraordinarily easy to prepare, we found that cooking the greens so that they are perfectly tender but not mushy can be tricky. The greens should be tender but retain a little character.

Swiss chard is an offshoot of the beet family and comes in several similar-tasting varieties, including red-veined or ruby chard, white (with white stems and veins), and Rainbow or Bright Lights (multicolored). Comparable in taste to spinach, chard is a bit earthier and more strongly flavored, and it has a chewier, coarser texture that requires slightly longer cooking.

The maturity of the chard affects how it must be prepared. If it is young, the thin, tender stems may be left in the leaves (the very thick bottom stems should be cut off and discarded). Tasters enjoyed the chewiness they added to the greens. If the stems are older and any thicker than a pencil, they must be removed because they will not cook thoroughly in the same time as the leaves. While too tough for a quick sauté, chard stems can be prepared in several ways, including simmering in soups and baking in a gratin.

Chard does not have the same high water content as spinach, so it needs a small amount of liquid to sauté effectively. As the dish's flavors are so assertive, we knew that water would be fine—stock or wine would be distracting. While it was easy enough to add a splash of water during cooking, it proved even easier just to not dry the greens after washing them. Enough moisture clung to the greens to aid in cooking, steaming the leaves as the water droplets hit the hot pan. The combination of steam and very hot, dry heat cooked the chard quickly and efficiently.

With the greens cooked, we tackled the details. For the best flavor, pine nuts must be toasted. Heat brings out the nuts' volatile oils and intensifies their flavor as well as their aroma. They tend to burn quickly because of their high fat content, so they must be cooked with a vigilant eye. Toasting them in the skillet before the chard kept dishwashing to a minimum.

Many recipes we found plumped the raisins in boiling water prior to adding them, but tasters felt they developed a slimy, off-putting texture when soaked. We discovered that adding them to the hot pan a minute before the chard softened them and improved their flavor by searing them in spots.

Breaking with tradition, we added red onions to intensify the overall flavor. The onions looked great, too; their pale pink color snakes through the dark green, glossy leaves.

As with many Italian vegetable preparations, we added a splash of vinegar off the heat just before serving. Used in moderation, acids like vinegar and lemon juice perk up and

PREPARING SWISS CHARD

Hold each leaf at the base of the stem over a bowl filled with water and use a sharp knife to slash the leafy portion from either side of the thick stem.

define flavors. Tasters agreed that with the vinegar, the chard tasted brighter and the sweetness of the raisins was highlighted.

Swiss Chard with Raisins and Pine Nuts

SERVES 4 TO 6

While the stems of mature chard must be excised prior to cooking (and saved for soup or baking in a gratin), tender young chard stems can be included in the sauté, adding a bit of chewiness. To remove thick stems, see the illustration on page 89. Spinach (well dried) and beet greens may be cooked in the same manner with delicious results. Depending on the age of the greens, cooking times may vary by a minute or two. Walnuts are a passable substitution for pine nuts. However, they must be toasted a couple of minutes longer than pine nuts.

¼	cup pine nuts
2	tablespoons extra-virgin olive oil
I	small red onion, halved and sliced thin
¼	cup raisins
I½	pounds Swiss chard, trimmed of tough stems, rinsed, and roughly chopped, but not drained
½	teaspoon salt
⅛	teaspoon ground black pepper
I	tablespoon balsamic vinegar

1. Place the pine nuts in a large skillet set over medium heat. Toast, stirring frequently, until they are light golden, 5 to 6 minutes. Transfer the nuts to a small bowl.

2. Increase the heat to medium-high and add the oil and onion to the empty pan. Cook, stirring occasionally, until the onion is soft and beginning to brown, about 4 minutes. Stir in the raisins and cook for 1 minute.

3. Add the chard and, using tongs, stir it

with the onion and raisin mixture (you will need to add the chard in batches—it quickly loses volume as it wilts). Sprinkle the salt and pepper over the chard and, stirring occasionally, cook until the leaves are completely wilted and the stems are easily pierced with a knife, 5 to 6 minutes. Remove the pan from the heat. Sprinkle the vinegar and pine nuts over the greens, stir, and serve immediately.

SLOW-ROASTED TOMATOES

ROASTING FLAWLESS, VINE-RIPENED tomatoes with garlic and olive oil takes them to a new level of perfection. The tomato's juices are concentrated by the steady heat and become one with the garlic and herb-scented olive oil. As a relish for grilled meats or topping for toasted bread, the dish is hard to beat. It is the distillation of summer in one easy-to-assemble and foolproof dish.

There are only five ingredients in this dish and, for the best results, each must be flawless. In other words, this is not a place to use pale, cardboardy supermarket tomatoes and cheap oil, as roasting merely magnifies their flaws. The tomatoes must be the best you can find, preferably from your local farmers' market—or your garden, if you are so lucky. In the heart of a New England winter, we used "vine-ripened" tomatoes from our gourmet market with some success, but we longed for the beauties of August, still warm from the sun's touch.

The oil should be the best you can find. We tried batches with varying oils and the differences were profound; the best-quality oil was in a league of its own, heady, with an herbaceous, peppery aroma and a taste that elevated the tomatoes beyond comparison.

(For recommendations about brands of olive oil, see page 33.)

For flavoring the tomatoes, garlic and basil were the only choices, according to our tasters. Oregano, mint, thyme, and rosemary all seemed inappropriate in this circumstance. Slivered garlic fared better than minced and looked much more attractive, too. The fine slivers practically melted during the slow bake, reduced to sweet and slightly chewy tidbits.

As this is a rustic dish, hand-torn basil leaves were the logical choice. Because they shrivel to mere shadows of themselves in the oven, we left the pieces large and left small leaves whole. Layering the leaves on both top and bottom of the tomatoes guaranteed potent flavor.

For seasoning, coarse salt (kosher or sea salt) was the unanimous choice of tasters, chosen for its crunchy texture and intense bursts of salinity. Regular table salt will do in a pinch, of course.

Preparation takes mere moments, but the roasting takes some time. These are not oven-dried tomatoes, which can take upwards of eight hours in a tepid oven, but they are also not classic oven-roasted tomatoes, heat-shriveled to a near candylike sweetness and intensity. Aiming for something in between, we set the baking temperature parameters between 300 and 400 degrees and began testing.

In a 400-degree oven, the garlic browned too quickly and turned acrid, ruining the dish. Erring on the side of caution, we lowered the temperature to 325 degrees and were pleased with the results. Within 1½ hours, the tomatoes were slightly wrinkled and touched with brown but, more importantly, their juices had largely evaporated and been replaced by the olive oil. A lower temperature yielded no better-tasting results and took longer, so we stuck with 325 degrees.

Slow-Roasted Tomatoes
SERVES 4 TO 6

For flavor and color contrast, feel free to mix and match varieties of tomatoes—Green Zebras, a relatively common heirloom variety, are stunning when interspersed with ruby-red beefsteaks. Use whatever tomatoes you can find, as long as they are flawlessly ripe. If you are left with a pool of olive oil in the pan, save it for flavoring a vinaigrette or brushing on bruschetta.

½	cup extra-virgin olive oil
4	medium cloves garlic, sliced thin
1	cup lightly packed fresh basil leaves, coarsely torn into large pieces
2	pounds vine-ripened tomatoes, cored and cut crosswise into ½-inch-thick slices
1	teaspoon coarse salt

1. Adjust the oven rack to the lower-middle position and heat the oven to 325 degrees. Lightly coat the bottom of a 9 by 13-inch baking dish with 2 tablespoons oil and evenly sprinkle half the garlic and basil leaves across the bottom of the dish. Lay the tomato slices in the pan, overlapping the edges if necessary to fit. Cover the tomatoes with the remaining garlic, basil, and oil, and sprinkle with the salt.

2. Roast until the tomatoes are slightly shriveled and their juices have been replaced with oil, about 1½ hours. Allow to cool at least 20 minutes or up to 1 hour before serving. Serve warm or at room temperature.

STUFFED TOMATOES

OUR PAST EXPERIENCES WITH OVEN-baked stuffed tomatoes have not been exactly great. Still, when we are presented with one, the thought of its potential juicy tenderness and warmth is too tempting to pass up. We succumb to the hope that maybe this time the stuffed tomato will live up to its potential, only to be let down by the first bite into sodden mediocrity.

What irks us is that the stuffed tomato's singular components hold forth the promise of perfection. What could be better than a ripe, sun-drenched summer tomato, garden-fresh herbs, garlicky bread crumbs, and a sprightly bite of sharp cheese? When these elements are brought together into one vessel, however, their divinity dissipates. The once buxom tomato becomes mealy and bland, and the flavor of the stuffing is drowned in the waterlogged texture of the bread. Determined to save this traditional dish from the bland and watery depths, we set out to prove that an oven-baked stuffed tomato can taste as good as we've always imagined.

We began testing by following the directions in most recipes: stuff a hollowed-out raw beefsteak tomato with a bread crumb filling and bake it at 375 degrees for 30 minutes. The outcome was a soggy mess. The tomato was bland and watery, and the stuffing tasted dull and overly moist. What's more, the tomato seemed to lack the structural strength to keep the filling intact. We concluded that perhaps the same element that lends majesty to a tomato, water, was the source of our failure.

Ridding the tomato of its excess liquid was our goal. First we tested oven drying, rationalizing that the slow, low heat would concentrate the tomato's sweetness and vaporize the water. The dried tomato was laden with rich flavor notes, but it was also shriveled and shrunken, a collapsed vessel that was in no condition to hold stuffing.

We then decided that if we chose a tomato with a naturally lower water content, such as a plum tomato, we might eliminate the water issue altogether. While we did end up with a meaty and sweet stuffed tomato, it lacked the complexity of flavor that the beefsteak possessed, and the effort required to stuff the smaller shell, coupled with the fact that we would have to make twice as many if we were substituting for beefsteak tomatoes, turned us off the plum variety.

Recalling how salt is used to sweat eggplant, we thought it might do the same for a tomato. We cored and seeded a beefsteak tomato, rubbed salt into its interior, and placed it upside down on a stack of paper towels. Within 30 minutes, our dry paper towels had absorbed a tremendous amount of liquid. Besides draining the tomato of its excess juices, the salt brightened and enhanced the tomato's flavor.

Now that we had the moisture problem solved, we moved on to stuffing, baking times,

To keep the stuffing light and crisp, draw excess moisture from the hollowed-out tomatoes with salt and then add the bread crumbs.

and temperatures. For the stuffing, we tested store-bought bread crumbs, homemade bread crumbs made from stale French bread, and variations in the ratio of crumbs to cheese to herbs. The fine store-bought crumbs were dry and gritty. Their homemade counterpart, on the other hand, absorbed the tomato's juices yet still provided an interesting chew and crunch, especially when paired with garlic, olive oil, and tangy Parmesan cheese.

Our previous oven-roasting experiment ruled out a low and long baking period, whereas experiments baking the tomato at an extremely high temperature (450 degrees) for a short time yielded burnt, crusty stuffing and a raw tomato. Baked at 375 degrees for 20 minutes, the tomatoes were tender and topped with a lovely golden crust. The result: a sweet and savory tomato triumph.

Stuffed Tomatoes with Parmesan, Garlic, and Basil

SERVES 6 AS A SIDE DISH

To make fresh bread crumbs, grind any hunk of stale country, Italian, or French bread in the food processor. See page 57 for details.

6	firm, ripe medium tomatoes (about 8 ounces each), 1/8 inch sliced off the stem end, cored, and seeded
1	teaspoon kosher salt
3/4	cup fresh bread crumbs
3	tablespoons plus 1 teaspoon extra-virgin olive oil
1/3	cup grated Parmesan cheese
1/3	cup chopped fresh basil leaves
2	medium cloves garlic, minced or pressed through a garlic press
	Ground black pepper

1. Sprinkle the inside of each tomato with salt and place it upside down on several layers of paper towels. Let stand to remove any excess moisture, about 30 minutes.

2. Meanwhile, toss the bread crumbs with 1 tablespoon oil and the Parmesan cheese, basil, garlic, and pepper to taste in a small bowl; set aside. Adjust an oven rack to the upper-middle position and heat the oven to 375 degrees. Line the bottom of a 13 by 9-inch baking dish with foil.

3. Roll several sheets of paper towels and pat the inside of each tomato dry. Arrange the tomatoes in a single layer in the baking dish. Brush the cut edges of the tomatoes with 1 teaspoon oil. Mound the stuffing into the tomatoes (about 1/4 cup per tomato); drizzle with the remaining 2 tablespoons oil. Bake until the tops are golden brown and crisp, about 20 minutes. Serve immediately.

➤ VARIATION
Stuffed Tomatoes with Goat Cheese, Olives, and Oregano

Follow the recipe for Baked Stuffed Tomatoes with Parmesan, Garlic, and Basil, substituting 3 ounces crumbled goat cheese for the Parmesan, omitting the basil, and adding 3 tablespoons minced fresh parsley, 1 1/2 teaspoons minced fresh oregano, and 3 tablespoons chopped black olives to the bread crumb mixture.

ZUCCHINI

ITALIAN GARDENS OVERFLOW WITH zucchini every summer. While American gardeners are often at a loss for ideas for using this bounty, Italians have countless ways to prepare zucchini. The biggest problem that confronts the cook when preparing zucchini is their wateriness. This vegetable is about 95 percent water and becomes soupy if just thrown into a hot pan. If zucchini cooks in its own juices it won't brown, and because it is fairly bland, zucchini really benefits from browning. Clearly, some of the water must be removed before sautéing.

We tested salting to draw off some water and found that sliced and salted zucchini sheds about 20 percent of its weight after sitting for 30 minutes. One pound of sliced zucchini threw off almost three tablespoons of liquid,

further confirmation that salting works. We tested longer periods and found that little additional moisture is extracted after 30 minutes.

Given that you don't always have 30 minutes, we wanted to develop quicker methods for cooking zucchini. We tried shredding the zucchini on the large holes of a box grater and then squeezing out excess water by hand. We were able to reduce the weight of shredded zucchini by 25 percent by wrapping it in paper towels and squeezing until dry. Because sliced zucchini has so much less surface area than shredded zucchini, the process works much more efficiently with the latter.

Another quick-prep option is the grill. The intense heat quickly expels excess moisture in zucchini, and that moisture harmlessly drops down on the coals rather than sitting in the pan. We found that so much evaporation occurs during grilling that salting is not necessary.

SHREDDING ZUCCHINI

1. For quick indoor cooking, shred trimmed zucchini or squash on the large holes of a box grater or in a food processor fitted with the shredding disk.

2. Wrap the shredded zucchini or squash in paper towels and squeeze out excess liquid. Proceed immediately with sautéing.

Sautéed Shredded Zucchini
SERVES 4

This recipe is best when you're pressed for time and want to cook zucchini indoors.

> 3   tablespoons extra-virgin olive oil
> 5   medium zucchini (about 2 pounds), trimmed, shredded, and squeezed dry (see illustrations at left)
> 3   medium cloves garlic, minced or pressed through a garlic press
> 2   tablespoons minced fresh parsley, basil, mint, tarragon, or chives
>   Salt and ground black pepper

Heat the oil in a large nonstick skillet over medium-high heat. Add the zucchini and garlic and cook, stirring occasionally, until tender, about 7 minutes. Stir in the herb and salt and pepper to taste. Serve immediately.

Sautéed Zucchini

SERVES 4

If you like browned zucchini, you must salt it before cooking. Salting drives off excess water and helps the zucchini sauté rather than stew in its own juices. Coarse kosher salt does the best job of driving off liquid and can be wiped away without rinsing. Do not add more salt when cooking or the dish will be too salty.

4	medium zucchini (about 1 ½ pounds), trimmed and sliced crosswise into ¼-inch-thick rounds
1	tablespoon kosher salt
3	tablespoons extra-virgin olive oil
1	small onion, minced
1	teaspoon grated zest and 1 tablespoon juice from 1 lemon
1–2	tablespoons minced fresh parsley, basil, mint, tarragon, or chives
	Ground black pepper

1. Place the zucchini slices in a colander and sprinkle with the salt. Set the colander over a bowl until about ⅓ cup water drains from the zucchini, about 30 minutes. Remove the zucchini from the colander and pat dry with a clean kitchen towel or several paper towels, wiping off any remaining crystals of salt.

2. Heat the oil in a large skillet over medium heat. Add the onion and sauté until almost softened, about 3 minutes. Increase the heat to medium-high and add the zucchini and lemon zest. Sauté until zucchini is golden brown, about 10 minutes. Stir in the lemon juice and herb and season with pepper to taste. Serve immediately.

VARIATIONS

Sautéed Zucchini with Walnuts and Herbs

Follow the recipe for Sautéed Zucchini, omitting the lemon zest and juice and adding 2 tablespoons toasted chopped walnuts along with the herb.

Sautéed Zucchini with Olives and Lemon

Follow the recipe for Sautéed Zucchini, adding ¼ cup pitted and chopped black olives along with the lemon juice and using 2 teaspoons minced fresh thyme or oregano as the herb.

Sautéed Zucchini with Pancetta and Parsley

Follow the recipe for Sautéed Zucchini, omitting the oil and lemon zest and juice. After salting the zucchini, cook 2 ounces diced pancetta in a large skillet over medium heat. When the fat renders, add the onion and continue with the recipe. Use parsley as the herb.

Grilled Zucchini

SERVES 4

Excess water evaporates over hot coals, so salting the zucchini before cooking is not necessary.

4	medium zucchini (about 1 ½ pounds), trimmed and sliced lengthwise into ½-inch-thick strips
2	tablespoons extra-virgin olive oil
	Salt and ground black pepper

1. Lay the zucchini slices on a large baking sheet and brush both sides with the oil. Sprinkle generously with salt and pepper to taste.

2. Grill the zucchini over a medium-hot fire, turning once, until marked with dark stripes, 8 to 10 minutes. Serve hot, warm, or at room temperature.

➤ VARIATION

Grilled Zucchini with Capers and Oregano

1   tablespoon red wine vinegar
1   tablespoon capers, chopped
1   medium clove garlic, minced or pressed
    through a garlic press
4   tablespoons extra-virgin olive oil
    Salt and ground black pepper
4   medium zucchini (about 1½ pounds),
    trimmed and sliced lengthwise into
    ½-inch-thick strips
1   tablespoon chopped fresh oregano leaves

1. Whisk the vinegar, capers, and garlic together in a small bowl. Whisk in 2 tablespoons oil until smooth and season with salt and pepper to taste.

2. Lay the zucchini slices on a large baking sheet and brush both sides with the remaining 2 tablespoons oil. Sprinkle generously with salt and pepper to taste. Grill the zucchini over a medium-hot fire, turning once, until marked with dark stripes, 8 to 10 minutes.

3. Remove the zucchini from the grill and cool slightly. Cut into 1-inch pieces and toss with the dressing and oregano. Serve warm or at room temperature.

INGREDIENTS: Zucchini

Although the Spanish are credited with introducing squash to Europe, believing them to be melons, it was the Italians who downsized the huge gourds into the delicate, green vegetable they termed *zucchini* in the 18th century. This dainty new vegetable, with its elegant flavor and tender flesh, was intended to be eaten before it matured and was immediately popular in France as well as Italy. The English acquired the vegetable through the French and therefore call them courgettes, whereas Italian immigrants brought them to the United States, so we call them by their Italian name.

According to Vincent Laurence of White Flower Farms in Litchfield, Conn., there is no noticeable difference in flavor among zucchini types, although different parts of the world prefer different shapes and shades of green. While consumers in the United States prefer straight, dark green zucchini, consumers in Syria prefer a tapered, pale gray zucchini, and the French often eat a round variety about the size of a tennis ball. In Italy, the long, dark green variety is the most common.

4

SOUPS

SOUPS MAINTAIN AN IMPORTANT PLACE in the Italian diet. They are often eaten as a first course (in place of pasta or rice) at multi-course meals. At other times, a hearty bowl of soup (usually accompanied by a hunk of crusty bread) is the entire meal.

Many of Italy's most popular soups have their roots in rural peasant cooking. For this reason, many Italian soups do not contain meat or chicken stock. Of course, there are times when a fine homemade chicken stock is required. For instance, few Italians would consider making passatelli (chicken soup with cheese dumplings) or tortellini soup with canned broth.

However, many bean and vegetable soups (and Italian cuisine seems to have an abundance of such recipes) build flavor slowly. Finely chopped vegetables are browned in olive oil, garlic is thrown into the pot (along with hot red pepper flakes, pancetta, or even anchovies, depending on the recipe), and water is added and followed by a handful of fresh herbs and maybe a Parmesan cheese rind. Each element adds complexity and depth.

As the recipes in this chapter demonstrate, Italian soups are easy to prepare and require few (if any) difficult techniques or unusual pieces of equipment. That said, Italian soups are carefully constructed. The recipes in this chapter offer a glimpse of the wide range of Italian soups.

CHICKEN STOCK

MOST STANDARD CHICKEN STOCKS ARE not flavorful enough for a robust chicken soup. They are fine if ladled into risotto or used as a base for vegetable soup, but they are not strong enough for a broth-based chicken soup such as straciatella or passatelli. Our goal was simple: to create a chicken stock with as much unadulterated chicken flavor as possible. We also wanted to streamline and speed the process as much as we could.

USING A CLEAVER

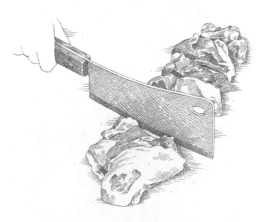

1. To hack through bone, place your hand near the far end of the meat cleaver's handle, curling your fingers securely around it in a fist. Handle the meat cleaver the way you would a hammer, with the motion in the arm rather than the wrist and the weight of the blade's front tip leading the force of the chop.

2. If you cannot chop the bone in one strike, place the cleaver in the groove of the first chop, then strike the blade's blunt edge with a heavy mallet.

We started with the most common technique for making stock—the simmering method. We placed all the ingredients (chicken, vegetables, aromatics, and water) in a pot, simmered everything for hours, then strained and defatted the stock. We tested a tremendous number of ingredients—everything from thyme and parsley to carrots and parsnips—and found that we preferred stock with fewer ingredients. Onions, salt, and bay leaves complement the flavor of the chicken; everything else is a distraction.

We tried making stock with a whole cut-up chicken, with whole legs, as well as with the more traditional necks and backs with the simmering method. While the necks and backs yielded a rich stock, tasters preferred stocks made with a cut-up chicken or whole legs, both of which had more flavor and body. Because whole legs are much less expensive, they are our first choice when using the traditional simmering method.

We uncovered several other findings during our testing. It is important to skim any impurities that rise to the surface as the water comes to a boil. We found that removing the foam gave our stock a clearer appearance. Also, it's important to reduce the heat once the stock comes to a boil. Boiling breaks the fat into tiny droplets that a gravy skimmer will not be able to trap. The result is greasy stock. While refrigerating the stock will allow the fat to congeal, at which point it can be removed, you may not always have time for this step. For the best results, gently simmer the stock (small bubbles will slowly and gently break through the surface).

Finally (and most importantly), we found that you must let the stock simmer as long as possible, up to five hours. We tried simmering stocks from one to six hours. When we tasted the various stocks, it was clear that more time yields a better stock. In fact, our favorite stock simmered for five hours. (After that, we could not taste any improvement; evidently the bones were spent, having given up all their flavor to the stock.) This long-cooked traditional chicken stock had a rich, intense chicken flavor, just what you want when making a simple chicken soup with a few tortellini. Although you may be tempted to shortcut this process, don't. While stocks simmered for at least 2½ hours were fine (stocks simmered for less time were insipid), they lacked the intensity and flavor of longer-cooked stocks. Time, and a lot of it, is needed to extract the full flavor from the chicken.

Our testing had produced a great stock, and we had reached some interesting conclusions about traditional stock making, but we wondered if there was a quicker route to good stock. While throwing everything into the pot and letting it simmer for hours is easy (the hands-on work is no more than 10 minutes), you do need to be around the house. More often than not, you need stock in a hurry or don't want to hang around the house for five hours. We were willing to try almost anything.

We tried blanching a whole chicken—submerging it briefly in boiling water—under the theory that blanching keeps the chicken from releasing foam during cooking. We then partially covered the blanched chicken with water and placed it in a heatproof bowl over a pan of simmering water. Cooked this way, the chicken never simmered, and the resulting stock was remarkably clear, refined, and full-flavored. The only problem: It took four hours to develop sufficient flavor. We also noted that our 4-pound chicken was good for nothing but the compost heap after being cooked for so long.

A number of recipes promote roasting chicken bones or parts and then using them to make stock. The theory, at least, is that roasted parts will flavor stock in minutes, not hours. We tried this several times, roasting chicken backs, necks, and bones with and without vegetables. We preferred the roasted stock with vegetables. The resulting stock was dark in color and had a nice caramelized onion flavor, but it still wasn't the full-flavored stock we were looking for. While the roasted flavor was quite strong, the actual chicken flavor was too tame.

We tried sautéing a chicken, hacked into small pieces, with an onion until the chicken was slightly browned. We then covered the pot and allowed the chicken and onion to cook over low heat until they released their juices, which took about 20 minutes. Only at this point did we add water, and the stock was simmered for just 20 minutes more.

We knew we were on to something when we smelled the chicken and onions sautéing, and the finished stock confirmed what our noses had detected. It tasted pleasantly sautéed, not boiled. We had some refining to do, though. For once, we had too much flavor.

We substituted chicken backs and wing tips for the whole chicken and used more water. This stock was less intense, but just the right strength to serve as a base for some of the best chicken soup we've ever tasted. We made the stock twice more, once without the onion and once with onion, celery, and carrot. The onion added a flavor dimension we liked; the extra vegetables neither added nor detracted from the final soup, so we left them out.

After much trial and error, we had a master recipe that delivered liquid gold in just 60

TWO WAYS TO DEFAT STOCK

Stock should be defatted before being used. The easiest way to do this is to refrigerate it until the fat rises to the surface and congeals. Use a spoon to scrape the fat off the surface of the stock. You may want to save the fat, which makes a flavorful replacement for oil or butter when cooking. Chicken fat can be kept refrigerated in an airtight container for several days.

If you don't have time to refrigerate the stock and allow the fat to congeal, use a gravy skimmer. Pour the stock into the gravy skimmer, then pour it back out through the spout attached to the bottom of the skimmer. The fat floating on top of the liquid will remain behind.

minutes. While this recipe requires some hands-on work (hacking up parts, browning an onion and then chicken parts), it is ready in a fraction of the time required to make a traditional, long-cooking stock.

The question before us now: How do you come up with these chicken parts for stock? The Buffalo chicken wing fad has made wings more expensive than legs and thighs. For those who can buy chicken backs, this is clearly an inexpensive way to make stock for soup. Our local grocery store usually sells the backs for practically nothing, but in many locations they are difficult to get. Luckily, we found that relatively inexpensive whole legs make incredibly full-flavored stocks for soup. In a side-by-side comparison of stocks, one made from backs and one from whole legs, we found the whole leg stock more full-flavored. Just don't try to salvage the meat once the stock is finished. After 5 minutes of sautéing, 20 minutes of sweating, and another 20 minutes of simmering, the meat is void of flavor.

One note about our recipe for quick stock. We found it necessary to cut the chicken into pieces small enough to release their flavorful juices in a short period of time (see "Hacking Up a Chicken for Stock," page 99). A cleaver or poultry shears speeds this process. Don't try to cut through chicken bones with a chef's knife. The blade isn't strong enough to cut through bone, and you may hurt yourself as the knife slips and slides. Even if you do manage to cut through the bone, your knife may become nicked in the process.

Quick Chicken Stock

MAKES ABOUT 2 QUARTS

Chicken pieces are sautéed and then sweated before being cooked in water for a rich but very quick stock. This is our favorite all-purpose stock; it takes less than an hour to prepare.

1	tablespoon vegetable oil
1	medium onion, chopped medium
4	pounds whole chicken legs or backs and wing tips, cut into 2-inch pieces (see "Hacking Up a Chicken for Stock" on page 99)
2	quarts boiling water
2	teaspoons salt
2	bay leaves

1. Heat the oil in a large stockpot or Dutch oven over medium-high heat. Add the onion; sauté until colored and slightly softened, 2 to 3 minutes. Transfer the onion to a large bowl.

2. Add half of the chicken pieces to the stockpot; sauté on both sides until lightly browned, 4 to 5 minutes. Transfer the cooked chicken to the bowl with the onions. Sauté the remaining chicken pieces. Return the onion and chicken pieces to the pot. Reduce the heat to low, cover, and cook until the chicken releases its juices, about 20 minutes.

3. Increase the heat to high; add the boiling water, salt, and bay leaves. Return to a simmer, then cover and barely simmer until the stock is rich and flavorful, about 20 minutes.

4. Strain the stock; discard the solids. Before using, defat the stock (see page 100). The stock can be refrigerated in an airtight container for up to 2 days or frozen for up to several months.

STRACIATELLA

WITH CHICKEN STOCK ON HAND, MANY soups are possible. Most Italian recipes rely on simple embellishments to turn homemade stock into great soups. Chicken soup with feathery bits of egg is perhaps the simplest choice of all.

Chinese egg drop soup is the most common form this soup takes in the United States, but the Italian version is equally simple and delicious. This soup is called *straciatella,* which translates as "little rags," referring to the shape of the egg pieces. While egg drop soup has long, ribbonlike pieces of egg, straciatella usually features elongated shredded rectangles that look like their namesake. Besides this difference, straciatella relies on typical Italian flavorings. The eggs are beaten with grated Parmesan cheese before being added to the soup. As for greens, minced basil or parsley or even spinach or chard is traditionally used, not scallions and cilantro, as is common in Chinese egg drop soup.

We figured that straciatella could be made just like egg drop soup. We heated the chicken stock in a saucepan, then started whisking the liquid and slowly drizzled in the egg-cheese mixture and continued to whisk. The results were disappointing—most of the egg mixture stuck to the wires of the whisk. Why does this technique work for egg drop soup and not for straciatella? The cheese added to the beaten eggs had to be the culprit.

We consulted a number of Italian sources and saw several possible solutions to this problem. Some cookbooks suggested tempering the egg-cheese mixture with the addition of cold chicken stock. Others suggested pouring the egg-cheese mixture through the large holes of a colander. Although both methods worked, in the end we found a simpler solution. It was the utensil (the whisk), not our technique (adding eggs gradually to moving stock), that was the problem. By using a fork rather than a whisk, we could use the same drizzling technique for straciatella and egg drop soup without losing too much egg to the utensil. The fork helped shape the egg mixture into elongated, shredded rectangles. (In contrast, a whisk turns eggs into long, smooth ribbons.)

Although we liked the idea of adding spinach or chard to this soup, in the end we preferred something less bulky. Chopped fresh basil or parsley adds a pleasing color and perfumes the stock nicely. It keeps this soup light and appropriate as a first course.

Straciatella

SERVES 6 TO 8 AS A FIRST COURSE

Straciatella is a sort of frittata soup—chicken stock with bits of Parmesan and egg floating in it. (See page 25 for more information about buying Parmesan cheese.) Fresh basil is a nice addition, but parsley works equally well.

2	quarts Quick Chicken Stock (page 101)
4	large eggs
1/4	cup freshly grated Parmesan cheese
1/4	cup finely chopped fresh basil or fresh parsley leaves
	Pinch freshly grated nutmeg
	Salt and ground black pepper

MAKING STRACIATELLA SOUP

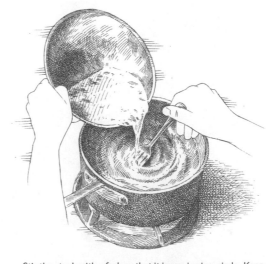

Stir the stock with a fork so that it is moving in a circle. Keep stirring as you pour the egg-cheese mixture in a slow, steady stream to form shreds of coagulated egg. Don't use a whisk; the egg-cheese mixture will cling to the wires.

1. Bring the stock to a simmer in a large saucepan over medium-high heat. Stir the eggs, Parmesan cheese, basil or parsley, and nutmeg together with a fork in a medium bowl.

2. Stir the stock with a fork so it is moving in a circle. Keep stirring as you pour the egg mixture into the stock in a slow, steady stream so that shreds of coagulated egg form, about 1 minute (see illustration on page 102). Let the egg shreds stand in the stock without mixing until they are set, less than 1 minute. Once they have set, break up the egg pieces with a fork. Season with salt and pepper to taste. Serve immediately.

Chicken Soup with Passatelli

PASSATELLI ARE ITALIAN DUMPLINGS made with Parmesan cheese and bread crumbs. They are similar to matzo balls and other European dumplings, although they are much less widely known, at least outside of Italy. That's a shame, given how simple and delicious these dumplings can be.

The combination of cheesy dumplings and chicken stock is irresistible. Dumplings made with bread crumbs, eggs, and grated cheese are cooked in chicken stock just until tender. The soup is often garnished with parsley and more grated cheese, but vegetables are not common additions.

We tried a variety of bread crumbs, including commercial crumbs from the supermarket, homemade crumbs from fresh bread, and homemade crumbs from stale bread. The commercial crumbs made bland-tasting, gummy dumplings. Homemade crumbs were better-tasting. The stale crumbs absorbed the eggs better and gave the dumplings a pleasing texture. We found that fresh crumbs could be used as long as they were dried out in a warm oven for five minutes. Because most cooks have a few slices of fresh bread on hand, we developed the recipe with this in mind.

With the bread crumb component decided, the other issues were easy to resolve. Good cheese (real Parmigiano-Reggiano) made a difference in this recipe. Dumplings made with domestic Parmesan were bland in comparison. (See page 25 for more information on Parmesan cheese.) A pinch of grated nutmeg added more flavor and highlighted the buttery, nutty flavor of the cheese.

As with matzo balls and other dumplings, we found it easier to shape cold batter. Just 15 minutes in the refrigerator is sufficient to firm this batter and make the shaping process much easier. In Italy, many cooks rely on a special tool to form the batter into thick, cylindrical strands. A food mill or ricer is another common option. The batter is pushed through the holes on the coarsest disk directly into a pot of simmering stock. We found that these authentic dumplings sometimes fall apart in the soup. Shaping the batter into small rounds (the size of grapes) ensures that the dumplings hold their shape. Although not strictly traditional, we think this modest change makes sense for cooks who have never made this soup before.

Chicken Soup with Passatelli

SERVES 6 TO 8 AS A FIRST COURSE

Make sure to use homemade bread crumbs in this recipe. Commercial crumbs are bland and too fine to make proper dumplings. For the Parmesan, we highly recommend Parmigiano-Reggiano.

2   slices white bread, torn into rough chunks
2   large eggs

1   cup freshly grated Parmesan cheese, plus
    more to pass at the table
    Pinch freshly grated nutmeg
    Salt and ground black pepper
2   quarts Quick Chicken Stock (page 101)
2   tablespoons minced fresh parsley leaves

1. Preheat the oven to 300 degrees. Grind the bread in a food processor. Measure ½ cup bread crumbs onto a small baking sheet. Toast until lightly dried, about 5 minutes. Cool completely.

2. Combine the bread crumbs, eggs, Parmesan cheese, nutmeg, and salt and pepper to taste in a medium bowl. Refrigerate this mixture until it firms, about 15 minutes.

3. With moistened hands, roll teaspoonfuls of the dumpling mixture into grape-sized balls.

4. Meanwhile, bring the stock to a boil in a large stockpot or Dutch oven over medium heat. Drop the dumplings into the gently simmering stock and cook until they float to the surface and are cooked through (taste one), 3 to 4 minutes. Stir in the parsley and adjust the

SHAPING TORTELLINI

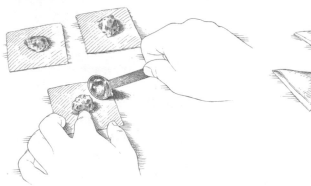

1. Use a pizza wheel or sharp knife to cut sheets of fresh pasta into 2-inch squares. Lift each square and place it on a clean part of the work surface (otherwise, squares may stick when stuffed). Place ½ teaspoon filling in the center of each square.

2. Fold each square diagonally in half to make a triangle. Make sure that the top piece of dough covers the filling, but leave a thin border of the bottom exposed. Seal the edges with your fingers.

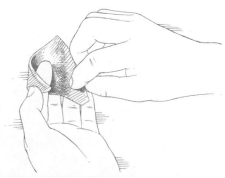

3. Lift the filled triangle from the counter and wrap the back of the triangle around the top of your index finger. Squeeze the two bottom corners of the triangle together.

4. As you pull back the top of the peak of the triangle, gently fold over the top ring of pasta so that the stuffing is completely enclosed. Slide the filled pasta off your finger.

seasonings with salt and pepper to taste. Ladle the soup and dumplings into bowls. Serve immediately, passing extra cheese at the table.

TORTELLINI SOUP

TORTELLINI IN BRODO, WHICH TRANSLATES as "tortellini in broth," is among Italy's most famous soups. Filled pastas are floated in a clear stock, usually flavored with greens. Although some recipes call for meat stock, we decided to use chicken stock because more cooks are likely to have this ingredient on hand. Because the stock portion of the recipe is so straightforward, we decided to focus on the tortellini first.

Some recipes call for cooking the tortellini right in the stock, although many suggest cooking them in salted water and then adding them to the stock. We tested both methods and preferred cooking the tortellini right in the stock. The pasta picked up more flavor this way, and tortellini didn't cloud the stock as we had feared they might.

Most commercially made tortellini are tough and doughy, not supple and tender, like homemade versions. We don't think the "fresh" tortellini sold in supermarket refrigerator cases are worth buying. These pastas are often quite old (many brands have sell-by dates that are weeks if not months away), and they don't have any of the delicacy we expect from fresh pasta. High-quality tortellini from a gourmet shop or pasta shop that makes fresh pasta every day is another matter. If you can find this product, by all means use it.

Because not everyone has access to handmade tortellini, we decided to figure out how to make them at home. After testing dozens of recipes, we can honestly say that filled pastas are not difficult to prepare. There is no question, however, that they are time-consuming.

Because most filled pastas have doubled edges where the pasta is folded over the filling and sealed, it is essential that the pasta sheets be rolled as thin as possible. Otherwise, the edges may remain too chewy when the rest of the pasta shape is already cooked through. Use the last setting on a manual pasta machine for the best results.

The biggest problem most home cooks encounter when making filled pastas is that the shapes open when boiled. There's nothing worse than seeing all the filling floating around the pot, so it's imperative to properly seal the edges on each piece of filled pasta. We tried brushing the edges of the dough with water and with lightly beaten egg. We found that both made the dough sticky and harder to handle, especially the egg.

We had the best results when we used the pasta sheet as quickly as possible, when it was still moist and pliable. Pasta sheets that have been left out to dry (even for just 20 to 30 minutes) are too brittle to manipulate. If your dough does become dry, brush the edges lightly with water. Be careful to brush lightly or the dough will become tacky. To guarantee that the pasta does not dry out, we recommend filling and shaping the tortellini as soon as the pasta is rolled out. This means the filling should be made first, then the pasta.

Take care not to overload the pasta with filling, which might cause the closed shape to burst in the boiling water. As an added precaution, cook the pasta in soup that is at a low boil. Highly agitated stock can rip open delicate shapes.

Tortellini fillings should be kept simple, especially as pasta making requires so much time. Ground meats enriched with cheese, or plain cheese flavored with herbs, are two classic choices. We found it best to add a little egg yolk (not the whole egg, as some sources suggested) to help bind filling ingredients.

With the tortellini made and stock on hand, the soup is easy to prepare. Most recipes call for some sort of greens, and we found that any tender leafy greens, including spinach, chard, escarole, and watercress, can be used. Just remove all tough stems and chop the leafy portion into small pieces that will fit on a soupspoon. A shower of grated Parmesan cheese at the table is all that's required to finish this soup.

Tortellini Soup

SERVES 6 TO 8 AS A FIRST COURSE

If you can find high-quality fresh tortellini at a local market, omit steps 1 and 2 and use about 50 small or medium tortellini in step 3. Once the fresh pasta is made (see recipe on page 185), use it immediately to make tortellini. Any extra scraps of pasta can be cut into long ribbons or rectangles, frozen on a baking sheet, transferred to a zipper-lock plastic bag, then added directly to pots of simmering soup and cooked until tender.

MEAT AND RICOTTA TORTELLINI

I	teaspoon extra-virgin olive oil
I	small clove garlic, minced
2	ounces ground beef, veal, or pork
1/3	cup ricotta cheese
I	tablespoon grated Parmesan cheese
I	tablespoon minced fresh basil or fresh parsley leaves
	Salt and ground black pepper
1/2	large egg yolk
1/2	pound Fresh Egg Pasta (page 185)

SOUP BASE

2	quarts Quick Chicken Stock (page 101)
4	cups stemmed and chopped spinach, chard, watercress, or escarole
	Salt and ground black pepper
	Freshly grated Parmesan cheese

1. FOR THE TORTELLINI: Heat the oil and garlic in a small skillet over medium heat. Cook until the garlic is golden, about 2 minutes. Add the meat and raise the heat to medium-high. Cook, using a wooden spoon to break up the larger pieces of meat, until the liquid evaporates and the meat browns, about 3 minutes. Spoon off the fat and transfer the meat mixture to a small bowl. Cool slightly. Stir in the cheeses, basil, and salt and pepper to taste. Stir in the egg yolk. (The filling can be covered and refrigerated for 1 day.)

2. Fill the pasta and shape the tortellini as directed in the illustrations on page 104. Place the filled tortellini on a large baking sheet lined with parchment or wax paper. (The tortellini can be refrigerated, uncovered, for up to 2 hours.)

3. FOR THE SOUP: Bring the stock to a boil in a large stockpot or Dutch oven. Drop the tortellini and greens into the pot. Simmer until the tortellini are al dente, about 4 minutes. Season the soup with salt and pepper to taste. Serve immediately, passing the Parmesan cheese at the table.

➤ VARIATION
Parsley-Cheese Tortellini in Chicken Stock

This filling requires no cooking and is quite simple to prepare.

Combine 1/3 cup ricotta cheese, 3 tablespoons freshly grated Parmesan cheese, 2 tablespoons minced fresh parsley leaves, 1/2 large egg yolk, and salt and pepper to taste in a small bowl. Follow the recipe for Tortellini Soup, omitting step 1. Use the ricotta mixture to fill the pasta in step 2. Proceed as directed.

MINESTRONE

MINESTRONE IS NOT A LIGHT UNDER-
taking. Any way you cut it, there is a lot of
dicing and chopping. Given the amount of
preparation, we thought it was important to
determine which steps and ingredients were
essential and which we could do without.
Could we simply add everything to the pot at
once, or would precooking some of the
vegetables be necessary? Was stock essential, or
could we use water, as many traditional recipes
do? How many vegetables were enough?
Which vegetables were best?

While we wanted to pack the soup with
vegetables, we were also determined to create
a harmonious balance of flavors. Minestrone
should be a group effort, with each element
pulling equal weight. From the start, we
decided to jettison vegetables that were too
bold (such as broccoli) as well as those that

were too bland and would contribute no
flavor to the soup (such as mushrooms).

But before tackling the issue of ingredients
(we had come up with a list of more than 35
to test), we wanted to devise a basic technique.
Our research turned up two possible paths.
The majority of recipes dump the vegetables
into a pot with liquid and simmer them until
everything is tender. A smaller number of
recipes call for sautéing some or most of the
vegetables before adding the liquid along with
those vegetables, such as spinach, that do not
benefit from cooking in fat.

Although we expected the soup with
sautéed vegetables to be more flavorful, it
wasn't. We then prepared three more pots
without sautéing any of the vegetables. We
added homemade vegetable stock to one pot,
homemade chicken stock to a second, and
water and the rind from a wedge of Parmesan
cheese to the third.

The results were unexpected. The soup
made with vegetable stock tasted one-
dimensional and overwhelmingly sweet;
because the vegetables were already sweet,
using vegetable stock, which is also fairly
sweet, did not help balance the flavors. We
realized we wanted the liquid portion of the
soup to add a layer of complexity that would
play off the vegetables. The soup made with
chicken stock seemed to fit the bill. It was rich,
complex, and delicious. However, the chicken
flavor overwhelmed the vegetables. Diluting
the stock with water wasn't the answer; this
resulted in a rather bland soup. Ultimately, we
preferred the soup made with water and the
cheese rind. The cheese gave the broth a buttery, nutty flavor that contrasted nicely with
the vegetables without overshadowing them.

We wanted the vegetables to soften
completely but not lose their shape, and an
hour of gentle simmering accomplished this.
Much longer, and the vegetables began to

*In addition to grated Parmesan, swirling pesto or a combination of
rosemary and garlic into the finished Minestrone builds flavor.*

107

break down. Less time over the flame, and the vegetables were too crunchy. We liked the concentrating effect of simmering without the lid on the pot.

We also saw several recipes that added some fresh vegetables at the end of the cooking time. It sounded like a nice idea, but the fresh peas and green beans added 10 minutes before the soup was done tasted uncooked and bland compared with the vegetables that had simmered in the flavorful stock for an hour. For maximum flavor, all of the vegetables, even those that usually require a brief cooking time, had to be added at the outset.

The addition of the cheese rind to the soup was an interesting find. During our research, we turned up two more flavor boosters that could be added up front: rehydrated porcini mushrooms with their soaking liquid, and pancetta (unsmoked Italian bacon). We made a batch of soup with the porcinis but felt that, like the chicken stock, they overpowered the flavor of the vegetables.

Pancetta must be sautéed to render its fat and release its flavor. We cooked a little pancetta until crisp in some olive oil, then added the water and vegetables. Like the cheese rind, the pancetta contributed depth. While the soup made with the cheese rind was buttery and nutty, the soup with pancetta had a subtle pork and spice flavor. We tried regular American bacon as well. It was stronger and lent the soup a smoky element. We preferred the subtler flavor of the pancetta, but either pancetta or smoked bacon is a significant improvement over water alone if you don't have a rind of Parmesan on hand.

To this point, we had focused on ingredients that went into the soup pot at the start. But many traditional recipes stir in fresh herbs or herb pastes just before the soup is served. Pesto is the most common choice. The first time we added pesto, we were hooked. The heat of the soup released the perfume of the basil and garlic and created another delicious layer of flavor. A simple mixture of minced fresh rosemary, garlic, and extra-virgin olive oil was also delicious. As with the pesto, the oil here adds some fat to a soup that is otherwise very lean. The rosemary and garlic combination is strong and must be used in smaller quantities than pesto.

Minestrone

SERVES 6 TO 8 AS A MAIN COURSE

The secret to this soup is adding the rind from a wedge of fresh Parmesan cheese, preferably Parmigiano-Reggiano, the Parmesan of Parmesans. It brings complexity and depth to a soup made with water instead of stock. (Rinds from which all the cheese has been grated can be stored in a zipperlock bag in the freezer to use as needed.) To experiment with different vegetables or beans, see the chart on page 109. For information on buying canned beans, see page 119.

2	small leeks (or 1 large), white and light green parts sliced thin crosswise (about ¾ cup)
2	medium carrots, chopped small (about ¾ cup)
2	small onions, chopped small (about ¾ cup)
2	medium stalks celery, chopped small (about ¾ cup)
1	medium baking potato, peeled and cut into ½-inch dice (about 1¼ cups)
1	medium zucchini, chopped medium (about 1¼ cups)
3	cups stemmed spinach leaves, cut into thin strips
1	(28-ounce) can whole tomatoes packed in juice, drained and chopped
8	cups water
1	Parmesan cheese rind, about 5 by 2 inches

Salt
1   (15½ ounce) can cannellini beans, drained and rinsed
¼   cup Classic Pesto (page 139) or 1 tablespoon minced fresh rosemary mixed with 1 teaspoon minced garlic and 1 tablespoon extra-virgin olive oil
    Ground black pepper

1. Bring the vegetables, tomatoes, water, cheese rind, and 1 teaspoon salt to a boil in a large stockpot or Dutch oven. Reduce the heat to medium-low and simmer, uncovered, stirring occasionally, until the vegetables are tender but still hold their shape, about 1 hour. Remove and discard the cheese rind. (Soup can be refrigerated in an airtight container for up to 3 days. Reheat before proceeding.)

2. Add the beans and cook just until heated through, about 5 minutes. Remove the pot from the heat. Stir in the pesto. Adjust the seasonings, adding pepper and more salt if necessary. Ladle the soup into bowls and serve immediately.

Varying the Vegetables and Beans in Minestrone

Our recipe for minestrone contains seven kinds of vegetables, plus tomatoes and cannellini beans. The aromatics—leeks, carrots, onions, and celery—are essential, as are the tomatoes. We like to add starchy potatoes, sweet zucchini, and leafy spinach, but this list is fairly subjective.

What follows are some notes on other vegetables that were tested in this soup and well liked by tasters. Bell peppers and broccoli were judged too distinctive, while eggplant and white mushrooms added little flavor, so none of those four vegetables is recommended.

When making substitutions, keep in mind that our minestrone recipe has 2½ cups solid vegetables (potatoes and zucchini) and 3 cups leafy spinach. Follow similar proportions when using the vegetables below. As for the beans, white kidney beans, called cannellini beans in Italy, are the classic choice. But other white beans may be used, as well as red kidney, cranberry, and borlotti beans, all of which appear in various traditional recipes for minestrone.

VEGETABLE	TESTING NOTES	HOW TO USE
Cauliflower	While broccoli is too intensely flavored for minestrone, milder cauliflower can blend in.	Cut into tiny florets and use in place of potatoes or zucchini.
Escarole	This slightly bitter green works well with white beans and pasta.	Chop and use in place of spinach.
Green Beans	A standard ingredient in French versions of this soup.	Cut into ½-inch pieces and use in place of zucchini.
Kale	This assertive green can be overwhelming on its own, but when combined with spinach it gives the soup a pleasant edge.	Remove ribs and chop. Use up to 1½ cups in place of 1½ cups of the spinach.
Peas	The delicate flavor of fresh peas is wasted in this soup, so use frozen.	Add up to ½ cup in place of ½ cup of the zucchini or white beans.
Savoy Cabbage	Adds an earthy note.	Shred fine and use in place of spinach.
Swiss Chard	Similar to spinach, with a slightly more earthy flavor.	Remove ribs and chop. Use in place of spinach.
Turnips	Modest bitter edge helps balance the sweetness of the some of the other vegetables.	Peel and cut into ½-inch dice. Use in place of potatoes.
Winter Squash	Butternut squash is sweet, but in small quantities it is especially colorful and delicious.	Peel and cut into ½-inch dice. Use in place of potatoes or zucchini.

Minestrone with Pancetta

Pancetta (unsmoked Italian bacon) can be used in place of a cheese rind to boost flavor in the soup. Because it has been smoked, American bacon can overwhelm the vegetables. To tone down some of the bacon's smokiness, cook bacon strips in simmering water for 1 minute.

Mince 2 ounces thinly sliced pancetta (or an equal amount of blanched bacon) and sauté in 1 tablespoon extra-virgin olive oil in a large stockpot or Dutch oven until crisp, 3 to 4 minutes. Proceed with the recipe for Minestrone, adding the vegetables, tomatoes, and water but omitting the cheese rind.

Minestrone with Rice or Pasta

Adding pasta or rice makes this soup hearty enough to serve as dinner. If the soup seems too thick after adding the pasta or rice, stir in a little water.

Follow the recipe for Minestrone or Minestrone with Pancetta until the vegetables are tender. Add ½ cup Arborio rice or small pasta shape, such as elbows, ditalini, or orzo. Continue cooking until the rice is tender but still a bit firm in the center of each grain, about 20 minutes, or until the pasta is al dente, 8 to 12 minutes, depending on the shape. Add the beans and proceed as directed.

TUSCAN TOMATO AND BREAD SOUP

THOUGH NOT AS FAMILIAR TO AMERICANS as minestrone, Tuscan tomato and bread soup (*pappa al pomodoro* in Italian) is a regional Italian favorite. On paper, pappa al pomodoro is a chicken stock and tomato soup finished with stale bread and basil, but in the pot, all of the ingredients meld to form a thick and fragrant porridgelike stew. Though the texture sets this recipe apart from conventional American soups, its soft luxuriousness combined with simple, pleasing flavors make it worth exploring.

No doubt owing to the dish's low profile in this country, we managed to dig up only two recipes from our collection of Italian cookbooks. The rest were mostly personal recipes that we uncovered during a search of the Web. Interestingly enough, each recipe had the same ingredient list: extra-virgin olive oil, red onion, garlic, chicken broth (canned), tomatoes (fresh or canned), Italian bread, and basil. Not one deviated. Some did differ in terms of preparation technique, though. In the case of the four recipes we chose to make, each had a base of onions and garlic sautéed in olive oil and was seasoned with salt and pepper and garnished with basil; here the similarities ended.

Two of the recipes called for canned, imported Italian whole tomatoes passed through a food mill to puree them and remove their seeds. The result, a red sea of thick tomato juice, was added to the aromatics and chicken broth and simmered for 20 minutes. At this point, the Italian bread, stale, crusty, and cubed, was mixed in and simmered for 20 minutes longer. Each soup (like the others to come) was then seasoned, garnished, and served with a healthy drizzle of good-quality extra-virgin olive oil. In terms of flavor, both soups were unanimously disliked for tasting tinny, acidic, and too tomatoey.

We next tested the recipes made with fresh tomatoes and learned a simple lesson: Don't make this soup with fresh tomatoes unless they are garden-fresh summer tomatoes. Store-bought off-season tomatoes were flavorless. If you do have access to garden-fresh tomatoes, by all means make the soup with them. Because we wanted to develop a recipe that can be used year-round, we decided to press ahead with the canned tomatoes; the recipe that uses fresh tomatoes would be a variation.

Abandoning the food mill was the first step to success with canned tomatoes. Processing the tomatoes through the mill turned out a highly acidic, just-plain-too-tomatoey slurry. Pappa al pomodoro should not be tomato soup dressed in bread clothing; it should be a brothy soup containing tomatoes and finished with stale bread. There is quite a difference. With this in mind, we set out to explore our options. We made three batches with canned tomatoes—left whole, chopped, and crushed by hand—each drained of their packing liquid. In all three, we added the tomatoes to the broth and let them simmer for 20 minutes. All three of these soups were much better than their predecessors. The tomatoes now dotted the soup and accompanied, not consumed, the other flavors in each bite.

The soup made with tomatoes crushed by hand (by gently squeezing them through our fingers until the pieces were small and uniform in size) got slightly higher marks for being more mellow-tasting than the soups made with whole or chopped tomatoes. This was because when we crushed the tomatoes, some of the seeds, which are notoriously bitter, escaped and never made it into the broth. The long, flat pieces of tomato (rather than three-dimensional chunks) were more smoothly incorporated into the soup and provided a nice contrast with the chunks of bread.

All canned tomatoes are not created equal (see page 145 for more information). We made two batches of soup: one with imported whole Italian tomatoes packed in puree, the other with Muir Glen whole tomatoes packed in tomato juice. Drained, squeezed, and simmered in the broth, the two kinds of tomatoes yielded a notable difference. The Muir Glen tomatoes packed in juice were sweeter, lighter, and fresher-tasting.

We now turned to the question of texture which, we found, was related to the treatment of the bread. In the two initial recipes we had made with canned tomatoes, one used the whole loaf, crust and all, while the other called for removing the crust. The soup made with crust-free bread came out thin and runny, with the bread all but disintegrating as it simmered in the tomatoey broth. The soup made with the whole loaf got better marks. As the dry, hard crusts absorbed the stock, they softened without breaking down completely, turning into voluptuously soft, chewy morsels. A few tasters were passionately drawn to this texture and commented that the soupy bread would never make it into bowls because they intended to stand there and pluck all of the "plump morsels" right out of the pot. Crusty bread was the way to go, but a little

CRUSHING TOMATOES

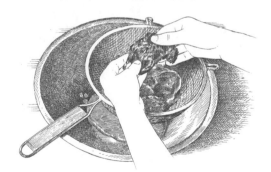

1. Empty the cans of whole tomatoes into a strainer and let the juice drain away in a bowl. With your fingertips, gently open each tomato and let the juice and seeds fall away.

2. Squeeze the opened tomato to break it into several rough pieces.

refinement still seemed to be in order.

While tasters liked biting into chunks of bread, they wanted the overall texture to be slightly more homogenous. In testing different methods of breaking down the bread beyond merely simmering it in the broth, we found that a wire whisk did the best job. The whisk, patiently but vigorously passed through the soup, broke down the crust-free pieces, incorporating them into the base of the soup. The whisk was no match for the crusty pieces, though. While some got caught in the wires (they were then tapped out), they largely retained their dumplinglike shape and texture, giving the soup some tooth.

To streamline the process, we also tested slicing techniques and found it best to slice and cube the loaf of bread while it was fresh. Cubing an already stale loaf was cumbersome and created excess crumbs that gave the soup a slimy texture. Slicing and cubing a fresh loaf and laying out the cubes to dehydrate for at least 24 hours eliminated the crumb issue. The cubes were solid and sturdy and held their own in the soup. If hard pressed for time, you can dry the cubes in a 250-degree oven for 30 minutes or until they are hard but not browned.

Adjusting the amounts of the few aromatics was easy; we knew they should complement one another, not do battle. Most of the recipes we looked at had similar ratios: 1 red onion to 3 cloves garlic to 2 cups chopped basil. The onion and garlic levels were just right—both flavors were subtle and soft. When we tested using red onion (which was part of every initial recipe) versus yellow onion, no one could detect a difference, so we decided to stick with tradition. Two cups basil, however, was too much; tasters found the flavor too potent. Working down in half-cup increments, we were all satisfied with a half cup. The clean, fresh taste of the basil perfumed the soup without overwhelming it.

For a complete, authentic experience, it is important to serve pappa al pomodoro as the Italians do: each bowl drizzled with high-quality extra-virgin olive oil. The oil's fruitiness brings out and heightens the flavors in the soup. Finally, remember that this is not minestrone—never sprinkle pappa al pomodoro with cheese. The strong flavor of cheese is quick to mute this soup's essential, unadulterated flavors.

Tuscan Tomato and Bread Soup

SERVES 6 AS A FIRST COURSE

This humble soup, known as pappa al pomodoro, requires good bread. We prefer to use Italian bread cubes staled for 1 to 2 days in this recipe, but you can stale fresh bread cubes quickly by putting them in a 250-degree oven until dry and hard but not browned, about 30 minutes. This soup does not hold and should be served as soon as it is ready.

¼	cup extra-virgin olive oil, plus extra for drizzling over individual bowls
I	large red onion, chopped fine
3	large cloves garlic, minced
5½	cups homemade chicken stock or canned low-sodium chicken broth
2	(28-ounce) cans whole tomatoes packed in juice, drained, tomatoes crushed by hand (see illustrations on page 111)
I	loaf good-quality Italian bread, cut into 1-inch square cubes, spread in an even layer on a rimmed baking sheet, and left to stale for 24 to 48 hours (about 9 heaping cups)
½	cup coarsely chopped fresh basil leaves Salt and ground black pepper

1. Heat the oil in a large stockpot or Dutch oven over medium-high until shimmering. Add the onion, reduce the heat to medium-

low, and cook, stirring frequently, until the onions are slightly softened and translucent, about 6 minutes. Add the garlic and cook, stirring frequently, until soft and fragrant, about 1 minute longer. Add the chicken stock, scraping the bottom of the pot with a wooden spoon; increase the heat to high and bring the mixture to a simmer. Add the tomatoes, cover, and simmer until the tomatoes soften and the stock turns red, about 20 minutes.

2. Stir in the bread cubes and press with a wooden spoon to submerge them in the liquid. Cover and simmer until the bread is softened, about 15 minutes. Stir the soup with a whisk to break down the bread until a thick, porridgelike texture is obtained.

3. Take the pot off the heat, stir in the basil, and season with salt and pepper to taste. Ladle the soup into individual bowls, drizzle with olive oil, and serve immediately.

➤ VARIATION

Fresh Tomato and Bread Soup

This soup is delicious when made with garden-fresh tomatoes. Italians serve it at room temperature when the weather is warm.

Core and roughly chop 2 pounds ripe fresh tomatoes. Follow the recipe for Tuscan Tomato and Bread Soup, adding the tomatoes with the stock in step 2. Proceed as directed.

TUSCAN WHITE BEAN SOUP

WE HAVE OFTEN THOUGHT OF WHITE bean soup as a choice between soup with mushy, exploded beans in an unmemorable liquid and soup filled with beans reminiscent of pebbles. But when made right (as is usually the case in Italy and always the case in Tuscany) white bean soup can be amazingly delicious, and it can be easy to make. This soup, a testament to restraint, is comprised of only two components: tender, creamy beans and a soup base perfumed with garlic and rosemary. We surmised that a soup so simple would be easy to duplicate. We had no idea.

We based our initial research on recipes that used navy, great Northern, or cannellini (white kidney) beans. After cooking a few batches, we found that we preferred the larger size and appearance of the cannellini beans, so we centered our testing on them. Many of these recipes came with tips and warnings on how to achieve a cooked bean with perfect texture. "Always soak the beans overnight to ensure even cooking" and "never salt the beans while they are cooking, or they will become tough or split open" were common counsel. Surely these "rules" were established for a reason. They couldn't be merely rural myths, could they?

We decided to find out and started with rule number one: Always soak the beans. We cooked up three batches of beans. Prior to cooking, we soaked one batch overnight and another according to the quick-soak method (water and beans simmer for two minutes, then are taken off the heat, covered, and allowed to sit in the water for one hour). We didn't soak the third batch at all. The results were altogether disappointing. Both batches of soaked beans split or exploded. The unsoaked beans looked better, but their texture was uneven; by the time half of the beans were tender, the other half had overcooked and disintegrated.

We wondered what would happen if we cooked unsoaked beans until just barely done, then let them sit off the heat in their still-hot cooking liquid. Would the residual heat from the liquid finish cooking the beans without any splitting or bursting? The answer was yes. This approach produced perfectly cooked beans that were creamy but not soggy.

INGREDIENTS: Commercial Chicken Broth

Few of the commercial broths in our tasting came close to the full-bodied consistency of a successful homemade stock. Many lacked even a hint of chicken flavor. Interestingly, the four broths we rated best were all products of the Campbell Soup Company, of which Swanson is a subsidiary. In order, they were Swanson Chicken Broth, Campbell's Chicken Broth, Swanson Natural Goodness Chicken Broth (with 33 percent less sodium than regular Swanson chicken broth), and Campbell's Healthy Request Chicken Broth (with 30 percent less sodium than regular Campbell's chicken broth.) The remaining broths were decidedly inferior and hard to recommend.

We tried to find out why Campbell's broths are superior to so many others, but the giant soup company declined to respond to questions, explaining that its recipes and cooking techniques are considered proprietary information. Many of the answers, however, could be found on the products' ingredient labels. As it turned out, the top two broths happened to contain the highest levels of sodium. Salt has been used for years in the food industry to make foods with less than optimal flavor tastier. The top two products also contained the controversial monosodium glutamate (MSG), an effective flavor enhancer.

Sadly, most of the products that had lower levels of salt and did not have the benefit of other food industry flavor enhancers simply tasted like dishwater. Their labels did indicate that their ingredients included "chicken broth" or "chicken stock," sometimes both. But calls to the U.S. Food and Drug Administration and the U.S. Department of Agriculture revealed that there are no standards that define chicken broth or stock, so an ingredient label indicating that the contents include chicken broth or chicken stock may mean anything as long as some chicken is used.

Ingredients aside, we found one more important explanation for why most commercial broths simply cannot replicate the full flavor and body of homemade stock. Most broths are sold canned, which entails an extended heating process carried out to ensure a sterilized product. The immediate disadvantage of this processing is that heat breaks down naturally present flavor enhancers found in chicken protein. Further, as it destroys other volatile flavors, the prolonged heating concentrates flavor components that are not volatile, such as salt.

A few national brands of chicken broth have begun to offer their products in aseptic packaging (special cartons). Compared with traditional canning, in which products are heated in the can for up to nearly an hour to ensure sterilization, the process of aseptic packaging entails a flash heating and cooling process that is said to help products better retain both their nutritional value and their flavor.

We decided to hold another tasting to see if we could detect more flavor in the products sold in aseptic packaging. Of the recommended broths in the tasting, only Swanson broths are available in aseptic packaging, and even these are not yet available nationwide. We tasted Swanson's traditional and Natural Goodness chicken broths sold in cans and in aseptic packages. The results fell clearly in favor of the aseptically packaged broths; both tasted cleaner and more chickeny than their canned counterparts. So if you are truly seeking the best of the best in commercial broths, choose one of the two Swanson broths sold in aseptic packaging. An opened aseptic package is said to keep in the refrigerator for up to two weeks (broth from a can is said to keep, refrigerated, for only a few days).

THE BEST CHICKEN BROTHS
Swanson Chicken Broth (left) and its reduced-sodium counterpart, Swanson Natural Goodness Chicken Broth (center), are our top choices in the test kitchen. In testing, we found that broth packaged in aseptic cartons (right) tastes better than canned broth.

Now we took on rule number two: Never salt the beans during cooking. Recipes that warned against salting stated that it would cause the outer shell of the bean to toughen. We tested beans cooked in salted water and in unsalted water, and the salted beans were indeed slightly more toothsome on the outside. However, these beans were not any less cooked on the inside than the unsalted beans. In addition, the small amount of resistance that the salted beans had developed on the outside seemed to keep them from bursting. The beans were now softly structured on the outside and tooth-tender on the inside.

One other advantage of using salted water is flavor. The seasoned beans were much tastier than those cooked in unsalted water. We reasoned that by adding other ingredients to the cooking liquid, we could improve the flavor of the beans that much more. In our initial testing, tasters preferred the beans flavored with pork rather than chicken, but because meat is not called for in the finished soup (only the extracted flavor of the meat is used), we didn't want to use expensive cuts of pork, such as loin chops, only to throw out the meat later. We reasoned that a ham hock or bacon would do the job, but smoked meats, we found out, added an unwanted sugary, smoky flavor reminiscent of canned soup. We tried an unsmoked ham hock, but the flavor lacked the punch that we were looking for. Finally, we tried pancetta, a salt-cured, unsmoked Italian bacon. The pancetta gave the beans a welcome sweet-and-sour flavor, and the rendered fat boosted the pork flavor of the broth. Cutting the pancetta into large cubes made it easy to remove once the beans were cooked. Onion, garlic, and a bay leaf are the other traditional additions; their flavors permeated the beans.

So now we had perfectly cooked beans, full of flavor from the pork and aromatics. Surely the finished soup would take little more than

rosemary and a light drizzling of olive oil to finish. Wrong. Although the beans were delicious enough to be eaten on their own, the liquid base lacked that bright, full garlic flavor we wanted. It was clear that we would have to add a second batch of vegetables toward the end of the cooking process.

We cooked another batch of beans with all of the accouterments, strained them from their cooking liquid, and allowed them to cool on the side while we proceeded. Sautéing was key to releasing the flavors from the aromatics quickly, and combining them with the bean water towards the end of cooking helped blend the flavors.

Now we needed to work in the flavor of rosemary, an herb traditional to white bean soup. We tried cooking the rosemary with the beans, but that produced a bitter, medicinal broth. Recalling a technique used in our shrimp bisque recipe, we allowed the herb to steep off the heat in the hot liquid for just a few minutes at the finish of our recipe. It worked—just the right amount of bright, fresh rosemary flavor was infused into the soup.

Tuscan White Bean Soup
SERVES 6 TO 8 AS A MAIN COURSE

For a more authentic soup, place a small slice of lightly toasted Italian bread in the bottom of each bowl and ladle the soup over it. To make this a vegetarian soup, omit the pancetta and add a piece of Parmesan rind to the pot along with the halved onion and unpeeled garlic in step 1.

6   ounces pancetta, one 1-inch-thick slice, cut into 1-inch cubes

1   pound (2¼ cups) dried cannellini beans, rinsed and picked over

1   large onion, unpeeled and halved pole to pole, plus 1 small onion, chopped medium

4   medium cloves garlic, unpeeled, plus
3 medium cloves garlic, peeled
and minced

1   bay leaf
Salt and ground black pepper

¼   cup extra-virgin olive oil, plus extra for
drizzling over individual bowls

1   sprig fresh rosemary

1. Cook the pancetta in a large stockpot or Dutch oven over medium heat until just golden, 8 to 10 minutes. Add 12 cups water and the beans, halved onion, unpeeled garlic, bay leaf, and 1 teaspoon salt. Bring to a boil over medium-high heat. Cover the pot partially, reduce the heat to low, and simmer, stirring occasionally, until the beans are almost tender, 1 to 1¼ hours. Remove the pot from the heat, cover, and let stand until the beans are tender, about 30 minutes. Drain the beans, reserving the cooking liquid. (You should have about 5 cups; if you don't, add water.) Discard the pancetta, onion, garlic, and bay leaf. Spread the beans in an even layer on a rimmed baking sheet and cool.

2. While the beans are cooling, heat the oil in the now-empty Dutch oven over medium heat until shimmering. Add the chopped onion and cook, stirring occasionally, until softened, 5 to 6 minutes. Stir in the minced garlic and cook until fragrant, about 30 seconds. Add the cooled beans and cooking liquid, increase the heat to medium-high, and bring to a simmer. Submerge the rosemary sprig in the liquid, cover the pot, and let stand off the heat for 15 to 20 minutes.

3. Discard the rosemary sprig and season to taste with salt and pepper. Ladle the soup into individual bowls and drizzle each bowl with olive oil. Serve immediately.

➤ VARIATIONS

White Bean Soup with Winter Vegetables

SERVES 10 TO 12 AS A MAIN COURSE

The addition of carrots, leeks, celery, tomatoes, and kale makes this soup much more substantial.

6   ounces pancetta, one 1-inch-thick slice,
cut into 1-inch cubes

1   pound (2¼ cups) dried cannellini beans,
rinsed and picked over

1   large onion, unpeeled and halved pole to
pole, plus 1 small onion, chopped medium

4   medium cloves garlic, unpeeled, plus
3 medium cloves garlic, minced

1   bay leaf
Salt and ground black pepper

¼   cup extra-virgin olive oil, plus extra for
drizzling over individual bowls

2   small carrots, chopped medium

2   stalks celery, chopped medium

2   small leeks, white and light green parts,
cut crosswise into ½-inch pieces

1   (14½-ounce) can diced tomatoes,
drained

8   ounces kale, stems discarded, leaves cut
into ½-inch strips (about 6 cups)

1   sprig fresh rosemary

1. Cook the pancetta in a large stockpot or Dutch oven over medium heat until just golden, 8 to 10 minutes. Add 12 cups water and the beans, halved onion, unpeeled garlic, bay leaf, and 1 teaspoon salt. Bring to a boil over medium-high heat. Cover the pot partially, reduce the heat to low, and simmer, stirring occasionally, until the beans are almost tender, 1 to 1¼ hours. Remove the pot from the heat, cover, and let stand until the beans are tender, about 30 minutes. Drain the beans, reserving the cooking liquid. (You should have about 5 cups. Add enough water to yield

9 cups.) Discard the pancetta, onion, garlic, and bay leaf. Spread the beans in an even layer on a rimmed baking sheet and cool.

2. While the beans are cooling, heat the oil in the now-empty Dutch oven over medium heat until shimmering. Add the chopped onion, carrots, celery, and leeks and cook, stirring occasionally, until softened but not browned, about 7 minutes. Stir in the minced garlic and cook until fragrant, about 30 seconds. Add the bean cooking liquid, increase the heat to medium-high, and bring to a boil. Cover, reduce the heat to low, and simmer for 30 minutes. Add the tomatoes, beans, and kale, increase the heat to medium-high, and bring to a simmer. Once simmering, submerge the rosemary sprig, cover the pot, and let stand off the heat for 15 to 20 minutes.

3. Discard the rosemary sprig and season to taste with salt and pepper. Ladle the soup into individual bowls and drizzle each bowl with olive oil. Serve immediately.

Quick Tuscan White Bean Soup

This quick variation uses canned beans and can be on the table in just 40 minutes. For information on buying canned beans, see page 119.

6	ounces pancetta, one 1-inch-thick slice, cut into 1-inch cubes
2	tablespoons extra-virgin olive oil, plus extra for drizzling over individual bowls
1	small onion, chopped medium
3	medium cloves garlic, minced
4	(15½-ounce) cans cannellini beans, drained and rinsed
	Salt and ground black pepper
1	sprig fresh rosemary

Cook the pancetta in a large stockpot or Dutch oven over medium heat until just golden, 8 to 10 minutes. Discard the pancetta and add the oil to the pot with the pancetta fat. Add the onion and cook, stirring occasionally, until softened, 5 to 6 minutes. Stir in the garlic and cook until fragrant, about 30 seconds. Add the beans, ½ teaspoon salt, and 3½ cups water. Increase the heat to medium-high and bring to a simmer. Submerge the rosemary in the liquid, cover the pot, and let stand off the heat for 15 to 20 minutes. Discard the rosemary and adjust the seasonings with salt and pepper. Ladle the soup into individual bowls and drizzle each bowl with olive oil. Serve immediately.

RIBOLLITA

IF YOU FIND YOURSELF WITH A PLETHORA of leftover bean and vegetable soup, have no fear. In Tuscany, where nothing is wasted, leftover soup is not seen as a problem but rather as the last step in creating a delicious, homey dish called *ribollita,* which means "reboiled" in Italian.

The leftover soup is warmed over medium-low heat. Slices of rustic day-old bread are submerged in the soup until completely softened, and then the mixture is blended or mashed until very thick. True ribollita connoisseurs say that it must be thick enough to eat with a fork.

We found that this classic recipe worked perfectly with our White Bean Soup with Winter Vegetables. As for the bread, either fresh or stale will work fine. We found it easier to mash bread that had been cut into large cubes rather than slices.

Don't be put off by the strange appearance of this dish—what ribollita lacks in beauty it more than makes up for in flavor. But do be sure to use a good-quality artisan or rustic bread when making ribollita; a fluffy supermarket bread will yield a mushy, sloppy mess.

Ribollita

SERVES 1

This recipe can be scaled up as desired to make multiple bowls of soup. Although traditionally made with stale bread, this recipe works just fine with fresh bread, too.

1   cup White Bean Soup with Winter Vegetables (page 116)

6   1-inch cubes country-style bread (about 1½ ounces)

    Extra-virgin olive oil

Place the soup in a medium saucepan and warm over medium-low heat until hot. Add the bread and, with a potato masher, break down the bread until the soup is creamy, about 1 minute. Ladle the soup into a warm, shallow soup bowl and drizzle with oil to taste. Serve immediately.

PASTA E FAGIOLI

PASTA E FAGIOLI (OR PASTA AND BEANS) is a hearty, nutritious peasant soup made throughout Italy. The beans and pasta shapes used vary from region to region, but the broad outlines of the dish are the same. This soup is loaded with ingredients and is quite thick. The orange-red color comes from tomatoes, and each spoonful should be laden with pasta and beans. The soup is full of harmonious flavors, with no single taste standing out. The vegetables are used as accents and cut small. A drizzle of olive oil and a dusting of grated Parmesan cheese are typical garnishes.

Most recipes follow a similar procedure. The aromatics (vegetables and, often, some pork product) are sautéed in olive oil. The tomatoes and broth go into the pot, followed by the beans and, lastly, the pasta. Our goal was to streamline the process and create a full-flavored soup that could be on the table in less than one hour.

Many authentic recipes call for pancetta, an unsmoked Italian bacon. (Americanized recipes call for regular bacon.) For our first test, we sautéed 4 ounces diced pancetta in ¼ cup olive oil prior to adding the aromatic vegetables. We found this amount of fat excessive, and the resulting soup had an oily texture. We reduced the pancetta to 3 ounces and the olive oil to 1 tablespoon, then compared this soup with one made with 3 tablespoons oil and no meat. All tasters felt that the pancetta added complexity to the soup. When diced small, the pancetta almost disappeared in the final soup. Its flavor lingered, though. Pancetta gave the soup a subtle pork flavor, but tasters did not mind the stronger, smokier flavor of regular bacon.

Most recipes use the same quartet of aromatic vegetables—onions, celery, carrots, and garlic. Tasters liked the onions, celery, and garlic but were divided about the sweetness imparted by the carrots. We decided to use carrots with the kidney bean variation—the sweetness of the carrots balances the earthiness of the beans—but to omit this ingredient from the master recipe.

Once the aromatics have been sautéed, most recipes use tomatoes or stock to deglaze the pan. We also wanted to try white wine. The wine proved a bad idea; the tomatoes

INGREDIENTS: Parmesan Rinds

Rinds from wedges of Parmigiano-Reggiano add a distinctive but hard-to-place flavor to many Italian soups and stews. We keep our leftover rinds in a sealed bag in the freezer, adding to the bag as we finish up wedges of Parmesan. If you do not happen to have any rinds, many Italian grocery stores and some supermarkets have them for the asking. They should be quite inexpensive.

provide plenty of acidity, and adding wine just made the soup sour. Both the tomatoes and stock worked fine, but we liked the way the tomatoes and aromatics blended, so we decided to add them to the pot first.

Pasta e fagioli usually starts with canned beans. The challenge is to get some flavor into them. We wondered if adding the beans to the tomato mixture (before the stock) would help infuse them with the flavors of the pancetta, oil, and vegetables. We prepared two batches of soup—one with beans and stock added simultaneously and one with beans added to the tomatoes and cooked for 10 minutes before the stock went into the pot. As we had hoped, simmering the beans in the thick tomato mixture infused them with flavor and was worth the extra step.

We next focused on the type of beans. Cranberry beans, a pink and white mottled variety, are especially popular in Italy. Because cranberry beans are hard to find in the United States, we tested two common substitutes, pinto beans and red kidney beans. Neither bean has the sweet, delicate flavor of the cranberry bean, but tasters felt that the red kidneys were a closer approximation. Cannellini beans, also known as white kidney beans, are the other common choice in this soup. These oval beans are sweet and creamy. Because they are widely available, we decided to use them in the master recipe.

Our recipe was coming together, but we had a few more points to consider. Many versions of this soup rely on chicken stock. However, many of our tasters complained that the chicken flavor was too strong. Was this chicken noodle soup with beans, they wondered? We decided some experiments were in order. First, we used water instead of chicken stock and added a Parmesan rind to pump up the flavor. This trick had worked well in our minestrone recipe. Tasters liked pasta e fagioli made this way. The cheese added flavor and

body. As a final test, we decided to keep the Parmesan rind and use half water and half chicken stock. This combination produced the best soup—the flavors were rich but not chickeny, and the liquid had better body.

Our last area of investigation was pasta. Our tests showed that smaller shapes are best in this soup. Larger shapes crowded out the other ingredients and soaked up too much liquid. Ditalini (small tubes), tubettini (very small tubes), and orzo (rice-shaped pasta) were favorites among our tasters. We also liked

INGREDIENTS: Canned Beans

Is it acceptable to use canned beans in soups? In recipes that put beans center stage, we find that there is a real difference in flavor and texture between dried beans that you cook yourself and those out of a can. Beans from a can are much less flavorful. They taste of salt and not much else, compared with beans you cook yourself, which can take on the flavors of garlic, bay leaves, and other seasonings added to the cooking water. Canned beans also tend to fall apart if simmered for any length of time.

In recipes where beans are not the focal point and the cooking time is short, we find canned beans an acceptable shortcut. For instance, canned beans are fine in pasta e fagioli and minestrone. These soups have so many other ingredients that most people won't notice any flavor deficiencies in the canned beans.

We tested six leading brands of canned beans—both traditional and organic—to see if any brands would outperform the others in a soup recipe. We found that creamy, well-seasoned beans were preferred by the majority of tasters, in part because canned beans generally don't spend much time in the soup pot. If you want beans that are tender and flavorful in your soup, they should come out of the can with these qualities.

Our tasting panel found organic beans to be quite firm and chalky and to taste underseasoned. Green Giant and Goya beans were the top choices because they were creamy (but not mushy) and well seasoned.

conchigliette (very small shells with ridges), but this shape is hard to find. Elbows were acceptable but a bit on the large side.

Pasta e Fagioli

SERVES 6 TO 8 AS A MAIN COURSE

This hearty pasta and bean soup is so simple and delicious, it is easy to understand why regional versions are found throughout Italy. We wanted ours to be quick-cooking; with canned beans, the soup is prepared in less than one hour. (For information about buying canned beans, see page 119.) Pancetta or bacon and the rind from a wedge of Parmesan infuse flavor into the broth. We preferred using half water and half chicken stock, but the bacon and cheese rind will flavor the soup nicely if stock is not available (use 2 quarts water and increase the salt to 2 teaspoons). This soup makes an excellent dinner when combined with a green salad and crusty bread. Because of the pasta and beans, however, it does not hold well and should be served as soon as it is ready.

3	tablespoons extra-virgin olive oil
3	ounces bacon or pancetta, chopped fine
1	medium onion, chopped fine
1	medium stalk celery, chopped fine
4	medium cloves garlic, minced
1	teaspoon dried oregano
1/4	teaspoon hot red pepper flakes
2	(14 1/2-ounce) cans diced tomatoes
1	Parmesan cheese rind, about 5 by 2 inches
2	(15 1/2-ounce) cans cannellini beans, drained and rinsed
4	cups homemade chicken stock or canned low-sodium chicken broth
1	teaspoon salt
8	ounces ditalini or other small pasta shape
1/4	cup chopped fresh parsley leaves Ground black pepper
1	cup freshly grated Parmesan cheese

1. Heat 1 tablespoon oil in a large stockpot or Dutch oven over medium-high heat. Add the bacon and sauté until browned, about 5 minutes. Add the onion and celery and cook, stirring occasionally, until the vegetables soften, 4 to 5 minutes. Add the garlic, oregano, and hot red pepper flakes and sauté until fragrant, about 1 minute.

2. Add the tomatoes and scrape any browned bits from the bottom of the pan. Add the cheese rind and the beans. Bring to a boil, reduce the heat to low, and simmer until the flavors meld, about 10 minutes. Add the chicken stock, 4 cups water, and salt. Raise the heat to high and bring to a boil. Add the pasta and cook until tender, about 8 minutes.

3. Off the heat, remove and discard the cheese rind. Stir in most of the parsley and season with pepper and additional salt, if needed. Ladle the soup into individual bowls. Drizzle some of the remaining 2 tablespoons oil over each bowl and then sprinkle with parsley. Serve immediately, passing the grated cheese at the table.

➤ VARIATIONS

Tubettini and Chickpea Soup

Follow the recipe for Pasta e Fagioli, substituting 1 tablespoon chopped fresh rosemary for the oregano, two 15 1/2-ounce cans chickpeas for the cannellini beans, and 8 ounces tubettini for the ditalini.

Orzo and Kidney Bean Soup with Carrots

Follow the recipe for Pasta e Fagioli, substituting 1 medium carrot, chopped small, for the celery, two 15 1/2-ounce cans kidney beans for the cannellini beans, and 8 ounces orzo for the ditalini. Proceed as directed, increasing the cooking time for the pasta to 13 to 15 minutes.

Chickpea Soup

ALTHOUGH A GOOD NUMBER OF DISHES from southern Italy were born of frugality, rarely do they taste like it. An intricate layering of assertively flavored elements makes for bold, bright dishes that belie the economical ingredients. Never is the ingenuity of southern Italian cooking more evident than in the preparation of soups. Humble ingredients like stale bread, beans, scraps of meat, and wild herbs and greens are transformed into extraordinary dishes.

Pasta e fagioli may be the most recognized soup from this region, but there are many others just as flavorful. While pasta e fagioli is generally made with cranberry or cannellini beans, chickpeas (also called garbanzo beans and *ceci*) are actually the most common legume used in southern Italian soups. We found dozens of soup recipes with chickpeas but were most interested in versions in which the humble bean played a starring role. Borrowing from several recipes, we set out to create a chickpea soup true to this bold style of cooking.

Chickpeas can be a challenge to cook properly. Our exhaustive research has proven to us that, contrary to popular belief, most beans may be cooked without being soaked first. Chickpeas, however, are an exception. We find that they must be soaked overnight; otherwise, they can develop a chalky texture and take almost four times as long to cook as soaked chickpeas. They must also be slowly simmered, or they cook unevenly and their skins toughen and grow fibrous (some traditional recipes have you peel the cooked chickpeas—an arduous process). When cooked properly, which means slowly over low heat, we find chickpeas take on a soft, creamy texture while retaining just a bit of chew. Unlike most other beans, they rarely break apart if overcooked—a quality that makes them perfect for soups.

Beans absorb a lot of flavor as they cook, so for the best-flavored beans, the cooking liquid should be well seasoned. We included onion, carrot, garlic, celery, a variety of herbs, hot red pepper flakes, and our secret ingredient, a Parmesan cheese rind—all of the flavors we wanted in the soup. While the aromatics season the beans, they also make the cooking liquid flavorful enough to serve as the soup's broth. The liquid was so flavorful that tasters could not believe it did not contain any stock.

While simmering a Parmesan rind with the beans may seem odd, cheese is a traditional flavoring agent for many Italian soups. Indiscernible as Parmesan per se, the rind adds a nutty richness and mysterious complexity that bolsters the chickpeas' own nuttiness.

With our beans tender and a flavorful broth with which to make our soup, we wanted to add texture and body with sautéed vegetables. Carrots and onions were naturals, as their flavors were already present in the broth. We also added fennel, which grows wild throughout much of the Mediterranean, and its mild anise bite complemented the chickpeas. A healthy dose of slivered garlic rounded out the aromatics, and diced tomato added brightness and color to the otherwise dowdy-looking soup. The final accents were minced anchovy, for briny richness, and orange peel, for a citrus punch. While the orange rind was not noticeable in the soup, it perked up the tomato's flavor with mild acidity and citrus bite. Fennel, orange, and anchovy are a classic combination used to flavor everything from salads to grilled fish and soups. Chopped parsley added just before serving brought freshness to the soup.

Many southern Italian soups are served with bread of some sort, be it *pane fritto* (fried bread), *pangrattato* (fried bread crumbs), or *crostini* and *bruschetta* (grilled or toasted bread rubbed with raw garlic and doused in good-quality olive oil). Tasters favored crostini over crumbs for their crisp texture and pungent bite of raw garlic. The crumbs also overwhelmed the flavors in the soup, whereas the raw garlic bite emphasized the garlic already present.

Chickpea Soup

SERVES 4 TO 6 AS A MAIN COURSE

Because its flavors improve with time, this is an excellent soup to make a day or two ahead. However, reserve the parsley until the soup is ready to serve. As the soup sits, the beans absorb the broth, so feel free to add additional liquid prior to reheating. Soaking beans takes a little forethought the night before. The soaking beans can be refrigerated or left on the kitchen counter (if it is cool in the kitchen; otherwise, they may begin to sprout or ferment). Just make sure the bowl is at least twice as deep as the beans and that you soak them in a lot of water. It can be surprising how much liquid they absorb.

CHICKPEAS AND BROTH

1	medium carrot, halved lengthwise
1	medium celery stalk
4	sprigs fresh parsley
4	sprigs fresh thyme
2	sprigs fresh oregano
1/2	pound (about 1 cup) dried chickpeas, soaked at least 8 hours or overnight in abundant water, drained, and rinsed
1	medium onion, halved from pole to pole
1	head garlic, top third cut off and discarded, loose outer skins removed and discarded
1/2	teaspoon hot red pepper flakes
2	bay leaves
1	Parmesan cheese rind, about 4 by 2 inches
1	teaspoon salt

SOUP

3	tablespoons extra-virgin olive oil, plus more for drizzling over bowls of soup
1	medium onion, diced small
1	medium fennel bulb (about 1/2 pound), feathery tops and stalks discarded, bulb diced small
1	medium carrot, diced small
4	large cloves garlic, sliced thin
2	anchovy fillets, minced
1	(14 1/2-ounce) can diced tomatoes, drained
1	(2 by 2-inch) piece orange rind, cleaned of all pith
2	tablespoons minced fresh parsley leaves Salt and ground black pepper
1	recipe Crostini for Soup (recipe follows)
1	cup freshly grated Parmesan cheese

1. FOR THE CHICKPEAS AND BROTH: Tie together the carrot, celery, and herbs with a length of kitchen twine and place them in a 6-quart Dutch oven. Add the remaining ingredients along with 10 cups water and bring to a boil over medium-high heat. Once boiling, reduce the heat to medium-low and simmer until the chickpeas are tender, about 1½ hours. Remove and discard the carrot and celery bundle, the onion halves, and the Parmesan rind (scraping off any cheese that has melted and adding it back to the pot). Remove the garlic and, using tongs, squeeze the cloves out of their skin and add them back to the beans; discard the skin. Keep the chickpeas and broth warm over low heat.

2. FOR THE SOUP: While the chickpeas are cooking, heat the oil, onion, fennel, and carrot in a medium skillet over medium-high heat. Cook, stirring frequently, until the vegetables have softened and begin to turn light brown around the edges, 7 to 9 minutes. Add the garlic and anchovies and cook until the garlic is

fragrant and softened, about 1 minute. Remove the pan from the heat and add the tomatoes. Use a wooden spoon to loosen any browned bits stuck to the bottom of the skillet.

3. When the chickpeas and broth are done, scrape the tomato mixture into the pot with the beans. Add the piece of orange rind. Increase the heat to medium-high and bring to a boil. Reduce the heat to low and simmer until the flavors have fully blended, about 1 hour. Stir in the parsley and adjust the seasonings with salt and pepper to taste. Allow to cool for 5 minutes. Place one crostini in each individual soup bowl, ladle the soup over the crostini, and serve immediately, accompanied by the freshly grated Parmesan, extra-virgin olive oil for drizzling, and additional crostini.

Crostini for Soup

MAKES ENOUGH FOR 4 TO 6 BOWLS OF SOUP

Choose a long loaf without seeds, preferably something hearty, with a chewy crumb.

- ½   baguette or long Italian loaf (6 to 8 ounces), cut into ½-inch-thick slices
- 1   large clove garlic, peeled
- ¼   cup good-quality extra-virgin olive oil
      Salt and ground black pepper

Adjust an oven rack to the middle position and heat the oven to 400 degrees. Arrange the bread slices in a single layer on a baking sheet and bake until they are dry and crisp, about 10 minutes, turning them over halfway through baking. While still hot, rub each slice of bread with the raw garlic clove. Liberally drizzle the olive oil over the slices. Sprinkle with salt and pepper. (Crostini are best straight from the oven, but they can be set aside on a plate for several hours.)

LENTIL AND ESCAROLE SOUP

LENTILS HAVE LONG BEEN IMPORTANT to Italian peasant cooking, with roots tracing back to the Roman Empire. Admittedly bland and boring on their own, lentils readily gain character when combined with hearty flavors, as they are in many dishes throughout Italy.

Lentil and escarole soup is a hearty but brothy soup with vegetables. While the supporting ingredients vary from town to town, the basic flavors of most versions are similar. The earthy, slightly sweet flavor of the lentils is supported by sautéed garlic and onions and balanced by the tomato's acidity and the escarole's bitterness. The textures are balanced, too; the lentils are cooked until just soft but retain some toothsomeness, which is complemented by the crisp, watery crunch provided by the escarole stems and the velvety softness of the leaves.

While vegetables and stock flavor this soup, lentils are its heart. Lentils have been cultivated throughout Europe and Asia for thousands of years and, consequently, come in many varieties and a rainbow of colors from pale yellow to pink, brown, gray, and green. Brown lentils are the most frequently used in Italy and what we chose for this soup. Dark green lentils from Castellucia, in Umbria, are also widespread in Italy, but they are comparatively expensive and tricky to find. (The French lentils du Puy are nearly identical and easier to locate.) Green lentils retain their shape and texture much better than brown lentils, which makes them ideal for salads and braised dishes when texture is crucial. Here, however, we found that brown lentils—the kind sold in almost every American supermarket—are just fine.

To lend this humble soup hearty, deep

flavor, we followed tradition and started with *soffritto*. This vegetable concoction, whose name literally means "underfried," is the keystone upon which many Italian dishes are built. Depending on the region of Italy—and who's making it—soffritto generally includes finely chopped onion, carrot, celery, parsley, and garlic cooked long and slow in fruity olive oil. The vegetables release their juices and develop a richness unattainable with briefer cooking methods. While time intensive, soffritto delivers robust flavor. For this soup, we included traditional ingredients for a soffritto with one minor change; we cut the carrots into dice large enough to retain some crunch through the long simmer. Tasters liked the texture and visual appeal of the larger dice.

For the soup's broth, we used a combination of chicken stock and water. Many Italian bean and vegetable soups use a weaker stock (called *brodo*) than American soups do so as not to overpower the other flavors. For this soup, we found that almost equal parts water and chicken stock lent the soup body but did not make it taste overwhelmingly of chicken, as all chicken stock had.

In addition to the soffritto and broth, we included canned diced tomatoes, which are classic, and bay leaves, for their warm, herbal flavor. After the first few batches tasted thin, we decided to add a Parmesan rind for more depth. As it does in many vegetable soups, the Parmesan rind contributed richness that supported the soup's flavors without calling attention to itself, as more chicken stock or olive oil would have. Although the cheese rind was definitely a plus, our tasters agreed the soup was still good without it. We decided to make the Parmesan rind optional.

While some versions we found simmered the escarole for quite a long time in the broth, tasters all agreed that a quick simmer after the lentils were cooked through was best. The lettuce's bitterness was muted, and the leaves and stem retained some crispness, which nicely contrasted with the softer lentils.

Lentil and Escarole Soup

SERVES 6 AS A MAIN COURSE

It is important to clean and sort lentils carefully because they are often sandy and loaded with small rocks. Sorting them in a white or stainless-steel bowl filled with plenty of water helps. Depending on the age of the lentils, they can cook at very different rates, so start checking them after one hour to be on the safe side. They can go from firm to mushy rather quickly. Serve the soup with fine olive oil and a hearty loaf of country bread, as you will want to soak up the last of the broth.

¼	cup extra-virgin olive oil, plus more for drizzling over bowls of soup
1	medium carrot, diced medium
1	medium onion, diced small
1	medium celery rib, diced small
6	medium cloves garlic, sliced thin
2	tablespoons minced fresh parsley leaves
	Salt
1	(14½-ounce) can diced tomatoes
8	ounces brown lentils, sorted and rinsed
4	cups homemade chicken stock or canned low-sodium chicken broth
2	bay leaves
1	Parmesan cheese rind, about 4 by 2 inches (optional)
1	head escarole (about 8 ounces), cut into ½-inch-wide strips
	Ground black pepper
	Freshly grated Parmesan cheese for garnish

1. Combine the oil, carrot, onion, celery, garlic, parsley, and ¾ teaspoon salt in a heavy-bottomed 6-quart Dutch oven over medium heat. Cook, stirring occasionally, until the vegetables are quite soft, dramatically reduced in

volume, and very lightly browned, 17 to 20 minutes. Increase the heat to medium-high and add the tomatoes, lentils, stock, 3 cups water, the bay leaves, and the Parmesan rind and bring to a boil. Once boiling, reduce the heat to low, partially cover, and simmer until the lentils are soft, 1 to 1¼ hours.

2. Stir in the escarole and cook until wilted, about 5 minutes. Season with salt and pepper to taste and serve immediately in warmed bowls, drizzled with olive oil and sprinkled with Parmesan cheese.

Savoy Cabbage Soup

ALONG THE NORTHERN BORDER OF Italy, high in the mountains, the food takes on a tone distinctly different from that of the southern regions. Swiss, Austrian, and Slavic influences become evident, and olive oil, tomatoes, and garlic are forsaken for butter, hearty vegetables, and lots of pork. Savoy cabbage soup is a fine example of this hearty cuisine. Cabbage and buttery caramelized onions are simmered in a rich broth and topped with melted cheese.

While we found many recipes for savoy cabbage soup that had similar ingredients, we wanted to create a recipe that showcased the subtle flavor of the cabbage and the mild, herbaceous flavor of Italian fontina cheese. Savoy cabbage, a mild, sophisticated cousin of standard green cabbage, is believed to have originated in Italy. Some food historians trace its origins to a cabbage eaten during the Roman period. It is easily differentiated from green cabbage by its pale color and characteristic wrinkled leaves. The leaves also tend to be more loosely gathered than green cabbage leaves.

Authentic fontina cheese comes only from the Val d'Aosta region of Italy, which is tucked in the Alps bordering Switzerland and France. While France, Denmark, and Sweden also produce fontina, it is entirely different. Italian fontina is made from raw cow's milk and has a grassy, earthy aroma and taste, whereas fontina produced outside the country is bland and flabby-tasting, and it pales in comparison to the original. While Italian fontina may be tricky to find, the search is worthwhile. If you are unsure about a cheese's origin, check its coating; it should be embossed with an illustration of a mountain bisected by the word "Fontina." You may also see the words "Val d'Aosta," indicating the origins of the cheese. If the cheese is wrapped in red wax, it is definitely not Italian and should be avoided.

After reviewing the recipes we gathered, we quickly decided that, for the best flavor, it would be crucial to keep the number of ingredients to a minimum and rely on slow, careful cooking. For the soup's base, we cooked onions and pancetta in butter until the mixture attained a rich golden hue. Pork is a traditional flavoring for cabbage throughout much of northern Europe, as the two share an earthy and complementary sweetness. Pancetta, which is cured and spiced meat taken from the pig's belly (just like American bacon), provided a deep pork flavor without being intrusive, which ham or bacon would have been. Caramelizing the onions brought out their sugars and provided depth to the soup. A little garlic added to the mixture just prior to the cabbage brought piquancy and contrast to the otherwise heavy onion flavor.

For the cabbage to have a soft, supple texture, we discovered, it was important to wilt it before adding the stock. When it was added raw to the simmering stock, it took on an unpleasant, rubbery texture. Very thinly sliced cabbage, as if for coleslaw or sauerkraut, also helped the texture and was the easiest to eat.

We tried different stocks for the soup and

were most pleased with slightly diluted chicken stock. Several of the recipes we tested used beef broth, but tasters felt that the meatiness was too rich and overpowered the cabbage's delicate flavor. All chicken stock was also too strong, but thinning it with a little water proved perfect. The soup was deep and balanced, tasting predominantly of the cabbage, with hints of the caramelized onion and pancetta noticeable in the background.

While all of the recipes we found included bread and fontina, they varied as to how it was incorporated. Some layered it with the cabbage (which nobody liked because the result was mushy), while others melted the cheese directly on top of the bread and soup, as for French onion soup. We liked the latter method, but the thought of sliding a steaming bowl of soup into the broiler made us nervous. Instead, we tried melting the cheese directly onto the bread in a hot oven and met with great success. For the bread, we used our garlic-rubbed crostini (page 123), which added bite from the raw garlic and crunch from the bread. The crostini could be easily floated on top of the soup and, for cheese lovers, additional crostini could be passed at the table. During testing, everyone came back for additional crostini.

Savoy Cabbage Soup

SERVES 4 TO 6 AS A MAIN COURSE

If you cannot find savoy cabbage at your market, regular green cabbage will suffice, but the soup's flavor will not be as delicate. Italian fontina cheese is buttery and nutty-tasting. It has a much better flavor than rubbery, bland Danish fontina. Taleggio, another semisoft cheese from northern Italy, is a better substitute. To thinly slice the cabbage, cut the cabbage head into quarters, remove the core, and separate the quarters into stacks of leaves. Press down on the stacks with your free hand and slice the leaves into thin strips with a chef's knife.

2	tablespoons unsalted butter
2	medium onions, halved and sliced thin
4	ounces pancetta, chopped fine
	Salt
4	medium cloves garlic, sliced thin
1	medium head savoy cabbage (about 1 1/2 pounds), cored and sliced thin
4	cups homemade chicken stock or canned low-sodium chicken broth
2	bay leaves
1	tablespoon minced fresh parsley leaves
	Ground black pepper
1	recipe Crostini for Soup (page 123)
6	ounces Italian fontina cheese, shredded (about 1 1/2 cups)

1. Melt the butter in a heavy-bottomed 6-quart Dutch oven over medium heat. Once the butter stops foaming, add the onions, pancetta, and 1 teaspoon salt. Cook, stirring occasionally, until the onions are completely soft and beginning to brown lightly, about 20 minutes. Add the garlic and cook until fragrant, about 30 seconds. Add the cabbage and cook, stirring occasionally, until it is completely wilted, about 10 minutes.

2. Add the chicken stock, bay leaves, and 3 cups water and increase the heat to medium-high. Once boiling, partially cover the pot and reduce the heat to medium-low. Simmer until the flavors are fully blended, 1 to 1¼ hours. Stir in the parsley and adjust the seasonings with salt and pepper to taste.

3. When the soup is nearly done, prepare the crostini. Rub the crostini with garlic and drizzle with oil as directed. Sprinkle the fontina cheese evenly over the crostini and return them (still on a baking sheet) to the oven and bake until the cheese is fully melted, about 5 minutes.

4. Ladle the soup into warmed shallow bowls. Float one crostini, cheese side up, in each bowl. Serve immediately, passing the remaining crostini at the table.

RISI E BISI

RISI E BISI (WHICH TRANSLATES AS "rice and peas") is a Venetian specialty that falls somewhere between soup and risotto. Depending on who's making it, it can be either thick enough to eat with a fork or loose enough to require a spoon. Whichever is the case, this simple dish is driven by the bright, vegetal sweetness of fresh green peas. The rest of the flavors—traditionally, garlic (just a hint), onion, pancetta or prosciutto, and Parmesan—are mere supporting players. The starchy, short-grained Arborio rice used for risotto is a must (see page 203 for more information on this rice).

Traditionally, this dish was made only in the spring with the freshest peas grown on the islands in the Venetian lagoon, the heart of Venice's agriculture. Knowing how difficult it is to get good-quality fresh peas, we set out to create an authentic recipe suited to American grocery store produce.

With pristinely fresh peas a rarity in most American markets, we knew that frozen peas were our best option. Unlike most frozen vegetables, frozen peas can actually be better than their fresh counterparts. Peas begin to lose flavor and nutrients as soon as they are picked, which accounts for the bland, starchy peas we often find in the market. Most of the frozen peas on the market are actually frozen within hours of picking, locking in freshness. In a side-by-side tasting, frozen peas held their own against fresh peas. The major brands—Birdseye and Green Giant included—all tasted nearly identical.

Because the flavor of this soup is so simple, a top-notch stock is of the utmost importance. We quickly found out that canned chicken stock on its own would not do; its flavor overwhelmed the peas. Vegetable stock muddied the flavor and made the soup taste predominantly of carrot. In our research, we discovered several recipes that made a quick stock with the shelled pods (others included the pods in the dish itself). Although we did not have the pods, we found another recipe that used snow peas—a resourceful substitution. As little as ½ pound snow peas contributed a robust pea flavor to the broth. To bring up the broth's sweetness, we added a carrot, and for depth, onion, garlic, and parsley sprigs went into the pot. A quick 30-minute simmer released the flavors of the vegetables. At this point, while the snow pea flavor was clear, the broth lacked body and depth. A small amount of homemade stock or canned chicken broth was all that was needed to round it out.

With our pea-flavored broth, we knew we were off to a good start. For the soup itself, we sautéed onion and pancetta and perked them up with just a hint of garlic. We chose pancetta over prosciutto because of its milder flavor and softer texture. Prosciutto can become tough if cooked too long, yet pancetta remains tender and pliant. Once the onions were soft, we sautéed the rice, just as we would for a risotto, which ensured plump, individual grains. (We found that uncooked rice simply simmered in the stock took on a chalky, bloated texture that was unpleasant to eat.) Because the texture should not be as creamy as a risotto, adding all the stock at once to the sautéed rice was fine.

Tasters favored smaller peas over large ones, as they were less starchy and provided a better contrast to the plumped grains of rice. The small peas cook almost instantaneously; any longer than four minutes and they began to lose color and turn mushy. Part of the appeal of this dish is the study in textures of the soft, creamy rice punctuated by the crisp peas.

Parsley was the only appropriate herb, as it added freshness without complicating the soup's clean flavor. A handful of grated

Parmesan stirred in at the very end brought creaminess and a mild nuttiness that tied everything together.

Risi e Bisi

SERVES 4 TO 6 AS A FIRST COURSE

The rice will quickly absorb the soup's liquid as it sits, so feel free to add more liquid if necessary. You may also add more liquid if you want a soupier texture than ours; we aimed for right in the middle between risotto and soup.

QUICK PEA BROTH

½	pound snow peas, chopped medium
1	small onion, chopped medium
1	medium carrot, chopped medium
1	medium clove garlic, smashed
2	teaspoons salt
2	bay leaves
1¾	cups homemade chicken stock or canned low-sodium chicken broth

SOUP

2	tablespoons unsalted butter
1	medium onion, chopped fine
2	ounces pancetta, chopped fine
1	medium clove garlic, minced
1	cup Arborio rice
1	(10-ounce) package frozen peas
4	teaspoons minced fresh parsley leaves
¾	cup freshly grated Parmesan cheese
	Salt and ground black pepper

1. FOR THE BROTH: Combine all the ingredients in a Dutch oven or large saucepan, add 1½ quarts water, and bring to a boil over medium-high heat. Once boiling, reduce the heat to medium-low, partially cover the pot, and simmer for 30 minutes. Strain the broth through a fine-mesh strainer into a medium saucepan, pushing on the solids with a wooden spoon to release as much liquid as possible. Cover and keep warm over low heat until ready to use.

2. FOR THE SOUP: Heat the butter in a 6-quart Dutch oven over medium heat. When the foaming subsides, add the onion and pancetta. Stirring occasionally, cook until the onion softens and just begins to turn light golden around the edges, about 9 minutes. Add the garlic and cook until fragrant, about 1 minute. Add the rice and cook, stirring frequently, until the rice begins to turn translucent, about 3 minutes.

3. Add the warm broth, increase the heat to medium-high, and bring to a boil. Once boiling, reduce the heat to medium-low, cover, and simmer, stirring occasionally, until the rice is just cooked, about 15 minutes. Add the peas and cook until warmed through, 3 to 4 minutes. Remove the pot from the heat, stir in the parsley and Parmesan cheese, and season with salt and pepper to taste. Serve immediately.

MUSSEL SOUP

MUSSEL SOUP (OR ZUPPA DI COZZE) is a staple found throughout the seaside towns and villages of southern Italy. While an ingredient or two may change from town to town, the basic ingredients are the same: garlic, a few tomatoes, herbs, maybe some wine and chiles, and, of course, the mussels. Simple stuff, but with a crusty loaf and a bottle of crisp Pinot Grigio, it's a light meal that's hard to beat.

While once shunned in the United States as unfit for eating, mussels are widely available today, both farm-raised and wild. Most mussels available in the United States are North Atlantic Blue mussels, although Mediterranean mussels (those indigenous to the waters of the Mediterranean) are farmed in California and Washington. We found they differ only slightly and are interchangeable in recipes. Wild mussels may have a more pronounced flavor, but we always choose farm-raised for ease of preparation. Soaking, scrubbing, and debearding wild mussels can triple the prep time and, as we have found, often produce a gritty bowl of soup anyway. Most farm-raised mussels come grit-free and scrubbed, requiring minimal cleaning.

Part of the allure of mussel soup is its quick cooking time from start to finish, less than 20 minutes. And the preparation is easy; only a few ingredients must be minced or sliced. For the soup's base, we turned to slivered and toasted garlic, which is a common ingredient throughout southern Italy. Toasting brings out the natural sweetness of the garlic. But it must be closely watched, as garlic burns quickly and attains an acrid bitterness that will completely ruin a dish. A light golden hue is perfect; anything darker is risking bitterness. A good rule of thumb is to have liquid ingredients close at hand to stop the garlic from cooking further once the desired color has been obtained.

Tomatoes and wine were the next additions to the pot. For the brightest tomato flavor, we knew a short simmer was in order. Countless tests have proven to us that anything more than about 20 minutes of simmering dulls freshness. We found that a mere 10 minutes of simmering softened the tomatoes enough so that they released some of their juices, but not so much for them to break down. A crisp white wine, like a Pinot Grigio or Côtes du Rhone, brought both acidity and sweetness to the dish, accenting the mussels' own sweetness and brininess.

After several tests, we found that we needed to add clam juice to the broth to round out the acidic flavors and to increase the soup's fishiness. The liquid released by the mussels was not enough on its own. We also found that a little minced anchovy increased the soup's depth without detracting from its elemental flavors.

The mussels themselves were the final addition, cooking in about five minutes. We found that they quickly turned rubbery and tough when cooked much longer. A sprinkling of basil and the soup was ready to eat, just 20 minutes after starting.

The soup, however, would not be complete without crostini for soaking up the flavorful broth and adding crunchy texture and a second dimension of garlic. We also added a garnish of slivered scallions, which brightened the other flavors and added visual appeal.

Mussel Soup

SERVES 4 TO 6 AS A MAIN COURSE

Like all shellfish, mussels must be thoroughly cleaned prior to cooking. With the aid of a paring knife, pull and trim the beard (see illustration on page 130), then scrub the mussel with a stiff-bristled brush to rid the shell's exterior of grit. Also, make absolutely certain that the mussels are completely closed; an open mussel that won't close is a dead mussel and should be promptly discarded. Our favorite mussels are from the Maine-based company Great Eastern. Readily available in many large markets, they are very clean, and the beards are easily removed. They are well marked and usually come in 2-pound bags. For the best results, refrain from debearding the mussels until shortly before cooking.

As with most shellfish, the cooking time of mussels is of the essence. Shellfish are done as soon as their shells open; any longer and they quickly toughen. If the meat falls from the shells, it is overcooked. Remember, the soup maintains a lot of heat, and the mussels will continue to cook off the stove.

¼	cup extra-virgin olive oil
6	medium cloves garlic, sliced thin
1	teaspoon hot red pepper flakes
1	(28-ounce) can diced tomatoes, drained
1	(8-ounce) bottle clam juice

1   cup dry white wine

2   bay leaves

4   anchovy fillets, minced

2   tablespoons minced fresh
     oregano leaves
     Salt

2   pounds mussels, debearded and well
     scrubbed (see illustration at right)

¼   cup thinly sliced fresh basil leaves
     Ground black pepper

1   recipe Crostini for Soup (page 123)

4   medium scallions, white and green parts,
     sliced thin on the bias (about ½ cup)

1. Combine the oil, garlic, and hot red pepper flakes in a heavy-bottomed 6-quart Dutch oven over medium heat. As the oil becomes hot, shake the pan back and forth so that the garlic does not stick (stirring with a spoon causes the garlic to clump). As the garlic begins to color, shake the pot more often. When the garlic turns light golden brown (this will take about 5 minutes), add the tomatoes, clam juice, wine, bay leaves, anchovies, oregano, ½ teaspoon salt, and 1 cup water. Increase the heat to medium-high and bring to a boil. Once boiling, reduce the heat to medium-low and simmer until the flavors have combined, about 10 minutes.

2. Add the mussels to the pot, stir, and cover. Cook until all the mussels have opened, about 5 minutes. Remove from the heat and stir in the basil. Adjust the seasonings, adding salt and pepper to taste.

3. Place a crostini in the center of each warmed shallow bowl. Using tongs, divide the mussels equally among the bowls, then ladle the broth over the mussels. Scatter the scallions over the top and serve immediately, passing the remaining crostini at the table.

CLEANING MUSSELS

Mussels often contain a weedy beard protruding from the crack between the two shells. It's fairly small and can be difficult to tug out. To remove it easily, trap the beard between the side of a small knife and your thumb and pull. The flat surface of a paring knife gives you some leverage to remove the beard.

5

PASTA

A WELL-KNOWN CHEF ONCE CONFESSED to us that he did not know what difference it made to add olive oil to the water when cooking pasta—but he always did it anyway, because that's what his Italian grandmother did. Like this chef, many of us follow pasta cooking methods blindly. So we decided to take a keen look at the method and rituals around cooking dried pasta. After collecting all the recipes we could find, the primary questions we ended up with were these: Do you have to start with cold water? Is salt necessary in the cooking water? How about oil? How thoroughly do you drain the pasta? What happens if you rinse after draining? Does the type of pan matter?

We had always been told that it is important to start with cold water when cooking pasta but confess that we haven't always followed that rule. Certainly the temptation to fill a pasta pot with hot tap water is strong.

Depending on how hot your tap water is, it can cut in half the time it takes the pot of water to reach a boil. But tradition holds that this is a bad idea, that it can make the pasta taste less fresh or give it an off taste.

But when we cooked side-by-side batches of pasta starting with cold tap water and hot tap water, no one on our tasting panel could tell the difference. So we talked to Darren Fitzgerald, general manager of Aqua Science, a water treatment consulting firm in Clifton Park, New York. Fitzgerald said that the common misconception is that hot tap water can pick up off tastes from a hot water heater. Hot tap water does have the potential to taste off, he said, but this depends more on the water itself than on your hot water heater. When being heated, organic compounds in water, such as iron and manganese, can oxidize; this oxidation has the potential to cause discoloring or an off taste. So we tried the side-by-side test again at

MATCHING PASTA SAUCES AND SHAPES

SHORT PASTAS

Short tubular or molded pasta shapes do an excellent job of trapping chunky sauces. Sauces with very large chunks are best with rigatoni or other large tubes. Sauces with small chunks make more sense with fusilli or penne. Clockwise from top right, the shapes shown are penne, shells, farfalle, orecchiette, rigatoni, and fusilli.

STRAND PASTAS

Long strands are best with smooth sauces or sauces with very small chunks. In general, wider noodles, such as pappardelle and fettuccine, can support slightly chunkier sauces (such as pasta primavera) than can very thin noodles. Clockwise from top right, the shapes shown are fettuccine, linguine, spaghetti, capellini, and pappardelle.

home, where the water is problematically hard. We still did not taste a difference.

Of course, the other nagging question around water, pasta, and corner cutting is how much water is enough? Many cooks tend to skimp, for the obvious reason that the less water you use, the faster it comes to a boil. To start testing this variable, we cooked a pound of pasta in two quarts of water and discovered two major problems straight off. First, the water tends to foam up and boil over the pan edges. Second, the pieces of pasta are more inclined to stick together.

Dr. Patricia Berglund, director of the Northern Crops Institute in Fargo, North Dakota, explained the reasons behind these problems. Pasta, Berglund explained, consists primarily of starch but also contains about 10 percent protein. For dried pasta to make the change from its brittle state to a tender, toothsome noodle, the starch granules must absorb enough hot water to make them burst, thereby giving pasta its tenderness, while the small amount of protein sets up to provide the noodle with its characteristic bite. We noticed that between absorption and evaporation,

---

EQUIPMENT: Pasta Paraphernalia

Nowadays, cookware stores and catalogs contain a mind-boggling array of pots, utensils, and gadgets for cooking pasta. We tried a wide variety and were surprised by what we found out.

POT WITH PERFORATED INSERT We have to confess that we don't understand the growing popularity of these pasta pots. We tried both the eight-quart Multi-Pot, which goes for about $45, and the All-Clad seven-quart Pasta Pentola, which sells for a steep $269.

To get four quarts of water into the Multi-Pot insert, you must fill the pan with six quarts of water. If you do that, we found, the pot is prone to boiling over. The All-Clad insert is an inch smaller in diameter than the 8½-inch-diameter pot and sits 6 inches below the pot edge. It has a deceptive 2½-inch lip that sits above the pot edge, making it look as if it has a much greater capacity. In fact, as it turns out, the insert to this expensive seven-quart pot has a capacity of just three quarts; add any more and the water begins to boil over.

MESH INSERTS The inexpensive mesh inserts sold in cookware stores proved much too small to be useful. They also tend to bob out of the water, which creates a suction at the bottom of the pan. When the suction releases, gurgles of boiling water are hurled from the pan.

PASTA PRONTO This pan takes a different approach to the issue of straining pasta. It has a perforated strainer lid with handles that swivel to hold the lid in place. It seems clever, but the handles do not actually lock the lid in place—your grip does. Once you tilt the pan to strain, the grip can become awkward. We lost our grip once, and the sink was not so clean that we dared try to salvage the fallen noodles.

STRAINER PLATE Similarly risky to the Pasta Pronto pan is a crescent-shaped perforated stainless-steel plate meant to fit around the pot edge for straining. We found that it fits comfortably only with pans of certain sizes—and, again, sureness of grip was essential.

PASTA RAKES The tines on the wooden versions of these rakes, designed to retrieve pasta, tend to fall out over time. The tines on the stainless-steel variety are welded in. But why spend $24 on a single-purpose utensil when a $5 pair of tongs works just fine?

PASTA TONGS Again, why pay $14 for a pasta-particular utensil when an inexpensive pair of all-purpose tongs will toss and serve just as well? In addition, the handle on this utensil is too short for fetching noodles out of hot cooking water.

PASTA FORKS This is the only pasta-specific tool that we found useful. It effectively combs through long, sticky strands of noodles to separate them. The wood variety tends to be clunky and is prone to splitting with use, but both the plastic and stainless-steel versions work fine.

a quart or more of water can be lost in the process of cooking one pound of pasta. During the cooking process, a lot of starch also leaches into the cooking water. Without enough water to dilute the leached starch, Berglund said, the pieces of pasta are more inclined to stick together and the water foams up, which is

INGREDIENTS: Dried Pasta

In the not-so-distant past, American pasta had a poor reputation, and rightly so. It cooked up gummy and starchy, and experts usually touted the superiority of Italian brands. We wondered if this was still the case.

To find out, we tasted eight leading brands of spaghetti—four American and four Italian. American brands took two of the three top spots, while two Italian brands landed at the bottom of the rankings. It seems that American companies have mastered the art of making pasta.

American-made Ronzoni was the top finisher, with tasters praising its "nutty, buttery" flavor and superb texture. Mueller's, another American brand, took third place. Tasters liked its "clean," "wheaty" flavor.

DeCecco was the highest-scoring Italian brand, finishing second in the tasting. It cooked up "very al dente" (with a good bite) and was almost chewy. Other Italian brands did not fare quite so well. Martelli, an artisanal pasta that costs nearly $5 a pound, finished in next-to-last place, with comments like "gritty" and "mushy" predominating on tasters' score sheets. Another Italian brand, Delverde, sank to the bottom of the ratings.

Our conclusion: Save your money and don't bother with most imported pasta—American pastas are just fine. If you must serve Italian pasta in your home, stick with DeCecco.

THE BEST PASTA

Ronzoni won tasters over with its firm texture and nutty, buttery flavor.

precisely what we observed. So we recommend that you not skimp on the water—use at least four quarts per pound of pasta.

While ample water proved key to preventing pasta from sticking, we also found (no great surprise) that frequent stirring makes a difference. It is particularly important to stir the moment the pasta goes into the water. Otherwise, pasta can get remarkably comfortable stuck to the pan bottom or nestled up against its kind. In most cases, any kind of spoon or even a pair of tongs will do for stirring. For long noodles, like spaghetti, we found the tines of a pasta fork to be most effective in separating the strands (see Pasta Paraphernalia on page 133).

Of course, what many people do to prevent sticking is add oil to the boiling water. We tried this repeatedly and determined that oil definitely did not minimize pasta's sticking potential while cooking. What best keeps noodles from sticking is not oil but cooking in a large quantity of water—and the method of saucing. Americans tend to fill a bowl with pasta and then glop the sauce on top. Italians toss the just-cooked pasta and the sauce together. This evenly distributes the sauce and, in effect, helps prevent sticking.

As with oil, opinions vary widely about whether or not salt should be added to the cooking water. Other than contributing to flavor, salt had no discernible effect on the pasta or the cooking process itself; in fact, the small amounts of salt we added to the water never increased the boiling point. As for flavor, every participating taster found the addition of two tablespoons of salt to be over the top once you tossed an already-seasoned sauce with the pasta. While a couple of tasters preferred 1½ teaspoons in the water, the overall opinion was that 1 tablespoon of salt to 4 quarts of water worked best to round out the pasta flavor.

Most important to the cooking process is

determining when the pasta is done, or al dente. We cooked up a number of pasta types made by a variety of manufacturers and found that, overall, the timing on the box instructions tends to be too long. We also found that the old, curious trick of tossing a noodle against the wall (which really only applies to spaghetti or fettuccine noodles) isn't very accurate. The surefire test is simply biting into the pasta about three minutes before the package directions indicate doneness. Undercooked pasta will have a clearly visible white core, making it crunchy in the center. When it's al dente, which translates as "to the tooth," it should have some bite to it but still be tender throughout. The white core may be just faintly visible.

While there is no exact science to determining doneness and each person has a different preference as to when pasta is done, taste-testing the pasta once or twice every minute within the last few minutes of cooking helps the cook gain a better sense for when the pasta is just right. The pasta will continue to soften a bit as you drain and sauce it, so pull it off the flame about 30 seconds before you think it will be perfectly cooked.

The only time you might want to rinse drained pasta is if you plan to make pasta salad. Rinsing flushes starch from the surface of the noodles, which causes two problems. First, starch helps the sauce adhere to the pasta; without it, the sauce can drain off and pool at the bottom of the bowl. Second, rinsing cools the noodles, which are best served hot.

Finally, some pasta aficionados warn against shaking the strainer after draining the pasta. As with the recommendation against rinsing, there is some cause for this. Shaking drains off some of the starchy moisture that helps the sauce cling to the pasta. But don't worry if by impulse you shake the strainer; it is no grave offense. We found that only about two tablespoons of liquid are lost.

INGREDIENTS: Garlic

Garlic falls into two primary categories, hardneck and softneck. The garlic that most of us cook with is softneck, so-called because its neck is soft and braidable. Softneck garlic contains a circle of plump cloves shrouding a second circle of smaller cloves, all enveloped by many papery layers. Because softneck garlic is heat tolerant and stores well, it has become the favored commercial garlic. Supermarket garlics are almost invariably softneck.

Hardneck, which is the original cultivated garlic variety, is distinguished by its stiff center staff, around which large uniform cloves hang. Hardneck garlic has a relatively sparse parchment wrapper that makes it easier to peel (and damage) than softneck. It is considered superior in flavor—more complex and intense than softneck. Its thinly wrapped cloves lose moisture quickly, however, and do not winter over, as do the cloves of the robust softneck.

We tasted eight garlic varieties, softneck and hardneck, raw and cooked, and found a wide range of flavors. We enjoyed several softneck and hardneck varieties. However, our two favorite varieties were Porcelain Zemo and Rocambole Carpathian, both of which are hardnecks.

HARDNECK GARLIC   SOFTNECK GARLIC

Hardneck garlic has a stiff center staff around which the large, uniformly-sized cloves hang. Softneck garlic, the kind found most commonly in supermarkets, has cloves of varying sizes (larger on the outside, smaller near the center) and no center staff.

In Italy, there is a fine art to matching pasta shapes and sauces. However, we find that there is only one important consideration—the texture of the sauce. A very chunky sauce is better with shells or rigatoni than spaghetti because the former shapes can trap and hold pieces of the sauce, while large chunks of vegetables, for instance, would just sit on top of long, thin strands. The idea is to eat sauce and pasta in the same mouthful. The illustrations on page 132 give some more specific examples.

Once the pasta has been sauced, it must served immediately. This is especially true when serving fresh pasta with cream and butter sauces, which tend to cool especially fast. You may want to warm serving bowls, either with the hot pasta cooking water or by placing the bowls in a very low oven.

A note about serving sizes. Most Americans would say that one pound of pasta serves four as a main course and, for the most part, we have followed this convention. In Italy, pasta is usually served as a first course, in smaller portions. In this case, one pound of sauced pasta yields six to eight servings. You may want to follow this practice, especially with rich pasta dishes with cream and butter, which can be overwhelming in large portions.

How to Cook Pasta

SERVES 4

This recipe summarizes our findings about cooking pasta. Refer to it when cooking pasta to go with your favorite sauces. It's best to combine pasta and sauce when both are hot and fresh, so if your sauce requires long cooking, have it nearly complete when you start cooking the pasta. Many simple sauces can be cooked simultaneously with the pasta.

4	quarts water
I	tablespoon salt
I	pound dried pasta

Bring the water to a rolling boil in a 6-quart (or larger) stockpot or Dutch oven. Add the salt and pasta; stir to separate the noodles. Cover the pot and return to a boil. Remove the cover and boil the pasta, stirring frequently

to keep the noodles separate. Taste for doneness 3 minutes short of the cooking time indicated on the box. If not done, taste every 30 seconds until the pasta is just shy of al dente—that is, the noodles are tender but resist slightly more than desired (an opaque white core should be faintly visible in the noodle you bit into). If necessary for the sauce, reserve ½ cup pasta cooking water (as suggested in many recipes in this chapter); drain the pasta in a large colander for 30 seconds without shaking. Transfer the pasta to the now-empty cooking pot or to a warm serving bowl; toss with the sauce and serve immediately.

PASTA WITH GARLIC AND OIL

PASTA WITH GARLIC AND OIL LOOKS guileless. It reads: "tangle of spaghetti flecked with parsley." But its subtext shouts garlic— garlic in every register, in every pitch, a virtual manifesto of bright garlic and deep green oil. Twirled hot on a fork and eaten without restraint, this is among the most satisfying (and simple) dishes on earth. It has the texture of innocence and a tyrant's bite.

At first, we wondered why anyone would need a recipe for this dish. You take spaghetti or capellini, perfume it straight from its bath with high-quality olive oil and as much fresh garlic as decency allows, add a dusting of hot red pepper flakes, a little fistful of parsley, and there it is, *pasta aglio e olio*. And yet, and yet. Who hasn't ordered it in a restaurant to find its fresh scent tormented by burnt garlic or its noodles gripped in a starchy skein dripping with oil? Clearly, there was much to learn.

Diving into Italian cookbooks, we found general agreement on ingredients: all those mentioned above, along with a splash of hot pasta cooking water to keep the components in motion. Beyond the basics were regional variations that included a selection of fresh herbs, savory accents such as capers and anchovies, and bread crumbs. We first pursued the perfect garlic flavor, working down the list of possibilities from whole crushed cloves to grated raw garlic and using one pound of pasta for all tests. We didn't care for sautéed whole or slivered garlic, whether ultimately removed from the dish or left in. In fact, no one cared for browned garlic at all—it was

PEELING GARLIC

Unless whole cloves are needed, we crush garlic cloves with the side of a large chef's knife to loosen the skins and make them easier to remove.

MINCING GARLIC TO A PASTE

If you have trouble mincing garlic very fine, salt crystals can be used to help break it down. Start by mincing the garlic as fine as you can. Sprinkle the minced garlic with salt, then drag the side of the knife over the garlic-salt mixture to form a fine puree. Continue to mince and drag the knife as necessary to obtain the desired texture. If possible, use kosher or coarse salt for this job; the larger crystals do a better job than fine table salt of breaking down the garlic.

acrid and one-dimensional. Raw minced or grated garlic alone was zingy and metallic. We needed another way.

We knew of a technique associated with Mexican cookery in which a large amount of minced garlic is sautéed slowly until it turns golden and becomes mellow, thus producing a garlic flavor far more complex than does a simple sauté. We tried this with a full head of garlic (about ¼ cup minced) and were delighted to discover that, given low heat and constant stirring, the garlic became sticky and straw-colored, with a flavor that was butter-nutty and rich, adding a pronounced depth to the dish. But alone, this slow-sautéed garlic lacked brightness. We decided to combine the forces of cooked and raw by reserving a tablespoon of raw garlic, then stirring it into the fully cooked, candied garlic off the heat to release its perfume and spicy sharpness. The effect of this one-two garlic punch was outstanding, causing waves of flavor to resonate within the dish.

While conducting garlic experiments, it became obvious that other ingredient ratios—for example, the amount of oil—had to be established contiguously. Too much oil removed the silky mouthfeel we wanted for the pasta, but too little left the garlic mute. The amount of oil necessary varied with the diameter of the pasta as well—thicker strands, such as spaghetti, required more oil, even when the total weight of each batch of pasta was the same. In fact, the diameter of the pasta strands altered the behavior of the recipe to such a degree that we decided to work with just one type of pasta—spaghetti, which, unlike some thinner pastas, is available in every grocery store.

The olive oil contributes much of the freshness and verve to this dish; extra-virgin is a must. We settled on 6 tablespoons: 3 to sauté the garlic, 3 tossed into the pasta at the end for flavor.

Parmesan cheese is not conventional in this

dish but, heathens that we are, we liked the nutty depth of flavor it added. Resist, by all means, an urge to pour the contents of a little green cylinder on this dish—it will be forever ruined. A very modest sprinkle of coarsely grated Parmigiano-Reggiano, on the other hand, improves it. (Be sure to do your grating on the larger holes of a box grater; this will discourage the cheese from getting into a sticking contest with the pasta.)

We liked parsley for its freshness but didn't want it slipping around on the noodles like mower clippings; 3 tablespoons did the trick. Gentle seasoning improvements were effected with a touch of lemon juice and sea salt flakes—the bright citrus notes and wee crunch made a big difference.

Finally, sequence and timing matter greatly with this dish. Perhaps to a larger degree than other pastas, pasta aglio e olio suffers from being dumped into cold serving bowls or waiting around for diners to make their way to the table. The most familiar pasta tool, a set of tongs, cannot be recommended for tossing; bits of garlic get stuck in its craw, right where

BRUISING HERB LEAVES

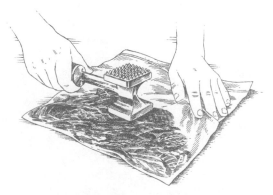

Bruising herb leaves, especially basil, in a zipper-lock plastic bag with a meat pounder (or rolling pin) is a quick but effective substitute for hand-pounding with a mortar and pestle, and it helps release the herbs' flavor.

you don't want them. We recommend that you toss the hot strands with a heatproof spatula or pasta rakes and use rakes or tongs only to transfer the pasta to bowls.

Pasta with Garlic and Oil
(Aglio e Olio)
SERVES 4 TO 6

For a twist on pasta with garlic and oil, try sprinkling toasted fresh bread crumbs (see page 57) over individual bowls, but prepare them before proceeding with the pasta recipe. We like the crunch of Maldon sea salt flakes for this dish, but ordinary table salt is fine as well.

	Salt (see note above)
1	pound spaghetti
6	tablespoons extra-virgin olive oil
¼	cup minced garlic (about 30 small, 20 medium, 10 large, or 5 extra-large cloves) from 1 to 2 heads
¾	teaspoon hot red pepper flakes
3	tablespoons chopped fresh parsley leaves
2	teaspoons juice from 1 lemon
½	cup coarsely grated Parmesan cheese (optional)

1. Adjust an oven rack to the lower-middle position, set a large heatproof serving bowl on the rack, and heat the oven to 200 degrees. Bring 4 quarts water to a rolling boil in a large pot. Add 1 tablespoon salt and the pasta to the boiling water, stir to separate the noodles, and cook until al dente; reserve ⅓ cup pasta cooking water and drain the pasta.

2. While the water is heating, combine 3 tablespoons oil, 3 tablespoons garlic, and ½ teaspoon salt in a heavy-bottomed non-stick 10-inch skillet. Cook over low heat, stirring constantly, until the garlic foams and is sticky and straw-colored, 10 to 12 minutes.

Off the heat, add the remaining tablespoon raw garlic, the hot red pepper flakes, parsley, lemon juice, and 2 tablespoons pasta cooking water and stir well to keep the garlic from clumping.

3. Transfer the drained pasta to a warm serving bowl; add the remaining 3 tablespoons olive oil and the remaining reserved pasta cooking water and toss to coat. Add the garlic mixture and ¾ teaspoon salt; toss well to combine. Serve immediately, sprinkling individual bowls with Parmesan cheese, if desired.

PESTO

IN OUR EXPERIENCE WITH PESTO, THE bright herbal fragrance of basil always hinted at more flavor than it really delivered. Also, although we love garlic, the raw article can have a sharp, acrid taste that overwhelms everything else in the sauce. So our goals were clear when developing a recipe for this simple sauce—heighten the flavor of the basil and subdue the garlic.

Traditionally, pesto is made in a mortar and pestle, which yields an especially silky texture and intense basil flavor. The slow pounding of the basil leaves (it takes 15 minutes to make pesto this way) releases their full flavor.

By comparison, both blender and food-processor pestos can seem dull or bland, but if required to choose between the two, we prefer a food processor for several reasons. In a blender, ingredients tend to bunch up near the blade and do not become evenly chopped. Also, to keep solids moving in a blender, it is necessary to add more oil than is really needed.

Because most Americans don't own a mortar and pestle (and those who do are unlikely to invest 15 minutes of pounding when the sauce can otherwise be made in seconds), we decided to focus on improving flavor in food-processor pesto. We tested chopping, tearing, and bruising

basil leaves to release more of their flavor before processing. In the end, we settled on packing basil leaves in a plastic bag and bruising them with a meat pounder or rolling pin (see illustration on page 138).

We tried several approaches to taming the garlic—roasting, sautéing, and infusing oil with garlic flavor—but found them all lacking. What we did like was toasting whole cloves in a warm skillet. This tamed the harsh garlic notes and loosened the skins from the cloves for easy peeling. We found that seven minutes over medium heat, or toasting the garlic until it is fragrant, gave us the best results.

To bring out the full flavor of the nuts, we toasted them in a dry skillet before processing. (We then toasted the garlic in the empty pan.) Almonds are sweet but fairly hard, so they give pesto a coarse, granular texture. Walnuts are softer but still fairly meaty in texture and flavor. Pine nuts yield the smoothest, creamiest pesto. The choice is yours, although pine nuts are traditional.

Classic Pesto

MAKES ABOUT ¾ CUP

Basil often darkens in pesto, but you can boost the color by adding parsley. For sharper flavor, substitute 1 tablespoon finely grated pecorino cheese for 1 tablespoon of the Parmesan.

¼ cup pine nuts, walnuts, or almonds
3 medium cloves garlic, unpeeled
2 cups packed fresh basil leaves
2 tablespoons packed fresh parsley leaves (optional)
7 tablespoons extra-virgin olive oil
Salt
¼ cup finely grated Parmesan cheese

1. Toast the nuts in a small, heavy skillet over medium heat, stirring frequently, until

EQUIPMENT: Garlic Presses

Most cooks dislike the chore of mincing garlic, and many turn to garlic presses. We know that many professional cooks sneer at this tool, but we have a different opinion. In hundreds of hours of use in our test kitchen, we have found that this little tool delivers speed, ease, and a comfortable separation of garlic from fingers.

The garlic press offers other advantages. First is flavor, which changes perceptibly depending on how the cloves are broken down. The finer a clove of garlic is cut, the more flavor is released from its broken cells. Fine mincing or pureeing, therefore, results in a fuller, more pungent garlic flavor. A good garlic press breaks down the cloves more than the average cook would with a knife. Second, a good garlic press ensures a consistently fine texture, which in turn means better distribution of the garlic throughout the dish.

The question for us, then, was not whether garlic presses work but which of the many available presses work best. Armed with 10 popular models, we pressed our way through a mountain of garlic cloves to find out.

Garlic press prices can vary by as much as a shocking 700 percent, from about $3 up to $25. Some are made from metal and others from plastic. Some offer devices to ease cleaning, and most show subtle differences in handle and hopper design.

Most garlic presses share a common design consisting of two handles connected by a hinge. At the end of one handle is a small, perforated hopper; at the end of the other is a plunger that fits snugly inside the hopper. The garlic cloves in the hopper get crushed by the descending plunger when the handles are squeezed together, and the puree is extruded through the perforations in the bottom of the hopper.

Some presses employ a completely different design—a relatively large cylindrical container with a tight-fitting screw-down plunger. These presses are designed for large capacity, but the unusual design failed to impress us. The screw-type plungers required both pressure and significant repetitive motion, which contributed to hand fatigue. This seemed like a lot of work just to press garlic. Matters did not improve when the hoppers were loaded with multiple garlic cloves. Even greater effort was required to twist down the plungers, and the texture of the garlic puree produced was coarse and uneven.

A good garlic press should not only produce a smooth, evenly textured puree but should also be easy to use. To us, this meant that different users should be able to operate it without straining their hands. With several notable exceptions, all of our presses performed reasonably well in this regard.

Several of our test cooks wondered if we could make an easy task even easier by putting the garlic cloves through the presses without first removing their skins. Instructions on the packaging of the Zyliss and Bodum presses specified that it was OK to press unpeeled cloves, and our tests bore out this assertion. Though the directions for several other presses did not address this issue specifically, we found that the Oxo and the Endurance also handled unpeeled garlic with ease. We did note, however, that the yield of garlic puree was greater across the board when we pressed peeled cloves. While we were at it, we also tried pressing chunks of peeled, fresh ginger. The Zyliss, Kuhn Rikon, and Oxo were the only three to excel in this department, and we found that smaller chunks, about ½ inch, were crushed much more easily than larger, 1-inch pieces.

When all was said and pressed, the traditionally designed, moderately priced Zyliss turned out to be comfortable and consistent, and it produced the finest, most even garlic puree. In addition, it handled unpeeled garlic and small chunks of fresh ginger without incident. While other presses got the job done, the Zyliss just edged out the field in terms of both performance and design.

THE BEST GARLIC PRESS
We found that this Zyliss press can handle two cloves at once, producing very finely pureed garlic in a flash.

just golden and fragrant, 4 to 5 minutes. Transfer the nuts to a plate.

2. Add the garlic to the empty pan. Toast, shaking the pan occasionally, until fragrant and the color of the cloves deepens slightly, about 7 minutes. Transfer the garlic to a plate; cool, peel, and chop.

3. Place the basil and parsley (if using) in a heavy-duty gallon-sized zipper-lock plastic bag. Pound the bag with the flat side of a meat pounder or rolling pin until all the leaves are bruised (see illustration on page 138).

4. Place the nuts, garlic, herbs, oil, and ½ teaspoon salt in the workbowl of a food processor. Process until smooth, stopping as necessary to scrape down the sides of the bowl. Transfer the mixture to a small bowl, stir in the Parmesan cheese, and adjust the salt. (The surface of the pesto can be covered with a sheet of plastic wrap or a thin film of oil and refrigerated for up to 3 days.)

➤ VARIATIONS

Mint Pesto

Follow the recipe for Classic Pesto, replacing the basil with an equal amount of mint leaves and omitting the parsley.

CLEANING A GARLIC PRESS

Garlic presses make quick work of garlic but are notoriously hard to clean. A toothbrush works well for this job. The bristles will clear bits of garlic from the press and are easy to rinse clean.

Creamy Basil Pesto

The addition of ricotta cheese makes pesto mild and creamy. The pesto is fairly thick and clings nicely to the curves on fusilli pasta.

Follow the recipe for Classic Pesto, adding ¼ cup ricotta cheese at the same time as the Parmesan.

Pasta with Pesto

SERVES 4

Serve with long, thin pasta or a shape, like fusilli, that can trap bits of the pesto. Pasta with pesto can be served immediately or allowed to cool and eaten at room temperature.

1	tablespoon salt
1	pound pasta (see note above)
1	recipe Classic Pesto

Bring 4 quarts water to a rolling boil in a large pot. Add the salt and pasta to the boiling water. Cook until al dente. Reserving ½ cup cooking water, drain the pasta and return it to the pot. Stir ¼ cup pasta cooking water into the pesto. Toss the pasta with the thinned pesto, adding the remaining reserved cooking water as needed. Serve immediately or let cool to room temperature.

PESTO BEYOND BASIL

IN THE UNITED STATES, THE CONCEPT of pesto has moved way beyond basil. Any pureed, highly flavorful oil-based sauce for pasta—including those made from herbs, spinach, arugula, dried mushrooms, nuts, olives, or roasted peppers—is given the name pesto. Although Italians generally reserve the term pesto for sauces made with basil, purees of roasted red peppers or, perhaps, ricotta and arugula are traditionally used to sauce pasta, especially when fresh basil is out of season.

We found the food processor to be the fastest way to produce a consistently good basil pesto. Three keys to a flavorful sauce included bruising the basil prior to pureeing, using extra-virgin olive oil, and finely grating a high-quality Parmesan. We found all three of these rules to hold true with these nonbasil pestos, and we added one of our own: Use toasted garlic rather than raw. Its mellowed and slightly sweetened flavor pairs better with the heartier flavors of toasted nuts and roasted vegetables.

Note that when adding any pesto to cooked pasta, it is important to include three to four tablespoons of the cooked pasta water for proper consistency and even distribution. These pestos can be kept in the refrigerator for up to three days if they are covered with a sheet of plastic wrap or a thin film of oil.

Arugula and Ricotta Pesto

MAKES ABOUT 1 1/2 CUPS,
ENOUGH TO SAUCE 1 POUND
COOKED PASTA

3	medium cloves garlic, unpeeled
1/4	cup pine nuts, walnuts, or almonds
1	cup packed fresh arugula leaves
1	cup packed fresh parsley leaves
7	tablespoons extra-virgin olive oil
1/3	cup ricotta cheese
2	tablespoons finely grated Parmesan cheese
	Salt and ground black pepper

1. Toast the garlic in a small, dry skillet over medium heat, shaking the pan occasionally, until softened and spotty brown, about 8 minutes; when cool, remove and discard the skins. While the garlic cools, toast the nuts in the same skillet over medium heat,

stirring frequently, until golden and fragrant, 4 to 5 minutes.

2. Place the arugula and parsley in a heavy-duty quart-sized zipper-lock plastic bag; bruise all the leaves with a meat pounder.

3. In the workbowl of a food processor fitted with a steel blade, process the garlic, nuts, arugula, parsley, and oil until smooth, stopping as necessary to scrape down the sides of the bowl. Transfer the mixture to a small bowl and stir in the cheeses; season to taste with salt and pepper.

Roasted Mushroom Pesto with Parsley and Thyme

MAKES ABOUT 1 1/2 CUPS,
ENOUGH TO SAUCE 1 POUND
COOKED PASTA

See illustrations on page 5 for tips on rehydrating porcini mushrooms.

10	ounces white mushrooms, sliced 1/4-inch thick
9	tablespoons extra-virgin olive oil
	Salt and ground black pepper
3	medium cloves garlic, unpeeled
1/2	ounce dried porcini mushrooms
1	small shallot, chopped coarse
1	tablespoon fresh thyme leaves
1/4	cup packed fresh parsley leaves
1/4	cup finely grated Parmesan cheese

1. Adjust the oven rack to the lowest position and heat the oven to 450 degrees; line a rimmed baking sheet with heavy-duty foil. Toss the sliced mushrooms with 2 tablespoons oil and salt and pepper to taste in a medium bowl; spread them evenly on the prepared baking sheet. Roast, stirring occasionally, until browned and crisp, about 25 minutes.

2. Meanwhile, toast the garlic in a small, dry skillet over medium heat, shaking the pan

occasionally, until softened and spotty brown, about 8 minutes; when cool, remove and discard the skins.

3. Mix the dried porcini mushrooms with ½ cup hot tap water in a small microwave-safe bowl. Cover with plastic wrap, cut several steam vents in the plastic wrap with a paring knife, and microwave on high power for 30 seconds. Let stand until the mushrooms soften, about 5 minutes. Lift the mushrooms from the liquid with a fork and mince. Pour the liquid through a small strainer lined with a single sheet of paper towel and placed over a measuring cup.

4. In the workbowl of a food processor fitted with a steel blade, process the roasted mushrooms, garlic, porcini and liquid, shallot, thyme, parsley, and remaining 7 tablespoons oil until smooth, stopping as necessary to scrape down the sides of the bowl. Transfer the mixture to a small bowl and stir in the Parmesan cheese; season to taste with salt and pepper.

Toasted Nut and Parsley Pesto

MAKES ABOUT 1½ CUPS,
ENOUGH TO SAUCE 1 POUND
COOKED PASTA

3	medium cloves garlic, unpeeled
1	cup pecans, walnuts, whole blanched almonds, skinned hazelnuts, unsalted pistachios, or pine nuts, or any combination thereof
¼	cup packed fresh parsley leaves
7	tablespoons extra-virgin olive oil
¼	cup finely grated Parmesan cheese
	Salt and ground black pepper

1. Toast the garlic in a small, dry skillet over medium heat, shaking the pan occasionally,

until softened and spotty brown, about 8 minutes; when cool, remove and discard the skins.

2. Toast the nuts in a medium, dry skillet over medium heat, stirring frequently, until golden and fragrant, 4 to 5 minutes.

3. In the workbowl of a food processor fitted with a steel blade, process the garlic, nuts, parsley, and oil until smooth, stopping as necessary to scrape down the sides of the bowl. Transfer the mixture to a small bowl and stir in the Parmesan cheese; season to taste with salt and pepper.

Roasted Red Pepper Pesto

MAKES ABOUT 1½ CUPS,
ENOUGH TO SAUCE 1 POUND
COOKED PASTA

See page 10 for information about how to roast and peel peppers.

3	medium cloves garlic, unpeeled
2	medium red bell peppers, roasted, peeled, and cut into rough 2-inch pieces
1	small shallot, chopped coarse
1	tablespoon fresh thyme leaves
¼	cup packed fresh parsley leaves
7	tablespoons extra-virgin olive oil
¼	cup finely grated Parmesan cheese
	Salt and ground black pepper

1. Toast the garlic in a small, dry skillet over medium heat, shaking the pan occasionally, until softened and spotty brown, about 8 minutes; when cool enough to handle, remove and discard the skins.

2. In the workbowl of a food processor fitted with a steel blade, process the garlic, peppers, shallot, thyme, parsley, and oil until smooth, stopping as necessary to scrape down the sides of the bowl. Transfer the mixture to a small bowl and stir in the Parmesan cheese; season to taste with salt and pepper.

QUICK TOMATO SAUCE

DAY IN, DAY OUT, WE FIND THAT CANNED tomatoes make the best sauce. (The exception might be at the height of the local tomato season, but even then, good canned tomatoes can compete.) To make our sauce, we wanted to use the fewest ingredients possible, so we selected the key players—tomatoes, oil, garlic, and salt—and eliminated nonessentials, such as carrots, meat, wine, and so forth. This immediately eliminated a whole category of longer-cooked, full-bodied sauces. The sauce we were looking for also had to be easy to make—done in 20 minutes or less from pantry to table. Finally, it had to taste first and foremost of tomatoes, with a hint of acidity and a light, fresh flavor.

With this fairly narrow mission statement formed, a number of fundamental issues came to mind. What sort of canned tomatoes are best: whole, chopped, or crushed, packed in puree or juice? How do you get a hint of garlic without overpowering the sauce? How does cooking time affect flavor? Do you need sugar to boost tomato flavor? What about tomato paste?

To get a better sense of the possibilities, we went into the kitchen and cooked up different sauces from our favorite Italian cooks. To our surprise, there was considerable agreement among the staff as to what worked and what didn't. Butter tended to dull the bright, slightly acidic flavor of the tomatoes. Nobody was enthusiastic about the rather one-dimensional flavor of tomato paste. More than two cloves of garlic and three tablespoons of olive oil for one 28-ounce can of tomatoes was too much.

In general, shorter cooking times of 10 to 15 minutes produced a fresher, brighter tomato flavor. A large sauté pan was preferred to a saucepan because it speeded the cooking.

We also came to some conclusions about overall flavor. The sauces we preferred tasted predominantly of tomatoes, not garlic, basil, or any other ingredient. The better recipes also had a nice balance between sweetness and acidity to give the sauce some depth. Sauces made with a little sugar (no more than ¼ teaspoon) tasted more complex and had a better balance between sweet and tart.

With these decisions made, we compiled a master recipe using one teaspoon of minced garlic, three tablespoons of olive oil, one can of diced tomatoes, eight chopped basil leaves, ¼ teaspoon of sugar, and salt to taste. This made enough to sauce one pound of pasta.

We also tested whether all of the olive oil should be added at the beginning of cooking or if some should be withheld and added at the end to provide a burst of fresh flavor. As we suspected, it was best to use two tablespoons of olive oil for cooking and a third tablespoon at the end to finish the sauce. Not surprisingly, we preferred a high-quality extra-virgin oil because it delivered a pleasant hint of fresh olives.

Now we were ready to taste the sauce on pasta. Much to our surprise, we found that it did not cling properly to the noodles. Our first fix was to return ¼ cup of the pasta cooking water to the drained pasta once it was back in the pot. This dramatically improved the ability of the sauce to cling to the pasta and, as an added bonus, also improved the flavor. As a final note, we found that adding the tomato sauce, stirring to coat the pasta, and then heating everything for one minute was the most effective saucing method, giving the sauce better distribution and overall consistency.

INGREDIENTS: Canned Tomatoes

Canned whole tomatoes are the closest product to fresh. Whole tomatoes, either plum or round, are steamed to remove their skins and then packed in tomato juice or puree. We prefer tomatoes packed in juice; they generally have a fresher, livelier flavor than tomatoes packed in puree, which has a cooked tomato flavor that imparts a slightly stale, tired taste to the whole can.

To find the best canned whole tomatoes, we tasted 11 brands, both straight from the can and in a simple tomato sauce. Muir Glen (an organic brand available in most supermarkets and natural foods stores) finished at the head of the pack, along with Progresso.

Diced tomatoes are simply whole tomatoes that have been roughly chopped during processing and then packed with juice. For pasta sauces, we prefer diced tomatoes because they save time and effort. Why chop canned tomatoes (a messy proposition at best) if you don't have to? There are not as many brands of diced tomatoes to choose from, although this seems to be changing as more companies realize that consumers want this product. Among the brands we tested, Muir Glen was our favorite.

THE BEST CANNED TOMATOES
Muir Glen diced tomatoes have a fresh, lively flavor (they are packed in juice, not puree) and are recipe-ready.

Pasta and Quick Tomato Sauce

SERVES 4

If you use whole canned tomatoes, avoid those packed in sauce or puree, which results in a dull, relatively flavorless sauce without the interplay of sweetness and acidity. If you choose Muir Glen Diced Tomatoes, use the can's entire contents, without discarding any liquid. The pasta and sauce quantities can be doubled, but you will have to simmer the sauce for an extra five to six minutes to thicken it. If you do not have a garlic press, mince the garlic very fine.

1	(28-ounce) can diced or whole tomatoes (not packed in puree or sauce)
2	medium cloves garlic, peeled
3	tablespoons extra-virgin olive oil
3	tablespoons coarsely chopped fresh basil leaves (about 8 leaves)
1/4	teaspoon sugar
	Salt
1	pound pasta (any shape)

1. If using diced tomatoes, go to step 2. If using whole tomatoes, drain and reserve the liquid. Dice the tomatoes either by hand or in the workbowl of a food processor fitted with a steel blade (three or four ½-second pulses). The tomatoes should be coarse, with ¼-inch pieces visible. If necessary, add reserved liquid to the tomatoes to total 2⅔ cups.

2. Process the garlic through a garlic press into small bowl (or mince very fine); stir in 1 teaspoon water. Heat 2 tablespoons oil and the garlic in a 10-inch sauté pan over medium heat until fragrant but not browned, about 2 minutes. Stir in the tomatoes; simmer until thickened slightly, about 10 minutes. Stir in the basil, sugar, and ½ teaspoon salt.

3. Meanwhile, bring 4 quarts water to a

rolling boil in large pot. Add 1 tablespoon salt and the pasta and cook until al dente. Reserve ¼ cup cooking water; drain the pasta and return it to the pot. Mix in the reserved cooking water, sauce, and remaining oil; cook together over medium heat for 1 minute, stirring constantly. Serve immediately.

➤ VARIATIONS

Pasta and Tomato Sauce with Bacon and Parsley

In a medium skillet, fry 4 ounces sliced bacon, cut into ½-inch pieces, over medium-high heat until crisp and brown, about 5 minutes. Transfer with a slotted spoon to a paper towel–lined plate; pour off all but 2 tablespoons fat from the pan. Follow the recipe for Pasta and Quick Tomato Sauce, omitting the olive oil and heating the garlic and ½ teaspoon hot red pepper flakes in the reserved bacon fat until fragrant but not brown, about 2 minutes. Continue with the recipe, substituting 2 tablespoons chopped fresh parsley leaves for the basil and adding the reserved bacon along with the parsley.

Pasta and Tomato Sauce with Vodka and Cream

Follow the recipe for Pasta and Quick Tomato Sauce, adding ¼ teaspoon hot red pepper flakes along with the garlic. Halfway through the 10-minute simmering time, add ½ cup vodka. Continue with the recipe, adding 1 cup heavy cream and ground black pepper to taste along with the remaining seasonings. Transfer the sauce to the workbowl of a food processor fitted with a steel blade; pulse to a coarse puree. Return the sauce to the pan; simmer over medium heat to thicken, 2 to 3 minutes.

RAW TOMATO SAUCE

AT THE HEIGHT OF SUMMER, RAW TOMATO sauces are a favorite choice in Italy. Of course, their quality depends on really ripe, really good tomatoes. Don't bother with this recipe if your tomatoes are less than stellar.

That said, how should the tomatoes be handled? Must they be peeled and/or seeded? What kind of tomatoes work best in a raw pasta sauce? Also, will the tomatoes be moist enough to sauce the pasta, or will they need some oil—and if so, how much? Also, what herbs and other seasonings are best in this kind of sauce?

We tested a basic recipe three ways: with chopped tomatoes; seeded and chopped tomatoes; and peeled, seeded, and chopped tomatoes. Peeling is a lot of work and, in this case, we did not feel that the work justified the effort. When fresh tomatoes are cooked, the skins tend to separate from the flesh and shrivel into tiny, unappealing bits. However, in this dish, the heat of the pasta is not sufficient to separate the peel from the flesh. We don't mind tomato peel as long as it stays attached to some flesh, so we opted not to peel tomatoes for this dish.

Seeding is another matter. The pasta tossed with chopped but not seeded tomatoes was watery. The pasta tossed with seeded tomatoes was much better, with no watery juices pooling in the bottom of each bowl. Seeding is quick (just cut the tomatoes in half through their equator and squeeze out the seeds), and the benefits are worth the minimal effort.

We had been conducting our tests with round (beefsteak) tomatoes. We wondered how other tomatoes would fare in this dish. We went to a local farmers' market and tried a half dozen kinds of tomatoes in various shapes and sizes. Our results are easily summarized: Any tomato that tastes good raw works well in a raw pasta sauce. In general, plum (Roma) tomatoes are a bit firmer than ripe round tomatoes; they don't soften quite as nicely when tossed with hot pasta and, given the choice, we recommend round tomatoes. We liked yellow tomatoes in this dish, although they lack some of the pleasing acidity of red tomatoes. If you want to use yellow tomatoes, we recommend using half red and half yellow tomatoes for the best flavor. (This combination also happens to look very good.)

As we suspected, olive oil is a must, both for moistening the pasta and flavoring the sauce. Because the oil is not cooked, extra-virgin oil is essential. In addition to tomatoes, oil, salt, and pepper, we like to add a little garlic to our raw tomato sauce. The heat of the pasta slightly tames the raw garlic flavor. However, don't use more than a clove of garlic, or the flavor will be too intense. Minced fresh basil completes our master recipe.

We recommend preparing raw tomato sauce in the time it takes to bring four quarts of water to a boil and cook the pasta. The salt in the sauce will cause the tomatoes to give up some of their flavorful juices, and the garlic flavor can become too harsh if this sauce is left to marinate for more than a half-hour or so.

Chunks of raw tomato work best with tubular shapes, like penne, or short, curly pasta shapes, such as fusilli. These shapes, along with small shells and orecchiette, trap bits of tomato better than long-strand pasta.

Pasta with raw tomato sauce is not meant to be served piping hot. The raw sauce cools the drained pasta, making it a palatable temperature even on the hottest summer day. We suggest serving this dish immediately (when warm but not hot), although it can be allowed to cool for 10 minutes or so and eaten when tepid if the weather is especially warm. Pasta with raw tomato sauce should not be served with grated cheese at the table, as there's not enough heat to melt it properly. Save grated cheese for dishes with cooked tomato sauce,

or add the cheese directly to the pot with the hot pasta and sauce.

Pasta with Raw Tomato Sauce

SERVES 4

Called salsa cruda *in Italy, this raw sauce depends on absolutely ripe summer tomatoes. The tomatoes are seeded (but not peeled), tossed with the finest olive oil and seasonings, and then used as a sauce for pasta. If you prefer, omit the garlic.*

1½	pounds ripe tomatoes, halved and seeded (see illustrations on page 149)
¼	cup extra-virgin olive oil
1	medium clove garlic, minced or pressed through a garlic press
2	tablespoons minced fresh basil leaves Salt and ground black pepper
1	pound penne or other short tubular pasta

1. Bring 4 quarts water to a rolling boil in a large pot.

2. Cut the seeded tomatoes into ¼-inch dice and place them in a medium bowl. Add the oil, garlic, basil, and salt and pepper to taste, and mix well.

3. Add 1 tablespoon salt and the pasta to the boiling water. Cook until al dente. Drain the pasta and transfer it back to the cooking pot. Mix in the sauce. Serve immediately.

➤ VARIATIONS

Pasta with Spicy Raw Tomato Sauce
Follow the recipe for Pasta with Raw Tomato Sauce, adding ½ teaspoon hot red pepper flakes to the tomato mixture.

Pasta with Raw Tomato Sauce and Mixed Herbs
Follow the recipe for Pasta with Raw Tomato Sauce, increasing the basil to 3 tablespoons

and adding 3 tablespoons minced parsley and 1 tablespoon each minced mint and thyme to the tomato mixture.

Pasta with Raw Tomato Sauce, Olives, and Capers

Consider this dish a summer version of the famed puttanesca sauce (see page 152), made with fresh tomatoes rather than canned. Go easy on the added salt, as the olives and capers already season the sauce.

Follow the recipe for Pasta with Raw Tomato Sauce, adding ⅓ cup black olives, pitted and chopped coarse, and 2 tablespoons rinsed capers to the tomato mixture.

FRESH TOMATO SAUCE

WHEN TOMATOES ARE GOOD, NOTHING quite compares with their taste, a study in subtly contrasting sweet and tart flavors. The best fresh tomato sauces for pasta capture this complexity. Another consideration when making fresh tomato sauce is texture; the best of them are hearty and dense. Too many fresh tomato sauces are watery or mealy and have little fresh tomato flavor. If you are going to bother with fresh tomatoes, the sauce should be at least as good (if not better) than one you could make by opening a can.

When we set out to make a really good fresh tomato sauce, we knew we would focus on two issues: preserving the fresh tomato flavor and handling the tomatoes in such a way that they would yield a sauce with the proper consistency.

We began by culling about 60 recipes for tomato sauce and analyzing the variables. Most sources followed a simple pattern: heat the oil (and, usually, garlic), add the tomatoes, simmer until the tomatoes have broken down into a thick sauce, add seasonings, and toss with pasta. In some cases, the tomatoes were simply chopped before being added to the oil, but most sources recommended peeling and seeding them before chopping. A few recipes called for seeding the tomatoes but leaving the skins on.

Working with a basic recipe that contained just olive oil, diced fresh tomatoes, and salt, we prepared three batches of sauce—one

PEELING TOMATOES

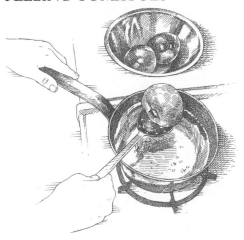

1. Place the cored tomatoes in a pot of boiling water, no more than five at a time. Boil until the skins split and begin to curl around the cored area of the tomato, about 15 seconds for very ripe tomatoes and up to 30 seconds for firmer tomatoes. Remove the tomatoes from the water with a slotted spoon and place them in a bowl of ice water to stop the cooking process and cool the tomatoes.

2. With a paring knife, peel the skins away using the curled edges at the core as your point of departure. (The bowl of ice water fulfills a helpful second function—the skins will slide right off the blade of the knife if you dip the blade into the water.)

with tomatoes that we peeled and seeded before dicing, one with tomatoes that we only seeded and diced, and one with tomatoes we neither seeded nor peeled. The results were surprisingly different. The sauce made with peeled and seeded tomatoes was by far the best. It had the best consistency—dense and hearty—as well as the brightest, freshest flavor. Both sauces made with unpeeled tomatoes contained hard, unappetizing bits of curled-up skin (the skin had separated from the individual tomato cubes as the tomatoes cooked). In addition, these sauces were less fresh-tasting.

We also found that the sauce made with peeled and seeded tomatoes cooked more quickly than the other two sauces. It took just 10 minutes in a sauté pan for peeled and seeded tomatoes to fall apart to the proper consistency. When we left the skins on the tomato cubes, they took 18 minutes to collapse; evidently, the skins helped the tomatoes hold their shape. Tasters did not object to the seeds themselves, but they made the chopped tomatoes more watery and thus increased the cooking time. We had uncovered a key element to great fresh tomato sauce: short cooking time. Peeling and seeding speeds cooking and is necessary for this reason, not to mention the fact that the skins mar the texture of the finished sauce.

We were pretty sure about our findings but felt that our hypothesis—that long cooking destroys fresh tomato flavor—needed more testing. After all, many Italian grandmothers (as well as countless Italian cookbook authors) insist on simmering tomato sauce for at least an hour, if not longer. We prepared three more sauces with peeled, seeded, and diced tomatoes. We cooked one for 10 minutes (the minimum time necessary for the tomatoes to break down into a sauce), one for 30 minutes, and one for an hour. The sauce that cooked

for 10 minutes had the best flavor. The others reminded tasters of tomato puree; they were dense and smooth but left us wondering where the tomato flavor had gone.

After making so many batches of this sauce, we were beginning to wonder if there was a way to get around peeling, seeding, and chopping before cooking. It was taking us longer to prepare the tomatoes than to cook the sauce.

Many recipes in Italian cookbooks call for peeling and seeding after the tomatoes have

SEEDING TOMATOES

Because of their different shapes, round and plum (also called Roma) tomatoes are seeded differently.

ROUND TOMATOES

Halve the cored tomato along the equator. Gently give each half a squeeze and shake out the seeds and gelatinous material. Use your finger to scoop out any seeds that remain.

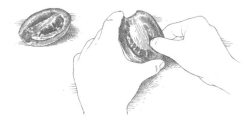

PLUM TOMATOES

Halve the cored tomato lengthwise, cutting through the core end. Scoop out the seeds and gelatinous material with your finger.

been cooked. The tomatoes are cut into quarters, stewed in a casserole until they collapse, then put through a food mill to remove the skins and seeds. The tomato pulp is then used to make sauce. A variation on this method calls for roasting the tomatoes, then putting them through a food mill. Either way, the food mill allows the skins and seeds to be removed after cooking.

We stewed tomatoes in a casserole with a bit of oil until they collapsed, then ran them through a food mill. The mill removed all the skins and a good amount of seeds. However, the tomato pulp was still pretty watery and had to be cooked down further, and the color of the pulp was an odd brick red. One taste and we recognized the flavor—the pulp had the strong scorched or roasted flavor we associate with Mexican cooking. (For many Mexican dishes, whole or sliced tomatoes are seared on a griddle, then peeled and made into sauce.) The same thing happened to tomatoes put in the oven. In both cases, the flesh of the tomato was exposed to the heat and acquired an almost burnt flavor that we did not want in this sauce. Tomato flavor is

delicate, and if you add burnt notes, the balance between sweetness and acidity will be lost.

In the process of doing this testing, we found that it worked best to use a wide pan (a 10-inch pan is right for a single batch of sauce) to promote quick evaporation. When we tried cooking two pounds of prepared tomatoes in a three-quart saucepan, we had to pile the tomatoes on top of one another because of the smaller surface area. As a result, they took an extra 10 minutes to thicken and did not taste as fresh. As for the type of pan, we prefer a sauté pan with relatively high three-inch sides rather than a skillet with sloped sides. The reason is splattering. Keep the cover off as the sauce cooks to allow the tomato liquid to evaporate, and cook the sauce over a brisk medium heat.

Now we knew how to handle the tomatoes to keep their flavor lively: peel, seed, and chop, then cook them quickly in a sauté pan with oil. Next we had to figure out the other components of the sauce. We tried sautéing various aromatic vegetables in the oil before adding the tomatoes and found that a little garlic (heated with the oil so it would not burn) was the best

KEEPING HERBS FRESH

In our tests, the combination of water and relatively little air kept herbs much fresher than other storage methods. Parsley and other fresh herbs with long stems can be kept fresh for at least a week, if not longer, if you follow this method.

1. Wash and dry the herbs thoroughly. Trim the stem ends just as you would trim the ends of cut flowers.

2. Place the herbs in a tall, airtight container with a tight-fitting lid. Add water up to the top of the stems, but don't cover the leaves. Seal the container tightly and refrigerate.

choice. Onion was good as well (especially when we wanted to play up the sweetness in the sauce), but garlic was our first choice. We found leeks, carrots, and celery too distracting.

Our recipe now contained olive oil (we found that extra-virgin oil makes a real difference here), garlic, and tomatoes. Of course, the sauce needed salt, and we thought an herb would round out the flavors. Basil is the natural choice, but parsley is appropriate as well.

As with our quick sauce from canned tomatoes, we saved some of the cooking water from the pasta to help spread the dense tomato sauce over the pasta, and we added a little olive oil to the pasta and sauce for a hit of fresh olive flavor. The result was a sauce that celebrated the flavor of tomatoes, plain and simple.

Pasta and Fresh Tomato Sauce with Garlic and Basil

SERVES 4

Any type of tomato may be used in this recipe—choose the ripest, most flavorful ones available. Short tubular or curly pasta shapes such as penne and fusilli are well suited to this chunky sauce. Alternately, before adding the basil, the sauce may be pureed in a blender or food processor so it will coat strands of spaghetti or linguine. The recipe may be doubled in a 12-inch skillet. The sauce freezes well, but add the basil when reheating. See the illustrations on page 148 for tips on peeling and on page 149 for tips on seeding tomatoes.

3	tablespoons extra-virgin olive oil
2	medium cloves garlic, minced or pressed through a garlic press
2	pounds ripe tomatoes, cored, peeled, seeded, and cut into ½-inch pieces
2	tablespoons chopped fresh basil leaves
	Salt
1	pound pasta (see note)

1. Bring 4 quarts water to a rolling boil in large pot.

2. Meanwhile, heat 2 tablespoons oil and the garlic in a medium skillet over medium heat until the garlic is fragrant but not browned, about 2 minutes. Stir in the tomatoes; increase the heat to medium-high and cook until any liquid given off by the tomatoes evaporates and the tomato pieces lose their shape to form a chunky sauce, about 10 minutes. Stir in the basil and salt to taste; cover to keep warm.

3. Add 1 tablespoon salt and the pasta to the boiling water. Cook until the pasta is al dente. Reserve ¼ cup cooking water; drain the pasta and transfer back to the cooking pot. Mix in the reserved cooking water, sauce, and remaining tablespoon oil; toss well to combine. Serve immediately.

> VARIATIONS

Pasta and Fresh Tomato Sauce with Chile Peppers and Basil

Follow the recipe for Pasta and Fresh Tomato Sauce with Garlic and Basil, heating ¾ teaspoon red pepper flakes with the oil and garlic.

Pasta and Fresh Tomato Cream Sauce with Onion and Butter

This rich sauce is especially good with fresh fettuccine or cheese ravioli.

Follow the recipe for Pasta and Fresh Tomato Sauce with Garlic and Basil, substituting melted butter for the olive oil and 1 medium onion, minced, for the garlic; sauté the onion until golden, about 5 minutes. Continue with the recipe, adding ½ cup heavy cream to the tomatoes after the chunky sauce has formed; simmer until the cream thickens slightly, 2 to 3 minutes longer. Toss the pasta with the sauce and cooking water, omitting the additional oil.

PUTTANESCA SAUCE

SAID TO HAVE BEEN CREATED BY Neapolitan ladies of the night, *puttanesca* is sauce with attitude. Most home cooks buy this lusty sauce by the jar or know it as restaurant fare—a slow-cooked tomato sauce with garlic, hot red pepper flakes, anchovies, capers, and black olives tossed with spaghetti. But those familiar with puttanesca are often disappointed. Chock-full of high-impact ingredients, puttanesca is often overpowered by one flavor; it is too fishy, too garlicky, too briny, or just plain salty. It can also be unduly heavy and stewlike or dull and monochromatic. We were searching for a satisfying sauce with aggressive but well-balanced flavors.

We started our testing by tossing all of the ingredients—minced garlic, minced olives, whole capers, minced anchovies, and hot red pepper flakes—into a base of canned tomatoes and simmering the lot for 25 minutes. The result was a dull sauce with undeveloped flavors. Our first revision began with sautéing the garlic in olive oil to deepen the garlic flavor—but, as we found out, the garlic should not be allowed to brown; when it did, the sauce quickly became bitter. We mixed a bit of water with the garlic before it went into the pan, which slowed the cooking, making the garlic less likely to brown.

Deciding how to prepare and cook the olives was the next task. After several tests, we decided to toss coarsely chopped olives into the sauce at the very last minute, allowing the residual heat of the tomatoes to warm them. This preserved their flavor, their texture, and their independence. As for which olives worked best, we started with Neapolitan gaeta olives—small, black, earthy, and herbaceous. For good measure, we also tested alfonso, kalamata, and canned black olives in place of the gaetas. Tasters unanimously rejected the "insipid," "springy" canned olives but liked

both the alfonso and kalamata olives for their "soft," "melting" qualities.

Capers were the least of our worries. Of all the ingredients, they were the most resilient, well able to retain their shape, texture, and flavor. Rinsing them thoroughly, whether salt- or brine-cured, and adding them at the end of cooking along with the olives proved best.

Up to this point, the anchovies in the sauce, added along with the tomatoes to simmer, tasted flat and salty and gave the sauce a funky, fishy taste. We tried mashing whole fillets into the oil with a fork and found the process tedious and ineffective; stray chunks were left behind and inevitably ended up offending anchovy-sensitive tasters. What worked best was mincing the anchovies to a fine paste and adding them to the oil in the pan with the garlic. In two to three minutes, the anchovies melted into the oil on their own (no fork necessary), and their characteristically full, rich flavor blossomed.

Blooming an ingredient in oil is a technique often used to develop flavor. Because it worked

Puttanesca is a quick tomato sauce enlivened with olives, capers, anchovies, pepper flakes, and garlic.

so well with the garlic and anchovies, we decided to try it with the hot red pepper flakes instead of simmering them with the tomatoes, as we had in the original test. As they cooked with the garlic and anchovies, their flavor permeated the oil.

As for the tomatoes, we tested crushed tomatoes, canned whole tomatoes (chopped by hand), canned diced tomatoes, and fresh. The canned diced tomatoes were the winner. They had a sweet flavor and clung nicely to the pasta. But we still weren't sure whether we should use the diced tomatoes along with their juices or not. Testing the two options head to head made the choice easy. When cooked with tomatoes and their juices, the sauce took 25 minutes to cook down to the right consistency; when cooked with the diced tomatoes alone, it reached the optimal consistency in a mere eight minutes. Tasters were also unanimously in favor of the lightly cooked sauce, finding its flavor fresh and "less stewed" as well as "sweet." They also liked the "meaty texture" and firm bite of the tomatoes in this version of the sauce.

One last discovery improved the sauce still further. In the test kitchen, we are in the habit of reserving a little pasta cooking water to toss with the finished pasta. On a whim, we decided to substitute some of the drained tomato juice for the water, which gave the sauce a brighter, livelier flavor.

MINCED VERSUS CHOPPED OLIVES

Minced olives (left) produced a muddy sauce and purple spaghetti. Coarsely chopped olives (right) won't dye the pasta and taste better.

Spaghetti Puttanesca
SERVES 4

The pasta and sauce cook in about the same amount of time. If you like the fruitiness of extra-virgin olive oil, toss 1 tablespoon into the sauced pasta before serving.

4	medium cloves garlic, minced to a paste or pressed through a garlic press
	Salt
1	pound spaghetti
2	tablespoons olive oil
1	teaspoon hot red pepper flakes
4	teaspoons minced anchovies (about 8 fillets)
1	(28-ounce) can diced tomatoes, drained, ½ cup juice reserved
3	tablespoons capers, rinsed
½	cup black olives (such as gaeta, alfonso, or kalamata), pitted and chopped coarse
¼	cup minced fresh parsley leaves

1. Bring 4 quarts water to a rolling boil in a large pot. Meanwhile, mix the garlic with 1 tablespoon water in a small bowl; set aside. When the water is boiling, add 1 tablespoon salt and the pasta; stir to separate the noodles. Immediately heat the oil, garlic mixture, hot red pepper flakes, and anchovies in a large skillet over medium heat. Cook, stirring frequently, until the garlic is fragrant but not browned, 2 to 3 minutes. Stir in the tomatoes and simmer until slightly thickened, about 8 minutes.

2. Cook the pasta until al dente. Drain, then return the pasta to the pot. Add ¼ cup reserved tomato juice and toss to combine.

3. Stir the capers, olives, and parsley into the sauce. Pour the sauce over the pasta and toss to combine, adding more tomato juice to moisten if necessary. Adjust the seasonings with salt to taste and serve immediately.

Spaghetti and Meatballs

MANY COOKS THINK OF MEATBALLS AS hamburgers with seasonings (cheese, herbs, garlic) and a round shape. This is partly true. However, unlike hamburgers, which are best cooked rare or medium-rare, meatballs are cooked through until well done—at which point they've often turned into dry, tough hockey pucks. When this is the case, the dish can be so heavy that Alka-Seltzer is the only dessert that makes sense.

Our goal was to create meatballs that were moist and light. We also wanted to develop a quick tomato sauce that was loaded with flavor. We focused on the meatballs first.

Meatballs start with ground meat but require additional ingredients to keep them moist and lighten their texture. Meatballs also require binders to keep them from falling apart in the tomato sauce.

A traditional source of moisture in meatballs is egg. We tested meatballs made with and without egg and quickly determined that the egg was a welcome addition. It made the meatballs both moister and lighter.

The list of possible binders included dried bread crumbs, fresh bread crumbs, ground crackers, and bread soaked in milk. We found that bread and cracker crumbs soaked up any available moisture, making the meatballs harder and drier when cooked to well done. In comparison, the meatballs made with bread soaked in milk were moist, creamy, and rich. Milk was clearly an important part of the equation.

We liked the milk but wondered if we could do better. We tried adding yogurt (which works well in our favorite meat loaf recipe) but had to thin it with milk in order to mix it with the bread. Meatballs made with thinned yogurt were even creamier and more flavorful than those made with plain milk. We also tried buttermilk; the results were just as good, with no need to thin the liquid.

With the dairy now part of our working recipe, we found the meatball mixture a tad sticky and hard to handle. By eliminating the egg white (the yolk has all the fat and emulsifiers that contribute smoothness), we eliminated the stickiness.

It was finally time to experiment with the crucial ingredient: the meat. Ground round was too lean; we preferred fattier chuck in this recipe. We tried blending in ground veal but decided it was not worth the bother; these meatballs tasted bland. Ground pork was another matter. It added a welcome flavor dimension.

With our ingredients in order, it was time to test cooking methods. We tried roasting, broiling, and the traditional pan-frying. Roasting yielded dry, crumbly meatballs, while broiling was extremely messy and also tended to produce dry meatballs. Pan-frying produced meatballs with a rich, dark crust and moist texture.

We wondered if we could save cleanup

Sandwich bread soaked in buttermilk is the key to great-tasting, moist meatballs.

time and build more flavor into the tomato sauce by making it in the same pan used to fry the meatballs. We emptied out the vegetable oil used to fry the meatballs (olive oil is too expensive for this task and doesn't add much flavor), then added a little fresh olive oil (olive oil is important to the flavor of the sauce) before adding garlic and tomatoes. Not only did this method prove convenient but it also gave the sauce depth, as the browned bits that had formed when the meatballs were fried loosened from the pan bottom and dissolved in the sauce.

Meatballs need a thick, smooth sauce—the kind produced by canned crushed tomatoes. Sauces made with whole or diced tomatoes were too chunky and liquidy; they didn't meld with the meatballs but did make them soggy.

Spaghetti and Meatballs

SERVES 4 TO 6

The shaped meatballs can be covered with plastic wrap and refrigerated for several hours ahead of serving time. Fry the meatballs and make the sauce at the last minute.

MEATBALLS

- 2 slices white sandwich bread (crusts discarded), torn into small pieces
- ½ cup buttermilk or 6 tablespoons plain yogurt thinned with 2 tablespoons whole milk
- 1 pound ground meat (preferably ¾ pound ground chuck and ¼ pound ground pork)
- ¼ cup finely grated Parmesan cheese
- 2 tablespoons minced fresh parsley leaves
- 1 large egg yolk
- 1 teaspoon finely minced garlic
- ¾ teaspoon salt
  Ground black pepper
- 1–1¼ cups vegetable oil for pan-frying

SMOOTH TOMATO SAUCE

- 2 tablespoons extra-virgin olive oil
- 1 teaspoon minced garlic
- 1 (28-ounce) can crushed tomatoes
- 1 tablespoon minced fresh basil leaves
  Salt and ground black pepper

- 1 pound spaghetti
  Freshly grated Parmesan cheese

1. FOR THE MEATBALLS: Combine the bread and buttermilk in a small bowl. Let sit for 10 minutes, mashing occasionally with a fork, until a smooth paste forms.

2. Place the ground meat, Parmesan cheese, parsley, egg yolk, garlic, salt, and pepper to taste in a medium bowl. Add the bread-milk mixture and combine until evenly mixed. Shape 3 tablespoons of the mixture into a 1½-inch-round meatball. (When forming meatballs, use a light touch. If you compact the meatballs too much, they can become dense and hard.) You should be able to form about 14 meatballs.

3. Pour vegetable oil into a 10- or 11-inch sauté pan to a depth of ¼ inch. Turn the heat to medium-high. After several minutes, test the oil with the edge of a meatball. When the oil sizzles, add the meatballs in a single layer. Fry, turning several times, until nicely browned on all sides, about 10 minutes (see the illustration on page 156). Regulate the heat as needed to keep the oil sizzling but not smoking. Transfer the browned meatballs to a plate lined with paper towels and set aside.

4. Meanwhile, bring 4 quarts water to a rolling boil in a large pot.

5. FOR THE SAUCE: Discard the oil in the pan, but leave behind any browned bits. Add the olive oil for the tomato sauce along with the garlic and sauté, scraping up browned bits, just until the garlic is golden, about 30 seconds. Add the tomatoes, bring to a simmer, and cook until the sauce thickens, about 10

minutes. Stir in the basil and salt and pepper to taste. Add the meatballs and simmer, turning them occasionally, until heated through, about 5 minutes. Keep warm over low heat.

6. Meanwhile, add 1 tablespoon salt and the pasta to the boiling water. Cook until al dente, drain, and return to the pot. Ladle several large spoonfuls of sauce (without meatballs) over the spaghetti and toss until the noodles are well coated. Divide the pasta among individual bowls and top each with a little more tomato sauce and 2 or 3 meatballs. Serve immediately, passing the Parmesan cheese separately.

➤ VARIATION
Spaghetti and Chicken Meatballs
If you want to trim some fat from this recipe, ground chicken is a decent alternative to ground beef and pork. We found that meatballs made from chicken are a tad soft, so they must be refrigerated for an hour before frying to keep them from sticking to the pan or falling apart.

BROWNING MEATBALLS

We found that meatballs taste best when browned evenly on all sides. Their round shape makes this a challenge. Our solution is to brown the two broader sides of the meatballs first, then use tongs to stand the meatballs on their sides. If necessary, lean the meatballs against one another as they brown.

Follow the recipe for Spaghetti and Meatballs, replacing the ground meat with 1 pound ground chicken. After shaping the meatballs in step 2, place them on a platter, cover with plastic wrap, and refrigerate until firm, about 1 hour. Proceed as directed.

BOLOGNESE SAUCE
SCORES OF DELICIOUS MEAT-BASED sauces are made in Italy and elsewhere, but slow-simmering Bolognese (it comes from the city of Bologna, hence the name) is perhaps the best. Unlike meat sauces in which tomatoes dominate (think jars of spaghetti sauce with flecks of meat in a sea of tomato puree), Bolognese sauce is about the meat, with the tomatoes in a supporting role. Bolognese also differs from many tomato-based meat sauces in that it contains dairy—butter, milk, and/or cream. The dairy gives the meat an especially sweet, appealing flavor.

Bolognese sauce is not hard to prepare (the hands-on work is less than 30 minutes), but it does require hours of slow simmering. The sauce must be worth the effort. Bolognese should be complex, with a good balance of flavors. The meat should be first and foremost, but there should be sweet, salty, and acidic flavors in the background.

All Bolognese recipes can be broken down into three steps. First, vegetables are sautéed in fat. Ground meat is then browned in the pan. The final step is the addition of liquids and slow simmering over very low heat.

After an initial round of testing in which we made five styles of Bolognese, we had a recipe we liked pretty well. We liked a combination of onions, carrots, and celery as the vegetables, and we liked them sautéed in butter rather than oil. We also discovered that a combination of ground beef, veal, and pork made this sauce especially complex and rich-tasting. The veal adds finesse and delicacy to the sauce, while the pork makes it sweet. Settling on the liquid element of the recipe, however, proved more difficult.

The secret to a great Bolognese sauce is the sequential reduction of various liquids over the sautéed meat and vegetables. The idea is to build flavor and tenderize the meat, which toughens during the browning phase. Many recipes insist on a particular order for adding these liquids. The most common liquid choices we uncovered in our research were milk, cream, stock, wine (both red and white), and tomatoes (fresh, canned whole, crushed, or paste). We ended up testing numerous combinations to find the perfect balance.

Liquids are treated in two ways. In the earlier part of the cooking process, liquids are added to the pan and simmered briskly until fully evaporated, the point being to impart flavor rather than to cook the meat and vegetables. Wine is always treated this way; if the wine is not evaporated, the sauce will be too alcoholic. Milk and cream are often but not always treated this way. Later, either stock or tomatoes are added in greater quantity and allowed to cook off very slowly. These liquids add flavor, to be sure, but they also serve as the cooking medium for the sauce during the slow simmering phase.

We tested pouring wine over the browned meat first, followed by milk. We also tried them in the opposite order—milk, then wine. We found that the meat cooked in milk first was softer and sweeter. As the bits of meat cook, they develop a hard crust that makes it more difficult for them to absorb liquid. Adding the milk first, when the meat is just barely cooked, works better. The milk penetrates more easily, tenderizing the meat and making it especially sweet.

We tried using cream instead of milk but felt that the sauce was too rich. Milk provides just enough dairy flavor to complement the meat flavor. (Some recipes finish the sauce with cream. We found that cream added just before the sauce was done was also overpowering.) So we settled on milk as the first liquid for the sauce. For the second liquid, we liked both white and red wine. White wine was a bit more delicate and is our choice for the basic recipe.

Then we moved on to the final element in most recipes, the cooking liquid. We did not like any of the recipes we tested with stock. As for tomato paste, we felt that it had little to offer; with none of the bright acidity of canned whole tomatoes and no fresh tomato flavor, it produced a dull sauce.

We tried tomatoes three more ways—fresh, canned whole, and canned crushed. Fresh tomatoes did nothing for the sauce and were a lot of work, as we found it necessary to peel them. (If not peeled, the skins would separate during the long cooking process and mar the texture of the sauce.) Crushed tomatoes were fine, but they did not taste as good as the canned whole tomatoes that we chopped. Whole tomatoes have an additional benefit—the packing juice. Because Bolognese sauce simmers for quite a while, it's nice to have all that juice to keep the pot from scorching.

Our recipe was finally taking shape, with all the ingredients in place. But we still wanted to know if it was necessary to cook Bolognese sauce over low heat and, if so, how long the sauce must simmer. When we tried to hurry the process by cooking over medium heat to evaporate the tomato juice more quickly, the meat was too firm and the flavors were not melded. Low simmering over the lowest possible heat—a few bubbles may rise to the surface of the sauce at one time, but it should not be simmering all over—is the only method that allows enough time for flavor to develop and for the meat to become tender.

As for the timing, we found that the sauce was too soupy after two hours on low heat, and the meat was still pretty firm. At three hours, the meat was much softer, with a melt-in-the-mouth consistency. The sauce was dense and smooth at this point. We tried simmering the sauce for four hours but found no benefit—some batches even overreduced and scorched a bit.

Fettuccine with Bolognese Sauce

SERVES 4

Don't drain the pasta of its cooking water too meticulously when using this sauce; a little water left clinging to the noodles will help distribute the very thick sauce evenly over the noodles, as will adding two tablespoons of butter along with the sauce. If doubling this recipe, increase the simmering times for the milk and the wine to 30 minutes each, and increase the simmering time once the tomatoes are added to 4 hours.

5	tablespoons unsalted butter
2	tablespoons minced onion
2	tablespoons minced carrot
2	tablespoons minced celery
¾	pound meat loaf mix or ¼ pound each ground beef chuck, ground veal, and ground pork
	Salt
I	cup whole milk
I	cup dry white wine
I	(28-ounce) can diced tomatoes with their juice
I	pound fresh or dried fettuccine
	Freshly grated Parmesan cheese

1. Heat 3 tablespoons butter in a large, heavy-bottomed Dutch oven over medium heat. Add the onion, carrot, and celery and sauté until softened but not browned, about 6 minutes. Add the ground meat and ½ teaspoon salt; crumble the meat into tiny pieces with the edge of a wooden spoon. Cook, continuing to crumble the meat, just until it loses its raw color but has not yet browned, about 3 minutes.

2. Add the milk and bring to a simmer; continue to simmer until the milk evaporates and only clear fat remains, 10 to 15 minutes. Add the wine and bring to a simmer; continue to simmer until the wine evaporates, 10 to 15 minutes longer. Add the tomatoes and their juice and bring to a simmer. Reduce the heat to low so that the sauce continues to simmer just barely, with an occasional bubble or two at the surface, until the liquid has evaporated, about 3 hours (if the lowest burner setting is too high to allow such a low simmer, use a flame tamer, shown in the illustration on page 159). Adjust seasonings with extra salt to taste. Keep the sauce warm. (The sauce can be refrigerated in an airtight container for several days or frozen for several months. Warm over low heat before serving.)

3. Bring 4 quarts water to a rolling boil in a large pot. Add 1 tablespoon salt and the pasta. Cook until al dente. Drain the pasta, leaving some water dripping from the noodles. Toss with the sauce and remaining 2 tablespoons butter. Distribute among individual bowls and serve immediately, passing the Parmesan cheese separately.

> VARIATIONS

Fettuccine with Beef Bolognese Sauce

There is something very appealing about the simplicity of an all-beef sauce. While it may lack some of the finesse and sweetness of the master recipe, its pure beef flavor is uniquely satisfying.

Follow the recipe for Fettuccine with Bolognese Sauce, substituting ¾ pound ground beef chuck for the meat loaf mix.

Fettuccine with Beef, Pancetta, and Red Wine Bolognese Sauce

All ground beef (rather than meat loaf mix) works best with the pancetta in this sauce. If you can't find pancetta, use prosciutto, but don't use American bacon, which is smoked and will overwhelm the beef. We found that red wine stands up to the more robust flavors in this sauce better than white wine.

Follow the recipe for Fettuccine with Bolognese Sauce, adding 2 ounces minced pancetta to the butter along with the vegetables, substituting ¾ pound ground beef chuck for the meat loaf mix, and substituting an equal amount of red wine for the white wine.

EQUIPMENT: Flame Tamer

A flame tamer (or heat diffuser) is a metal disk that can be fitted over an electric or gas burner to reduce the heat transfer. This device is especially useful when trying to keep a pot at the barest simmer. If you don't own a flame tamer (it costs less than $10 and is stocked at most kitchenware stores), you can fashion one from aluminum foil. Take a long sheet of heavy-duty foil and shape it into a 1-inch-thick ring that will fit on your burner. Make sure that the ring is an even thickness so that a pot will rest flat on it. A foil ring elevates the pot slightly above the flame or electric coil, allowing you to keep a pot of Bolognese sauce at the merest simmer.

HOMEMADE FLAME TAMER
A homemade flame tamer made with aluminum foil keeps sauces, such as Bolognese, from simmering too briskly, even on a stovetop that runs fairly hot.

MEATY TOMATO SAUCE

BOLOGNESE IS THE KING OF ITALIAN meat sauces, but making it can be a labor of love. Many Italian cooks prefer a simpler, more rustic sauce made from canned tomatoes and a stray piece of meat. The meat (often a pork chop) is browned, the fat drained, and the sauce built in the empty pan. Then the browned meat is added back to the sauce, the pan covered, and the sauce simmered slowly until the meat is fall-off-the-bone tender. Finally, the meat is shredded and stirred into the sauce, which is then served over rigatoni with a good sprinkling of grated cheese.

When we began testing this sauce, it soon became clear that the choice of meat was the most important issue. We tried pork chops from the blade, loin, and sirloin. Even the fattiest chops were dry and tough after braising. We wanted the meat to almost melt when added to the tomato sauce. We needed a piece of meat with more marbling so that it would not dry out during braising.

We thought about a cut from the shoulder—either picnic or Boston butt—because this part of the pig has more fat than the loin, where most chops come from. The problem with these shoulder roasts was their size; the smallest at the market was four pounds. Nevertheless, we cut a pound of this meat into stewlike chunks and proceeded. This meat was more yielding when cooked and had a better flavor. However, the sauce tasted a bit wan; the meat had not done a really good job of flavoring the tomato sauce.

At this point, we turned to spareribs, which are fattier than roasts from the shoulder. The braised meat from spareribs was better than the Boston butt—it was unctuous, almost gelatinous. Best of all, the tomato sauce really tasted meaty. The bones had flavored the sauce in a way that meat alone couldn't. But spareribs are sold in an entire rack that weighs three or more pounds. We needed only four or five ribs for a batch of sauce. That meant spending $9 on a rack of ribs and using half for the sauce and freezing the rest. Was there a more economical way to make this peasant sauce?

We paid $1.99 per pound for country-style ribs and were able to find a small packet with just 1½ pounds of ribs—enough for one batch of sauce, with no leftovers. The sauce made with country-style ribs was similar to the spareribs sauce.

Next, we wondered if this sauce could be made with beef. Short ribs are roughly equivalent to spareribs and country-style ribs. (On the cow, ribs cut from the belly, called the plate, as well as those cut from the back are called short ribs.) The sauce made with short ribs was delicious, too. It's just important to remember that short ribs must be simmered longer than pork ribs because they are thicker.

PORK RIBS

SPARERIBS

COUNTRY-STYLE RIBS

Spareribs come from the belly of the hog. Country-style ribs come from the backbone of the animal, where the shoulder and loin meet. Either can be used in our meaty tomato sauce, although country-style ribs are usually sold in packets with four or five ribs and are more convenient to use than spareribs, which are sold in racks of ten or more ribs.

Pasta and Rustic Slow-Simmered Tomato Sauce with Meat

SERVES 4

This sauce can be made with either beef or pork ribs. Depending on their size, you will need 4 or 5 ribs. To prevent the sauce from becoming greasy, trim all external fat from the ribs and drain off most of the fat from the skillet after browning. This thick, rich, robust sauce is best with tubular pasta, such as rigatoni, ziti, or penne. Pass grated pecorino (especially nice with pork) or Parmesan cheese at the table. The sauce can be covered and refrigerated for up to 4 days or frozen for up to 2 months.

1	tablespoon olive oil
1½	pounds beef short ribs, or pork spareribs or country-style ribs, trimmed of fat
	Salt and ground black pepper
1	medium onion, minced
½	cup red wine
1	(28-ounce) can diced tomatoes with their juice
1	pound pasta (see note above)
	Freshly grated Pecorino Romano or Parmesan cheese

1. Heat the oil in a heavy-bottomed 12-inch skillet over medium-high heat until shimmering. Season the ribs with salt and pepper and brown on all sides, turning occasionally with tongs, 8 to 10 minutes. Transfer the ribs to a plate; pour off all but 1 teaspoon fat from the skillet. Add the onion and sauté until softened, 2 to 3 minutes. Add the wine and simmer, scraping the pan bottom with a wooden spoon

to loosen the browned bits, until the wine reduces to a glaze, about 2 minutes.

2. Return the ribs and accumulated juices to the skillet; add the tomatoes and their juices. Bring to a boil, then reduce the heat to low, cover, and simmer gently, turning the ribs several times, until the meat is very tender and falling off the bones, 1½ hours (for pork spareribs or country-style ribs) to 2 hours (for beef short ribs).

3. Transfer the ribs to a clean plate. When cool enough to handle, remove the meat from the bones and shred it with your fingers, discarding the fat and bones. Return the shredded meat to the sauce in the skillet. Bring the sauce to a simmer over medium heat and cook, uncovered, until heated through and slightly thickened, about 5 minutes. Adjust the seasoning with salt and pepper.

4. Meanwhile, bring 4 quarts water to a rolling boil in a large pot. Add 1 tablespoon salt and the pasta. Cook until al dente. Toss the pasta with the sauce. Serve immediately, passing the cheese separately.

➤ VARIATIONS

Pasta and Tomato-Pork Sauce with Rosemary and Garlic

Follow the recipe for Pasta and Rustic Slow-Simmered Tomato Sauce with Meat, using pork spareribs or country-style ribs. Substitute 3 medium garlic cloves, minced, for the onion, and add 2 teaspoons minced fresh rosemary to the skillet along with the garlic; sauté until softened and fragrant, about 30 seconds. Continue with the recipe.

Pasta and Tomato-Beef Sauce with Cinnamon, Cloves, and Parsley

Follow the recipe for Pasta and Rustic Slow-Simmered Tomato Sauce with Meat, using beef short ribs and adding ½ teaspoon ground cinnamon, pinch ground cloves, and

2 tablespoons minced fresh parsley leaves to the softened onion; sauté until the spices are fragrant, about 30 seconds longer. Continue with the recipe.

AMATRICIANA SAUCE

PASTA ALL'AMATRICIANA IS ARGUABLY Rome's most famous dish. This lusty pasta dish starts with bucatini, an extralong tube pasta that looks like a drinking straw. The sauce contains tomato, bacon, onion, dried chile, and pecorino cheese. Like most Roman cooking, this dish is bold and brash. The recipe comes from Amatrice, a town outside of Rome, but it has become one of those classics, like pesto and carbonara, available in restaurants from Milan to Los Angeles.

What makes Amatriciana so popular? First, most cooks have all the ingredients on hand. Second, the sauce can be made in the time it takes to boil the water and cook the pasta. Third, although the recipe is simple, the flavors are complex and perfectly balanced—acidity from the tomatoes, sweetness from the sautéed onions, heat from the dried chile, meatiness and salt from the bacon, and tangy dairy from the cheese. Our goals in developing our version were to stay faithful to the traditional recipes but to use ingredients available to Americans. The biggest challenge was the bacon. Romans use guanciale, which is bacon made from pork jowls. In the rest of Italy, pancetta (bacon made from pork belly) is used. We wondered how American bacon would compare.

Our first tests revolved around the choice of bacon. We tested pancetta, American bacon, Canadian bacon, Irish bacon (both of the latter are cured pork loin), and salt pork (unsmoked pork belly). Tasters preferred the pancetta, which was the meatiest. The pure pork and salt flavors of the pancetta worked best with the sauce. All three bacons were good, but most tasters felt that the smoke flavor and sweetness were distracting. The Canadian bacon and the Irish bacon (also called Irish back bacon) were meatier than the American bacon, although both were deemed a bit "hamlike." Regular American bacon was excessively fatty. If using it, you will need to drain off the rendered fat (up to ⅓ cup), an unnecessary step when using pancetta, Canadian bacon, or Irish bacon.

The only product not recommended is the salt pork. Although it comes from the belly and is not smoked, it is much too fatty to use in a pasta sauce. Whatever kind of bacon you use, make sure it is sliced thick. When we used thinly sliced pancetta or regular American bacon, the meat nearly disappeared in the sauce.

Our next tests focused on technique. About half of the recipes we consulted called for sautéing the bacon and onion together, then building the tomato sauce on top of them. In the remaining recipes, the bacon was fried until crisp, removed from the pan, and then the onion was cooked in the bacon fat. Once the onion softened, it was time to make the tomato sauce. The crisped bacon was added back just before tossing the sauce with the pasta.

When we simmered the bacon with the tomatoes, it lost its crisp texture. By the time the sauce was done, the bacon was leathery and lacking in flavor. We much preferred bacon that was fried and then removed from the pan. It was crisp and chewy when tossed with the pasta and retained its salty, meaty flavor.

The next issue was the tomato. Crushed tomatoes made the worst sauce—the tomato flavor was weak, and the consistency of the sauce was too thin. We missed the chunks of tomato, which give this sauce some character. Fresh tomatoes were good, but tasters liked canned diced tomatoes even better. They were

a tad juicier, and the preparation was certainly easier—no peeling, seeding, or chopping. Whole tomatoes packed in juice—which must be diced by hand or in a food processor—were just as good, but less convenient.

We tried simmering a small dried red chile in the sauce as an alternative to hot red pepper flakes. The hot red pepper flakes won out, as they provide a more consistent heat level and are more likely to be on hand.

Some Amatriciana recipes call for Parmesan cheese, although pecorino is traditional. We found the taste of Parmesan too subtle to stand up to the chile's heat. Sharp, robust pecorino works better.

Pasta with Tomato, Bacon, and Onion
(Pasta all'Amatriciana)
SERVES 4

This dish is traditionally made with bucatini, also called perciatelli, which appear to be thick, round strands but are actually thin, extralong tubes. Linguine works fine, too. When buying pancetta, ask the butcher to slice it ¼ inch thick; if using bacon, buy slab bacon and cut it into ¼-inch-thick slices yourself. If the pancetta that you're using is very lean, it's unlikely that you will need to drain off any fat before adding the onion. Use 1½ small (14½ ounce) cans of diced tomatoes, or dice a single large (28 ounce) can of whole tomatoes packed in juice.

2	tablespoons extra-virgin olive oil
6	ounces ¼-inch-thick sliced pancetta or bacon cut into strips about ¼ inch wide and 1 inch long
1	medium onion, chopped fine
½	teaspoon hot red pepper flakes, or to taste
2½	cups canned diced tomatoes with juice
	Salt
1	pound bucatini, perciatelli, or linguine
⅓	cup grated pecorino cheese

1. Bring 4 quarts water to a rolling boil in a large pot.

2. Meanwhile, heat the oil in a large skillet over medium heat until shimmering but not smoking. Add the pancetta or bacon and cook, stirring occasionally, until lightly browned and crisp, about 8 minutes. Transfer the pancetta or bacon with a slotted spoon to a paper towel–lined plate; set aside. If necessary, drain all but 2 tablespoons fat from the skillet. Add the onion to the skillet; sauté over medium heat until softened, about 5 minutes. Add the hot red pepper flakes and cook to release their flavor, about 30 seconds. Stir in the tomatoes and salt to taste; simmer until slightly thickened, about 10 minutes.

3. While the sauce is simmering, add 1 tablespoon salt and the pasta to the boiling water. Cook until pasta is al dente; drain and return the pasta to the empty pot.

4. Add the pancetta to the tomato sauce and adjust the seasonings with salt. Add the sauce to the pot with the pasta and toss over low heat to combine, about 30 seconds. Add the pecorino cheese and toss again; serve immediately.

INGREDIENTS: Pancetta

Pancetta and American bacon come from the same part of the pig—the belly—but the curing process is different. American bacon is cured with salt, sugar, and spices (the mix varies from producer to producer) and smoked. Pancetta is not smoked, and the cure does not contain sugar—just salt, pepper, and usually cloves. Pancetta is usually cured for two weeks, rolled up tightly like a jelly roll, and packed into a casing.

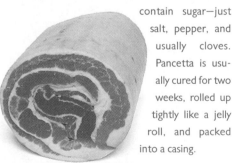

SPAGHETTI ALLA CARBONARA

CARBONARA IS ANOTHER POPULAR Roman pasta dish, but unlike Amatriciana this one taunts us with food taboos. It begins with a sauce made from eggs and cheese that cook into a velvety consistency only from the heat of the just-drained pasta that it drapes. Shards of Italian bacon punctuate the dish with enough presence to make one give silent thanks to the pig. And just when you think that it can't get any better, the bright punch of hot garlic kicks in. This is no diet food, but the indulgent nature of carbonara is one reason it is featured on every trattoria menu.

Far from this heavenly marriage of sauce and pasta, the run-of-the-mill carbonara is a lackluster dish of spaghetti smothered in a heavy, dull, cream-laden sauce that makes you wonder if you ordered Alfredo by mistake. Even worse are variations loaded with cheese that refuses to melt and sticks to the pasta in dry, abrasive pieces. Even a well-made carbonara can be destroyed by a waitperson. If the dish is not brought to the table immediately, the sauce congeals, and the carbonara turns sticky and rubbery.

Searching Italian cookbooks for the solutions to these problems provided little help. Most recipes deviated little in the ingredient list, and the technique was similar throughout: Make a raw sauce with eggs and cheese, render bacon, cook pasta, add hot pasta to sauce and bacon, and toss until the mixture is hot and creamy. The only noticeable difference we found was in the ratio of ingredients, especially the eggs and cheese. That ratio, we reasoned, must be the key to a successful carbonara.

Eggs form the base of the lush, silky sauce that binds the other ingredients to the slender strands of pasta. Only the heat from the cooked pasta is necessary to cook the eggs to the right consistency, so we knew a precise amount of egg would be critical to both the texture and the richness of the dish. Basing our recipe on one pound of pasta, we started out with two eggs. Mixed with one cup grated cheese, this sauce was thick and clumped when introduced to the hot pasta. Four eggs made a sauce too soupy and wet to stick to the pasta. Three eggs were just right. The sauce was silky in texture, had the fortitude to cling to the spaghetti, and was moist and rich.

Next, the cheese. When in Rome, the cheese of choice is Pecorino Romano, an aged sheep's-milk cheese with a distinctly sharp, tangy flavor. On its own, one cup of Pecorino Romano proved too strong for our taste, but reducing the amount of cheese in hopes of buffering the strong flavor yielded a dish that lacked richness.

We tried substituting one cup of Parmigiano-Reggiano for the Pecorino Romano. While the Parmigiano-Reggiano gave the dish a sweet, nutty flavor that was well received, tasters now longed for a little of the potency of the Pecorino Romano. We found that a blend of cheeses—¼ cup Pecorino Romano and ¾ cup Parmesan—brought out just the right amount of flavor from both. It also made for a perfect ratio of cheese to eggs to create the smooth, creamy sauce we'd been looking for.

Many carbonara recipes dictate the addition of ½ cup heavy cream to the sauce. Our tasters immediately rejected this lack of discretion. The heavy cream dulled the mouth with a fatty coating, and it deadened the flavor of the cheeses. Tablespoon by tablespoon, we reduced the amount of cream in the recipe, but tasters were satisfied only when the cream was omitted altogether.

On the other hand, the sweet punch of garlic was a welcome addition. At first, we sautéed a few minced cloves in a little olive oil before adding it to the sauce, but this sautéed garlic lacked the fortitude to shoulder the heavy weight of the eggs and cheese. Adding raw garlic to the mixture was just the trick. With just a brief introduction to heat via the hot pasta, the garlic flavor bloomed and gave the dish a pleasing bite.

In Rome, carbonara is traditionally made with guanciale—salt-cured pork jowl. You can't buy this product in the United States, so we centered the testing around available bacons—pancetta (Italian bacon) and American bacon. Pancetta, like American bacon, comes from the belly of the pig, but rather than being smoked, pancetta is cured only with salt, pepper, and spice, usually cloves. American bacon is recognizably smoked and has a distinct sweetness from the sugar that's added during the curing process.

The pancetta gave the carbonara a substantial pork flavor, plus seasoning with the salt and pepper of the cure, but tasters weren't crazy about its texture. Even though the pancetta was thinly sliced and fried until crisp, the pieces became chewy after a short time in the sauce. The American bacon managed to

Pouring the eggs and cheese over the hot pasta, tossing, and then adding the bacon ensures that the spaghetti is evenly coated with the carbonara ingredients.

retain much of its crisp texture, and it added a pleasantly sweet and smoky flavor to the dish that tasters preferred overwhelmingly.

In Italy, you can start a heated argument over whether or not to use wine in carbonara. In an effort to find the absolutely best carbonara, we tried a dry red wine (a common ingredient in authentic recipes), vermouth (which appeared in only one recipe but piqued our interest), and a dry white wine, which was favored by the majority of the recipes we had found.

The red wine wasn't unpleasant, but the overall flavor wasn't bright enough to stand up to the smoky flavor of the bacon. The vermouth offered a distinct herbal flavor that

EQUIPMENT: Cheese Graters

In the old days, you grated cheese on the fine teeth of a box grater. Now, cheese graters come in several distinct designs. Unfortunately, many of them don't work all that well. With some designs, you need Herculean strength to move the cheese over the teeth with sufficient pressure for grating; with others, you eventually discover that a large portion of the grated cheese has remained jammed in the grater instead of going where it belongs: on your food. Whether you are dusting a plate of pasta or grating a full cup of cheese to use in a recipe, a good grater should be easy to use and efficient.

We rounded up 15 models and set about determining which was the best grater. We found five basic configurations. Four-sided box graters have different-sized holes on each side to allow for both fine grating and coarse shredding. Flat graters consist of a flat sheet of metal that is punched through with fine teeth and attached to some type of handle. With rotary graters, you put a small chunk of cheese in a hopper and use a handle to press it down against a crank-operated grating wheel. Porcelain dish graters have raised teeth in the center and a well around the outside edge to collect the grated cheese. We also found a model that uses an electric motor to push and rotate small chunks of cheese against a grating disk.

After grating more than 10 pounds of Parmesan cheese, we concluded that success was due to a combination of sharp grating teeth, a comfortable handle or grip, and good leverage for pressing the cheese onto the grater. Our favorite model was a flat grater based on a small, maneuverable woodworking tool called a rasp. Shaped like a ruler, but with lots and lots of tiny, sharp

raised teeth, the Cheese Grater (as it is called) can grate large quantities of cheese smoothly and almost effortlessly. The black plastic handle, which we found more comfortable than any of the others, also earned high praise. Other flat graters also scored well.

What about traditional box graters? Box graters can deliver good results and can do more than just grate hard cheese. However, if grating hard cheese is the task at hand, a box grater is not our first choice.

We also had good results with rotary graters made from metal, but we did not like flimsy versions made from plastic. A metal arm is rigid enough to do some of the work of pushing the cheese down onto the grating drum. The arms on the plastic models we tested flexed too much against the cheese, thus requiring extra pressure to force the cheese down. Hand strain set in quickly. A rotary grater can also chop nuts finely and grate chocolate.

The two porcelain dish graters we tested were duds; the teeth were quite ineffective. And the electric grater was a loser of monumental proportions. True, the grating effort required was next to nothing, but so were the results.

THE BEST GRATER
This Microplane grater has very sharp teeth and a solid handle, which together making grating cheese a breeze.

tasters voted down. White wine created the most impact and resonance. It was full-flavored, and its acidic nature cut through the taste of the bacon, brightening the flavor of the dish. Testing how much to add, we found that a modest amount wouldn't do. To bring the wine's full presence to the table, we needed to use at least ½ cup. We also found that adding the white wine to the bacon as it sautéed deepened the overall flavor of the dish.

Up to this point, we had been making the carbonara by the traditional method. We mixed the eggs and cheese in the bottom of the serving bowl along with the fried bacon, then dumped the hot, drained pasta on top and tossed the mixture thoroughly. But this method had flaws. It was difficult to distribute the egg and cheese mixture evenly throughout the pasta, and, try as we might to keep the bacon pieces afloat, gravity pulled them back to the bottom of the bowl.

Mixing the eggs and cheese together in a separate bowl, then pouring the mixture over the hot pasta, ensured even coverage. This also meant that the serving bowl could be preheated—a step that keeps the pasta warm. Finally, we found that tossing the hot pasta with the egg mixture first, then gently tossing in the bacon, worked best. The bacon adhered nicely to the sticky coating of sauce.

We found that carbonara will not maintain its creamy consistency if the cooked pasta is allowed too much time to drain. We ultimately allowed it to sit in the colander for only a few seconds before mixing it with the sauce. (To ensure that proper moisture from the pasta was not lost, we found it a good practice to reserve ⅓ cup of the pasta cooking water to add if the noodles became dry or sticky.) Even with these precautions, the carbonara thickened considerably if left to cool for even a short time. It's best for hungry diners to wait for the carbonara, not the other way around.

Spaghetti alla Carbonara
SERVES 4 TO 6

Add regular table salt to the pasta cooking water but use sea salt flakes, if you can find them, to season the dish. We like the full flavor they bring to the carbonara. Note that while either table salt or sea salt can be used when seasoning in step 3, they are not used in equal amounts.

¼   cup extra-virgin olive oil

½   pound bacon (6 to 8 slices), slices halved lengthwise, then cut crosswise into ¼-inch pieces

½   cup dry white wine

3   large eggs

¾   cup finely grated Parmesan (about 2 ounces)

¼   cup finely grated Pecorino Romano (about ¾ ounce)

3   small cloves garlic, minced to paste or pressed through a garlic press

I   pound spaghetti
  Salt and ground black pepper

1. Adjust an oven rack to the lower-middle position, set a large heatproof serving bowl on the rack, and heat the oven to 200 degrees. Bring 4 quarts water to a rolling boil in a large pot.

2. While the water is heating, heat the oil in a large skillet over medium heat until shimmering but not smoking. Add the bacon and cook, stirring occasionally, until lightly browned and crisp, about 8 minutes. Add the wine and simmer until the alcohol aroma has cooked off and the wine is slightly reduced, 6 to 8 minutes. Remove from the heat and cover to keep warm. Beat the eggs, cheeses, and garlic together with a fork in a small bowl; set aside.

3. When the water comes to a boil, add 1 tablespoon salt and the pasta; stir to separate the noodles. Cook until al dente; reserve ⅓ cup

pasta cooking water and drain the pasta for about 5 seconds, leaving the pasta slightly wet. Transfer the drained pasta to the warm serving bowl; if the pasta appears dry, add some reserved cooking water and toss to moisten. Immediately pour the egg mixture over the hot pasta, sprinkle with 1 teaspoon sea salt or ¾ teaspoon table salt, and toss well to combine. Pour the bacon mixture over the pasta, season generously with black pepper to taste, and toss well to combine. Serve immediately.

SPAGHETTI WITH CLAM SAUCE

TOO OFTEN, SPAGHETTI WITH CLAM sauce is a soggy mess of canned clams tossed with overcooked pasta. We knew we could do better, especially if we used fresh clams.

First, we decided to identify the best clams and figure out the best way to cook them. In Italy, tiny clams are often used for this dish, but we couldn't find these clams in the United States unless we begged them from chefs. So we began by buying the tiniest littlenecks we could find. This helped somewhat, but with clams selling for about $5 a dozen regardless of size, a simple pasta dish for four quickly became an extravagance.

We tried the larger cherrystones and even giant quahogs (they're all the same species, just increasingly bigger specimens), lightly steamed and chopped into pieces. But no matter how long or short we cooked them, they were tough, and they lacked the distinctive, fresh brininess of littlenecks. However, we did learn something: Large, less palatable, and far less expensive clams gave us the same kind of delicious clam juice—the backbone of this dish—as small clams.

Then we found cockles, which are almost as small as the baby clams you find in Italy. Because they are sold by the pound, not the dozen, and because they are small, cockles are less expensive than littlenecks. They are also quite delicious. Unfortunately, they're not nearly as widely available as littlenecks. The alternative is littlenecks, the littler the better, and at least six (preferably eight or more) per person.

Because we still favored using all littlenecks, our dish remained quite expensive. So we resolved that if we were going to pay a small fortune for the dish, we would make sure that it would be uniformly wonderful each time we cooked it. There were three problems with our original recipe, we thought. One was that the clam meat tended to become overcooked in the time it took to finish the sauce; one was that there was often not enough clam juice; finally, we thought that the sauce itself could use another dimension of flavor.

Solving the first problem was easy: We cooked the clams first, just until they gave up their juices. Then we recombined the clams with the sauce at the last minute, just enough to reheat them.

Next we turned to the occasional dearth of clam juice. When we were too cheap to buy enough littlenecks or couldn't find cockles, we combined a couple dozen littlenecks with about six large quahogs, which we could often buy for just a few dollars. Because it was the juice we were after—not the clam meat—this

TWO TYPES OF CLAMS

Quahogs (left) flavor the broth, but littlenecks (right) provide the meat for the pasta sauce.

worked out fine; we simply discarded the quahog meat after cooking it.

We liked the flavor of white wine mixed with clam juice, but we did not like using more than ½ cup or so because its distinctive flavor was somewhat overwhelming. Cutting back on the wine, though, robbed the dish of needed acidity. We experimented with lemon juice but felt that the flavor was too strong. Vinegar, of course, was even worse. Finally, we

added just a little bit of diced plum tomato, barely enough to color the sauce. The benefits were immediate: Not only was the flavor balanced, but another welcome texture was added to the dish.

Satisfied at last, we pronounced ourselves done. With the final recipe, you can steam the clams open while bringing the pasta water to a boil and preparing the other ingredients. Once the clams are done, begin browning the garlic; five minutes later, put in the pasta and finish the sauce. The timing is perfect and perfectly easy.

PREPARING CLAM SAUCE

1. Scrub clams with a soft brush under running water to remove any sand from their shells.

2. To remove any grit from the clam cooking liquid, strain it through a sieve lined with a single layer of paper towel and set over a measuring cup. If desired, moisten the towel first so that it does not absorb any precious clam juices.

Pasta with Fresh Clam Sauce

SERVES 4

You can save money by using large, inexpensive quahogs, which provide plenty of liquid for a briny, brothy dish, for about half the price of littlenecks. Because quahogs are so cheap, discard the steamed meat without guilt and dine on the sweet, tender littlenecks with the pasta.

24	littleneck clams (the smaller the better), scrubbed thoroughly (see illustration at left)
6	quahog or chowder clams (the larger the better), scrubbed thoroughly
½	cup dry white wine
	Pinch cayenne pepper
¼	cup extra-virgin olive oil
2	medium cloves garlic, minced or pressed through a garlic press
I	large or 2 small plum tomatoes, peeled, seeded, and minced
	Salt
I	pound spaghetti, linguine, or other long-strand pasta
⅓	cup chopped fresh parsley leaves

1. Bring 4 quarts water to a rolling boil in a large pot.

2. Meanwhile, bring the clams, wine, and cayenne to a boil in a deep 10- to 12-inch covered skillet over high heat. Boil, shaking the pan occasionally, until the littlenecks just begin to open (try to catch clams before they open completely), 3 to 5 minutes. Transfer the littlenecks with a slotted spoon to a medium bowl; set aside. Re-cover pan and continue cooking the quahogs until their liquid is released, about 5 minutes longer. Discard the quahogs; strain the liquid in the pan through a paper towel–lined sieve into a large measuring cup (see illustration 2 on page 168). Add enough water to make 1 cup; set aside.

3. Heat the oil and garlic in the cleaned skillet over medium-low heat until the garlic turns pale gold, about 5 minutes. Add the tomatoes, raise the heat to high, and sauté until the tomatoes soften, about 2 minutes longer. Add the littlenecks and cover; cook until all the clams open completely, 1 to 2 minutes longer.

4. Meanwhile, add 1 tablespoon salt and the pasta to the boiling water; cook until al dente, 7 to 9 minutes. Drain the pasta, transfer it to the skillet with the sauce, and toss. Add the reserved clam liquid and cook until the flavors meld, about 30 seconds. Stir in the parsley and adjust the seasonings. Serve immediately.

PASTA WITH TUNA

WHAT COOK HASN'T COME HOME FROM a long day, tired and hungry, to find the refrigerator bare, offering poor prospects for a good, quick dinner? Yet a simple can of tuna paired with a box of dried pasta can come to the rescue even faster than the pizza delivery guy. The trick is to choose the right can of tuna and use it properly to make a fast,

satisfying dinner; otherwise, the sauce can be murky, mealy, and unappetizing.

A side-by-side tasting of different types of tuna made into sauces got us going. The lineup was comprised of water-packed solid white StarKist (which won our tasting of leading brands of canned tuna packed in water), its vegetable oil–packed counterpart, and a tuna packed in olive oil (after the Italian style), which, like the other tunas, is available on many supermarket shelves. The surprise winner was the water-packed tuna, preferred for its toothsome texture and light, clear flavor. Several dissenters favored the rich flavor of the tuna packed in olive oil, but everyone frowned on the off flavor and mushy texture of the tuna packed in vegetable oil. (If you like the stronger flavor of tuna packed in olive oil, we found it best to drain the tuna and use fresh oil to make pasta sauces.)

Draining the tuna well prevents it from tasting waterlogged and diluting the sauce. We also found it useful to use our fingers to shred large chunks to a fine and uniform texture, thereby ensuring even distribution of the tuna. These techniques add but a minute to the preparation time yet make real improvements to the overall consistency of the final dish. We wondered about the right time to add the tuna to the other sauce ingredients and found that adding it late in the game was best. If sautéed from the start, the tuna dried out and became gritty, dragging down the texture of the whole dish with it. If the tuna is added to the sauce at the last minute and allowed to just heat through, it remains moist and tender.

Because these sauces are relatively thick, we pair them with stubby, open, or tubular pasta shapes that can trap the sauce effectively. Penne, fusilli, radiatore, and gemelli are particularly good choices.

Pasta and Garlic-Lemon Tuna Sauce with Capers and Parsley

SERVES 4 TO 6

3	tablespoons olive oil
6	medium cloves garlic, minced or pressed through a garlic press (about 2 tablespoons)
1/2	teaspoon hot red pepper flakes
3	tablespoons capers, rinsed and drained
1/2	cup dry white wine
2	(6-ounce) cans solid white tuna in water, drained well and chunks broken up with fingers
	Salt
1	pound penne or fusilli
1/4	cup chopped fresh parsley leaves
1	teaspoon grated zest from 1 lemon
3	tablespoons unsalted butter, cut into 6 pieces
	Ground black pepper

1. Bring 4 quarts water to a rolling boil in a large pot.

2. Meanwhile, heat the oil, 1 tablespoon garlic, hot red pepper flakes, and capers in a 12-inch skillet over medium-high heat, stirring frequently, until fragrant and sizzling but not browned, 1 to 2 minutes. Add the wine and bring to a simmer; simmer until aroma bears no trace of alcohol, about 1 minute. Add the tuna and 2 teaspoons salt and cook, stirring frequently, until tuna is heated through, about 1 minute.

3. Add 1 tablespoon salt and the pasta to the boiling water. Cook until al dente. Drain, reserving 1/4 cup cooking water. Return the pasta to the pot and toss with the tuna mixture, remaining garlic, parsley, zest, butter, and reserved pasta water to coat. Adjust the seasonings with salt and pepper to taste. Serve immediately.

Pasta and Tomato Tuna Sauce with Garlic and Mint

SERVES 4 TO 6

4	tablespoons olive oil
6	medium cloves garlic, minced or pressed through a garlic press (about 2 tablespoons)
1	(28-ounce) can diced tomatoes, drained
1/2	cup dry red wine
2	(6-ounce) cans solid white tuna in water, drained well and chunks broken up with fingers
	Salt
1	pound penne or fusilli
1	tablespoon balsamic vinegar
2	tablespoons chopped fresh mint or fresh parsley leaves
	Ground black pepper

1. Bring 4 quarts water to a rolling boil in a large pot.

2. Heat 2 tablespoons oil and 1 tablespoon garlic in a 12-inch skillet over medium-high heat, stirring frequently, until fragrant and sizzling but not browned, 1 to 2 minutes. Add the tomatoes and cook, stirring constantly, until combined, about 30 seconds. Add the wine and bring to a simmer; simmer until the aroma bears no trace of alcohol, about 1 minute. Add the tuna and 2 teaspoons salt and cook, stirring frequently, until the tuna is heated through, about 1 minute.

3. Add 1 tablespoon salt and the pasta to the boiling water. Cook until al dente. Drain, reserving 1/4 cup cooking water. Return the pasta to the pot and toss with the tuna mixture, remaining oil and garlic, vinegar, mint, and reserved pasta water to coat. Adjust the seasonings with salt and pepper to taste. Serve immediately.

Pasta and Red Pepper Tuna Sauce with Anchovies, Garlic, and Basil

SERVES 4 TO 6

6	tablespoons olive oil
6	medium cloves garlic, minced or pressed through a garlic press (about 2 tablespoons)
½	teaspoon hot red pepper flakes
2	anchovy fillets, minced
I	cup (about 7 ounces) jarred roasted red bell peppers, cut into ½-inch pieces
½	cup dry white wine
2	(6-ounce) cans solid white tuna in water, drained well and chunks broken up with fingers
	Salt
I	pound penne or fusilli
I	tablespoon juice from I lemon
2	tablespoons chopped fresh basil or fresh parsley leaves
	Ground black pepper

1. Bring 4 quarts water to a rolling boil in a large pot.

2. Heat 3 tablespoons oil, 1 tablespoon garlic, and the hot red pepper flakes in a 12-inch skillet over medium-high heat, stirring frequently, until fragrant and sizzling but not browned, 1 to 2 minutes. Add the anchovies and roasted red peppers and cook, stirring constantly, until slightly dry, about 30 seconds. Add the wine and bring to a simmer; simmer until the aroma bears no trace of alcohol, about 1 minute. Add the tuna and 2 teaspoons salt and cook, stirring frequently, until the tuna is heated through, about 1 minute.

3. Add 1 tablespoon salt and the pasta to the boiling water. Cook until al dente. Drain, reserving ¼ cup cooking water. Return the pasta to the pot and toss with the tuna mixture, remaining oil and garlic, lemon juice, basil, and reserved pasta water to coat. Adjust the seasonings with salt and pepper to taste. Serve immediately.

PASTA ALLA NORMA

PASTA ALLA NORMA IS A GUTSY TOMATO sauce studded with chunks of eggplant. The tomato sauce part is easy—just make a basic sauce and use plenty of garlic and hot red pepper flakes. It's the eggplant that causes so much worry.

Many people complain that their eggplant dishes are either tough, pithy, and astringently bitter or oil-soaked, slimy, and tasteless. This is not inevitable. Eggplant can—and should—be firm and meaty, with a rich, sweet, nutty flavor. We find that most eggplant (as long as they are not huge) are rarely bitter. Our early tests did show that much eggplant cooks up slimy and soft. We decided to focus our energies here.

The problem most cooks face when preparing eggplant is how to rid the vegetable of its excess moisture. Eggplant is full of water, and even when cooked in a very hot skillet, it steams in its own juices. The result is lifeless flavor and squishy texture.

Salt is often used for drawing moisture out of eggplant before cooking. We salted eggplants with regular table salt and kosher salt and prefer kosher salt for its large crystals, which can be easily wiped away after salting. Table salt dissolves into the eggplant flesh and must be thoroughly rinsed away with water. The eggplant must then be thoroughly dried, which can take some time, especially if the eggplant has been diced for a pasta sauce.

Although many classic recipes suggest salting eggplant for hours, we found that 30 minutes did the trick. The salted eggplant then can be sautéed until it becomes tender and lightly browned. Some recipes for Pasta alla Norma suggest building the tomato sauce in a separate pan and adding the sautéed eggplant to the sauce right before it is tossed with the pasta. This seemed like extra work that such a simple recipe should not require. We wondered if we could build the tomato sauce right on top of the eggplant.

We added garlic and hot red pepper flakes to the pan with the cooked eggplant, then diced canned tomatoes. The tomatoes were fairly watery and had a detrimental effect on the texture of the eggplant. By the time the sauce was done (it took about 10 minutes of simmering), the eggplant was mushy. We wondered if a smooth, thick tomato product, such as crushed tomatoes, would work better here. Sure enough, after just two to three minutes in the pan, the crushed tomatoes had thickened to a sauce consistency without injuring the eggplant. For the freshest flavor, choose a brand of crushed tomatoes that lists tomatoes rather than tomato puree first.

Pasta alla Norma

SERVES 4

Add crushed tomatoes to sautéed eggplant, toss with rigatoni, and you have Pasta alla Norma. Grated ricotta salata is optional. If you do use it, hold off on adding salt to the sauce; between the eggplant and the cheese, the finished dish will probably have enough salt.

- 2   medium eggplant (about 2 pounds), ends trimmed, cut into ¾-inch cubes
       Kosher salt
- 3   tablespoons extra-virgin olive oil
- 3   medium cloves garlic, minced or pressed through a garlic press (about 1 tablespoon)
- ¼   teaspoon hot red pepper flakes, or to taste
- 1¼   cups canned crushed tomatoes
- 1   pound rigatoni or other short tubular pasta
- 1   cup shredded ricotta salata cheese
- ¼   cup minced fresh parsley or fresh basil leaves

1. Place the eggplant in a large colander and sprinkle with 1 tablespoon salt. Let stand 30 minutes. Using paper towels or a large kitchen towel, wipe the salt off and pat the excess moisture from the eggplant.

2. Heat the oil in a large heavy-bottomed skillet over medium-high heat until it shimmers and becomes fragrant. Add the eggplant; sauté until it begins to brown, about 4 minutes. Reduce the heat to medium-low and cook, stirring occasionally, until the eggplant is fully tender and lightly browned, 10 to 15 minutes. Stir in the garlic and hot red pepper flakes; cook to blend the flavors, about 2 minutes. Add the tomatoes, bring to a simmer, and cook until slightly thickened, 2 to 3 minutes. Season with salt and pepper to taste.

3. Meanwhile, bring 4 quarts water to a rolling boil in a large pot. Add 1 tablespoon salt and the pasta. Cook until al dente. Reserve ½ cup cooking liquid, then drain. Return the pasta to the cooking pot and toss with the eggplant, ricotta salata cheese, parsley or basil, and ¼ cup cooking liquid. Stir in more cooking liquid, 1 tablespoon at a time, if the sauce seems dry. Divide among 4 pasta bowls and serve immediately.

ORECCHIETTE WITH BROCCOLI RABE

ITALIANS LOVE BROCCOLI RABE AND commonly use this bitter, spicy green in pasta sauces. Ear-shaped orecchiette pasta often teams up with broccoli rabe, garlic, and hot red pepper flakes to create a simple pasta dish.

If you are not familiar with broccoli rabe, it can seem tricky to cook. Broccoli rabe contains thick stalks, tender leaves, and small florets. If all the stalks were removed, there would be little left to this plant. We had to devise a cooking method that would soften the stalks but keep the florets and leaves from becoming mushy.

We tested boiling and steaming and found that steaming cooks this tough green unevenly. By the time the thick stalks soften, the tender florets were mushy. Boiling did a better job of cooking the various parts of this plant evenly, if only because it is faster and there is less time for the florets to become mushy. Because the florets still tend to over-cook, however, we found it necessary to drain and refresh the broccoli rabe in a bowl of cold water to stop the cooking process. It's also a good idea to pull broccoli rabe off the flame before it is completely tender, especially as it will be cooked again in the pasta sauce.

The thick ends of each stalk never softened properly, even when boiled, so we decided they should be removed before cooking. The remaining portion of the stalks and the florets should be cut into bite-sized pieces (about 1 inch long) for use in pasta sauces.

With the broccoli rabe blanched, the sauce comes together rather quickly. Garlic—and lots of it—should be cooked in olive oil. Tasters voted for four cloves, and we found it best to keep the heat at a moderate level so that the garlic would not burn and become

acrid. Once the garlic is golden, it's time to add the broccoli rabe. Some recipes suggest adding stock to the pan (without liquid, the broccoli, oil, and garlic will be dry on the pasta). However, we had better luck just reserving some of the pasta cooking water to moisten the pasta.

~≈

Orecchiette with Broccoli Rabe

SERVES 4

You can substitute other hearty greens, such as kale or collards, for the broccoli rabe. However, you may need to increase the blanching time in step 1.

Salt
1   pound broccoli rabe, trimmed and cut into 1-inch pieces (see illustrations on page 62)
1/3 cup extra-virgin olive oil
4   medium cloves garlic, minced or pressed through a garlic press
1/2 teaspoon hot red pepper flakes
1   pound orecchiette or other shell-shaped pasta
1/2 cup grated Parmesan cheese

1. Bring 1 quart water to a boil in a large pot. Add salt to taste and the broccoli rabe. Return to a boil and cook until the broccoli rabe is bright green and almost tender, 2 to 3 minutes. Drain the broccoli rabe and plunge into cold water to stop the cooking process; drain the broccoli rabe and set aside.

2. Heat the oil with the garlic in a large skillet over medium heat until the garlic is golden, 1 to 2 minutes; add the pepper flakes and broccoli rabe. Sauté until heated through, 3 to 4 minutes.

3. Meanwhile, bring 4 quarts water to a boil in a large pot. Add 1 tablespoon salt and the

EQUIPMENT: Manual Can Openers

Like many gadgets, can openers aren't something most cooks give much thought to until they're using one. But with several new types on the market, all boasting superior operation and safety features, we wanted to see if there were notable differences among leading brands.

We purchased four safety can openers and six standard can openers with varying grips and features. Prices ranged from $6.99 to $24.95. A standard can opener attaches to the side of the can and punctures the lid just inside the rim. When the can is open, both the lid and the edges are often jagged and rough. A safety can opener attaches to the top of the can and punctures the outside of the can just below the rim. When the can is open, both the lid and the edges are perfectly smooth.

We tested all 10 models on standard 14½-ounce cans of beans and 6-ounce cans of tuna. We judged each opener on its comfort, ease of operation, and safety.

In terms of comfort, we took into account both the grip and the turning mechanism. Can openers with an ergonomic grip and a comfortable turning mechanism were preferred over models that pinched our fingers or forced an uncomfortable hand angle.

Ease of operation hinged on time—if more than one rotation around the can was necessary, or if we had to pause and restart turning, the opener was downgraded.

Determining safety was clear-cut. If the opened can had smooth edges and little handling of sharp-edged tops was necessary, the opener earned the top rating. If the operation endangered fingers or produced ragged edges on the can or its top, the opener received a lower rating.

In the end, our testers preferred the standard can openers to the safety models. Perhaps it was our lifelong familiarity with standard can openers, but we simply could not get used to the different hand position required, the two-part operation, or the locking handles on the safety openers. Many of the safety can openers were stiff and difficult to operate, and all caused liquid to spill out of the side of the can because the entire top was removed. Standard models may not result in perfectly smooth edges, but we are willing to use a bit of extra caution in exchange for ease, speed, and comfort.

Our favorite standard can openers were the Oxo Good Grips ($9.95), with a great grip and comfortable turning mechanism, and the Swing Away ($6.99), a classic stainless-steel opener with plastic-coated handles for extra comfort. If safety is your prime concern, our testers had the best luck with the Culinare MagiCan Auto Release ($9.99).

THE BEST STANDARD CAN OPENERS

The Oxo Good Grips (left) earned top marks for its great plastic grip and comfortable turning mechanism. Operation was fast, easy, and secure. The Swing Away (right) is probably what your grandmother has in her drawer. The plastic-coated handles are especially easy on your hands.

THE BEST SAFETY CAN OPENER

The Culinare MagiCan Auto Release is exceedingly safe but liquid spills from cans while opening. This all-plastic option is friendly for lefties as well as righties.

pasta to the boiling water. Cook until al dente. Reserve ½ cup cooking liquid, then drain. Return the pasta to the cooking pot and toss with the sauce. Stir in the cooking liquid, 1 tablespoon at a time, if the sauce seems dry. Stir in the Parmesan cheese and divide among 4 pasta bowls. Serve immediately.

PASTA PRIMAVERA

UNLIKE MOST DISHES, PASTA PRIMAVERA has a clear pedigree—and despite the name, this popular recipe originated in the United States, not Italy. Pasta primavera was created at Le Cirque, New York's famed French restaurant, in the 1970s. Patrons told restaurateur Sirio Maccioni that they wanted healthier, lighter dishes, so he created a pasta dish loaded with fresh vegetables. He dubbed his invention spaghetti primavera—*primavera* is Italian for "spring"—and it quickly became a

Our streamlined pasta primavera comes together in about half the time of the original restaurant recipe.

New York sensation.

If you've ever made this dish, you probably loved the flavor. It's a sure winner with company, but for the cook, this recipe is a labor of love. For one thing, it calls for blanching each green vegetable in a separate pot to retain its individual character; if the same pot is used for each vegetable, this first step takes almost an hour. If that weren't enough bother, once the vegetables are blanched, you need five more pots: one to cook the vegetables in garlicky olive oil, one to sauté mushrooms, one to make a fresh tomato sauce flavored with basil, one to make a cream sauce with butter and Parmesan, and one to cook the pasta.

None of the tasks involved is difficult, but the timing is complicated and better suited to a professional kitchen, where several cooks can handle different jobs. But we love this dish. We wanted to find out if we could simplify the cooking process while keeping the fresh vegetable flavors.

We began combing through Italian cookbooks, both those written in English and those in Italian. We were intrigued by a couple of older Italian recipes for pasta dishes with the word *primavera* in the title. These dishes were substantially different from the version we now know. The directions read like those used to make a slow-simmering meat sauce. In these old-fashioned recipes, the vegetables were either sautéed or stewed together in just one pot. How sensible and how Italian, we thought. We were sure we had discovered the secret to simpler, home-style primavera. We prepared several of these recipes, some in which the vegetables were stewed and others in which they were sautéed.

When we cooked the vegetables in a covered pan, they quickly dissolved into a thick porridge. The lid trapped moisture, and the vegetables, instead of browning and gaining flavor, just fell apart—they tasted like over-cooked minestrone. Sautéing the vegetables in an open pan was better, but tasters felt that freshness was missing from this dish. Yes, this was pasta with lots of produce, but it didn't have the crisp-tender vegetables, each with its own distinct shape and flavor, that everyone expects from a dish called pasta primavera.

Having reached a dead end, we returned to Le Cirque's original recipe. We would still blanch the vegetables to keep them crisp, but we knew we could do better than six pots and two hours.

The first issue was to decide which vegetables were essential for primavera sauce and which could be dropped. Despite its name, this dish as originally conceived contains many nonspring vegetables, including broccoli, green beans, and zucchini. Only the peas, snow peas, and asparagus are truly spring vegetables.

We began testing other spring vegetables and soon realized why they were not included. Artichokes were way too much work to prepare, and leeks tasted better when sautéed rather than blanched, which meant an extra pan and more work. We usually like fennel, but its sweet, anise flavor overwhelmed that of the other vegetables. We also decided to jettison the broccoli (tasters liked this vegetable the least in this sauce) and snow peas (the pea family was already represented by shelled peas). We were left with four spring/summer vegetables—asparagus, peas, zucchini, and green beans. We went still further and tried eliminating a couple of these vegetables and increasing the quantity of those remaining, but this compromise did not save any time, and tasters felt that the name "primavera" connotes many vegetables, not just two or three.

We found we could blanch all the green vegetables together in a single pot. We had to add them at different times to make sure each was properly cooked, but after some trial and error we devised a cooking regimen—adding the green beans first, followed by the asparagus, then the zucchini, and ending with the

SHREDDING BASIL

For larger herb leaves such as basil or mint, a cut called a chiffonade is the most attractive and bruise-free way to chop.

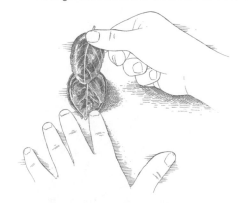

1. Stack 3 or 4 clean dry leaves.

2. Roll the leaves tightly like a cigar and then slice thinly.

peas. Because we were cooking all the vegetables together, we needed a larger pot, which we found we could reuse (without washing) to cook the mushrooms and tomatoes.

We tried adding the cooked vegetables directly to the drained pasta, but they were watery and bland. Clearly, they needed to be sautéed to build flavor. A few minutes in a hot skillet with garlicky butter proved essential.

In the original recipe, the mushrooms are sautéed, then added to the green vegetables, then sautéed again. We wondered if we could instead keep the mushrooms in the pan and build the tomato sauce on top of them. This worked fine. We tried cooking the mushroom-tomato sauce (as well as the green vegetables) in butter and in olive oil. Tasters preferred the sweet, rich flavor of the butter, which worked better with the cream.

Next, we focused on the tomatoes. We concluded that this dish would need fresh tomatoes for flavor and juiciness. Plum tomatoes are not as watery as fresh round tomatoes and are best in this dish. We found it unnecessary to seed them, but the peels had to go because they separated from the chopped tomatoes and curled up into unappetizing bits.

Finally, we found that the separate cream sauce (with butter, cheese, and cream) could be combined with the mushroom-tomato sauce. We reduced some cream over the mushroom-tomato mixture and discovered that this worked perfectly well. There was plenty of butter in the sauce already, and we found that cheese could just as easily be sprinkled on at the table. So instead of three pans—one for mushrooms, one for tomato sauce, and one for cream sauce—we had cooked them together in one pan.

At this point, our recipe was just as delicious as the original, and we were down to just three pans, not six. We had also reduced total preparation and cooking time by more than half. This pasta primavera may not be Tuesday night supper, but when you want a fancy pasta dish, there's no reason to run when someone suggests primavera sauce.

Pasta Primavera
SERVES 6 AS A MAIN COURSE OR 8 TO 10 AS A FIRST COURSE

This dish requires careful timing so that the three main elements—the cooked pasta, the green vegetables, and the sauce—come together at the right time.

	Salt
6	ounces green beans, cut into ³⁄₄-inch pieces (about 1 ¹⁄₄ cups)
12	medium asparagus spears, tough ends snapped off (see illustration on page 59), halved lengthwise, and cut diagonally into ³⁄₄-inch pieces
1	medium zucchini, cut into ¹⁄₂-inch dice
1	cup frozen peas, thawed
6	tablespoons unsalted butter
8	ounces white mushrooms, sliced thin (about 4 cups)
4	large plum tomatoes (about 1 pound), cored, peeled, and chopped medium (about 2 cups)
¹⁄₄	teaspoon hot red pepper flakes (optional)
¹⁄₂	cup heavy cream
1	pound dried egg fettuccine (see page 192)
2	medium cloves garlic, minced or pressed through a garlic press
¹⁄₄	cup shredded fresh basil leaves
1¹⁄₂	tablespoons juice from 1 lemon
	Freshly grated Parmesan cheese

1. Bring 6 quarts water to a rolling boil in a large stockpot for the pasta. Bring 3 quarts water to a boil in a large saucepan for the green vegetables; add 1 tablespoon salt. Fill a large bowl with ice water; set aside. Add the green beans to

the boiling water in the saucepan; cook 1½ minutes. Add the asparagus; cook 30 seconds. Add the zucchini; cook 30 seconds. Add the peas; cook 30 seconds. Drain the vegetables and immediately plunge them into the ice water bath to stop cooking; let sit until chilled, about 3 minutes. Drain well and set aside.

2. Heat 3 tablespoons butter over medium-high heat until foamy in the now-empty saucepan. Add the mushrooms and sauté until browned, 8 to 10 minutes. Add the tomatoes and hot red pepper flakes (if using), reduce the heat to medium, and simmer until the tomatoes begin to lose their shape, about 7 minutes. Add the cream and simmer until slightly thickened, about 4 minutes; cover to keep warm and set aside.

3. Add 1 tablespoon salt and the pasta to the boiling water in the stockpot and cook until the pasta is al dente. While the pasta is cooking, heat the remaining 3 tablespoons butter in a large skillet over medium heat until foamy. Add the garlic and sauté until fragrant and very lightly colored, about 1 minute. Add the blanched vegetables and cook until heated through and infused with garlic flavor, about 2 minutes. Season to taste with salt; set aside. Meanwhile, bring the mushroom-tomato sauce back to a simmer over medium heat.

4. Drain the pasta and add it back to the now-empty stockpot. Add the mushroom-tomato sauce to the pot with the pasta and toss well to coat over low heat. Add the vegetables, basil, and lemon juice; season to taste with salt and toss well. Divide portions among individual pasta bowls. Serve immediately, passing the Parmesan cheese separately.

➤ VARIATION

Lighter Pasta Primavera

While not as delectably rich as the version above, this primavera, with considerably less saturated fat, is still delicious.

Follow the recipe for Pasta Primavera, replacing 4 tablespoons butter with olive oil, using 2 tablespoons to sauté the mushrooms in step 2 and 2 tablespoons to sauté the garlic in step 3. Substitute canned low-sodium chicken broth for the heavy cream, swirling 2 tablespoons softened butter into the mushroom-tomato sauce before pouring it over the pasta.

BAKED ZITI

WHAT CHURCH SUPPER OR POTLUCK dinner would be complete without baked ziti? The dish sounds simple enough. Take cooked pasta; add tomato sauce, cheese, and maybe some meatballs, sausage, or even eggplant. If this dish is so easy to prepare, then why are most versions so dry, so bland, and so downright unappealing? We knew good baked ziti, an Italian-American classic, was possible. We just had to figure out how to make it.

Mozzarella binds noodles together and makes this baked casserole rich and gooey. We found that fresh mozzarella packed in water makes the texture of the finished dish especially moist and creamy; we recommend it. Besides adding moisture, we found that fresh mozzarella lent this dish far more flavor than bland, rubbery supermarket mozzarella.

Eight ounces of mozzarella was just right for a pound of pasta. More made the dish too heavy and too rich. In fact, we realized that many American recipes for baked ziti simply add too much cheese, sauce, and other goodies. These ingredients overwhelm the noodles and make the casserole too thick, which extends the cooking time and makes the pasta mushy. We were learning that less is more when it comes to baked ziti.

Even good mozzarella is a bit bland. We found that adding ¼ cup of Parmesan perks up the flavor. To ensure that the cheese is evenly distributed throughout the casserole, layer half the pasta into the baking dish, sprinkle with half the cheeses, then add the remaining pasta and cheeses.

The mozzarella is really the binder in baked ziti, but it's the tomato sauce that must keep the dish moist. We found that a smooth sauce made with crushed tomatoes was best. Diced tomatoes tasted good, but tasters did not like the chunks of tomato, which tended to dry out in the oven. Crushed tomatoes coated evenly and thoroughly.

Although it seems obvious, the pasta for these dishes should be slightly undercooked (it softens further in the oven). Too many recipes start with al dente or, worse still, overcooked pasta. By the time the pasta is baked, it's soft and squishy. We also found it helpful to reserve some of the pasta cooking water to help spread the tomato sauce and keep the pasta moist.

We tested a variety of baking dishes and found that a relatively shallow 9 by 13-inch dish was best because it allowed the pasta to heat through quickly. More time in the oven only dries out the noodles or makes them overly soft. With that in mind, we found that a hot 400-degree oven was best. Just 20 minutes in the oven (not the hour called for in many recipes with too much cheese, sauce, and other filling ingredients) yields a casserole with pasta that you still want to eat.

Although the dish needs only cheese and sauce, many recipes throw in the kitchen sink, adding sliced sausage, meatballs, sautéed eggplant, and more. Our tasters rejected these additions. Although they tasted good, most everyone in the kitchen preferred the simpler versions with good fresh mozzarella, tomatoes, garlic, and basil. When loaded down with meatballs and sausage, the baking time increases, which causes the pasta to soften excessively. In the end, this Italian-American dish is best made with restraint.

Baked Ziti with Tomatoes and Mozzarella

SERVES 4 TO 6

In this baked pasta dish, melted mozzarella cheese provides the binding for the pasta and other ingredients. Use fresh mozzarella if possible; it will provide extra creaminess and moisture, which are important in the dish.

2	medium cloves garlic, minced or pressed through a garlic press
3	tablespoons extra-virgin olive oil
I	(28-ounce) can crushed tomatoes
2	tablespoons coarsely chopped fresh basil leaves
	Salt
I	pound ziti or other short tubular pasta
8	ounces mozzarella cheese, shredded
¼	cup grated Parmesan cheese

1. Preheat the oven to 400 degrees. Heat 2 tablespoons oil and the garlic in a medium sauté pan over medium heat until fragrant but not brown, about 2 minutes. Stir in the tomatoes; simmer until thickened slightly, about 10 minutes. Stir in the basil and salt to taste.

2. Meanwhile, bring 4 quarts water to a boil in a large pot. Add 1 tablespoon salt and the pasta. Cook until almost al dente but still a little firm to the bite. Reserve ¼ cup cooking water, drain the pasta, and return it to the pot with the reserved liquid. Stir in the tomato sauce.

3. Brush a 9 by 13-inch baking dish with the remaining tablespoon oil. Pour half the pasta into the dish. Sprinkle with half the mozzarella and half the Parmesan cheese. Pour the remaining pasta into the dish and sprinkle with the remaining mozzarella and Parmesan.

4. Bake until the cheeses turn golden brown, about 20 minutes. Remove the dish from the oven and let rest for 5 minutes before serving.

VEGETABLE LASAGNE

VEGETABLE LASAGNE SOUNDS wonderful, but the reality can be quite disappointing. Too often, the dish is bland and watery, nothing like the rich, hearty version with meat. But Italians certainly make vegetable lasagne, and this dish has great appeal for Americans, especially as lasagne is typically served as an "entertaining dish," and cooks need to satisfy growing numbers of guests who don't eat meat. We knew it was possible to make a great—and quick—vegetable lasagne.

We knew from past experience that precooking the vegetables not only drives off excess liquid but gives the cook a chance to boost their flavor, either by caramelizing their natural sugars or by adding ingredients such as olive oil, garlic, hot red pepper flakes, or herbs. The moisture content of the vegetable determines which cooking technique should be used. For example, high-moisture mushrooms are best sautéed or roasted, but low-moisture broccoli must be blanched, chopped, and sautéed. While it is possible to combine two (or more) vegetables in one lasagne, choose vegetables that can be cooked in the same fashion to keep prep time to a minimum.

It was time to get serious about the noodles. We decided to try using the no-boil noodles that have become so popular in recent years. The first no-boil lasagne noodles appeared on supermarket shelves about a decade ago. We tried them in a favorite lasagne recipe with tomato sauce, tiny meatballs, and mozzarella cheese and were unimpressed. The noodles sucked all the moisture out of the sauce, leaving tiny bits of dried-out tomato pulp behind. Even so, the noodles were way too stiff, almost crunchy in places. The label on one brand suggested pouring stock over the lasagne just before it went into the oven. The result was a watery mess. We thought no-boil noodles would be a passing fad.

Preparing Vegetables for Lasagne

Use the following vegetables, either singly or in combination, in the master recipe. You need a total of 3 cups cooked and seasoned vegetables. Toss the vegetables with enough olive oil to coat them lightly before roasting, or sauté them in a few tablespoons of olive oil. Season the vegetables with salt and pepper as well as fresh herbs, garlic, or hot red pepper flakes, if desired.

VEGETABLE	PREPARATION AND COOKING METHOD
Asparagus	Trim tough ends, slice in half lengthwise, and cut into $1/2$-inch pieces. Blanch until crisp-tender, about 1 minute. Drain well and sauté until tender, about 3 minutes.
Broccoli/Cauliflower	Cut into florets; blanch until crisp-tender, about 2 minutes. Drain well, chop into $1/4$-inch pieces, and sauté until tender, about 4 minutes.
Eggplant	Cut into $1/2$-inch dice; roast until tender, about 35 minutes at 400 degrees.
Fennel	Cut bulb into very thin strips; sauté or roast until tender, about 15 minutes for sautéing or 30 minutes at 400 degrees for roasting.
Mushrooms	Trim and slice or dice; sauté or roast until golden, 8 minutes for sautéing or 20 minutes at 400 degrees for roasting.
Onions	Peel and cut into thin slices; sauté or roast until soft and golden, 5 to 7 minutes for sautéing or 20 minutes at 400 degrees for roasting.
Spinach/Swiss Chard	Wash, stem, and chop; sauté until wilted, about 5 minutes.
Zucchini	Cut into $1/2$-inch dice; sauté or roast until tender, about 7 minutes for sautéing or 35 minutes at 400 degrees for roasting.

Fast-forward several years. No-boil lasagne noodles are now standard items in most supermarkets. We figured someone must be using these noodles successfully—or maybe the noodles themselves (there are now American as well as Italian brands) had improved. So we tried them again.

Some recipes we ran across in our current research suggested soaking the noodles in either cold or hot tap water before layering them with the sauce and cheese. We found that this step made the pasta too soft after baking.

As we had observed several years ago, just layering the noodles and vegetable sauce into the pan and then baking is not acceptable. The sauce dries out, and the noodles are too crispy. In an attempt to keep the sauce from drying out, we wrapped the lasagne pan with foil and then baked it. This step was clearly an improvement. The noodles were tender, not crunchy, and the sauce was not overly reduced.

It also helped to use more sauce than we ordinarily use with boiled noodles. We found

Cooking the spinach and mushrooms in garlicky olive oil adds flavor to this quick vegetable lasagne.

that leaving the tomato sauce fairly watery (we simmered it for just five minutes and then added a little water) was a benefit. The no-boil noodles soaked up some of the excess liquid, and the sauce reduced to the proper consistency.

Covering the lasagne with foil as it bakes does present a couple of problems. First, the foil tends to stick to the top layer of cheese. Spraying the foil with vegetable oil is an easy solution. The other issue is browning the top layer of cheese. When you bake a conventional lasagne uncovered in the oven, the top layer of cheese becomes golden and chewy in spots. We found that by removing the foil during the last 15 minutes of baking, we were able to achieve the color and texture we wanted.

Master Recipe for Vegetable Lasagne with Tomato Sauce

SERVES 6 TO 8

Smoked mozzarella, Gruyère, or fontina can be substituted for the mozzarella and Pecorino Romano for the Parmesan. Also, 3½ cups of your favorite prepared tomato sauce can be substituted for the sauce in this recipe. Because no-boil noodles come 12 to 16 in a box, we suggest buying two boxes to ensure that you'll have the 15 required for this lasagne.

2 tablespoons olive oil
2 medium cloves garlic, minced or pressed through a garlic press
1 (28-ounce) can crushed tomatoes
2 tablespoons chopped fresh basil or fresh parsley leaves
Salt and ground black pepper
15 dried 7 by 3½-inch no-boil lasagne noodles
3 cups cooked and seasoned vegetables (see "Preparing Vegetables for Lasagne," page 180, or the variations that follow)

1   **pound mozzarella cheese, shredded
    (about 4 cups)**
²/₃ **cup grated Parmesan cheese**

1. Heat the oil and garlic in a 10-inch skillet over medium heat until the garlic is fragrant but not browned, about 2 minutes. Stir in the tomatoes; simmer until thickened slightly, about 5 minutes. Stir in the basil or parsley and salt and pepper to taste. Pour into a large measuring cup. Add enough water to make 3½ cups.

2. Spread ½ cup sauce evenly over the bottom of a greased 9 by 13-inch lasagne pan. Lay three noodles crosswise over the sauce, making sure they do not touch each other or the sides of the pan. Spread ¾ cup prepared vegetables evenly over the noodles, ½ cup sauce evenly over the vegetables, and ¾ cup mozzarella and 2 generous tablespoons Parmesan evenly over the sauce. Repeat the layering of the noodles, vegetables, sauce, and cheeses three more times. For the fifth and final layer, lay the final three noodles crosswise over the previous layer and top with the remaining 1 cup tomato sauce, 1 cup mozzarella, and 2 tablespoons Parmesan. (Lasagne can be wrapped with plastic and refrigerated overnight or wrapped in plastic and aluminum foil and frozen for up to 1 month. If frozen, defrost in refrigerator.)

3. Adjust the oven rack to the middle position and heat the oven to 375 degrees. Cover

---

INGREDIENTS: No-Boil Lasagne Noodles

No-boil (also called oven-ready) lasagne noodles use a couple of neat tricks to work in lasagne recipes without precooking. First, the noodles are thinner than conventional dried lasagne noodles. Second, they are rippled. The accordion-like pleats relax as the pasta rehydrates in the oven, allowing the noodles to elongate. Lastly, the noodles are precooked at the factory. The extruded noodles are run through a water bath, then dried. The moisture from the sauce (as long as enough is used) softens the noodles, especially if you trap steam by covering the pan as the lasagne bakes.

Most supermarkets stock American brands, which are long and narrow. Three of these noodles, which measure 7 inches across and 3½ inches wide, make a single layer in a conventional 9 by 13-inch lasagne pan when they swell in the oven. We found two brands, Ronzoni and DeFino. They were equally thin (usually 14 noodles per pound but, inexplicably, sometimes fewer), and both worked well. Ronzoni is made by Hershey Foods, which sells the same product under the American Beauty, Skinner, and San Giorgio labels in other parts of the country.

In terms of texture and flavor, our favorite brand was Delverde from Italy. However, these 7-inch-square noodles are designed to fit into an 8-inch-square pan. (The noodles are sold with two disposable pans.) Most Americans make lasagne for a crowd and will find this size inconvenient. To be used in a 9 by 13-inch pan, these noodles must be soaked in hot water until tender and then cut to fit with scissors. The slight advantage they have in flavor and texture over domestic products is outweighed by their odd size.

DOMESTIC NOODLE   IMPORTED NOODLE

Most domestic no-boil noodles are rectangular, and three noodles will fit crosswise in a standard 9 by 13-inch lasagne pan. Imported no-boil noodles may taste better, but their square shape makes them awkward to use in most American recipes, which are written for larger pans.

the pan with a large sheet of aluminum foil greased with cooking spray. Bake 25 minutes (30 minutes if chilled); remove the foil and continue baking until the top turns golden brown in spots, about 15 minutes. Remove the pan from the oven and let rest 5 minutes. Cut and serve immediately.

➤ VARIATIONS

Roasted Zucchini and Eggplant Lasagne

Adjust the oven racks to the upper- and lower-middle positions and heat the oven to 400 degrees. Toss 1 pound each zucchini (about 2 medium) and eggplant (about 2 small), cut into ½-inch dice, with 3 tablespoons olive oil, 4 minced garlic cloves, and salt and pepper to taste. Spread the vegetables on two greased baking sheets; roast, turning occasionally, until golden brown, about 35 minutes. Set the vegetables aside. Follow the Master Recipe for Vegetable Lasagne with Tomato Sauce, using the roasted zucchini and eggplant for the vegetables.

Spinach and Mushroom Lasagne

Cremini mushrooms are particularly good in this dish, but any fresh mushroom is fine.

Heat 2 tablespoons olive oil over medium heat in a Dutch oven. Add 1 minced medium onion; sauté until translucent, about 5 minutes. Add 1 pound mushrooms, trimmed and sliced; sauté until golden, about 8 minutes. Season with salt and pepper to taste. Remove the mushrooms; set aside. In the same pan, heat 1 tablespoon olive oil over medium heat; add 10 ounces (12 cups) washed, stemmed, and chopped spinach leaves. Cook, stirring often, until the spinach is wilted, about 5 minutes. Season with salt and pepper to taste. Set the vegetables aside. Follow the Master Recipe for Vegetable Lasagne with Tomato Sauce, using the mushrooms and spinach for the vegetables.

FRESH PASTA

SOME SAUCES (ESPECIALLY THOSE WITH cream) require fresh egg pasta. Filled pasta (such as ravioli) starts with homemade pasta. We wanted to develop a foolproof recipe for basic fresh egg pasta. This meant figuring out the proper ratio of eggs to flour as well as the role of salt and olive oil in the dough. Most recipes start with all-purpose flour, but we figured it was worth testing various kinds of flour. Perhaps most important, we wanted to devise a kneading method that was easy.

Before beginning to develop our pasta dough recipe, we wanted to settle on a basic technique. Pasta dough can be made three ways. Traditionally, the dough is made by hand on a clean counter. The flour is formed into a ring, the eggs are cracked into the center, and the flour is slowly worked into the eggs with a fork. When the eggs are no longer runny, hand-kneading begins. The whole process takes at least 20 minutes and requires a lot of hand strength.

Another option is an electric pasta maker that kneads the dough and cuts it into various shapes. Although these machines have some limited appeal, they are quite expensive. We find that a food processor makes pasta dough much more quickly than the old-fashioned hand method. As most cooks already own a food processor, we recommend it for making fresh pasta dough.

Most recipes for fresh egg pasta start with three eggs and then add various amounts of flour. A three-egg dough will produce about one pound of fresh pasta, so this seemed like a good place to start our working recipe. We saw recipes that called for as little as ½ cup of flour per egg. Other recipes called for as much as ¾ cup of flour per egg. After several tests, we settled on ⅔ cup of flour per egg, or 2 cups of all-purpose flour for 3 eggs.

In most tests, this ratio produced perfect

pasta dough without adjustments. However, on a few occasions the dough was a bit dry. This seemed to happen on dry days, but it also could be that slight variations in egg size threw off the ratio. It was easy enough to add a little water to bring the dough together. The dough was almost never too wet, which was a good thing. It's much harder to add flour to a sticky dough than it is to add a little water to a dry, crumbly dough.

Once the dough came together, we found it beneficial to knead it by hand for a minute or two. The motor on our food processor started to labor before the dough was smooth enough. Taking the dough out as soon as it came together prevented our food processor from overheating.

At this point, we had a recipe and a method for making pasta dough that we liked a lot. It seemed time to start testing additional flavorings. We found no benefit from adding salt to the dough. If the pasta is cooked in salted water or stock, it will taste well seasoned. Adding olive oil makes fresh pasta a bit slick, and the olive oil flavor seems out of place in many recipes.

We had been using unbleached all-purpose flour in our tests. We then tested several brands of bleached all-purpose flour and found only minimal differences in the way each flour absorbed the egg. We could not detect any significant differences in flavor. On the other hand, high-protein bread flour and low-protein cake flour had disastrous effects. Bread flour produced a very tough dough that was hard to handle. At the opposite end of the spectrum, pasta made with cake flour was too soft and crumbly. Cake flour also has a sour chemical flavor that is obscured by sugar and butter in cake but comes through loud and clear in pasta.

With our dough made, it was time to test rolling techniques. Many Italian sources tout the superiority of hand-rolled pasta. However,

PASTA DOUGH DONE RIGHT

Pasta dough can be a bit tricky to get just right. Higher-protein flour will absorb the eggs more readily than lower-protein flour, and the resulting dough may be dry. During the summer, flour holds more moisture, so the dough may turn out a bit wet. Here's how to judge the consistency of the pasta dough and make adjustments in the food processor.

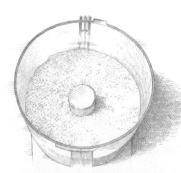

DRY DOUGH

If after 30 seconds of processing the dough resembles small pebbles, it is too dry. With the motor running, add ½ teaspoon water. Repeat one more time if necessary.

WET DOUGH

If the dough sticks to the sides of the workbowl, it is too wet. Add 1 tablespoon flour at a time until the dough is no longer tacky.

PERFECT DOUGH

Dough that has the right amount of moisture will come together in one large mass. If some small bits remain unincorporated, turn the contents of the workbowl onto a floured surface and knead them together.

every time we rolled pasta dough with a pin, it was too thick. Although thick fettuccine is not an abomination, pasta for tortellini, with its doubled edges, must be thin. Perhaps after years of practice we could roll pasta thin enough, but for now we prefer a hand-cranked manual pasta machine. We tested the Imperia and Atlas pasta machines—the two major brands in Italy and widely available in cookware shops in the United States—and found them equally good at turning dough into thin, smooth, satiny sheets of pasta.

Fresh Egg Pasta

MAKES ABOUT 1 POUND

Although the food processor does most of the work, finish kneading this dough by hand. Keep pressing and folding the dough until it is extremely smooth.

2   cups (10 ounces) unbleached
    all-purpose flour
3   large eggs, beaten

1. Pulse the flour in the workbowl of a

ROLLING OUT AND CUTTING PASTA DOUGH

1. Cut about one-sixth of the dough from the ball and flatten it into a disk. (Re-cover remaining dough with plastic.) Run the disk through the rollers set to the widest position.

2. Bring the ends of the dough toward the middle and press down to seal.

3. Feed the open side of the pasta through the rollers. Repeat steps 1 and 2.

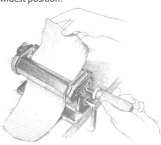

4. Without folding again, run the pasta through the widest setting twice or until the dough is smooth. If the dough is at all sticky, lightly dust it with flour.

5. Roll the pasta thinner by putting it through the machine repeatedly, narrowing the setting each time. Roll until the dough is thin and satiny. You should be able to see the outline of your hand through the pasta. Lay the sheet of pasta on a clean kitchen towel and cover it with a damp cloth to keep it from drying out. Repeat with the other pieces of dough.

6. To make fettuccine, run each sheet through the wide cutter on the pasta machine. Each noodle will measure $\frac{1}{8}$ to $\frac{1}{4}$ inch across.

185

food processor fitted with a steel blade to evenly distribute and aerate it. Add the eggs; process until the dough forms a rough ball, about 30 seconds. (If the dough resembles small pebbles, add water, ½ teaspoon at a time; if the dough sticks to the side of the work-bowl, add flour, 1 tablespoon at a time, and process until the dough forms a rough ball.)

2. Turn out the dough ball and small bits onto a dry work surface; knead until the dough is smooth, 1 to 2 minutes. Cover with plastic wrap and set aside for at least 15 minutes and up to 2 hours to relax.

3. Using a manual pasta machine, roll out the dough (see illustrations 1–5 on page 185). Leave the pasta as is for use in filled pastas. Cut the pasta sheets into long strands to make fettuccine (see illustration 6 on page 185).

PASTA WITH BUTTER AND CHEESE

SAUCES THAT DERIVE MOST OF THEIR flavor from butter and/or cheese are among the simplest in any cook's repertoire. They require minimal work and can usually be prepared in the time it takes to bring four quarts of water to a boil and cook the pasta.

It goes without saying that pasta with butter and cheese is the simplest version of this sauce. We recommend using unsalted butter in this pasta dish (and all your cooking). Salted butter does not have the same fresh dairy flavor as sweet butter. Also, manufacturers add varying amounts of salt, which makes it difficult to judge how much more salt a dish might require. We prefer to add salt directly to a dish, not through the butter.

Many butter and cheese sauces are traditionally served over fresh pasta. To understand the logic behind the recommendation, we tested a simple butter and Parmesan sauce with both fresh and dried pasta. We felt that fresh pasta was far superior to dried pasta. Fresh noodles absorbed some of the butter, which slid off dried noodles. Also, the egg flavor of good fresh pasta melded better with the butter and cheese, making for more complex dishes.

Unless you plan to flavor the butter (with herbs, for instance), there's no reason to melt it. Simply toss the drained pasta and sauce over low heat to give the noodles a chance to absorb the butter and cheese. Softened butter is a must, but otherwise this sauce requires no planning or cooking. As for the ratio of ingredients, our tests found that 6 tablespoons butter and ½ cup grated Parmesan made the best sauce.

Fettuccine with Butter and Parmesan
SERVES 4

One of the simplest and best pasta dishes, this should be made with fresh egg noodles. When we tested this dish with dried pasta, we were quite disappointed. The sauce slid off the dried noodles and pooled in the bottom of each serving bowl. In contrast, the fresh noodles absorbed some sauce (and thus tasted better), and the remaining sauce clung to these noodles much more tenaciously.

	Salt
1	pound Fresh Egg Pasta (page 185), cut into fettuccine
6	tablespoons unsalted butter, softened
½	cup grated Parmesan cheese, plus more for the table

Bring 4 quarts water to a rolling boil in a large pot. Add 1 tablespoon salt and the pasta to the boiling water. Cook just until al dente. Drain the pasta and return it to the cooking pot. Add the butter and Parmesan cheese and cook over low heat, tossing to combine the ingredients, for 1 minute. Adjust the seasonings, adding salt to taste. Serve immediately, passing more cheese at the table.

Fettuccine with Sage Butter

Other fresh, highly aromatic herbs, such as rosemary and thyme, may be used similarly. We found it best to let the herbs steep in the melted butter for 5 minutes, enough time for the butter to be perfumed with—but not overwhelmed by—the flavor of the sage.

Place 5 tablespoons butter and 2 tablespoons minced fresh sage in a sauté pan large enough to accommodate the cooked pasta. Heat over low until the butter is melted. Turn off the heat and set aside for 5 minutes to allow the sage to flavor the butter. Cook pasta as directed in the recipe for Fettuccine with Butter and Parmesan. Drain the pasta and add it to the sauté pan. Add ½ cup grated Parmesan cheese and cook over low heat, tossing to combine the ingredients and flavors, 1 to 2 minutes. Adjust the seasonings and serve immediately, passing more cheese at the table.

PASTA WITH FOUR CHEESES

PASTA QUATTRO FORMAGGI (OR PASTA with four cheeses) is another popular dairy-based sauce that requires almost no cooking. The pasta, typically penne, is tossed with a blend of four Italian cheeses, usually fontina, Gorgonzola, mascarpone, and Parmesan. Most recipes melt the cheese in cream and/or butter to form a thick, super-cheesy sauce.

We had several basic questions about this classic sauce. How much cheese (and in what proportions) would deliver the best results? What's the best way to melt the cheese—in cream, butter, or a mixture of the two?

We started with the issue of cream and butter first. Most recipes melt the cheeses in cream to smooth the consistency of the sauce (alone, melted cheeses are too thick) and to

help blend their flavors. We found recipes that called for as much as 1½ cups of cream and others that called for just ¼ cup. We found that less cream was better. With a cup or more of cream, the sauce was simply too rich. In the end, we found that ½ cup of cream was the right amount for 12 ounces of cheese. A small pat of butter added another layer of flavor and helped the cheeses melt.

Many recipes call for equal amounts of all four cheeses, but our tasters wanted the stronger cheeses (the fontina and Gorgonzola) to take center stage. Therefore, we reduced the amounts of mascarpone and Parmesan to keep the amount of cheese at 12 ounces. (With more than 12 ounces of cheese, the sauce became too rich.)

We wondered if cooking the cheese and cream together would improve their flavor. In fact, just the opposite happened. Simmering the sauce seemed to rob the cheese of flavor. We found it best to heat the cheeses just until they had melted and then remove the pan from the heat to prevent scorching.

Pasta with Four Cheeses
SERVES 4

This rich dish—called pasta quattro formaggi, *or pasta with four cheeses—showcases the cheeses of Italy: buttery fontina, piquant Gorgonzola, creamy mascarpone, and nutty Parmesan. The cream and small pat of butter help smooth the consistency of the sauce and keep the cheeses from sticking to the pan as they melt. This dish can also be served in smaller portions as a first course.*

	Salt
1	pound penne or other short tubular pasta
1	tablespoon unsalted butter
½	cup heavy cream
1	cup shredded Italian fontina cheese (about 4 ounces)

1   cup crumbled Gorgonzola cheese (about
     4 ounces)
½   cup mascarpone cheese (about
     2 ounces)
½   cup grated Parmesan cheese (about
     2 ounces)
     Ground black pepper

1. Bring 4 quarts water to a rolling boil in a large pot. Add 1 tablespoon salt and the pasta. Cook until al dente.

2. Meanwhile, heat the butter and cream in a small saucepan over low heat. Add the cheeses and stir until melted and well combined, 2 to 3 minutes. Remove the pan from the heat and cover to keep warm.

3. Drain the pasta and return it to the cooking pot. Stir in the cheese sauce. Season with salt and pepper to taste. Serve immediately.

FETTUCCINE ALFREDO

THE MOST FAMOUS CREAM SAUCE FOR pasta is commonly called *Alfredo*. This rich sauce of cream, butter, and Parmesan cheese is named for a restaurant in Rome that popularized the dish at the 1939 World's Fair in New York.

When fettuccine Alfredo is good, it is worth every calorie, but the sauce is often thick and gloppy; at other times, it is too runny and just sits at the bottom of the bowl. We wanted to develop a foolproof sauce that was thick enough to coat pasta from end to end without becoming dry or gloppy.

We had a number of questions about alfredo. First of all, what is the right ratio of ingredients? Does the type of cream matter? Should the cream be reduced? Must this sauce be used with fresh pasta only?

We started out with a composite recipe

and decided to test cooking methods first. Some sources suggest reducing the cream to thicken its texture. Others merely heat the cream. Some just pour room-temperature cream over drained pasta. We found problems with all three methods.

If all the cream is reduced, the sauce becomes too thick and does not easily coat the noodles. However, if the cream is just warmed, it remains too liquidy and pools around the pasta. We decided to test reducing part of the cream to give the sauce enough body to cling to the pasta, then adding the remaining cream to the sauce along with the cooked pasta. This worked beautifully. After several tests, we settled on a total of 1⅔ cups cream for one pound of pasta and bringing most of the cream (1⅓ cups) to a simmer to reduce it slightly. Once the cream comes to a bare simmer, remove the pan from the heat to prevent the cream from cooking down too much.

In the spirit of trying weird suggestions, we experimented with a few recipes that called for whipping the cream lightly instead of reducing it to give it body. As might be expected, this did not work. The sauce was fluffy and odd on pasta. Save whipped cream for dessert.

Because the butter must be melted for this sauce, we decided to add it directly to the cream. We tested as little as two tablespoons and as much as two sticks. Five tablespoons was just right, providing the right amount of lubrication to the pasta and a good, buttery flavor. To round out the sauce, we settled on a cup of grated Parmesan cheese and some salt, pepper, and nutmeg.

We tested our working recipe with ultra-pasteurized and pasteurized cream. Ultra-pasteurized cream is the standard in most markets. It is subjected to high temperatures during pasteurization to promote longer shelf life. This process gives the cream a slightly cooked flavor, which we could taste in a blind test against a sauce made with pasteurized cream.

Pasteurized cream is heated during processing to a temperature that kills bacteria but doesn't prolong shelf life. In our tests, it had a fresher, sweeter cream flavor. We think it is worth searching out this product when making cream sauces. (It also makes great whipped cream.) Many organic creams are pasteurized, so check out the organic dairy section in your supermarket or visit a natural foods store.

Until this point, we had been using our own homemade fettuccine in tests. We decided to test store-bought fresh fettuccine as well as dried fettuccine with our alfredo sauce.

Dried fettuccine was a disappointment. When cooked, dried pasta is much less porous than fresh, and the cream sauce did not adhere well to the noodles. When we finished eating, there still was sauce in the bottom of the bowls.

The package of mass-market fresh fettuccine from the supermarket refrigerator case cooked up a bit gummy (a common problem with these products) and did not have much flavor. This pasta would do in a pinch, but it was a far cry from homemade. On the other hand, store-bought fettuccine that had been freshly made at a local gourmet shop was quite good, holding on to every drop of sauce and adding a nice egg flavor to the dish.

Some sources suggest cooking the fresh pasta a little firmer than usual and then finishing the cooking process right in the cream sauce. We tested this method against pasta that was fully cooked and sauced and much preferred it. The sauce really penetrates the noodles, and the combination of creamy sauce and fresh egg pasta is unbeatable.

Some final observations. The dish may look a bit soupy as you divide it among individual serving bowls. However, the pasta will continue to absorb sauce as it sits in the bowls. In fact, pasta that looks perfect going into bowls will be too dry by the time you start eating. Lukewarm cream sauces are not appetizing, so heating the pasta bowls is a must. Lastly, fettuccine alfredo is quite rich. We prefer to serve it in small portions as an appetizer. A few bites more than satisfy any longing for creamy richness.

Finally, this basic sauce lends itself to numerous variations. We tested several possibilities, and tasters responded most favorably to lemon, Gorgonzola, and prosciutto (separately, not together). We developed variations for each of these ingredients.

Fettuccine Alfredo

SERVES 6 AS AN APPETIZER

Do not cook the sauce over too high a flame or for too long, or it will be gluey instead of creamy. Fresh egg pasta is a must here; dried pasta can't stand up to the richness of the Alfredo ingredients. You can substitute one pound of high-quality purchased fresh fettuccine for our homemade pasta. Make sure to cook your pasta extra-firm, as it will cook further (and absorb some of the butter and cream) when added to the sauce.

1⅔ cups heavy cream, preferably not ultrapasteurized

5 tablespoons unsalted butter
  Salt

1 pound Fresh Egg Pasta (page 185), cut into fettuccine

1 cup freshly grated Parmesan cheese
  Ground black pepper
  Pinch ground nutmeg

1. Bring 4 quarts water to a rolling boil in a large pot.

2. Combine 1⅓ cups cream and the butter in a sauté pan large enough to accommodate the cooked pasta. Heat over low until the butter is melted and the cream comes to a bare simmer. Turn off the heat and set aside.

3. When the water comes to a boil, add 1 tablespoon salt and the pasta. Cook until almost al dente. Drain the pasta and add it to the sauté pan. Add the remaining ⅓ cup cream, the Parmesan cheese, ½ teaspoon salt, pepper to taste, and the nutmeg. Cook over very low heat, tossing to combine ingredients, until the sauce is slightly thickened, 1 to 2 minutes. Serve immediately.

> VARIATIONS

Fettuccine with Lemon and Cream

Follow the recipe for Fettuccine Alfredo, heating ¼ cup lemon juice with the cream and butter in step 2 and tossing 2 teaspoons grated lemon zest with the pasta and sauce in step 3.

Fettuccine with Gorgonzola and Cream

Sweet Gorgonzola, sometimes labeled Gorgonzola dolce, is milder than the harder, drier aged Gorgonzola and makes for a slightly piquant but still creamy variation on alfredo sauce. It is available at cheese shops, Italian delis, and many supermarkets.

Follow the recipe for Fettuccine Alfredo, stirring 4 ounces crumbled sweet Gorgonzola cheese into the heated cream and butter mixture in step 2.

Fettuccine with Prosciutto and Cream

For this recipe, we like prosciutto cut in ¼-inch-thick slices and then diced; prosciutto sliced paper-thin seems to disappear into the sauce and noodles.

Follow the recipe for Fettuccine Alfredo, cooking ¼ pound prosciutto, cut into ¼-inch dice, in the 5 tablespoons butter just until softened, about 2 minutes. Add the cream and bring to a bare simmer. Proceed as directed.

RAVIOLI

RAVIOLI, AS ALL FILLED PASTAS, ARE among the rare treats that the home cook is best equipped to execute properly. Commercial ravioli are tough and doughy, not supple and tender like homemade versions. Ravioli made by hand at a gourmet pasta shop or Italian market can be every bit as good as those made at home but, in our experience, you are well advised to walk past packages of ravioli in the supermarket refrigerator case.

Of course, making filled pasta strikes fear into many home cooks, who expect the job to be impossibly difficult and time-consuming. After making countless batches of ravioli, we must admit that these fears are at least partially true. Ravioli need not be difficult to prepare, but they are time-consuming. Each piece must be shaped by hand, and that takes time.

We don't make this statement lightly. We're certainly not purists and were more than willing to try the various ravioli-making gadgets sold in any well-stocked kitchen shop. Sadly, we must report that the gimmicks we tried for making quick ravioli don't really work.

We began with the attachments that can be fitted onto a manual pasta machine to turn out ravioli. It looks so easy. Take two sheets of pasta, some filling, and turn out hundreds of ravioli in minutes. Unfortunately, we had problems with the pasta sticking together and can't recommend these attachments. We threw away at least half the ravioli we made because they were misshapen or broken. Such waste just isn't acceptable.

Likewise, we were disappointed with the metal molds sometimes used by pasta shops. They seemed more trouble than they are worth, as the pasta sheets must be cut precisely to fit in the molds. The other choice is to waste a lot of fresh pasta but, given the amount of time and effort it takes to make the pasta, that doesn't make much sense. In the end, we found that cutting and shaping the pasta dough by hand is the most straightforward and foolproof way to make ravioli pasta.

Because ravioli have doubled edges where the pasta is folded over the filling and sealed together, we found that the pasta sheets must be rolled as thin as possible. Otherwise, the edges may remain too chewy when the rest of the pasta shape is already cooked through. Use the last setting on a manual pasta machine for the best results.

The biggest problem most home cooks encounter when making ravioli is that the pastas sometimes open up when they are boiled. There's nothing worse than seeing all the filling floating around the pot, so it's imperative to seal the edges of each piece of filled pasta properly. We tried brushing the edges of the dough with water and with lightly beaten egg. We found that both made the dough sticky and harder to handle. We had the best results when we used the pasta sheet as quickly as possible, when it was still moist and pliable. Pasta sheets that have been left out to dry (even for just 20 to 30 minutes) will be too brittle to manipulate. If your dough has become dry, brushing the edges lightly with water is best. (Eggs just make a sticky mess.) Just be careful to brush the edges lightly, or the dough will become very tacky.

To guarantee that the pasta does not dry out, we recommend that you roll one sheet of dough at a time, then fill and shape it. Once the first batch of ravioli is made, start over again with another piece of pasta dough, running it through the pasta machine and then cutting and filling it as directed.

Don't overload the pasta with filling, which might cause the pasta shape to burst in the boiling water. A rounded teaspoon of filling is more than enough for a medium ravioli. As an added precaution, cook the pasta in water that is at a low boil. Highly agitated water may actually rip open delicate pasta shapes.

To prevent the ravioli from sticking together in the pot, we found it necessary to cook the pasta in two batches. While the second batch is in the pot, you can sauce the first batch and bring it to the table. Warmed pasta bowls will keep the pasta hot while you finish cooking the remaining pasta. If you prefer, bring two pots of water to a boil and divide the pasta between the two pots to cook it all at one time.

Given the work involved, we wanted to be able to shape the ravioli in advance and then cook them as desired. (You don't want to be shaping ravioli while dinner guests wait.) We found it best to transfer shaped ravioli to a lightly floured baking sheet. (The flour helps prevent sticking.) If you are not going to cook the pasta right away, put the baking sheets in the refrigerator for up to two hours. After two hours, we found, the pasta dried out.

For longer storage, we discovered that the freezer is the best place for ravioli. Place the floured baking sheets with ravioli in the freezer until the pasta shapes are frozen solid, about two hours. Transfer the frozen pastas to a large zipper-lock plastic bag and freeze them for up to a month. Don't defrost frozen pasta; simply drop it into boiling water and add a minute or two to the cooking time.

Most any finely chopped or ground meat, seafood, poultry, or vegetable can be turned into a filling for ravioli, but there are a couple of guidelines. Most fillings have cheese to add flavor and a creamy texture. Fillings also contain egg yolk, which helps bind the ingredients. When we tested fillings without egg yolk, they tended to be runny and thin. We found it best to add just the yolk, which has most of the egg's thickening powers, and omit the watery white.

A liquidy filling will become even runnier when the pasta is cooked, so juices from vegetables should be cooked off, and some very loose ingredients, such as tomatoes, are best not included in fillings. For these reasons, we

INGREDIENTS: Egg Pasta

In recent years, the selection of pasta shapes, types, and sizes readily available to the American cook has become mind-boggling. One of the more beguiling options is the so-called fresh pasta found in the refrigerator cases of many supermarkets these days. With the growing enthusiasm among consumers for fresh, natural foods, these packages may cause shoppers to pause and take a second look. But the price of such products, usually about twice that of dried pasta, can provide enough impetus to push the shopping cart on.

We wanted to know when it is more appropriate or advantageous to cook with fresh egg pasta. Also, in such instances, just how much work do you have to put into it? While you cannot get any fresher than homemade—which is surprisingly simple—few home cooks are willing to make pasta from scratch. The alternatives include shopping at a market that makes pasta fresh on site or purchasing the "fresh" packaged pasta at the supermarket. You can also forgo the fresh approach and purchase dried egg pasta, which is manufactured under numerous brand names and sold in supermarkets and specialty stores. Which option, we wondered, is the best?

Typically, dried pasta is made with semolina flour and water. Made from a hard wheat called durum, semolina flour is high in protein, which makes it perfect for creating an elastic dough and springy, resilient noodles. This pasta is dried under specific humidity and temperature controls so that it is shelf-stable for up to or beyond one year. Like dried pasta, homemade fresh pasta is made of just two ingredients. Instead of semolina, however, it is made with softer all-purpose flour and is bound with egg instead of water. As a result, fresh pasta is more delicate than its resilient dried counterpart, with a texture that is not mushy but certainly soft. Fresh homemade egg pasta is rarely dried and is typically used within a couple of hours of being made.

The differences in resilience and texture between fresh egg pasta and dried semolina pasta translate into differences in the ways they are meant to be served. Fresh egg pasta is supposed to be porous as well as delicate so as to absorb the accompanying sauce. For this reason, it is meant to be paired with a butter- or cream-based sauce, such as the famous alfredo sauce. Dried semolina pasta is not absorbent, which makes it better suited to tomato- or oil-based sauces; each dried pasta shape is better suited to a different consistency of sauce.

There is also a third option for those who want the flavor and softer texture of egg pasta: dried egg pasta. Made with ingredients similar to fresh pasta, this product might, we thought, be a more convenient way to benefit from the advantages of its fresh cousin.

For our blind tasting, we purchased samples of fresh and dried egg pastas cut in the form of fettuccine. We also made our own homemade fettuccine with whole eggs and flour.

As expected, the homemade pasta in our tasting stood out for its soft, delicate chew and clean flavor. It was the absolute favorite. Also relatively agreeable to our panel of tasters, which included magazine staff and several local chefs, were a couple of brands of fresh refrigerator pasta and a common supermarket brand of dried egg pasta. Tasters gave decent marks to refrigerated fresh fettuccine made by Contadina Buitoni (which is available nationwide) as well as Monterey Pasta Company (available mostly in California). They also liked Ronzoni dried egg fettuccine, which is available nationwide.

In the process of doing this tasting, though, we found that fresh is a relative term. Unlike homemade fresh pasta, with its two ingredients, the "fresh" refrigerator egg pasta found in supermarkets, as well as the dried egg pasta, are hybrids, made with the semolina flour and water ordinarily used for dried pasta, but with eggs added in. The higher-protein semolina flour, which can absorb more liquid than all-purpose flour, automatically compromises the delicacy of the noodles' consistency. That is not to say, however, that they had the chew of eggless dried pasta; they simply could not compare with the delicacy of homemade. Also, the addition of water to these pastas (and the fact that some contain egg whites rather than whole eggs) seemed to dilute the fresh egg flavor usually associated with homemade pasta. This was particularly true with the dried egg pasta. One that we tasted was a surprising disappointment because it was inferior in taste and texture to the semolina pasta made by the same company, which is a favorite of many of our tasters.

Perhaps our biggest quibble with fresh refrigerator pasta, though, is that it is not really fresh at all. Unless your supermarket has a high rate of turnover, you may be buying a product that has been sitting on the shelf for weeks.

Fresh pastas are extremely perishable because they are high in moisture, which provides an ideal breeding ground for bacteria. Naturally occurring enzymes also exist that will, over time, discolor the pasta as well as modify its fats. These changes in the fats produce off flavors, according to Jim Jacobs, technical director at Northern Crops Institute, a learning center in Fargo, N.D., devoted to the study of the use of wheats, including durum, in food products. Consequently, the majority of fresh pasta products sold in supermarkets are both pasteurized and sealed in something called modified atmosphere packaging so as to extend their shelf life. This packaging method involves extracting air from inside the package and substituting it with another gas, typically a mix of carbon dioxide and nitrogen. This inhibits the growth of bacteria and helps extend the pasta's shelf life by 25 to 120 days, depending on the product as well as the specific technology used. Consequently, there is really no way of knowing the age of the pasta you buy.

Even though a fresh refrigerated pasta product can be safe to eat for as many as four months after its manufacture, this does not mean that time does not take its toll. So if you are not absolutely sure of the relative freshness of the supermarket product you are buying, it is possible that the pasta will have sat long enough for its texture to degrade from somewhat tender and soft to mushy.

One last point, regarding the price. The packaging size of fresh refrigerator pastas is curiously awkward. Most packages are just 9 ounces. Because most recipes call for either 12 or 16 ounces of fresh pasta, you end up buying two packages and spending nearly $6. Besides the expense, you inevitably have a few ounces left over. A 1-pound package of dried pasta serves four to six for about $1. If money is really a concern, set aside a few hours on a Saturday afternoon to make your own homemade noodles (the actual hands-on time is less than an hour) and serve your guests genuinely fresh pasta for pennies.

THE BEST EGG PASTAS

Homemade pasta (far left) was the clear favorite, with springy yet resilient texture and pure flavor. Contadina Buitoni (second from left) is a decent second choice with good chew but little egg flavor. Monterey Pasta Co. (second from right) is found mostly in supermarkets in California. It is a bit thicker than the others and tastes more like wheat than eggs. Ronzoni dried pasta (right) is made with eggs and has a clean, almost sweet flavor. The noodles are thicker and heartier than homemade.

think a plain cheese and herb filling, or one made with ground meat, is the easiest to work with. We decided to offer both choices.

We find that simple sauces are best with filled pastas. You don't want to overwhelm the filling, which you have worked hard to make and should be the focal point for your taste buds. Ravioli is delicious with melted butter and a sprinkling of grated Parmesan cheese. When you want to sauce the pasta a bit more elaborately, a fairly smooth tomato sauce that will stick to the pasta (not slide off) is best. Tasters liked a tomato sauce made with butter; the butter flavor complemented the fresh egg pasta. Minced carrot and onion give this sauce a sweetness that contrasts nicely with both the cheese and the meat filling.

Ravioli

SERVES 4 TO 6 AS A MAIN COURSE
OR 8 AS A FIRST COURSE

This recipe produces 2-inch-square ravioli with three cut edges and one folded edge. The folded edge may be trimmed with a fluted pastry wheel, if you like. For a smooth, more refined sauce, puree the mixture in a food processor or blender, return the pureed sauce to the pan, and stir in ½ cup heavy cream, and cook, stirring constantly, until the sauce thickens, about 2 minutes.

RAVIOLI

1	pound Fresh Egg Pasta (page 185)
2½	cups Parsley and Ricotta Filling or Meat and Ricotta Filling (recipes follow)

SIMPLE TOMATO SAUCE

3	tablespoons unsalted butter
1	small onion, minced
1	medium carrot, peeled and minced
1	(28-ounce) can diced tomatoes with their juice
	Salt

2	tablespoons minced fresh basil or fresh parsley leaves
	Freshly grated Parmesan cheese

1. FOR THE RAVIOLI: Follow the illustrations on page 195 to form and fill the ravioli.

2. FOR THE SAUCE: Melt the butter in a medium saucepan. Add the onion and carrot; cook over medium heat until the vegetables soften but are not browned, about 10 minutes. Stir in the tomatoes and ½ teaspoon salt; simmer until thickened slightly, about 10 minutes. Stir in the basil and adjust the seasonings.

3. TO COOK AND SAUCE THE PASTA: Bring 4 quarts water to a boil in a large pot. Add 1 tablespoon salt and half the pasta. Cook, lowering the heat if necessary to keep the water at a gentle boil, until the doubled edges are al dente, 4 to 5 minutes. With a slotted spoon, transfer the ravioli to warmed bowls or plates; add some sauce. Meanwhile, put the remaining ravioli in the boiling water and repeat the cooking and saucing process. Serve immediately, passing the Parmesan cheese separately.

Parsley and Ricotta Filling

MAKES ABOUT 2½ CUPS

This is the simplest pasta filling, as it requires no cooking. Other fresh herbs—try basil or mint—can be substituted.

1	cup ricotta cheese
¾	cup grated Parmesan cheese
1	large egg yolk
½	cup minced fresh parsley leaves
½	teaspoon salt
	Ground black pepper

Combine the ricotta, Parmesan cheese, egg, parsley, salt, and pepper to taste in a medium bowl. (The filling can be covered and refrigerated overnight.)

Meat and Ricotta Filling

MAKES ABOUT 2 ½ CUPS

This filling is delicious with ground beef, veal, and/or pork. Use any combination of these meats.

1	tablespoon extra-virgin olive oil
2	medium garlic cloves, minced
½	pound ground meat (see note)
1	cup ricotta cheese
¼	cup grated Parmesan cheese
1	large egg yolk

¼	cup minced fresh basil leaves
½	teaspoon salt
	Ground black pepper

1. Heat the oil in a medium skillet. Add the garlic and sauté until lightly colored, about 1 minute. Add the meat; cook over medium-high heat, stirring to break up larger pieces, until the liquid evaporates and the meat browns, 3 to 4 minutes. Drain off the fat; transfer the meat mixture to a medium bowl. Cool the meat slightly.

2. Stir in the remaining ingredients, including pepper to taste. (The filling can be covered and refrigerated overnight.)

MAKING RAVIOLI

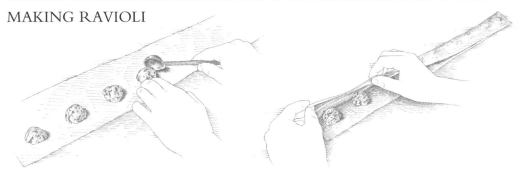

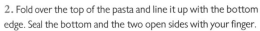

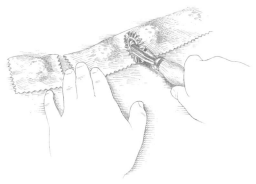

1. Use a pizza wheel or sharp knife to cut pasta sheets into long rectangles measuring 4 inches across. Place small balls of filling (about 1 rounded teaspoon each) in a line 1 inch from the bottom of the pasta sheet. Leave 1 ¼ inches between each ball of filling.

2. Fold over the top of the pasta and line it up with the bottom edge. Seal the bottom and the two open sides with your finger.

3. Use a fluted pastry wheel to cut along the two sides and bottom of the sealed pasta sheet.

4. Run the pastry wheel between the balls of filling to cut the ravioli.

Gnocchi

GNOCCHI, IN ONE FORM OR ANOTHER, have been eaten since Roman times. At one time, the most basic recipe for this Italian dumpling called for just flour and water; the result was, in effect, soft pieces of boiled dough. Other versions, which are still made today, use ricotta cheese and spinach or a mixture of semolina, milk, butter, eggs, and Parmesan cheese. However, potato gnocchi began to gain wide culinary acceptance in the 18th century and have since become the dominant kind of Italian dumpling. While many potato dumplings, especially those from Germany and other Central European regions, are heavy, stick-to-your-ribs fare, gnocchi should be light, airy, and fluffy.

Our mission was simple: to figure out what makes potato dumplings heavy and then develop a recipe that avoids these pitfalls. After conducting 36 tests, we concluded that the real culprit behind leaden gnocchi is the flour, not the potatoes. While it is important to use the right kind of potato (see "Which Potato Is Best?" on page 200), even the right potato will make terrible gnocchi if too much flour is added. The trick is prepare the potatoes so they require the least possible amount of flour to form a coherent dough.

Before we started our kitchen work, we gathered about 75 gnocchi recipes and analyzed them for ingredients and cooking methods. The majority called for boiling the potatoes with their skins on, peeling and mashing them, and then combining them with flour and salt. A smaller number advocated peeling the potatoes before boiling, or steaming them either with or without skins. We also ran across a few recipes that suggested baking potatoes in their skins. After working with four kinds of potatoes (reds, Yukon Golds, Idaho baking, and russets), we concluded that all potatoes respond best to baking.

Boiled peeled potatoes made the worst gnocchi in our tests, followed by boiled unpeeled potatoes. Steamed potatoes (either with or without skin) made less doughy gnocchi, but they were no match for gnocchi formed from baked potatoes. We attributed these results to the presence or absence of moisture during cooking. Boiling and steaming are wet cooking methods that theoretically leave potatoes quite moist. Baking in a hot oven, however, dries the potatoes. This theory was supported by our observation that dry baked potatoes needed far less flour to form a coherent dough.

To see if our hunch was correct, we weighed several kinds of potatoes before and after cooking. Boiling and steaming had a negligible effect; boiling increased weight by about 0.5 percent, while steaming decreased weight by about 2 percent. However, baked potatoes shed between 15 and 20 percent of their weight, depending on the variety, after 50 minutes in the oven. This weight loss was caused by the evaporation of water. As an added benefit, gnocchi made with baked potatoes have a stronger potato flavor. The release of water during cooking not only makes the potatoes drier but concentrates the flavor so much that we could pick out gnocchi made with baked potatoes by taste alone.

After settling on baking, we experimented with a number of methods for peeling and mashing potatoes. While it would be more convenient to peel cool potatoes, we found that the skin, which lifts and separates from the flesh during baking, reattaches fairly quickly. It is possible to peel cooled potatoes, but you lose more flesh than if you peel potatoes as soon as they come out of the oven. To prevent scorching your hand, wear an oven mitt and hold the hot potato in your protected hand. A swivel vegetable peeler can be used to lift the skin, while fingers are best equipped to carefully peel and remove it.

Once the potatoes are peeled, they must be mashed. It became quickly clear that lumps caused the gnocchi to come apart when cooked and had to be avoided at all costs. The shredding disk on the food processor, a hand-held masher, and a fork all left lumps; the food processor also made the potatoes slightly gummy. We found that a $9 ricer was the best tool for mashing potatoes without lumps. This device gets its name from the tiny rice-shaped pieces it produces. Simply place peeled potatoes in the round compartment fitted with the fine disk. Press down on the clamp, and perfectly

riced potatoes are extruded through the disk.

The next step is to add the salt and flour to make the dough. Again, working from the premise that less flour makes better gnocchi, we found it helpful to allow the steam from the riced potatoes to dissipate. By adding flour to room-temperature or only slightly warm potatoes, we could prevent the gumminess that sometimes resulted when flour was sprinkled over steaming hot potatoes.

Kneading is the enemy of light gnocchi. When we combined the potatoes and flour in a standing mixer, the dough was incredibly tacky, and the gnocchi cooked up like little

MAKING POTATO GNOCCHI

1. Break off a portion of the dough and roll it into a rough rope. Glide your hands over the dough to thin the rope evenly to about ³/₄-inch thick.

2. If the rope won't hold together when it's rolled, there is not enough flour in the dough. Return the rope to the bowl with the remaining dough and work in more flour as needed.

3. Use a sharp knife to cut the dough rope into ³/₄-inch lengths.

4. Hold a wooden butter paddle in one hand and press each piece of dough against its ridged surface with your finger to make an indentation in the center. Roll the dough down and off the ridges and let it drop to the work surface.

5. If you would rather use a fork. hold the fork so that the tines are parallel to the work surface. Place the gnocchi under the tines of the fork. Flip the gnocchi off the ends of the fork to imprint the ridges, applying some pressure as you do this in order to make a shallow indentation in the center.

Superballs that bounced right off the plate. Working the dough by hand until it just comes together is the easiest and safest way to combine the flour and potatoes.

As a side note, we felt compelled to try potato gnocchi made with an egg, a common addition to northern European dumplings and a trick espoused by some Italian cookbook authors to bind the dough more tightly. (Several usually reliable sources argued that eggs were anathema to light gnocchi, so we had doubts from the start.) After trying whole eggs, whites, and yolks, we concluded that while eggs make firmer gnocchi, the dumplings are also gummier and heavier. We also felt that the egg overwhelmed the delicate potato flavor.

Throughout most of our testing, we concentrated on adding as little flour as possible to the potatoes. However, when we began to roll and shape the gnocchi, we realized it was possible to add too little flour. The potatoes need enough flour to make a dough that is not sticky and that will roll easily. If the dough comes apart (see illustration 2 on page 197), add more flour.

There also were times when we added enough flour, just barely, to bind the dough and allow it to be rolled and shaped. While the dough looked fine, the gnocchi cooked up a bit soft and mushy. We realized we were taking our obsession with flour too far and that our gnocchi would have been more resilient if we had added a few more tablespoons of flour after the dough seemed to first come together.

Because the moisture level of each potato varies according to how long it has been out of the ground and with the variety, it is impossible to write a recipe with an exact ratio of potatoes to flour. We found that two pounds of baked potatoes could require as little as 1¼ cups of flour and as much as 1½ cups. As a general rule, we worked 1¼ cups of

flour into the riced potatoes. In most cases, the dough seemed to be just barely bound, so we added another two tablespoons of flour as a kind of insurance policy. First-time gnocchi cooks may also want to boil a few quickly shaped gnocchi to evaluate their texture before shaping and rolling out dozens.

With the dough made, it was time to focus on forming the gnocchi. A fair amount of mystique surrounds the cutting and shaping of gnocchi. Traditionally, the dough is rolled into long ropes that are cut into small pieces and then imprinted with ridges as the center is gently indented. The final result looks like a slept-on pillow on one side and has several thin grooves on the other.

Rolling the dough into long ropes (we found a thickness of ¾ inch ideal) and then slicing them into individual gnocchi seems unavoidable. In any case, the process is fairly quick. However, we wondered if the final shaping process—which can become tedious when 100 gnocchi are involved—was necessary. The answer is yes.

We cooked traditionally formed gnocchi and compared them to gnocchi that were simply cut from the dough ropes and then dropped into the boiling water. The indentation in the center of the gnocchi has two purposes. First, it decreases the width of the gnocchi in the middle and allows the center to cook through more evenly. Gnocchi without this indentation often were a bit underdone in the center. Second, the indentation traps sauce on the otherwise smooth surface. As for the grooves, traditionally formed gnocchi did a better job of holding onto the sauce in our tests than did gnocchi without creases or crevices.

Although we judged the traditional shape essential, we wanted to see if we could improve on the process. Most sources use the tines of the fork to imprint ridges. We found that simply pressing the fork against the cut gnocchi, much like you press a fork against peanut butter cookie dough, squashes them and is not advised. Holding the tines of a fork parallel to a work surface and flipping little balls of dough off the tines imprints ridges and gives gnocchi their characteristic indentations if pressure is applied to the dough as it is flipped. The problem is that the dough tends to stick to the metal fork.

After looking around the kitchen for a better solution, we noticed the ridges on a wooden mallet and wooden butter paddle. When we rolled/flipped gnocchi off these surfaces, we were pleasantly surprised. Not only was it easier because the surfaces we were working against were so much bigger but also the gnocchi did not stick. The bigger surfaces also meant the entire length of the gnocchi was covered by thin grooves, as opposed to fork-rolled gnocchi, which had only a few crevices. More grooves translates into a more attractive appearance and better sauce retention.

Potato Gnocchi with Butter, Sage, and Parmesan Cheese

SERVES 4 TO 6 AS A MAIN COURSE
OR 8 AS FIRST COURSE

To ensure that gnocchi are the right texture, bring a small saucepan of water to simmer while mixing the dough. Roll a small piece of the dough into the rope shape. Cut off a small piece or two from the rope, shape into gnocchi, then drop into the simmering water. If the gnocchi are too mushy, put the dough rope back into the potato mixture and add in another tablespoon or two of flour. It's better to take the time to test one or two gnocchi than to ruin the whole batch. Also, be careful not to overwork or overknead the dough; you simply want to incorporate the flour into the potatoes. Avoid

cooking the gnocchi at a rolling boil, as violently churning water makes it difficult to determine when the gnocchi are floating. Even gently boiling gnocchi may bob temporarily to the surface, but don't lift them out until they float. This recipe makes about 100 gnocchi.

We like the simplicity of the sage butter sauce (you can really taste the potatoes), but gnocchi can also work well with tomato sauce (use about 2 cups of any smooth sauce) or pesto (¾ cup is enough to sauce 100 gnocchi).

GNOCCHI
2 pounds russet or baking potatoes, washed
1¼ cups unbleached all-purpose flour, plus more as needed
Salt

SAGE BUTTER SAUCE
6 tablespoons unsalted butter
12 fresh sage leaves, cut into thin strips
½ cup grated Parmesan cheese, plus extra for passing at the table

1. FOR THE GNOCCHI: Heat the oven to 400 degrees. Bake the potatoes until a metal skewer slides easily through them, 45 minutes to 1 hour, depending on size.

2. Hold a potato with a potholder or kitchen towel and peel it with a vegetable peeler or paring knife; rice the peeled potato into a large bowl. Peel and rice the remaining potatoes. Cool until the potatoes are no longer hot, about 15 minutes.

3. Sprinkle 1¼ cups flour and 1 teaspoon salt over the warm potatoes. Using your hands, work the mixture into a soft, smooth dough. If the dough is sticky (which is often the case), add more flour as needed, up to 1½ cups total.

4. Roll about one-quarter of the dough into a long ¾-inch-thick rope (see illustration 1 on page 197). If the rope won't hold together

(see illustration 2 on page 197), return it to the bowl with the remaining dough and work in more flour as needed. Repeat until all the dough is rolled.

5. Cut each rope of dough into ¾-inch lengths (see illustration 3 on page 197). Holding a butter paddle or fork in one hand, press each piece of cut dough against the ridged surface with your index finger to make an indentation in the center. Roll the dough down and off the ridges and allow it to drop to the work surface (see illustrations 4 and 5 on page 197). (Gnocchi can be placed in a single layer on a baking sheet and refrigerated for several hours. Alternatively, the baking sheet can be placed in the freezer for about 1 hour. Partially frozen gnocchi can be transferred to a plastic bag or container, sealed, and frozen for up to 1 month.)

6. FOR THE SAUCE: Melt the butter in a small skillet. When the butter foams, add the sage. Remove the pan from the heat and set aside. Cover to keep warm.

7. TO COOK AND SAUCE THE GNOCCHI: Bring 4 quarts water to a low boil in a large pot. Add 2 teaspoons salt or to taste. Add about one-third of the gnocchi and cook until they float, 1½ to 2 minutes (about 3 minutes for frozen gnocchi). Retrieve the gnocchi with a slotted spoon and transfer to a warm, shallow serving bowl or platter. Spoon about one-third of the butter sauce and one-third of the Parmesan cheese over the cooked gnocchi. Repeat the cooking process with the remaining gnocchi and top each batch with butter sauce and Parmesan cheese. When the last batch has been sauced, gently toss the gnocchi and serve immediately, passing more Parmesan cheese separately.

INGREDIENTS: Which Potato Is Best?

Some trusted cookbooks swear that only boiling potatoes can make good gnocchi, while others tout baking or russet potatoes. After a number of experiments with red boiling potatoes, Yukon Golds, russets, and Idaho baking potatoes, we found that russet and baking potatoes consistently make the best gnocchi. So why the confusion and misinformation, even in some usually reliable sources?

After some research, we have a tentative explanation. Our tests proved that a relatively dry, starchy potato makes the best gnocchi and that a waxy potato should be avoided. We found that red boiling potatoes (not tiny new potatoes but those about the size of a tangerine) make gummy, heavy gnocchi, as did freshly dug Yukon Golds. Both potatoes seem to have too much moisture in them.

In *The Essentials of Classic Italian Cooking* (Knopf, 1992), Marcella Hazan notes that knowledgeable shoppers in Italy ask produce vendors for "old" boiling potatoes when making gnocchi. She says new potatoes should be avoided. Our theory is that old boiling potatoes simply don't exist in this country. Given Americans' passion for potatoes, we think there is too much turnover in our supermarkets. We also seem to remember from our cooking experience in Italy that their boiling potatoes are less waxy than ours.

Although we are fairly confident you could make fine gnocchi from boiling potatoes that were dug long ago, figuring out how long potatoes have been out of the ground is impossible, and storing them for the express purpose of someday making gnocchi seems a waste of effort when there is an easier option: Use starchy russet or baking potatoes.

6

RISOTTO, POLENTA, AND BEANS

WHEN IT COMES TO STARCHES AND Italian cuisine, we tend to think of pasta first and foremost. While Italians do consume tremendous amounts of pasta, other options enjoy strong regional popularity.

For instance, risotto is nearly as common as pasta on many restaurant menus in Milan. (Arborio rice, the special rice used to make creamy risotto, grows in the nearby Po River Valley.) Risotto can be modestly flavored, with just sautéed onion, butter, and cheese, and served as a side dish with osso buco or another main course. However, like pasta, risotto is a neutral canvas that can be flavored in countless ways. When asparagus, mushrooms, or seafood is added, risotto becomes a substantial first course in Italy (followed by a small portion of meat, fish, or chicken). Many Americans will be happy to serve these heartier risotto dishes as a main course. Risotto is an especially good choice for vegetarians.

Polenta (cornmeal cooked in water to form a soft mush) is also popular in northern Italy. Polenta can be simply flavored with just butter and salt and served as the starch base for a juicy stew, braise, or sauté. When dusted with grated Parmesan cheese or topped with a slice of Gorgonzola, polenta can also become a hearty first course or light entrée.

Beans are popular throughout Italy. Each region seems to have its favorite bean and several favorite preparations. Many of these beans can be hard to find in the United States; however, two favorite Italian legumes—cannellini beans and chickpeas—are widely available. For each of these, we have chosen a dish from the region where it is most popular, which means cannellini beans prepared Tuscan-style with tomatoes and garlic and chickpeas Sicilian-style with escarole, garlic, and raisins.

PARMESAN RISOTTO

RISOTTO IS A SIMPLE RICE DISH ELEVATED to ambrosia by the presence of a simple starchy sauce. Encouraged by judicious additions of wine and stock, the starch in the rice is transformed into a velvety, creamy sauce that clings to the toothsome grains. Risotto is one of the highlights of Italian cooking and, unsurprisingly, the myths surrounding it abound. In the matters of cooking technique and equipment, ingredients, and even how to eat it, every Italian cookbook author and chef has a firm opinion. As is our custom in the test kitchen, we set out to separate fact from fiction and get to the heart of risotto.

Obviously, the rice is the key element to a texturally flawless risotto. When buying rice, it is imperative that you pay attention to the size of the grains. Rice can be classified as long-grain, medium-grain, or short-grain. Long-grain rice is about four times as long as it is wide. Medium-grain rice is twice as long as it is wide. Short-grain rice is round. In general, long-grain rice cooks up fluffy and separate, while medium- and short-grain rice tend to cling or become starchy. This is owing to the ratio of the two main starches in rice, amylose and amylopectin.

Long-grain rice contains between 23 and 26 percent amylose, the starch that does not gelatinize during cooking. With such a high amylose content, properly cooked long-grain rice remains dry and separate. Medium-grain has an average amylose content between 18 and 26 percent, and short-grain falls between 15 and 20 percent. As these numbers indicate, individual lots of rice will behave differently, and our tests with different brands proved this.

We found that medium-grain rice is the best choice for risotto, in which we want some starchiness but not too much. But not all medium-grain rice is the same. In our kitchen tests, we found that the risotto technique may be used with non-Italian medium-grain rice, but the finished texture will pale in comparison to risotto made with Italian rice, which provides the best contrast between supple sauce and firm, toothsome rice. We think Italian rice is a must.

Italian rice comes in four varieties: *superfino, fino, semifino,* and *commune.* The top two grades include Arborio (the most widely available), Carnaroli, and Vialone Nano. There are even more varieties, like Baldo and the newly developed quick-cooking Poseidone, but they can be difficult to find outside of Italy.

In a side-by-side taste test of Arborio, Carnaroli, and Vialone Nano, tasters were split evenly between the Arborio and Carnaroli; those liking firmer rice grains chose Arborio, and those liking softer, creamier rice chose Carnaroli. Vialone was deemed too soft and had a pasty texture; the grains lacked a firm center. One source suggested that Vialone Nano is most popular in and around Venice, where a decidedly loose, soupy texture is the desired consistency for risotto. On a whim, we also tried an Arborio integrale, or whole-grain (brown) Arborio. While it did take nearly twice as long to cook and was not quite as creamy as fully processed white Arborio, some tasters appreciated its distinctly nutty taste and chewy texture.

Luckily, risotto is so popular that most markets carry at least one brand of Italian rice, generally Arborio. Because this rice is so widely available, we call for it in our recipes. If you like a softer, creamier rice and can find Carnaroli, buy it; it can be used in all the recipes in this chapter. In any case, do not be swayed by fancy "rustic" or gimmicky packaging with inflated price tags. We purchased Arborio from a variety of stores—from supermarkets to upscale Italian markets in Boston's North End—and found little difference in the finished dish. However, be wary of the rice's age because, like most grains, rice does go stale. Risotto made with rice past its prime turns mealy and chalky, loses its al dente core, and lacks the thick creaminess of fresh rice. To be on the safe side, we generally purchase rice in vacuum-packed bags, about one to two pounds at a time. Rice from bulk bins of unquestionable vintage is a dicey proposition; who knows how long it has sat exposed to air?

Having good-quality rice is only half the battle; cooking is the rest. After countless batches with minute variations, we were certain about a few points. First, slowly cooking the diced onions until they yielded their juices and firm form was imperative to the final flavor and texture. The sweetness of properly cooked onions lent depth to this dish, and the softened onion melted into the risotto by serving time. The next step was sautéing the rice, which prompted the starches in the rice to turn translucent—a good visual clue for adding liquid. When we did not cook the rice prior to adding liquid, the risotto was mushy and chalky, and the rice grains lacked their distinctive toothsomeness.

Once the rice is toasted, the liquids are added. The wine must be added before the stock so that the boozy flavor has a chance to cook off. Otherwise, we found the alcohol punch was too much. Virtually all risottos are made with a light, dry white wine, although some regional specialties are made with red wine. Risotto made without wine lacked dimension and tasted bland, so don't skip this ingredient.

The recipes we researched offered a wide range of options for broth, from plain water to veal stock. Water didn't impress us, and veal stock is rare in all but the best-provisioned professional kitchen. Straight beef stock and chicken stock proved too intense, but diluting chicken stock with an equal amount of water was just right. The chicken broth added richness and depth without taking over. We found that homemade stock was preferable to commercial broth, but the latter still makes a good risotto.

On an interesting note, several prominent cookbook authors suggested using bouillon cubes, but we found the cubes muddied the risotto's clean flavor. We can only assume that the quality of Italian bouillon cubes is superior to what we found on our grocers' shelves.

Although this is contrary to conventional wisdom and the instructions in most cookbooks, we discovered that constant stirring is unnecessary. We added half the broth once the wine had cooked off and allowed the rice to simmer for about 10 minutes, or half the cooking time, with little attention. The rice floated freely, individual grains suspended by the bubbling broth. During this period, we stirred the rice infrequently—about every three minutes—to ensure that it was not sticking to the bottom of the pan. Once all the broth was absorbed by the rice, we added more, a scant half-cup at a time. For this period, stirring every minute or so was important; if we did not, the rice stuck to the bottom of the pan.

There is quite a bit of controversy surrounding the doneness of risotto. Some insist it should have a chalky, solid bite, while others feel it should be soft to the core. Tasters expressed individual preferences quite strongly, so you must taste as the rice nears completion and decide for yourself. Generally, we began tasting our rice after about 20 minutes of cooking; you can always cook it longer for a softer texture, but you can never bring back bite.

For the final touch, Parmesan goes in at the very end to preserve its distinctive flavor and aroma. Grated cheese proved best, as it melted almost instantaneously. The quality of the cheese was paramount, as its taste is so prominent. This is the perfect occasion for buying the authentic Parmesan freshly cut from the wheel, boldly displaying its branded trademark on the rind.

Parmesan Risotto
SERVES 6 AS A FIRST COURSE OR SIDE DISH

This is risotto at its simplest. It can accompany a variety of meals, from grilled or braised meat to a melange of roasted vegetables. Parmesan risotto is also appropriate as a first course. Don't fret if you have stock left over once the rice is finished cooking; different brands of rice all cook differently, and we prefer to err on the side of slightly too much stock rather than too little. If you do use all the stock and the rice has not finished cooking, add hot water. Reheated risotto will never have the same texture as the dish did the first time around, so we prefer to turn leftovers into risotto cakes (see page 215).

3½   cups homemade chicken stock or canned low-sodium chicken broth
4   tablespoons unsalted butter
1   medium onion, diced fine
   Salt
2   cups Arborio rice
1   cup dry white wine
1   cup finely grated Parmesan cheese
   Ground black pepper

1. Bring the stock and 3 cups water to a simmer in a medium saucepan over medium-high heat. Reduce the heat to the lowest possible setting to keep the broth warm.

2. Melt the butter in a 4-quart saucepan over medium heat. Once the foaming subsides, add the onion and ½ teaspoon salt and cook, stirring occasionally, until the onion is

very soft and translucent, about 9 minutes. Add the rice and cook, stirring frequently, until the kernel edges are transparent, about 4 minutes. Add the wine and cook, stirring frequently, until the wine is completely absorbed by the rice, about 2 minutes. Add 3 cups warm stock and, stirring infrequently (about every 3 minutes), simmer until the liquid is absorbed and the bottom of the pan is dry, 10 to 12 minutes.

3. Add more stock, ½ cup at a time, as needed to keep the pan bottom from drying out (every 3 to 4 minutes); cook, stirring frequently, until the grains of rice are cooked through but still somewhat firm in the center, 10 to 12 minutes. Stir in the Parmesan cheese, season with salt and pepper to taste, and serve immediately in warmed shallow bowls.

SAFFRON RISOTTO

CALLED RISOTTO ALLA MILANESE IN honor of the city of Milan, saffron risotto by any name is one of the simplest and best variations on basic risotto. The creamy rice is the perfect vehicle for saffron's heady flavor and aroma, and the threads dye the rice a spectacular gold. While saffron risotto is the traditional accompaniment to osso buco (page 306), it is just as good on its own or with roasted pork, veal, or poultry.

Saffron risotto is nothing more than Parmesan Risotto (page 204) with saffron included as a flavoring. The trick is to add the saffron to the risotto such that the best flavor is obtained. (Using the best-tasting saffron is also important; see page 207 for details.) While some recipes we tried dissolved the saffron threads in hot broth or wine prior to adding them to the risotto, we found this superfluous. Tasters could not tell the difference between risotto flavored with presoaked saffron and

risotto in which the saffron had been added dry to the pot.

Other recipes suggested toasting the saffron in oil, which we found did magnify its flavor. As with many other dried spices, saffron needs the dry heat to activate its volatile oils. Toasting the saffron with the rice helped further break up the saffron and distribute its flavor throughout the dish.

Saffron Risotto

SERVES 6 AS A FIRST COURSE OR SIDE DISH

If you prefer seeing some of the threads weaving through the risotto, as some of our tasters did, lightly crumble the saffron between your fingers—the flavor will not be altered. If not, crumble the saffron more thoroughly, and it will disintegrate during cooking.

3½	cups homemade chicken stock or canned low-sodium chicken broth
4	tablespoons unsalted butter
1	medium onion, diced fine
	Salt
2	cups Arborio rice
¼	teaspoon saffron threads
1	cup dry white wine
1	cup finely grated Parmesan cheese
	Ground black pepper

1. Bring the stock and 3 cups water to a simmer in a medium saucepan over medium-high heat. Reduce the heat to the lowest possible setting to keep the broth warm.

2. Melt the butter in a 4-quart saucepan over medium heat. Once the foaming subsides, add the onion and ½ teaspoon salt and cook, stirring occasionally, until the onion is very soft and translucent, about 9 minutes. Add the rice and crumble the saffron threads with your fingers into the pot. Cook, stirring

EQUIPMENT: Large Saucepans

Whether we are blanching vegetables, cooking beans, or making risotto, we reach for a large (by which we mean three- to four-quart) saucepan. Which begs an obvious question: Does the brand of pan matter? With prices for large saucepans ranging from $24.99 for a Revere stainless-steel model with thin copper cladding at the base up to $140 for an All-Clad pan with a complete aluminum core and stainless-steel interior and exterior cladding, a lot of money is riding on the answer. To offer guidance, we tested eight models, all between three and four quarts in size, from well-known cookware manufacturers.

The tests we performed were based on common cooking tasks and designed to highlight specific characteristics of the pans' performance. Sautéing minced onions illustrated the pace at which the pan heats up and sautés. Cooking white rice provided a good indication of the pan's ability to heat evenly as well as how tightly the lid sealed. Making pastry cream let us know how user-friendly the pan was—was it shaped such that a whisk reached into the corners without trouble, was it comfortable to pick up, and could we pour liquid from it neatly? These traits can make a real difference when you use a pan day in and day out.

Of the tests we performed, sautéing onions was the most telling. In our view, onions should soften reliably and evenly (and with minimal attention and stirring) when sautéed over medium heat. In this regard, the All-Clad, Calphalon, KitchenAid, and Sitram pans all delivered. The Chantal and Cuisinart pans sautéed slightly faster, necessitating a little more attention from the cook, but still well within acceptable bounds. Only the Revere and Farberware Millennium sautéed so fast that we considered them problematic.

Incidentally, the Revere and Farberware pans that sautéed onions too fast for us were the lightest pans of the bunch, weighing only 1 pound 10 ounces and 2 pounds 6 ounces respectively. This indicates that they were made from thinner metal, which is one reason they heat quickly. On the flip side of the weight issue, however, we found that too heavy a pan, such as the 4-pound Calphalon, could be uncomfortable to lift when full. We felt that around 3½ pounds was the ideal weight; pans near this weight, including the All-Clad, KitchenAid, Chantal, Sitram, and Cuisinart, balanced good heft with easy maneuverability.

While none of the pans failed the rice test outright, there were performance differences. In the Sitram, Revere, and Farberware pans, the rice stuck and dried out at the bottom, if only a little bit. Although this did not greatly affect the texture, the flavor, or the cleanup, we'd still choose a pan for which this was not an issue.

Every pan in the group turned out perfect pastry cream. During this test, we did observe one design element that made it easy to pour liquid from the pan neatly, without dribbles and spills. A rolled lip that flares slightly at the top of the pan helped control the pour. Only two pans in the group did not have a rolled lip: the All-Clad and the Calphalon.

So which pan do you want to buy? That depends largely on two things: your budget and your attention as a cook. Based on our tests, we'd advise against really inexpensive pans—those that cost less than $50. For between $50 and $100, you can get a competent pan such as the Chantal, Sitram, or Cuisinart. The only caveat is that you have to watch them carefully; they offer less room for error than our favorite pans made by All-Clad, Calphalon, and KitchenAid.

THE BEST SAUCEPANS

The All-Clad (left), Calphalon (center), and KitchenAid (right) saucepans are our favorites, but they are not flawless. The Calphalon ($110) is heavy, both it and the All-Clad pan ($140) lack rolled lips, and the KitchenAid pan ($119) has a relatively short curved handle. However, these three pans provide moderate, steady heat.

frequently, until the kernel edges are transparent, about 4 minutes. Add the wine and cook, stirring frequently, until the wine is completely absorbed by the rice, about 2 minutes. Add 3 cups warm stock and, stirring infrequently (about every 3 minutes), simmer until the liquid is absorbed and the bottom of the pan is dry, 10 to 12 minutes.

3. Add more stock, ½ cup at a time, as needed to keep the pan bottom from drying out (every 3 to 4 minutes), and cook, stirring frequently, until the grains of rice are cooked through but still somewhat firm in the center, 10 to 12 minutes. Stir in the Parmesan cheese, season with salt and pepper to taste, and serve immediately in warmed shallow bowls.

INGREDIENTS: Saffron

While most cooks know that saffron is the world's most expensive spice, few are aware that it is grown in many locations and that price and quality can vary considerably. Though the bulk of commercially produced saffron comes from Spain and Iran, it is also harvested on a small scale in India, Greece, France—and, closer to home, in Lancaster County, Pa.

We decided to toss saffron from different places purchased at different prices into a few pots and set up a test. We prepared three batches of risotto alla Milanese and flavored one with Spanish saffron, one with Indian, and one with American.

The finished risottos were similar in hue, though the Indian Kashmir saffron threads were darkest prior to cooking. Surprisingly, no one cared for the Indian saffron, although it was almost twice as costly as the other two and is generally regarded as one of the best in the world. Despite its heady aroma, floral tones, and earthy scent, many tasters found it "tinny" and "bland" when cooked. The risotto made with the Spanish saffron was better, but we overwhelmingly favored the risotto made with the Pennsylvania-grown saffron, judging it the "most potent" and "perfumed" of the three samples.

WILD MUSHROOM RISOTTO

THE COMBINATION OF EARTHY WILD mushrooms and risotto is hard to beat. The creamy, slightly nutty risotto provides a perfect foil for the chewy intensity of the mushrooms. Italians are fond of mushrooms of all sorts, from humble portobellos and cremini to exotica like porcini and black trumpets. Outside of upscale restaurants and the Pacific Northwest, where they grow abundantly, wild mushrooms are rarely given due credit in the United States. Most markets carry a limited selection, if any, and at exorbitant prices. With these limitations in mind, our goal was to develop intense mushroom flavor without a trip to a specialty store or breaking the bank.

After developing a long list of mushroom dishes, we were familiar with coaxing big mushroom flavor from grocery store staples. For this risotto, dried mushrooms seemed the best route and dried porcinis the best choice. Called *cèpes* in France, porcini (*boletus edulis*) are large-capped, fat-stemmed mushrooms that are as exaggerated in appearance as they are in flavor. They have a robustly funky, woodsy taste and aroma unparalleled by anything short of truffles. When available fresh in the United States—which is rare—porcini fetch exorbitant prices, upwards of $30 a pound.

Luckily for those of us without expansive bank accounts, porcini dry exceptionally well and retain their earthy flavor—in fact, it is intensified by the drying process. Dried porcini are available in almost all supermarkets. A quick soak in hot water rehydrates them and makes them ready to be incorporated into any number of dishes. The soaking water also becomes strongly flavored and should definitely be used. We found that just ⅓ ounce of dried porcini, rehydrated and finely chopped, was enough to add deep flavor and musky aroma to our risotto.

Tasters, however, requested fresh mushrooms to lend form to flavor. Because we already had an intense flavor, we knew we would not have to use expensive wild mushrooms like shiitake or chanterelles. White button mushrooms, however, failed to impress; their bland flavor and spongy texture left tasters unhappy. Only nominally more expensive, cremini mushrooms—also known as baby bellas—proved to be the answer. (As their nickname suggests, cremini are baby portobellos.) When sautéed, the cremini developed a significantly more intense flavor than their paler siblings, and they had a firmer, meatier texture.

To make the most of their flavor, we sautéed the cremini over high heat in butter, which prompted stronger browning than olive oil. Garlic and minced thyme added definition to the deep earthiness of the browned mushrooms.

Most recipes simply build the risotto on top of the sautéed mushrooms. However, tasters were disappointed with this approach. The texture of the mushrooms suffered as they simmered for more than 20 minutes in the stock. After several attempts to add the mushrooms at various points in the process, we decided to stir the sautéed mushrooms into the risotto at the very end, along with the cheese. In effect, we treated the mushrooms like meat. We even deglazed the pan they were sautéed in and made this liquid part of the stock used to cook the rice.

Wild Mushroom Risotto

SERVES 4 AS A MAIN COURSE
OR 6 AS A FIRST COURSE

Using a regular skillet (not nonstick) for cooking the mushrooms encourages the development of a fond, the flavorful layer of browned bits that adheres to the pan bottom. The fond is packed full of flavor and will enrich the risotto, so be sure to completely deglaze the pan. See the illustrations on page 5 for tips on rehydrating dried mushrooms.

⅓	ounce dried porcini mushrooms
3½	cups homemade chicken stock or canned low-sodium chicken broth
6	tablespoons unsalted butter
I	pound cremini mushrooms, stem bottoms trimmed, mushrooms cut into 6 wedges
	Salt
2	medium cloves garlic, minced or pressed through a garlic press
½	teaspoon minced fresh thyme leaves
I	medium onion, diced fine
2	cups Arborio rice
I	cup dry white wine
I	cup finely grated Parmesan cheese
	Ground black pepper

1. Mix the dried porcini with ½ cup hot tap water in a small microwave-safe bowl. Cover with plastic wrap, cut several steam vents in the plastic wrap with a paring knife, and microwave on high power for 30 seconds. Let stand until the mushrooms soften, about 5 minutes. Lift the mushrooms from the liquid with a fork. Mince the mushrooms and reserve. Pour the liquid through a small strainer lined with a single sheet of paper towel and placed over a medium saucepan. Add the chicken stock and 2½ cups water to the saucepan and bring to a simmer over medium-high heat. Reduce the heat to the lowest possible setting to keep the broth warm.

2. Heat the oven to 200 degrees. Melt 2 tablespoons butter in a 12-inch skillet over medium-high heat. Once the foaming subsides, add the cremini and ½ teaspoon salt and cook, stirring occasionally, until the mushrooms have shed their liquid and browned, 5 to 6 minutes. Add the garlic and

thyme and cook until fragrant, about 1 minute. Transfer the mushrooms to an oven-safe bowl and keep them warm in the oven. Off the heat, add ½ cup warm broth to the pan and scrape with a wooden spoon to loosen any browned bits. Once the pan is deglazed, return the liquid to the saucepan with the remaining broth.

3. Melt the remaining 4 tablespoons butter in a 4-quart saucepan over medium heat. Once the foaming subsides, add the onion and ½ teaspoon salt and cook, stirring occasionally, until the onion is very soft and translucent, about 9 minutes. Add the rice and cook, stirring frequently, until the kernel edges are transparent, about 4 minutes. Add the wine and cook, stirring frequently, until the wine is completely absorbed by the rice, about 2 minutes. Add the minced porcini and 3 cups warm stock and, stirring infrequently (about every 3 minutes), simmer until the liquid is absorbed and the bottom of the pan is dry, 10 to 12 minutes.

4. Add more stock, ½ cup at a time, as needed to keep the pan bottom from drying out (every 3 to 4 minutes), and cook, stirring frequently, until the grains of rice are cooked through but still somewhat firm in the center, 10 to 12 minutes. Stir in the cremini mushrooms (and any juices that accumulated in the bowl) and the Parmesan cheese, season with salt and pepper to taste, and serve immediately in warmed shallow bowls.

ASPARAGUS RISOTTO

RISOTTO IS THE PERFECT VEHICLE FOR asparagus. The starches soak up and intensify its elusive flavor, and the creamy texture provides a sharp contrast to its crisp snap. Most Italian asparagus dishes treat the vegetable with a light hand, allowing it to shine on its own. We

hoped to honor this approach and coax as much flavor as we could out of the asparagus, using the simplest method we could find.

Asparagus are available in a variety of sizes, from thumb thick to chopstick thin. For risotto, we preferred asparagus about the width of a pencil because it cooked quickly and had little chance of being woody. Thicker asparagus was sometimes tough; it is not right for this recipe.

To lend as much asparagus flavor as we could to the risotto, we simmered its fibrous ends (snapped off before the tender portion of the spear is sliced) in the chicken broth that would be used to cook the rice. The trimmings may be indigestible, but they are still packed with flavor. We found that as little as 15 minutes of simmering was enough to infuse the broth with a pleasant vegetal flavor. The trimmings were then strained, and the asparagus-flavored chicken broth was used to make the risotto.

While we are fond of roasting asparagus (the high heat concentrates the flavors in this delicate-tasting vegetable), tasters found the withered, darkened asparagus unappealing when set against the stark white rice. Instead, we opted for cooking the asparagus in the risotto itself. The gentle heat from the rice preserved the crispness and delicate flavor of the asparagus. Small slices cut on the bias cooked quickly, looked attractive, and fit on a fork with the rice.

To round out the flavors in this risotto, we tried a variety of herbs, but most of them muddied or detracted from the clean impact of the simply cooked asparagus. Mint, however, added a refreshing lightness. The final touch was a little lemon zest for a hint of lemon without the brash acidity of lemon juice. Some tasters enjoyed an additional spritz of lemon, but others dissented, so we decided to serve lemon wedges at the table and let each diner decide for himself.

Asparagus Risotto

SERVES 4 AS A MAIN COURSE
OR 6 AS A FIRST COURSE

If you purchase the asparagus more than a day ahead of time, store them standing upright in a small amount of water and blanketed with moist paper towels to prevent them from drying out. If they come bound by a rubber band, snip it off; the band can encourage rotting. The flavors in this dish are light, making it a suitable accompaniment to broiled or poached salmon or a simple roast chicken.

1	pound thin asparagus, tough ends snapped off (see illustration on page 59) and reserved, spears cut on the bias into ½-inch lengths
3½	cups homemade chicken stock or canned low-sodium chicken broth
4	tablespoons unsalted butter
1	medium onion, diced fine
	Salt
2	cups Arborio rice
1	cup dry white wine
1	cup finely grated Parmesan cheese
½	teaspoon grated lemon zest from 1 small lemon, plus 1 medium lemon, cut into wedges
2	tablespoons minced fresh mint leaves
	Ground black pepper

1. Bring the tough asparagus ends, stock, and 3 cups water to a boil in a medium saucepan over medium-high heat. Reduce the heat to low, partially cover, and simmer for 15 minutes. Strain the broth through a fine-mesh strainer into another saucepan, pushing on the solids to extract as much liquid as possible. Discard the asparagus and return the saucepan to the lowest possible heat to keep the broth warm.

2. Melt the butter in a 4-quart saucepan over medium heat. Once the foaming subsides, add the onion and ½ teaspoon salt and cook, stirring occasionally, until the onion is very soft and translucent, about 9 minutes. Add the rice and cook, stirring frequently, until the kernel edges are transparent, about 4 minutes. Add the wine and cook, stirring frequently, until the wine is completely absorbed by the rice, about 2 minutes. Add 3 cups warm stock and, stirring infrequently (about every 3 minutes), simmer until the liquid is absorbed and the bottom of the pan is dry, 10 to 12 minutes.

3. Add more stock, ½ cup at a time, as needed to keep the pan bottom from drying out (every 3 to 4 minutes); cook, stirring frequently, for 5 minutes. Stir in the sliced asparagus and continue cooking, adding stock in ½-cup increments and stirring frequently, until the grains of rice are cooked through but still somewhat firm in the center, 5 to 7 minutes. Stir in the Parmesan cheese, lemon zest, and mint. Season with salt and pepper to taste and serve immediately in warmed shallow bowls, accompanied by the lemon wedges.

BUTTERNUT SQUASH RISOTTO

VIVIDLY COLORED AND RICHLY FLAVORED, butternut squash is an ideal addition to risotto. The hearty, sweet flavor of this risotto stands well on its own and pairs well with pork, veal, or poultry. Parmesan risotto was the perfect starting point for this dish because the nutty flavor of the cheese complements the flavors of the squash. All we needed to do was figure out the best method for incorporating the squash into the risotto.

We found that recipes added the squash to the risotto in one of two ways, either as a puree or diced. While tasters appreciated the golden hue that the puree tinted the rice, they felt the squash flavor was faint at best. Diced squash, on the other hand, maintained its flavor and contrasted well (both in terms of texture and color) with the creamy rice.

After developing a recipe for squash with sage and browned butter for the vegetable chapter (page 88), we knew that roasting was the best cooking method for squash. The high heat evaporated the excess moisture in the squash, concentrating its sweetness and flavor. During testing, the roasted squash was so sweet that tasters were surprised to find that no sugar had been added prior to cooking. The only trick to roasting was not overcooking the squash, which quickly turned mushy when left in the oven for too long. This was especially important when adding the squash to the risotto because we wanted to be able to stir the roasted cubes into the rice without them breaking apart. After experimenting with different-sized pieces of squash, we settled on ½-inch dice. The pieces maintained their shape, and the small size meant it was easy to fit both rice and squash in one forkful.

Although the neutral flavor of butternut squash can stand up to any number of seasonings and herbs, sage is easily the best choice. Its sharp bite balances the squash's sweetness and enhances its distinctive taste. Sage is best used with discretion. We have ruined many dishes with too much sage. Tasters agreed that only the mildest hint of sage should season the risotto; the squash flavor should predominate. We tried adding the sage at various points as the risotto cooked; tasters favored it added at the very end so that it cooked only lightly and did not turn bitter.

Butternut Squash Risotto with Sage

SERVES 4 AS A MAIN COURSE OR 6 AS A FIRST COURSE

Peeling butternut squash requires a sturdy, very sharp vegetable peeler (see page 60). If you have a thin-bladed model, you might have better luck with a very sharp knife. Simply cut the squash in half, place the bottom on a cutting board, and cut toward the board. Be careful; it can be slippery work. Dried sage is not an acceptable substitute for fresh sage in this instance; its flavor is dusty and vague at best.

1	medium butternut squash (2½ to 3 pounds), peeled, seeded, and cut into ½-inch cubes
6	tablespoons unsalted butter, 2 tablespoons melted
	Salt and ground black pepper
3½	cups homemade chicken stock or canned low-sodium chicken broth
1	medium onion, diced fine
2	cups Arborio rice
1	cup dry white wine
1	cup finely grated Parmesan cheese
1	tablespoon minced fresh sage leaves
	Pinch freshly grated nutmeg

1. Adjust an oven rack to the lower-middle position and heat the oven to 475 degrees. In a large bowl, combine the squash, melted butter, ¼ teaspoon salt, and ¼ teaspoon pepper, and toss with a rubber spatula to uniformly coat the squash cubes. Spread the squash evenly on a rimmed baking sheet and place it in the oven. After 15 minutes, remove the baking sheet from the oven and shake it to redistribute the squash. Return it to the oven and roast until the squash is lightly browned and the tip of a paring knife easily pierces the flesh, about 15 minutes longer. Remove the squash from the oven and keep warm until needed.

2. Bring the stock and 3 cups water to a simmer in a medium saucepan over medium-high heat. Reduce the heat to the lowest possible setting to keep the broth warm.

3. Melt the remaining 4 tablespoons butter in a 4-quart saucepan over medium heat. Once the foaming subsides, add the onion and ½ teaspoon salt and cook, stirring occasionally, until the onion is very soft and translucent, about 9 minutes. Add the rice and cook, stirring frequently, until the kernel edges are transparent, about 4 minutes. Add the wine and cook, stirring frequently, until the wine is completely absorbed by the rice, about 2 minutes. Add 3 cups warm stock and, stirring infrequently (about every 3 minutes), simmer until the liquid is absorbed and the bottom of the pan is dry, 10 to 12 minutes.

4. Add more stock, ½ cup at a time, as needed to keep the pan bottom from drying out (every 3 to 4 minutes); cook, stirring frequently, until the grains of rice are cooked through but still somewhat firm in the center, 10 to 12 minutes. Stir in the Parmesan cheese, sage, and nutmeg until evenly incorporated. Gently fold in the cooked squash. Season with salt and pepper to taste and serve immediately in warmed shallow bowls.

SEAFOOD RISOTTO

SEAFOOD RISOTTO IS PERHAPS THE king of all Italian rice dishes. With several kinds of seafood, it certainly can cost a king's ransom. An ideal seafood risotto is a glamorous mix of flavors, shapes, and textures. The seafood is nestled in the creamy risotto, perfectly cooked and richly flavored; the surrounding rice is bathed with the seafood juices. But making a perfect seafood risotto is harder than it sounds. From choosing the right mix of seafood, making the broth, and cooking the seafood so it

doesn't become tough, there are many potential problems with this recipe.

Our first step was to choose the seafood. Most of the recipes we found were from Venice and capitalized on the seemingly endless variety of seafood caught in the nearby lagoon. Even the best American fishmonger offers only a fraction of what is routinely available in Venetian markets, so we had to make do with what we could find. We set the parameters to include seafood that could cook in the risotto during the last few moments—the last thing we wanted to do was introduce additional pots and pans. This ruled out lobster and crab, both common to Venetian seafood risotto. We also chose to skip flaky fish that would fall apart easily.

For their color and firm, meaty texture, shrimp were a must. After trying several sizes, small shrimp (around 40 to a pound) were the favorite. Squid was our next addition, liked by tasters for its mild flavor and chewy, toothsome texture. At first, we used just the bodies cut into small rings, but several tasters demanded that tentacles be included as well. They do add a unique texture and presence to the risotto.

For a big, briny hit of flavor, we hoped to add shellfish like clams and mussels, but their inclusion posed a riddle: what to do about the shells? They were attractive nestled into the creamy rice, where they added striking visual appeal, but eating the risotto proved difficult. The rice tenaciously clung to the shells, and even the most uninhibited taster felt awkward sucking it from the shell crevices. We tried steaming the shellfish ahead of time and removing the meat from the shells, but this proved too much work for a dish that was already labor-intensive. In the end, we excluded clams and mussels and used scallops for their whiff of brininess and characteristic sweetness. Scallops certainly were far less work. As with the shrimp, we chose small bay scallops over large sea scallops because they cooked quickly and easily fit on a fork with a bite of rice.

With the seafood chosen, we turned our attention to the broth. Diluted chicken stock—what we normally use for making risotto—was quickly ruled out because it muddied the subtle flavor of the seafood. We came across one noted cookbook author who suggested that plain water was the best choice for seafood risotto, but our tasters disagreed, arguing that the resulting risotto tasted thin and bland. Bottled clam juice diluted with water tasted bland, too, but was more promising. To add body to the clam juice, we simmered it with shrimp shells (from the shrimp for the risotto) as well as carrot, onion, bay leaves, and peppercorns. Just 15 minutes on the stovetop infused the broth with a light but distinct seafood flavor.

After we made several batches of risotto with this broth, we realized that a little more depth and an acidic note was needed to balance the sweetness of the seafood. The combination of seafoods reminded one taster of bouillabaisse, which is strongly flavored with saffron. A small pinch of this proved just what the risotto needed; it tied together the flavors and imparted a lush golden hue to the rice. Again borrowing from bouillabaisse, we added fresh basil; the anise bite did wonders for the flavor of the shrimp, scallops, and squid. For acidity, we added tomato to the quick stock.

With the flavors in order, we aimed to refine the cooking time to achieve perfectly cooked seafood. Throughout testing, we had been adding the seafood roughly five minutes before we thought the rice would be cooked through, but occasionally this led to overcooking, as Arborio rice, from batch to batch, may take several minutes longer than expected to soften. Then one taster remembered a restaurant trick she had learned and suggested allowing the fish to cook solely in

the residual heat of the finished rice, essentially poaching it in gentle heat. Once the rice was cooked, we added the seafood, covered the pot, and let the risotto rest off the heat just until the seafood was cooked through (this took about five minutes). This technique produced flawlessly cooked fish every time, without the risk of overcooking.

Except in the rarest situations, fish and cheese are never combined in Italian cooking. To add richness and body to this cheeseless risotto, we employed an Italian technique called *mantecare*, which roughly translates as "to beat" and involves rigorously stirring in butter once the rice has finished cooking. The grains become freshly lacquered with the fat and take on a voluptuous mouthfeel. Although we found that the additional butter is superfluous in cheese-enriched risotto recipes, it made a real difference in this dish.

Seafood Risotto

SERVES 6 AS A MAIN COURSE
OR 8 AS A FIRST COURSE

In contrast to the other risotto recipes in this chapter, tasters preferred this one cooked in the Venetian style called all'onda—literally, "wavy." The lyrical name simply means that the risotto is looser in texture—loose enough to be poured from the pot. Feel free to cook it to the consistency you prefer, but take into consideration that as the seafood cooks, it releases juices that will loosen the final texture of the risotto. We like whole small bay scallops in this dish, but you can substitute larger sea scallops, cut into ½-inch dice.

QUICK SEAFOOD BROTH
1   medium onion, unpeeled and quartered through the root end
1   medium carrot, cut into 2-inch lengths
10 black peppercorns
2   bay leaves

½ teaspoon salt

Shells from ½ pound shrimp (see below)

2 cups bottled clam juice

1 (14½-ounce) can diced tomatoes, drained

RISOTTO

5 tablespoons unsalted butter

1 medium onion, diced fine

Salt

2 cups Arborio rice

Small pinch saffron threads

1 cup dry white wine

½ pound small shrimp (about 40 per pound), shells (including tails) removed and reserved

½ pound small bay scallops

½ pound squid, bodies cut crosswise into ½-inch-thick rings, tentacles left whole

¼ cup roughly chopped fresh basil leaves

Ground black pepper

1. FOR THE BROTH: Combine all of the ingredients and 5½ cups water in a large saucepan and bring to a boil over medium-high heat. Reduce the heat to medium-low and simmer for 15 minutes. Strain the broth through a fine-mesh strainer into another saucepan, pushing on the solids to extract as much liquid as possible. Discard the solids and return the saucepan to the lowest possible heat to keep the broth warm.

2. FOR THE RISOTTO: Melt 4 tablespoons butter in a 4-quart saucepan over medium heat. Once the foaming subsides, add the onion and ½ teaspoon salt and cook, stirring occasionally, until the onion is very soft and translucent, about 9 minutes. Add the rice and crumble the saffron threads with your fingers into the pot. Cook, stirring frequently, until the kernel edges are transparent, about 4 minutes. Add the wine and cook, stirring frequently, until the wine is completely absorbed by the rice, about 2 minutes. Add 3 cups warm broth and, stirring infrequently (about every 3 minutes), simmer until the liquid is absorbed and the bottom of the pan is dry, about 10 to 12 minutes.

3. Add more liquid, ½ cup at a time, as needed to keep the pan bottom from drying out (every 3 to 4 minutes); cook, stirring frequently, until the grains of rice are cooked through but still somewhat firm in the center, about 10 to 12 minutes. Vigorously stir in the remaining 1 tablespoon butter until melted, then gently fold in the shrimp, scallops, squid, and basil. Cover the pot and remove it from the heat. Let stand until the seafood is cooked through, 5 to 6 minutes. Season with salt and pepper to taste and serve immediately in warmed shallow bowls.

RISOTTO CAKES

REHEATED RISOTTO, WHETHER WARMED on the stovetop, in the oven, or in the microwave, never has quite the same texture as freshly made. The grains of rice turn mushy, and the velvety sauce, the heart and soul of risotto, becomes downright gluey. The butter can also leach from the rice and make a greasy mess.

Instead of suffering through mediocre leftover risotto or relinquishing it to the garbage, Italians turn it into something entirely new: risotto cakes. Breaded and pan-fried, the cakes become browned and crunchy on the exterior and soft and creamy on the inside, especially when stuffed with soft, stringy cheese. There are several variations on this dish, including *arancini* and *suppli al telefono*. Literally "little oranges," arancini take their name from their color, not their flavor—they are tinted orange with a spoonful of tomato paste. Suppli al telefono, or "telephone wires," are a Roman specialty named for the cheese stuffing that, when bitten into, stretches into strings resembling telephone cables.

While both of these versions are delicious, we wanted a more substantial cake, something that could serve as a meal rather than just a snack. Increasing the size from the traditional small ball to a larger patty or cake was an easy step. However, we needed to keep the size of the cake small enough so that the interior would heat through in the same time that the exterior would brown. When the cakes were too thick, the inside was barely warm by the time the exterior was deeply browned.

Borrowing from suppli al telefono, we stuffed the center of each cake with a soft cheese that would melt, like mozzarella or provolone. We started off using grated cheese but found that bits of cheese worked their way to the exterior and burned in the oil. Diced cheese proved easier to manage and melted just as thoroughly.

We hoped to simply dust the cakes with flour prior to frying, but we found that the cakes absorbed a great quantity of oil and turned sodden. A thicker coating of beaten egg and bread crumbs was substantial enough to shield the rice from the oil and turned quite crisp when fried. Seasoning the bread crumbs with black pepper, cayenne, and minced parsley improved the flavor and appearance of the coating.

For frying the cakes, we had expected to use olive oil, but tasters preferred vegetable oil, which produced a lighter-flavored and less greasy-tasting cake.

Risotto Cakes
MAKES 2 CAKES (SERVING 1)

Parmesan and saffron risotto are the best bets for this recipe, but just about any risotto works as long as its components are not too large, as in seafood or asparagus risotto. (The chunky bits will stick out of the cake and burn.) Spraying the measuring cup with nonstick cooking spray before measuring the risotto facilitates easy removal. To use the minimal amount of oil for frying, choose a pan just large enough to accommodate the risotto cakes without them touching. Two cakes can be fried in an 8-inch skillet. Although a spritz of lemon cuts the richness of the risotto cakes and sharpens the flavors, feel free to serve the cakes with tomato sauce (page 145) or even a smear of pesto (page 139) or olivada (page 22). Depending on how much leftover

SHAPING RISOTTO CAKES

1. Using both hands, shape ½ cup chilled risotto into a uniform disk roughly 3 inches wide and 1 inch thick.

2. With your thumb, make an indentation in the center of the disk and pack it with 1 tablespoon finely diced cheese.

3. Carefully cover the cheese with the risotto mounded around the edges of the indentation. Pat the surface smooth, making sure that no cheese is exposed.

risotto you have, the ingredients can be easily multiplied for more servings. Note that four cakes will require a 12-inch skillet and more oil, which should reach halfway up the sides of the cakes as they cook.

½   **cup fresh bread crumbs (page 57)**
       Pinch salt
       Pinch ground black pepper
       Small pinch cayenne pepper (optional)
1   **teaspoon minced fresh parsley leaves**
1   **large egg**
1   **cup leftover risotto, chilled**
2   **tablespoons finely diced mozzarella, fontina, or provolone cheese**
½–⅔ **cup vegetable oil for frying**
       Lemon wedges for garnish

1. Mix the bread crumbs, salt, ground black pepper, cayenne pepper (if using), and parsley together in a small shallow dish. Beat the egg in another small shallow dish. Measure ½ cup chilled risotto and shape and fill it with 1 tablespoon cheese as directed in the illustrations on page 215. Repeat with the remaining risotto and cheese to form a second cake. Dip each cake into the egg, allowing excess to drip back into the bowl. Dip both sides of the cake in the bread crumb mixture, pressing the crumbs with your fingers to form an even, cohesive coat.

2. Pour enough oil into an 8-inch nonstick skillet to reach a depth just under ½ inch. Turn the heat to medium-high and heat until the oil is shimmering but not smoking, about 2 minutes. With a spatula, gently lower each cake into the pan and cook until golden brown, about 3 minutes. Flip the cakes with the spatula and cook until browned on the other side, about 3 minutes. Transfer the cakes to a paper towel–lined plate, blot any excess oil, and serve immediately with lemon wedges.

POLENTA

IF YOUR MOTHER EVER COMPLAINED about slaving over a hot stove, she may have been talking about making *polenta*. Nothing more than cornmeal mush, polenta is made from dried, ground corn cooked in liquid until the starches in the corn hydrate and swell. For many purposes, this soft stage is the most delicious way to serve polenta.

The stiff polenta you often see in restaurants starts out as a soft mass but is spread into a thin layer on a baking sheet or marble surface, cooled until stiff, sliced, and then sautéed, fried, or grilled until it resembles a crouton. These crisp rectangles are rarely more than a garnish. However, a smooth, piping-hot mound of soft polenta can be the base of a meal. More commonly, soft polenta is used as a filler to stretch dishes made with meager game birds like quail or to cut the richness of sausages. Most stews and braised dishes—everything from osso buco to braised rabbit—can be ladled over a bowl of soft polenta.

Although making polenta sounds easy, the traditional Italian method for cooking it is a lot of work. The polenta must be slowly added to boiling salted water and stirred constantly (to prevent scorching) during the entire 30- to 40-minute cooking time. Within five minutes, you'll feel like you've been arm-wrestling Arnold Schwarzenegger. Thirty minutes of such constant stirring can seem like an eternity.

Of course, this assumes that you have avoided the biggest pitfall of all, the seizing problem at the beginning of the cooking process. Cornmeal is a starch, and starch thickens when mixed with water and heated. If this happens too quickly, the cornmeal seizes up into a solid, nearly immovable mass.

We tested adding cornmeal to cold water, using more water, using less water, and using different grinds of cornmeal, all to no avail. Yes, we learned to prevent seizing (add the cornmeal very slowly), but we still needed to stir constantly for at least 30 minutes to prevent scorching.

This testing did, however, reveal some important information. We found that medium-grind cornmeal makes the best polenta. Finely ground cornmeal, such as the Quaker brand sold in many supermarkets, is too powdery and makes gummy polenta. Cornmeal with a texture akin to granulated sugar, not table salt, makes the best polenta. We also discovered that a ratio of 4 parts water to 1 part cornmeal delivers the right consistency. As for salt, 1 teaspoon is the right amount for 1 cup of cornmeal.

At this point in our testing, we started to explore alternative cooking methods. The microwave was a bust, yielding sticky, raw-tasting polenta. The pressure cooker was even worse; the polenta took a long time to cook and then stuck firmly to the pot. We finally got good results when we prepared polenta in a double boiler. The polenta is cooked over simmering water so it cannot scorch or seize

up the way it can when cooked over direct heat. It emerges with a soft, light texture and sweet corn flavor. There is only one drawback, and it is a big one: time.

While a double boiler produced undeniably rich, creamy polenta, the cooking time was prohibitively long. Even with the minimum attention that the technique required, 1½ hours of cooking was simply impractical. We wondered whether we could produce similar results by more conventional methods. The double boiler method proved to us that slow, very gentle heat was the key to unlocking cornmeal's smooth texture, not vigilant stirring. Could we approximate a double boiler's low heat with a conventional saucepan?

Luckily, we could. A heavy-bottomed saucepan on the stove's lowest possible setting (or in conjunction with a heat tamer; see headnote) shielded the polenta from cooking too rapidly and allowed for the starches to be released and the flavor of the cornmeal to develop. Keeping the cover on the pot held in

---

INGREDIENTS: Cornmeal

Large commercial mills use huge steel rollers to grind dent corn (a hard, dry corn) into cornmeal. This is how Quaker cornmeal, the leading supermarket brand, is produced. But some smaller mills scattered around the United States grind with millstones; this product is called stone-ground cornmeal. (If water is used as an energy source, the cornmeal may be labeled water-ground.) Stone-ground cornmeal is usually a bit coarser than cornmeal processed through steel rollers. The difference is like that between granulated sugar (which is a tiny bit coarse) and table salt (which is smooth and fine).

In addition, smaller millers often choose not to degerm, or remove all the germ, cleanly. This makes their product closer to whole-grain cornmeal. If the color is uniform, the germ has been removed. A stone-ground cornmeal with some germ has flecks that are both lighter and darker than

the predominant color, whether yellow or white.

In our tests, we found the texture of polenta made with stone-ground meal more interesting, as the grind of the cornmeal was not uniform. More important, we found that polenta made with stone-ground cornmeal tasted much better than that made with the standard Quaker cornmeal. Stone-ground cornmeal gives polenta a sweeter, more intense corn flavor. Yellow cornmeal is traditional for polenta making and was the first choice among our tasters.

The higher moisture and oil content of stone-ground cornmeal causes it to go rancid rather quickly. Wrap stone-ground cornmeal tightly in plastic or put it into a moisture-proof container, then refrigerate or freeze it to prolong freshness. Degerminated cornmeals, such as Quaker, keep for a year if stored in a dry, cool place.

moisture and reduced the risk of scorching the polenta, even when we stirred infrequently rather than constantly. Within ½ hour, a third of the time it took in the double boiler, we had creamy polenta ready for the table. We did find, however, that with the slightly higher temperature, stirring was a more significant issue. When we left the polenta unheeded for more than seven minutes, it tended to stick to the pot bottom and corners, where it remained immovably until washing. Stirring vigorously every five minutes prevented such mishaps.

Basic Polenta
SERVES 4 TO 6

If you do not have a heavy-bottomed saucepan, you may want to use a flame tamer to manage the heat. A flame tamer can be purchased at most kitchen supply stores, or one can be fashioned from a ring of foil (see the illustration on page 159). It's easy to tell whether you need a flame tamer or not. If the polenta bubbles or sputters at all after the first 10 minutes, the heat is too high, and you need one. Properly heated polenta will do little more than release wisps of steam. When stirring the polenta, make sure to scrape the sides and bottom of the pan to ensure even cooking. Use this polenta as base for any stew or braise, especially lamb shanks (page 325) or osso buco (page 306). Roasted quail (page 253) or cooked leafy greens also make excellent toppings for soft polenta.

Salt
1½ cups medium cornmeal, preferably stone-ground
3 tablespoons unsalted butter, cut into large chunks
Ground black pepper

1. Bring 6 cups water to a boil in a heavy-bottomed 4-quart saucepan over medium-high heat. Once boiling, add 1½ teaspoons salt and pour the cornmeal into the water in a very slow stream from a measuring cup, all the while stirring in a circular motion with a wooden spoon (see the illustration on page 219).

2. Reduce the heat to the lowest possible setting and cover. Cook, vigorously stirring the polenta once every 5 minutes for about 10 seconds and making sure to scrape clean the bottom and corners of the pot, until the polenta has lost its raw cornmeal taste and becomes soft and smooth, about 30 minutes. Stir in the butter, season with salt and pepper to taste, and serve immediately.

➤ VARIATIONS
Polenta with Parmesan and Butter
SERVES 4 TO 6 AS A FIRST COURSE OR SIDE DISH
Follow the recipe for Basic Polenta, stirring in ¾ cup grated Parmesan cheese with the butter. Divide the polenta among individual bowls and top each with a small pat of butter. Sprinkle generously with more grated Parmesan cheese to taste and serve immediately.

Polenta with Meat Ragù
SERVES 4 TO 6 AS A MAIN COURSE
Instead of tossing slow-simmering Bolognese sauce with pasta, ladle it over mounds of soft polenta, sprinkle it with grated Parmesan cheese, and serve it as a hearty main course.

Prepare Bolognese Sauce (page 158) and keep it warm over low heat. Follow the recipe for Basic Polenta, dividing the finished polenta among individual bowls. Ladle some Bolognese sauce into each bowl and sprinkle with grated Parmesan cheese to taste. Serve immediately, passing more grated Parmesan at the table.

Polenta with Gorgonzola
SERVES 4 TO 6 AS A SUBSTANTIAL FIRST COURSE OR LIGHT ENTRÉE
Choose a Gorgonzola dolce or other mild, creamy blue cheese such as Saga Blue. Do not use an aged

Gorgonzola for this dish. Other aged blue cheeses will also be too salty, crumbly, and pungent.

Follow the recipe for Basic Polenta, dividing the finished polenta among individual bowls. Top each bowl with a 1-ounce slice of Gorgonzola cheese and serve immediately.

POLENTA WITH WILD MUSHROOMS

MUSHROOMS HAVE A NATURAL AFFINITY with polenta, as their chewy, meaty texture and flavor is sharply contrasted by the creamy cornmeal. We wanted to create a mushroom topping for polenta that offered all the rich flavor of exotic wild mushrooms but was made with supermarket domesticated mushrooms.

In the hills of Tuscany, mushrooms are easily foraged, but such wild mushrooms can cost a small fortune in the United States. Luckily, rich, earthy mushroom flavor may be attained without breaking the bank. Through the judicious use of dried porcini mushrooms, which are readily available in most markets, we have elicited a deep, earthy flavor from such moderately priced mushrooms as cremini and portobellos. The dried mushrooms lend surprising robustness to these milder mushrooms.

For the richest flavor, we sautéed the mushrooms in a mix of olive oil and butter over relatively high heat so that they shed their liquid quickly and browned well. We found that the butter helped the mushrooms achieve a deep, caramel-colored crust that was both delicious and visually appealing. The olive oil kept the butter from burning and added flavor. For seasoning the mushrooms, rosemary and garlic were a natural combination. If used too liberally, rosemary can overpower the heartiest dish with its piney taste and woodsy aroma. Borrowing a technique we often use with

soups, we cooked the mushrooms with a whole rosemary sprig, which we removed before serving. Just enough rosemary flavor was imparted to the mushrooms and, as a bonus, there was no tedious mincing. To prevent the garlic from burning in the hot pan, we added it at the very end of cooking and quickly reduced the heat under the pan.

Although the mushrooms were delicious on their own, tasters felt that they were too dry for the polenta; they wanted juices for the cornmeal to soak up. Simply adding wine and stock to the mushrooms was not successful; the mushrooms took on an unappetizingly spongy texture as they simmered. It then occurred to us that we could treat the mushrooms like seared meat, so we removed the browned mushrooms from the pan before building a pan sauce from the fond (the browned bits that adhere to the bottom of the pan when cooking foods over high heat). We deglazed the pan with red wine (tasters favored it over white) and the reserved liquid from rehydrating the dried mushrooms, then reduced the liquid to a highly flavored syrup. With a little butter whisked in, we had a sauce worthy of a fine steak as well as sautéed mushrooms and polenta.

MAKING POLENTA

When the water comes to a boil, add the salt, then pour the polenta into the water in a very slow stream from a measuring cup, all the while stirring in a circular motion with a wooden spoon to prevent clumping.

Polenta with Wild Mushroom Sauté

SERVES 4 TO 6 AS A MAIN COURSE

See page 5 for tips on rehydrating dried mushrooms. Start the polenta before beginning to cook the mushrooms. If the polenta is ready before the mushrooms are, keep it warm over very low heat; leave the cover on and stir every five minutes or so. The polenta can be held this way for 15 minutes.

⅓	ounce dried porcini mushrooms
3	tablespoons unsalted butter
2	tablespoons extra-virgin olive oil
1	sprig fresh rosemary
1	pound portobello mushrooms, stems removed and discarded, caps halved and cut crosswise into ½-inch-thick slices
1	pound cremini mushrooms, stem ends trimmed, mushrooms halved
	Salt
2	medium cloves garlic, minced or pressed through a garlic press
1	tablespoon minced fresh parsley leaves
	Ground black pepper
½	cup red wine
	Basic Polenta (page 218)

1. Mix the dried porcini mushrooms with ½ cup hot tap water in a small microwave-safe bowl. Cover with plastic wrap, cut several steam vents in the plastic wrap with a paring knife, and microwave on high power for 30 seconds. Let stand until the mushrooms soften, about 5 minutes. Lift the mushrooms from the liquid with a fork and mince. Pour the liquid through a small strainer lined with a single sheet of paper towel and placed over a measuring cup. Reserve the mushrooms and strained soaking liquid separately.

2. Heat 1 tablespoon butter with the oil and the rosemary sprig in a large skillet over medium-high heat. Once the foaming subsides, add the portobello and cremini mushrooms and ½ teaspoon salt and cook, stirring occasionally, until the mushrooms have shed their liquid and the cut surfaces have browned, about 10 minutes. Reduce the heat to medium-low and add the garlic and minced porcini. Cook, stirring frequently, until aromatic, about 1 minute. Remove and discard the rosemary, stir in the parsley, and season with salt and pepper to taste. Transfer the mushrooms to a bowl and tent with foil to keep warm.

3. Return the pan to the stove and increase the heat to medium-high. Add the porcini liquid and the wine to the skillet and scrape the pan bottom to loosen any browned bits. Simmer until the liquid has reduced to about ⅓ cup, 6 to 8 minutes. Remove the pan from the heat and whisk in the remaining 2 tablespoons butter until completely incorporated. Season with salt and pepper to taste.

4. Divide the polenta among individual bowls. Divide the mushrooms among the bowls and drizzle a little sauce over each portion. Serve immediately.

INGREDIENTS: Instant Polenta

After testing dozens of ways to prepare polenta, we still had one question: what about quick-cooking, or instant, polenta? We tested several brands (all imported from Italy) and found that instant polenta is a great way to make polenta in a hurry. The flavor is good (although not nearly as good as our basic polenta), and it takes no more than 10 minutes. When time really matters, this product is a decent alternative.

Quick polenta, like quick grits and instant rice, has been cooked, then dried. All you need to do is reconstitute it with boiling water. Quick polenta costs at least three times as much as regular cornmeal and doesn't have the smooth texture and full corn flavor of regular polenta. However, instant polenta is easy to prepare (just add to boiling water and simmer for several minutes), and the result is pretty good.

White Beans with Tomatoes, Garlic, and Sage

CALLED CANNELLINI ALL'UCCELLETO, or "beans cooked like little birds" in Italian, white beans with tomatoes, garlic, and sage is a ubiquitous dish in Florence, much like Boston and its trademark baked beans. The colorful name comes from the cooking method and flavorings; game birds are traditionally stewed in a combination of tomatoes, garlic, and sage. While we found the combination of flavors delicious, we thought that this traditional dish could benefit from a little fine-tuning of both technique and flavor.

Tuscans, who are notorious bean eaters, are nicknamed *mangiafagiole,* "the bean eaters." While a variety of beans are consumed in the region, cannellini beans are the most prevalent. Their creamy texture and sweet, neutral flavor is used to great effect in soups and stews. Cannellini beans can be simply dressed with nothing more than fine extra-virgin olive oil and herbs and eaten on their own (perhaps with slices of bruschetta), over salad greens, or as an accompaniment to roast meat or fish.

The traditional Tuscan method for cooking beans is romantic but impractical for the modern home cook. The dried beans are placed in a *fiasco,* the bulbous wine bottle used for Chianti, with some liquid, a sprig of sage, and a few garlic cloves, and then the bottle is sealed and nestled into the embers of the household fire to cook slowly through the night. By the morning, the beans are plump and ready to eat.

Needless to say, we did not try cooking our beans in a fiasco or dying embers. A large heavy-bottomed saucepan or Dutch oven was our choice as it retained heat well, an important attribute when cooking beans. After exhaustively testing different methods, we knew we could cook them unsoaked (contrary to what most sources say) and that a relatively low temperature yielded the creamiest beans. Anything more than a slow simmer yielded unevenly cooked beans; some beans were falling apart soft while others were still chalky. (For more information about cooking beans, see page 113 and read about our tests concerning Tuscan White Bean Soup.)

To add flavor to the beans as they cooked, we added an onion and a carrot as well as a whole head of garlic with its top lopped off so that its flavor would permeate the liquid. According to most tasters, the traditional handful of garlic cloves added little flavor. While the carrot and onion were discarded after cooking, the garlic cloves were squeezed from their skins and returned to the beans, lending a sweet, mild garlic flavor. We saved a portion of the highly seasoned cooking liquid to moisten the beans (the cooking liquid can also be used as a foundation for soup, as in Tuscan White Bean Soup).

With the beans cooked, it was time to combine them with the tomatoes, garlic, and sage. Not out to reinvent the wheel, we did not change the flavorings outside of how they were added to the beans. Traditionally, the flavorings are stirred directly into the cooked beans and briefly simmered, but we found that garlic and sage had a better flavor if they were first sautéed in olive oil. When the garlic was lightly toasted, it had a mellower flavor that emphasized the sweetness of the beans. Cooking the sage with the garlic tempered the brash herb to a pleasant background note.

Diced canned tomatoes were preferred over pureed, which made the beans too soupy. Once the juices of the tomatoes evaporated, we added the beans and some of their cooking liquid and simmered until the flavors melded and the bean cooking liquid evaporated.

White Beans with Tomatoes, Garlic, and Sage

SERVES 6 AS A MAIN DISH
OR 8 TO 10 AS A SIDE DISH

Traditionally, the beans receive a liberal dousing of the finest extra-virgin olive oil prior to serving, but use your discretion; some tasters felt the beans were overwhelmed by the pungency of the oil. The amount of oil also depends on its flavor. Although this recipe yields a large quantity, the beans keep for several days and reheat well. Mixed with additional olive oil and a spritz of lemon juice, the beans are an outstanding topping for bruschetta (page 19). The grilled bread and beans can also be topped with sautéed spinach (page 86) for a nutritious vegetarian meal. Although we strongly recommend cooking dried beans for the best flavor, we do offer a canned bean version below.

1	pound dried cannellini beans (or great Northern or navy beans), rinsed and picked over
1	medium onion, unpeeled and halved through the root end
1	medium carrot, cut into 2-inch lengths
1	head garlic, top quarter cut off and loose papery skins removed, plus 4 medium cloves, sliced thin
	Salt
2	bay leaves
¼	cup extra-virgin olive oil, plus additional for the table
¼	cup roughly chopped fresh sage leaves
1	(28-ounce) can diced tomatoes, drained
2	tablespoons minced fresh parsley leaves
	Ground black pepper

1. Bring the beans, onion, carrot, garlic head, 1 teaspoon salt, bay leaves, and 6 cups water to a boil in a large saucepan or Dutch oven over medium-high heat. Reduce the heat to low, partially cover, and simmer, stirring occasionally, until the beans are almost tender, 1 to 1¼ hours, adding more liquid if necessary. Remove the pot from the heat, completely cover, and let stand until the beans are fully tender, 30 to 60 minutes. Drain the beans, reserving 1 cup cooking liquid. Remove and discard the onion, carrot, and bay leaves. With a slotted spoon, transfer the head of garlic to a cutting board. Using tongs, squeeze the cloves out of the skins and return the softened cloves to the pot with the beans; discard the skins.

2. Heat the olive oil, thinly sliced garlic, and sage in a 12-inch skillet over medium heat. As the oil begins to sizzle, shake the pan back and forth so that the garlic does not stick (stirring with a wooden spoon will cause the garlic to clump). Cook until the garlic turns very pale gold and the sage darkens, about 4 minutes. Add the tomatoes and ½ teaspoon salt and simmer, stirring occasionally, until the tomato juices have evaporated and the tomatoes look shiny, about 10 minutes.

3. Stir in the beans and reserved cooking liquid. Simmer, stirring occasionally, until the liquid has evaporated, 18 to 20 minutes. Off the heat, stir in the parsley and season with salt and pepper to taste. Serve immediately, accompanied by extra-virgin olive oil for drizzling at the table.

➤ VARIATION

Quick White Beans with Tomatoes, Garlic, and Sage

With canned beans, this variation can be made start to finish in about half an hour.

Follow the recipe for White Beans with Tomatoes, Garlic, and Sage, omitting step 1. In step 3, add 4 (15½-ounce) cans cannellini beans, drained and rinsed, along with 1 cup chicken stock or canned low-sodium chicken broth. Proceed as directed.

SICILIAN CHICKPEAS AND ESCAROLE

A SEEMINGLY ENDLESS VARIETY OF dishes with beans and greens stewed together are found throughout southern Europe. They are a prime example of what Italians call *cucina povera*, or "cuisine of the poor," as they combine readily available, inexpensive (or free, in the case of wild greens) ingredients in a highly nutritious meal.

Sicily's beloved chickpeas (ceci) shine when paired with leafy escarole. Their sweetness and firm, chewy texture is complemented by the bitterness and supple smoothness of the wilted greens. Coated with a drizzle of extra-virgin olive oil and served with crusty bread, this dish makes an irresistible one-pot main course. However, like many cucina povera dishes, we discovered that it needed a little updating to suit our modern palates.

Chickpeas are the heart of this dish. While we normally prefer dried beans over canned, we have found that canned chickpeas are perfectly acceptable in some instances, as their texture and flavor are little compromised by the canning process. And admittedly, cooking dried chickpeas takes some effort; they must be soaked overnight (in contrast to most other beans), and they take a minimum of 1½ hours to cook. When they were combined with the other assertive ingredients in this dish, tasters had a hard time telling if the beans were canned or dried.

Aromatics, such as onions, carrots, and garlic, are traditional flavorings for this dish. Tasters favored red onion over yellow for their sweetness, and the firm texture of the carrots added a pleasing crunch. As is common throughout southern Italy, we lightly toasted the garlic in the olive oil prior to adding the other aromatics. Toasting mellowed the garlic's fierce bite to a nutty sweetness that contributed body and depth to the dish. We toasted hot red pepper flakes at the same time, as the dry heat activates their volatile oils for a deeper, roasted flavor—an improvement noted by tasters.

With the aromatics cooked, the beans and some liquid can be added to the pot. Although the escarole can be washed and shaken dry so the leaves are still damp, more liquid is needed for steaming it. Water was a bit bland; tasters preferred chicken stock (or the bean cooking liquid, if dried beans are used).

Raisins appear in numerous savory dishes throughout southern Italy, including caponata (page 12). The savory use of dried fruit is a vestige of the Arab influence on Italian cooking. In this case, the raisins balance the dish, tying together the beans and greens and tempering the chile heat. The raisins are usually plumped so that their texture acts as a counterpoint to the beans; they literally burst in your mouth. For this reason, we found it best to add them to the pot along with the chickpeas and stock.

As the beans are already cooked through, actual cooking time—outside of sautéing the aromatics—was just long enough to wilt the escarole and blend the flavors. After wrestling with wilting the awkward escarole in a skillet, we discovered that a deep Dutch oven made for hassle-free cooking. All of the escarole could be added at once, and the pot could be covered. As the escarole wilted in the enclosed steam, we stirred it into the chickpea mixture. Once all of the escarole had wilted, we found it necessary to simmer the dish uncovered briefly to concentrate the watery liquid shed by the greens. Parsley and lemon juice brightened the appearance and flavor of the final dish.

223

Sicilian Chickpeas with Escarole

SERVES 4 TO 6 AS A MAIN COURSE
OR 6 TO 8 AS A SIDE DISH

If you would like to use dried chickpeas, follow the cooking instructions for the beans in the Chickpea Soup recipe (page 122), but reduce the amount of cooking liquid by half. You will have double the amount of beans necessary for this recipe. If you like, replace the chicken stock with 1 cup of the chickpea cooking liquid. If you have problems locating escarole, substitute chicory, although its flavor is stronger. The overall sweetness of this dish stands up well to a fair amount of spiciness, but you can adjust the amount of hot red pepper flakes to taste. For a vegetarian main course, serve this dish with bruschetta or polenta. This is also an excellent side dish with roast pork or fish.

¼	cup extra-virgin olive oil, plus additional for the table
4	medium cloves garlic, sliced thin
½	teaspoon hot red pepper flakes
1	large red onion, diced medium
1	medium carrot, diced medium
	Salt
2	(15½-ounce) cans chickpeas, drained and rinsed, or 3 cups cooked chickpeas
⅓	cup raisins
1	cup homemade chicken stock or canned low-sodium chicken broth
1	head escarole (about 1 pound), washed, shaken dry, and cut into 1-inch lengths
2	tablespoons minced fresh parsley leaves
2	teaspoons lemon juice
	Ground black pepper

1. Combine the oil, garlic, and hot red pepper flakes in a large Dutch oven over medium-high heat. As the oil begins to sizzle, shake the pan back and forth so that the garlic does not stick (stirring with a wooden spoon will cause the garlic to clump). Cook until the garlic turns very pale gold, 2 to 2½ minutes. Add the onion, carrot, and ½ teaspoon salt and cook, stirring frequently, until the vegetables are softened and lightly browned, 7 to 8 minutes.

2. Reduce the heat to medium and stir in the chickpeas, raisins, and stock. Mix thoroughly, then add the damp escarole and cover the pan. Every 2 minutes, uncover the pot and stir. Once all the escarole has wilted (this should take about 8 to 10 minutes), uncover the pot and simmer until the liquid is reduced to a light coating on the bottom of the pan, about 5 minutes. Remove the pan from the heat, stir in the parsley and lemon juice, and season with salt and pepper to taste. Serve immediately, accompanied by extra-virgin olive oil for drizzling at the table.

7

POULTRY

LIKE AMERICANS, ITALIANS PREPARE chicken in countless ways. Cutlets can be breaded and sautéed or simply seared and sauced. Whole chickens are often butterflied (the cook removes the backbone with poultry shears, then opens the bird and flattens it) and grilled or cooked in a skillet under weights. Whole chickens are roasted, usually with typical Italian flavorings such as lemon or, perhaps, rosemary and garlic.

Unlike Americans, Italians also cook a number of little birds and rabbit (which is not, of course, a member of the poultry family, but shares many flavor and cooking properties with chicken). We have chosen two simple dishes, roast quail and braised rabbit, as representatives of this distinctive branch of Italian cooking.

CHICKEN MILANESE

TENDER BONELESS CHICKEN BREAST, pan-fried with a cloak of mild-flavored crumbs, has universal appeal. Almost every cuisine has such a dish. In Italy, grated Parmesan is added to the coating, and the dish is called chicken Milanese. Though simple, this dish, which is perhaps the most popular chicken preparation in Italy, can fall prey to a host of problems. The chicken itself may be rubbery and tasteless, and the coating—called a bound breading and arguably the best part of the dish—often ends up uneven, greasy, pale, or even burnt.

For a breaded chicken cutlet to be great, the chicken itself must hold up its end of the bargain. Because the test kitchen is fiercely devoted to the benefits of brining poultry, we wondered what effect soaking the cutlets in a mixture of salt, sugar, and water would have. The brined cutlets were a hit, exceptionally juicy and seasoned all the way to the center. The brining

step is easy to execute and takes just 30 minutes, during which time you can pull together other components of the recipe. It's not often that so little work yields such big benefits. (For cutlet recipes with a sauce, such as Marsala and piccata, the sauce adds plenty of moisture, and there's no need to brine the chicken.)

Throughout the first series of tests, we noticed that the thin tip of the cutlet and the opposite end, which was much more plump, cooked at different rates. This problem was a cinch to fix; all we had to do was pound the chicken breasts gently to an even ½-inch thickness with a meat pounder (see page 231) or the bottom of a small saucepan. To promote even cooking, we also found it best to remove the floppy tenderloin from the underside of each cutlet before pounding.

The ideal breading should taste mild and comforting but not dull and certainly not greasy. To explore the possibilities, we pan-fried cutlets coated with fine, fresh bread crumbs (made from fresh sliced white sandwich bread ground fine in the food processor) and dry bread crumbs. The dry bread crumbs had an unmistakably stale flavor. The fresh bread crumbs swept the test, with a mild, subtly sweet flavor and a light, crisp texture. We went on to test crumbs made from different kinds of white bread, including premium sliced sandwich bread, Italian, French, and country-style. The sliced bread was the sweetest and appealed to tasters in this recipe. That said, fresh crumbs made from all of these breads were good. (See page 57 for more information on homemade bread crumbs.)

During the crumb testing, we made several important observations about the breading process. First, we learned that the cutlets had to be thoroughly dried after brining. We also learned that we could not dispense with the coating of flour that went onto the chicken before the egg wash and crumbs. If the cutlets were even slightly moist, or if we skipped the flour coat, the breading would peel off the finished cutlets in sheets. Dry cutlets also produced the thinnest possible coating of flour, which eliminated any floury taste when the cutlets were cooked and served. In addition, we found that it was essential to press the crumbs onto the cutlets to assure an even, thorough cover. Finally, we discovered that it was best to let the breaded cutlets rest for about five minutes before frying them, again to help bind the breading to the meat.

The bread crumbs are attached to the floured cutlets by means of a quick dip into beaten egg. But beaten eggs are thick and viscous, and they tend to form too heavy a layer on the meat, giving the breading a thick, indelicate quality. Thinning the egg with oil, water, or both is a common practice that allows excess egg to slide off the meat more easily, leaving a thinner, more delicate coat. We tried all three routines, and honestly, we couldn't detect much difference in the flavor or texture of the finished breading. In repeated tests, we did notice that the breading made with oil-thinned egg wash seemed to brown a little

more deeply than that made with water-thinned wash, so we added a tablespoon of oil to our two beaten eggs and moved on.

Last, we explored the details of pan-frying. In any breaded preparation, the oil in the pan should reach one-third to one-half the way up the food for thorough browning. Which fat should be used for sautéing the cutlets? Cutlets sautéed in olive oil were markedly better than those sautéed in vegetable oil.

Chicken Milanese
SERVES 4

When coating the cutlets with the bread crumb and cheese mixture, use your hands to pat a thorough, even coating onto the chicken to make sure the crumbs adhere. The chicken is cooked in batches of two because the crust is noticeably more crisp if the pan is not overcrowded. See the illustrations on page 228 for tips on breading cutlets.

4	boneless, skinless chicken breasts (5 to 6 ounces each), tenderloins removed and reserved for another use, fat trimmed (see illustration at left)
½	cup kosher salt or ¼ cup table salt
½	cup sugar
	Ground black pepper
1¼	cups homemade bread crumbs (page 57)
¼	cup finely grated Parmesan cheese
¾	cup unbleached all-purpose flour
2	large eggs
1	tablespoon plus ¾ cup olive oil
	Lemon wedges for serving

1. Use a meat pounder, rubber mallet, or rolling pin to pound the chicken breasts to an even ½-inch thickness. Dissolve the salt and sugar in 1 quart cold water in a gallon-sized zipper-lock plastic bag. Add the cutlets and seal the bag, pressing out as much air as

TRIMMING CUTLETS

Most cutlets have a little yellow or white fat still attached to the breast meat. Lay each cutlet tenderloin side down and smooth the top with your fingers. Any fat will slide to the edge of the cutlet, where it can be trimmed with a knife.

possible. Refrigerate until the cutlets are fully seasoned, 30 minutes. Line a baking sheet with a triple layer of paper towels.

2. Remove the cutlets and lay them in a single layer on the baking sheet. Cover with another triple layer of paper towels and press firmly to absorb moisture. Allow the cutlets to dry for 10 minutes. Carefully peel the paper towels off the cutlets; sprinkle the cutlets with pepper to taste and set them aside.

3. Adjust an oven rack to the lower-middle position, set a large heatproof plate on the rack, and heat the oven to 200 degrees. Combine the bread crumbs and Parmesan cheese in a shallow dish or pie plate. Spread the flour in a second shallow dish. Beat the eggs with 1 tablespoon oil in a third shallow dish.

4. Working with one at a time, dredge the cutlets thoroughly in the flour, shaking off the excess. Using tongs, dip both sides of the cutlets in the egg mixture, taking care to coat them thoroughly and allowing the excess to drip back into the dish to ensure a very thin coating. Dip both sides of the cutlets in the bread crumb mixture, pressing the crumbs with your fingers to form an even, cohesive coat. Place the breaded cutlets in a single layer on a wire rack set over a baking sheet and allow the

BREADING CUTLETS

1. Dredge the cutlets thoroughly in flour, shaking off the excess.

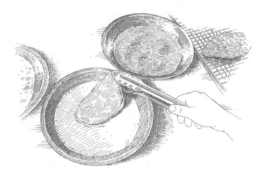

2. Using tongs, dip both sides of the cutlets in the egg mixture, taking care to coat them thoroughly and allowing the excess to drip back into the dish to ensure a very thin coating. Tongs keep the breading from coating your fingers.

3. Dip both sides of the cutlets in the bread crumbs, pressing the crumbs with your fingers to form an even, cohesive coat.

4. Place the breaded cutlets in a single layer on a wire rack set over a baking sheet and allow the coating to dry for about 5 minutes. This drying time stabilizes the breading so that it can be sautéed without sticking to the pan or falling off.

coating to dry for about 5 minutes.

5. Meanwhile, heat 6 tablespoons of the remaining oil in a heavy-bottomed 10-inch nonstick skillet over medium-high heat until shimmering but not smoking, about 2 minutes. Lay two cutlets gently in the skillet and cook until deep golden brown and crisp on the first side, gently pressing down on the cutlets with a wide metal spatula to help ensure even browning, about 2½ minutes. Using tongs, flip the cutlets, reduce the heat to medium, and continue to cook until the meat feels firm when pressed gently and the second side is deep golden brown and crisp, 2½ to 3 minutes. Line the warmed plate with a double layer of paper towels and set the cutlets on top; return the plate to the oven.

6. Discard the oil in the skillet and wipe the skillet clean using tongs and a large wad of paper towels. Repeat step 5, using the remaining 6 tablespoons oil and the now-clean skillet to cook the remaining cutlets. Serve immediately along with the first batch and the lemon wedges.

➤ VARIATIONS

Breaded Chicken Cutlets with Garlic and Oregano

Follow the recipe for Chicken Milanese, increasing the bread crumbs to 1½ cups and omitting the Parmesan cheese. Beat 3 tablespoons very finely minced fresh oregano leaves and 8 medium garlic cloves, minced to puree or pressed through a garlic press, into the egg mixture in step 3.

Basic Breaded Chicken Cutlets

This variation works well for Chicken Parmesan (page 230).

Follow the recipe for Chicken Milanese, increasing the bread crumbs to 1½ cups and omitting the Parmesan cheese.

CHICKEN PARMESAN

CHICKEN PARMESAN—BREADED CHICKEN cutlets topped with cheese and tomato sauce—is beloved by many American families. Although the dish has its roots in Italy, the execution and the excess are purely American. The chicken is usually covered with way too much cheese and sauce, and it is served with a full portion of spaghetti.

We wanted to remain true to the hearty nature of this dish, but we also wanted to use some restraint. At the outset, we made several decisions. First, the chicken would take center stage, and the pasta portions would be modest. (We figured on eight ounces of dried spaghetti for four servings, not the pound called for in many recipes.) Second, we would cover the chicken with a modest amount of cheese and tomato sauce. You spend a lot of time breading and cooking the chicken; why bury it under a mountain of molten cheese and sauce? We also wanted to avoid a problem common with this dish—soggy cutlets.

Based on our experience with chicken Milanese, we knew the best way to bread and cook a cutlet. However, we wondered if sautéing would be the right route here, as the cheese that coats the cooked cutlets would be melted under the broiler or in the oven. We figured it was worth trying to cook the chicken under the broiler and save a step. Unfortunately, broiling resulted in inconsistently and unimpressively browned cutlets. In contrast, sautéing produced a beautiful, evenly golden-brown color and rich, satisfying flavor.

Some recipes, especially older ones, instruct the reader to top cooked cutlets with mozzarella cheese and bake them on a bed of tomato sauce, covered, until the cheese melts. As far as we are concerned, this step not only added several minutes to the preparation time, it also destroyed the crisp, delicious coating and turned the cutlets into soggy mush. We simply sprinkled the cooked cutlets with mozzarella and Parmesan (3 tablespoons mozzarella and 1 tablespoon Parmesan per cutlet was sufficient) and broiled them until the cheeses melted and turned spotty brown. They were now ready for tomato sauce and the accompanying pasta.

As for the sauce, chicken Parmesan requires a smooth, thick sauce that goes together in a flash. Crushed tomatoes were the obvious choice. We found that a little garlic and herbs enlivened their flavor and kept the recipe simple.

Chicken Parmesan

SERVES 4

For more information about breading and cooking the chicken, see the chicken Milanese recipe on page 227. Timing is key here. The spaghetti should go into the boiling water at the same time the first batch of breaded cutlets goes into the oil.

SMOOTH TOMATO SAUCE

2	medium cloves garlic, minced or pressed through a garlic press
¼	cup extra-virgin olive oil
1	(28-ounce) can crushed tomatoes
½	teaspoon dried basil
¼	teaspoon dried oregano
¼	teaspoon sugar
	Salt and ground black pepper

1	recipe Basic Breaded Chicken Cutlets (page 229)
2	teaspoons salt
8	ounces spaghetti or linguine
¾	cup (3 ounces) grated mozzarella cheese
¼	cup grated Parmesan cheese, plus extra for passing at the table

1. **FOR THE SAUCE:** Heat the garlic and oil together in a large saucepan over medium-high heat until the garlic starts to sizzle. Stir in the tomatoes, basil, oregano, sugar, a pinch of salt, and two grinds of pepper and bring to a simmer. Continue to simmer until the sauce thickens a bit and the flavors meld, 10 to 12 minutes. Taste the sauce, adjusting the salt if necessary. Cover and keep warm.

2. Bring 3 quarts water to a boil in a large pot. Adjust the oven rack to the top position and heat the broiler.

3. Bread the chicken cutlets, place them in a single layer on a wire rack set over a baking sheet, and allow the coating to dry about 5 minutes (see step 4 of the recipe on page 228).

4. Add 2 teaspoons salt and the spaghetti to the boiling water. At the same time, cook the chicken cutlets according to step 5 of the recipe on page 229. When the cutlets are done, transfer them a clean wire rack set over a clean baking sheet. Top each cutlet with 3 tablespoons mozzarella and 1 tablespoon Parmesan cheese. Place the baking sheet under the broiler and broil until the cheeses melt and are spotty brown, about 3 minutes.

To keep the coating on the chicken cutlets crisp, the tomato sauce is not added until serving time.

5. Drain the spaghetti. Transfer a chicken cutlet and a portion of spaghetti to each of four plates. Spoon 1 to 2 tablespoons sauce over part of each cutlet, then sauce the spaghetti as desired. Serve immediately, passing extra Parmesan separately at the table.

CHICKEN MARSALA

MARSALA, NEVER A GLAMOROUS WINE, bears the name of its hometown, a seaport on the western coast of Sicily once mockingly dubbed "the dump" by Italians from neighboring wine-making regions. In the early 1800s, a marketing campaign touted Marsala as a less expensive alternative to Madeira and sherry. As sales soared, it quickly made its way into Italian kitchens, where classic dishes such as chicken Marsala were created. Nowadays, chicken Marsala is an Italian restaurant staple. After several disappointing encounters with this dish that involved watery sauces, flaccid mushrooms, and pale, stale chicken, we realized that chicken Marsala was being taken for granted. It was in need of a rescue.

While all of the recipes we found listed the same three ingredients—breast of chicken, mushrooms, and Marsala—the cooking methods differed. Some called for simmering the chicken and mushrooms in Marsala, which resulted in flavors that were waterlogged and bland. Others recommended cooking everything in separate pans, creating not only a messy kitchen but a dish with disjointed flavors. Yet others had the cook sauté everything in the same pan, but sequentially. The clear winner turned out to be the classic approach, in which the meat is sautéed first, then moved to a warm oven while the browned bits left in the pan are splashed with wine and enriched with butter to create a sauce. With this decided, we focused on perfecting the sautéed chicken

and developing the sauce.

When sautéing, the most important steps include getting the skillet as hot as possible and patting the chicken dry with paper towels before dusting with a light coating of flour. Using these pointers as a guide, we sautéed with a variety of oils and with butter to find that vegetable oil was the least likely to burn and splatter.

Our next task was to figure out how to get the mushrooms crisp and brown without burning the drippings left from the sautéed chicken. One way to do this, we thought, would be to add more fat to the pan and scrape the browned bits off the bottom before cooking the mushrooms. We tried adding both fat and flavor by cooking small pieces of

---

EQUIPMENT: Meat Pounder

When developing our recipes for chicken Parmesan and chicken Milanese, we tried several pounding gadgets—makeshift as well as purchased—and found that the best chicken breast pounders were relatively lightweight, with large flat surfaces. A disk-style pounder with a handle in the center was our favorite. As long as we pounded lightly, its relatively large, round surface quickly and efficiently transformed breasts into cutlets. If you don't have this kind of

pounder, we suggest pounding gently with what you have on hand, which is likely heavier than our disk-style pounder. A rubber mallet or rolling pin would be our second choice, but the bottom of a small saucepan will work in a pinch.

THE BEST MEAT POUNDER
We tested several styles of meat pounders and found that a disk-style pounder with a handle in the center is the gentlest on delicate chicken cutlets; it is our top choice.

pancetta (Italian bacon that has been cured but not smoked) directly after the chicken. Just as we thought, the fat rendered from the pancetta prevented the chicken drippings from burning while providing the oil necessary for sautéing the mushrooms—not to mention adding a meaty, pepper-flavored punch to the sauce.

Because several types and grades of Marsala wine can be found on the market, we conducted a taste test before doing any cooking, trying imported and California brands of both the sweet and dry varieties. We favored an imported wine, Sweet Marsala Fine, for its depth of flavor, smooth finish, and reasonable price tag. By reducing the wine, we found the silky, plush texture we were looking for in the final sauce. Knowing that stock is traditionally added to pan sauces for depth of flavor and body, we tested a variety of stock-to-Marsala ratios. Again and again, tasters preferred a sauce made only from wine, slightly reduced. The stock simply got in the way of the Marsala's distinctive zip.

Mushrooms, pancetta, and tomato paste add depth, complexity, and color to chicken Marsala.

SCIENCE: How Brining Works

Soaking chicken in a brine—a solution of salt (and often sugar) and a liquid (usually water)—provides it with a plump cushion of seasoned moisture that will sustain it throughout cooking. The chicken will actually gain a bit of weight (call it, for lack of a better term, water retention) which stays with it throughout cooking. This weight gain translates into moist flesh; the salt and sugar in the brine translate into seasoned, flavorful flesh.

Brining responds to two rules of nature, diffusion and osmosis, that like things to be kept in equilibrium. For instance, when brining chicken, there is a greater concentration of salt and sugar outside of the chicken (in the brine) than inside the chicken (in the cells that make up its flesh). Following the law of diffusion, the salt and sugar naturally flow from the area of greater concentration (the brine) to that of lesser concentration

(the cells). There is also a greater concentration of water, so to speak, outside of the chicken than inside. Here, too, the water naturally flows from the area of greater concentration (the brine) to that of lesser concentration (the cells). When water moves in this fashion, the process is called osmosis.

Once inside the cells, the salt and, to a lesser extent, the sugar, cause the cell proteins to unravel, or denature. As the individual proteins unravel, they become more likely to interact. This interaction results in the formation of a sticky matrix that captures and holds moisture. Once exposed to heat, the matrix gels and forms a barrier that keeps much of the water from leaking out as the meat cooks. The result is chicken that is both better seasoned and much moister than when you started.

All we had to do now was round out the final flavors. Lemon juice tempered the Marsala's sweetness, while one clove of garlic and a teaspoon of tomato paste rounded out the other flavors. Last, we found that 4 tablespoons of unsalted butter whisked in at the end added a dreamlike finish and beautiful sheen. Here was a chicken Marsala Sicilians could be proud of.

Chicken Marsala

SERVES 4

Our wine of choice for this dish is Sweet Marsala Fine, an Italian wine that gives the sauce body, soft edges, and a smooth finish. See page 234 for more information about making a pan sauce. Because these cutlets spend about 15 minutes in the oven while the sauce is being prepared, there's no need to pound the cutlets or remove the tenderloins.

4	boneless, skinless chicken breasts (5 to 6 ounces each), fat trimmed (see illustration on page 227)
I	cup unbleached all-purpose flour
	Salt and ground black pepper
2	tablespoons vegetable oil
2½	ounces pancetta (about 3 slices), cut into pieces I inch long and ⅛ inch wide
8	ounces white mushrooms, sliced (about 2 cups)
I	medium clove garlic, minced or pressed through a garlic press
I	teaspoon tomato paste
I½	cups sweet Marsala
I½	tablespoons lemon juice
4	tablespoons unsalted butter, cut into 4 pieces
2	tablespoons minced fresh parsley leaves

1. Adjust an oven rack to the lower-middle position, place a large heatproof dinner plate on the rack, and heat the oven to 200 degrees.

2. Pat the chicken breasts dry. Place the flour in a shallow baking dish or pie plate. Season both sides of the chicken cutlets with salt and pepper to taste. Working with one cutlet at a time, coat both sides with flour. Lift the breast from the tapered end and shake to remove excess flour; set aside.

3. Meanwhile, heat the oil in a 12-inch heavy-bottomed skillet over medium-high heat until shimmering. Place the floured cutlets in a single layer in the skillet and cook until golden brown, about 3 minutes. Using tongs, flip the cutlets and cook on the second side until golden brown and the meat feels firm when pressed with a finger, about 3 minutes longer. Transfer the chicken to the heated plate and return the plate to the oven.

4. Return the skillet to low heat and add the pancetta. Sauté, stirring occasionally and scraping the pan bottom with a wooden spoon to loosen browned bits, until the pancetta is brown and crisp, about 4 minutes.

CHOOSING MARSALA

The choice of wines does matter in chicken Marsala. We found that imported Marsala (from Italy) had more complex flavors than domestic wines. We had the best results with sweet Marsala (left), which produced a smoother, rounder sauce than dry Marsala (right).

With a slotted spoon, transfer the pancetta to a paper towel–lined plate.

5. Add the mushrooms to the pan and increase the heat to medium-high. Sauté, stirring occasionally and scraping the pan bottom, until the liquid released by the mushrooms evaporates and the mushrooms begin to brown, about 8 minutes. Add the garlic, tomato paste, and cooked pancetta and cook, stirring constantly, until the tomato paste begins to brown, about 1 minute. Off the heat, add the Marsala. Return the pan to high heat and simmer vigorously, scraping the browned bits from the pan bottom, until the sauce is slightly syrupy and reduced to about 1¼ cups, about 5 minutes. Off the

heat, add the lemon juice and any accumulated juices from the chicken. Whisk in the butter, 1 tablespoon at a time. Stir in the parsley and season with salt and pepper to taste. Pour the sauce over the chicken and serve immediately.

SCIENCE: Making Pan Sauces

Ever wonder how restaurants make thick, rich sauces to accompany sautéed cutlets and steaks? Chances are they use a pan sauce, made with the delicious caramelized browned bits that sit on the bottom of the pan after the meat has been sautéed or pan-seared.

Pan sauces are usually made by adding liquid (stock, wine, or juice) to the pan once the cooked cutlets or steaks have been transferred to a plate to rest. The liquid dissolves the browned bits (a process known as deglazing) and incorporates them into the sauce.

What makes those browned bits so delicious, so valuable? When meat or chicken browns, something called the Maillard reaction occurs. This process is named after the French chemist who first described this reaction about 100 years ago. When the amino acids (or protein components) and natural sugars in meat are subjected to intense heat, like that found in a skillet, they begin to combine and form new compounds. These compounds in turn break down and form yet more new flavor compounds, and so on and so on. The process is like rabbits multiplying. The browned bits left in the pan once the meat has been cooked are packed with complex flavors that are carried over to the pan sauce once the liquid is added.

CHICKEN PICCATA

CHICKEN PICCATA–SAUTÉED CUTLETS with a lemon-caper sauce—is a restaurant classic that translates easily to the home kitchen. We imagined that piccata would be easy to perfect—and it was, after we realized that most recipes miss the point. To begin with, many cookbook authors add extraneous ingredients and thereby ruin the pure simplicity of the dish. The other major problem is blandness. Many recipes contain just a tablespoon of lemon juice and a teaspoon of capers, neither of which provides much flavor. Our goals were simple: to cook the chicken properly and to make a streamlined sauce that really tastes of lemons and capers.

We started with the chicken. Many piccata recipes suggest pounding the cutlets, even thin ones. We found this step unnecessary; cutlets less than ½ inch thick cook quickly enough. Pounding not only makes the cutlets thinner but increases their surface area, making it harder to fit them in the pan. Then you're forced to cook them in three batches to make enough for four people, dramatically increasing your chances of burning the pan drippings. Without pounding, you can cook 1½ pounds of small cutlets in a 12-inch skillet in two batches.

Many piccata recipes call for flouring or breading the cutlets. As in past tests, we found that floured cutlets browned better and were less likely to stick to the pan. Tasters did not like breaded cutlets—what's the point of developing a crisp crust only to douse it with sauce? We also tried dipping the cutlets in milk as well as beaten eggs before flouring them. Although the crust was a bit thicker when cooked, tasters felt that there was little advantage to this extra step.

With our chicken tests completed, we turned our attention to the sauce. We wanted a strong lemon flavor that wasn't harsh or overly acidic. We also wanted a sauce that was thick enough to nap the sautéed cutlets. We knew we wanted to deglaze the empty skillet used to cook the chicken with some liquid to loosen the flavorful browned bits, then reduce the liquid and thicken it.

Most of the recipes we uncovered in our research called for 1 or 2 tablespoons of lemon

---

INGREDIENTS: Capers

Many people associate capers with anchovies and assume that they come from the sea. Others assume that they must be related to peas or beans because of their shape. Capers are actually pickles made from the unopened flower buds of the caper shrub, which grows in the Mediterranean region. These briny morsels are used in countless Italian, Spanish, and Greek recipes.

Capers can be preserved in two ways. Most often, the flower buds are soaked in a saltwater brine, then packed in brine or a mixture of brine and vinegar. This is how capers are sold in most supermarkets. The other option is to cure them with salt. This kind of caper costs more and is available only in specialty markets.

In addition to differences in preservation technique, capers vary in size. The smallest capers—no larger than small peas—are called nonpareils. There are several more grades, the largest being the size of small olives and called gruesas. If you drink martinis, you may also have seen caperberries. These oval berries form if the flower buds are allowed to open and set fruit. Caperberries are pickled in brine, just like capers.

To make sense of these variables, we purchased six brands of capers and held a small tasting. We tasted small and large capers packed in brine and vinegar as well as one brand of salted capers. For cooking, tasters agreed that small capers are best because they can be used as is; larger capers are too potent to eat whole and should be chopped. Besides adding an extra step, chopped capers disintegrate when added to sauces.

The taste differences among the various brands were subtle, although most tasters felt that the brand packed in wine vinegar was the least harsh and therefore the most flavorful. (Labels on the other bottles just said "vinegar.")

Capers packed in salt were unbearably salty straight from the bottle. Rinsing didn't do much to lessen their sting. Soaking in cool water for at least 20 minutes (and preferably an hour) washed out enough of the salt to reveal the flavor of the capers. Without the salt (and because there's no vinegar), we picked up hints of herbs (especially oregano) and mustard that we never tasted in the brined capers. These salted capers were delicious, but once we used them in piccata, their subtle traits faded behind other ingredients.

Many sources suggest rinsing brined capers, too. We think you can skip this step. Drain the capers well and taste one. If they seem very salty or vinegary, you can rinse them. In most cases, this step won't be necessary.

CAPERBERRIES   GRUESAS   NONPAREILS   SALT-CURED CAPERS

juice. All of our tasters agreed that these sauces weren't lemony enough. We found that ¼ cup delivered a nice lemon punch. Recipes that instructed the cook to deglaze the hot pan with lemon juice and then simmer the sauce for several minutes tasted flat. Adding the lemon juice toward the end of the cooking time helped keep it tasting fresh.

Our caper testing led us to a similar conclusion. You need to use a lot of capers— 2 tablespoons is just right—and they should be added when the sauce is nearly done so they retain their structural integrity.

We next focused on the liquid for deglazing the pan. Chicken stock and white wine were the most obvious candidates. The wine seemed like a good idea, but it contributed more acid to the sauce, which it did not need. Stock proved a more neutral base for the lemon juice and capers.

Before deglazing the pan, we sautéed some aromatics in the pan drippings. We tested shallots, onions, scallions, and garlic separately. All were fine, although tasters preferred the shallots and garlic. Just make sure to watch the pan carefully so that the aromatics don't burn. Add the broth to the pan as soon as the garlic or shallots start to color.

At this point, our sauce was quite good, but we wondered if there was another way to add lemon flavor. In our research, we uncovered several recipes that called for lemon slices. We halved a lemon, then cut it into very thin half-circles. We tried adding the lemon slices with the lemon juice, but the slices were too crunchy and numerous. For the next test, we used just half a lemon and added the slices with the broth. They simmered for five minutes and softened considerably. The longer simmering time also allowed oils from the peel to flavor the sauce. We tried replacing the sliced lemons with grated zest but found the sliced lemons more appealing and less work.

The last remaining issue for testing was thickening the sauce. Some recipes called for a roux (stirring flour into fat before adding the liquid) while others added either softened butter or softened butter mixed with flour once the sauce was cooked. A roux made the sauce too thick. Thickening the sauce at the end seemed more practical. The butter-flour paste gave the sauce a floury taste that dulled the flavors of lemon and capers. Plain butter proved best. Parsley, added with the butter, gave the sauce some color.

Chicken Piccata

SERVES 4

Because this sauce is so light, we find that each person should be served 1½ small cutlets. Serve the cutlets and sauce on a single platter and let each person help himself.

- 2   large lemons
- 6   boneless, skinless chicken breasts (5 to 6 ounces each), tenderloins removed and reserved for another use, fat trimmed (see illustration on page 227)
  Salt and ground black pepper
- ½   cup unbleached all-purpose flour
- 4   tablespoons vegetable oil
- 1   small shallot, minced (about 2 tablespoons), or 1 small clove garlic, minced or pressed through a garlic press (about 1 teaspoon)
- 1   cup homemade chicken stock or canned low-sodium chicken broth
- 2   tablespoons drained small capers
- 3   tablespoons unsalted butter, softened
- 2   tablespoons minced fresh parsley leaves

1. Adjust an oven rack to the lower-middle position, set a large heatproof plate on the rack, and heat the oven to 200 degrees.

2. Halve one lemon pole to pole. Trim the

ends from one half and cut it crosswise into slices ⅛ to ¼ inch thick; set aside. Juice the remaining half and whole lemon to obtain ¼ cup juice; reserve.

3. Sprinkle both sides of the cutlets generously with salt and pepper. Measure the flour into a shallow baking dish or pie plate. Working with one cutlet at a time, coat with the flour and shake to remove the excess.

4. Heat 2 tablespoons oil in a heavy-bottomed 12-inch skillet over medium-high heat until shimmering. Lay half of the chicken cutlets in the skillet. Sauté the cutlets until lightly browned on the first side, 2 to 2½ minutes. Turn the cutlets and cook until the second side is lightly browned, 2 to 2½ minutes longer. Remove the pan from the heat and transfer the cutlets to the plate in the oven. Add the remaining 2 tablespoons oil to the now-empty skillet and heat until shimmering. Add the remaining chicken cutlets and repeat.

5. Add the shallot or garlic to the now-empty skillet and return the skillet to medium heat. Sauté until fragrant, about 30 seconds for shallot or 10 seconds for garlic. Add the stock and lemon slices, increase the heat to high, and scrape the pan bottom with a wooden spoon or spatula to loosen the browned bits. Simmer until the liquid reduces to about ⅓ cup, about 4 minutes. Add the lemon juice and capers and simmer until the sauce reduces again to ⅓ cup, about 1 minute. Remove the pan from the heat and swirl in the butter until the butter melts and thickens the sauce. Stir in the parsley and season with salt and pepper to taste. Spoon the sauce over the chicken and serve immediately.

➤ VARIATIONS
Peppery Chicken Piccata
Follow the recipe for Chicken Piccata, adding ½ teaspoon coarsely ground black peppercorns along with lemon juice and capers.

Chicken Piccata with Prosciutto
Follow the recipe for Chicken Piccata, adding 2 ounces thinly sliced prosciutto, cut into pieces 1 inch long and ¼ inch wide, along with the shallot or garlic; sauté just until the prosciutto is lightly crisped, about 45 seconds.

Chicken Piccata with Black Olives
Follow the recipe for Chicken Piccata, adding ¼ cup pitted and chopped black olives along with the lemon juice and capers.

CHICKEN CACCIATORE

CACCIATORE, WHICH MEANS "HUNTER-style" in Italian, originally referred to a simple method of cooking fresh-killed game. Game hen or rabbit was sautéed along with wild mushrooms, onions, and other foraged vegetables, then braised with wine or stock. Unfortunately, when applied to chicken and translated by American cooks, cacciatore mutated into a generic pasty "red sauce" dish, often featuring sauces that were greasy and overly sweet along with dry, overcooked chicken. We thought it was time for a resurrection. We knew there was a really good version of this dish to be found, and we were determined to discover it.

From the beginning, we knew that we wanted a sauce that was just substantial enough to cling to the chicken; we didn't want the chicken to be swimming in broth, nor did we want a sauce reminiscent of spackle. Another thing we wanted was a streamlined cooking method. This cacciatore would be easy enough to prepare on a weeknight and, we hoped, would necessitate the use of only one pot.

We began our work with a blind taste test.

We gathered an abundance of recipes (every Italian cookbook seems to include some form of cacciatore), then selected what seemed to be the more authentic versions (no boneless, skinless chicken breasts, no jarred tomato sauces) written by prominent Italian cooks. All four of the recipes we chose started with the same basic preparation, one that we would also use for our working recipe. Chicken (a whole chicken cut up, in all but one of the recipes) was dredged in flour and sautéed in olive oil, then removed from the pan, which was then deglazed—a process in which a liquid is used to lift the browned bits from the pan bottom—with either wine or stock. Vegetables (most often tomatoes, onions, and mushrooms) were added to the braise, and the dish was then left to cook until the meat was fall-apart tender.

As we reviewed the tasters' notes on this trial run, we noticed that two problems were common to all the recipes. For one, tasters found the dishes too greasy (nearly an inch of oil floated at the top of one dish); for another, they disliked the presence of chicken skin in the final product. The skin, which was crisp after the initial sauté, had become soggy and unappealing.

All of the recipes except one had other serious problems as well. One was too vegetal, another included black olives that proved too dominant a flavor, and a third had no tomatoes, an omission that tasters thought took the dish too far from what Americans consider a classic cacciatore. The fourth recipe was much more promising. It started off with chicken thighs rather than a whole cut-up chicken and used a mixture made from equal parts flour and softened butter, known as beurre manié, to thicken the sauce. The dark thigh meat remained much more moist and plump than the fibrous, flavorless breast meat we had ended up with in the other recipes. (It was also much easier to simply buy a package of thighs than to cut up a whole chicken.) The thighs also gave the braising liquid a more intense flavor. Unfortunately, the beurre manié overthickened the sauce, giving it a gravylike consistency.

From the test results, we derived a few conclusions and devised a working recipe. Chicken thighs were in, but the flabby skin was out—and this, we hoped, would reduce the overabundance of grease in the dish. Wine (whether red or white was still to be determined) was the liquid of choice for braising, and the additional vegetables needed to be kept to a minimum. A combination of onions, mushrooms, and tomatoes was all that was needed.

We thought that the flabby skin problem could be solved by using skinless chicken thighs, but that assumption proved untrue. A batch made with skinless thighs, while good, lacked the intense flavor of the batches made with skin-on chicken. The rendered fat and

A Parmesan rind gives the tomato-based sauce for chicken cacciatore a robust, savory flavor.

juice from the chicken skin caramelized on the pan bottom; this fond, when deglazed, made a big contribution to the flavor of the sauce. In addition, the skin protected the flesh of the chicken from direct contact with the high heat, thereby preventing the formation of a fibrous crust. We needed to lose the chicken skin after its fat had been rendered.

We found that pulling the skin off the thighs after the initial sauté cost the dish none of its flavor while allowing us to serve the dish skinless. Removing the skin before braising also eliminated the problem of excess grease. The fat from the skin is first rendered at a high heat, which helps keep the skin from sticking to the pan bottom. The extra fat is disposed of, but the caramelized bits are left behind for deglazing.

Next came the braising medium. Preliminary testing suggested that red wine would prevail. Most tasters liked its bold presence, although some thought its hearty flavor was a bit too harsh. We tried cutting the wine with small amounts of water, dry vermouth, and chicken stock and found that the latter buffered the strong presence of the wine and rounded out the flavors. (Because some tasters preferred the lighter, brothier taste of the version made with white wine, we decided to offer that as a variation on the master recipe.)

At this point, the sauce was rich in flavor but lacking in substance. Truthfully, it was more like a broth; the vegetables and chicken were lost in the liquid. We remembered that the flour used to dredge the chicken thighs had been thrown away with the skin. We would have to reintroduce it somewhere else. A beurre manié was too complicated for this streamlined dish, so we ended up adding a little flour directly to the vegetables as they were finishing their sauté. The sauce was now silky and robust. On a whim, we threw in a piece of a Parmesan cheese rind, an option we had noticed in one of the recipes tested earlier.

The sauce, very good before, now surpassed all of our expectations. It was now substantial, lavish, and amply flavored.

We were finally down to the details of finishing. Portobello mushrooms, bursting with the essence of red wine, added an earthy flavor and meaty chew. We also found that just about any herb would complement the recipe; we chose sage for its woodsy flavor.

≺━

Chicken Cacciatore with Portobellos and Sage

SERVES 4

The Parmesan cheese rind is optional, but we highly recommend it for the robust, savory flavor it adds to the dish. An equal amount of minced fresh rosemary can be substituted for the sage.

8 bone-in chicken thighs (about 3 pounds), trimmed of excess skin and fat
   Salt and ground black pepper
1 teaspoon olive oil
1 medium onion, chopped
6 ounces (about 3 medium) portobello mushroom caps, wiped clean and cut into ¾-inch dice
4 medium cloves garlic, minced or pressed through a garlic press
1½ tablespoons all-purpose flour
1½ cups dry red wine
½ cup homemade chicken stock or canned low-sodium chicken broth
1 (14½-ounce) can diced tomatoes, drained
2 teaspoons minced fresh thyme leaves
1 Parmesan cheese rind, about 4 by 2 inches (optional)
2 teaspoons minced fresh sage leaves

1. Preheat the oven to 300 degrees. Season the chicken liberally with salt and pepper to taste. Heat the oil in a large ovenproof Dutch

oven over medium-high heat until shimmering but not smoking, about 2 minutes. Add 4 chicken thighs, skin side down, and cook, not moving them until the skin is crisp and well-browned, about 5 minutes. Using tongs, flip the chicken and brown on the second side, about 5 minutes longer. Transfer the browned chicken to a large plate. Brown the remaining chicken thighs, transfer them to the plate, and set aside. When the chicken has cooled, remove and discard the skin (see illustration below). With a spoon, remove and discard all but 1 tablespoon fat from the pan.

2. Add the onion, mushrooms, and ½ teaspoon salt to the now-empty Dutch oven. Sauté over medium-high heat, stirring occasionally, until the moisture evaporates and the vegetables begin to brown, 6 to 8 minutes. Add the garlic and sauté until fragrant, about 30 seconds. Stir in the flour and cook, stirring constantly, for about 1 minute. Add the wine, scraping the pot bottom with a wooden spoon to loosen the brown bits. Stir in the stock, tomatoes, thyme, Parmesan cheese rind (if using), ½ teaspoon salt (omit salt if using cheese rind), and pepper to taste. Add the chicken pieces and accumulated juices, submerging the

SKINNING BROWNED CHICKEN

Once the chicken thighs have been browned and cooled, grasp the skin from one end and pull to separate the skin from the meat. Discard the skin.

chicken in the liquid. Bring to a simmer, cover, and place the pot in the oven. Cook until the chicken is done, about 30 minutes. Remove the pot from the oven. (The stew can be covered and refrigerated for up to 3 days. Bring to a simmer over medium-low heat.)

3. Discard the cheese rind, stir in the sage, and adjust the seasonings. Serve immediately.

➤ VARIATION

Chicken Cacciatore with White Wine and Tarragon

Mince 3 large shallots; clean 10 ounces white mushrooms and quarter if large, halve if medium, or leave whole if small. Follow the recipe for Chicken Cacciatore with Portobellos and Sage, substituting shallots for onions, white mushrooms for portobellos, dry white wine for red wine, and 2 teaspoons minced fresh tarragon for sage.

CHICKEN ALLA DIAVOLO

THERE ARE MANY THEORIES ON HOW this "chicken of the devil" got its name. Some say it is in reference to the fiery coals over which the chicken is grilled; others claim it is for the diabolical amount of black pepper or hot red pepper flakes that are used. But name aside, most recipes for this classic grilled chicken are quite similar; the chicken is butterflied and grilled with a heavy dousing of either black pepper or hot red pepper flakes and lots of lemon. As simple as it sounds, we found that grilling a whole butterflied chicken is tricky, and it is difficult to get the lemon and pepper seasonings to shine through.

Saving the issue of flavor for later, we first focused on the obvious problem of how to grill a butterflied chicken. Most recipes call for weights to be placed on top of the bird as it is grilled, to promote fast and even cooking. Covered with a cast-iron pan or old baking sheet, the flattened chicken is then weighted down with bricks or heavy cans. After cooking two chickens, with and without weights, it became obvious why the weights were necessary. When pounded, then weighted flat, the chicken not only cooked more quickly and evenly but also achieved beautiful grill marks. The unweighted chicken, by comparison, had a less evenly colored skin and took longer to cook through.

We found the chicken skin was quick to tear when overhandled, and we wanted to find a cooking method that involved a minimum of flipping. When cooked over a single level medium-hot grill, the chicken cooked in about 30 minutes, flipped once halfway through. Interestingly, we found cooking on a charcoal grill required a different method from a gas grill. On charcoal, it is important to cook the chicken skin side up first, or else the bright, hot coals will burn the skin. For a gas grill, the bird must be grilled skin side down first, or else the grill will cool, making it difficult to get decent grill marks on the skin.

Moving on to flavor, we tested several ways to make the chicken taste robust and spicy. Immediately, we found that marinating the chicken before grilling was essential. Although marinating does little to enhance the texture of the meat, it does a lot in terms of flavor. Marinating in lemon juice, black pepper, and olive oil offered a good base, but we wanted more flavor. In an effort to bring out the black pepper, we found it better to rub the chicken vigorously first before dousing it with the lemon juice and olive oil. To make the chicken a bit spicier, we added hot red pepper flakes and smashed garlic cloves to the marinade.

Although our recipe was coming along, we still had problems getting the lemon to shine through. Lemon has an ethereal flavor that can disappear quickly when cooked. Adding zest to the marinade helped the lemon flavor permeate the meat, yet we still wanted more. Basting the chicken with marinade helped a little, but the smoke from the grill dulled the lemon flavor as it continued to cook. To prevent the grill from stealing our flavor, we discovered that a last-minute brush of fresh marinade and a quick revisit to the coals to fuse the marinade to the skin was the key. The result is a perfectly grilled butterflied chicken with potent lemon and pepper flavor.

Chicken alla Diavolo on a Charcoal Grill

SERVES 4

You will need four large lemons for this recipe.

1	whole chicken (3 to 3½ pounds), butterflied (see illustrations on page 244)
1½	tablespoons coarsely ground black pepper
½	cup extra-virgin olive oil
¾	cup lemon juice
1	teaspoon grated lemon zest
3	medium cloves garlic, skins left on, smashed
¼	teaspoon hot red pepper flakes
1¼	teaspoons salt

1. Rub the chicken all over with 1 tablespoon black pepper. Place the chicken in a gallon-size zipper-lock plastic bag and add the oil, ½ cup lemon juice, zest, garlic, hot red pepper flakes, and 1 teaspoon salt. Gently massage the bag to mix the marinade around chicken and refrigerate for 2 hours. Mix the remaining ½ tablespoon black pepper, ¼ cup lemon juice, and ¼ teaspoon salt together in a small bowl and set aside.

2. Light a large chimney starter filled three-quarters with hardwood charcoal (about 2

INGREDIENTS: Chicken

Picking out a high-quality chicken at the supermarket is a guessing game. The terms fresh, organic, free-range, all-natural, and lean rarely indicate good flavor or texture, and neither does price. In our 1994 chicken tasting, the only dependable sign of quality we found was brand, with Bell & Evans and Empire taking top honors. Eight years later, we wondered if these companies would win a second tasting and if, at long last, we could find a reliable, nonbranded measure of quality.

We identified and investigated a long list of genetic and environmental factors that might help the consumer purchase a high-quality, tasty bird. Our first stop was genetic engineering. Birds are bred to meet the goals of a particular producer. Murray's chickens, for example, are engineered for a high yield of breast meat and a low yield of fat. (Tasters found them "tough" and "dry.") Perdue chickens are bred for a high ratio of meat to bone. (We found this means big breasts but scrawny legs.) It seemed to us, at least at first pass, that few, if any, producers were engineering birds for flavor.

More toothsome meat can simply be the result of a chicken's age. The older the chicken (an older broiler/fryer is seven to nine weeks old rather than the more typical six to seven weeks), the more distinct its flavor. Free-range birds, whose diet is less intense and less controlled than that of indoor chickens (because free-range birds have unrestricted access to the outdoors, it is impossible to keep them from eating random grasses and insects), take longer to reach their proper weight and are older when they are processed. Yet the free-range moniker is no indication of superior flavor. The two free-range birds we tasted, Eberly and D'Artagnan, had both fans and critics.

Our first solid clue to any possible connection between processing method and flavor emerged when we discovered that Empire, the only kosher chicken in our tasting, was also the best-tasting. (Murray birds are not kosher but are processed under similar conditions in accordance with Muslim law.) Both Empire and Murray birds are hand-slaughtered rather than killed by machine, which ensures both a clean kill and a quick and efficient bleed-out. Industry experts indicated that machine-processed chickens are more likely to be subject to improper slaughtering, which can cause blood to clot, resulting in tough meat or a livery flavor.

Because tasters far preferred the Empire chicken to Murray's, however, it followed that more was at work here than slaughtering technique. For one thing, kosher chickens like Empire's are dunked in cold water to remove feathers after slaughter. Cold water firms both the skin and the fat layer beneath it. In contrast, most other producers scald birds in hot water to remove the feathers. The experts we talked to said that scalding can "solubilize" the chicken's fat, leading to excessive moisture loss and a wrinkled appearance in the skin after cooking. Uneven scalding can also cause barking, a blotchy appearance, in the skin.

Appearance aside, perhaps the most noticeable difference between the Empire bird and the others we tasted is that the Empire bird tasted juicy and well seasoned. In keeping with kosher law, the chickens are buried in salt for one hour to draw out impurities and are then rinsed in cold spring water. The combination of salt and water acts like a brine, encouraging the fiber in the meat to open and trap the salt and water, leading to a juicier, more flavorful bird. This single factor, more than any other, seems to have put the Empire bird ahead of the pack. (If using a kosher chicken, don't brine it, or the resulting dish will be too salty.)

If you are looking for advice on purchasing a high-quality, good-tasting chicken, we recommend kosher. All the other adjectives—free-range, natural, lean, organic, and the like—don't necessarily translate into a better-tasting chicken. Empire, the brand that won our contest, was followed by Bell & Evans, winner of our 1994 tasting. You can't go wrong with either. Let it also be noted that Tyson, a mass-produced bird priced at just $1.29/pound, came in third, ahead of birds costing more than twice as much. One last word of advice. Out of eight birds in the tasting, Perdue finished dead last, with tasters describing the meat as "pithy," "chalky," and "stringy," with sour notes as well.

pounds) and allow to burn until all the charcoal is covered with a layer of fine gray ash. Build a single-level fire by spreading the coals evenly over the bottom of the grill. Set the cooking rack in place, cover with the lid, and let the rack heat, about 5 minutes. Use a wire brush to scrape clean the cooking rack. The grill is ready when the coals are medium-hot (you can hold your hand 5 inches above the cooking rack for 3 to 4 seconds).

3. Remove the chicken from the marinade and discard the marinade. Place the chicken, bone side down, on the cooking rack. Set a rimmed baking sheet (or other flat pan) on top of the chicken and put two bricks in the pan (see the illustration on page 245). Grill until the chicken is deep brown, about 12 minutes. Turn the chicken skin side down with tongs. Replace the baking sheet and bricks and continue cooking until the chicken juices run clear and an instant-read thermometer inserted deep into the thigh registers 165 degrees, 12 to 15 minutes longer.

4. Remove the bricks and pan, turn the chicken skin side up, and brush the skin with the reserved lemon mixture. Carefully flip the chicken skin side down and allow the skin to crisp, 1 to 2 minutes. Transfer the chicken to a cutting board and allow to rest for 10 minutes. Carve according to the illustrations on page 246 and serve hot.

➤ VARIATION

Chicken alla Diavolo on a Gas Grill
Because this chicken is cooked skin side down first, we found it best not to replace the bricks on top of the crisp skin.

Follow the recipe for Chicken alla Diavolo through step 1. Preheat the grill with all burners set to high and the lid down until the grill is very hot, about 15 minutes. Use a wire brush to scrape clean the cooking rack. Turn all burners to medium. Place the chicken skin side down on the cooking rack. Set a rimmed baking sheet (or other flat pan) on top of the chicken and put two bricks in the pan (see the illustration on page 245). Cover and grill until the chicken skin is deep brown and shows grill marks, 12 to 15 minutes. Turn the chicken with tongs and continue to cook (without replacing the pan or the bricks on top) until the chicken juices run clear and an instant-read thermometer inserted deep into the thigh registers 165 degrees, about 15 minutes more. Brush the skin with the reserved lemon mixture. Carefully flip the chicken skin side down and allow the skin to crisp, 1 to 2 minutes. Transfer the chicken to a cutting board and allow to rest for 10 minutes. Carve according to the illustrations on page 246 and serve.

CHICKEN UNDER A BRICK

THE POINT OF COOKING A CHICKEN under a brick (*pollo alla mattone*) is not simply to impress your friends and neighbors (although it does look cool) but rather to achieve a stunningly crisp skin. After the chicken is butterflied and pounded flat, it is pressed into a hot pan under the weight of a brick (which, for hygiene reasons, is usually wrapped in foil). The brick helps keep the chicken flat as it cooks, forcing all of the skin to make contact with the pan. Usually marinated with garlic and rosemary, this flavorful chicken cooks in about 45 minutes.

After trying a few recipes, however, we noted two big problems. First, the beautiful, crisp skin often turned soggy or greasy as the chicken finished cooking. Second, the marinade burned in the hot pan, making the chicken taste scorched. We also took notice of a few problems that could be immediately rectified. The weight of two bricks is much better than just one. Also, the bricks offered a more even distribution of weight when placed on a baking sheet or cast-iron skillet. We also found that chickens much larger than 3 pounds were difficult to fit into a 12-inch skillet.

To start, we set the rosemary and garlic marinade aside and focused on the cooking method. Using two unmarinated butterflied chickens, we tested the difference between pounding the chicken to an even thickness using a mallet versus simply pressing the chicken flat by hand. When pounded with a mallet, the super-flat chicken cooked evenly, and more of the skin was able to make contact with the pan and turn crisp. By comparison, only portions of skin on the chicken flattened by hand were nicely browned.

We cooked these chickens according to most of the recipes we researched: skin-side down first with bricks on top, then flipped over to cook the underside, replacing the bricks to help keep the chicken flat. We found, however, that this method didn't work. After the chickens were flipped and the weight was replaced on top, the skin (which was now crisp and delicate) tore in places and began to steam, turning shaggy and flaccid. We then

tried not replacing the bricks after the chicken was flipped, but the skin still turned rubbery from the steam and splattering oil.

Next, we tried cooking the underside of the chicken first, finishing with the breast side down, but this didn't work either. By the time it was ready to flip, the pan was loaded with so much grease and nasty burned bits that the skin ended up greasy, spotty, and slightly bitter. We then decided to try a different approach altogether. We cooked the chicken skin side down, underneath the weights, until it had a beautiful color. We then removed the bricks, flipped the bird over, and finished it in a hot oven. The hot, dry air of the oven ensured that the skin remained crisp as it finished cooking through.

With the method nailed down, we moved our attention to flavor. As we do most poultry, we liked the chicken when it was brined (soaked in a salt solution). The brine ensured that the meat remained tender and juicy, but we missed the herb and garlic flavors in our original marinade. We discovered an easy way to include the marinade without letting it burn: brush the marinade onto the chicken before it goes into the oven. The flavors of

BUTTERFLYING A CHICKEN

 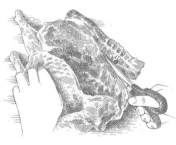 

1. With the breast side down and the tail of the chicken facing you, use poultry shears to cut along the entire length of one side of the backbone.

2. With the breast side still down, turn the neck end to face you and cut along the other side of the backbone and remove it.

3. Turn the chicken breast side up. Open the chicken out on the work surface. Use the palm of your hand to flatten the chicken, then pound it with the flat side of a mallet to a fairly even thickness.

the marinade remained fresh and potent while the heat of the oven fused the marinade to the skin instantly without ruining its crisp texture.

Tasters preferred a simple olive oil–based marinade flavored with garlic, rosemary (or oregano), hot red pepper flakes, and black pepper. Emerging from the oven fragrant and stunningly gorgeous, the chicken simply needs to rest for 5 to 10 minutes, allowing the juices to redistribute, before serving.

Chicken Under a Brick

SERVES 4

Our favorite weights are a small baking sheet (it should fit inside the 12-inch skillet) and two bricks. If you don't have a small baking sheet and two bricks handy, other heavy objects can be used in their place, such as a cast-iron pan loaded with several cans or a large stockpot filled partially with water. If using a kosher chicken, skip step 1, season with pepper, and begin at step 2. Be careful when removing the pan from the oven; the handle will be very hot.

I	cup kosher salt or ¹/₂ cup table salt
I	small whole chicken (3 pounds), butter-flied (see illustrations on page 244) Ground black pepper
I	teaspoon vegetable oil
¹/₄	cup extra-virgin olive oil
I	medium clove garlic, minced or pressed through a garlic press
¹/₂	teaspoon minced fresh rosemary or fresh oregano leaves Pinch hot red pepper flakes

1. Dissolve the salt in 3 quarts water in a large container or bowl. Submerge the chicken pieces in the brine and refrigerate until fully seasoned, 3 hours. Remove the chicken from brine, rinse under running water, and pat dry with paper towels. Season the chicken with black pepper to taste.

2. Adjust an oven rack to the lowest position and heat the oven to 450 degrees. Heat the vegetable oil in a heavy-bottomed, ovenproof 12-inch skillet over medium-high heat until it begins to smoke. Swirl the skillet to coat evenly with the oil. Place the chicken skin side down in the hot pan and turn the heat down to medium. Place a small baking sheet and two bricks on top of the chicken and cook, checking every 5 or so minutes, until evenly browned, about 25 minutes. (After 20 minutes, the chicken should be fairly crisp and golden; if it is not, turn the heat up to medium-high and continue to cook until well browned.)

3. Meanwhile, mix the olive oil, garlic, rosemary, and hot red pepper flakes together in a small bowl and reserve.

4. Remove the baking sheets and bricks. Using tongs, carefully flip the chicken skin side up. (If more than 3 tablespoons fat have accumulated in the skillet, transfer the chicken to a clean plate and pour most of the fat out of skillet. Return the chicken to the

WEIGHTING A BUTTERFLIED CHICKEN

To weight a butterflied chicken while it grills or cooks in a skillet, set a rimmed baking sheet on top and put two bricks in the pan.

skillet skin side up and continue.) Brush the skin with the marinade and place the skillet in the oven. (Be careful handling the pan once it is in the oven, as the handle will be very hot.) Cook until the thickest part of the breast registers 160 degrees on an instant-read thermometer and the thickest part of thigh registers 170 degrees, 7 to 10 minutes longer. Transfer the chicken to a platter and let rest 5 to 10 minutes. Carve according to the illustrations below and serve.

CARVING A BUTTERFLIED CHICKEN

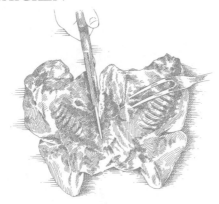

1. Place the chicken skin side down and use kitchen shears to cut through the breastbone. (Because the breastbone is broken and the meat is flattened during pounding, this should be easy.)

2. Once the breast has been split, only the skin holds the portions together. Separate each leg and thigh from each breast and wing.

ROAST CHICKEN WITH LEMON

ROAST CHICKEN LIGHTLY PERFUMED with the clean, simple flavor of lemon is a basic Italian dish. As with most things basic, there is little room for error. With no exotic combinations of flavors or unique presentations to hide behind, the chicken must be roasted to perfection and infused with pure lemon flavor. But after making several recipes we had researched, we were grossly disappointed. They produced dry, overcooked breast meat that tasted bitter and pithy, not lemony. Wanting to figure out how to make this dish right, we set aside the issue of lemon flavor and worked first on finding the best way to roast a chicken.

To begin, we tried simply roasting the birds, breast side up, on a rack at 350 degrees, but the results were dismal. By the time the inner thighs finished cooking, the breast meat was far overdone and dried out. To boot, the skin was flabby. To combat the problem of undercooked thighs, we tried roasting the chicken breast side down for the first half of the cooking, then flipping it right side up for the remaining half. When the chicken was breast side down, the delicate breast meat was self-basted and protected from the oven heat, while the inner thigh joint was directly exposed to the oven heat. Although this helped cook the chicken more evenly, the skin still didn't brown right.

To deal with this, we began to vary the oven temperatures. Roasting the birds at 425 and 450 degrees produced good skin color, but the oven smoked profusely and set off the smoke alarms. Adding water to the pan prevented the smoke, but the steam it produced turned the breast soggy as it hung upside down and prevented it from browning properly. After all this testing, we realized that it

EQUIPMENT: Pepper Mills

In this test, we sought top performers that would make great kitchen partners; appearance was pretty much beside the point. We rounded up 12 mills, each close to 8 inches high. Prices ranged from $14.99 to $45.

Most pepper mills work by similar means. Peppercorns are loaded into a central chamber through which runs a metal shaft. Near the bottom of the mill, the shaft is connected to a grinding mechanism that consists of a rotating, grooved "male" head that fits into a stationary, grooved "female" ring. Near the top of the male piece, the large grooves crack the peppercorns, then feed the smaller pieces downward to be ground between the finer grooves, or teeth, of the male and female components.

To a reasonable point, the finer the grind, the more evenly the pepper will be distributed throughout a dish. Likewise, the coarser the grind, the better for dishes like chicken alla diavolo or steak au poivre, which have assertive flavors. Thus, the quality of a pepper mill's fine and coarse grinds (are all the bits fine or coarse, or does the mill yield a mix of fine and coarse bits at the same time?) is more important than options for an endless range of grinds beyond fine, medium, and coarse.

The industry experts we queried explained that the specifics of the grinding mechanism are key to grind quality. Jack Pierotti, president of Chef Specialties, maker of the Windsor mill, named the size, number, and angle of teeth in both male and female grinder components as factors in performance. A related consideration, according to Tom David, president of Tom David, Inc., maker of the Unicorn Magnum Plus mill, is how well the male and female grinding pieces are machined. Sharper teeth combined with a very tight tolerance between the pieces yield a finer grind. Unfortunately, none of these details are evident on inspecting a pepper mill in a kitchen store.

In addition to having an excellent grind quality, Unicorn Magnum Plus managed an awesome output. In one minute of grinding, the Magnum produced an amazing average of 7.3 grams, or about 3½ teaspoons, of fine-ground pepper. By comparison, honors for the next-highest average output went to the Oxo Good Grips Grind It, at 5.1 grams, while about half the pack came in around the 2-grams or less mark (which, at roughly 1 teaspoon in volume, is perfectly acceptable).

Grind quality and speed are only half the battle—especially if most of your peppercorns land on the floor when you try to fill the mill. So we appreciated mills with wide filler doors that could accommodate the tip of a wide funnel or, better yet, the lip of a bag or jar so that we could dispense with the funnel altogether. The East Hampton Industries (EHI) Peppermate took high honors in this category, with a lid that snaps off to create a gaping 3-inch opening, followed by the Zyliss, with a 2-inch opening, and the Oxo Grind It, with a wide-open 1⅜-inch mouth. With its sliding collar door, the Unicorn Magnum Plus was also easy to fill. Along the same lines, the more peppercorns a mill can hold, the less often it has to be filled. The Zyliss held a full cup, and the Unicorn Magnum Plus trailed behind by just 1 tablespoon.

The ease of adjusting the grind was another factor we considered. Changing the grind from fine to coarse involves changing the distances between the male and female grinding components. The more space between them, the larger the pepper particles and the coarser the grind. Traditionally, a knob at the top of the mill, called the finial, is used to adjust the grind. This was our least favorite design for two reasons. First, the finial must be screwed down very tight for a fine grind, which not only requires significant finger strength but also makes the head (or the crank) of the mill more difficult to turn. Second, the finial usually has to be removed entirely to fill the mill, which means you have to readjust the grind with each filling. We preferred mills like the Unicorn Magnum Plus, which use a screw or dial at the base of the grinding mechanism.

More than half of the mills tested did their jobs well, but the Unicorn Magnum Plus was the superstar. Its grind quality is exemplary, its output astounding, and its capacity huge. If that weren't enough, it's also easy to fill and comfortable to use. At $45, however, this mill was one of the two most expensive in the test (the second-place EHI Peppermate was $40). If your budget is restricted, we recommend both the Oxo Good Grips Grind It ($19.99) and the Zyliss Large Pepper Mill ($27.50).

would take a combination of these ideas to produce the perfectly roasted chicken. To start, we needed to roast the chicken breast side down at a temperature low enough not to smoke for the first half of the cooking time. Then, we needed to flip the bird breast side up, raise the temperature to brown the skin, and add water to the pan to prevent the drippings from smoking. Using this combination of techniques, we were able to get the best roast chicken.

Moving on to flavor, we found the tasters preferred the chicken when it was brined (soaked in a salt solution) for several hours. The salt thoroughly seasoned the meat, while several lemons squeezed into the brine provided citrus flavor. Although the brine gave the chicken a good, mild base of lemon flavor, we wanted more. We tried putting whole lemons, halved lemons, and lemons that were poked several times with a skewer inside the cavity of the chicken as it roasted. Although all of these birds emerged from the oven with a beautiful aroma, we were disappointed with their flavor. The purest flavor came from chicken that had half a lemon squeezed and thrown into its cavity. The others simply tasted pithy and sour.

With a solid lemon flavor still eluding us, we tried another idea. We made both a lemon butter (softened butter mixed with grated zest) and a lemon oil (grated zest steeped in olive oil) and rubbed chickens thoroughly with each after they were brined. Although both added good flavor, the butter helped the chicken brown to a deeper golden color than the oil. Believe it or not, however, we still were not satisfied. Even with lemons in the brine, in the cavity, and in the butter that was rubbed all over the chicken, the lemon flavor was not potent enough.

Lemon has an ethereal flavor that is quick to dissipate. Noting that the drippings in the pan were beautiful and nicely flavored, we realized how to get that last, fresh bite of clean lemon flavor: by making a sauce with the pan drippings. Changing the liquid in the pan from water to chicken stock, it was easy to make a bright, lemony sauce to serve alongside the chicken. Finally, we had achieved the perfect roast chicken with lemon.

Roast Chicken with Lemon
SERVES 4

Lemon flavor is added at several points in this recipe—juice and spent lemon halves go in the brine, more juice and a spent lemon half is placed in the cavity of the chicken before roasting, and zest is mixed with butter and rubbed under and over the skin before roasting. Lemon juice added to taste to the finished sauce gives a final citrus kick. If using a kosher chicken, skip step 1 but note that the lemon flavor will be tamer.

1	cup kosher salt or ½ cup table salt
4	lemons
1	whole chicken (about 3 pounds), giblets removed and discarded
	Oil for basket or V-rack
4	tablespoons unsalted butter, softened
	Ground black pepper
1	(14½-ounce) can low-sodium chicken broth
¼	cup dry white wine
	Salt

1. Dissolve the salt in 3 quarts water in a large container. Add the juice of 3 lemons, then add the spent lemon halves. Submerge the chicken in the brine and refrigerate until fully seasoned, 3 hours.

2. Adjust an oven rack to the lower-middle position and heat the oven to 375 degrees. Oil the basket or V-rack and place the rack in a roasting pan. Grate the zest from the remaining lemon (reserve the lemon) and mix the

zest with the softened butter in a small bowl.

3. Remove the chicken from the brine and pat dry with paper towels inside and out. Squeeze the juice from half of the zested lemon into the cavity of the chicken and place the lemon half inside. Slip 2 tablespoons lemon butter under the breast skin (see illustrations below). Rub 1 tablespoon lemon butter over the breast side of the chicken and sprinkle liberally with pepper to taste. Place the chicken breast side down in the roasting rack. Rub the remaining tablespoon lemon butter over the back of the chicken and sprinkle liberally with pepper to taste.

4. Place the roasting pan in the oven and roast the chicken for 25 minutes. Remove the chicken from the oven and increase the temperature to 450 degrees. Rotate the chicken breast side up in the rack and pour 1 cup chicken broth into the bottom of the roasting pan. Return the roasting pan with the chicken to the oven and continue to roast until an instant-read thermometer inserted in the breast registers 160 degrees and the thigh registers between 165 and 170 degrees, about 35 minutes. Remove the roasting pan from oven and tip the rack on end, allowing the

chicken juices to pour into the roasting pan. Transfer the chicken to a cutting board and let rest for 10 minutes.

5. Tip the roasting pan on end and use a large spoon to remove as much fat as possible from the pan drippings. Set the pan on a stovetop burner set to high heat and add the remaining ¾ cup broth and wine. Simmer, scraping the pan bottom to loosen any browned bits, until the mixture is slightly thickened and reduced to about ½ cup, about 5 minutes. Season the sauce to taste with salt, pepper, and lemon juice from the remaining lemon half. Carve the chicken and serve immediately with the sauce.

ROAST CHICKEN WITH ROSEMARY AND GARLIC

CHICKEN ROASTED WITH GARLIC AND rosemary is a classic preparation in Tuscany, where huge bushes of rosemary are grown as hedges. But much like our roast lemon chicken, a dish this basic must be done well or

SLIPPING FLAVORED BUTTER UNDER CHICKEN SKIN

Softened butter mixed with lemon zest adds flavor to the breast meat and keeps it from drying out. Here's how to get the butter under the skin.

1. Slip your fingers between the skin and the breast meat, loosening the membrane.

2. Scoop some of the lemon butter onto a spoon and slide it under the skin. Push the butter off the spoon with your finger.

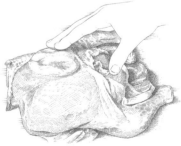

3. Work the butter under the skin to cover the breast evenly.

not at all. Because we had already figured out how to perfectly roast a chicken while developing our recipe for lemon chicken, we needed only to focus on how to bring out and balance the two bold flavors of garlic and rosemary.

Taking a close look at our roasting technique, we tried to figure out where in the process we could insert the flavors of garlic and rosemary. To ensure that the meat is thoroughly seasoned and stays tender as it roasts, we first soaked the chicken in a brine (saltwater solution). Wanting the flavors of both the garlic and rosemary to penetrate deep into the meat, we tried including both with the brine. To amplify the flavors, we used a mallet to smash the garlic and rosemary with the salt in a zipper-lock bag before adding the water. Although this flavored brine was successful at building a solid base of the two flavors, we noted a lack of freshness in both flavor and aroma of the finished chicken.

Next, we tried placing both garlic and rosemary in the cavity of the bird as it roasted, but tasters only liked the aroma of the rosemary. The garlic added little beyond a slightly bitter, steamed flavor. Omitting the garlic from the cavity, we tried rubbing the skin with garlic oil and garlic butter but found both potent and overwhelming. The pan juices, however, were beautiful, with light hints of both the garlic and the rosemary, and we decided it would be best to make a sauce.

After the chicken finished roasting, we set it aside to rest and used the roasting pan to create a sauce that offered the fresh kick of flavor we were looking for. Pouring out the potent rosemary-scented drippings from within the cavity of the chicken, we simply needed a way to bring out the flavor of garlic. Adding freshly sliced or minced garlic to the pan drippings did not work; they made the sauce taste steamed and harsh. We wanted a potent, smooth garlic flavor to shine through, as though it had been roasting alongside the chicken the entire time. It occurred to us that we could simply roast a head of garlic alongside the chicken and use it in the sauce.

The chicken roasted in about an hour, and this was the perfect length of time to roast the garlic as well. We found that a whole head of roasted garlic was too much for the small

ROASTING GARLIC

1. Cut ½ inch from the tip end of the head of garlic so that the clove interiors are exposed.

2. Place the garlic, cut side up, in the center of an 8-inch square of aluminum foil. Sprinkle the garlic with a pinch of salt and drizzle with 1 tablespoon melted butter, then gather and twist foil to seal.

3. After the garlic has roasted, open the foil package and cool. With your hand or the flat edge of a chef's knife, squeeze the garlic from the skins, starting from the root end and working up.

amount of sauce, so we added just half the cloves to the sauce and saved the rest for spreading on toasted bread.

Roast Chicken with Garlic and Rosemary

SERVES 4

A whole head of garlic is wrapped in foil (see illustrations on page 250) and roasted alongside the chicken. Use just half the roasted cloves for the sauce (more will make it too strong) and smear the extra on slices of grilled and oiled bread. If using a kosher chicken, skip step 1, but note that the garlic and rosemary flavors will be tamer.

1	cup kosher salt or ½ cup table salt
5	large sprigs fresh rosemary
2	whole heads garlic
1	whole chicken (about 3 pounds), giblets removed and discarded
	Oil for basket or V-rack
	Salt
3	tablespoons unsalted butter, melted
	Ground black pepper
1	(14½-ounce) can low-sodium chicken broth
¼	cup dry white wine

1. Place the salt, 2 sprigs rosemary, and 1 head garlic inside a heavy-duty zipper-lock plastic bag. Using a large rubber mallet or the bottom of a skillet, pound the bag until the garlic is smashed and the rosemary is bruised. Transfer the salt mixture to a large container, add 3 quarts water, and stir to dissolve. Submerge the chicken in the brine and refrigerate until fully seasoned, 3 hours.

2. Adjust an oven rack to the lower-middle position and heat the oven to 375 degrees. Oil the basket or V-rack and place it in a roasting pan. Cut the tip end from the remaining head of garlic, sprinkle with salt to taste, drizzle

EQUIPMENT: Roasting Racks

A rack keeps a roast chicken above the pan juices and grease, which helps prevent the skin from cooking up soft or flabby. A rack also allows air to circulate underneath so the bottom of a chicken can brown.

There are several types of roasting racks, each with a different use. In our tests, we found that a U-shaped basket rack cradles a chicken perfectly, keeping the wings and legs in good position so the birds are easy to turn. We also found that a perforated nonstick finish conducts heat better than other racks, so the skin browns especially well. Basket racks are solid and stable but too small to accommodate turkeys.

For these larger birds, a nonadjustable V-rack is recommended. Unlike adjustable V-racks, the nonadjustable version is made from thick metal bars, not flimsy wires. We found that this kind of rack stays put in the pan and doesn't bend when holding heavy birds. While you can use a V-rack to roast a chicken, the wings and/or legs may slip through the bars. When you turn the bird, you may have to lift the dangling limbs back over the bars.

Basket and V-racks keep birds well above the roasting pan so that the skin on the underside browns well. In our tests, a vertical rack didn't lift the chicken far enough off the pan to brown the skin on the bottom end of the bird. A vertical rack also splatters fat all over the oven. Likewise, a regular flat rack didn't lift the chicken far enough off the pan and, as a result, the skin suffered.

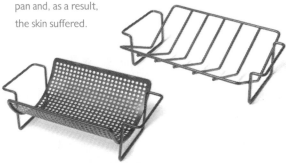

THE BEST ROASTING RACKS
A basket rack (bottom) is stable and solid and browns the skin more thoroughly than other racks. Its U-shaped design cradles the chicken snugly, keeping the wings and legs close to the body. A nonadjustable V-rack (top) is another good choice. It will stay put on the roasting pan, but the wings and legs may slip through the wires.

with 1 tablespoon melted butter, and wrap in foil (see illustrations 1 and 2 on page 250).

3. Remove the chicken from the brine and pat dry with paper towels inside and out. Place the remaining 3 sprigs rosemary in the cavity of the chicken, brush 1 tablespoon melted butter over the breast side, and sprinkle liberally with pepper to taste. Place the chicken breast side down in the roasting rack. Brush the remaining tablespoon melted butter over the back of the chicken and sprinkle liberally with pepper to taste.

4. Place the garlic package on the rack toward the back of oven. Place the roasting pan in the oven and roast for 25 minutes. Remove the chicken from the oven and increase the temperature to 450 degrees. Rotate the chicken breast side up in the rack and pour 1 cup chicken broth into the bottom of the roasting pan. Return the roasting pan with the chicken to the oven and continue to roast until an instant-read thermometer inserted in breast registers 160 degrees and the thigh registers between 165 and 170 degrees, about 35 minutes. Remove the roasting pan from the oven and tip the rack on end, allowing the chicken juices to pour into the roasting pan. Transfer the chicken to a cutting board and let rest for 10 minutes. Remove the foil package with the garlic from the oven and open it. When cool enough to handle, squeeze out the roasted cloves (see illustration 3 on page 250).

5. Tip the roasting pan on end and use a large spoon to remove as much fat as possible from the pan drippings. Set the pan on a stovetop burner set to high heat and add the remaining ¾ cup broth, wine, and half the roasted garlic cloves. Simmer, scraping the pan bottom to loosen any browned bits, until the mixture is slightly thickened and reduced to about ½ cup, about 5 minutes. Season with salt and pepper to taste. Carve the chicken and serve immediately with the sauce.

ROAST QUAIL

THESE TINY GAME BIRDS ARE REVERED for their sweet, delicate flavor. One bird makes a nice-sized appetizer, while two are required for a dinner-sized portion. Although quail can be cooked in a variety of ways, in Italy they are most commonly roasted. The problem, however, is that the birds are so small that they cook very quickly, and it is difficult to get the skin golden and crisp without overcooking the tender breast meat.

To start, we tried several roasting methods. Using a range of oven temperatures, we noted that these birds required high heat to crisp the skin. Yet, even when we roasted them at 500 degrees, we still couldn't get the skin crisp before the tiny portion of breast meat overcooked and dried out. Roasting the birds upside down did help protect the breast meat, but it also cast a shadow over the skin and caused it to emerge from the oven rubbery. We needed to give the skin direct contact with the heat.

Using a large skillet, we found it easy to brown the birds in a little oil before placing them on a rack in a roasting pan and finishing them in a hot oven. Although this ensured that the skin was beautifully browned, we noted that the birds emerged from the oven with slightly underdone thighs. The roasting pan, as it turned out, acted as a sort of heat shield and prevented the underside of the quail from cooking through. Not wanting to mar the crisp skin we had finally achieved, roasting them upside down at this point was not an option. But it occurred to us that we could preheat the roasting pan so that when the rack of birds was placed in the oven to finish, heat would radiate from the hot pan and help cook the thighs through faster. This trick worked, resulting in lovely, crisp skin along with perfectly cooked dark and light meat.

We found that the quail tasted best when soaked for 30 minutes in brine and then stuffed with an ample amount of fresh herbs. The brine enhanced the delicate flavor of the quail while ensuring that the breast meat remained juicy. The herbs (our tasters liked a combination of rosemary and sage) lightly perfumed the meat from the inside as it cooked.

Delicate and sophisticated, these roasted quail are not meant to be served with gravy but rather a more distinguished sauce. We found that a simple reduction of balsamic vinegar, bay leaf, and peppercorns made a quick syrupy glaze that added the perfect balance of flavors to the quail. Taking less than an hour to make, these impressive little birds are not only good for company but easy enough to make for a weeknight supper.

PREPARING QUAIL

1. Using the tip of a paring knife, make an incision all the way through the meat of one drumstick, about ½ inch from the end of the drumstick bone.

2. Carefully insert the other drumstick through the incision so that the legs are securely crossed.

Roast Quail with Balsamic Glaze

SERVES 4

A single quail served over arugula or mesclun makes an excellent appetizer. Two quail, served with polenta, makes a fine main course. If you don't have a roasting rack that's the right size for this recipe, try the top of a broiler pan. For the meatiest portions, use large quail that weigh 5 ounces each.

1	cup kosher salt or ½ cup table salt
8	whole quail (about 5 ounces each)
¾	cup balsamic vinegar
1	bay leaf
5	whole black peppercorns
	Pinch sugar
	Ground black pepper
4	sprigs fresh rosemary, cut in half
16	fresh sage leaves
2	tablespoons extra-virgin olive oil

1. Dissolve the salt in 2½ quarts water in a large container or bowl. Submerge the quail in the brine and refrigerate until fully seasoned, 30 minutes.

2. Meanwhile, bring the vinegar, bay leaf, peppercorns, and sugar to a simmer in a small nonstick skillet over medium heat. Cook until the mixture is syrupy and measures 3 tablespoons, about 20 minutes. Remove the pan from the heat, discard the bay leaf, and reserve the syrup.

3. Rinse the quail under running water and pat dry with paper towels. Season with pepper to taste. Place half a rosemary sprig and 2 sage leaves in the cavity of each quail and secure the legs (see the illustrations at left).

4. Adjust an oven rack to the middle position, place a roasting pan on the oven rack, and heat the oven to 450 degrees. Heat the oil in a large skillet over high heat until just smoking, about 2 minutes. Reduce the heat to medium

and place 4 quail, breast side down, in the skillet. Cook, turning the quail on their sides occasionally, until the breast skin is a golden brown, 2 to 4 minutes. Transfer the browned quail to a flat roasting rack that will fit inside the roasting pan. Repeat with the remaining quail.

5. Place the rack with the quail in the preheated roasting pan and roast until the juices run clear when a fork pierces the breast just above the wing, 7 to 10 minutes. Remove the quail from the oven and arrange them on a large platter or individual plates. Drizzle with the balsamic syrup and serve immediately.

BRAISED RABBIT

BROWSE THROUGH REGIONAL ITALIAN cookbooks and you will find plenty of recipes for rabbit braised in white wine. Although the various regions add their own local ingredients, the basic recipe remains the same. However, as we soon found out, these braises often produce tough, dry pieces of rabbit and a relatively thin, bland sauce.

Rabbit is not as common in the United States as it is abroad, and we visited several grocery stores to see how it is most often butchered and sold. At most stores, the rabbit was sold whole; however, we saw a few packages with cut-up pieces. Although the packages of cut-up pieces are appealing (there's no need to butcher the rabbit at home), we found that they made a much less flavorful braise. When compared to a whole rabbit cut into seven pieces (including the neck, backbone, and liver), the packaged pieces simply didn't offer enough variety in terms of meat, bones, or gizzards to help flavor the sauce. Luckily, we found cutting up a rabbit was easy; the parts are easy to identify, the bones are relatively small, and there is no slippery skin to deal with.

With the rabbit cut into seven pieces, we turned our attention to getting all these pieces properly cooked. Braising involves cooking meat partially covered in liquid for a substantial period, after which the cooking liquid is reduced to a sauce. (For more about the science of braising, see page 287.) The beauty of this method is that tough pieces of meat are rendered tender and flavorful, while the entire process is contained to just one pot. All braises follow the same basic process: Brown the meat, then remove it from the pan, sauté the aromatics in the rendered meat fat, then add liquid and the meat back to the pan and cook at a gentle simmer until the meat is tender. The liquid is then reduced to a sauce while the meat rests off to the side.

We braised a rabbit using this simple technique and noted that it took the hindquarters and forequarters nearly an hour to become tender. By this time, the loin had overcooked and turned dry. The muscles of the loin, including the tenderloin and sirloin, are more delicate than the quarters and don't require the long braising time. Leaving the loin pieces out of the braise until the last 10 minutes of cooking solved this problem and resulted in perfectly cooked meat across the board.

Next, we tried a few tricks to improve (and thicken) the texture of the sauce. Using flour to thicken the sauce is common in braises, and we tested dredging the rabbit in flour before browning it versus adding the flour straight to the pan. The rabbit dredged in flour did thicken the sauce, but the surface of the meat turned slightly gummy. Adding a small amount of flour to the sautéed aromatics before adding the braising liquid worked much better. Noting that three cups of liquid was the right amount to braise a whole rabbit, we found one tablespoon of flour was enough to thicken the final sauce.

EQUIPMENT: Sauté Pans

With some kitchen equipment, the difference between pricey and inexpensive models just isn't that big a deal—either will get the job done. But sauté pans are another story, primarily because of the nature of sautéing. When you sauté, you cook food quickly, with minimal fat, in a very hot pan. As it cooks, the food develops a nice, dark, flavorful crust, which is the glory of sautéing.

But there is a thin line between crusty and burnt—and it's a line that you definitely don't want to cross. To sauté successfully, you need a pan that distributes heat evenly, without hot spots that can cause food to scorch or burn outright. We opened our wallet and chose eight popular models in the three-quart size, then headed off to the test kitchen for a two-week sauté-a-thon.

The popularity of nonstick pans compelled us to consider several in our tests. By and large, the nonstick pans performed on a par with the other pans in our tests. Yet for all of their virtues, the nonsticks had, in our opinion at least, what amounted to a serious flaw: They resist the development of a fond, the sticky, brown, caramelized bits that form on the pan bottom as the food cooks. When released from the pan bottom with the addition of liquid, which is then boiled to dissolve those bits (called deglazing), the fond provides the savory underpinnings of sauces, stews, and braises. Fond develops because the drippings from the food stick to the pan—no sticking, no fond. As a result, when we used nonstick pans to make the sauce for a braised chicken dish, the sauce looked light and tasted weak. We advise you to stick with a traditional nonreactive cooking surface.

Differences in the pans' sautéing and browning performance were not as significant as we had imagined they would be. All of the pans in our price range were thick enough to allow good conduction with no significant hot spots that could cause food to burn.

While variations in the sautéing and browning performance of the pans turned out to be relatively undramatic, certain aspects of pan design made a much bigger difference to us than we had anticipated. For example, each pan was rated at or very close to three quarts, but their diameters varied by more than an inch, from about 11 inches for the Look and All-Clad pans to about 10 inches for the KitchenAid, Analon, and Mauviel. A little larger diameter was a big advantage for the cook. For instance, the 11-inch All-Clad accommodated the chicken in our braised chicken test more comfortably than the smaller KitchenAid, Analon, and Mauviel, which were snug. This meant it was easier to slide tongs or a spatula into the All-Clad to move the chicken pieces without accidentally gouging or damaging them or splashing the sauce. It also meant more favorable conditions for sautéing turkey cutlets, which are wide and flat and need space around them to brown properly.

Hot handles turned out to be a problem with only two of the pans, the Le Creuset and the Mauviel copper. The stainless-steel handles of the All-Clad and KitchenAid pans and the cast-steel handle of the Calphalon stayed cool (though the KitchenAid tended to heat near the base), as did the phenolic (heat-resistant plastic) handles of the Look and Analon pans. All of the pans except for the Look and Mauviel have a helper handle, usually consisting of a small loop opposite the long handle so that the cook can use two hands to lift the pan when desired. We find the helper handle especially useful when we're hoisting full pans in and out of the oven.

For our money, the All-Clad pan, with a traditional cooking surface, provided the best combination of great design, ample proportions, and reliable performance. The Calphalon, KitchenAid, Analon, and Look pans all performed well, too, and some cost a few dollars less, but each had a design flaw that caused it to fall behind the All-Clad.

THE BEST SAUTE PAN
The All-Clad Stainless Steel 3-Quart Sauté Pan was our top choice. It promoted a beautiful brown crust on foods, developed an impressive fond, and handled batches easily. This pan is also quite spacious.

Focusing last on flavor, we tested various types of braising liquids and found a combination of chicken stock and white wine to taste best. Beef broth was too heavy for the light, poultrylike flavor of rabbit, while red wine was too tannic and turned the meat a strange garnet color.

Looking for even more flavor, we tried cooking the aromatics, in this case onions, to a sweet, lightly caramelized stage before adding the liquid. The complex flavor of the caramelized onion carried through and made a deeper-tasting sauce. A few recipes we researched called for adding the rabbit liver to the braise, and we found that it did indeed make a big difference. It added a meaty, intense rabbit flavor without tasting metallic or, for lack of a better word, livery. A small amount of tomato paste, some bay leaves, a sprig of rosemary, and a pinch of hot red pepper flakes helped round out the flavors.

Most Italian recipes for braised rabbit call for tomatoes and olives, and we found canned diced tomatoes worked well when incorporated into the braising liquid. Good brined black olives, such as kalamatas, also added welcome flavor and texture, but they were better stirred in at the end. Finished with a sprinkle of fresh parsley, this simple braise offers tender, juicy pieces of meat and a rich, brothy sauce, leaving no doubt as to why it is such a classic.

CUTTING UP A RABBIT

1. Using a sharp chef's knife, cut the hind-quarters from the loin.

2. Cut the hindquarters in half, down through the spine, to yield two pieces.

3. Trim and discard the thin flap that hangs between the rib cage and loin.

4. To remove the loin from the forequarters, cut through the spine at the point where the rib cage is attached, right behind the forequarters.

5. Cut the loin in half crosswise to yield two pieces.

6. To separate the two forequarters from the neck, cut down through the rib cage on either side of the neck. You should have two forequarter pieces plus the neck, a bony piece that contributes flavor to the sauce and also contains some meat you can eat.

EQUIPMENT: Chef's Knives

A good chef's knife is the most useful tool any cook owns. Besides chopping vegetables, it can be used for myriad tasks, including cutting up poultry, mincing herbs, and slicing fruit. So what separates a good knife from an inferior one? To understand the answer to this question, it helps to know something about how knives are constructed.

The first pieces of cutlery were made about 4,000 years ago with the discovery that iron ore could be melted and shaped into tools. The creation of steel, which is 80 percent iron and 20 percent other elements, led to the development of carbon steel knives—the standard for 3,000 years. Although this kind of steel takes and holds an edge easily, it also stains and rusts. Something as simple as cutting an acidic tomato or living in the salt air of the seacoast can corrode carbon steel.

Today, new alloys have given cooks better options. Stainless steel, made with at least 4 percent chromium and/or nickel, will never rust. Used for many cheap knives, stainless steel is also very difficult to sharpen. The compromise between durable but dull stainless steel and sharp but corrodible carbon steel is high-carbon stainless steel. Used by most knife manufacturers, this blend combines durability and sharpness.

Until recently, all knives were hot drop forged—that is, the steel was heated to 2000 degrees, dropped into a mold, given four or five shots with a hammer, and then tempered (cooled and heated several times to build strength). This process is labor-intensive (many steps must be done by hand), which explains why many chef's knives cost almost $100.

A second manufacturing process feeds longs sheets of steel through a press that punches out knife after knife, much like a cookie cutter slicing through dough. Called stamped blades, these knives require some hand finishing but are much cheaper to produce because a machine does most of the work.

While experts have long argued that forged knives are better than stamped ones, our testing did not fully support this position. We liked some forged knives and did not like others. Likewise, we liked some stamped knives and did not like others. The weight and shape of the handle (it must be comfortable to hold and substantial but not too heavy), the ability of the blade to take an edge, and the shape of the blade (we like a slightly curved blade, which is better suited to the rocking motion often used to mince herbs or garlic than a straight blade) are all key factors in choosing a knife.

When shopping, pick up the knife and see how it feels in your hand. Is it easy to grip? Does the weight seem properly distributed between the handle and blade? In our testing, we liked knives made by Henckels and Wüsthof. An inexpensive knife by Forschner, with a stamped blade, also scored well.

Buying a good knife is only half the challenge. You must keep the edge sharp. To that end, we recommend buying an electric knife sharpener. Steels are best for modest corrections, but all knives will require more substantial sharpening at least several times a year, if not more often if you cook a lot. Stones are difficult to use because they require that you maintain a perfect 20-degree angle between the stone and blade. An electric knife sharpener (we like models made by Chef's Choice) takes the guesswork out of sharpening and allows you to keep edges sharp and effective.

THE BEST CHEF'S KNIVES

The Henckels Four Star (left) and Wüsthof-Trident Grand Prix (center) are top choices, but expect to spend about $80 for one of these knives. The Forschner (Victorinox) Fibrox (right) is lighter but still solid and costs just $30.

Braised Rabbit

SERVES 4

The liver is usually loose in the cavity and should be reserved. It looks like a large chicken liver. Some rabbits may also contain the kidneys, which are shaped like large jelly beans; if they are present, remove and discard them. Serve braised rabbit with polenta (page 218).

3   tablespoons extra-virgin olive oil
1   whole rabbit (about 3 pounds), cut into
    7 pieces (see illustrations on page 256),
    liver reserved and cut into 1/8-inch pieces
    Salt and ground black pepper
1   medium onion, chopped medium
5   medium cloves garlic, minced or pressed
    through a garlic press
1   tablespoon tomato paste
1   tablespoon all-purpose flour
1   cup dry white wine
1   (14 1/2-ounce) can low-sodium
    chicken broth
1   (14 1/2-ounce) can diced tomatoes,
    drained
    Pinch hot red pepper flakes
3   bay leaves
1   sprig fresh rosemary
1/4 cup black olives, such as kalamatas, pitted
    and slivered lengthwise
1   tablespoon minced fresh parsley leaves

1. Heat 2 tablespoons oil in a large sauté pan over high heat until just smoking, about 2 minutes. Sprinkle the pieces of rabbit liberally with salt and pepper to taste. Add half the rabbit pieces to the pan and reduce the heat to medium-high. Cook, turning the meat once, until nicely browned on both sides, about 4 minutes. Transfer the browned rabbit to a clean plate and repeat with the remaining pieces.

2. Return the empty pan to medium heat, add the remaining tablespoon oil, and swirl to coat the pan bottom with the oil. Add the onion and cook until soft and light brown, about 15 minutes. Add the garlic and tomato paste and cook until aromatic, about 30 seconds. Add the flour and stir until it is incorporated, about 1 minute. Raise the heat to high, add the wine, broth, tomatoes, hot red pepper flakes, bay leaves, and rosemary, and stir to incorporate. Return the forequarters, hindquarters, and neck to the pan (leave the loin pieces out for now) and bring to a gentle simmer. Reduce the heat to low, cover, and cook until the meat is almost tender, about 45 minutes. Add the two loin pieces and continue to cook until all the meat is tender, about 10 minutes longer.

3. Remove the lid and transfer the rabbit pieces to a clean plate. Remove and discard the bay leaves and rosemary. Bring the sauce to a simmer over high heat, add the liver, and, using a potato masher or the back of a spoon, work the liver into the sauce. Cook the sauce until slightly thickened, about 5 minutes. Stir in the olives and parsley and season with salt and pepper to taste. Return the rabbit to the sauce, heat briefly, and serve.

MINESTRONE WITH CLASSIC PESTO **PAGE 108**

TOMATO, MOZZARELLA, AND BASIL TART **PAGE 393**

MARINATED BLACK AND GREEN OLIVES **PAGE 3**

CHARCOAL-GRILLED TUSCAN STEAK WITH OLIVE OIL AND LEMON   PAGE 278

PASTA WITH TOMATO, BACON, AND ONION (PASTA ALL'AMATRICIANA)   **PAGE 162**

263

POLENTA WITH GORGONZOLA **PAGE 218**

GRILLED VEAL CHOPS ON A BED OF ARUGULA   **PAGE 301**

PASTA WITH FRESH CLAM SAUCE   **PAGE 168**

CHICKEN PARMESAN **PAGE 230**

RISOTTO CAKES **PAGE 215**

PARMESAN RISOTTO **PAGE 204**

FOCACCIA WITH BLACK OLIVES AND THYME **PAGE 356**

GRILLED PEPPER SALAD WITH GREEN OLIVES AND CAPERS   **PAGE 43**

PASTA AND RED PEPPER TUNA SAUCE WITH ANCHOVIES, GARLIC, AND BASIL **PAGE 171**

CHICKEN CACCIATORE WITH PORTOBELLOS AND SAGE   **PAGE 239**

273

NECTARINES, PLUMS, AND BERRIES IN PROSECCO   **PAGE 401**

8
MEAT

ITALIANS ENJOY A WIDE VARIETY OF dishes made with beef, veal, pork, and lamb. Typically, these dishes are served after pasta or risotto, and the portions are fairly small. Seasonings are simple, bold, and direct. The recipes that follow offer a good selection of our favorite Italian meat dishes. Some are lightning-fast sautés (such as veal scaloppine and Parmesan-breaded lamb chops), while others are slow-simmering braises (such as beef in barolo and osso buco). Together they offer an accurate snapshot of Italian meat cookery.

STEAK FIORENTINA

WHEN AMERICANS GARNISH A STEAK, it's often with A.1. sauce. The French use a fla-vored compound butter. But the Italians have something even better—and, arguably, easier too: olive oil and lemon. *Bistecca alla Fiorentina,* as it is called in Tuscany, couldn't be simpler; a thick, juicy steak is grilled rare, sliced, and served with a drizzle of extra-virgin olive oil and a squeeze of lemon. For most of us here in the test kitchen, this unexpected combina-tion was a revelation, and we expect that any steak lover who gives it a whirl will become a convert, too. The fruity, peppery olive oil amplifies the savory nature of the beef, while the lemon provides a bright counterpoint that cuts right through the richness to sharpen the other flavors.

In a dish this direct, though, good tech-nique can mean the difference between mediocre and magical, so we grilled our way through more than 30 pounds of steak to per-fect both the grilling technique and the details of the olive oil and lemon garnish—that is, when and how to introduce it.

Thick T-bone and porterhouse steaks are recommended most often for bistecca alla Fiorentina. Both steaks feature a T-shaped bone with meat from the top loin (also known as the strip) on one side and from the tenderloin on the other side. The primary difference between the two is the size of the tenderloin piece, which is larger on the porterhouse. Of course, we sampled both steaks and found them equally appealing—tender, with a robust, well-balanced flavor. There was no reason to test additional cuts. The suggested thickness, around 1½ inches, also worked well, allowing for an appealing textural contrast between the smoky crust that formed on the outside of the steak and the rare, tender interior.

The flavor of that smoky, crisp, brown, caramelized crust is a primary reason to cook the steak over a charcoal fire. A few rounds at the grill quickly proved that plenty of heat was necessary to achieve a sufficient crust. Anything cooler than medium-hot would not get the job done. But there was a problem: The interior had not cooked enough by the time the crust was perfectly done. Leaving the

Steak Fiorentina is grilled, sliced off the bone, drizzled with extra-virgin olive oil, and served with lemon wedges.

steak in place until the interior reached 120 degrees on an instant-read thermometer (rare) torched the exterior. Obviously, we needed a more reliable method.

A little pyro-experimentation helped solve the problem. We needed a two-level fire, with more coals on one side of the grill than on the other to create hotter and cooler areas. Starting the steaks over the hotter part of the fire allowed the exterior to sear deeply; finishing them over the cooler area allowed the inside to cook through without charring the outside.

The recipes we turned up in our research shared an odd voodoo when it came to seasoning the steaks. Several recommended using olive oil to marinate the raw steaks, a few more suggested rubbing the steaks with olive oil just before grilling them, while one passionately declared that oiling the meat before

cooking would cause it to "taste greasy and be nauseating." Another recipe insisted that the steaks be both salted and drizzled with olive oil after they had cooked but before they were removed from the grill.

To see if any of these techniques could really work magic, we evaluated steaks treated with oil in five different ways: The oil was used as a marinade before cooking, brushed on the meat before grilling, brushed on the meat as it grilled, drizzled on the whole cooked steaks before slicing, and drizzled over the sliced steak at serving time.

We preferred drizzling the oil over the sliced steak for a few reasons. It was the easiest, least fussy method; it flavored the meat most effectively, bringing the full fruity, peppery impact of the raw oil to the fore; and it guaranteed a hit of oil with each bite of steak. Although the steaks that were oiled prior to or during grilling were not nauseating, as one author had predicted, the heat of the grill did mitigate the nuances of the oil, in a sense deadening its flavor. The oiled steaks also caused more flare-ups on the grill.

We tried both pure and extra-virgin olive oils, and the extra-virgin was far and away the best for its distinctive character and bold flavor. We went on to try several brands of extra-virgin oil and preferred those with bolder, fuller-bodied flavor to the milder oils. We also experimented with the lemon and found it easiest and best to squeeze it over the sliced steak at the last minute. Juicing the lemon and brushing the juice on the steaks any earlier relieved the lemon of some of its freshness and tang.

The use of garlic was a matter of debate in the original recipes. Some included it, while others decried it as nontraditional. The idea appealed to us nonetheless, so we tried four ways of working it into the program. We made a sauce with pureed fresh garlic, olive oil, and

T-BONE AND PORTERHOUSE STEAKS

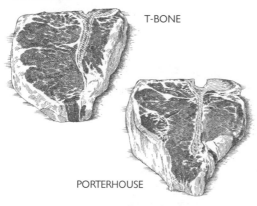

T-BONE

PORTERHOUSE

The T-bone and porterhouse contain a nice balance of chewy strip steak (on the left side of the bone in these illustrations) and buttery tenderloin (on the right side of the bone in these illustrations). The porterhouse, cut from farther back in the animal, has a larger piece of tenderloin than the T-bone, while the grain of the strip piece on a porterhouse is rougher than that on a T-bone. Although some experts say that the T-bone is preferable to the porterhouse (because the grain of its strip meat is finer), we found the two steaks equally delicious, if slightly different.

lemon juice and poured it over the sliced steak, but the garlic was overpowering. We tried rubbing both fresh and toasted garlic cloves over the cooked steak, but tasters were not impressed. Last, we rubbed a fresh-cut

SLICING T-BONE AND PORTERHOUSE STEAKS

1. After allowing the steaks to rest, cut along the bone to remove the large strip section.

2. Cut the smaller tenderloin section off the bone.

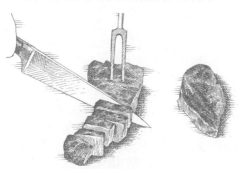

3. Cut each large piece crosswise into ½-inch-thick slices for serving.

garlic clove over the bone and then the meat of the raw steak. The bone scraped the surface of the garlic, allowing small bits to cling to the meat. Once this steak was grilled, it had a faint suggestion of toasted garlic flavor that was a hit with the tasters. This became a variation on the basic recipe.

Charcoal-Grilled Tuscan Steak with Olive Oil and Lemon
(Bistecca alla Fiorentina)
SERVES 4

T-Bone and porterhouse steaks are large enough to serve two. We prefer to season the steaks with kosher salt because its coarse grains are easier than fine table salt to sprinkle evenly over the meat. If you use charcoal briquettes instead of hardwood charcoal, one chimney-full will weigh close to 6 pounds. Also, you may have to increase the searing time by about 30 seconds on each side. There is no need to build a two-level fire if you can adjust the level of the charcoal rack on your grill; crank the rack up high to sear the steaks, then drop it down a couple of levels for less intense heat to finish cooking them.

2   T-bone or porterhouse steaks, each 1½ inches thick (about 3½ pounds total), patted dry
2   teaspoons kosher salt
1   teaspoon ground black pepper
3   tablespoons extra-virgin olive oil
     Lemon wedges for serving

1. Light a large chimney starter filled with hardwood charcoal (about 2½ pounds) and burn until covered with a layer of fine gray ash. Build a two-level fire by stacking most of the coals on one side of the grill and arranging the remaining coals in a single layer on the other side. Set the cooking grate in place,

cover the grill with the lid, and let the grate heat, about 5 minutes. Use a wire brush to scrape the grate clean. The grill is ready when the thicker layer of coals is medium-hot (you can hold your hand 5 inches above the cooking grate for 3 to 4 seconds).

2. Meanwhile, sprinkle each side of each steak with ½ teaspoon salt and ¼ teaspoon pepper. Cook the steaks, uncovered, over the hotter part of the grill until well browned on each side, about 2½ minutes per side. (If the steaks start to flame, move them to the cooler side of the grill and/or extinguish the flames with a squirt bottle). Move the steaks to the cooler side of the grill and continue cooking, turning once, to the desired doneness, 5 to 6 minutes more for rare (120 degrees on an instant-read thermometer), 6 to 7 minutes for rare medium-rare (125 degrees), 7 to 8 minute for medium medium-rare (130 degrees), or 8

EQUIPMENT: Charcoal

Would you ever have guessed that Henry Ford was to thank for charcoal-grilled steak? That's right. Ford pioneered the charcoal briquette industry as a way to profit from the scrap wood generated by manufacturing all those Model Ts in the 1920s.

Generally speaking, charcoal is the carbonized remains of wood that has been burned in the absence of oxygen. Without oxygen, resins and moisture in the wood evaporate, leaving behind light, easily lit, combustible charcoal.

Three types of charcoal dominate the market. They are hardwood charcoal (also called charwood, lump charwood, and lump hardwood), which, like the wood used to make it, consists of irregularly shaped pieces and is additive-free; square, pillow-shaped briquettes made from scrap wood and sawdust that is burned and then compacted along with chemicals and other binders that help them ignite and burn evenly; and a Kingsford product called Match Light, which are briquettes that have been permeated with lighter fluid and thereby promise to ignite with the touch of a lit match. (Match Light did live up to its name, quickly producing a spectacular 3-foot column of flame on the windy day we conducted our tests.)

We were anxious to test the common assertion that hardwood charcoal burns hotter and faster than briquettes, so we hooked up a sophisticated, high-range temperature sensor to the cooking grate above fires made from each of the three types of charcoal. We recorded temperatures after 5 minutes, 15 minutes, and 25 minutes to gauge the drop-off in heat. Sure enough, the hardwood fire was the hottest initially at just above 700 degrees, compared with 660 degrees for the briquettes and 550 degrees for the Match Light. The hardwood also dropped off the most dramatically—by almost 450 degrees—after 25 minutes.

We were also curious to see if we could detect flavor differences in foods grilled with the three types of charcoal, so we sampled steak (because it's hearty) and zucchini (because it's delicate). Though the hardwood charcoal fire formed the thickest, most deeply brown crust on the steaks, tasters did not detect any significant flavor differences in the three steaks. It was another story, however, with the zucchini. The zucchini grilled over hardwood charcoal colored the fastest and tasted smokier than the others. The briquette-grilled zucchini had the lightest grilled flavor (but no off flavors), and the Match Light—grilled sample demonstrated a faint but odd bitterness.

So where does this leave us? We'd just as soon avoid any off flavors in delicate foods, so we'll pass on the Match Light charcoal. For grill-roasting over a longer period at a lower temperature, we'll opt for briquettes because they burn a little cooler and a lot longer than hardwood. But for straight-ahead grilling applications, especially when there's meat on the menu that cries out for a deep sear, we'll take hardwood. Grilling is all about high heat, and we'll take every extra degree we can get.

to 9 minutes for medium (135 to 140 degrees).

3. Transfer the steaks to a cutting board and let rest 5 minutes. Following the illustrations on page 278, cut the strip and tenderloin pieces off the bones and slice them crosswise about ½ inch thick. Arrange the slices on a platter, drizzle with the olive oil, and serve immediately with the lemon wedges.

➤ VARIATIONS

Gas-Grilled Tuscan Steak with Olive Oil and Lemon

Turn all burners on a gas grill to high, close the lid, and heat until very hot, about 15 minutes. Scrape the cooking grate clean with a wire brush; leave one burner on high and turn the other burner(s) down to medium. Follow the recipe for Charcoal-Grilled Tuscan Steak with Olive Oil and Lemon, beginning with step 2 and cooking with the lid down.

Grilled Tuscan Steak with Garlic Essence

Follow the recipe for Charcoal- or Gas-Grilled Tuscan Steak with Olive Oil and Lemon, rubbing a halved garlic clove over the bone and meat on each side of each steak before seasoning with salt and pepper.

STEAK PIZZAIOLA

SUPPOSEDLY INVENTED BY THE WIVES of Neapolitan pizza makers, this weeknight favorite is nothing more than steak cooked with pizza sauce—tomato sauce flavored with garlic and herbs. After making several authentic recipes, it became clear that although this classic steak dish is easy to make, it is not necessarily easy to make well.

Our first job was to find the best cut of meat, so we cooked our way around the meat counter until we found just the right one. While older recipes use steaks cut from the round, we found that round steaks were too tough and dry even after they were simmered in the sauce for a long time. More modern recipes, on the other hand, call for expensive steaks such as New York strip, rib eye, and tenderloin. Although these steaks cooked up tender, their delicate flavors and fancy prices simply didn't pair well with the potency of the accompanying pizza sauce. We then tried flank steak as well as skirt steak, and we finally discovered the meat we were looking for. With a strong, beefy flavor and a reasonable weekday price tag, these steaks cooked in only a few minutes and sliced up perfectly to feed a family of four.

To cook the steaks, we tried the classic technique of browning then simmering in the pizza sauce but found that they easily overcooked. Flank steak and skirt steak are quite thin, and we learned it was better to brown them in a hot pan and keep them warm in the oven while we made a pizza sauce from the pan drippings.

With the steak nailed down, we turned our focus to the sauce. We found that diced tomatoes tasted great but were just too chunky for this recipe. We preferred the thick, smooth sauce made from crushed tomatoes. The problem, however, is that crushed tomatoes are generally sold in 28-ounce cans, which are simply too big. We decided to crush our own tomatoes by pulsing a small (14½-ounce) can of diced tomatoes in a food processor. Now the texture of the tomatoes was correct, and we had no leftovers. In addition, the diced tomatoes gave the sauce a lively, fresh flavor.

Keeping the other flavors of the sauce simple, we added only the basics, including onions, garlic, oregano, red wine, and a sprinkling of fresh parsley to finish. Although the sauce was perfect for pizza, it still needed a bigger flavor to stand up to the steak. To boost the tomatoes, we found it necessary to round out the sauce with a tablespoon of tomato paste. The paste gave our sauce a richer, more complex flavor.

Taking just 20 minutes from start to finish, this simple, perfectly cooked steak and potent pizza sauce will quickly become a favorite dish in your weeknight repertoire.

Steak Pizzaiola

SERVES 4

Skirt steak is richer and beefier than flank steak, but it tends to fall apart when sliced. The flank steak is firmer and slices better. Both are good choices for this recipe.

1	(14½-ounce) can diced tomatoes
1½	pounds flank or skirt steak (if using skirt steak, cut it into several 8-inch lengths)
	Salt and ground black pepper
2	tablespoons extra-virgin olive oil
1	medium onion, sliced thin
5	medium cloves garlic, minced or pressed through a garlic press
	Pinch hot red pepper flakes
1	tablespoon tomato paste
¼	cup dry red wine
1	sprig fresh oregano
1	tablespoon minced fresh parsley leaves

1. Pulse the tomatoes and their juices in the workbowl of a food processor fitted with a steel blade to a coarse puree, about five 1-second pulses. Set the tomatoes aside.

2. Adjust an oven rack to the middle position and heat the oven to 300 degrees. Season the meat liberally with salt and pepper to taste. Heat 1 tablespoon oil in a heavy bottomed 12-inch skillet over high heat until it just starts to smoke. Reduce the heat to medium, add the meat, and cook, not moving, until well browned, 4 to 5 minutes. Turn the meat with tongs and cook until well browned on the second side, 4 to 5 minutes longer. Transfer the meat to a clean plate and place the plate in the warm oven while assembling the sauce.

3. Return the empty pan to medium heat, add the remaining tablespoon oil, and swirl to coat the pan. Add the onion and cook until slightly browned around the edges, 2 to 3 minutes. Add the garlic, hot red pepper flakes, and tomato paste and cook until aromatic, about 30 seconds. Add the wine, pureed tomatoes, and oregano, scraping any browned bits from the bottom of the pan with a wooden spoon. Cook until the sauce is slightly thickened and measures about 1½ cups, about 5 minutes. Remove the pan from the heat and stir in the parsley.

4. As the sauce finishes cooking, remove the meat from the oven and transfer it to a cutting board, adding any accumulated juices to the sauce. Slice the steak on the bias against the grain into ½-inch-thick pieces. To serve, pour the sauce onto individual plates or a large warmed serving platter and top with the sliced steak. Serve immediately.

BRACIOLE

BEEF BRACIOLE IS A CLASSIC SUNDAY dinner in many Italian-American households. The recipe has its roots in southern Italy. For braciole, thin slices of meat are filled with aromatics, rolled, and braised in a tomato sauce often referred to as Sunday gravy or Sunday sauce. Although recipes for braciole call for a range of fillings from sausage and prosciutto to spinach and provolone, the classic (and, we think, best) filling consists of raisins, pine nuts, herbs, grated cheese, and garlic. We began our testing with an authentic recipe from an editor's Italian grandmother who is known for her good food. (The editor also swore by this family recipe.) This treasured recipe immediately set the parameters for our testing.

A good braciole doesn't require the use of a knife at the table; it should fall apart under the light pressure of a fork. Although most recipes call for thin slices of meat cut from the round, we tried making braciole using two other common cuts of beef. Chuck steaks turned out to be too fatty, leaving a greasy slick on top of the sauce, while steaks cut from the loin turned tough and dry after being simmered in the tomato sauce. Returning to thin steaks cut from the round, we then tested whether or not they should be pounded. The unpounded steaks turned out dense and a bit too chewy, while the pounded steaks emerged from the sauce absolutely tender. For the best results, we discovered that the meat should be pounded to a thickness of ¼ inch.

For the filling, we tried several approaches using the basic mixture of raisins, pine nuts, parsley, basil (tasters liked both herbs rather than just one), pecorino cheese (which tasters preferred over milder Parmesan), and garlic. Some recipes call for binding the mixture with oil, eggs, fresh bread crumbs, or cubes of bread soaked in milk. However, our tasters preferred the clean, herbaceous flavor of the mixture without any binding. The oil-soaked stuffing added unnecessary fat to the sauce, while the egg, bread crumbs, and milk-soaked cubes turned it heavy, soggy, and leaden. Left alone, the loose, dry mixture of herbs, nuts, and raisins acted like an aromatic paste, infusing flavor into both the meat and the sauce.

To help this loose mixture of fruit and nuts stick to the meat, we brushed the pounded steaks with a little oil before sprinkling the mixture evenly over the meat. We also found it helpful to press the mixture lightly into the meat with our hands.

Several recipes call for a slice of provolone to be rolled up in the braciole, but the result was met with mixed reviews. Many of the tasters liked the texture and flavor of gooey cheese in the filling, while others preferred it without (we made it optional). Just 1½ tablespoons of the mixture was needed to fill one braciola, and we noted that a total of 12 braciole served six people.

Cooking braciole is a straightforward procedure. The rolls are browned and removed from the pan. A simple tomato sauce is then built using the drippings left behind in the pan. Finally, the rolls are simmered in the sauce until they are fork-tender. The recipes we researched called for a range of simmering times from 15 minutes to several hours, but our grandmother's recipe nailed the time perfectly. The beef rolls took exactly two hours to cook through. When cooked less, the braciole required a sharp knife and a strong jaw to eat, while more time in the pan simply caused the beef (and the rolls) to fall apart.

To make the simple tomato sauce, we first discarded the spent oil left over from browning the braciole. Using fresh extra-virgin olive oil, we sautéed onion and garlic, then added two large cans of crushed tomatoes along with some red wine. (The sauce for braciole is traditionally smooth, so crushed tomatoes are the best choice here.) Seasoned with fresh basil, hot red pepper flakes, and a bay leaf, the sauce turned out flavorful and ample for both our authentic braciole and a pound of freshly cooked pasta, its classic accompaniment.

Braciole

SERVES 6

Many supermarkets sell meat specifically labeled "for braciole." If yours does not, the butcher should be able to cut it for you. Steaks that measure 5 inches across by 7 inches long are ideal. This recipe makes enough extra sauce to coat one pound of pasta. We like to serve braciole with a hearty pasta shape, such as ziti or rigatoni.

BRACIOLE

2	medium cloves garlic, minced or pressed through a garlic press
½	cup raisins
½	cup pine nuts, toasted in a dry skillet until fragrant
½	cup minced fresh parsley leaves
¼	cup minced fresh basil leaves
⅓	cup grated Pecorino Romano cheese
6	½-inch-thick steaks cut from the widest part of a top round roast (about 2 pounds total)
5	tablespoons extra-virgin olive oil
	Salt and ground black pepper
6	thin slices provolone cheese, cut in half (optional)

SIMPLE TOMATO SAUCE

2	tablespoons extra-virgin olive oil
½	small onion, minced
5	medium cloves garlic, minced or pressed through a garlic press
¼	teaspoon hot red pepper flakes
⅓	cup red wine
2	(28-ounce) cans crushed tomatoes
I	bay leaf
2	tablespoon minced fresh basil leaves
	Salt and ground black pepper

1. FOR THE BRACIOLE: Combine the garlic, raisins, pine nuts, herbs, and Pecorino Romano cheese in a medium bowl. Cut each steak in half crosswise to yield 12 pieces in total. Place the meat between two sheets of parchment or wax paper and pound to a thickness of ¼ inch. Lay the meat flat on a cutting board, brush the top of each piece with a little oil (use 3 tablespoons oil in total), and season with salt and pepper. If using, lay a slice of provolone on top of each piece of meat. Sprinkle 1½ tablespoons filling evenly over each piece of meat, leaving a clean ½-inch border. Press the filling lightly into the meat to help it adhere. Starting at the narrow end, roll each piece of meat to form a tidy bundle; secure the end with a metal turkey trussing skewer, long toothpick, or bamboo skewer cut to a 4-inch length. Season the outside of the braciole with salt and pepper to taste.

2. Heat the remaining 2 tablespoons oil in a large sauté pan or Dutch oven over medium-high heat until shimmering with wisps of smoke, about 2 minutes. Add half the braciole to the pan, reduce the heat to medium, and cook, turning several times, until well browned on all sides, 5 to 6 minutes. Transfer the braciole to a clean plate and reserve. Add the remaining braciole to the pan and cook as before, adjusting the heat as necessary to prevent the pan drippings from burning. Transfer the second batch to the plate.

3. FOR THE SAUCE: Discard any oil left in the pan, retaining any browned bits. Add 2 tablespoons oil to the pan and return the pan to medium heat. When the oil is hot, add the onion and sauté, scraping up any browned bits, until the onion is soft, about 2 minutes. Add the garlic and hot red pepper flakes and cook until aromatic, about 30 seconds. Add the wine, scraping up any browned bits from the pan. Add the tomatoes and bring to a simmer. Stir in the bay leaf and basil and return the braciole to the pan. Bring to a simmer, cover, and reduce the heat to low. Cook, turning the braciole occasionally, until the meat is

fork-tender, about 2 hours.

4. Transfer the braciole to a large serving platter. Bring the sauce to a boil over medium-high heat. Cook until the sauce is thickened and measures 5 cups, 10 to 15 minutes. Season with salt and pepper to taste. Pour 3 cups sauce around the braciole on the platter and serve. The remaining 2 cups tomato sauce will coat 1 pound of cooked pasta.

STRACOTTO

STRACOTTO IS AN ITALIAN POT ROAST with wine and tomatoes. As for any good pot roast, the goal is to transform a tough (read cheap), nearly unpalatable cut of meat into a tender, rich, flavorful main course by means of a slow, moist cooking process called braising. But this is not as easy as it sounds. Like other pot roasts, stracotto is often tough and stringy and so dry that it must be drowned with the merciful sauce that accompanies the dish. Stracotto should not be sliceable; rather, the tension of a stern gaze should be enough to break it apart. Nor should it be pink or rosy in the middle; save that for prime rib or steak.

The meat for stracotto should be well marbled with fat and connective tissue to provide the dish with the necessary flavor and moisture. Recipes typically call for roasts from the sirloin (or rump), round (leg), or chuck (shoulder). When all was said and done, we cooked a dozen cuts of meat to find the right one. The sirloin roasts tested—the bottom rump roast and top sirloin—were the leanest of the cuts and needed a longer cooking period to break down the meat to a palatable texture. The round cuts—top round, bottom round, and eye of round—had more fat running through them than the sirloin cuts, but the meat was chewy. The chuck cuts—shoulder roast, boneless chuck roast, cross rib, chuck mock tender, seven-bone roast, top-blade roast, and chuck eye roast—cooked up the most tender, although we gave preference to three of these cuts (see "Three Chuck Roasts" on page 286). The high proportion of fat and connective tissue in these chuck cuts gave the meat much-needed moisture and superior flavor.

Tough meat can benefit from the low, dry heat of oven roasting, and it can be boiled. With pot roast, however, the introduction of moisture by means of a braising liquid is thought to be integral to the breakdown of the tough muscle fibers. (We also tried dry-roasting and boiling pot roast just to make sure. See page 287 to find out why braising was the winner.) It was time to find out what kind of liquid, and how much, was needed to best cook the roast and supply a good sauce.

Before we began the testing, we addressed the aesthetics of the dish. Because stracotto is traditionally cooked with liquid at a low temperature, the exterior of the meat will not brown sufficiently unless it is first sautéed in a Dutch oven on the stovetop. High heat and a little oil were all that were needed to caramelize the exterior of the beef and boost both the flavor and appearance of the dish.

Using water as the braising medium, we started with a modest ¼ cup, as suggested in a few recipes. This produced a roast that was unacceptably fibrous, even after hours of cooking. After increasing the amount of liquid incrementally, we found the moistest meat was produced when we added liquid halfway up the sides of the roast (depending on the cut, this amount could be between two and four cups). The larger amount of liquid also accelerated the cooking process, shaving nearly one hour off the cooking time needed for a roast cooked in just ¼ cup of liquid. Naively assuming that more is always better, we continued to increase the amount of water, but to no better effect. We also found that it was necessary to cover the Dutch oven with a piece of foil before placing the lid on top. The added seal of the foil kept the liquid from escaping (in the form of steam) through the cracks of a loose-fitting lid and eliminated any need to add liquid to the pot.

Next we tested different liquids, hoping to add flavor to the roast and sauce. Along with our old standby, water, we tested red wine, canned tomatoes, low-sodium canned chicken broth, and low-sodium canned beef broth. Red wine had the most startling effect on the meat, penetrating it with a potent wine flavor. Tomatoes were an important addition, and we liked a single can of diced tomatoes with their juice. Each of the broths on their own failed to win tasters over completely; the chicken broth was rich but gave the dish a

poultry flavor, while the beef broth tasted sour when added solo. In the end, we found an equal amount of each did the job, with the beef broth deepening the flavor and the chicken broth tempering any sourness. Because different amounts of liquid are needed depending on the size and shape of the individual roast, we chose to use water to bring the liquid level halfway up the roast.

Trying to boost the flavor of the sauce even more, we added the basic vegetables—carrot, celery, onion, and garlic—to the pot as the meat braised. Unfortunately, the addition of raw vegetables made the stracotto taste too much like a vegetable stew. We tried sautéing the vegetables until golden brown and found that the caramelized flavor of the vegetables added another layer of flavor to the sauce.

HOW TO TIE A TOP-BLADE ROAST

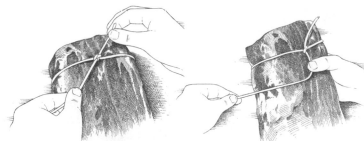 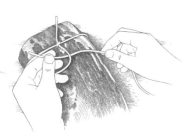

1. Slip a 6-foot piece of twine under the roast and tie a double knot.

2. Hold the twine against the meat and loop the long end under and around the roast.

3. Run the long end through the loop.

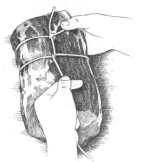 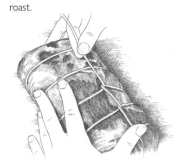 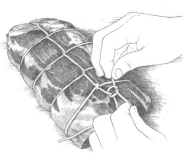

4. Repeat the procedure down the length of the roast.

5. Roll the roast over and run the twine under and around each the loop.

6. Wrap the twine around the end of the roast, flip the roast, and tie the twine to the original knot.

Many stracotto recipes call for mushrooms, and tasters felt that they added heft and depth to this dish. A little sugar (2 teaspoons) added to the vegetables as they cooked gave the sauce the sweetness tasters were looking for.

Some recipes thicken the sauce with a mixture of equal parts butter and flour (beurre manié); others use a slurry of cornstarch mixed with a little braising liquid. Both techniques made the sauce more gravylike than we preferred, and we didn't care for the dilution of flavor. We chose to remove the roast from the pot, then reduce the liquid over high heat until the flavors were concentrated and the texture substantial. A final hint of rosemary (we added a whole sprig as the sauce reduced), and the flavors were perfect.

We were nearly done but needed to refine the cooking location, temperature, and time. When it comes to how to cook the roast, the schools of thought are divided neatly into two camps: on the stove or in the oven. After a few rounds of stovetop cooking, we felt that it was too difficult to maintain a steady, low temperature, so we began pot-roasting in the oven, starting at 250 degrees. This method required no supervision, just a turn of the meat every 30 to 40 minutes to ensure even cooking. We then tested higher temperatures to reduce the cooking time. Heat levels above 350 degrees boiled the meat to a stringy, dry texture because the exterior of the roast overcooked before the interior was cooked and tender. The magic temperature turned out to be 300 degrees—low enough to keep the meat at a low simmer while high enough to shave a few minutes off the cooking time.

As expressed before, stracotto is well-done meat—meat cooked to an internal temperature above 165 degrees. Up to this point, we were bringing the meat to an internal temperature of 200 to 210 degrees, the point at which the fat and connective tissue begin to melt. In a 300-degree oven, we found that the roast came up to that temperature in a neat 2½ hours, by no means a quick meal but still a relatively short

THREE CHUCK ROASTS

We tested a dozen roasts from all parts of the cow and found that three roasts, all from the chuck, were the best choice for stracotto.

SEVEN-BONE ROAST

This is a well-marbled cut with an incredibly beefy flavor. It gets its name from the bone found in the roast, which is shaped like the number seven. Because it is only 2 inches thick, less liquid and less time are needed to braise the roast. Do not buy a seven-bone roast that weighs more than 3½ pounds, as it will not fit into a Dutch oven. This roast is also sometimes referred to as a seven-bone steak.

TOP-BLADE ROAST

This cut is well marbled with fat and connective tissue, which makes the roast juicy and flavorful. Even after thorough braising, this roast retains a distinctive strip of connective tissue that is not unpleasant to eat. This roast may also be sold as a blade roast. You should tie the roast to keep it from falling apart as it cooks.

CHUCK-EYE ROAST

This cut is the fattiest of the three roasts and the most commonly available. The high proportion of fat gives the stracotto great flavor and tenderness. Because of its thickness, this roast takes the longest to cook. It's usually tied by the butcher; if it is not, do this yourself.

time in which to cook a pot roast. But we still had not achieved the desired fall-apart-tender stracotto, so we went back and reviewed our prior testing to see what we might have missed.

Once in a great while in the test kitchen, we happen on a true "Eureka!" moment, when a chance test result leads to a breakthrough cooking technique. Some days before, we had forgotten to remove one of the roasts from the oven, allowing it to cook an hour longer than intended. Racing to the kitchen with an instant-read thermometer, we found the internal temperature of the roast was still 210 degrees, but the meat had a substantially different appearance and texture. The roast was so tender that it was starting to separate along its muscle lines. A fork poked into the meat met with no resistance and nearly disappeared into the flesh. We took the roast out of the pot and "sliced" into it. Nearly all the fat and connective tissue had dissolved into the meat, giving each bite a soft, silky texture and rich, succulent flavor.

SCIENCE: The Mystery of Braising

Braising—searing meat, partially submerging it in liquid in a sealed pot, then cooking it until fork-tender—is a classic technique used with tough cuts of meat. A variety of cooks have put forward theories about why and how braising works to tenderize such meats (and why roasting and boiling do not). We devised a series of experiments that would explain the mystery of braising.

Before kitchen testing began, we researched meat itself to better understand its behavior in the kitchen. Meat (muscle) is made up of two major components: muscle fibers, the long thin strands visible as the grain, and connective tissue, the membranous, translucent film that covers the bundles of muscle fiber and gives them structure and support. Muscle fiber is tender because of its high water content (up to 78 percent). Once meat is heated beyond about 120 degrees, the long strands of muscle fiber contract and coil, expelling moisture in much the same way that it's wrung out of a towel. In contrast, connective tissue is tough because it is composed primarily of collagen, a sturdy protein that is in everything from the cow's muscle tendons to its hooves. When collagen is cooked at temperatures exceeding 140 degrees, it starts to break down to gelatin, the protein responsible for the tender meat, thick sauces, and rich mouthfeel of braised dishes.

In essence, then, meat both dries out as it cooks (meat fibers lose moisture) and becomes softer (the collagen melts). That is why (depending on the cut) meat is best either when cooked rare or pot-roasted—cooked to the point at which the collagen dissolves completely. Anything in between is dry and tough, the worst of both worlds.

This brings us to why braising is an effective cooking technique for tough cuts of meat. To determine the relative advantages of roasting, braising, and boiling, we constructed a simple test. One roast was cooked in a 250-degree oven, one was braised, and one was simmered in enough liquid to cover it. The results were startling. The roast never reached an internal temperature of more than 175 degrees, even after four hours, and the meat was tough and dry (see "Roasting versus Braising" on page 291). To our great surprise, both the braised and boiled roasts cooked in about the same amount of time, and the results were almost identical. Cutting the roasts in half revealed little difference; both exhibited nearly full melting of the thick bands of connective tissue. With respect to the taste and texture of the meat, tasters were hard pressed to find any substantial difference between the two. Both roasts yielded meat that was exceedingly tender, moist, and infused with rich gelatin.

The conclusion? Dry heat (roasting) is ineffective because the meat never gets hot enough. It does not appear that steam heat (braising) enjoys any special ability to soften meat over boiling. Braising has one advantage over simmering and boiling, however—half a pot of liquid reduces to a sauce much faster than a full pot does.

We "overcooked" several more roasts. Each had the same great texture. The conclusion? Not only do you have to cook stracotto until it reaches 210 degrees internally, but the meat has to remain at that temperature for a full hour. In other words, cook the stracotto until it's done—and then keep on cooking!

Stracotto
(Pot Roast with Mushrooms, Tomatoes, and Red Wine)
SERVES 6 TO 8

Chuck-eye roast is our first choice for this recipe. Most markets sell this roast with twine tied around the center (see photo on page 286). If necessary, do this yourself. Seven-bone and top-blade roasts are also good choices. Add only enough water to come halfway up the sides of these thinner roasts, and begin checking for doneness after 2 hours. If using a top-blade roast, tie it before cooking (see the illustrations on page 285). Serve with Parmesan Mashed Potatoes (page 82).

I	boneless chuck-eye, seven-bone, or boneless top-blade roast (about 3½ pounds)
	Salt and ground black pepper
2	tablespoons vegetable oil
I	medium onion, chopped medium
I	small carrot, chopped medium
I	small celery rib, chopped medium
10	ounces white button mushrooms, quartered
2	medium cloves garlic, minced or pressed through a garlic press
2	teaspoons sugar
½	cup canned low-sodium chicken broth
½	cup canned low-sodium beef broth
½	cup dry red wine
I	(14½-ounce) can diced tomatoes
I	sprig fresh thyme
I–I½	cups water
I	sprig fresh rosemary

1. Adjust an oven rack to the middle position and heat the oven to 300 degrees. Thoroughly pat the roast dry with paper towels; sprinkle generously with salt and pepper to taste.

2. Heat the oil in a large ovenproof Dutch oven over medium-high heat until shimmering but not smoking. Brown the roast thoroughly on all sides, reducing the heat if the fat begins to smoke, 8 to 10 minutes. Transfer the roast to a large plate; set aside.

3. Reduce the heat to medium, add the onion, carrot, celery, and mushrooms to the pot, and cook, stirring occasionally, until the vegetables begin to brown, 6 to 8 minutes. Add the garlic and sugar and cook until fragrant, about 30 seconds. Add the chicken and beef broths, wine, tomatoes and their juices, and thyme, scraping the bottom of the pan with a wooden spoon to loosen the browned bits. Return the roast and any accumulated juices to the pot. Add enough water to come halfway up the sides of the roast. Bring the liquid to a simmer over medium heat, then place a large piece of foil over the pot and cover tightly with the lid. Transfer the pot to the oven. Cook, turning the roast every 30 minutes, until fully tender and a meat fork or sharp knife easily slips in and out, 3½ to 4 hours.

4. Transfer the roast to a carving board and tent with foil to keep warm. Allow the liquid in the pot to settle for about 5 minutes, then use a wide spoon to skim fat off the surface. Add the rosemary and boil over high heat until reduced to about 1½ cups, about 8 minutes. Discard the thyme and rosemary sprigs. Season to taste with salt and pepper.

5. Using a chef's or carving knife, cut the meat into ½-inch-thick slices or pull it apart into large pieces. Transfer the meat to a warmed serving platter and pour the sauce and vegetables over it. Serve immediately.

EQUIPMENT: Dutch Ovens

We find that a Dutch oven (also called a lidded casserole) is almost essential to making stews and braises, such as stracotto and osso buco. A Dutch oven is nothing more than a wide, deep pot with a cover. It was originally manufactured with ears on the side (small, round tabs used to pick up the pot) and a top that had a lip around the edge. The latter design element was important because a Dutch oven was heated by coals placed both underneath and on top of the pot. The lip kept the coals on the lid from falling off. One could bake biscuits, cobblers, beans, and stews in this pot. It was, in the full sense of the word, an oven. This oven was a key feature of chuck wagons and essential in many Colonial American households, where all cooking occurred in the fireplace. This useful pot supposedly came to be called "Dutch" because at some point the best cast iron came from Holland.

Now that everyone in the United States has an oven, the Dutch oven is no longer used to bake biscuits or cobblers. However, it is essential for dishes that start on top of the stove and finish in the oven, as many stews do. To make recommendations about buying a modern Dutch oven, we tested 12 models from leading makers of cookware.

We found that a Dutch oven should have a capacity of at least six quarts to be useful. Eight quarts is even better. As we cooked in the pots, we came to prefer wider, shallower Dutch ovens because it's easier to see and reach inside them, and they offer more bottom surface area to accommodate larger batches of meat for browning. This reduces the number of batches required to brown a given quantity of meat and, with it, the chances of burning the flavorful pan drippings. Ideally, the diameter of a Dutch oven is twice as great as its height.

We also preferred pots with a light-colored interior finish, such as stainless steel or enameled cast iron. It is easier to judge the caramelization of the drippings at a glance in these pots. Dark finishes can mask the color of the drippings, which may burn before you realize it. Our favorite pot is the eight-quart All-Clad Stainless Stockpot (despite the name, this pot is a Dutch oven). The seven-quart Le Creuset Round French Oven, which is made of enameled cast iron, also tested well. These pots are quite expensive, costing at least $150 even on sale. A less expensive alternative is the seven-quart Lodge Dutch Oven, which is made from cast iron. This pot is extremely heavy (making it a bit hard to maneuver), it must be seasoned (wiped with oil) regularly, and the dark interior finish is not ideal, but it does brown food quite well and costs just $45.

THE BEST DUTCH OVENS

Our favorite pot is the eight-quart All-Clad Stainless Stockpot (left). Despite the name, this pot is a Dutch oven. Expect to spend nearly $200 for this piece of cookware. A less expensive alternative is the seven-quart Lodge Dutch Oven (about $45) (right), which is made from cast iron.

Beef Braised in Barolo

ALTHOUGH SIMILAR TO STRACOTTO, this pot roast doesn't use stock in the braising liquid, only fine Barolo wine. Barolo is made from the Nebbiolo grape and is produced in the northern region of Piedmont. This red wine is known for its hearty aromas of oak, licorice, plum, roses, and violets. As the meat slowly cooks in the Barolo, the flavors meld and mellow; the dish emerges from the oven with a heady aroma and potent flavor unlike any pot roast you've ever had. The problem, however, is that Barolo is a tannic, full-bodied wine that produces a harsh, astringent-tasting pot roast if not handled correctly.

Starting with our recipe for stracotto, we focused our attention on the best way to add the Barolo and eliminate the stock and water. Many recipes we researched soaked the roast in the wine for several hours before braising it, however, we found this made the meat taste musty and fermented. Simply replacing the three cups of stock, wine, and water in our stracotto recipe with a bottle of Barolo was quicker and better. However, our work was not done. This second method produced a raw-tasting sauce with mouth-puckering intensity.

To temper the Barolo, we tried increasing the amount of vegetables—onions, carrots, and celery. Although this helped round out the flavor of the roast itself, the sauce was still a bit overpowering. Tasters wanted a smoother, rounder sauce, which we finally achieved by using a little tomato paste and a few spices. Cinnamon, cloves, bay leaves, thyme, and parsley added complexity to the sauce and helped bring the big flavors in the wine under control.

Lastly, unlike in stracotto, the spent vegetables and spices are strained out of the beautiful, dark sauce before serving. The sauce for beef in Barolo is usually thickened slightly and glossy. We found that adding flour to the sautéed vegetables as well as reducing the sauce once the meat was removed from the pot helped achieve the correct consistency.

Beef Braised in Barolo

SERVES 6 TO 8

There is no such thing as a cheap Barolo (prices start at $30 a bottle at our local wine shops), but there's no need to spend more for a reserve wine. Chuck-eye roast is our choice for this recipe because the meat holds together nicely and slices better than similar cuts. Most markets sell this roast with twine tied around the center (see photo on page 286). If necessary, do this yourself.

1	boneless chuck-eye roast (about 3½ pounds)
	Salt and ground black pepper
2	tablespoons vegetable oil
2	medium onions, chopped medium
2	medium carrots, chopped medium
2	medium celery stalks, chopped medium
3	medium cloves garlic, minced or pressed through a garlic press
½	teaspoon sugar
1	tablespoon tomato paste
1	tablespoon unbleached all-purpose flour
1	(750-milliliter) bottle Barolo wine
3	bay leaves
1	cinnamon stick
3	whole cloves
2	sprigs fresh thyme
10	sprigs fresh parsley

1. Adjust an oven rack to the middle position and heat the oven to 300 degrees. Thoroughly pat the roast dry with paper towels; sprinkle generously with salt and pepper to taste.

2. Heat the oil in a large ovenproof Dutch oven over medium-high heat until shimmering but not smoking. Brown the roast thoroughly on all sides, reducing the heat if the fat begins to smoke, 8 to 10 minutes. Transfer the roast to a large plate; set aside.

3. Reduce the heat to medium, add the onions, carrots, and celery to the pot, and cook, stirring occasionally, until the vegetables begin to brown, 6 to 8 minutes. Add the garlic, sugar, tomato paste, and flour and cook until fragrant, about 30 seconds. Add the wine, scraping the bottom of the pan with a wooden spoon to loosen the browned bits. Return the roast and any accumulated juices to the pot. Add the bay leaves, cinnamon, cloves, thyme, and parsley. Bring the liquid to a simmer over medium heat, then place a large piece of foil over the pot and cover it tightly with the lid. Transfer the pot to the oven. Cook, turning the roast every 30 minutes, until fully tender and a meat fork or sharp knife easily slips in and out, 3½ to 4 hours.

4. Transfer the roast to a carving board and tent with foil to keep warm. Allow the liquid in the pot to settle for about 5 minutes, then use a wide spoon to skim the fat off the surface. Bring to a boil over high heat. Cook, whisking vigorously to help the vegetables dissolve, until the sauce is well thickened and measures about 2 cups, 5 to 6 minutes. Strain the sauce through a fine-mesh sieve and season with salt and pepper to taste (you should have about 1 cup sauce).

5. Using a chef's or carving knife, cut the meat into ½-inch-thick slices or pull it apart into large pieces. Transfer the meat to a warmed serving platter and pour about half the sauce over it. Serve immediately, passing the remaining sauce separately.

BOLLITO MISTO

SERVED ON MANY SPECIAL OCCASIONS, *bollito misto* is a large platter of various boiled meats accompanied by salsa verde—a bright green sauce made of chopped parsley, olives, capers, lemon juice, and olive oil. All of the meat—tender, juicy, and tasty—is simmered together in a large pot of flavorful broth. We set out to discover how American home cooks could make a good bollito misto.

We began with the ingredient list. The authentic recipes we found read more like a butcher's daily chalkboard than a recipe: beef tongue, brisket, veal breast, pigs' feet, chicken, pork sausage—and the list goes on. To update

ROASTING VERSUS BRAISING

A distinctive pattern of fat and connective tissue runs through the meat of a chuck roast (left). When cooked in dry heat, or roasted (middle), the fat and sinew do not break down sufficiently, even after many hours in the oven. Cooking the meat in moist heat, or braising (right), promotes a more complete breakdown of the fat and connective tissue, yielding very tender meat.

this recipe for the American palate (and supermarket), we decided to include only mainstream meats such as beef brisket, veal breast, chicken, and pork sausage.

The cooking method for all these meats, however, is universal. A water-based broth is seasoned and brought to a simmer. The meat is then added to the broth and poached until it is fully cooked and tender. Because the different meats require different cooking times, they are added to the pot sequentially so that they are all done at the same time. Figuring out this timing, we realized, is the trick to a good bollito misto.

Beginning with the broth, we figured we needed five to six quarts of liquid to be able to cook the brisket, veal, and chicken together in the same pot. (The fatty sausage is always cooked separately so as not to ruin the flavor of the broth.) To make the broth, all the recipes we found added just one carrot, one celery stalk, and one onion to the water. Realizing that this small amount of vegetables would not add enough flavor to five or six quarts of water, we doubled the amount of carrot and celery, tripled the amount of onion, and added a head of garlic, some parsley, bay leaves, peppercorns, and salt. With five to six quarts of this flavorful broth brought to a simmer in a 10- to 12-quart pot over medium-high heat, we were ready to start adding the meat.

To ensure that all the meat emerges from the broth perfectly cooked at the same time, all the recipes we found cooked the various items according to the following schedule: Cook the brisket for two hours, add the veal breast and cook for half an hour longer, then add the chicken for a final hour. The result of this classic bollito misto schedule, however, was disappointing. All of the meat was far overcooked; the brisket began to shred apart on its own, while the veal and chicken turned bone dry. To correct this, we needed to find

out exactly how long it would take each of the meats to cook. Cooking them separately, we determined that a 2-pound piece of brisket requires about two hours, a 2-pound veal roast about one hour, and a 3½-pound chicken about 30 minutes. Combining these times, it was easy to organize an accurate cooking schedule for the bollito misto. The sausage, which we cooked off to the side in a small pot of water, required 15 to 20 minutes to cook through.

We next focused on making enough sauce (called *salsa verde,* or green sauce) to accompany the meat. The sauce, made mostly from parsley and olive oil, is seasoned with green olives, capers, garlic, anchovies, and lemon juice. We found that sweet, mellow basil was a lovely addition. Salsa verde is usually hand chopped to yield a slightly chunky texture, but due to the volume we needed, it was easier to make the sauce in a food processor. To achieve evenly sized pieces, we processed the delicate herbs with the oil and the tougher olives, capers, garlic cloves, and anchovies separately with the lemon juice. Seasoned lightly with pepper, this clean, crisp sauce is the perfect accompaniment to the tender, juicy meats.

Bollito Misto
SERVES 10 TO 12

The leftover broth used to cook the meat should not be discarded but rather strained and reserved for use as a stock or soup base. (The liquid used to cook the sausage is very fatty and should be discarded.) If you want to prepare this recipe in advance, follow the recipe through step 1, then remove the meat from the broth and refrigerate both separately for up to 2 days. When reheating, bring the broth to a simmer, then return the cooked brisket and veal to the broth and continue with steps 2 and 3. Ask your butcher to tie the veal roast so it won't fall apart as it cooks.

3   medium onions, chopped coarse
2   medium carrots, chopped coarse
2   medium celery stalks, chopped coarse
1   head garlic, smashed, with loose, papery
       skins discarded
3   bay leaves
5   sprigs fresh parsley
5   black peppercorns
1   tablespoon salt
2   pounds beef brisket
2   pounds boneless veal breast roast, tied
1   whole chicken (about 3½ pounds)
2   pounds cotechino, garlic-pork sausage, or
       sweet Italian sausage
       Salsa Verde (recipe follows)

1. Place the onions, carrots, celery, garlic, bay leaves, parsley, peppercorns, and salt in a 10- or 12-quart stockpot and fill halfway with water. Bring to a boil over high heat and add the beef brisket. Bring the pot back to a simmer, cover, and reduce the heat as necessary to maintain the simmer. Cook for 1 hour. Add the veal roast, return the pot to a simmer, cover, and cook for 30 minutes.

2. Add the chicken and return the pot to a simmer. Cover and cook until an instant-read thermometer inserted in the chicken breast registers 160 degrees, 25 to 30 minutes.

3. Meanwhile, bring 2 quarts water to a boil in a separate pot. Prick the sausages several times with the tines of a fork and add them to the water. Bring to a simmer and cook over medium-low heat until the sausage is cooked through, 15 to 20 minutes.

4. To serve, remove the meats from the hot broth, slice, and arrange them on a large platter. Sprinkle the sliced meats with several tablespoons cooking liquid to help keep them moist. (Alternatively, you can strain the broth, place it in a tureen large enough to hold all the meats, and slice to order at the table.) Serve immediately with the salsa verde.

Salsa Verde

MAKES ABOUT 2½ CUPS

This sauce can be refrigerated in an airtight container for up to several days.

4   cups lightly packed fresh parsley leaves
2   cups lightly packed fresh basil leaves
1   cup extra-virgin olive oil
1   cup pitted green olives
½   cup capers, rinsed and dried
8   medium cloves garlic, peeled
8   anchovy fillets
½   cup lemon juice
       Ground black pepper

Pulse the parsley, basil, and oil in the workbowl of a food processor fitted with the steel blade and process until the mixture resembles pesto, about ten 1-second pulses. Transfer the herb paste to a medium bowl. Add the olives, capers, garlic, anchovies, and lemon juice to the workbowl. Pulse until uniformly sized, about ten 1-second pulses. Add these finely chopped ingredients to the bowl with the herb paste and mix to combine. Season with pepper to taste.

VEAL SCALOPPINE

THIS CLASSIC DISH IS FAST, EASY, AND tastes impressive when done right. Thin pieces of veal are quickly sautéed, leaving tasty drippings in the pan that are perfect for building an accompanying sauce. The problem, however, is that the cutlets are so thin that it is difficult for them to acquire a brown crust without overcooking. Also, we noted that many cutlets buckle and turn tough as they cook, while others remain flat and tender.

Beginning our testing at the meat counter, we found most packaged cutlets inaccurately butchered. Proper scaloppine should be cut from the top round, the upper portion of the leg, which is lean and has no muscle separation. The packaged cutlets we found were obviously cut from the shoulder and other parts of the animal, resulting in shaggy, fatty pieces that fell apart and cooked unevenly.

We also found that many of these cutlets were cut with the grain of the muscle instead of against it (see the illustrations on page 297). When cut with the grain of the muscle, the cutlet contracts and puckers as it cooks, turning tough. If cut across the grain of the muscle, the cutlet remains flat as it cooks and stay tender. Although most butchers were obliging when we asked them to slice cutlets for us in this manner, we also found the cutlets easy to cut ourselves from a veal top round roast (see the illustrations at left).

Before hitting the pan, we had one last issue to test—pounding. Although both pounded and unpounded cutlets worked well, tasters preferred the lightly pounded cutlets for their delicate texture and elegant thinness.

Next, we focused on how to get a crust on the cutlets without overcooking them. Using a hot pan, we were surprised to find that pounded cutlets cooked in merely two minutes—one minute on each side. When cooked for any longer, the meat turned dry and stringy. In an effort to get some sort of brown crust within that short cooking time, we tried flouring the cutlets. Compared to cutlets that were unfloured, the floured pieces browned in spots and had a crisp exterior that nicely contrasted with the soft interior. The flour also acted as a barrier that helped protect the delicate meat as it cooked. We tried using a nonstick pan but found the floured cutlets didn't brown as readily and produced almost no drippings with which to make a sauce.

We then put the cutlets in a warm oven to help them retain their heat while we made a quick pan sauce. We found, however, that the five minutes it took to make the sauce was too long for the thin cutlets to rest in the oven, and they overcooked. To correct this, we simply set them off to the side, covered, while we focused our attention on the sauce. Using only onions, lemon juice, parsley, butter, and either white wine or Marsala (both are traditional), we were able to make a simple, classic sauce, turning the veal cutlets into an authentic veal scaloppine.

CUTTING VEAL CUTLETS

1. With a boning knife, remove the silver skin (the white membrane that covers the meat in places) from a piece of veal top round.

2. Once the silver skin has been removed, use a long, inflexible slicing knife to cut slices—on the bias and against the grain—that are between 1/4 and 1/2 inch thick.

Veal Scaloppine

SERVES 4

White wine or Marsala can be used in this recipe. When made with white wine, the sauce is light and crisp. With Marsala, the sauce is dark and sweet. Refer to the illustration on page 297 for tips on buying veal cutlets, or see the illustrations on page 294 if you want to cut your own cutlets from a roast.

6	½-inch-thick veal cutlets (about 1½ pounds), cut from the round
	Salt and ground black pepper
½	cup unbleached all-purpose flour
3	tablespoons extra-virgin olive oil
½	small onion, minced
½	cup white wine or Marsala
2	tablespoons unsalted butter, cut into 2 pieces
1	tablespoon lemon juice
1	tablespoon minced fresh parsley leaves

1. Place the cutlets between two sheets of parchment or wax paper and pound to a thickness of ¼ inch. Season both sides of the cutlets liberally with salt and pepper. Measure the flour into a shallow dish or pie plate. Working with one at a time, dredge the cutlets in flour and shake to remove the excess.

2. Heat 1 tablespoon oil in a heavy-bottomed 12-inch skillet over high heat until just smoking. Lay 3 cutlets in the pan, making sure they do not overlap. Reduce the heat to medium-high and cook, not moving, until browned, about 1 minute. Turn the cutlets with tongs and sauté until the meat feels firm when pressed, about 30 seconds. Remove the pan from the heat and transfer the cutlets to a clean plate and cover with foil. Add another tablespoon oil to the pan, return the heat to medium-high, and allow the oil to heat for 5 to 10 seconds. Cook the remaining 3 cutlets as before, transferring them to the foil-covered plate to keep warm while making the sauce.

3. Add the remaining 1 tablespoon oil to the empty skillet and return the pan to medium heat. Add the onion and cook, scraping the browned bits from the bottom of the pan with a wooden spoon, until softened, about 1 minute. Add the wine and cook, scraping up the browned bits, until well reduced and syrupy, 3 to 4 minutes. Whisk in the butter, lemon juice, parsley, and any accumulated juices from the cutlets. Remove the pan from the heat and season the sauce with salt and pepper to taste. To serve, arrange the cutlets on either a large platter or individual plates and pour the sauce over them. Serve immediately.

VEAL SALTIMBOCCA

ITS NAME LITERALLY MEANING "JUMP in the mouth," *saltimbocca* is a simple variation on veal scaloppine that hails from Rome. Thinly sliced pieces of prosciutto and leaves of sage are pressed into the cutlet and secured with a toothpick before the cutlets are quickly sautéed. The simple combination of these three flavors is so good that the cutlets jump into your mouth.

Having figured out how to buy and cook veal cutlets properly for scaloppine, it was easy to add prosciutto and sage to our basic sautéed veal cutlet recipe. Although many recipes pound the prosciutto and sage into the cutlets, we found this didn't work very well. The pounding simply tore the thin prosciutto and fragile sage to shaggy pieces. Instead, we simply pressed the tacky prosciutto into the already pounded cutlet with our hands. Laying the sage leaf on top of the prosciutto, we secured the trio with a toothpick.

Just like scaloppine, these cutlets browned better when they were floured, and they cooked quickly—in less than two minutes. Finished with a simple white wine pan sauce, veal saltimbocca is both incredibly simple and elegant. It's also amazingly delicious.

Veal Saltimbocca

SERVES 4

See the illustration at right for hints on making sure the prosciutto and sage attach firmly to the cutlets.

6	½-inch-thick veal cutlets (about 1½ pounds), cut from the round
6	thin prosciutto slices (about 3 ounces)
6	large fresh sage leaves
	Salt and ground black pepper
½	cup unbleached all-purpose flour
3	tablespoons extra-virgin olive oil
½	small onion, minced
½	cup white wine
2	tablespoons unsalted butter, cut into 2 pieces
1	tablespoon lemon juice
1	tablespoon minced fresh parsley leaves

1. Place the cutlets between two sheets of parchment or wax paper and pound to a thickness of ¼ inch. Place 1 slice of prosciutto on top of each cutlet and lay 1 sage leaf in the center of each cutlet, pressing them into the veal with the palm of your hand. Secure the prosciutto and sage with a toothpick (see the illustration at right). Season both sides of the cutlets liberally with salt and pepper. Measure the flour into a shallow dish or pie plate. Working with one at a time, dredge each cutlet in flour and shake to remove the excess.

2. Heat 1 tablespoon oil in a heavy-bottomed 12-inch skillet over high heat until just smoking. Lay 3 cutlets, prosciutto side down, in the pan, making sure they do not overlap. Reduce the heat to medium-high and cook, not moving, until browned, about 1

MAKING VEAL SALTIMBOCCA

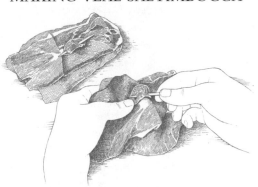

Using a toothpick as if it were a stickpin, secure the sage and prosciutto to the veal cutlet by poking the toothpick down through the three layers, then back out again. The toothpick should be parallel to the cutlet and as flat as possible.

minute. Turn the cutlets with tongs and sauté until the meat feels firm when pressed, about 30 seconds. Remove the pan from the heat and transfer the cutlets to a clean plate and cover with foil. Add another tablespoon oil to the pan, return the heat to medium-high, and allow the oil to heat for 5 to 10 seconds. Cook the remaining 3 cutlets as before, transferring them to the foil-covered plate to keep warm while making the sauce.

3. Add the remaining 1 tablespoon oil to the empty skillet and return the pan to medium heat. Add the onion and cook, scraping the browned bits from the bottom of the pan with a wooden spoon, until softened, about 1 minute. Add the wine and cook, scraping up the browned bits, until well reduced and syrupy, 3 to 4 minutes. Whisk in the butter, lemon juice, parsley, and any accumulated juices from the cutlets. Remove the pan from the heat and season the sauce with salt and pepper to taste. To serve, arrange the cutlets, prosciutto side up, on either a large platter or individual plates and pour the sauce over them. Serve immediately.

VITELLO TONNATO

THIS UNUSUAL, LIGHT SUMMER DISH of thinly sliced veal "marinated" in a tuna and garlic mayonnaise may sound odd at first, but it makes sense when you picture eating it seaside in Italy with a chilled glass of white wine. Wanting to reproduce this warm-weather classic here in the United States, we set out to uncover its secrets in our test kitchen.

All of the authentic recipes we found called for the same cut of veal and cooked it similarly. Using a top round veal roast, these recipes poached the meat for hours in a watery broth, then pulled the pot off the heat, letting the roast cool until it could be sliced and layered with the sauce. Although this method sounded strange to us (and chancy), we gave it a whirl. While the tuna sauce tasted surprisingly good, the veal turned out as we expected—dry and bland, leaving much of its

GOOD VEAL CUTLETS, BAD VEAL CUTLETS

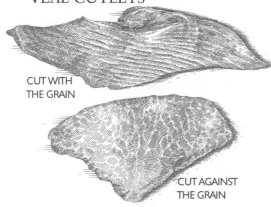

CUT WITH
THE GRAIN

CUT AGAINST
THE GRAIN

Veal cutlets should be cut from the top round. Most super-markets use the leg or sirloin and do not butcher the meat properly—it is cut with the grain, not against the grain, as is best. When shopping, look for cutlets in which no linear striation is evident. The linear striation in the top cutlet is an indication that the veal has been cut with the grain and will be tough. Instead, the cutlet should have a smooth surface, like the cutlet on the bottom, in which no lines are evident.

moisture and flavor behind in the broth.

Focusing our attention on the meat, we decided not to try other cuts of veal but rather to use the traditional top round roast and work on improving the poaching technique. First, we noted that most recipes threw only a handful of vegetables into the poaching liquid. Thinking that the liquid needed more flavor if the veal were to emerge from it tasting like anything, we added several carrots, stalks of celery, and onions along with garlic, bay leaves, parsley, and peppercorns. Although this made a huge difference in the flavor of the veal, its texture was still too dry and chewy.

Turning our attention to the cooking time, we wondered if we could correct the tough meat problem by cooking the veal less. We wondered if poaching the veal for several hours was necessary. Poaching two roasts side by side, we pulled one out of the liquid when it reached an internal temperature of 155 degrees (after about 55 minutes in the simmering water), and cooked the other for the standard two hours (it reached an internal temperature in excess of 200 degrees). After they were cooled and sliced, we found the veal cooked to 155 degrees was far more tender and juicy.

But we weren't finished. All the old recipes let the veal cool in its poaching liquid, allowing the moisture to soak into the meat as it comes to room temperature. Wanting to try this technique but worried that the residual heat from the poaching liquid would raise the temperature of the veal above 155 degrees, we tried cooking the roast to 125 degrees before pulling the pot off the heat. This final trick worked like a charm, and the veal roast emerged from an hour in the cooling liquid with an internal temperature of 155 degrees. Not only did the veal have a full, round flavor, it was moist and tender, with only the slightest toothsome bite.

Last, we turned our attention to the tuna

sauce. Based on a mayonnaise-like emulsion, the tuna sauce is classically made by blending a raw egg yolk slowly with olive oil (making an emulsion), then flavoring it with tuna, anchovies, capers, and lemon juice. Although this sounds strange, the resulting flavor is mild and elegant, and it pairs amazingly well with the poached veal. We tried making the sauce with extra-virgin olive oil but found its flavor was overly bitter and fruity, preferring instead the simple flavor of regular olive oil. As for the tuna, we vastly preferred the flavor of olive oil–packed tuna to any of the water-packed varieties, and good-quality tuna made all the difference.

As for the assembly method, we tried several techniques and wound up liking the easiest one best. After making a loose emulsion in the food processor with a whole egg and 1 cup of olive oil, we simply pulsed in the tuna and flavorings along with some water to adjust the consistency. Rather than making the sauce with just a yolk, as most recipes do, we found that it was easier to use a whole egg. The yolk slipped under the blades of the processor, making it difficult to process, while the whole egg blended easily, with no discernible difference in either the texture or the flavor.

Last, we combined the thinly sliced veal and tuna sauce and let it sit until the flavor of the tuna and moisture of the olive oil permeated the veal. It took at least 4 hours for the veal to take on the flavor of the sauce, but the dish tasted much better when allowed to "marinate" overnight. Garnished with lemon wedges, capers, and minced parsley, this unusual dish is light, refreshing, and elegant. It requires only a glass of crisp, white wine and a warm, sunny day to be complete.

Vitello Tonnato
SERVES 4

Tying the roast makes it easier to carve uniform slices after it has cooled—ask your butcher to do this for you. Although the poaching liquid has no use in this recipe after the veal is cooked, it has a great flavor and could be used as a base for soups. If saving the broth, strain it after removing the veal, then refrigerate or freeze it until needed.

2	medium carrots, diced medium
2	medium celery stalks, diced medium
3	medium onions, diced medium
I	head garlic, smashed, with loose, papery skins removed
2	bay leaves
5	fresh parsley stems
5	black peppercorns
I	top round veal roast (about 1½ pounds), tied
	Cold Tuna Sauce (recipe follows)
I	lemon
I	tablespoon capers, rinsed and patted dry
I	teaspoon minced fresh parsley leaves

1. Bring the carrots, celery, onions, garlic, bay leaves, parsley, peppercorns, and 5 quarts water to a boil in a large stockpot over high heat. Add the veal and bring to a gentle simmer. Reduce the heat to low, cover, and cook until the internal temperature on an instant-read thermometer registers 125 degrees, 25 to 30 minutes. Remove the pot from the heat, place it on a sturdy cooling rack on the counter, uncover, and allow the veal to cool in its broth, about 1 hour.

2. When the meat has cooled, remove it from the cooking liquid and slice it as thinly as possible using either a sharp slicing or serrated knife. Reserve the cooking liquid for another use (see headnote).

3. To assemble, spread a thin layer of sauce

on a large serving platter. Lay slices of veal, side by side but not overlapping, on top of the sauce. Repeat with the remaining sauce and veal (the number of layers will depend on the size of the platter). When topping the final layer with sauce, leave ¼ inch of the outer edge of the meat unsauced. Cover with plastic wrap and refrigerate for at least 4 hours or overnight.

4. Just before serving, cut the lemon into quarters. Slice 2 quarters into very thin slices and arrange them around the edge of the platter. Sprinkle the capers and parsley over the top as a garnish and spritz with lemon juice to taste from the remaining 2 lemon quarters. Serve immediately.

Cold Tuna Sauce

MAKES A GENEROUS 2 CUPS

We prefer the mellow flavor of regular olive oil (as opposed to extra-virgin oil) in this recipe. See page 50 for recommendations when buying tuna packed in olive oil. To minimize the risk of salmonella, be sure to use a very fresh egg for this recipe.

1	large egg
	Salt and ground black pepper
1	cup olive oil
3	tablespoons lemon juice
1	(6-ounce) can tuna packed in olive oil, drained
6	anchovy fillets
3	tablespoons capers, rinsed and patted dry

Place the egg, ¼ teaspoon salt, and a pinch of pepper in the workbowl of a food processor fitted with a steel blade. Process until the mixture turns light yellow, about 30 seconds. With the motor running, pour the oil in a thin steady, stream through the feed tube until fully incorporated, about 1 minute. Turn the machine off and add the lemon juice, tuna, anchovies, capers, and ½ cup water. Pulse until the tuna is well broken up and the sauce is loose but well mixed, about ten 1-second pulses. Transfer the sauce to a clean bowl and season with salt and pepper to taste. (The sauce can be refrigerated in an airtight container for up to 1 day.)

GRILLED VEAL CHOPS

ITALIANS KNOW THAT THE COMBINATION of smoky flavor and intense browning does expensive veal chops justice. That said, you need the right grilling technique. Should the chops be cooked over direct heat, or do they need a two-level fire? And what about the various choices at the market? There are chops from the shoulder, loin, and rib as well as milk-fed and natural veal.

We began by testing various types of veal chops on the grill. We quickly dismissed inexpensive shoulder chops, which were tough and chewy and seemed better suited to braising or stewing. Both the loin and rib chops were exceptionally tender and expensive— $14 to $16 per pound in our local markets. The rib chops were a touch juicier and richer in flavor than the loin chops, so they are our first choice. However, if your market carries only loin chops, don't worry. They are good and can be grilled just like rib chops.

With our chop type chosen, we focused on size. We found that thin chops are hard to cook correctly because they dry out before the exterior gets any color. Likewise, very thick chops can overbrown by the time the meat near the bone is done. We had the best luck when we grilled chops about 1¼ inches thick. Slightly thicker chops (up to 1½ inches) are fine and will take just an extra minute or so to grill.

It was now time to perfect our grilling technique. Quickly we realized that veal chops do not fare well when cooked solely over hot coals; the exterior burns before the center is done. Cooking over a two-level fire produced chops that were evenly cooked and nicely caramelized on the exterior. Our tasters preferred chops pulled off the grill when the internal temperature reached 130 degrees. At this stage, the chops have just a tinge of pink in the center. Do not cook veal chops past this point or they will be tough and dry.

We did have problems with flare-ups. When we trimmed away excess fat, flare-ups were reduced but not eliminated. We also decided not to oil the chops to further reduce the risk of flare-ups. Keep a spray bottle close at hand while grilling to tame any flare-ups that occur.

Grilled veal chops are delicious with a simple seasoning of salt and pepper. If you choose to add more flavors, we suggest herbs or something relatively mild. There's no sense masking the delicate veal flavor with too many spices or chiles.

Charcoal-Grilled Veal Rib Chops
SERVES 4

Be sure to trim the veal chops of excess fat to prevent flare-ups on the grill. Keep a squirt bottle on hand filled with water to spray on flare-ups that may still occur. Veal chops need to be cooked over a two-level fire to ensure a nicely caramelized crust and a center perfectly cooked to medium. Use an instant-read thermometer to ensure that the chops aren't overcooked.

4   1¼-inch-thick bone-in rib veal chops, excess fat trimmed
      Salt and ground black pepper

1. Light a large chimney starter filled with hardwood charcoal (about 2½ pounds) and allow to burn until all the charcoal is covered with a layer of fine gray ash. Build a two-level fire by stacking most of the coals on one side of the grill for a medium-hot fire. Arrange the remaining coals in a single layer on the other side of the grill for a medium-low fire. Set the cooking rack in place, cover the grill with the lid, and let the rack heat, about 5 minutes. Use a wire brush to scrape the rack clean.

2. Sprinkle the chops with salt and pepper to taste.

3. Grill the chops, uncovered, over the hotter part of the grill until browned, about 2 minutes on each side. (If the chops start to flame, move them to the cooler part of the grill for a moment and/or extinguish the flames with a squirt bottle.) Move the chops to the cooler part of the grill. Continue grilling,

RIB VERSUS LOIN VEAL CHOPS

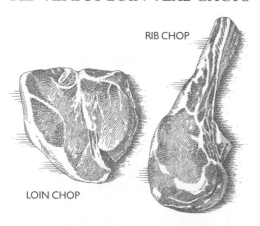

RIB CHOP

LOIN CHOP

The best veal chops come from the rib area and the loin. (We find that shoulder chops can be tough and are best braised or cut off the bone and used in stews.) A loin chop looks like a T-bone steak, with the bone running down the center and the meat on both sides. We find that rib chops are juicier and more flavorful than loin chops. The bone runs along the edge of a rib chop, with all the meat on one side.

turning once, until the meat is still rosy pink at the center and an instant-read thermometer inserted through the side of the chops and away from the bone registers 130 degrees, 10 to 11 minutes.

4. Remove the chops from the grill and let rest for 5 minutes. Serve immediately.

➤ VARIATIONS

Gas-Grilled Rib Veal Chops

Cooking on gas is pretty much the same as on charcoal, except that the grill should be covered.

Turn all burners on a gas grill to high, close the lid, and heat until very hot, about 15 minutes. Scrape the cooking grate clean with a wire brush; leave one burner on high and turn the other burner(s) down to medium. Follow the recipe for Charcoal-Grilled Veal Rib Chops, beginning with step 2 and cooking with the lid down.

Grilled Veal Chops with Herb Paste

Because of the oil in the herb paste, these chops are prone to flare-ups, so be vigilant.

Combine 1 tablespoon chopped fresh parsley leaves, 2 teaspoons each chopped fresh sage, thyme, rosemary, and oregano leaves, 3 minced garlic cloves, and ¼ cup extra-virgin olive oil in a small bowl. Follow the recipe for Charcoal-Grilled or Gas-Grilled Rib Veal Chops, rubbing the chops with the herb paste and then sprinkling them with salt and pepper to taste. Grill as directed and serve with lemon wedges.

Porcini-Rubbed Grilled Veal Chops

Dried porcini mushrooms can be ground to a powder and moistened with oil to form a thick paste. When spread on veal chops, the mushroom paste imparts an especially meaty flavor. If you don't have a spice grinder, use a blender to grind the mushrooms to a fine powder.

Grind ½ ounce dried porcini mushrooms to a powder in a spice grinder. Mix the ground mushrooms in a small bowl with 2 minced garlic cloves, 6 tablespoons extra-virgin olive oil, 1 teaspoon salt, and ¼ teaspoon ground black pepper. Follow the recipe for Charcoal-Grilled or Gas-Grilled Rib Veal Chops, rubbing the chops with the mushroom paste. Do not sprinkle with salt and pepper. Grill as directed.

Grilled Veal Chops on a Bed of Arugula

The balsamic vinegar not only dresses the arugula in this recipe, it also offsets the meaty richness of the veal. The heat of the chops wilts the arugula slightly and softens its texture.

I	recipe Charcoal-Grilled or Gas-Grilled Rib Veal Chops
1½	tablespoons balsamic vinegar
I	small clove garlic, minced very fine or pressed through a garlic press
5	tablespoons extra-virgin olive oil
	Salt and ground black pepper
8	cups lightly packed stemmed arugula, washed and thoroughly dried

1. Grill the chops as directed.

2. While the chops are cooking, whisk together the vinegar, garlic, and oil in a small bowl. Season with salt and pepper to taste. Toss the arugula and dressing in a large bowl. Transfer the arugula to a platter or divide it among individual plates.

3. As soon as the chops are done, transfer them to the platter or plates, then let them rest for 5 minutes. Serve immediately.

BREADED VEAL CHOPS

NOT MEANT FOR A WEEKNIGHT SUPPER, delicate and pricey veal chops are usually reserved for special occasions and good company. However, their mild flavor is often disappointing when they are merely sautéed or broiled, especially when they cost anywhere from $14 to $16 a pound. Breading the chops before quickly pan-frying them, as cooks do in Milan, adds flavor and texture as well as a protective coating that shields the delicate meat. Of course, this recipe is not without its pitfalls. The breading often turns soggy, falls off the meat, or, worse, tastes stale and old.

As we did for grilled chops, we found rib chops preferable to shoulder chops, which are tough and chewy, and loin chops, which have a bone in the middle and two smaller portions of meat on either side (see the illustration on page 300). Cooking chops of varying thickness, we found medium-thick chops (roughly 1 inch thick) fried up best. Thinner chops overcooked before the breadcrumbs had a chance to brown, while thicker chops were simply too bulky and took too long to cook through. We found several recipes that called for pounding the meat around the bone with a mallet; however, our tests showed that this step was unnecessary.

Moving on to the breading, we far preferred the flavor of homemade bread crumbs to any we could buy. Compared to the light flavor of fresh bread processed into crumbs, the packaged commercial varieties tasted stale and of plastic. A thin coat of beaten egg (mixed with a bit of oil to help the excess slide off the meat) acted as a glue between the meat and crumbs, and a sheer film of flour applied to the meat just beforehand allowed the egg to cling. We tried to do without the initial flour coating, but the egg would not adhere to the meat without it, leading to a flimsy coating.

The highlight of these chops, besides the rare and delicate flavor of the veal, is the crisp, golden crust that results from the pan-frying. After cooking these chops several times, we realized that the key to a good crust is using enough hot oil. It is crucial that the oil reach halfway up the chops as they cook, ensuring an evenly colored, crisp coating. When less is used, the chops turn out blotchy with both charred and blond spots. A 12-inch skillet requires about ½ cup of oil to pan-fry 1-inch chops. The large skillet can cook only two chops at a time, and we found it necessary to use fresh oil when frying the second batch. When we didn't change the oil, small crumbs fell off the chops in the first batch, burned, then stuck to the coating of the second batch, making them taste scorched. Last, we found that letting the breaded chops rest for at least 30 minutes before they were cooked helped the coating stick better.

Using enough heat is also important when frying breaded veal chops. When the oil was not hot enough, the crust turned greasy and took too long to brown, overcooking the meat. Cooking the chops so that the meat at the very center retained some of its rosy hue (medium to medium-rare) took only five to six minutes. To get the oil hot enough to brown the crumbs within this time frame, we found it necessary to heat it in the pan over high heat for about two minutes before adding the chops.

To prevent the first batch of chops from getting soggy or cold while the second batch fried, we found it best to let them rest in a warm oven. Served with wedges of lemon, these crisp, delicate veal chops are an interesting and welcome change of pace that will leave you looking for special occasions on which to justify their cost.

Breaded Veal Chops

SERVES 4 TO 6

Good sliced sandwich bread works best in this recipe. For uniformity in color and crumb texture, we found it necessary to remove the crust.

3   cups fresh bread crumbs (page 57)
½   cup unbleached all-purpose flour
2   large eggs
1   tablespoon plus 1 cup vegetable oil
4   (12-ounce, 1-inch-thick) bone-in rib veal chops, excess fat trimmed
    Salt and ground black pepper
1   lemon, cut into wedges

1. Place the bread crumbs in a shallow dish or pie plate. Spread the flour in a second dish. Beat the eggs with 1 tablespoon oil in a third dish.

2. Blot the chops dry with paper towels and sprinkle generously with salt and pepper. Working with one at a time, dredge the chops thoroughly in the flour, shaking off the excess. Using tongs, dip both sides of the chops in the egg mixture, allowing the excess to drip back into the dish to ensure a very thin coating. Dip both sides of the chops in the bread crumbs, pressing the crumbs with your fingers to form an even, cohesive coat. Place the breaded chops in a single layer on a wire rack set over a baking sheet and refrigerate for at least 30 minutes or up to 4 hours.

3. Adjust an oven rack to a lower-middle position, set a large heatproof plate on the rack, and heat the oven to 200 degrees. Heat ½ cup oil in a 12-inch nonstick skillet over medium-high heat until shimmering. Place 2 chops in the skillet and fry until they are crisp and deep golden brown on the first side, gently pressing down on them with a wide metal spatula to help ensure even browning and checking partway through, about 3 minutes. Using tongs, flip the chops and reduce the heat to medium.

Continue to cook until the meat feels firm when pressed gently and the second side is deep golden brown and crisp, again checking partway through, 2 to 3 minutes longer. Line the warmed plate with a double layer of paper towels and set the chops on top; return the plate to the oven.

4. Discard the used oil and wipe the skillet clean using tongs and a large wad of paper towels. Repeat step 3, using the remaining ½ cup oil and the now-clean skillet and preheating the oil 2 minutes to cook the remaining 2 chops. Blot the second batch of chops with paper towels. Serve immediately along with first batch, with lemon wedges.

INGREDIENTS: Milk-Fed versus Natural Veal

Many people are opposed to milk-fed veal because the calves are confined to small stalls before being butchered. "Natural" is the term used to inform the consumer that the calves are allowed to move freely, without the confines of the stalls. Natural veal is also generally raised on grass (the calves can forage) and without hormones or antibiotics.

Moral issues aside, the differences in how the calves are raised create differences in the texture and flavor of the veal. Natural veal is darker, meatier, and more like beef. Milk-fed is paler in color, more tender, and milder in flavor. When we grilled both types of veal chops in the test kitchen, each had its supporters.

Several tasters preferred the meatier, more intense flavor of the natural veal. They thought the milk-fed veal seemed bland in comparison. Other tasters preferred the softer texture and milder flavor of the milk-fed veal. They felt that the natural veal tasted like "wimpy" beef and that the milk-fed chops had the mild, sweet flavor they expected from veal.

Both natural and milk-fed veal chops grill well, so the choice is really a personal one. Milk-fed veal is sold in most grocery stores, while natural veal is available at butcher shops, specialty markets, and natural foods markets.

OSSO BUCO

OSSO BUCO, OR ITALIAN BRAISED VEAL shanks, is too venerable a recipe to fiddle with. With humility, we headed into the kitchen. We decided the best way to approach the dish was to perfect (and simplify, if possible) the cooking technique and to extract the most flavor from the simple ingredients: veal shanks (which are browned), aromatics (onions, carrots, and celery, all sautéed), and liquids (a blend of wine, stock, and tomatoes).

To start, we gathered three classic recipes and prepared each in the test kitchen. At the tasting, there was little consensus about the recipes, although white wine was clearly preferred to red wine. Tasters did, however, offer similar ideas as to what constituted the perfect osso buco; it would be rich in flavor and color and somewhat brothy but not stewy. This first goal is the reason why we prefer osso buco to veal stews made with boneless shoulder meat. While shoulder meat can be a bit wan, the shank is robust, and the bone adds tremendous flavor to the stewing liquid. With these traits in mind, we created a rough working recipe and set out to explore the two main components in this dish—the veal shanks and the braising liquid.

Most recipes we reviewed called for shanks from the upper portion of the hind leg, cut into pieces between 1 and 1½ inches thick. We found that purchasing shanks is tricky, even when we special-ordered them. From one market, we received stunning shanks with a lovely pinkish blush, which were ideal except for the weight. Each shank weighed between 12 and 16 ounces—too large for individual servings. Part of the charm of osso buco is receiving an individual shank as a portion. We concluded that shanks should weigh 8 to 10 ounces (with the bone) and no more. At another market, the shanks were generally in the ideal weight range, but the butchering job was less than perfect. In the same package, shank widths varied from 1 to 2½ inches and were occasionally cut on an extreme bias, making tying difficult (see explanation below) and searing uneven.

The first step, then, is to shop carefully. We found a thickness of 1½ inches and a weight of 8 ounces ideal. Make sure all the shanks you buy are close to these specifications. Each shank should have two nicely cut, flat sides to facilitate browning.

Preparing the meat for braising was the first step. Most recipes called for tying the shanks and dredging them in flour before searing. We found that tying a piece of butcher's twine around the equator of each shank does prevent the meat from falling apart and makes for a more attractive presentation. When we skipped this step, the meat fell off the bone and floated about in the pot.

Although we do not generally dredge meat in flour before browning, we felt we should at least try it, considering that the majority of osso buco recipes include this step. Tasters felt that the meat floured before searing was gummy and lacked depth. The flour on the meat browns rather than the meat itself, and the flour coating may peel off during the long braising time.

To develop the best flavor in the shanks, we seasoned them heavily with salt and pepper and seared them until a thick, golden brown crust formed. We seared the shanks in two batches (even if they could all fit in the pan at the same time) so that we could deglaze the pan twice with wine, thereby enriching the braising liquid doubly.

The most difficult part of developing this recipe was attaining an ideal braising liquid and sauce. Braising, by design, is a relatively inexact cooking method because the rate at which the liquid reduces can vary greatly. Some of the initial recipes we tried yielded far too much liquid, which was thin in flavor and texture. In other cases, the liquid nearly evaporated by the time the meat was tender. We needed to create a foolproof, flavorful braising liquid and cooking technique that produced a rich sauce in a suitable volume and did not need a lot of last-minute fussing.

We experimented with numerous techniques to attain our ideal liquid, including reductions before braising and after braising (with the aromatics and without) and a reduction of the wine to a syrup during the deglazing process. In the end, we settled on the easiest method: natural reduction in the oven. The seal on most Dutch ovens is not perfectly tight, so the liquid reduces as the osso buco cooks. We found further simmering on the stovetop unnecessary as long as we started with the right amount of liquid in the pot.

The braising liquid traditionally begins with meat stock and adds white wine and tomatoes. As few cooks have homemade meat stock on hand and canned versions are often unappealing, we knew that canned chicken broth would be our likely starting point. Two cups (or one can) seemed the right amount, and tests confirmed this. To enrich the flavor of the broth, we used a hefty amount of diced onion, carrot, and celery. Tasters liked the large amount of garlic in one recipe, so we finely minced about five cloves and added it in to the pot prior to the stock. We rounded out the flavors with two bay leaves.

We hoped to write the recipe in even amounts, using whole vegetables, one can of stock, one bottle of wine, etc. But an entire bottle of wine proved overwhelming. The resulting sauce was dominated by acidity. Some testers also felt that the meat was tougher than previous batches with less wine. We scaled the wine back to 2½ cups, about two-thirds of a bottle, and were happy with

the results. More than half of the wine is used to deglaze the pot between searing batches of veal shanks and thus the final dish is not as alcoholic or liquidy as it might seem.

With the wine and stock amounts settled, we needed to figure out how to best incorporate tomatoes. Most tasters did not like too much tomato because they felt it easily overwhelmed the other flavors. Fresh tomatoes are always a gamble outside of the summer months, so we chose canned diced tomatoes, thoroughly strained of their juice. This approach worked out well, and the tomatoes did not overwhelm the sauce.

We still needed to determine the ideal braising time. Several sources suggested cooking osso buco almost to the consistency of pulled pork. Tasters loved the meat cooked this way, but it was less than attractive—broken down and pot roast–like. We wanted compact meat firmly attached to the bone, so we cooked the meat just until it was fork tender but still clinging to the bone. Two hours in the oven produced veal that was meltingly soft but still affixed to the bone. With some of the larger shanks, the cooking time extended to about 2½ hours.

We experimented with oven temperature and found that 325 degrees reduced the braising liquid to the right consistency and did not harm the texture of the meat. While beef stews are best cooked at 300 degrees, veal shanks have so much collagen and connective tissue that they can be braised at a slightly higher temperature.

Just before serving, osso buco is sprinkled with gremolata, a mixture of minced garlic, parsley, and lemon zest. We were surprised to find variations on this classic trio. A number of recipes included orange zest mixed with lemon zest or on its own. Other recipes included anchovies. We tested three gremolatas: one traditional, one with orange zest mixed equally with lemon zest, and one with anchovies. Tasters liked all three but favored the traditional version.

In some recipes the gremolata is used as a garnish, and in others it is added to the pot just before serving. We chose a compromise approach, stirring half the gremolata into the pot and letting it stand for five minutes so that the flavors of the garlic, lemon, and parsley permeated the dish. We sprinkled the remaining gremolata on individual servings for a hit of freshness.

Osso Buco

SERVES 6

To keep the meat attached to the bone during the long simmering process, tie a piece of twine around the thickest portion of each shank before it is browned. Use a zester, vegetable peeler, or paring knife to remove the zest from a single lemon, then mince it with a chef's knife. Osso buco is traditionally served with risotto alla Milanese (saffron risotto; see page 205). Parmesan mashed potatoes (page 82) and polenta (page 218) are excellent options as well.

OSSO BUCO

- 6 tablespoons vegetable oil
- 6 (8- to 10-ounce, 1½-inch-thick) veal shanks, dried thoroughly with paper towels and tied around the equator with butcher's twine

  Salt and ground black pepper
- 2½ cups dry white wine
- 2 medium onions, cut into ½-inch dice (about 2 cups)
- 2 medium carrots, cut into ½-inch dice (about 1½ cups)
- 2 medium stalks celery, cut into ½-inch dice (about 1 cup)
- 6 medium cloves garlic, minced or pressed through a garlic press

- 2 cups homemade chicken stock or canned low-sodium chicken broth
- 2 small bay leaves
- 1 (14½-ounce) can diced tomatoes, drained

GREMOLATA

- 3 medium cloves garlic, minced or pressed through a garlic press
- 2 teaspoons minced lemon zest
- ¼ cup minced fresh parsley leaves

1. FOR THE OSSO BUCO: Adjust the oven rack to the lower-middle position and heat the oven to 325 degrees.

2. Heat 2 tablespoons oil in a large ovenproof Dutch oven over medium-high heat until shimmering. Meanwhile, sprinkle both sides of the shanks generously with salt and pepper. Swirl to coat the pan bottom with the oil. Place 3 shanks in a single layer in the pan and cook until they are golden brown on one side, about 5 minutes. Using tongs, flip the shanks and cook on the second side until golden brown, about 5 minutes longer. Transfer the shanks to a bowl and set aside. Off the heat, add ½ cup wine to the Dutch oven, scraping the bottom with a wooden spoon to loosen any browned bits. Pour the liquid into the bowl with the browned shanks. Return the pot to medium-high heat, add 2 tablespoons oil, and heat until it is shimmering. Brown the remaining shanks, about 5 minutes for each side. Transfer the shanks to the bowl with the other shanks. Off the heat, add an additional 1 cup wine to the pot, scraping the bottom to loosen the browned bits. Pour the liquid into the bowl with the shanks.

3. Set the pot over medium heat. Add the remaining 2 tablespoons oil and heat until it is shimmering. Add the onions, carrots, and celery and cook, stirring occasionally, until soft and lightly browned, about 9 minutes. Add the garlic and cook until lightly browned, about

1 minute longer. Increase the heat to high and stir in the chicken stock, remaining 1 cup wine, juices from the veal shanks, and bay leaves. Add the tomatoes and veal shanks to the pot (the liquid should just cover the shanks). Cover the pot and place it in the oven. Cook the shanks until the meat is easily pierced with a fork but not falling off the bone, about 2 hours. (Osso buco can be refrigerated for up to 2 days. Bring to a simmer over medium-low heat.)

4. FOR THE GREMOLATA: Combine the garlic, lemon zest, and parsley in a small bowl. Stir half of the gremolata into the pot, reserving the rest for garnish. Adjust the seasonings with salt and pepper to taste. Let the osso buco stand, uncovered, for 5 minutes.

5. Using tongs, remove the shanks from the pot, cut off and discard the twine, and place 1 veal shank in each of 6 bowls. Ladle some braising liquid over each shank and sprinkle with the remaining gremolata. Serve immediately.

CALF'S LIVER AND ONIONS, VENETIAN STYLE

LIVER AND ONIONS MAY NOT HAVE A huge audience here in the United States, but they would, no doubt, be much more popular if made in the Venetian style. Delicate pieces of calf's liver are quickly sautéed and served with plenty of lightly caramelized onions and a squirt of lemon. Yet the common distaste for liver and onions is well founded, as the dish is most often poorly made, with rubbery, gray pieces of potent-tasting liver surrounded by soggy, steamed onions. Wanting to emulate the Venetian knack for cooking this unpopular offal, we set out to uncover the secret to good liver and onions.

Finding the delicate, pink calf's liver already sliced into ½-inch-thick pieces at the supermarket, we noted that four slices were plenty for four people and easily fit into a 10- or 12-inch skillet. Although the recipes we researched called for a wide range of cooking times, these thin pieces actually cooked very quickly; they retained the rosy interior we desired when cooked in two to three minutes total. When cooked any longer, they turned a uniform gray hue and tasted dry. However, due do this short cooking time, it was difficult to achieve a good golden crust on the outside. By preheating the skillet and oil for several minutes over high heat, we were able to get a beautiful golden rim of crust around the edges without overcooking the inside.

Sweet golden onions are important for the success of this dish; however, the process of caramelization can be confusing, and recipes offer varying techniques and tricks. To determine which method works best, we tried them all. To start, we cooked onions in all butter, all oil, or a combination of the two. Tasters far preferred the combination of oil and butter, finding all butter too rich and overpowering and the flavor of all oil too lean.

Some recipes call for cooking the onions over low heat the entire time, while others claim the process is best done quickly over high heat. In three pans, we tried cooking onions over high, medium, and low heat. The onions cooked over medium heat turned out best, with a solid, caramelized flavor and slightly crunchy texture. The onions cooked over low heat simply took too long, while the high heat produced onions with a scorched flavor—yet we were impressed with the rate at which the high-heat onions caramelized. Using high heat for just the first five minutes of cooking to get the process going, we then turned the heat to medium so as not to scorch the flavor. Adding salt to the onions as they caramelized did not speed the process (contrary to popular belief), but the resulting onions did have a better flavor than those that were salted postcaramelization.

The usual technique for making a sauté involves cooking the meat first, then using the drippings for a sauce—or, in this case, the onions. We found, however, this recipe worked better when cooked the other way around—the onions first and the meat last. The onions took nearly 20 minutes to cook properly, at which time the delicate calf's liver would either overcook in a warm oven or turn cold if left to wait on the counter. We also found that a nonstick pan worked better than a regular pan, as the slippery surface repelled any juices or browned bits that would otherwise stick and burn. Finished with fresh butter, parsley, and lemon juice, the Venetian version of liver and onions is light, elegant, and tastes unlike any liver and onions you've eaten before.

Sautéed Calf's Liver and Onions

SERVES 4

A nonstick pan will keep the onions from burning as they cook. Use the same pan to cook the liver.

3	tablespoons extra-virgin olive oil
3	tablespoons unsalted butter
3	medium onions, sliced thin (about 4 cups)
	Salt
4	(½-inch-thick) slices calf's liver (about 1 pound)
	Ground black pepper
2	tablespoons lemon juice
2	tablespoons minced fresh parsley leaves

1. Heat 2 tablespoons oil and 1 tablespoon butter in a large nonstick skillet over high heat. When the butter foams, add the onions and ¼ teaspoon salt and cook until their juices are released, about 5 minutes. Reduce the heat to medium and cook until lightly browned and sticky, 10 to 12 minutes longer. Transfer the onions to a medium bowl and reserve.

2. Return the pan to medium-high heat, add the remaining tablespoon oil, and heat until shimmering. Season the liver liberally with salt and pepper and lay the pieces in pan. Cook until the first side is browned around the edges, 1 to 1½ minutes. Flip the liver and cook on the second side until the edges are browned, 1 to 1½ minutes. Transfer the liver to a plate and reserve.

3. To the warm skillet, add the remaining 2 tablespoons butter, lemon juice, parsley, and reserved onions. Toss to mix, stirring in any accumulated juices from the liver. Place the onions on a large platter or individual plates and lay the liver on top. Serve immediately.

PORK CHOPS WITH VINEGAR PEPPERS

THIS SIMPLE, RUSTIC DISH FEATURES pan-seared pork chops smothered in a silky, caramelly sauce of bell peppers. Although the flavors are complex, the execution of this dish is quick and straightforward, making it easy enough for a weeknight dinner. The chops are usually browned and removed from the pan, and the vinegar and pepper sauce is built on the pan drippings.

Of course, the success of this recipe begins with properly cooked chops. But when was the last time you had a really juicy, tender, thick pork chop? These days, it is likely to be something you remember but not something that you've recently enjoyed. In response to American demands for low-fat meat, the pork industry has systematically trimmed down the hefty fat-producing hogs of the past to create today's newer pig, sleek of silhouette and lean of flesh. In fact, today's pork has at least 30 percent less fat than that of 20 years ago.

In our experience, thick-cut pork chops are less likely to dry out than thinner chops. After testing several options, we settled on rib loin chops 1½ inches thick (see page 311 for details of this testing). Thick chops require a bit more finesse than simple sautéing because the exterior will brown long before the interior comes up to temperature. Our research uncovered two options: cook the chops on the stovetop the entire time (using the cover and regulating the heat levels to produce fully cooked chops that do not burn), or start the chops on the stove and transfer them to the oven to finish cooking through to the bone.

A high-heat sear for two to three minutes per side (depending on the number of chops in the pan) followed by about 10 minutes per side of covered stovetop cooking over reduced heat yielded very good results. But we found these chops to be just slightly less tender than those that we started in the frying pan and finished in the oven. There was no demonstrable advantage to using a lower oven temperature (we tried 450, 350, and 250 degrees); the chops simply took longer to cook. In the end, purely for the sake of expediency, we settled on searing the chops in a sauté pan, then transferring them to a preheated sheet pan in a 450-degree oven to finish cooking.

We had found the best cooking method, but the chops were still lacking in flavor and moisture. Owing to their relative absence of fat or collagen (those classic suppliers of flavor and moisture), these chops were clearly perfect candidates for brining. Soaking the chops for an hour in a salt-and-sugar brine yielded a significant improvement in flavor and moisture.

Our final step was to determine the exact relationship between flavor and the internal temperature of the meat. The best-tasting chops we had tried had an internal reading of 140 to 145 degrees. But medium-rare pork? What would our mothers say?

One of the reasons so much pork today reaches the table dry and overcooked is the public's residual fear of the trichinosis parasite. But there is actually little cause for concern, because the United States now sees few trichinosis cases (only 230 cases nationwide from 1991 to 1996, some 40 percent of them caused by eating wild game). Moreover, the parasites that cause this disease are destroyed when the pork reaches an internal temperature of 137 degrees. So the notion of medium-rare pork needn't be met with a shudder of horror or revulsion.

After fiddling with various options, we committed to the bold maneuver of cooking the chops to a temperature of 125 to 127 degrees. We were able to do this by letting the chops complete their cooking outside the oven, covering them with aluminum foil while they rested to allow the juices to redistribute throughout the meat. After this five-minute rest, the chops' temperature went up to a perfect 140 to 145 degrees. Relinquishing a minimum of juice—it mostly stayed in the chop—and retaining the barest whisper of pink on their interior, the chops were succulent and highly flavorful. This was largely due, we felt, to the fact that cooking by residual

BUY THE RIGHT PORK CHOP

Supermarket chops are often cut thick at the bone and thinner at the outer edge, like the one on the left. With such chops, the thinner periphery will overcook before the thicker meat near the bone is finished. Make sure you get chops that are of even thickness, like the one on the right.

heat is a gentler and more precise method of reaching the final serving temperature. Chops left to rest uncovered, on the other hand, not only lost heat but showed little escalation in their internal temperature between pan and plate.

To ensure perfectly cooked chops, an instant-read thermometer is absolutely essential. Time estimates will be just that—estimates—and no amount of prodding or poking with your finger will give you a true reading of doneness.

Our next challenge was to create a flavorful, heady pan sauce that would contrast with the substantial and yet tender pork. In almost all the traditional recipes, the peppers of choice are raw, skin-on red bell peppers that have been bottled and submerged in white vinegar and labeled "vinegar peppers," "Italian-style peppers," or "Greek-style peppers."

Some recipes called for using the liquid from the bottle, but we found the flavor to be tinny and inconsistent from manufacturer to manufacturer (some were packed mostly in vinegar, others mostly in water), which made writing a recipe almost impossible. When we drained the peppers and replaced the vinegar mixture in the bottle with white wine vinegar, we found there was no comparison; the white wine vinegar was far brighter and clearer. (Because the traditional dish calls for white wine vinegar, we rejected both red wine and balsamic vinegar from the start, as we felt they would transform it into an entirely different dish.)

Although the combination of drained bottled peppers and fresh vinegar was a big step forward, some tinniness remained in the peppers, and their texture was slightly stiff and rubbery. We decided to try replacing the bottled peppers with fresh red and yellow bell peppers. Sure enough, this was a huge improvement. Using the combination of two colors (both red and yellow peppers) made for a much more vibrant-looking dish.

We cooked the fresh peppers down twice, first in white wine vinegar and water and then again in plain water. This technique gave the peppers their caramel flavor and silky texture. When we quickly cooked the peppers in vinegar alone, they were raw and too crunchy, and simmering the peppers in a covered pan made them taste boiled and bland. Cooking the peppers and liquid in an open pan allowed the natural sugars in the peppers to caramelize and provided a nice balance to the tartness of the vinegar.

Our research recipes indicated that we had several optional ingredients to test. In the end, we found that garlic, anchovies, and herbs were essential, as they made the dish both fuller and richer. The final dish was aromatic, impressive looking, juicy, and slightly sweet, with sour, almost tart undertones. In short, it was just what we were looking for.

Thick pork chops are best browned in a skillet and then finished in the oven so they can cook through to the bone.

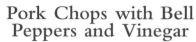

Pork Chops with Bell Peppers and Vinegar

SERVES 4

Be sure to buy chops of the same thickness so that they cook consistently. See page 309 for details.

PORK CHOPS

1½	cups kosher salt or ¾ cup table salt
1½	cups sugar
4	(12-ounce, 1½-inch-thick) bone-in rib loin pork chops
2	tablespoons olive oil
½	teaspoon ground black pepper

PEPPERS AND VINEGAR

2	medium cloves garlic, minced or pressed through a garlic press
2	anchovy fillets, minced
1	medium red bell pepper, stemmed, seeded, and cut into ½-inch dice
1	medium yellow bell pepper, stemmed, seeded, and cut into ½-inch dice
1	sprig fresh rosemary
½	cup white wine vinegar

1. FOR THE CHOPS: Dissolve the salt and sugar in 3 quarts water in a large container. Submerge the chops in the brine and refrigerate until fully seasoned, 1 hour. Remove the chops from the brine, rinse, and thoroughly dry with paper towels.

2. Adjust an oven rack to the lower-middle position, place a shallow roasting pan or rimmed baking pan on the rack, and heat the oven to 450 degrees. When the oven reaches 450 degrees, heat the oil in a heavy-bottomed 12-inch skillet over high heat until shimmering but not smoking, about 2 minutes. Swirl the skillet to coat evenly with oil. Sprinkle the chops with the pepper and place them in the skillet. Cook until well browned and a nice crust has formed on the surface, about 3

minutes. Turn the chops over with tongs and cook until well browned and a nice crust has formed on the second side, about 3 minutes longer. Using tongs, transfer the chops to the

INGREDIENTS: Pork Chops

In many supermarkets, all pork chops from the loin are simply labeled "loin chops." However, there are significant differences in the four types of chops that come from the loin. Two—the blade chop and the sirloin chop—are less common and more likely to be labeled correctly. The two chops that you are most likely to run into labeled simply "loin chop" are the center-cut chop and the rib chop.

As their name implies, center-cut chops are cut right out of the center of the loin. You can identify them by the bone that divides them into two sections, giving them a close resemblance to a T-bone steak. Like a T-bone, they have meat from the loin on one side of the bone and a small portion of the tenderloin muscle on the other side. Some people prefer these center-cut chops because the tenderloin portion in particular is extremely tender. However, our top choice is the rib chop, cut from the rib section of the loin, which is slightly closer to the shoulder. It has a somewhat higher fat content, which makes it more flavorful and less likely to dry out during cooking. The rib pork chop can be distinguished by the section of rib bone along one side. Sometimes rib and center-cut chops are sold boneless, making it much more difficult to tell them apart. However, because we find bone-in meat juicier when cooked, we suggest you look for bone-in chops.

CENTER-CUT CHOP   RIB CHOP

A bone runs through the middle of the center-cut chop, with meat on either side. The meat on the left side of the bone is from the tenderloin. The bone on a rib chop runs along one edge of the chop, with all the meat on one side of the bone.

preheated pan in the oven. Roast the chops until an instant-read thermometer inserted into the center of a chop registers 125 to 127 degrees, 8 to 10 minutes, turning the chops over once halfway through the cooking time. Set the chops aside, covered with foil, while the peppers finish cooking.

3. FOR THE PEPPERS AND VINEGAR: As soon as you place the chops in the oven, return the skillet to medium-high heat, add the garlic, anchovies, peppers, and rosemary, and cook until the peppers begin to soften, 4 to 5 minutes. Add ½ cup water and the vinegar and bring to a boil, stirring and scraping any browned bits from the pan bottom. Cook until the liquid has almost evaporated, about 6 minutes. Add the remaining ½ cup water and cook until the mixture is syrupy, 3 to 4 minutes. Remove and discard the rosemary.

4. Add the pork chops to the pan and simmer, turning the chops once, until heated through and the internal temperature of the chops registers 145 degrees, about 2 minutes. Serve immediately.

PORK BRAISED IN MILK

MAIALE AL LATTE (PORK LOIN BRAISED in milk), a humble and intriguing dish, is considered one of the best illustrations of regional northern Italian cooking—and yet, there are those in Naples who claim it as their own, while still others say it's a Tuscan classic. Most of the recipes we found originated with women who gave them to neighbors who gave them to their daughters who have continued to pass them on. Regardless of geographic origin, all recipe writers profess that "my mother's version is best."

The basic recipe remains the same: A pork loin is slow-cooked in milk long enough for the milk to coagulate into delicious (but inelegant) little clumps of browned milk protein. The simplest recipe was really just that—a pork loin browned in olive oil, then covered and slowly simmered in milk. Although the pork itself was tender and sweet, our tasters found the sauce bland. We wanted a meatier flavor in the sauce and thought that salt pork (suggested in several recipes) rather than olive oil might fit the bill. Sure enough, browning the pork in salt pork (which had first been diced and rendered) yielded a much more flavorful dish.

Next, we tried rubbing the pork with garlic and herbs, which added much-needed flavor but produced little burnt bits on the crust. Instead, we added the same ingredients along with carrots, celery, and onion to the salt pork. Once the roast was done, we strained out these aromatic vegetables and the salt pork, and the resulting sauce was more complex and better-tasting. In our research, we had seen several versions of this recipe with nutmeg, cinnamon, and Parmesan cheese. However, tasters found the sweet spices almost cloying, and the Parmesan was, well, too cheesy for the pork. We decided to pass on all three of these embellishments.

Most recipes call for cooking the dish on the stovetop, but we found that the meat cooked somewhat unevenly. Once the meat is browned and the braising liquid brought to a simmer, we generally like to braise meat in the oven. As we expected, the more even heat of the oven yielded a more evenly cooked roast.

Rosy-colored pork struck several tasters as odd in this dish, where the pork is usually cooked until well done. We found that because the pork braises in so much liquid, the meat will not dry out if cooked to a slightly higher than usual (at least by our custom) internal temperature of 150 degrees. At this temperature, the pork was still juicy, and its pale gray color was deemed more traditional.

This is a dish that experienced eaters love, whether they have fond memories of sitting down to their grandmother's table or have braved their guests' doubtful stares and made it themselves time after time. If you are new to this recipe, you must suspend your aesthetic ideas; as the milk cooks down, it turns into little pale brownish clumps that, frankly, look like a broken mess of unappetizing curds. Most traditional recipes say to serve the pork either on top of or alongside the curds. For those who want a less rustic look, we discovered that the sauce can be smoothed out by blending or straining it (for less quantity and thickness).

In the end, we found that pork braised in milk is especially moist, juicy, and flavorful. Both main ingredients, even the skeptics agreed, are transformed by this exceptional method.

Pork Loin Braised in Milk

SERVES 6

Although the sauce is traditionally served as is (with the unattractive milk clumps floating in it), it can be pureed in a blender or poured through a fine-mesh strainer for a more refined look. Use leftover meat in sandwiches.

¼	pound salt pork, cut into ½-inch dice
1	boneless center-cut pork loin (2¼ to 2½ pounds)
1	teaspoon kosher salt
1	teaspoon ground black pepper
1	medium onion, halved
8	medium cloves garlic, peeled and left whole
1	medium carrot, halved lengthwise
1	medium celery stalk, halved lengthwise
1	bay leaf
1	sprig fresh rosemary or fresh thyme
3½	cups whole milk
⅓	cup white wine

1. Adjust an oven rack to the middle position and heat the oven to 325 degrees.

2. Place the salt pork in a large, heavy-bottomed Dutch oven over medium-high heat and cook until the fat begins to render, about 4 minutes. Sprinkle the pork loin with the salt and pepper and place it in the pot, fat side down. Cook, turning occasionally, until the roast begins to brown, 5 to 6 minutes. Add the onion, garlic, carrot, celery, bay leaf, and rosemary and continue cooking until the pork is well browned on all sides, about 6 minutes longer. Add the milk and bring to a simmer.

3. Transfer the pot to the oven, partially cover with the lid, and cook, turning occasionally, until the pork is tender and registers about 150 degrees on an instant-read thermometer, the milk is reduced by half, and light brown clumps of milk solids appear, about 1 hour.

4. Transfer the pork loin to a platter and cover it with aluminum foil. Using a slotted spoon, remove and discard the salt pork, onion, carrot, celery, bay leaf, and rosemary. Set the pot over high heat, add the wine, and cook, scraping up any browned bits with a wooden spoon, until the sauce reduces to about 2 cups, 7 to 10 minutes. If you are straining the sauce, pour it through a fine-mesh strainer into a serving bowl. If you are pureeing it, transfer it to a blender and puree until smooth, then transfer to a serving bowl. If you are leaving it chunky, simply transfer it to a serving bowl. Cut the pork crosswise into ½-inch-thick slices and arrange them on the platter. Drizzle ½ cup sauce over the sliced pork and serve immediately, with more sauce passed separately.

TUSCAN PORK ROAST WITH GARLIC AND ROSEMARY

TUSCAN-STYLE ROAST PORK IS A DISH with lore reaching back to the 15th century. This simple roasted pork loin is served boneless and sliced thick, often accompanied by the pan juices. The meat is succulent, the crust crisp, and the roast is infused with the appealing flavor combination of rosemary and garlic. It's great hot from the oven or cold sliced in sandwiches, and it is surprisingly inexpensive. This is a roast that can be a showpiece for a special occasion or a family meal with leftovers.

But for such a simple roast, problems abound. The meat can be dry, tough, and unevenly cooked; the crust can be absent, resulting in a pale and unappealing dish; and the rosemary and garlic flavors can be either too bland or too harsh. Our research revealed that there is no consensus on the cut of meat, the best way to flavor the pork, or the oven temperature at which to roast it.

We began by testing the cut of meat. Recipes called for a wide range of choices, the most popular being a boneless center-cut pork loin. Preparing and tasting 12 recipes convinced us to use a bone-in loin. These roasts had a richer pork flavor and were noticeably juicier. The boneless loins, in comparison, failed on the taste test, but we noted that they were easier to carve. We also observed that the boneless roasts cooked on a rack, assuring that the meat on the bottom roasted rather than steamed. With this information in hand, we continued testing to determine which of the bone-in choices was best.

Visualizing pig anatomy helps in understanding the choices. Working from shoulder to midsection, first comes the blade roast, then the rib roast, next the loin roast, and finally the sirloin roast. We eliminated the blade roast and the sirloin roast, both of which are composed of many separate muscles and fatty deposits. Tests showed that these cuts were difficult to cook evenly, flavor well, and carve.

Both the rib roast and the loin roast seemed worthy candidates. Each of these roasts consists largely of the same single, uniformly shaped muscle, so we prepared them side by side. You can imagine our delight at discovering that the cut of choice, the rib roast, provided not just the tastiest meat but also the most natural and ideal rack to cook the loin on—the rib bones.

We asked several butchers to explain why the meat was so much better from the rib roast despite the similarity of the loin roast. We learned that the meat on the rib roast includes a protective cap of fat and muscle and is marbled with more fat than the loin roast. The marbling (threads of intramuscular fat) and the fat in the cap melt during cooking and flavor the meat as well as ensure juiciness. The loin roast has less marbling, lacks a protective cap of fat and muscle, and does not have as many rib bones.

The bones of the rib roast make an important contribution to the success of this dish. They protect the meat, which helps keep it moist, and they enhance the pork flavor. The rib bones also lift the meat off the floor of the roasting pan, which allows for the circulation of air and, hence, even cooking, and prevents mushy bottom meat. The backbone, called the chine bone, is sometimes attached to the rib bones, and it also provides stability. After much testing, we concluded that the cut of choice was a rib roast with the chine bone attached.

Purchasing a rib roast requires an understanding of the distinction between the rib roast and the loin roast because sometimes these roasts are labeled exactly the same: "center cut, bone-in roast." If you are looking in a meat case, refer to the photographs on page

316, or simply ask your butcher. Know that this is the same prized cut of meat sold as rack of lamb or prime rib of beef—it just comes from a pig.

With the cut of meat decided, we turned our attention to the traditional Tuscan flavors. Rosemary, garlic, and olive oil are strong characters, and we were determined to harness and marry their flavors so that the roast would be perfumed with their essence. We identified the classic approaches and began testing.

Stuffing slivers of garlic, with or without rosemary, into slits on the outside of the roast failed to impress. The flavors did not permeate deeply (even when we refrigerated the loin overnight before cooking), and the garlic and rosemary were not pleasant to eat. Garlic and rosemary rubbed on the outside tended to burn and become bitter. Rosemary sprigs tied to the outside looked appealing, but the flavor

---

S C I E N C E : What Is Enhanced Pork?
Our obsession with fat has prompted the pork industry to breed a leaner pig. Today's pork is much leaner than its 1950s counterpart. The industry has addressed the issue that less fat means less flavor and moisture by introducing a product called enhanced pork—meat injected with a solution of water, salt, and sodium phosphate. The idea is to both season the pork and prevent it from drying out.

We wondered if we could skip brining and save time by using enhanced pork. We tested side by side enhanced pork, unenhanced pork, and unenhanced pork that had been brined. The enhanced pork was salty and had a somewhat artificial flavor. The unenhanced pork that was not brined was dry and bland. The unenhanced and brined pork was juicy and well seasoned—the clear winner. The benefit of brining pork is that you can control the salt and seasoning and avoid an artificial aftertaste. During our research, it seemed that some stores carry enhanced pork roasts only. If you have no other choice, skip the brining step to keep the meat from tasting overly salty.

---

did not penetrate and the crust did not brown evenly. In an attempt to flavor the center of the meat, some recipes called for creating a hole in the middle of the loin and then stuffing it, while other recipes have you slit open the loin and spread a rosemary garlic mixture on the inside. These approaches held promise, but the garlic was often undercooked and harsh and the rosemary overpowering.

We were convinced that putting a paste in the center of the meat was the answer. We tried using a mini food processor to make the paste, but the garlic did not break down into small enough pieces. The bigger chunks were undercooked and sharp-tasting in the cooked pork. Making the paste by hand with the help of a garlic press gave the best results. Equal parts rosemary and garlic was most pleasing, and tests showed that including olive oil helps heat and cook the garlic and rosemary paste, which facilitates the infusion of flavor.

We were on our 26th roast and still having problems using the paste to infuse the meat with flavor. Our search for creative solutions led us to remove the meat from the bone, cut it open in the center, and open it like a book, a technique called butterflying. We placed the paste in the cut and then tied the roast back together. This roast was very flavorful, but there was too much paste, which was unpleasant and overpowering to eat. We tried another butterflied loin with the intention of spreading less of the paste into the cut when the naked bones gave us an idea. We slathered the bones with two-thirds of the paste and spread the rest in the cut, then tied the meat back onto the bones. This technique worked like a charm. The rosemary and garlic flavors infused the meat, but the paste stayed on the bones when the roast was sliced and served. The bonus of deconstructing the roast to apply the paste was that carving was no longer an issue. By simply cutting the twine after cooking, the bone-in roast was now as easy to slice and serve as the boneless roasts we had tried at the beginning. Our search for flavor had served up convenience as well.

We now had a very good-tasting roast, but we were looking for the best. We wanted to address the fact that pigs are bred leaner these days, and less fat means less flavor and less moisture. We decided to try brining—soaking the pork (both the meat and the bones) in a saltwater solution. Brining causes the protein cells within the meat to unravel and thus capture and retain both moisture and seasoning. Sure enough, tests confirmed that this technique produced a roast that was better seasoned and juicer. We added rosemary and garlic to the brine along with brown sugar for depth and caramelization. This created a terrific and aromatic roast, with complex flavors that were both strong and savory.

We were in the home stretch and ready to experiment with roasting methods. Our goal— a crispy and flavorful crust combined with tender and moist morsels of meat—was in sight.

Older recipes call for cooking the loin until the internal temperature reaches 160 degrees. Especially with today's lean pork, this produces a roast that is dry and gray. With concerns about the trichinosis parasite largely eliminated, the Pork Board now recommends cooking pork until it is just slightly rosy in the center and registers 150 degrees on an instant-read thermometer. The test kitchen suggests a final temperature of 145 degrees—the meat will be juicier and the temperature is sufficient to kill trichinosis, however remote the possibility that the parasite is present. Because the internal heat will keep cooking the meat and cause the temperature to rise while the roast is resting, the meat should be removed from the oven at 140 degrees.

Roasting at a constant temperature was not ideal. A low temperature (325 degrees or lower) produced the best meat, while high heat (400 degrees or higher) produced the best crust. A moderate oven temperature produced neither delectable meat nor an appealing crust.

We resisted dividing the cooking between the stovetop and the oven, trying every imaginable combination of high heat and low heat in the oven instead. But this approach also failed. The high heat dried out the meat or even worse; occasionally, the high heat resulted in billows of smoke pouring out of the oven from the pork fat.

The answer came easily once we let go of our resolve to limit cooking to the oven. Restaurant training taught us that searing on the stovetop and then cooking in the oven is a fail-safe method for producing an excellent crust and perfectly cooked meat. A constant 325-degree oven subsequent to stovetop searing gave the best results.

Finally, we had developed a recipe for a Tuscan-style roast pork loin that lives up to its reputation. The approach of using a bone-in roast, removing the meat to brine it and flavor

RIGHT PORK ROAST, WRONG PORK ROAST

RIB ROAST   LOIN ROAST

Both the rib roast and loin roast can be labeled "center-cut roast" at the market, but they are not the same. The meat on the pork rib roast includes a protective cap of fat and muscle and is marbled with more fat than the loin roast. The marbling (threads of intramuscular fat) and the fat in the cap melt during cooking and flavor the meat as well as ensure its juiciness. The loin roast has less marbling, lacks a protective cap of fat and muscle, and does not have as many rib bones, so the meat is more likely to dry out in the oven. For these reasons, we recommend a rib roast, not a loin roast.

it, then tying the meat back to the bone for roasting is a bit unconventional—but the process is easy and ensures a roast that reveals why the love affair with Tuscan-style roast pork began 600 years ago.

Tuscan-Style Roast Pork Loin with Garlic and Rosemary

SERVES 6 TO 8

The roasting time is determined in part by the shape of the roast; a long, thin roast will cook faster than a roast with a large circumference. Though not traditionally served, the ribs are rich with flavor. If you'd like to serve them or enjoy them yourself, after untying the roast and removing the loin, scrape the excess garlic-rosemary paste from the ribs, set the ribs on a rimmed baking sheet, and put them in a 375-degree oven for about 20 minutes or until they are brown and crisp.

ROAST

2	cups kosher salt or 1 cup table salt
2	cups packed dark brown sugar
10	large cloves garlic, lightly crushed and peeled
5	(6-inch-long) sprigs fresh rosemary
1	bone-in, center-cut 4-pound pork loin roast with chine bone cracked, preferably from the rib end (see page 316), prepared according to illustrations 1 and 2 on page 318

GARLIC-ROSEMARY PASTE

8–10	cloves garlic, pressed through a garlic press or minced to a paste (1½ tablespoons)
1½	tablespoons finely chopped fresh rosemary leaves
1	teaspoon ground black pepper
1	tablespoon extra-virgin olive oil
⅛	teaspoon kosher salt
1	cup dry white wine
1	teaspoon ground black pepper
1	medium-large shallot, minced (about 3 tablespoons)
1½	teaspoons minced fresh rosemary leaves
1¾	cups homemade chicken stock or canned low-sodium chicken broth
2	tablespoons unsalted butter, cut into 4 pieces and softened

1. FOR THE ROAST: Dissolve the salt and brown sugar in 1½ quarts hot tap water in a large stockpot or clean bucket. Stir in the garlic and rosemary. Add 2½ quarts cold water and submerge the meat and bones in the brine. Refrigerate until fully seasoned, about 3 hours. Rinse the meat and ribs under cold water and dry thoroughly with paper towels.

2. FOR THE PASTE: While the roast brines, mix the garlic, rosemary, pepper, olive oil, and salt in a small bowl to form a paste; set aside.

3. FOR COOKING THE ROAST: When the roast is out of the brine, adjust an oven rack to the middle position and heat the oven to 325 degrees. Heat a heavy-bottomed 12-inch skillet over medium heat until hot. Place the roast, fat side down, in the skillet and cook until well browned, about 8 minutes. Transfer the roast, browned side up, to a rimmed baking sheet and set aside. Pour off the fat from the skillet and add the wine. Increase the heat to high and bring to a boil, scraping the skillet with a wooden spoon until the browned bits are loosened. Set the skillet with the wine aside.

4. Make a lengthwise incision in the pork loin and rub with one-third of the garlic-rosemary paste (see illustrations 3 and 4 on page 318). Rub the remaining paste on the cut side of the ribs where the meat was attached (see illustration 5). Tie the meat to the ribs (see illustration 6); sprinkle the browned side of the roast with the pepper. Pour the reserved wine

and browned bits from the skillet into the roasting pan. Roast, basting the loin with the pan drippings every 20 minutes, until the center of loin registers about 140 degrees on an instant-read thermometer, 65 to 80 minutes. (If the wine evaporates, add about ½ cup water to the roasting pan to prevent scorching.) Transfer the roast to a carving board and tent loosely with foil. Let stand until the center of the loin registers about 145 degrees on an instant-read thermometer, about 15 minutes.

5. While the roast rests, spoon most of the fat from the roasting pan and place the pan over 2 burners at a high heat. Add the shallot and rosemary. Using a wooden spoon, scrape up the browned bits with a wooden spoon and boil the liquid until reduced by half and the shallot has softened, about 2 minutes. Add the chicken stock and continue to cook, stirring occasionally, until reduced by half, about 8 minutes. Add any accumulated pork juices and cook 1 minute longer. Off the heat, whisk in the butter. Strain the jus into the gravy boat.

6. Cut the twine on the roast and remove the meat from the bones. Set the meat, browned side up, on a board and cut it into ¼-inch thick slices. Serve immediately, passing the jus separately.

PREPARING A BONE-IN PORK ROAST

1. Position the loin so that the rib bones are perpendicular to the cutting board. Using a sharp knife and starting from the far end and working toward you, separate the meat from the rib bones by pressing—almost scraping—the knife along the rib bones.

2. Use a series of small, easy strokes to cut all along the bones, following the rib bones along the curve to the backbone until the meat is free of the bones. You will have a compact eye of the loin, with a small flap attached to the side.

3. Slice through the center of the entire length of the eye, stopping 1 inch shy of the edge.

4. Open the eye up so it is spread flat like butterfly wings and rub one-third of the rosemary mixture in an even layer on one side of the cut, leaving ½ inch on each end bare.

5. Spread the remaining rosemary mixture evenly along the bones from where the meat was cut, leaving ½ inch on each end bare. Fold the eye back together and secure the meat on the bones exactly from where it was cut.

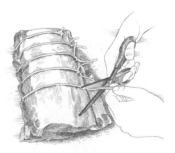

6. Use seven lengths of twine to tie the meat back onto the bones.

Tuscan-Style Roast Pork Loin with Potatoes

Instead of making a jus from the roasting pan drippings, use them to flavor roasted potatoes to serve with the pork.

Follow the recipe for Tuscan-Style Roast Pork Loin with Rosemary and Garlic, reducing the wine to ¾ cup and omitting the shallot, chicken stock, and butter. When the pork has roasted 15 minutes, quarter 2 pounds 2½-inch red potatoes; toss the potatoes with 2 tablespoons olive oil in a medium bowl and season generously with salt and pepper to taste. After the pork has been roasting for 30 minutes, add the potatoes to the roasting pan; stir to coat the potatoes with the pan juices. After transferring the roast to a carving board, turn the potato pieces with a wide metal spatula and spread them in an even layer. Increase the oven temperature to 400 degrees, return the potatoes to the oven, and continue to roast until tender and browned, 5 to 15 minutes longer. Serve the potatoes with the roast.

Tuscan-Style Roast Pork Loin with Fennel

Fennel is a common addition to the classic garlic-rosemary flavored pork roast. Fennel seeds and the delicate, wispy fronds are used in the paste, and fennel bulbs are roasted in the pan alongside the pork.

1. Trim 2 medium fennel bulbs of stalks and fronds; finely chop 2 teaspoons fronds. Cut each bulb lengthwise into eighths. Toss the fennel with 1 tablespoon olive oil in a medium bowl and season generously with salt and pepper to taste.

2. Follow the recipe for Tuscan-Style Roast Pork Loin with Garlic and Rosemary, adding 1 teaspoon finely chopped fennel seeds and the chopped fennel fronds to the garlic-rosemary paste. Reduce the wine to ¾ cup and omit

the shallot, chicken broth, and butter. Add the fennel to the roasting pan along with the wine. After transferring the roast to the carving board, return the fennel to the oven and continue to roast until tender, 5 to 15 minutes. Serve the fennel with the roast.

GRILLED LAMB CHOPS

ITALIANS ENJOY LAMB IN A VARIETY OF forms. Braised shanks are popular winter fare (see recipe on page 325), and a whole roasted baby lamb is traditional at Easter. Grilled chops are a favorite summertime dish; this is perhaps the easiest way to make lamb at home.

Lamb chops don't have to be a rare (and expensive) treat. True, loin and rib chops (together, the eight rib chops form the cut known as rack of lamb) can cost upward of $14 a pound. But we love the meaty flavor and chewy (but not tough) texture of shoulder chops (see page 320 for more information). We also like that they cost only about $4 per pound.

In a side-by-side taste test, we grilled loin, rib, and shoulder chops to medium-rare and let them stand about 5 minutes before tasting. The rib chop was the most refined of the three, with a mild, almost sweet flavor and tender texture. The loin chop had a slightly stronger flavor, and the texture was a bit firmer (but not chewier) than the rib chop. The shoulder chop had a distinctly gutsier flavor than the other two. While it was not at all tough, it was chewier. If you like the flavor of lamb (and we do) and are trying to keep within a budget, then try shoulder chops.

We also tried a second test in which we grilled the chops to medium, a stage at which many people prefer lamb. Both the rib and

Shoulder Lamb Chops

Lamb shoulder is sliced into two cuts, blade and round-bone chops. You'll find them sold in a range of thicknesses (from about ½ inch to more than 1 inch thick), depending on who's doing the butchering. (In our experience, supermarkets tend to cut them thinner, while independent butchers cut them thicker.) Blade chops are roughly rectangular in shape, and some are thickly striated with fat. Each blade chop includes a piece of the chine bone (the backbone) and a thin piece of the blade bone (the shoulder blade).

Round-bone chops, also called arm chops, are more oval in shape and, as a rule, are substantially leaner than blade chops. Each contains a round cross-section of the arm bone so that the chop looks a bit like a small ham steak. In addition to the arm bone, there's also a tiny line of riblets on the side of each chop.

As to which type is better, we didn't find any difference in taste or texture between the two except that blade chops generally have more fat. We grill both blade and round-bone chops. We like the way the fat in the blade chop melts on the grill, flavoring and moistening the meat, and we love the grilled riblets from the round bone chop.

BLADE CHOP

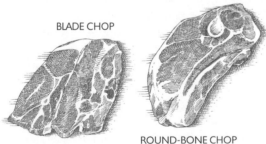

ROUND-BONE CHOP

There are two kinds of lamb shoulder chops. The blade chop (left) is roughly rectangular in shape and contains a piece of the chine bone and a thin piece of the blade bone. The arm, or round-bone, chop (right) is leaner and contains a round cross-section of the arm bone. The extra fat in blade chops melts on the grill, flavoring and moistening the meat. The arm bone chop has a tiny line of delicious riblets on the side of each chop. Either chop takes well to grilling.

loin chops were dry and less flavorful and juicy than they were at medium-rare. The shoulder chop held its own in both taste and texture, displaying another advantage besides price.

Shoulder chops can range in thickness from ½ to 1 inch. We prefer the thicker chops, and you should ask your butcher to cut them for you if necessary. Loin and rib chops are usually thicker, often close to 1½ inches.

In our testing, we found that all of these chops should be cooked over a two-level fire to bring the inside up to temperature without charring the exterior. A two-level fire also makes sense because lamb tends to flame; drag the chops to the cooler part of the grill and wait for the flames to die down. Even when cooking thinner chops, we found that the flames often became too intense on a single-level fire. A squirt bottle filled with water is a handy item to keep near the grill.

Charcoal-Grilled Shoulder Lamb Chops
SERVES 4

Try to get shoulder lamb chops that are at least ¾ inch thick, as they are less likely to overcook. If you can only find chops that are ½ inch thick, reduce the cooking time over the medium-low fire by about 30 seconds on each side. See left for information about the different kinds of shoulder chops.

4	shoulder lamb chops (blade or round bone), ¾ to 1 inch thick
2	tablespoons extra-virgin olive oil
	Salt and ground black pepper

1. Light a large chimney starter filled with hardwood charcoal (about 2½ pounds) and allow it to burn until all the charcoal is covered with a layer of fine gray ash. Build a two-

level fire by stacking most of the coals on one side of the grill for a medium-hot fire. Arrange the remaining coals in a single layer on the other side of the grill for a medium-low fire. Set the cooking rack in place, cover the grill with the lid, and let the rack heat, about 5 minutes. Use a wire brush to scrape clean the rack.

2. Rub the chops with oil and sprinkle with salt and pepper to taste.

3. Grill the chops, uncovered, over the hotter part of the grill, turning them once, until well browned, 4 minutes. (If the chops start to flame, drag them to the cooler part of the grill and/or extinguish the flames with a squirt bottle.) Move the chops to the cooler part of the grill and continue grilling, turning once, to the desired doneness, about 5 minutes for rare (about 120 degrees on an instant-read thermometer), about 7 minutes for medium (about 130 degrees), or about 9 minutes for well done (140 to 150 degrees).

4. Remove the chops from the grill and let rest for 5 minutes. Serve immediately.

➤ VARIATIONS
Gas-Grilled Shoulder Lamb Chops
SERVES 4
To make sure that your lamb chops aren't flaming up under the grill cover, watch for substantial smoke coming through the vents. This indicates that flare-ups are occurring and must be extinguished.

Turn all burners on a gas grill to high, close the lid, and heat until very hot, about 15 minutes. Scrape the cooking grate clean with a wire brush; leave one burner on high and turn the other burner(s) down to medium. Follow the recipe for Charcoal-Grilled Shoulder Lamb Chops, beginning with step 2 and cooking with the lid down. You may need to increase the cooking time on the cooler side of the grill by a minute or so.

Grilled Shoulder Lamb Chops with Garlic and Rosemary
Garlic and rosemary are classic accompaniments with lamb.

Combine 2 tablespoons extra-virgin olive oil, 2 large garlic cloves, minced very fine or put through a press, 1 tablespoon minced fresh rosemary leaves, and a pinch cayenne pepper in a small bowl. Follow the recipe for Charcoal-Grilled or Gas-Grilled Lamb Chops, rubbing the chops with the garlic-rosemary mixture instead of plain olive oil. Marinate in the refrigerator for at least 20 minutes or up to 1 day. Sprinkle the chops with salt and pepper and grill as directed.

Charcoal-Grilled Loin or Rib Lamb Chops
SERVES 4
While loin and rib chops are especially tender cuts of lamb, they tend to dry out if cooked past medium because they have less intramuscular fat than shoulder chops. To make these chops worth their high price, keep an eye on the grill to make sure the meat does not overcook. These chops are smaller than shoulder chops; you will need two for each serving.

8   loin or rib lamb chops, 1¼ to 1½ inches thick
2   tablespoons extra-virgin olive oil
     Salt and ground black pepper

1. Light a large chimney starter filled with hardwood charcoal (about 2½ pounds) and allow it to burn until all the charcoal is covered with a layer of fine gray ash. Build a two-level fire by stacking most of the coals on one side of the grill for a medium-hot fire. Arrange the remaining coals in a single layer on the other side of the grill for a medium-low fire. Set the cooking rack in place, cover the grill with the

lid, and let the rack heat, about 5 minutes. Use a wire brush to scrape clean the rack.

2. Rub the chops with the oil and sprinkle with salt and pepper to taste.

3. Grill the chops, uncovered, over the hotter part of the grill, turning them once, until well browned, 4 minutes. (If the chops start to flame, drag them to the cooler part of the grill for a moment and/or extinguish the flames with a squirt bottle.) Move the chops to the cooler part of the grill and continue grilling, turning once, to the desired doneness, about 6 minutes for rare (about 120 on an instant-read thermometer) or about 8 minutes for medium (about 130 degrees).

4. Remove the chops from the grill and let rest for 5 minutes. Serve immediately.

➤ VARIATIONS

Gas-Grilled Loin or Rib Lamb Chops

SERVES 4

With the cover down, it can be hard to detect flames. Watch for excessive smoking and extinguish flames with a squirt bottle as soon as they erupt.

Turn all burners on a gas grill to high, close the lid, and heat until very hot, about 15 minutes. Scrape the cooking grate clean with a wire brush; leave one burner on high and turn the other burner(s) down to medium. Follow the recipe for Charcoal-Grilled Loin or Rib Lamb Chops, beginning with step 2 and cooking with the lid down. You may need to increase the cooking time on the cooler side of the grill by a minute or so.

Grilled Loin or Rib Lamb Chops with Herbs and Garlic

Combine 1 tablespoon chopped fresh parsley leaves, 2 teaspoons each chopped fresh sage, thyme, rosemary, and oregano leaves, 3 minced garlic cloves, and ¼ cup extra-virgin olive oil in a small bowl. Follow the recipe for Charcoal-Grilled or Gas-Grilled Loin or Rib Lamb Chops, rubbing the chops with the herb paste instead of oil. Marinate for at least 20 minutes or up to 1 day in the refrigerator. Sprinkle with salt and pepper and grill as directed.

PARMESAN-BREADED LAMB CHOPS

THIS EMBLEMATIC ITALIAN DISH IS savored throughout Italy and can be easily, elegantly, and authentically reproduced at home. The idea and the execution are quite simple. Take the finest lamb chops, coat them with Parmesan cheese and bread crumbs, and sauté the breaded chops until the coating turns golden brown and crisp. At $14 to $16 per pound for lamb, there is almost no entrée so costly to prepare. After making it numerous times, our conclusion is that it is more than worth the price. But if you don't follow some basic rules, you can make costly mistakes along the way.

There was no question that a dish of this delicacy needed the youngest and smallest loin or rib chops we could find; such chops are more widely available at butchers and natural foods markets than at grocery stores. While many of the recipes we saw in Italian books called for flattening the lamb chops, we discovered that it was not necessary with the single-rib chops less than 1 inch thick. However, it is essential to buy chops of the same thickness so that they will cook consistently. When we bought chops of different sizes, we ended up with some perfectly cooked chops and some that were either overcooked or undercooked.

For this recipe, the lamb chops are prepared in the classic breading style (first dredged in flour, then dipped in eggs and then in bread crumbs)—except here, true to the tradition of the recipe, we dusted them with finely grated Parmesan cheese instead of flour. After almost grinding Parmesan cheese into butter in the food processor, we realized that it needed to be grated by hand with either a microplane or a box grater in order to get the cheese fine enough. We did try coating the chops with the coarser Parmesan and, although we liked it, all the tasters preferred the delicacy of more finely grated cheese. We determined that ½ cup of cheese was enough to coat lightly 12 chops. (Because these chops are so thin, tasters agreed that three chops, rather than the standard two, made a generous serving.)

After determining the right amount of cheese, our next task was to work on the bread crumbs. As we expected, dry bread crumbs did not do justice to the lamb. Fresh homemade crumbs are a must here. Toasting the crumbs first didn't work, as we were then essentially retoasting and therefore burning them when we cooked the chops—yet we found the fresh bread crumbs a tad bland. Adding more Parmesan cheese to the crumbs produced a burnt crust, whereas the addition of rosemary and mint, classically paired with lamb, enhanced the dish and made it more striking.

LOIN AND RIB LAMB CHOPS

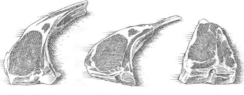

RIB CHOP   FRENCHED   LOIN CHOP
            RIB CHOP

A rib chop often contains a lot of fat on the bone. Have your butcher french the chop by scraping away this fat. Like a T-bone steak, a loin chop has meat on either side of the bone. The small piece on the right side of the bone is very tender and fine-grained. The larger piece of meat on the other side of the bone is chewier.

Last, we found it essential to let the chops rest after being breaded. When we sautéed the chops right away parts of the coating peeled off, taking with them flavor and beauty. When we let the chops rest, refrigerated, for as little as ½ hour and as much as 4 hours, the coating stayed on, producing a tastier and more attractive dish. The succulent and delicate chops had a crisp crust and a tender and slightly pink interior.

The actual cooking procedure turned out to be quite simple. The chops should be sautéed in enough oil to come halfway up their sides. A 12-inch skillet can accommodate six chops and requires 4 tablespoons of oil. For the best results, the oil should be very hot before the chops are added. Cooking time is just five minutes. As for serving the chops, we could find nothing to beat the classic choice—lemon wedges.

Parmesan-Breaded Lamb Chops

SERVES 4

Make sure the oil is good and hot before adding the chops. You want them to brown quickly because these thin chops will overcook if left in the pan too long.

½	cup finely grated Parmesan cheese
2	large eggs
1	tablespoon plus ½ cup extra-virgin olive oil
1½	cups fresh bread crumbs (page 57)
1	teaspoon finely chopped fresh rosemary leaves
2	teaspoons finely chopped fresh mint leaves
12	loin or rib lamb chops, ¾ to 1 inch thick
½	teaspoon salt
¼	teaspoon ground black pepper
1	lemon, cut into wedges

1. Place the cheese in a shallow dish or pie plate. Beat the eggs and 1 tablespoon oil in a second shallow dish. Combine the bread crumbs, rosemary, and mint in a third shallow dish. Sprinkle the chops with the salt and pepper.

2. Working with one at a time, dredge the chops in the cheese, patting them to make the cheese adhere. Using tongs, dip both sides of the chops in the eggs, taking care to coat thoroughly and allowing the excess to drip back into the dish to ensure a very thin coating. Dip both sides of the chops in the bread crumb mixture, pressing the crumbs with your fingers to form an even, cohesive coat. Place the breaded chops in a single layer on a wire rack set over a baking sheet and refrigerate for at least 30 minutes or up to 4 hours.

3. Adjust an oven rack to lower-middle position, set a large heatproof platter on the rack, and heat the oven to 200 degrees.

4. Heat ¼ cup oil in a 12-inch nonstick skillet over medium-high heat until it is shimmering but not quite smoking. Add half the chops (the oil should go halfway up the chops) and cook, turning once, until well browned on both sides and medium-rare in the center (the internal temperature should register 125 degrees on an instant-read thermometer), about 5 minutes. Line the heated platter with paper towels, transfer the chops to the platter, and keep them warm in the oven.

5. Discard the used oil. Wipe the skillet clean using tongs and a large wad of paper towels. Repeat step 4, using the remaining ¼ cup oil and the now-clean skillet to cook the remaining chops. Blot the second batch of chops with paper towels. Serve immediately along with first batch, with lemon wedges.

BRAISED LAMB SHANKS

ITALIANS ARE MASTERS AT TURNING relatively tough cuts of meat into meltingly tender dishes. Among the most richly flavored of these tougher cuts is the lamb shank, which is simply the bottom portion of the fore or hind leg of a lamb.

Like other cuts of meat that come from the joints of animals, such as oxtails or short ribs, lamb shanks are extremely flavorful when properly cooked. This is because they contain a high proportion of connective tissue and fat, which break down during cooking and add flavor to the meat.

However, the presence of all this connective tissue and fat means that shanks can only be cooked using a long, slow, moist cooking method that will cause the connective tissue to disintegrate and render the fat without drying out the meat. The only practical cooking method for achieving this goal is braising, which means cooking the meat partially covered in liquid, usually in a closed container. Braising keeps the temperature of the meat relatively low—around the boiling point of water—for a long period, which is exactly what is needed to convert the tough collagen to tender gelatin.

While we obtained satisfactory results by braising shanks on top of the stove, we preferred braising in an oven because of its unique heating properties. With the heat coming from all directions, the meat cooks more evenly. This is a particular advantage, given that many pans have hot spots that cause them to heat unevenly on a burner.

Because of the high fat content of this cut, several straightforward precautions are necessary to keep the level of fat in the final product to a minimum. First, if your butcher has not already done so, take the time to trim the lamb shanks of the excess fat that encases the meat. Even a long, slow braise will not successfully render all of the exterior fat on a lamb shank. Trimming it helps you get a jump on that potential problem.

Browning the shanks well before braising them also helps render some of the exterior fat. Browning also offers the advantage of providing a great deal of flavor to the dish. Be sure to drain the fat from the pan after browning.

The third important step is to remove the fat from the braising liquid after the shanks have been cooked. To do this, take the shanks out of the braising liquid, strain out the vegetables, and allow the sauce to rest undisturbed for a short while. Then, using a ladle, carefully skim the fat that has risen to the surface and discard it. This process can be facilitated by transferring the sauce to a taller, narrower container before setting it aside to rest. If, after skimming the liquid, you find that it still has too much fat, you may repeat this step after 10 more minutes, although with most shanks, this will not be necessary. Further, if the braise is prepared well in advance of serving, you may refrigerate the braising liquid, then simply lift the solidified fat from the top of the liquid.

The braising liquid, along with the aromatics you add to it, will greatly enhance the flavor of the entire dish. Stock is the traditional braising liquid because it adds textural richness as well as depth of flavor. We recommend using chicken stock in the braise rather than beef or veal stock, because we found that these heartier stocks compete with the flavor of the lamb and tend to make the sauce overly rich. A good chicken stock will complement the flavor of the lamb shanks.

Wine is a particularly good addition to the braising liquid, adding complexity and acid to the sauce. The acid is particularly important because of the richness of the lamb. Too little acid creates a dull, rather flat-tasting dish. On the other hand, too much acid results in a harsh, off-putting flavor. After trying different ratios, we found that 2 parts wine to 3 parts stock gives the best flavor.

We found that either white wine or red works well, the difference being that red wine will give you a richer, deeper finish. You may also vary the choice of herbs and spices according to your taste; in the following recipes, we have included suggestions.

Whatever liquid you use for braising, we discovered, it should cover all but the top inch of the shanks. This differs somewhat from classic braising, in which only a small amount of liquid is used. We adopted this method after leaving shanks braising in the oven, then returning some time later to find that the liquid had boiled away and the shanks were burned. Unless you are using a true braising pan with an extremely tight-fitting lid, a fair amount of liquid will escape. Using more liquid prevents the pan from drying out, no matter how loose the seal is.

Lamb shanks need not be served whole, though we prefer them this way for their dramatic appeal. Once the shanks are cooked and cooled, you may remove the meat from the bone before reincorporating it with the vegetables and sauce. The resulting stew-type dish will be less dramatic in presentation but equally delicious.

Lamb Shanks Braised in Red Wine

SERVES 6

If you're using smaller shanks than the ones called for in this recipe, reduce the braising time from 1½ hours to 1 hour. Serve braised shanks over mashed potatoes or polenta. If you prefer, prepare the recipe through step 3, then cool and refrigerate the shanks and braising liquid (still in the pot) overnight. When ready to serve, skim the congealed fat from the surface of the pot and warm over medium heat.

1	tablespoon extra-virgin olive oil
6	(¾- to 1-pound) lamb shanks, trimmed of excess fat
	Salt and ground black pepper
2	medium onions, sliced thick
3	medium carrots, cut crosswise into 2-inch pieces
2	celery stalks, cut crosswise into 2-inch pieces
4	medium cloves garlic, peeled
2	tablespoons tomato paste
2	teaspoons minced fresh thyme leaves
2	teaspoons minced fresh rosemary leaves
2	cups dry red wine
3	cups homemade chicken stock or canned low-sodium chicken broth

1. Adjust an oven rack to the lower-middle position and heat the oven to 350 degrees. Heat the oil in a large ovenproof Dutch oven over medium-high heat until it is shimmering. Meanwhile, sprinkle both sides of the shanks generously with salt and pepper. Swirl to coat the pan bottom with the oil. Place 3 shanks in a single layer in the pan and cook, turning once, until they are nicely browned all over, about 7 minutes. Transfer the shanks to a plate and set aside. Brown the remaining shanks and transfer them to the plate.

2. Drain all but 2 tablespoons fat from the pot. Add the onions, carrots, celery, garlic, tomato paste, herbs, and a light sprinkling of salt. Cook until the vegetables soften slightly, 3 to 4 minutes. Add the wine, then the stock, stirring with a wooden spoon to loosen the browned bits from the bottom of the pan. Bring the liquid to a simmer. Add the shanks and season with salt and pepper to taste.

3. Cover and transfer the pot to the oven. Braise the shanks for 1½ hours. Uncover and continue braising until the shank tops are browned, about 30 minutes. Turn the shanks and braise until the other side is browned and the shanks are fall-off-the-bone tender, 15 to 30 minutes longer.

4. Remove the pot from the oven and let the shanks rest in the sauce for at least 15 minutes. With tongs, carefully transfer the shanks to individual plates. Arrange a portion of the vegetables around each shank. With a spoon, skim the excess fat from the braising liquid and adjust the seasonings. Spoon some braising liquid over each shank and serve immediately.

➤ VARIATION

Braised Lamb Shanks with Lemon and Mint

Grate the zest from 1 lemon, then cut the lemon in quarters. Follow the recipe for Lamb Shanks Braised in Red Wine, replacing the thyme and rosemary with 1 tablespoon fresh mint leaves and replacing the red wine with white wine. Add the quartered lemon to the braising liquid. Proceed as directed, stirring the lemon zest and an additional 1 tablespoon minced fresh mint leaves into the sauce just before serving.

9

FISH AND SHELLFISH

AS A COOK MIGHT EXPECT, ITALIANS stress simplicity and freshness in their seafood preparations. Recipes can be as basic as a grilled whole sea bass or red snapper flavored with nothing more than extra-virgin olive oil, salt, pepper, and lemon. Even more complex recipes, such as Sicilian fish stew with tomatoes, capers, olives, pine nuts, and raisins, go together rather quickly and easily.

Because Italy is surrounded by water, seafood plays a major role in the local diet. Each region has its own specialties, many based on fish or shellfish available only in that area. As a result, these dishes are not easily reproduced in other parts of Italy, let alone other parts of the world. For this reason, we have chosen dishes that rely on widely available fish and shellfish and other ingredients available to American cooks.

Two important seafood-based dishes—linguine with clam sauce and seafood risotto—appear elsewhere in this book. See the pasta and risotto chapters for these recipes. A recipe for stuffed clams appears in the antipasto chapter and one for mussel soup in chapter 4.

FISH IN "CRAZY WATER"

PESCE ALL'ACQUA PAZZA IS ONE OF the more evocatively named Italian dishes. The name literally translates as "fish in crazy water." While romantic (with many a story behind it), the title does little to define the dish, which is fish simmered in a tomato-laced broth. Like many Italian standards, acqua pazza is made with simple ingredients readily at hand and intuitively combined.

The older recipes we researched included little more than fish, water, salt, and a tomato or two. The impeccable flavor of the just-caught fish needed little improvement. Through the

years, however, the recipe has become more elaborate, with some recipes including everything from wine and herbs to a list of fish rivaling bouillabaisse's lengthy roster. While the primitive versions left us wanting, the upscale versions were over the top, mocking the simple roots of this dish. We hoped to strike a happy medium that was refined and let the flavor of the fish shine without a long list of ingredients.

The first step was choosing the fish. Small whole fish are traditional, as the heads and bones lend deep flavor and rich collagen to the broth. Unfortunately, whole fish, besides trout, are hard to find in most American markets, and trout are too soft-fleshed to be simmered. Fillets would have to do the trick, so we turned to semifirm and firm fish that would withstand the rigors of simmering. Oily fish, like salmon and bluefish, were out of the question, as their potent flavor overpowered the broth. Monkfish, a fish touted in several sources, turned rubbery. In the end, red snapper proved the best choice, although halibut, sea bass, and grouper all worked as well. We found that large fillets held up best during simmering (to be portioned after cooking), and leaving the skin on was crucial to prevent the fish from falling apart.

A *soffritto* (aromatics sautéed in olive oil) of garlic and red onion laid a solid foundation for the broth, which must be prepared before the fish goes into the pan. For the tomato element, we found that both halved cherry tomatoes and canned diced tomatoes had their merits. Cherry or grape tomatoes are the authentic choice and gave the dish a decidedly rustic appearance, but ripe, sweet tomatoes are not always available. Using canned tomatoes guaranteed dependable flavor.

Despite its name, acqua pazza needs a more flavorful liquid than plain water. Without the fish heads and bones lending flavor, the broth lacked body. White wine added just the right note, providing depth to the dish without overwhelming the other flavors the way bottled clam juice did. To add an herbal presence to the broth, tasters favored parsley and oregano. We found that simmering herb sprigs in the broth added plenty of flavor without the effort of mincing. A mere 10-minute simmer married the flavors in the broth while maintaining the bright, fresh appeal of the tomatoes.

Cooking the fish could not have been any easier. We gently slid the fillets into the skillet (skin side down to keep the flesh from falling apart) and piled the onion slices and tomatoes on top to help flavor the flesh. We put the cover on the skillet and simmered until the fish was just done, about 10 minutes. The fish absorbed the heady flavor of the broth, and the broth was enriched by the fish. With garlicky crostini to soak up the broth, dinner was served.

Fish in "Crazy Water"
SERVES 4

If you choose cherry tomatoes, use the ripest ones you can find. If they are not perfectly ripe, you may need to balance their acidity with some sugar. Taste the broth right before adding the fish and add ½ teaspoon sugar if it tastes too harsh. Although we included only a modest amount of hot red pepper flakes, feel free to add more to suit personal preferences. (Some sources suggested that "crazy water" was actually a reference to the broth's spiciness.) We like to serve this dish in wide, shallow bowls that will accommodate both the fish and the broth. We rest the fish on top of crostini, which soak up the flavorful broth and add a bit of heft to this otherwise light dish.

4	stems parsley, plus 1 tablespoon minced fresh leaves
2	sprigs fresh oregano
2	tablespoons extra-virgin olive oil
2	medium cloves garlic, sliced thin
¼	teaspoon hot red pepper flakes
1	small red onion, halved through root end and sliced thin
	Salt
1	(14½-ounce) can diced tomatoes, drained, or 1½ cups lightly packed cherry tomatoes, halved
1	cup dry white wine
2	large skin-on red snapper fillets (each about 1 pound)
	Ground black pepper
1	small lemon, cut into wedges
1	recipe Crostini for Soup (page 123)

1. Tie together the parsley stems and oregano sprigs with a short piece of kitchen twine. Heat the oil, garlic, and hot red pepper flakes in a 12-inch skillet over medium-high heat. As the oil begins to sizzle, shake the pan back and forth so that the garlic does not stick (stirring with a wooden spoon will cause the garlic to clump). Once the garlic turns pale gold, about 2 to 2½ minutes, add the onion and ½ teaspoon salt and cook, stirring frequently, until the onion is translucent and lightly browned, 3 to 4 minutes. Add the tomatoes, wine, herb bundle, and 2 cups water and bring to a boil. Reduce the heat to medium and simmer until the flavors have blended, about 10 minutes.

2. Gently slide the fish fillets, skin side down, into the liquid. With tongs, arrange the onion slices and tomatoes over the fish. Reduce the heat to low, cover, and simmer until the fish is cooked through and just beginning to flake, about 10 minutes. Sprinkle the minced parsley over the fish and season the broth with salt and black pepper to taste. With the edge of a spatula, cut each fillet into two portions.

3. Place one crostini in the center of each individual serving bowl, set a piece of fish on each crostini, then ladle some broth over the top. Serve immediately, passing the lemon wedges and extra crostini at the table.

ROASTED SEA BASS WITH WILD MUSHROOMS

WHILE NOT THE FIRST COMBINATION that comes to the mind, fish and mushrooms work surprisingly well together. Italians routinely combine them, usually pairing mild, flaky fish with robust wild mushrooms, especially porcini. Mushrooms have an almost winey, tart finish that accents the flavor of the fish, much as lemon juice or a splash of vinegar does. The combination is also a study in contrasts: The oceanic, briny fish is set in sharp relief against the earthy mushrooms. Our goal was to find the best way to marry the flavors of fish and mushrooms and the simplest method for roasting the fish.

We started with the choice of fish. In Italy, this dish would most likely be made with *branzino*, or sea bass. We tried this mild, flaky fish, and tasters felt that its delicate texture was less than ideal in this dish. In addition, European sea bass (which is also caught in Atlantic waters off the United States) is not always available. We wanted to try other options.

A dozen fish later, we made this conclusion: For the sharpest contrast between the flavor and texture of the fish and mushrooms, a mild-flavored, firm-bodied fish is the best choice. Strong-tasting oily fish, such as mackerel, bluefish, and salmon, overpowered the mushrooms. Flaky, tender fish, such as red snapper, lacked enough presence to stand up to the mushrooms. Halibut, cod, and even swordfish were passable in this dish, but Chilean sea bass was perfect. Texturally speaking, Chilean sea bass is akin to salmon. When cooked, it divides into large, firm, moist flakes, not dry, small flakes like European sea bass. The mouthfeel of this rich fish is reminiscent of beef tenderloin. The chewy mushrooms were a perfect complement. As for its flavor, Chilean sea bass is oily but much milder than salmon. As we discovered during testing, Chilean sea bass is surprisingly forgiving; a minute or two extra cooking won't ruin it.

Chilean sea bass tastes best thoroughly cooked. Unlike salmon and tuna, which are at their finest with a translucent core, Chilean sea bass must be well cooked to release its light flavor and buttery texture. We found recipes that roasted the fish at temperatures ranging from 375 degrees to 500 degrees. The lower temperatures yielded much drier fish than the high temperatures, although 500 degrees overcooked the exterior before the interior was finished. A little less heat, 475 degrees, proved accurate, yielding perfectly cooked bass at about 10 minutes per inch of thickness—the standard cooking time advocated by most seafood experts. A thin coating of olive oil protected the exterior from drying out, and a liberal coating of salt and ground black pepper sharpened the mild fish flavor.

Wild mushrooms are traditional in this dish, but we found them hard to come by and prohibitively expensive when we could find them. Fortunately, dried porcini mushrooms can infuse even the mildest mushrooms with woodsy, deep flavor reminiscent of fresh (and pricey) exotica. The dried porcini flavor is potent; as little as $\frac{1}{3}$ ounce can add intensity to a large skillet of fresh mushrooms. For a mixture of shapes and textures, we chose both cremini and portobello mushrooms. They have a fuller flavor than white button mushrooms, at only a slight premium. We cooked the mushrooms over relatively high heat with a mixture of butter and olive oil for depth of flavor and butter's browning abilities. For seasoning, garlic and rosemary were a natural combination. Despite rosemary's penetrating pine flavor, Italians regularly combine it with seafood to great effect.

At first, we roasted the fish as the mushrooms sautéed, but cooking the two components separately led to a finished dish lacking unity. It then occurred to us that we could treat the dish as a pan roast and cook the fish and mushrooms together so that their flavors would blend better. We simply added the fish to the sautéed mushrooms in the hot skillet and slid the pan into the oven. The overall flavor was markedly improved; the fish was imbued with a hit of the mushrooms and vice versa. We did find that the mushrooms dried out in the high heat, but adding the liquid used to rehydrate the dried porcini prevented this. As a bonus, in the oven this liquid boiled down to a light, flavorful sauce.

Roasted Sea Bass with Wild Mushrooms

SERVES 4

Chilean sea bass is available cut into a variety of shapes and sizes. For this dish, skinless fillets about 1½ inches thick are the best choice; the center of each fillet will cook through without the edges drying out. Avoid pieces that are much thicker. Make sure the pieces are relatively square and avoid tail end pieces, as they cook too quickly. Although Chilean sea bass is resistant to overcooking, it is not impervious; pay close attention to the clock and check the fish as needed. As with roasted meats and poultry, the fish will continue to cook from residual heat once removed from the oven, so remove the skillet from the oven when the fish is just shy of perfectly cooked. See the illustrations on page 5 for tips on rehydrating dried porcini mushrooms.

⅓	ounce dried porcini mushrooms
2	tablespoons unsalted butter
2	tablespoons extra-virgin olive oil, plus additional for fish
1	sprig fresh rosemary
1	small red onion, halved through the root end and sliced thin
1	pound portobello mushrooms, stems removed, caps halved and cut into ½-inch-thick slices
1	pound cremini mushrooms, halved
	Salt
2	medium cloves garlic, minced or pressed through a garlic press
	Ground black pepper
4	skinless fillets Chilean sea bass, each about 1½ inches thick (about 1½ pounds total)
1	tablespoon minced fresh parsley leaves
1	small lemon, cut into wedges

1. Mix the dried porcini mushrooms with ½ cup hot tap water in a small microwave-safe bowl. Cover with plastic wrap, cut several steam vents in the plastic wrap with a paring knife, and microwave on high power for 30 seconds. Let stand until the mushrooms soften, about 5 minutes. Lift the mushrooms from the liquid with a fork and mince. Pour the liquid through a small strainer lined with a single sheet of paper towel and placed over a measuring cup.

2. Adjust an oven rack to the lower-middle position and heat the oven to 475 degrees. Heat the butter, olive oil, and rosemary in an ovenproof 12-inch skillet over medium-high heat until the foaming subsides. Add the onion, fresh mushrooms, and ½ teaspoon salt. Cook, stirring occasionally, until the mushrooms have shed their liquid and their cut surfaces have browned, 8 to 10 minutes. Reduce the heat to medium-low and add the garlic and minced porcini. Cook, stirring frequently, until aromatic, about 1 minute. Remove the pan from the heat and season the vegetables with salt and pepper to taste.

3. Using a wooden spoon, clear 4 spaces in the skillet for the fish fillets. (The spaces should

be equidistant from one another so that the fillets don't touch.) Rub each fillet with enough oil to coat lightly and sprinkle generously with salt and pepper to taste. Nestle one fillet into each space in the skillet. Drizzle the reserved porcini liquid over the mushrooms (avoiding the fish) and immediately set the pan in the oven. Cook until the fish is opaque and cooked through, 11 to 12 minutes. Sprinkle with the parsley. Divide the mushrooms among individual plates and place a piece of fish on top of the mushrooms on each plate. Drizzle the fish with any juices remaining in the pan as well as a little olive oil. Serve immediately with lemon wedges.

GRILLED SWORDFISH SKEWERS WITH SALMORIGLIO SAUCE

CONSIDERED ONE OF THE ESSENTIAL sauces of Sicilian cookery, *salmoriglio* is a potent dressing composed of extra-virgin olive oil, lemon juice, and abundant amounts of fresh oregano. It is the traditional accompaniment to grilled fish, especially swordfish, on which it is liberally slathered once the fish is removed from the fire. The residual heat of the fish "cooks" the sauce, releasing an intoxicating aroma and rich flavor.

Although this sauce is traditionally used with swordfish steaks, we wanted to adapt it for use with kebabs. We like swordfish kebabs better than steaks because there is more surface area for caramelization. In addition, swordfish is ideal for kebabs because the flesh is firm and has a steaklike quality. Because this fish is cut into small pieces (we found that 1-inch chunks are ideal), it cooks quickly and does not dry out. We found that coating the

fish with olive oil helps keep it moist, too.

Although thick swordfish steaks are best grilled over a two-level fire, we found that skewers can be cooked over a medium-hot single-level fire. Turning the skewers every two minutes or so ensures that all sides of the swordfish cubes have a chance to face the fire. Oiling the grill rack is also essential to prevent the fish from sticking. Unlike salmon and tuna, swordfish should be cooked until medium—no more, no less. Even when cooked to medium, swordfish kebabs are done in just seven minutes.

For such a simple sauce, we were surprised to find a variety of recipes for salmoriglio. The core ingredients—olive oil, lemon juice, and oregano—were unvarying, but some recipes included additional herbs, such as parsley and mint. We found the simplest version the best; the other versions were not unpleasant, but the unmitigated force of the oregano was refreshing. Garlic was another variable that we did like; its pungent taste and aroma lent depth and body to the sauce.

Although a mortar and pestle are the traditional tools for combining the sauce, we found that a food processor works just as well with a fraction of the effort. Some versions whisk the sauce over low heat to encourage emulsification, but we found this step unnecessary.

Charcoal-Grilled Swordfish Skewers with Salmoriglio Sauce
SERVES 4

As soon as the fish is removed from the grill, liberally brush the sauce over it. The heat "cooks" the sauce, releasing a heady aroma that is hard to resist. If you have extra sauce, pass it at the table. While salmoriglio sauce is traditional on swordfish, it works equally well on other firm white fish as well as grilled chicken.

SALMORIGLIO SAUCE

1	medium clove garlic, coarsely chopped
2	tablespoons lemon juice
¼	teaspoon salt
¼	teaspoon coarsely ground black pepper
3	tablespoons packed fresh oregano leaves
½	cup extra-virgin olive oil

SWORDFISH SKEWERS

2	(1-inch-thick) swordfish steaks (about 2 pounds total), skin removed, cut into 1-inch cubes
3	tablespoons extra-virgin olive oil
	Salt and ground black pepper
	Vegetable oil for grill rack

1. FOR THE SAUCE: Place the garlic, lemon juice, salt, pepper, and oregano in the workbowl of a food processor fitted with a steel blade. Process, scraping down the sides of the bowl as necessary, until the garlic and oregano are finely chopped, 30 seconds. With the motor running, pour the oil through the feed tube in a slow, steady stream and process until the sauce is thoroughly combined, about 30 seconds. Scrape the sauce into a small bowl, cover, and set aside at room temperature until needed.

2. FOR THE FISH: Toss the swordfish cubes and olive oil in a large bowl. Season with salt and pepper to taste. Thread the swordfish onto skewers.

3. Meanwhile, light a large chimney starter filled with hardwood charcoal (about 2½ pounds) and allow it to burn until all the charcoal is covered with a layer of fine gray ash. Build a single-level fire by spreading the coals evenly over the bottom of the grill for a medium-hot fire. Set the cooking rack in place, cover the grill with the lid, and let the rack heat, about 5 minutes. Use a wire brush to scrape the rack clean. Lightly dip a small wad of paper towels in vegetable oil. Holding the wad with tongs, wipe the rack.

4. Grill the swordfish skewers, uncovered, giving each a one-quarter turn every 1¾ minutes, until the center of the swordfish is no longer translucent, about 7 minutes. Transfer the skewers to a serving platter and liberally brush them with the sauce. Serve immediately, passing any extra sauce at the table.

➤ VARIATION

Gas-Grilled Swordfish Skewers

To keep the heat from dissipating, work quickly when you open the lid to turn the kebabs.

Preheat the grill with all burners set to high and the lid down until very hot, about 15 minutes. Use a wire brush to scrape the cooking grate clean. Leave all burners on high. Follow the recipe for Charcoal-Grilled Swordfish Skewers with Salmoriglio Sauce, grilling the skewers with the lid down.

GRILLED WHOLE SEA BASS

GRILLING A WHOLE FISH IS ONE OF those dazzling acts that looks harder than it really is. While Americans rarely cook fish this way, Italians almost always grill fish whole rather than in steaks or fillets. Most Americans don't want to bother with whole fish, but the rewards are ample. When cooked on the bone, the flesh is especially flavorful and juicy. Italians know that grilled whole fish rarely needs a sauce or seasonings beyond salt, pepper, good olive oil, and lemon wedges.

Branzino (sea bass) is a favorite fish for grilling in Italy and a good choice for novice fish grillers because of its small size. That said, sea bass, like all whole fish, can stick to the grill. This is perhaps the main reason why Americans don't grill whole fish, and we were determined to reduce this anxiety.

SLASHING THE SKIN

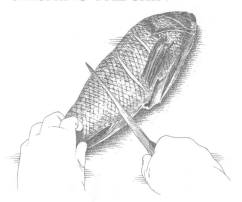

Use a sharp knife to make shallow diagonal slashes every 2 inches along both sides of the scaled and gutted sea bass from top to bottom, beginning just behind the dorsal fin. This helps ensure even cooking and allows the cook to peek into the flesh to see if it is done.

In our testing, we discovered a number of general techniques that make grilling whole fish much easier. Make sure your cooking rack is very hot before placing the fish on the grill. If using charcoal, heat the cooking rack for 10 minutes rather than the standard 5 minutes. We found that oiling the fish as well as the rack helped prevent sticking.

Most cooks encounter trouble when it comes time to turn the fish. Try to position the fish on the grill initially so it can be turned by rolling. Lifting a whole fish off the grill is risky. The fish can snap in half so do this only when you must—that is, when the fish is done. When turning the fish, lift it gently at first to make sure that it is not sticking to the grill. If the fish is sticking, gently pull it from the rack, working the sticking skin off the grill grates. The skin may break, but at least you won't split the fish itself. To remove the whole fish from the grill once it's done, we found that two metal spatulas give the proper support and greatly reduce the risk of breaking the fish in half on the way to the platter. Ask someone to hold the platter right next to the grill for an easy transfer.

Whole fish are fairly oily, making flare-ups a major concern. The oil rubbed into the skin to keep it from sticking also increases the chance of flare-ups. Be prepared to move the fish to another part of the grill if flare-ups occur. Better yet, keep a spray bottle filled with water nearby (whole fish can tear and fall apart if moved too much). Dousing the flames with a spritz of water makes more sense.

Sea bass is almost completely black. Once scaled, it has a black-and-white houndstooth appearance. The flesh is firm and the flavor is quite mild. The skin on this delicious fish crisps when grilled, which is one reason it is so popular in Italy.

Chilean sea bass is not a true sea bass and cannot be used in this recipe. This cold-water fish is much too large and the flesh is oily, making it more akin to salmon. Red snapper is a better alternative to sea bass. It is white-fleshed, firm, and lean; when purchased, it should be bright silvery red. Its flavor is mild and clean, and its skin crisps nicely.

MOVING GRILLED WHOLE FISH

Once the sea bass is done, slide two metal spatulas under the belly, lifting gently to make sure that the skin is not sticking to the grill. Quickly lift the fish and place on a nearby platter. (Ask someone to hold the platter for you.)

We found that fish, whether sea bass or red snapper, weighing between 1½ and 1¾ pounds are best for grilling. Fish any larger than 2 pounds are hard to turn and remove from the grill. In addition, larger fish take a long time to cook through, and the skin is more likely to char. A 1½-pound fish will feed two people. You should be able to fit two fish on the grill at the same time.

Grilled Whole Sea Bass or Red Snapper

SERVES 4

If your fish are between 1½ and 2 pounds, simply grill them a minute or two longer on each side. Fish weighing more than 2 pounds will be hard to maneuver on the grill and should be avoided. Ask your fishmonger to scale and gut the fish.

> 2 whole sea bass or red snapper (about 1½ pounds each), scaled, gutted, and skin slashed on both sides (see the illustration on page 334)
> 3 tablespoons extra-virgin olive oil
> Salt and ground black pepper
> Vegetable oil for the grill rack
> Lemon wedges

1. Light a large chimney starter filled with hardwood charcoal (about 2½ pounds) and allow it to burn until all the charcoal is covered with a layer of fine gray ash. Build a single-level fire by spreading the coals evenly over the bottom of the grill. Set the cooking rack in place, cover the grill with the lid, and let the rack heat, about 10 minutes. Use a wire brush to scrape the rack clean. The grill is ready when the coals are medium-hot (you can hold your hand 5 inches above the grate for 3 to 4 seconds).

2. Rub the fish with the olive oil and season generously with salt and pepper on the outside as well as the inside of the fish.

3. Lightly dip a small wad of paper towels in vegetable oil; holding the wad with tongs, wipe the grill rack. Place the fish on the rack. Grill, uncovered, until the side of the fish facing the charcoal is browned and crisp, 6 to 7 minutes. Gently turn the fish over using two spatulas and cook until the flesh is no longer translucent at the center and the skin on both sides is blistered and crisp, 6 to 8 minutes more. (To check for doneness, peek into slashed flesh or into the interior through the open bottom area of the fish to see whether

FILLETING GRILLED WHOLE FISH

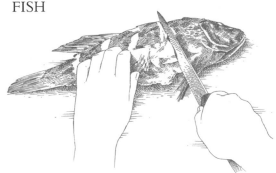

1. Using a sharp knife, make a vertical cut just behind the head from the top of the fish to the belly. Make another cut along the top of the fish from the head toward the tail.

2. Use a metal spatula to lift the meat from the bones, starting at the head end and running the spatula over the bones to lift out the fillet. Repeat on the other side of the fish. Discard the fish head and skeleton.

the flesh is still translucent.) Use two metal spatulas to transfer the fish to a platter (see the illustration on page 334).

4. Fillet the fish according to the illustrations on page 335 and serve with lemon wedges.

➤ VARIATIONS

Gas-Grilled Whole Sea Bass or Red Snapper

Make sure the grill is as hot and clean as possible.

Preheat the grill with all burners set to high and the lid down until very hot, about 15 minutes. Use a wire brush to scrape the cooking rack clean. Leave all burners on high. Follow the recipe for Charcoal-Grilled Whole Sea Bass or Red Snapper, grilling with the lid down and increasing the cooking time by 1 to 2 minutes.

Grilled Whole Sea Bass or Red Snapper with Tomato-Basil Relish

Use this recipe in the summer when tomato season is at its peak.

1	pound ripe tomatoes, cored, seeded, and cut into ¼-inch dice
1	medium shallot, minced
1	medium clove garlic, minced or pressed through a garlic press
2	tablespoons extra-virgin olive oil
1	teaspoon red wine vinegar
2	tablespoons chopped fresh basil leaves Salt and ground black pepper
1	recipe Charcoal-Grilled or Gas-Grilled Whole Sea Bass or Red Snapper (without lemon wedges)

1. Mix the tomatoes, shallot, garlic, olive oil, vinegar, basil, and salt and pepper to taste in a medium bowl. (The relish can be covered and refrigerated for up to two days.)

2. Grill the fish as directed. Serve the filleted fish with the relish.

SICILIAN FISH STEW

IN SICILY, FISH IS OFTEN COMBINED with tomatoes and favorite local seasonings—olives, capers, raisins, and pine nuts—to create a heady, simple stew. Although easy to prepare, this recipe requires a careful balancing act; add too much tomato and the dish feels like a pasta sauce. Finding the right mix of tomatoes and fish stock (the other liquid element) is key.

The other challenge is to create just the right blend of sweet, sour, and salty flavors. Many Sicilian dishes, including this one, demonstrate the strong influence of Arabic cooking in the region. The use of dried fruits and nuts in savory dishes is a telltale sign of Arab inspiration. Although these flavors are delicious, they must be used judiciously to keep them from upstaging each other and the fish.

We started our work on this recipe with the fish. Several sources suggested firm, white-fleshed fillets, such as snapper. Others pointed to swordfish or tuna. We prepared a batch of stew with each kind of fish. Tasters felt that the mild flavor of snapper was lost amid the bold flavors of the stew. Swordfish and tuna have more flavor; both are well suited to this dish. In addition, the meaty texture of swordfish and tuna works better here—these fish stay firm and hold their shape, especially when cut into large chunks.

Most everyone in the test kitchen liked the beefy texture and meaty appearance of the tuna, although a few dissenters complained about the "fishy" flavor. Swordfish has a great texture and mild, sweet flavor that pleased everyone. We decided to use swordfish in the recipe and give tuna as an option. Either way, we found that 1½-inch cubes of fish offered the best combination of texture and appearance in the final dish. Smaller pieces of fish tended to fall apart, and larger chunks looked ungainly in serving bowls.

As for cooking the fish, we found it best to add the chunks once the stew is nearly done. To prevent overcooking, we simmered the fish until partially cooked, then turned off the heat and covered the pot. The fish finished cooking by residual heat, thus greatly reducing its potential to dry out. Needless to say, the stew must be served the second the fish is properly cooked. If it is held or reheated, the texture of the fish declines dramatically.

With the fish chosen, we moved on to the liquid portion of the stew. Most every recipe we ran across when researching this dish called for canned tomatoes and fish stock. (A few recipes used water instead of stock, but we quickly dismissed this idea.) Ideally, we wanted the briny taste of the sea offset by the sweetness and acidity of the tomatoes.

We started out with 2 cups of canned diced tomatoes and 4½ cups of stock. The resulting stew was too brothy and souplike. We cut back on the tomatoes, which helped reduce the volume but made the stew even more watery. For the next test, we increased the tomatoes to 3 cups and cut the stock way back to just 2 cups. The finished stew looked better (it was red, not pale pink), and the texture was thicker. To our surprise, the briny flavor of the stock was still present. We had hit upon the right mix. The texture was thinner than tomato sauce but thicker than fish stock, with a few bits of tomato, and the flavors of the tomato and stock harmonized.

Although the stew tasted great when made with fish stock, we wondered if there was some way to get around the time-consuming process of making homemade stock. Given the presence of tomatoes and other strong flavors in this dish, we figured we had a fighting chance.

After much trial and error, we successfully developed a cheater's stock (page 338), which starts with bottled clam juice. We found that simmering the clam juice with aromatic vegetables and herbs enhances its salty, briny flavor. A splash of white wine rounds out the other flavors and gives the impression of depth. Unlike real fish stock, cheater's stock is thin because it contains no dissolved gelatin from bones. However, with so many tomatoes and other chunky ingredients in this recipe, this stock substitute was more than adequate.

It was time to examine the seasonings that give the stew its characteristic sweet, sour, and piquant flavors. Tasters preferred yellow raisins to black and found that their texture was improved by simmering them in the stew rather than adding them at the end of the cooking process.

Pine nuts added a welcome crunch, and mint provided sweetness and fragrance. Some sources stirred these ingredients right into the stew, while others used them as a garnish. We found that the texture of the nuts and fresh flavor of the mint was better preserved by using them as a garnish. For maximum flavor, we found it worthwhile to toast the nuts in a dry skillet until lightly colored.

We ran across several recipes that called for cayenne pepper or hot red pepper flakes. Most tasters felt that the heat was not necessary; the sweet and sour elements provide more than enough complexity. If you like, you can add some hot red pepper flakes, but we left this ingredient optional.

Capers and green olives provide the sour, piquant elements in this recipe. We found that fair amounts of both ingredients are needed. Recipes with a teaspoon of capers and a half dozen olives just didn't cut it. In the end, we added 2 tablespoons of capers and ½ cup of sliced green olives. Although some recipes called for adding these ingredients with the garnish, we felt they had more impact on the stew when simmered with the other ingredients.

Sicilian Fish Stew

SERVES 6 TO 8

Sweet and sour flavor combinations are at the heart of this stew and stand up well to strong-flavored fish like swordfish. Tuna is another favorite in Sicily and can be used with excellent results in this tomato-based stew. Add a pinch of hot red pepper flakes for heat, if desired. Serve with crusty bread or bruschetta (see page 19).

2	tablespoons extra-virgin olive oil
2	medium onions, chopped coarse
3	large cloves garlic, minced or pressed through a garlic press
½	cup dry white wine
2	(14½-ounce) cans diced tomatoes
2	large bay leaves
	Salt and ground black pepper
2	cups homemade fish stock or Cheater's Fish Stock (at right)
¼	cup golden raisins
3	pounds swordfish steaks (1 to 1½ inches thick), trimmed of skin and cut into 1½-inch cubes
2	tablespoons drained capers
18	medium green olives, pitted and quartered lengthwise (about ½ cup)
¼	cup pine nuts, toasted in a dry skillet until fragrant
¼	cup coarsely chopped fresh mint leaves

1. Heat the oil in a large stockpot or Dutch oven. Add the onions and cook over medium heat until softened, about 5 minutes. Stir in the garlic and cook until aromatic, about 30 seconds. Add the wine and simmer until reduced by half, 2 to 3 minutes. Add the tomatoes, bay leaves, ½ teaspoon salt, and pepper to taste. Bring to a boil over high heat, reduce the heat, and simmer until the mixture has thickened to the consistency of tomato sauce, 15 to 20 minutes.

2. Add the fish stock and golden raisins and bring to a boil over high heat. Reduce the heat and simmer until the flavors meld, about 10 minutes.

3. Stir in the swordfish cubes, capers, and olives and bring back to a simmer over medium heat. Simmer for 7 minutes, stirring a few times to ensure even cooking. Remove the pot from the heat, cover, and let stand until the fish is just cooked through, 2 to 3 minutes. Discard the bay leaves and adjust the seasonings. Serve immediately, garnishing each bowl with pine nuts and mint.

Cheater's Fish Stock

MAKES ABOUT 2 CUPS

Clam juice is very salty, so don't add any salt to the stew until you have tasted it. We tested several brands of bottled clam juice and found Doxsee to have the cleanest, truest flavor.

½	small onion, chopped coarse
1	small carrot, chopped coarse
½	stalk celery, chopped coarse
4	sprigs fresh parsley
¼	cup dry white wine
3	(8-ounce) bottles clam juice
1	bay leaf
4	whole black peppercorns
¼	teaspoon dried thyme

Bring all ingredients to a boil in a medium saucepan. Simmer to blend the flavors, about 20 minutes. Strain, pressing on the solids with the back of a spoon to extract as much liquid as possible. Use immediately.

SHRIMP SCAMPI

ALMOST EVERY ITALIAN RESTAURANT menu in the United States features shrimp scampi. The name sounds Italian but, in reality, it doesn't make much sense. The word *scampi* refers to a species of crayfish found in the Adriatic, not the buttery, herby, garlicky, lemony sauce we think of as a natural partner to sautéed shrimp. Despite the questionable origins of this dish, we love its simplicity and bold flavors.

The perfect shrimp scampi is surrounded by an ample amount of sauce flavored with garlic and lemon. We find that most recipes are too oily and that the garlic (which generally goes into the pan first) burns by the time the shrimp have cooked through. Most sauces are too thin, and there's not near enough to sop up with a chewy piece of bread. In addition, most recipes overcook the shrimp.

To start, we sautéed the shrimp quickly in batches. This prevented them from overcooking and becoming rubbery while helping retain their natural juices so they would not dry out. With the shrimp cooked and reserved, we built a sauce in the empty pan. Beginning with butter, we simply heated the garlic through before adding the lemon juice and a little vermouth, which gave the sauce a nice depth of flavor. Adding the liquid also kept the garlic from burning and turning bitter.

The sauce was delicious but thin. For body, we added more butter and finished it with parsley, then added a pinch of cayenne. We returned the shrimp and their juices to the pan, and the dish was done. Nothing complicated, but perfect nonetheless.

PEELING SHRIMP

1. Holding the tail end of the shrimp with one hand and the opposite end with the other, bend the shrimp side to side to split the shell.

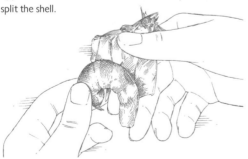

2. Lift off the tail portion of the shell, then slide your thumb under the legs of the remaining portion and lift it off as well.

Shrimp Scampi

SERVES 4 TO 6

Serve scampi with plenty of chewy bread to soak up extra juices.

2	tablespoons extra-virgin olive oil
2	pounds large shrimp (21 to 25 per pound), peeled and deveined, if desired
3	tablespoons unsalted butter
4	medium cloves garlic, minced or pressed through a garlic press
2	tablespoons lemon juice
1	tablespoon dry vermouth
2	tablespoons minced fresh parsley leaves
	Pinch cayenne pepper
	Salt and ground black pepper

1. Heat 1 tablespoon oil in a 12-inch skillet over high heat until shimmering. Swirl to coat the pan bottom with the oil. Add half the shrimp and cook, stirring occasionally, until opaque and just cooked through, about

2 minutes. Transfer the shrimp to a medium bowl. Repeat the process with the remaining oil and shrimp.

2. Return the now-empty skillet to medium-low heat. Melt 1 tablespoon butter in the pan. When the foaming subsides, add the garlic and cook, stirring constantly, until fragrant, about 30 seconds. Off the heat, add the lemon juice and vermouth. Whisk in the remaining 2 tablespoons butter, add the parsley and cayenne pepper, and season to taste with salt and pepper. Return the shrimp and accumulated juices to the skillet. Toss to combine. Serve immediately.

SHRIMP FRA DIAVOLO

FRA DIAVOLO, WITH ITS ABUNDANCE of hot red pepper and attendant fiery nature, may be named for the devil—its literal translation from the Italian is "brother devil"—but it can do an angel's work for home cooks. How so? Shrimp fra diavolo, a seriously garlicky, spicy, winey tomato sauce studded with shrimp and served over pasta, takes less than 30 minutes to prepare from start to finish. It's a standard restaurant dish that easily makes the transition to home cooking.

That's not to say that this dish doesn't have its challenges, as we discovered after dining on shrimp fra diavolo in restaurants all over Boston's Italian neighborhood, the North End, and then trying published recipes back in the test kitchen. Overall, the sauces we sampled lacked depth and unity of flavor— backbone, if you will. The shrimp contributed little to the overall flavor of the sauce, serving merely as a bulky, lifeless garnish. Ditto the garlic, the flavor of which was often unpleasantly sharp, even acrid. In our ideal fra diavolo, not only would the shrimp themselves be firm, sweet, and well seasoned, but they would commit their flavor to the sauce as well.

Determined as we were to maximize the flavor of the shrimp, they seemed like the natural starting point for our investigation. We made sauces with several species of shrimp (all medium-large, or 31 to 35 shrimp to the pound) and, as we had found in earlier tests with other shrimp dishes, we preferred Mexican Whites and Gulf Whites equally, followed by Black Tiger shrimp, which are the most widely available.

We learned during testing that the way the shrimp are cooked does have a tremendous effect not just on their texture and flavor but also on the overall flavor of the sauce. Most fra diavolo recipes we encountered add plain raw shrimp to the almost finished sauce; in effect, this means the shrimp are braised in the sauce. While these shrimp do remain tender, our tasters agreed that their flavor was barely developed. We tried seasoning the shrimp with olive oil, salt, and hot red pepper flakes, searing them quickly in a very hot pan, then adding them to the sauce just before serving. Every taster noted that the shrimp themselves—and therefore the sauce—had a stronger, more unified flavor. The sear also benefited the hot red pepper flakes, as they now contributed an earthy, toasty note to the sauce in addition to heat.

Though the searing helped, we wanted to coax still more flavor from the shrimp. Several of the fra diavolo recipes we consulted included cognac. We added cognac to the pan with the seared shrimp and flambéed it for a minute until the flame petered out. The combined forces of cognac and flame made a difference in the flavor. Not only did many tasters detect the spirit's own complexity but also they felt that the shrimp tasted a little stronger. This sauce had backbone, which we'd missed in the restaurant versions. All this and drama, too, in an easy, one-minute step.

Curious about why the shrimp flambéed in cognac tasted better, we contacted Dr. Susan Brewer in the department of food science and human nutrition at the University of Illinois in Urbana. She noted that brandy contains hundreds of compounds that undergo profound changes at the roughly 400-degree temperatures of a flambé. The reason for this change is isomerization, a process in which heat changes the structure of sugar molecules. A session with the infrared thermometer in our test kitchen confirmed that the flame does burn at more than 400 degrees. We went on to test Brewer's suggestion by tasting side-by-side sauces in which the shrimp and cognac had been flambéed and not. Indeed, tasters noted a slightly fuller, sweeter flavor in the sauce in which the shrimp and cognac had been flambéed.

Fra diavolo's satanic associations arise from its liberal doses of garlic and spicy chile heat.

We wanted enough garlic to make the devil proud, and we were frankly surprised to find that tasters agreed, preferring sauces that packed the wallop of almost an entire head, or about eight large cloves, over those with lesser amounts. But there was a caveat: Though we wanted the flavor of browned garlic, we had to mitigate the bitterness that often comes with it. We experimented with cutting the garlic in slices and slivers, grating it, pureeing it, and adding it to the sauce at various times, none of which eliminated the bitterness completely. Then we borrowed the stellar technique from our recipe for Pasta with Garlic and Oil (page 138), wherein a similar quantity of garlic is sautéed slowly over low heat until it becomes golden, sticky, mellow, and nutty. What was good for aglio e olio proved good for fra diavolo; the bitterness was gone, and the sauce acquired a sweeter, deeper dimension. Taking another cue from the aglio e olio recipe, we

---

INGREDIENTS: Hot Red Pepper Flakes

Lending both name and fire to shrimp fra diavolo, dried, crushed red chile pepper (nicknamed *diavolochino* in Italian and referred to as hot red pepper flakes in this book) is fundamental to this dish. As we finished one bottle and opened the next during testing, we began to wonder just what, exactly, was in those bottles and whether brand mattered. We purchased four samples of crushed pepper and blind-tasted our way to a surprise answer.

Nearly identical in color and consistency, our lineup included three national brands—McCormick, Durkee, and Spice Islands—and a mail-ordered sample from Penzeys. We infused each sample in vegetable oil, which we tasted plain and sprinkled on rice. Even the most astute tasters on our staff failed to detect appreciable differences, although several participants had a slight preference for the Penzeys brand, in which they detected a fresher flavor. Each sample tasted bright, with a clear, direct heat.

The manufacturing process is straightforward. Before the dried chiles are crushed, they are roasted to attain their characteristic ruddy tone and mildly smoky flavor. Research revealed that the varieties used most often for crushed red pepper are the California or New Mexico chiles. Both are relatively mild, rating between 16,000 and 20,000 units on the Scoville heat scale, which is used to measure chiles' heat. (By comparison, jalapeños rate between 3,000 and 5,000 Scoville units, while superhot habaneros and Scotch bonnets score above 200,000.) Penzeys was the only product in our lineup to note the variety—California—on its label.

According to our tests, then, brand makes little or no difference when it comes to hot red pepper flakes. What does make a difference, as we've discovered in the past, is freshness. Stale pepper flakes that have been sitting in your pantry for a year or more just won't provide the same bite as those from a newly opened bottle.

---

reserved a tablespoon of raw garlic to add to the sauce at the end of cooking, along with a splash of raw olive oil. The tasters appreciated the bright, fruity, high flavor notes of these raw ingredients, which complemented the bass notes grounding the sauce.

Chile adds fiery heat to fra diavolo. Traditionally, hot red pepper flakes get the job

---

INGREDIENTS: Shrimp

It's safe to say that any shrimp you buy have been frozen (and usually thawed by the retailer), but not all shrimp are the same—far from it. The Gulf of Mexico supplies about 200 million pounds of shrimp annually to the United States, but three times that amount is imported as well, mostly from Asia and Central and South America.

After tasting all of the commonly available varieties of shrimp several times, we had little trouble declaring two winners. Mexican whites (*Panaeus vannamei*), from the Pacific coast, are usually the best. A close second, and often just as good, are Gulf whites (*P. setiferus*). Either of these may be wild or farm-raised. Unfortunately, these are rarely the shrimp you're offered in supermarkets. The shrimp most commonly found in supermarkets is Black Tiger, a farmed shrimp from Asia. Its quality is inconsistent, but it can be quite flavorful and firm. Even if you go to a fishmonger and ask for white shrimp, you may get farm-raised, less expensive, and decidedly inferior shrimp from China (*P. chinensis*). (There are more than 300 species of shrimp and not nearly as many common names.)

All you can do is try to buy the best shrimp available, and buy it right. Beyond choosing the best species you can find, consider these factors as well.

Because almost all shrimp are frozen after the catch and thawed shrimp start losing their flavor in just a couple of days, buying thawed shrimp gives you neither the flavor of fresh nor the flexibility of frozen. We recommend you buy frozen shrimp rather than thawed. We found that shrimp stored in the freezer retain peak quality for several weeks, deteriorating very slowly after that until about the three-month point, when we detected a noticeable deterioration in quality. If you do buy thawed shrimp, they should smell of saltwater and little else, and they should be firm and fully fill their shells.

Avoid peeled and deveined shrimp; cleaning before freezing unquestionably deprives shrimp of some of their flavor and texture; everyone we asked to sample precleaned shrimp found them nearly tasteless. In addition, precleaned shrimp may have added tripolyphosphate, a chemical that aids in water retention and can give shrimp an off flavor.

Shrimp should have no black spots, or melanosis, on their shells, which indicate that a breakdown of the meat has begun. Be equally suspicious of shrimp with yellowing shells or those that feel gritty. Either of these conditions may indicate the overuse of sodium bisulfite, a bleaching agent sometimes used to retard melanosis.

Despite the popularity of shrimp, there are no standards for size. Small, medium, large, extra-large, jumbo, and other size classifications are subjective and relative. Small shrimp of 70 or so to the pound are frequently labeled "medium," as are those twice that size and even larger. It pays, then, to judge shrimp size by the number it takes to make a pound, as retailers do. Shrimp labeled "16/20," for example, require 16 to 20 (usually closer to 20) individual specimens to make a pound. Those labeled "U-20" require fewer than 20 to make a pound. Large shrimp (21 to 25 per pound) usually yield the best combination of flavor, ease of preparation, and value (really big shrimp usually cost more).

One more note about size: Larger shrimp generally have larger veins, which should be removed. The veins in smaller shrimp are often so negligible that it's not worth removing them. Either way, we find the issue of removing the vein one of aesthetics; it neither harms nor improves flavor. We tested several shrimp deveiners and found that some models work better than others, but none beats a regular paring knife. We recommend that you save money (and drawer space) and live without this gadget, which is of little real use.

done, but we also tested cayenne and hot pepper sauce, alone and in various combinations. Though tasters did not detect significant flavor differences, neither cayenne nor pepper sauce bested the traditional pepper flakes, so we stuck with the tried and true.

Our last tests focused on fra diavolo's two remaining major components: tomatoes and wine. We tested canned diced tomatoes (drained of excess liquid), canned crushed tomatoes, canned whole tomatoes (which we chopped by hand), and fresh tomatoes. The winner was drained canned diced tomatoes. The tasters were likewise united behind white wine over its rivals, red wine and white vermouth. The red wine was judged "muddy" and "sour" and the vermouth too herbal. We had been bothered by the compounded acidity of the tomatoes and wine, so we tried adding a little bit of sugar, which balanced the acidity perfectly. We finally had a top-notch shrimp fra diavolo—and the devil by the nose.

Flambéing the shrimp in cognac brings out its sweetness and provides a nice balance to the spicy, garlicky tomato sauce.

Shrimp Fra Diavolo with Linguine
SERVES 4 TO 6

One teaspoon of hot red pepper flakes will give the sauce a little kick, but add more to suit your taste.

1	pound medium-large shrimp (31 to 35 per pound), peeled and deveined, if desired
1	teaspoon hot red pepper flakes
6	tablespoons extra-virgin olive oil
1½	tablespoons salt
¼	cup cognac or brandy
4	tablespoons minced or pressed (through a garlic press) garlic (about 12 medium, 8 large, or 5 extra-large cloves)
½	teaspoon sugar
1	(28-ounce) can diced tomatoes, drained
1	cup medium-dry white wine, such as Sauvignon Blanc
¼	cup minced fresh parsley leaves
1	pound linguine or spaghetti

1. Bring 4 quarts water to a rolling boil in a large pot.

2. While the water is heating, heat a heavy-bottomed 12-inch skillet over high heat until the pan is very hot. Meanwhile, toss the shrimp, ½ teaspoon hot red pepper flakes, 2 tablespoons oil, and ¾ teaspoon salt in a medium bowl. Add the shrimp to the skillet and quickly spread in a single layer. Cook without stirring until the bottoms of shrimp turn spotty brown, 30 to 45 seconds. Off the heat, stir to turn the shrimp, then add the cognac. Let stand off the heat until the cognac warms slightly, about 5 seconds, and return the pan to high heat. Wave a lit match over the skillet until the cognac ignites. Shake the skillet until the flames subside, then transfer the shrimp to a medium bowl and set aside.

3. Off the heat, cool the now-empty skillet

for 2 minutes. Return the skillet to a burner and reduce the heat to low. Add 3 tablespoons oil and 3 tablespoons garlic. Cook, stirring constantly, until the garlic foams and is sticky and straw-colored, 7 to 10 minutes. Add the remaining ½ teaspoon hot red pepper flakes, ¾ teaspoon salt, sugar, tomatoes, and wine. Increase the heat to medium-high and simmer until thickened and fragrant, about 8 minutes.

4. Stir in the reserved shrimp and accumulated juices, remaining 1 tablespoon garlic, and parsley and simmer until the shrimp are heated through, about 1 minute longer. Off the heat, stir in the remaining 1 tablespoon oil.

5. While the sauce simmers, add the linguine or spaghetti and remaining 1 tablespoon salt to the boiling water. Stir to separate the pasta and cook until al dente. Reserve ⅓ cup pasta cooking water and drain the pasta. Return the drained pasta to the now-empty pot, add about ½ cup sauce (without shrimp) and 2 to 3 tablespoons reserved pasta cooking water, and toss to coat. Divide the pasta among warmed individual bowls, top with a portion of the sauce and shrimp, and serve immediately.

➤ VARIATIONS

Scallops Fra Diavolo with Linguine

The scallops, as well as the monkfish in the following variation, leave more flavorful drippings in the skillet than the shrimp, and these drippings can make the garlic appear straw-colored before it is done cooking. Make sure that the garlic is fragrant, looks sticky, and has cooked for the full 7 to 10 minutes.

Follow the recipe for Shrimp Fra Diavolo with Linguine, replacing the shrimp with 1 pound sea scallops, tendons removed.

Monkfish Fra Diavolo with Linguine

Don't be alarmed if the monkfish sticks to the pan initially; it will loosen after the cognac has been added and flamed.

Follow the recipe for Shrimp Fra Diavolo with Linguine, replacing the shrimp with a 1-pound monkfish fillet, cut into 1-inch pieces.

SHRIMP AND WHITE BEANS

NORTHERN ITALIANS COMBINE THEIR beloved white beans (called cannellini beans) with a seemingly infinite variety of ingredients. Shrimp and white beans may seem an unusual combination to Americans, but it is utterly traditional. Essentially, this dish consists of beans lightly cooked with shrimp, vegetables, and herbs until the flavors blend. It is eaten either chilled as a salad or antipasto or warm as a main course. The combination works to great effect; the sweetness of the beans emphasizes the flavor of the shrimp and helps extend this expensive seafood without diluting its impact.

We prefer the warm version, as the subtle flavor of the beans is more apparent. After making several batches from the recipes we researched, we found that the major issues lay in choosing the best flavors to accent the shrimp and finding the ideal method to cook it. To our taste, traditional versions were decidedly bland.

Plump, white cannellini beans are the bean of choice here. Their mild, creamy flesh serves as a foil to the chewy, briny shrimp. Ideally, the beans should start as dried beans, which are gently simmered with aromatics until tender (see page 113 for information about our favorite bean cooking method). Tasters, however, felt that canned beans passed muster in this case. The aromatics and shrimp mediated the mildly tinny flavor of canned cannellini beans. With respect to texture, there was little we could do to resurrect it. Canned beans have a decidedly mushier texture than freshly cooked beans. Surprisingly, the price of canned beans is not necessarily an indicator of quality. We have had good luck with Goya beans, while organic beans at three times their cost have paled in comparison in taste and texture. (For more information on buying canned beans, see page 119.)

The beans are the heart of the dish, but the shrimp play the starring role. Recipes ran the gamut here, employing shrimp ranging from tiny fingernail-sized specimens to huge prawns that are rare in the United States. Tasters felt that large shrimp, while delicious, seemed out of place, as if they were a garnish rather than integral to the dish. We then experimented with different sizes of smaller shrimp, and tasters agreed on medium shrimp as they blended into the beans without wholly disappearing. While we often like to leave the shrimp tails attached for visual appeal, they were annoying and messy in this case, so we removed them.

Most recipes boil or poach the shrimp before tossing them with the beans, but we found this approach made the shrimp too bland. We wanted a cooking method that boosted the flavor of the shrimp so that they would stand out from the beans. Grilling would have been ideal, but it seemed like too much hassle for so few shrimp. Broiling would have worked, but it can be tricky to find the ideal rack height for the shrimp to cook properly. Then it occurred to us that searing the shrimp would deliver all the flavor of high-heat cooking in a matter of seconds right on the stovetop. We followed the method we developed for our shrimp fra diavolo recipe, coating the shrimp with olive oil, salt, and hot red pepper flakes, then searing them in an extremely hot skillet. Within 45 seconds, the shrimp were speckled with browned seared spots as if they had been grilled. Within a minute and a half, they were perfectly cooked, seared on the outside and moist on the inside.

With a hot skillet ready to go, it was quick work to finish the dish. We experimented with various aromatics and settled on red onion, red bell pepper, and garlic. The sweetness of the onion and bell pepper intensified the shrimp flavor, and the garlic added much-needed punch. Although we would normally cook the vegetables until lightly browned to improve their flavor, we found that the caramelization muddied the flavors in this delicate dish. Briefer cooking kept their flavors fresh and their texture appealingly crunchy.

For herbs, we revisited the traditional recipes and discovered that the sky was the limit; everything from rosemary and sage to basil, mint, and arugula could be used. We found rosemary and sage too strong; they overpowered the delicate flavors of the beans and the shrimp. Tasters liked basil, but some felt that the combination of lemon juice and basil made the dish overly tart. Everyone in the test kitchen loved arugula in this dish. Rarely used as an herb in the United States, arugula lends a gentle peppery bite that successfully marries with the other flavors in this dish. Copious amounts were needed, as the arugula wilted to a shadow of its raw self.

Shrimp and White Beans
SERVES 4 TO 6

Leftovers may be eaten cold, enlivened with additional lemon juice, or spooned on top of crostini (see page 123). If you want to cook cannellini beans yourself (rather than using canned beans), prepare ½ pound dried beans according to step 1 in the recipe for White Beans with Tomatoes, Garlic, and Sage (see page 222). Cut the quantities of water and vegetables in half and discard all the cooking liquid and the vegetables, including the garlic, when the beans are done. Although this recipe calls for serving the shrimp and beans hot, some tasters felt that the flavors were better developed when the dish was served warm.

1 pound medium shrimp (40 to 50 per pound), peeled and deveined, if desired

6 tablespoons extra-virgin olive oil
Salt

¼ teaspoon hot red pepper flakes

1 medium red bell pepper, stemmed, seeded, and diced small

1 small red onion, diced small

2 medium cloves garlic, minced or pressed through a garlic press

3 cups cooked cannellini beans or 2 (15½-ounce) cans cannellini beans, drained and rinsed

2 cups lightly packed coarsely chopped arugula

2 tablespoons lemon juice, plus 1 small lemon, cut into wedges
Ground black pepper

1. Heat a heavy-bottomed 12-inch skillet over high heat until the pan is very hot. Meanwhile, toss the shrimp with 2 tablespoons oil, ¾ teaspoon salt, and the hot red pepper flakes in a medium bowl. Add the shrimp to the skillet and quickly spread in a single layer. Cook without stirring until the bottoms of shrimp turn spotty brown, about 45 seconds. Using tongs, flip the shrimp and cook until spotty brown on the other side, about 45 seconds. Transfer the shrimp to a bowl and cover to keep warm.

2. Off the heat, let the pan cool for 30 seconds. Return the pan to medium heat and add the remaining 4 tablespoons oil, bell pepper, onion, and ½ teaspoon salt. Cook, stirring frequently, until the onion is translucent and the bell pepper has softened, about 4 minutes. Add the garlic and cook until fragrant, about 30 seconds. Stir in the beans and cook until heated through and the flavors have blended, about 5 minutes.

3. Add the shrimp, followed by the arugula, and stir until the arugula is wilted, about 1 minute. Remove the pan from the heat and sprinkle with the lemon juice. Season with salt and pepper to taste. Serve immediately in shallow bowls, accompanied by lemon wedges.

STEAMED CLAMS AND MUSSELS

NOTHING COULD BE SIMPLER, OR more Italian, than a big bowl of steamed clams and/or mussels in a white wine broth flavored with garlic and herbs. Add some crusty bread (to soak up all those juices), and you have a light meal.

Clams and mussels are both bivalves, and they can be prepared in the same fashion. The main challenge when preparing clams and mussels is getting rid of the grit. These two-shelled creatures are easy to cook: When they open, they are done. However, perfectly cooked clams and mussels can be made inedible by lingering sand. Straining their juices through cheesecloth after cooking removes the grit, but it's a pain. Besides being messy, solids such as garlic and herbs are removed. Worse still, careful straining may not remove every trace of grit, especially bits still clinging to the meat.

After much trial and error in the test kitchen, we concluded that it is impossible to remove all the sand from dirty clams or mussels before cooking. We tried various soaking regimens, such as soaking in cold water for two hours, soaking in water with flour, soaking in water with cornmeal, and scrubbing and rinsing in five changes of water. None of these techniques worked. Dirty clams and mussels must be rinsed and scrubbed before cooking, and any cooking liquid must be strained after cooking. Rinsing the cooked clams and mussels is a final guarantee that the grit is removed, but flavor is washed away as well.

During the course of this testing, we noticed that some varieties of clams and mussels were extremely clean and free of grit. A quick scrub of the shell exterior and these bivalves were ready for the pot. Best of all, the cooking liquid could be served without straining. After talking to seafood experts around the country, we came to this conclusion: If you want to minimize your kitchen work and ensure that your clams and mussels are free of grit, you must shop carefully.

Clams can be divided into two categories: hard-shell varieties (such as littlenecks and cherrystone) and soft-shell varieties (such as steamers and razor clams). Hard-shells grow along sandy beaches and bays, soft-shells in muddy tidal flats. A modest shift in location makes all the difference in the kitchen.

When harvested, hard-shells remain tightly closed. In our test, we found that the meat inside was always free of sand. The exterior should be scrubbed under cold running water to remove any caked-on mud, but otherwise, these clams can be cooked without further worry about gritty broth.

Soft-shell clams gape in their natural habitat. We found that they almost always contain a lot of sand. While it's worthwhile to soak them in several batches of cold water to remove some of the sand, you can never get rid of it all. In the end, you must strain the cooking liquid, and sometimes you must rinse the cooked clams after shucking as well.

We concluded that hard-shell clams (that is, littlenecks and cherrystones) are worth the extra money at the market. Gritty clams, no matter how cheap, are inedible. Buying littlenecks or cherrystones ensures that the clams will be clean.

A similar distinction can be made with mussels based on how and where they are grown. Most mussels are now farmed either on ropes or along seabeds. (You may also see wild mussels at the market. These mussels are caught the old-fashioned way—by dredging along the sea floor. In our tests, we found them extremely muddy and basically inedible.) Rope-cultured mussels can cost twice as much as wild or bottom-cultured mussels, but we found them to be free of grit in our testing. As mussels are generally inexpensive (no more than a few dollars a pound), we think clean mussels are worth the extra money. Look for tags, usually attached to bags of mussels, that indicate how and where the mussels were grown.

When shopping, look for tightly closed clams and mussels (avoid any that are gaping, which may be dying or dead). Clams need only be scrubbed. Mussels may need scrubbing as well as debearding, which involves simply grabbing the weedy protrusion and pulling it out from between the shells. Don't debeard mussels until you are ready to cook them, as debearding can cause them to die. Mussels or clams kept in sealed plastic bags or underwater will also die. Keep them in a bowl in the refrigerator and use them within a day or two for best results.

We tested the four most common cooking methods for cooking clams and mussels: steaming in an aromatic broth (usually including wine), steaming over an aromatic broth, roasting in the oven, and sautéing in oil on the stove. We found that clams or mussels that were sautéed, roasted, or steamed over a broth tasted of pure shellfish, but they also tasted flat and one-dimensional; they cooked in their own juices and not much else. In contrast, clams and mussels that were steamed in a flavorful broth picked up flavors from the liquid. They tasted more complex and, in our opinion, better.

With steaming in broth as our preferred all-purpose cooking method, we started to test various amounts and types of liquids, including fish stock, water, and white wine. We found white wine the best choice. The bright acidity of white wine balances the briny flavor of clams and mussels. Fish stock and water (even when seasoned with garlic and herbs) were dull by comparison. While it is possible to steam 4 pounds of bivalves in just ½ cup of liquid (the pot tightly sealed), we like to have extra broth for soaking into bread. We settled on using 2 cups of white wine to cook 4 pounds of clams or mussels.

We also refined the cooking broth. Garlic and a bay leaf enrich the flavor of the shellfish. Simmering for three minutes before adding the shellfish is sufficient time for these seasonings to flavor the wine broth. We found that adding the parsley at the end preserves its color and flavor. Although the broth can be served as is, our tasters preferred it enriched and thickened with butter.

Steamed Clams or Mussels
SERVES 4

The basic flavorings in this recipe work with mussels and either littleneck or cherrystone clams. (Note that really large cherrystones may require 9 to 10 minutes of steaming to open.) Serve with plenty of crusty bread.

2	cups white wine
6	medium cloves garlic, minced or pressed through a garlic press
1	bay leaf
4	pounds clams or mussels, well scrubbed and mussels debearded (see the illustration on page 130)
4	tablespoons unsalted butter
½	cup chopped fresh parsley leaves

1. Bring the wine, garlic, and bay leaf to a simmer in a large pot. Continue to simmer to blend flavors, about 3 minutes. Increase the

heat to high and add the clams or mussels. Cover and cook, stirring twice, until the clams or mussels open, 4 to 8 minutes, depending on the size of the shellfish and the pot.

2. Use a slotted spoon to transfer the clams or mussels to a large serving bowl. Swirl the butter into the liquid in the pan to make an emulsified sauce. Stir in the parsley. Pour the broth over clams or mussels and serve immediately.

VARIATION

Mussels with Tomato and Basil

This is our version of mussels marinara. The mussels are cooked in the white wine broth (made with less wine so the final sauce isn't soupy), removed from the pot, and set aside while tomatoes and olive oil are simmered with the wine broth to produce a thick, smooth sauce. A handful of minced basil added just before serving perfumes the sauce. The mussels and sauce may be served with bread or over 1 pound cooked linguine.

1	cup white wine
6	medium cloves garlic, minced or pressed through a garlic press
1	bay leaf
4	pounds mussels, well scrubbed and debearded (see the illustration on page 130)
2	cups crushed canned tomatoes
¼	cup extra-virgin olive oil
½	cup minced fresh basil leaves
	Salt and ground black pepper

1. Bring the wine, garlic, and bay leaf to a simmer in a large pot. Continue to simmer to blend flavors, about 3 minutes. Increase the heat to high and add the mussels. Cover and cook, stirring twice, until the mussels open, 4 to 8 minutes, depending on the size of the mussels and the pot.

2. Use a slotted spoon to transfer the mussels to a large serving bowl. Add the tomatoes

and oil to the pot and simmer until the mixture reduces to a sauce consistency, about 10 minutes. Stir in the basil and season with salt and pepper to taste. Return the mussels to the pot, heat briefly, and serve immediately.

FRIED CALAMARI

ONCE RARE IN THE UNITED STATES outside of the most authentic Italian restaurants, fried calamari now appears in restaurants of all stripes almost as frequently as nachos and onion rings do. Crunchy, chewy, and mildly fishy, fried calamari is hard to resist and thoroughly addictive. But few restaurants seem to get it right. Too often, the coating is greasy and gummy, or the squid itself is as chewy as an old tire. What is so difficult about such a simple snack?

Traditionally, Italians do little beyond tossing the squid with seasoned flour prior to frying. Because of its newfound popularity outside of Italian restaurants, calamari now comes garbed in a variety of more complicated, highly seasoned coatings that, by our standards, are too heavy. The goals of the coating are to protect the fish as it fries and to add a textural counterpoint to the tender, slightly chewy flesh—not to bury it in doughy breading.

This said, we were disappointed by the traditional recipes we tried. The simple flour coating lacked flavor and quickly turned gummy if not eaten within a minute or two out of the hot oil. Further, the coating was so thin that the squid overcooked within moments if not carefully watched. What we needed was a slightly thicker coating that would stay crisp and better shield the fish.

A standard breading of flour, then beaten eggs, and bread crumbs proved too heavy—close to the gummy, overseasoned restaurant fare we wanted to avoid. Eliminating the bread crumbs was a step in the right direction,

but the fried squid still turned gummy if not consumed immediately. Mixing the flour with cornstarch—the secret to tempura's brittle crispness—did little good. We then tried separating the eggs and coating the squid with only yolks or only whites. The whites-only batch was a revelation; the coating was airy crisp and stayed crunchy long enough to eat all the fried calamari.

The only problem was the pale color of the fried calamari. When we fried the rings until the coating was golden brown, the squid was unpleasantly rubbery. Herein lay the problem with squid: The color of the breading cannot be the indicator of doneness, as the squid itself cooks much faster than the coating. Within 1½ minutes, the squid was perfectly cooked, but the breading was only light brown. Boosting the oil temperature to 400 degrees from the more conventional 375 degrees improved browning, but the rings were still on the pale side.

To improve the coating's color, we added cornmeal to the flour. Although cornmeal is not traditional in Italian recipes, tasters appreciated both the color and crunch it contributed. Cayenne pepper helped the color as well, and the mild spiciness sharpened the squid's mild flavor.

Fried Calamari
SERVES 4 AS A FIRST COURSE

This recipe yields calamari lighter in color than most restaurant versions, so keep this in mind when frying. Follow the cooking time, not the color, and you will have perfectly cooked squid. While we love the texture and visual appeal of the tentacles, not everyone does; most fishmongers will gladly sell only bodies if you so desire. Before slicing the squid, check the bodies for beaks the fishmonger might have missed. They look and feel like pieces of transparent plastic. For a specialty native to Federal

Hill, the Italian neighborhood in Providence, Rhode Island, toss the fried calamari with thinly sliced rings of jarred pepperoncini. The spicy bite of the peppers and the tanginess of the brine are surprisingly good with fried squid. For the best results, clip a candy/deep-fry thermometer to the side of the saucepan to monitor the temperature of the oil.

1¼	cups unbleached all-purpose flour
¼	cup fine-ground cornmeal
½	teaspoon ground black pepper
½	teaspoon cayenne pepper
	Salt
2	large egg whites
1	pound squid, bodies sliced crosswise into ½-inch-thick rings, tentacles left whole
4	cups vegetable oil for frying
1	small lemon, cut into wedges

1. Thoroughly combine the flour, cornmeal, black pepper, cayenne, and ½ teaspoon salt in a medium bowl. In another medium bowl, beat the egg whites with a fork until frothy, about 10 seconds. Add half the squid to the bowl with the egg whites, toss to coat, and remove with a slotted spoon or your hands, allowing the excess whites to drip back into the bowl. Add the squid to the bowl with the seasoned flour and, using your hands or a large rubber spatula, toss to coat. Place the coated squid in a single layer on a wire rack set over a rimmed baking sheet, allowing the excess flour to fall free of the squid. Repeat the process with the remaining squid.

2. Meanwhile, heat the oil in a heavy-bottomed 4-quart saucepan over medium heat until it reaches 400 degrees. Carefully add one-quarter of the squid and fry until light golden (do not let the coating turn golden brown, or the squid will toughen), about 1½ minutes, adjusting the heat as necessary to maintain a temperature of 380 to 400 degrees. With a slotted spoon or mesh skimmer, transfer the fried squid to a paper towel–lined plate. Fry the remaining batches of squid and add them to the plate. Sprinkle the fried squid lightly with salt to taste and serve immediately with lemon wedges.

10

BREAD AND PIZZA

WE KNOW AND LOVE ITALIAN CUISINE because of pasta, first and foremost. But pizzas and breads are probably Italy's second most important culinary export. Americans have adopted pizza as their own, adding odd toppings (pineapple) and creating new styles (such as crust filled with cheese).

For this chapter, we've taken a look at the most popular kind of pizza in Italy, which originated in Naples and is now made throughout the country (and the world). Pizza made this way has a thin, crisp crust and light, flavorful toppings. Italians believe that pizza is a bread, not just a vehicle for excessive amounts of cheese and sauce. Real Italian pizza is never soft or greasy.

In addition, this chapter looks at several popular breads that can be made at home, including focaccia, a rustic country loaf, olive-rosemary bread, and ciabatta. They offer a real taste of the fine art of Italian bread making.

FOCACCIA

MANY OF THE FOCACCIA RECIPES WE tried in the past produced a crusty, crisp bread that was only slightly thicker than pizza. These dense, hard breads were often loaded with toppings. They were more a meal than a snack or an accompaniment to Sunday dinner.

We wanted something quite different. Good focaccia has a soft, chewy texture and a high rise. The crumb is filled with small to medium-sized air pockets, which give the bread a good rise and create an overall impression of lightness and chewiness. As for the toppings, they should be minimal. Focaccia is a bread, not a meal.

We began our investigations with a composite recipe of yeast, warm water, olive oil, flour, and salt that was similar to our pizza dough (see page 369). After more than a dozen initial tests, we were not much closer to a solution. We tried reducing the salt, which can inhibit the action of yeast, and ended up with a better rise but bland bread. We tried bread flour, all-purpose flour, whole wheat flour, and all possible combinations of these three. Bread flour makes focaccia chewy but also dry and tough. Whole wheat flour is at cross-purposes with our stated goal of a soft texture and high rise. Unbleached all-purpose flour turned out to be the right choice, but we still had a lot of work to do.

We tried milk instead of water and got better browning and a softer dough, but the bread was kind of flat. Increasing the yeast produced a high focaccia, but the flavor of the yeast was too dominant. We tried letting the dough ferment in the refrigerator for a day. This lightened the texture and produced larger holes in the dough but seemed like a lot of work for a relatively small improvement. We wanted to be able to make and enjoy focaccia on the same day.

In our research, we ran across two recipes from southern Italy that added riced potatoes to the dough. When we tried one of them, from Carol Field's *The Italian Baker* (Harper & Row, 1985), we liked the moistness, high rise, and soft texture of this bread. However, the crumb was fairly dense and compact, like a cake. This bread had several appealing traits but still was not quite what we wanted.

We knew that sponges (relatively thin mixtures of yeast, water, and flour that are allowed to ferment briefly) are often used to lend flavor to and create air holes in breads. We were not terribly concerned about flavor. With olive oil, salt, and herbs, we were sure that any flavor boost from a sponge would be hard to detect. But we did want those air holes, so we tried a quick sponge.

We stirred the yeast, half the water, and a small portion of the flour together in a small bowl, covered the bowl with plastic wrap, and let the sponge rest before adding the remaining water, flour, oil, and salt. The difference was remarkable. The extra half-hour of fermentation produced wonderfully large bubbles. The result was a bread that rose very high but still had a nice, light texture. We tried longer sponges and found that 30 minutes was enough time for the yeast to work its magic.

With the sponge having been successful in our basic composite recipe, we now tried it with Carol Field's potato focaccia, which we had liked so much. The result was perfect. The sponge transformed the crumb from dense and cakelike to chewy and airy. The bread rose higher than the version made with just flour, and the crumb was softer and more moist. As a final adjustment, we tried rapid-rise yeast to see if we could cut the rising times. This yeast works fine in this recipe and shaves off more than an hour from the process.

MEASURING FLOUR

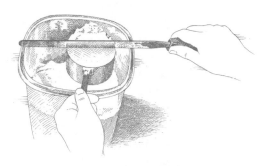

No matter the type or brand, we measure all flour by the dip-and-sweep method. Dip a metal or plastic dry measure into a bag of flour so that the cup is overflowing, then use the flat side of a knife or an icing spatula to level the flour, sweeping the excess back into the bag. Short of weighing flour (which is what professional bakers do), this measuring method is your best guarantee of using the right amount of flour. Spooning the flour into the measuring cup aerates it, and you might end up with as much as 25 percent less flour by weight.

A couple of notes about working with this dough. The moisture from the potatoes helps keep the crumb soft but also makes the dough very sticky. Adding extra flour makes the dough easier to handle, but the results are not as good because the wet dough helps produce bread with air pockets and chewiness.

Sticky doughs are best kneaded in a standing mixer or a food processor. You can make

SCIENCE: How Yeast Works

Yeast is a plantlike living organism. Its function in a bread dough is to consume sugars and starches in the flour and convert them into carbon dioxide and alcohol, which give bread its lift and flavor. This process is known as fermentation. Flavor compounds and alcohol—byproducts of fermentation—give yeasted bread its characteristic aroma and flavor.

A small amount of honey or sugar is sometimes added to bread dough to enhance the fermentation process; yeast grows faster and better when it has enough food (sugar) to feed on. Warm water (about 110 degrees) is also necessary to activate dry yeast; very hot or cold water may impair its functioning. In fact, very warm water (in excess of 125 degrees) will kill the yeast, and yeast will not activate well in cool water.

Heat is generated during fermentation and rising, and punching the dough down mixes the warmer dough (in the center) with the cooler dough (on the outside edges), thus normalizing the overall temperature. Punching down also releases any excess carbon dioxide, breaks apart yeast particles that are clinging together, and redistributes the sugars, giving the yeast a refreshed food source. After punching down, the dough is often given a second rise, which happens more quickly because more yeast is at work.

During the first few minutes of baking, the alcohol (formed earlier during fermentation) evaporates, gases expand, and bubbles enlarge, fostering more rise. This is referred to as oven spring. The yeast cells are killed during this process.

the dough by hand, but you will probably end up incorporating slightly more flour.

When it comes time to shape the dough, moisten your hands with a little water. This will prevent the dough from sticking to your fingers. If you try to stretch the dough to fit into a rectangular pan, you may need to let it rest before completing the final shaping. The dough is quite elastic and will put up a good fight without this rest.

An oven temperature of 425 degrees bakes the focaccia quickly without any burning. Lower temperatures produce an inferior crust, and higher temperatures can cause the bottom to burn. Keep the focaccia away from the bottom of the oven to prevent the crust from scorching. Once the bread is golden brown, immediately transfer it to a cooling rack to keep the bottom crust from becoming soggy. Focaccia tastes best warm, so wait about 20 minutes and then serve.

SCIENCE: What Potatoes Do in Bread Dough

Boiled potatoes in focaccia dough had a distinct effect on its flavor and texture. The result: a moister, more tender, sweeter, and softer dough than one made with just wheat flour. We wanted to know why the boiled potatoes made such a difference in the focaccia dough.

According to Dr. Al Bushway, professor of food science at the University of Maine, potatoes contain more starch than wheat flour. Because starch traps moisture during baking, this makes for a moister dough. Potatoes also contain less protein than flour. This results in less gluten being formed in the dough, which in turn produces a softer, more tender product. Finally, potatoes add another dimension of flavor in two ways. First, the free sugars in the potatoes cause faster fermentation, resulting in a more complex flavor in a shorter period of time. Second, the sugars that are not consumed by the yeast in the fermentation process add sweetness to the final dough.

Rosemary Focaccia

MAKES ONE 15½ BY 10½-INCH RECTANGLE

Rapid-rise yeast reduces the preparation time by more than an hour. If you use an equal amount of regular active dry yeast instead, let the sponge in step 2 develop for 30 minutes rather than 20, and increase the first and second rises to 1½ hours each.

DOUGH

1	medium baking potato (about 9 ounces), peeled and quartered
1½	teaspoons rapid-rise yeast
3½	cups (17½ ounces) unbleached all-purpose flour
1	cup warm water (105 to 115 degrees)
2	tablespoons extra-virgin olive oil, plus more for oiling the bowl and pan
1¼	teaspoons salt

TOPPING

2	tablespoons extra-virgin olive oil
2	tablespoons fresh rosemary leaves
¾	teaspoon coarse sea salt (or 1¼ teaspoons kosher salt)

1. FOR THE DOUGH: Bring 1 quart water to a boil in a small saucepan. Add the potato and simmer until tender, about 25 minutes. Drain the potato well. When cool, put the potato through a ricer (fitted with the fine disk) or grate it on the large holes on a box grater. Reserve 1⅓ cups lightly packed potato.

2. Meanwhile, in the bowl of a standing mixer or the workbowl of a food processor fitted with a steel blade, mix or pulse the yeast, ½ cup flour, and ½ cup warm water until combined. Cover tightly with plastic wrap (or put the workbowl lid on) and set aside until bubbly, about 20 minutes. Add the remaining dough ingredients, including the reserved potato. If using a mixer, fit it with a paddle attachment and mix on low speed until the

dough comes together. Switch to a dough hook attachment and increase the speed to medium; continue kneading until the dough is smooth and elastic, about 5 minutes. If using a food processor, process the dough until it is smooth and elastic, about 40 seconds.

3. Transfer the dough to a lightly oiled bowl, turn to coat with oil, and cover tightly with plastic wrap. Let rise in a warm, draft-free area until the dough is puffy and doubled in volume, about 1 hour.

4. With wet hands (to prevent sticking), press the dough flat into a generously oiled 15½ by 10½-inch rimmed baking sheet. If the dough resists going into the corners (and it probably will), cover it with a damp cloth and let it relax for 15 minutes before trying to stretch it again. Cover the dough with lightly greased or oil-sprayed plastic wrap and let rise in a warm, draft-free area until puffy and doubled in volume, 45 minutes to 1 hour.

5. Meanwhile, adjust an oven rack to the lower-middle position and heat the oven to 425 degrees. With two wet fingers, dimple the risen dough at regular intervals (see the

DIMPLING FOCACCIA DOUGH

After the dough has risen for the second time, wet two fingers and use them to make indentations at regular intervals. The dimples should be deep enough to hold small pieces of topping, herbs, and/or pools of olive oil. There should be about two dozen dimples.

illustration below). The dimples (make about 2 dozen) should be deep enough to hold small pieces of topping, herbs, and/or pools of olive oil.

6. FOR THE TOPPING: Drizzle the dough with the oil and sprinkle evenly with the rosemary and coarse salt, landing some in the pools of oil.

7. Bake until the focaccia bottom is golden brown and crisp, 23 to 25 minutes. Transfer to a wire rack to cool slightly. Cut into squares and serve warm. (Focaccia can be kept on the counter for several hours and reheated just before serving. Alternatively, wrap the cooled focaccia in plastic and then foil and freeze for up to 1 month; unwrap and defrost in a 325-degree oven until soft, about 15 minutes.)

➤ VARIATIONS
Hand-Kneaded Focaccia
Follow the recipe for Rosemary Focaccia through step 1. In step 2, mix the starter ingredients with a wooden spoon in a large bowl; cover and let stand 20 minutes. Add 1½ cups flour to the starter, then beat with a wooden spoon for 5 minutes. Add 1¼ cups flour along with the remaining dough ingredients; continue beating until the dough comes together. Turn the dough onto a floured surface; knead in the remaining ¼ cup flour until the dough is elastic and sticky, 4 to 5 minutes. Transfer the dough to an oiled bowl as in step 3 and follow the remaining instructions.

Parmesan Focaccia
Follow the recipe for Rosemary Focaccia, substituting ⅔ cup grated Parmesan cheese for the rosemary and coarse sea salt.

Sage Focaccia
Follow the recipe for Rosemary Focaccia, adding 1 tablespoon chopped fresh sage leaves with the other dough ingredients in step 2

and substituting 24 whole fresh sage leaves (one per oil-filled dimple) for the rosemary.

Focaccia with Black Olives and Thyme

Follow the recipe for Rosemary Focaccia, substituting 1 teaspoon fresh thyme leaves and 24 pitted large black olives (one per oil-filled dimple) for the rosemary.

RUSTIC ITALIAN BREAD

A SIMPLE, RUSTIC WHITE BREAD IS AS much a staple in Italy as pasta. It is served with dinner, sliced for sandwiches, toasted for bruschetta, mixed with leftover soup to create a new meal, or soaked in water for a quick summer salad with tomatoes. Unfortunately, the loaves offered at most American supermarkets are of poor quality, with a fluffy, flavorless crumb and a thin, blond crust. A good rustic Italian loaf has a thick, hearty crust that contrasts with the soft yet toothsome white crumb within. The flavor should be easy and well-rounded, neither sour nor yeasty. Although this simple, hearty bread requires only four ingredients—flour, water, yeast, and salt—the amount of each and manner in which they are put together determine the difference between good, artisanal-quality bread and a disappointing waste of time.

Beginning with the ingredients, we first decided to use unbleached all-purpose flour. Although wheat and bread flours do make great loaves of bread, they are too hearty for the light, airy crumb and simple flavor of the traditional Italian loaf. Many recipes we researched called for special bottled or purified water; however, we found that tap water worked just fine. Rapid-rise yeast, a relative newcomer in the baking world (it

was introduced within in the last 20 years), was easiest to use because it requires no special proofing or hydrating but rather can simply be put into the mixer with the other ingredients. For salt, we preferred the smaller, more uniform crystal size of table salt over kosher salt. With the ingredients chosen, we focused next on their amounts.

Wanting to produce a large, round loaf that would serve a table of 8 to 10 people (or 4, with leftovers for sandwiches the next day), we knew that 6 cups of flour was the right amount to begin with. We accurately figured that 6 cups of flour required 2 teaspoons of salt and roughly one teaspoon of rapid-rise yeast. The water, on the other hand, was a more difficult variable to nail down. Most white bread recipes call for around 2¼ cups of water for 6 cups of flour, but we found this produced a dry, mediocre crumb that lacked the chewiness we wanted. After doing some research, we noted that most artisan bakers use a bit more water to enhance the crumb texture. We then baked off several loaves using various amounts of water until we achieve just the right texture—2½ cups of water to the 6 cups of flour made the light, airy crumb and toothsome chew of a true rustic loaf.

The next issue was whether or not to use a starter (a fermented piece of dough), called a *biga* in Italian. A biga is simply a small, wet dough made of flour, water, and yeast that is allowed to ferment overnight. The fermentation develops gas, gluten, and a wheaty characteristic, which in turn adds leavening, structure, and flavor to the final bread. Making two loaves side by side, one with and one without a biga, we found the loaf with the biga tasted much better. Not only did it offer a deeper flavor but also its chewy, hearty texture was both authentic and satisfying. To figure out how much biga we needed, we baked several loaves with varying amounts, keeping

INGREDIENTS: All-Purpose Flour

We wanted to know if there was a single all-purpose flour that would be best for those cooks who keep only one kind of flour in the pantry. So we stocked our test kitchen shelves with nine brands of all-purpose flour and started a bake-off that eventually stretched over some six months. We ended up preparing two kinds of cookies, pie pastry, biscuits, cake, muffins, and bread with each brand of flour, often making several batches of each item.

When milling all-purpose flour, a flour company must make a number of choices that influence the way its product performs in recipes. For starters, there is the essence of the flour, the wheat itself. All-purpose flour is typically made from hard red winter wheat, soft red winter wheat, or a combination of the two. Of the flours we used in the taste tests, five were made from hard winter wheat, one was made of soft wheat, and three were a mix of soft and hard.

Perhaps the primary difference between these types of wheat—and, consequently, the flours made from them—is in their protein content. Hard winter wheat is about 10 to 13 percent protein, soft wheat about 8 to 10 percent. Mixtures of the two are somewhere in between. You can actually feel this difference with your fingers; hard wheat flours tend to have a subtle granular feel while soft wheat flours feel fine but starchy, much like cornstarch.

A second important difference in flours is whether they are bleached or not. Technically, all-purpose flours are all bleached. Carotenoid pigments in wheat lend a faint yellowish tint to freshly milled flour, but in a matter of about 12 weeks these pigments oxidize, undergoing the same chemical process that turns a sliced apple brown. In this case, yellowish flour changes to a whiter hue (though not stark white). Early in the 20th century, as the natural bleaching process came to be understood, scientists identified methods to chemically expedite and intensify it. Typically, all-purpose flours are bleached with either benzoyl peroxide or chlorine gas. The latter not only bleaches the flour but also alters the flour proteins, making them less inclined to form strong gluten. Today, consumers prefer chemically bleached flour over unbleached because they associate the whiter color with higher quality. In our tests, some of the baked goods made with bleached flour were such a pure white that they actually looked startlingly unnatural and "commercial" versus homemade.

While the protein guidelines make eminently good sense, to our surprise, the results of our tests did not always correspond. The biscuit test did reveal a certain progression from light, cakelike biscuits produced by the lowest-protein flours to coarser, heavier biscuits produced by the higher-protein flours. But our tasters liked all of the biscuits, except for one that had stale flavors. Another trend we noticed was that lower-protein flours spread more in tests of chocolate chip cookies and muffins.

Overall, the four bleached flours we tested did not perform as well as the unbleached flours and were regularly criticized for tasting flat or carrying off flavors, often described as metallic. These characteristics, however, were more difficult to detect in recipes that contained a high proportion of ingredients other than flour. Our cake tests and chocolate chip cookie tests (both sugary recipes) were the two tests in which off flavors carried by the bleached flour went undetected or were considered faint.

Despite the subtleties, however, the good news is that we did end up with two flours we can recommend wholeheartedly. Both King Arthur and Pillsbury unbleached flours regularly made for highly recommended baked goods, producing a more consistent range of preferred products than the other seven flours in the taste tests.

THE BEST ALL-PURPOSE FLOURS
In our testing of nine leading brands of all-purpose flour, we preferred unbleached flour made by King Arthur (left) and Pillsbury (right). If you are going to have only one flour in the kitchen, our advice is to choose one of these two.

the total percentage of each ingredient the same. We learned that too much biga sours the otherwise simple flavor of a rustic loaf. We determined that biga made with 1 cup of flour, ½ cup of water, and a tiny amount of yeast was enough.

Although recipes make and ferment bigas differently, we found it was fine when left out on the counter covered with plastic wrap. To help promote its fermentation and build gluten, we found we need to mix the biga for about four minutes. Although many starters do not require this, we noted the extra mixing was necessary to help develop flavor and gluten, as the bread was made with all-purpose flour only.

Until now, we had been using a straightforward mixing procedure; we combined the biga with the remaining ingredients and kneaded until the dough was soft and firm, about 10 minutes. Yet the resulting loaves were a bit too dense and rose little in the oven. Taking a closer look at the crumb, it seemed as though we hadn't built up enough gluten strength to produce a taller loaf. We tried kneading the dough longer in the mixer, but the results were disappointing. The longer the dough was kneaded, the warmer it became, turning from a pale yellow to a grayish white. Although this dough did have a higher rise in the oven, it had an odd, chopped-looking crumb structure and far less flavor than our previous loaves. We learned, after a little research, that we had overmixed the dough. Overmixing, although nearly impossible to do by hand, is quite easy when using a standing mixer. Although mixing the dough is necessary to hydrate and combine the ingredients and to develop gluten, overmixed dough (which is often overheated) pushes the gluten into small, tight, tough strands that are pale in both color and flavor.

Wanting to develop long, golden strands of gluten without overmixing, we tried a technique called autolysis. Setting the biga aside, we mixed the remaining flour and water and let the mixture sit for 30 minutes, allowing the flour to hydrate fully before being mixed. We then combined this flour and water mixture with the remaining ingredients and kneaded until it was smooth and tight, about 10 minutes. The resulting bread was wonderful, with a beautifully textured crumb and a hearty crust that shattered as it was cut. The key was that the hydrated flour mixed to a tight, glutinous dough in less time, producing a far superior crust and a crumb with a full, clean flavor.

Shaping the dough and baking it turned out to be relatively simple. To shape the dough, we found it best to handle it as little as possible so as not to disturb any of the air bubbles that developed during fermentation. When the dough was overhandled, these bubbles were forced out, and the resulting crumb was dense and even. After gently pulling the edges of the dough together to form a round, we turned it smooth side up and continued to tuck the dough underneath itself until the outer surface was smooth and taut. Transferring this delicate, somewhat sticky dough was a challenge, but we figured out a solution: place it on a sheet of parchment as it's shaped and slide the parchment and dough onto the hot baking stone together.

We baked bread at temperatures ranging from 400 to 500 degrees and found a combination of temperatures yielded the best result. Starting at 500 degrees for the first 10 minutes, we found it necessary to turn the oven down to 450 to finish baking. The initial burst of high heat ensured the loaf would rise as much as possible, while the lower temperature baked the bread through without burning the crust. The addition of steam also was key for a good rise in the oven (known as oven spring) as well as a good crust. The steam, which we made by pouring water on a preheated baking sheet placed on the bottom rack of the oven, helped keep the surface of the dough moist and pliable. The pliable crust allowed the bread to rise as much as possible during its first few minutes of baking before it set. We found the bread took about 45 minutes to bake through. Although the warm loaf, fresh from the oven, is tempting, it is best to let it cool thoroughly before slicing.

Rustic Italian Bread

MAKES I LARGE LOAF

We found parchment paper to be key when shaping and baking the bread. Shaping the dough is easy but does take practice. Be careful not to overwork the dough as it is being turned into a round, but make sure the final loaf has a taut surface.

BIGA

I	cup (5 ounces) unbleached all-purpose flour
⅛	teaspoon rapid-rise yeast
½	cup water, at room temperature

DOUGH

5	cups (25 ounces) unbleached all-purpose flour, plus more for dusting work surfaces and hands
2	cups water, at room temperature
I	teaspoon rapid-rise yeast
2	teaspoons salt
	Olive oil or nonstick cooking spray for oiling bowl
2	cups hot water for adding steam in the oven

1. FOR THE BIGA: Place the flour, yeast, and water in the bowl of a standing mixer fitted with a paddle attachment. Mix on the lowest setting until the ingredients form a uniform, sticky mass, about 1 minute. Scrape down the sides of the bowl with a rubber spatula and turn the mixer to the second-lowest setting. Mix until the biga becomes a glutinous mass, about 4 minutes. Transfer the biga to a clean bowl, cover it tightly with plastic wrap, and allow it to sit at room temperature (60 to 70 degrees) for 12 hours or overnight.

2. FOR THE DOUGH: Place the flour in the bowl of a standing mixer and add the water. Stir with a wooden spoon until just combined. Cover with plastic wrap and set aside for 30 minutes. Add the biga and yeast to the bowl with the flour and water mixture and place the bowl in a standing mixer fitted with a dough hook. Knead on the lowest setting until the ingredients come together to form a dough, about 4 minutes (the dough should clear the sides of the bowl as it is being kneaded but should stick to the very bottom). Add the salt and continue to mix on medium-

INGREDIENTS: Rapid-Rise Yeast

Yeast is a plant, and different varieties have quite different qualities, as do different varieties of, say, roses. Rapid-rise yeast (also called instant yeast) has been genetically engineered to reproduce the best characteristics of yeasts from around the world. Although genetic engineering often results in loss of flavor, our blind taste tests over the past several years have confirmed that in this case, genetic engineering has produced an excellent product.

This yeast works faster for two primary reasons. Rapid-rise yeast has superior enzyme activity when compared to regular active dry yeast. This enzyme activity converts starches to sugars faster then regular-rise varieties. Rapid-rise yeast also has an open, porous structure, which means that it can absorb liquid instantly.

For these reasons, we prefer rapid-rise yeast. You can use active dry yeast in any of our recipes, however the rising times will be slightly longer.

low speed until the dough is smooth, about 6 minutes longer (do not knead the dough for more than 12 minutes in total). Transfer the dough to a large, lightly oiled bowl, cover with plastic wrap, and let rise until nearly tripled in volume, about 3 hours.

3. Gently slide the dough onto a lightly floured surface with its rough side (the side that was touching the bowl) facing up. Dust the dough and your hands with flour. Gently pull the dough into a round by gathering its edges into a bundle and pinching to close, like a beggar's purse. Carefully transfer the dough, smooth side up, to a large sheet of parchment paper and gently tuck the edges of the dough underneath until the loaf is taut across the top. Dust with flour and cover loosely with plastic wrap. Let rise until doubled in size, about 1 hour.

4. Meanwhile, adjust an oven rack to the lower-middle position and place baking tiles or a large baking stone on the rack. On a second rack, set in the lowest position, place a small baking pan or cast-iron skillet to hold water. Heat the oven to 500 degrees.

5. Use a razor blade or sharp knife to cut a large X about ½ inch deep into the top of the dough. Gently transfer the loaf (still on the parchment) to a peel or the back of a baking sheet. Remove the plastic wrap and slide the dough into the center of the baking tiles or stone. Pour 2 cups hot water into the heated pan underneath the stone, being careful to avoid the steam. Bake for 10 minutes, then reduce the oven temperature to 450 degrees. Continue baking until an instant-read thermometer inserted in the bottom of the bread registers 210 degrees and the crust is dark golden brown, 30 to 35 minutes longer. Remove the bread from the oven; let it cool to room temperature before slicing, about 2 hours. To crisp the crust, bake the cooled bread in a 450-degree oven for 10 minutes.

OLIVE-ROSEMARY BREAD

OLIVE-ROSEMARY BREAD IS A HEFTY, rustic country loaf. Armored with the thickest of crusts and full of incredible chew, this bread is pure substance. After making a few of these loaves, however, we found the same problems again and again. Flimsy, anemic crusts, fluffy, tasteless interiors with little sign of olive or rosemary—this bread needed help.

We wanted to develop a loaf with a substantial crust that would challenge the sturdiest bread knife. This bread would have a fabulous tug-and-pull texture that made us want to rip it apart with our hands. Last, we wanted it to be brimming with the flavor of olives and perfumed with rosemary, a whiff of yeast, and a hint of sourness.

There are many ways of leavening a country bread, but we wanted to find one that was both convenient for the home cook and allowed for maximum flavor development. We ended up using a biga—a mixture of flour, water, and yeast is left to ferment, then additional flour, water, and other ingredients are added. We found that allowing the biga to sit overnight produced a great-tasting loaf with more flavor than one made with a quick rise using more yeast. In fact, we only used ½ teaspoon of rapid-rise yeast for 6 cups of flour. We also tried varying the biga recipe by using equal amounts of whole wheat and white flour. The whole-wheat flour added texture and flavor, and we liked the results.

The next test was water. Professional bakers know that a high water content produces more texture and chew. After some research, we figured that a water content of 68 percent should work. The theory was that the higher percentage of water—most bread recipes run around 60 percent—would improve the chew. We tried this formula and got mediocre results. It was good bread, but it lacked the big chew we wanted.

After visiting a professional bakery, we were inspired to push the water level even higher. The dough in the bakery was a sticky mass and made bread with big chew, big crust, and big flavor. Back in the test kitchen, we increased the water to 2½ cups per 6 cups of flour, which brought the proportion of water up to a whopping 76 percent. We tried to knead the sticky dough by hand, but this was almost impossible without adding lots of additional flour. At the end of the day, the bread was vastly improved and had cavernous airholes and real chew.

Until now, we had been using a professional baker's bread flour, which has a very high level of protein (about 14 percent). Because this flour is not readily available to the public, we tried two lower-protein flours: a regular bread flour and an all-purpose flour. Both flours produced a chewier, crustier loaf, although the dough was nearly too wet to work with. We reduced the amount of water to 2⅓ cups to accommodate the lower-protein flours, which can't absorb as much water as higher-protein flour, and the results were even better. Because regular bread flour is sold in supermarkets, we decided to use it in our recipe.

The type of olives to add was next on our list, and a quick testing of green versus black varieties led tasters to choose the latter, mostly for their piquant flavor and dramatic color. When it came to brined versus oil-cured, there was no debate. Tasters overwhelmingly preferred the oil-cured olives. Their potent flavor brought olive impact to every bite.

The other main flavor ingredient in this bread is rosemary, and here we found that more is definitely better. Tasting after tasting, tasters asked that the rosemary level be increased. Finally, we found that ¼ cup of chopped fresh rosemary filled the loaf with its potent flavor.

Tweaking the flavor of the bread at this point, we tested the amount of salt. Most recipes using 6 cups of flour use 2 teaspoons of salt. We thought that the added salt from the olives would lower the amount of salt needed, but we were wrong. Even with the salty olives, 2 teaspoons of salt was just right. Next, we tried a little sweetness to both boost flavor and promote browning of the crust. When we added 2 tablespoons of honey, the flavor was improved, and the crust turned a rich nut brown.

Kneading such wet dough at length by hand was not our first choice. We tried using a food processor fitted with a steel blade but found that the heavy dough was too much for all but the heaviest-duty processor. The best solution was a heavy-duty standing mixer with a dough hook. After 15 minutes of kneading at the lowest speed, we turned our dough into an oiled bowl to rise for about 2 hours or until tripled in volume. Allowing the dough to triple in volume both improves flavor and helps the loaf retain its shape when baked.

Getting the olives into the dough begat a new set of problems. Adding them to the dough in the mixer turned the dough an unattractive shade of gray. We found it better to gently knead the olives in by hand. We also found that it was important not to chop the olives. Cut into pieces, the olives leached their black liquid into the dough. Tasters wanted distinct pieces of olives, so unless they were extremely large (bigger than 1 inch), we left them alone once pitted.

Because the dough is still very wet at this point, it can be difficult to handle and shape. To avoid excess handling (too much ruins the irregular, airy holes in the crumb), we found the best solution was to turn the dough out onto a lightly floured surface, flour hands and the top of the dough very lightly, and gently press into a round. Next, fold the dough into a ball, then transfer it to a basket or colander lined with inexpensive 100 percent cotton muslin or linen that has flour worked into the fabric. Cover the dough with aluminum foil (a damp dishtowel stuck to the dough, while plastic wrap caused it to proof too much and yielded a fluffy-textured dough). It is then easy to invert the dough onto a cornmeal-dusted or parchment-lined peel.

The last major issue was the crust. Steam is often identified as the key to a good crust, and after baking one loaf with no steam (which yielded a paper-thin crust), we agreed. We tested ways to introduce the steam: spritzing the bread with water, adding ice cubes to the oven, and adding a pan of hot water to the oven. Of the three, we found that the hot pan of water worked, but only if the pan was preheated. Two cups of water generates both instant steam and enough residual water to maintain a steamy atmosphere throughout baking. It is important, though, to use caution when working with steam. Use thick oven mitts and a long-sleeved shirt when pouring the hot water into the pan.

Most recipes state that the bread should be baked to an internal temperature of 190 degrees, but this produces undercooked bread with our recipe. This bread must reach 210 degrees, which can be measured by inserting an instant-read thermometer halfway into the bottom of the loaf. If you do not have an instant-read thermometer, bake the bread until the crust starts to turn brownish-black in spots.

Finally, we tested oven temperature. We thought that starting the bread in a 500-degree oven, then dropping the temperature to 400 degrees, would compensate for the heat lost when the oven door was opened. The crust on this dough was thin and disappointing. Baking the dough at 500 degrees for the first 15 minutes, then dropping the temperature to 400 degrees led to a scorched crust with an undercooked interior. The best baking temperature turned out to be a constant 450 degrees.

Olive-Rosemary Bread

MAKES 1 LARGE LOAF

Because of its high water content, the bread will be gummy if pulled from the oven too soon. To ensure the bread's doneness, make sure the internal temperature reaches 210 degrees by inserting an instant-read thermometer into the bottom of the loaf. Also, look at the crust; it should be very dark brown, almost black. Keep in mind that rising times vary depending on the kitchen temperature (the times listed below are minimums). For the second rising, we used a basket that was 4 inches high, 7 inches wide across the bottom, and 12 inches wide across the top. A colander of similar proportions works equally well. For coarser, chewier bread, decrease the bread flour by ¼ cup. You will need muslin or linen, baking tiles or a stone, and a pizza peel for this recipe.

BIGA

½	teaspoon rapid-rise yeast
1	cup water, at room temperature
1	cup (5 ounces) bread flour
1	cup (5 ounces) whole wheat flour

DOUGH

4	cups (20 ounces) bread flour, plus more for dusting on work surfaces and hands
1⅓	cups water, at room temperature
2	tablespoons honey
¼	cup chopped fresh rosemary leaves
2	teaspoons salt
12	ounces oil-cured black olives, pitted and cut in half widthwise if larger than 1 inch (about 9 ounces pitted olives)

	Olive oil or nonstick cooking spray for oiling bowl
	Coarse cornmeal for sprinkling on the peel
1	tablespoon coarse sea salt for sprinkling into the dough
2	cups hot water for adding steam in the oven

1. FOR THE BIGA: Stir the yeast into the water in a medium bowl until dissolved. Mix in the flours with a rubber spatula to create a stiff, wet dough. Cover with plastic wrap. Let sit at room temperature for at least 5 hours or, preferably, overnight. (The biga can be refrigerated up to 24 hours; return it to room temperature before continuing with the recipe.)

2. FOR THE DOUGH: Mix the flour, water, honey, rosemary, and biga in the bowl of a

---

EQUIPMENT: Kitchen Scales

Every serious cook needs an accurate scale for weighing fruits, vegetables, and meats. When making bread, a scale is even more critical. Professional bakers know that measuring flour by volume can be problematic. A cup of flour can weigh between 4 and 6 ounces depending on its type, the humidity, whether or not it has been sifted, and the way it has been put into the cup. Weight is a much more accurate way to measure flour.

There are two basic types of kitchen scales. Mechanical scales operate on a spring and lever system. When an item is placed on the scale, internal springs are compressed. The springs are attached to levers, which move a needle on the scale's display (a ruler with lines and numbers printed on paper and glued to the scale). The more the springs are compressed, the farther the needle moves along the ruler.

Electronic, or digital, scales have two plates that are set at a fixed distance. The bottom plate is stationary, the top plate is not. When food is placed on the platform attached to the top plate, the distance between the plates changes slightly. The movement of the top plate (no more than 1/1,000 inch) causes a change in the flow of electricity through the scale's circuitry. This change is translated into a weight and expressed in numbers displayed on the face of the scale.

We tested 10 electronic scales and 9 mechanical scales. As a group, the electronic scales were vastly preferred. Their digital displays are much easier to read than the measures on most mechanical scales, where the lines on the ruler are so closely spaced it's impossible to nail down the precise weight within 1 ½ ounce. Also, many mechanical scales could weigh items only within a limited range—usually between 1 ounce and 5 pounds. What's the point of owning a scale that can't weigh a large chicken or roast? Most electronic scales can handle items that weigh as much as 10 pounds and as little as ¼ ounce. Among the electronic scales we tested, we found that several features make the difference between a good electronic scale and a great one.

Readability is a must. The displayed numbers should be large. Also, the displayed numbers should be steeply angled and as far from the weighing platform as possible. If the display is too close to the platform, the numbers can hide beneath the rim of a dinner plate or cake pan.

An automatic shut-off feature will save battery life, but this feature can be annoying, especially if the shut-off cycle kicks in at under two minutes. A scale that shuts off automatically after five minutes or more is easier to use.

A large weighing platform (that detaches for easy cleaning) is another plus. Last, we preferred electronic scales that display weight increments in decimals rather than fractions. The former are more accurate and easier to work with when scaling a recipe up or down.

THE BEST SCALES
Despite its high price tag ($125) and some minor quirks, the Soehnle Cyber Electronic Scale (left) was the runaway winner in our testing. It has a detachable glass measuring platform that is especially easy to clean. The Salter Electronic Aquatronic Scale (right) is our second choice. It is half the price ($60) of the Soehnle, but food can become trapped between the weighing platform and base.

standing mixer with a rubber spatula. Knead, using a dough hook attachment, on the lowest speed until the dough is smooth, about 15 minutes, adding the salt during the final 3 minutes. Transfer the dough to a lightly floured countertop. Lightly flour your hands and, working quickly but gently, knead in the olives in three batches, making sure to handle the dough as little as possible. Transfer the dough to a large, lightly oiled bowl. Cover with plastic wrap. Let rise until tripled in volume, at least 2 hours.

3. Turn the dough onto a lightly floured surface. Dust the dough top and your hands with flour. Lightly press the dough into a round by folding its edges into the middle from top, right, bottom, and left, sequentially, then gathering it loosely together. Transfer the dough, smooth side down, to a colander or basket lined with heavily floured muslin or linen. Cover loosely with a large sheet of aluminum foil. Let the dough rise until almost doubled in size, at least 45 minutes.

4. Meanwhile, adjust an oven rack to the lower-middle position and place baking tiles or a large baking stone on the rack. On a second rack, set in the lowest position, place a small baking pan or cast-iron skillet to hold water. Heat the oven to 450 degrees.

5. Liberally sprinkle coarse cornmeal over the entire surface of a peel or place a large sheet of parchment on the peel. Invert the dough onto the peel and remove the muslin. Use a razor blade or sharp knife to cut a large X about ½ inch deep into the top of the dough, then sprinkle the coarse salt into the X.

6. Slide the dough (with parchment, if using) from the peel onto the tiles or stone; remove the peel with a quick backward jerk. Pour 2 cups hot water into the heated pan underneath the stone, being careful to avoid the steam. Bake until an instant-read thermometer inserted in the bottom of the bread registers 210 degrees and the crust is very dark brown, 35 to 40 minutes, turning the bread around after 25 minutes if it is not browning evenly. Turn the oven off, open the door, and let the bread remain in the oven 10 minutes longer. Remove the bread from the oven; let it cool to room temperature before slicing, about 2 hours. To crisp the crust, bake the cooled bread in a 450-degree oven for 10 minutes.

CIABATTA

FOUND THROUGHOUT ITALY, CIABATTA is a flattened, flour-streaked loaf whose rough appearance speaks of its rustic roots. The name, which translates as "slipper," is an apt description, as long as you envision a threadbare bedroom scuff, not a dainty silk number. Despite its unappetizing name, ciabatta is a delicious bread characterized by a crisp, full-flavored crust and a spongy, tart crumb punctuated by irregular bubbles. As we quickly found out, achieving this distinctive texture and flavor requires an eccentric dough and a leap of faith.

Our preliminary attempts at baking ciabatta revealed that ciabatta dough is unlike anything we had ever worked with. First, it is stunningly wet. We thought we were making grave mistakes in measuring the flour and water, but every recipe we tried produced dough closer in texture to thick cake batter than bread dough. Confused by this inexplicably gooey dough, we dug deeper and started our research from the ground up.

Ciabatta dough starts off with a sponge (called a *biga* in Italian). A biga is nothing more than a mixture of flour, water, and yeast that is allowed to ferment overnight. The fermentation develops the wheat's character and gluten, which in turn add flavor, leavening, and structure to the bread. (Biga traditionally was used in Italy to contribute structure to the notoriously low-protein flour available there. Therefore, bread made with biga often does not need high-protein bread flour for structure. In fact, we found that ciabatta should be made with all-purpose flour so that the crumb remains spongy and soft.) The sourness results from acid (lactic and acetic) buildup in the biga, a byproduct of fermentation. Because ciabatta is characteristically sour, a large amount of biga is used. Milder-tasting loaves, like the olive-rosemary bread (page 362), use smaller amounts.

While the recipes we consulted urged strict guidelines for making and fermenting the biga, we found that much of the fuss was unnecessary. We mixed everything together with the aid of a standing mixer, then covered the bowl and left it out on the counter overnight. By the morning, 12 hours later, it bubbled with

SHAPING CIABATTA

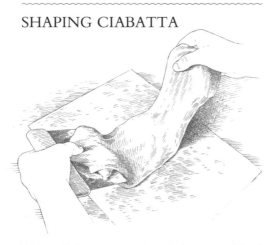

With one fluid motion, grasp the end of one piece of dough with the bench scraper and the other end with your free hand (well dusted with flour) and lift the dough over a large sheet of parchment paper. Allow the middle of the dough to drop to the parchment paper and fold the ends of the dough over like a business letter.

activity and smelled sour. We found that as long as the ambient temperature was between 60 and 70 degrees—standard room temperature—it was okay to leave the biga unrefrigerated. Higher temperatures yielded an overly fermented biga that tasted too sour and produced a poorly leavened loaf. Lower temperatures fermented too slowly, and the biga was not ready for use the following morning.

Unlike most bread doughs, ciabatta dough is barely kneaded—just enough to activate the flour's gluten and make a smooth, elastic dough, albeit a very wet one. Anything longer than five minutes in a standing mixer made for a uniform crumb, which is not desirable in a ciabatta.

Because of its short knead, ciabatta dough is often turned (gently folded onto itself) as it rises to increase flavor and gluten development. We were initially skeptical of the technique but were surprised by the results; unturned dough paled in comparison, producing a loaf with a milder flavor and a less interesting crumb than dough that had been turned.

Turning is a simple technique. During the first rise, the dough is typically emptied onto a floured work surface and folded onto itself—gently enough that the dough's pent-up gases are not expressed. Our ciabatta dough was so sticky that this resulted in a gummy mess. However, we found we could turn the dough in the bowl with the aid of a large rubber spatula. The technique felt similar to folding egg whites into a batter, requiring a similar gentle touch and circular motion.

After several turns and tripling in bulk, the dough was ready to be shaped, the step we feared the most. Because of its high moisture content, ciabatta dough cannot be shaped using conventional methods. Instead, it is stretched and folded with quick, decisive movements and liberal amounts of flour.

There are two distinct ways to shape ciabatta: a simple stretch and a more complicated trifold, which starts with a stretch but also involves folding the ends of the dough over each other. Both shapes produced ungainly-looking loaves, but we preferred the trifold as it lent more structure to the loaf, making it slightly taller. Traditional bakers employ clouches, flour-infused heavy muslin cloths, for shaping and proofing the dough, but we found parchment paper served well too. Further, the dough can be baked directly on the parchment, avoiding more tricky maneuvers.

After experimenting with oven temperature, we found that the higher the temperature, the better the bread's crust and crumb. We baked ciabatta at temperatures ranging from 400 to 500 degrees, and 500 degrees yielded superior bread. The crust was darker in color (like a dark caramel), crisper, and more flavorful. The crumb was more uneven—liberally pockmarked with big air bubbles. Water in the oven improved the crumb and assisted in oven spring, the quick expansion of the loaf during the first moments of baking.

While the top crust was ideal, the bottom crust was lacking. The parchment paper—essential for moving the fragile dough into the oven—blocked the evaporation of moisture and prevented the crust from browning. We found that once the dough had firmed, the loaf could be flipped over and the parchment paper removed. Finishing the loaf upside down colored the bottom to the desired crisp brown, just a shade lighter than the top.

Ciabatta

MAKES 2 LOAVES

As you make this bread, keep in mind that the dough is unique; it is wet and very, very sticky. The key to manipulating it is working quickly and gently; rough handling will result in flat, tough bread. Use a large rubber spatula and a dough scraper rather than your hands to move the dough. Make sure to keep the uncooked loaf well covered as the other loaf bakes. Ciabattas are best eaten within a day or two. Because of the amount of flour, this dough must be prepared in a standing mixer. You will also need baking tiles or a stone for this recipe.

BIGA

2½	cups (12½ ounces) unbleached all-purpose flour
¼	teaspoon rapid-rise yeast
1½	cups water, at room temperature

DOUGH

4	cups (20 ounces) unbleached all-purpose flour, plus more for dusting work surfaces and hands
1	teaspoon rapid-rise yeast
2	teaspoons salt
1½	cups water, at room temperature
4	cups hot water for adding steam in the oven

1. FOR THE BIGA: Place the flour, yeast, and water in the bowl of a standing mixer fitted with a paddle attachment. Mix on the lowest setting until the ingredients form a uniform, sticky mass, about 1 minute. Scrape down the sides of the bowl with a rubber spatula and turn the mixer to the second-lowest setting. Mix until the biga becomes a glutinous mass, about 4 minutes. Remove the bowl from the mixer, cover it tightly with plastic wrap, and

allow it to sit at room temperature (60 to 70 degrees) overnight.

2. FOR THE DOUGH: Add all of the ingredients to the bowl with the biga. Place the bowl in a standing mixer fitted with a paddle attachment. Mix on the lowest speed until a roughly combined, shaggy dough forms, about 1 minute; scrape down the sides of the bowl as necessary. Continue mixing on low until the dough becomes shiny and uniform (unlike most bread dough, this dough will never clear the sides of the bowl), about 5 minutes. Turn the dough into a large mixing bowl, cover tightly with plastic wrap, and keep at room temperature.

3. After 1 hour, uncover the dough, liberally dust the top with flour, and slide a rubber spatula between the bowl and the dough, about 3 inches straight down the side of the bowl, and gently lift and fold the edge of the dough toward the middle. Repeat the process around the circumference until all of the dough has been turned over. Tightly re-cover the bowl with plastic wrap. Repeat the process in 1 hour.

4. Within 2½ to 3 hours, the dough should be have roughly tripled in volume. Heavily dust a countertop with flour and, using a rubber spatula, gently turn the dough out onto the countertop. Liberally dust the top of the dough with flour. Using a dough scraper dipped in water, cut the dough into 2 roughly equal pieces. With one fluid motion, grasp the end of one piece of dough with the bench scraper and the other end with your free hand (well dusted with flour) and lift the dough over a large sheet of parchment paper. Allow the middle of the dough to drop to the parchment paper and fold the ends of the dough over like a business letter (see the illustration on page 365). With well-floured hands, gently stretch the dough to approximately 10 by 5 inches. Repeat with the remaining dough and a second sheet of parchment. Cover each loaf loosely with plastic wrap and allow to rest until roughly doubled in bulk and the dough feels relatively firm to the touch, about 1 hour.

5. Meanwhile, adjust an oven rack to the middle position and place baking tiles or a large baking stone on the rack. On a second rack, set in the lowest position, place a small baking pan or cast-iron skillet to hold water. Heat the oven to 500 degrees.

6. Gently transfer one shaped loaf (still on the parchment) to a peel or the back of a baking sheet. Remove the plastic wrap and slide the dough into the center of the baking tiles or stone. Pour 2 cups hot water into the heated pan underneath the stone, being careful of the steam. Bake for 20 minutes, then remove the bread from the oven and remove the parchment paper from the bottom of the loaf. Return the bread to the oven, bottom side up. Bake until the crust is dark golden brown, 15 to 20 minutes longer. Remove the bread from the oven, set right side up on a cooling rack, and cool for at least 1 hour. Repeat the process with the remaining loaf and remaining 2 cups hot water. Before serving, brush excess flour off the loaf with a pastry brush.

PIZZA DOUGH

THE DOUGH IS PROBABLY THE TRICKIEST part of pizza making at home. While pizza dough is nothing more than bread dough with oil added for softness and suppleness, we found in our testing that minor changes in the ingredient list can yield dramatically different results.

Our goal in testing was threefold. We wanted to develop a recipe that was simple to put together; the dough had to be easy to shape and stretch thin; and the crust needed to bake up crisp and chewy, not tough and leathery.

After initial tests, it was clear that bread

flour delivers the best texture. Bread flour makes pizza crust that is chewy and crisp. Unbleached all-purpose flour can be used in a pinch, but the resulting crust is less crisp.

The second key to perfect crust is water. We found that using more water makes the dough softer and more elastic. It stretches more easily than a stiffer, harder dough with less water. We prefer to jump-start the yeast in a little warm water for five minutes. We then add more room-temperature water and oil.

For combining the dry ingredients (flour and salt) with the wet ingredients, the food processor is our first choice. The liquid is evenly incorporated into the dry ingredients, and the blade kneads the dough in just 30 seconds. Of course, the dough can be kneaded by hand or with a standing mixer. If making the dough by hand, resist the temptation to add a lot of flour as you knead.

Use plastic wrap to cover the oiled bowl with the rising dough. We found that the tight seal offered by plastic wrap keeps the dough moist and protects it from drafts better than the standard damp cloth. We reserve the damp cloth for use when the dough has been divided into balls and is waiting to be stretched.

To stretch dough to its maximum diameter, let it rest once or twice during the shaping process. Once you feel some resistance, cover the dough with a damp cloth and wait five minutes before going at it again. Fingertips and hands generally do a better job of stretching dough than a rolling pin, which

KEY PIZZA STEPS

1. Working with one ball of dough at a time and keeping the rest covered with a damp cloth, flatten the dough ball into a disk using the palms of your hands.

2. Starting at the center of the disk and working outward, use your fingertips to press the dough to about ½ inch thick.

3. Holding the center in place, stretch the dough outward. Rotate the dough a quarter-turn and stretch again. Repeat until the dough reaches a diameter of 12 inches.

4. Use your palm to press down and flatten the thick edge of the dough.

5. Carefully lift the dough round and transfer it to a peel dusted with semolina or cornmeal.

6. If the dough loses its round shape, adjust it on the peel to return it to the original shape.

7. Brush the entire dough round with a little olive oil. Add the toppings. To make it easier to hold pizza slices when eating, leave a ½-inch border of dough uncovered.

8. Use a quick jerking action to slide the topped dough off the peel and onto the hot tiles or stone. Make sure that the pizza lands far enough back so that the front edge does not hang off the tiles or stone.

presses out air from the risen dough and makes it tough. Our low-tech method is also superior to flipping dough into the air and other frivolous techniques that may work in a pizza parlor but can lead to disaster at home.

Even if baking just one medium pizza, make a full dough recipe. After the dough has risen and been divided, place the extra dough in an airtight container and freeze it for up to several weeks. Defrost and stretch the dough when desired.

Pizza Dough

MAKES ENOUGH FOR
3 MEDIUM PIZZAS

We find that the food processor is the best tool for making pizza dough. However, only a food processor with a capacity of at least 11 cups can handle this much dough. You can also knead this dough by hand or in a standing mixer (see the directions that follow). Unbleached all-purpose flour can be used in a pinch, but the resulting crust will be less crisp.

½	cup warm water (105 to 115 degrees)
1	envelope (2¼ teaspoons) rapid-rise yeast
1¼	cups water, at room temperature
2	tablespoons extra-virgin olive oil
4	cups (20 ounces) bread flour, plus more for dusting work surfaces and hands
1½	teaspoons salt
	Olive oil or nonstick cooking spray for oiling the bowl

1. Measure the warm water into a 2-cup measuring cup. Sprinkle in the yeast and let stand until the yeast dissolves and swells, about 5 minutes. Add the room-temperature water and oil and stir to combine.

2. Pulse the flour and salt in the workbowl of a large food processor fitted with a steel blade to combine. Continue pulsing while pouring the liquid ingredients (holding back a few tablespoons) through the feed tube. If the dough does not readily form into a ball, add the remaining liquid and continue to pulse until a ball forms. Process until the dough is smooth and elastic, about 30 seconds longer.

3. The dough will be a bit tacky, so use a rubber spatula to turn it out onto a lightly floured work surface. Knead by hand for a few strokes to form a smooth, round ball. Put the dough into a deep oiled bowl and cover with plastic wrap. Let rise until doubled in size, 1½ to 2 hours.

➤ VARIATIONS

Pizza Dough Kneaded by Hand
Follow the recipe for Pizza Dough through step 1. Omit step 2 and instead combine the salt and half the flour in a deep bowl. Add the liquid ingredients and use a wooden spoon to combine. Add the remaining flour, stirring until a cohesive mass forms. Turn the dough onto a lightly floured work surface and knead until smooth and elastic, 7 to 8 minutes, using as little dusting flour as possible while

---

EQUIPMENT: Pizza Peels

We like to transfer stretched dough to a peel that has been dusted with semolina. The long handle on the peel makes it easy to slide the dough onto tiles or a stone in a hot oven. Although a rimless metal baking sheet can be used in this fashion, the lack of a handle means your hands are that much closer to the oven heat.

When shopping for a pizza peel, note that there are two choices. Aluminum peels with heat-resistant wooden handles are probably the better bet because they can be washed and cleaned easily. Peels made entirely of wood can mildew when washed, so it's best just to wipe them clean. Either way, make sure your peel measures at least 16 inches across so that it can accommodate a large dough round with room left around the edges.

---

kneading. Form the dough into a ball, put it in a deep oiled bowl, cover with plastic wrap, and proceed with the recipe.

Pizza Dough Kneaded in a Standing Mixer

Follow the recipe for Pizza Dough through step 1. Omit step 2 and instead place the flour and salt in the deep bowl of a standing mixer. With a paddle attachment, briefly combine the dry ingredients at low speed. Slowly add the liquid ingredients and continue to mix at low speed until a cohesive mass forms. Stop the mixer and replace the paddle with a dough hook. Knead until the dough is smooth and elastic, about 5 minutes. Form the dough into a ball, put it in a deep oiled bowl, cover with plastic wrap, and proceed with the recipe.

EQUIPMENT: Baking Tiles and Stones

If you like pizza with a thin, crisp crust, we recommend that you invest $15 to $20 to line the bottom rack of your oven with unglazed quarry tiles made of terra cotta. These porous tiles absorb heat better than a metal baking sheet and thus transfer more heat to whatever food is cooked on them. Pizza crust becomes especially crisp and well browned on the bottom when cooked on tiles. In our test kitchen, we have found that these tiles are good for most bread as well. The tiles come in 6-inch squares and can be cut at a tile store to fit your oven rack perfectly. Look for ½-inch-thick tiles.

A large rectangular pizza stone (circular stones are generally smaller and not recommended) is also a good option. The chief drawback here is size. In most home ovens, you can fit two medium pizzas on a tile-lined rack. However, most pizza stones can accommodate only one pizza at a time. If using a stone, be careful when sliding the pizza into the oven. You don't want part of the pizza to hang off the stone, dumping toppings onto the oven floor.

PIZZA BASICS

UNLESS YOU BUILD A BRICK OVEN IN your kitchen, it's not possible to duplicate thin pizzeria-style pies at home. Commercial pizza ovens can reach 800 degrees; home ovens just can't compete. That said, homemade thin-crust pizza is delicious even if different from the pies you get when you eat out. The crust is chewier, crisper, and not nearly as greasy.

While American pizza parlors weigh down their crusts with pounds of toppings, Italians use a restrained hand when topping a thin-crust pizza. After all, you are making home-made bread, and pizza should be about the crust as well as the cheese and sauce.

In our testing, we found that baking pizza on tiles or a pizza stone is a must. We found that crusts baked on a pizza screen (a perforated pan) or a baking sheet were not as crisp and chewy. (See left for more information on tiles and stones.) Our testing revealed that an oven temperature of 500 degrees is your best bet. When cooked at a lower temperature, the crust was not as crisp.

We find that a pizza peel is the best tool for

PRICKING THE PIZZA DOUGH

Some pizzas are baked without toppings. To keep the dough from ballooning in the oven, prick the dough all over with a fork before it goes into the oven. If bubbles form during baking, prick them before they become too large.

getting topped pizza dough onto a preheated stone. With its fine, sandy texture, semolina keeps pizza dough from sticking to peels. Cornmeal can be used, but we find that its coarser texture can make the bottom of the crust a bit gritty.

Remember to preheat the oven (and stone or tiles) for at least 30 minutes. Depending on your oven, the type of stone or tiles used, and the amount of topping, thin-crust pizzas may be done in as little as 6 minutes or may take as long as 12 minutes. Don't pull a pizza out of the oven until the edge of the crust is golden brown and the toppings are sizzling.

Pizza Bianca with Garlic and Rosemary

MAKES 3 MEDIUM PIZZAS, SERVING 6

This simple pizza is best as part of an antipasto or as a bread accompaniment to dinner. Pizza bianca translates as "white pizza," referring to the fact that there are no tomatoes—just garlic, oil, rosemary, and salt—in this recipe.

I	recipe Pizza Dough (page 369)
¼	cup extra-virgin olive oil, plus extra for brushing on the stretched dough
6	medium cloves garlic, minced or pressed through a garlic press
4	teaspoons minced fresh rosemary leaves
	Salt and ground black pepper
	Semolina or cornmeal for dusting on the pizza peel

1. Prepare the dough as directed in the dough recipe. Place a pizza stone on a rack in the lower third of the oven if oven is not lined with tiles. Preheat the oven to 500 degrees for at least 30 minutes. Turn the dough out onto a lightly floured work surface. Use a chef's knife or dough scraper to divide the dough into three pieces. Form

each piece of dough into a smooth, round ball and cover it with a damp cloth. Let the dough relax for at least 10 minutes but no more than 30 minutes.

2. While preparing the dough, combine ¼ cup oil, garlic, rosemary, and salt and pepper to taste in a small bowl. Set the herb oil aside.

3. Working with one piece of dough at a time and keeping the others covered, shape the dough as directed in illustrations 1 through 4 on page 368, then transfer it to a pizza peel that has been lightly dusted with semolina or cornmeal (see illustrations 5 and 6 on page 368).

4. Lightly brush the dough round with plain olive oil. Prick the dough round all over with a fork to prevent ballooning in the oven (see the illustration on page 370).

5. Slide the dough onto the heated stone or tiles (see illustration 8 on page 368). Bake until the crust begins to brown in spots, 6 to 10 minutes. Brush the crust with one-third of the herb oil and continue baking until the garlic is fragrant, 1 to 2 minutes. Remove the pizza from the oven, cut into wedges, and serve immediately. Repeat steps 3, 4, and 5 with the remaining two pieces of dough and the remaining herb oil.

➤ VARIATIONS
Pesto Pizza
Follow the recipe for Pizza Bianca with Garlic and Rosemary through step 4, omitting the herb oil in step 2. Bake the dough as directed until golden brown in spots, 8 to 10 minutes. Remove the crust from the oven and spread with ¼ cup Pesto (page 139), leaving a ½-inch border. Cut into wedges and serve.

Lemon–Sea Salt Pizza
Follow the recipe for Pizza Bianca with Garlic and Rosemary through step 3. Brush the dough round with plain olive oil as directed in step 4. Arrange 1 small lemon, sliced paper-

thin, over the dough round, leaving a ½-inch border uncovered. Sprinkle with coarse sea salt to taste. (Do not prick the dough.) Bake and brush with the herb oil as directed in step 5.

White Pizza with Spinach and Ricotta

MAKES 3 MEDIUM PIZZAS, SERVING 6

Ricotta cheese and garlicky sautéed spinach flavor this tomatoless pizza.

I	recipe Pizza Dough (page 369)
2	tablespoons extra-virgin olive oil, plus more for brushing on the stretched dough
4	medium cloves garlic, minced or pressed through a garlic press
¼	teaspoon hot red pepper flakes
I½	pounds spinach, stemmed, washed, shaken to remove excess water, and chopped coarse
	Salt and ground black pepper
	Semolina or cornmeal for dusting on the pizza peel
2	cups ricotta cheese
6	tablespoons grated Parmesan cheese

1. Prepare the dough as directed in the dough recipe. Place a pizza stone on a rack in the lower third of the oven if oven is not lined with tiles. Preheat the oven to 500 degrees for at least 30 minutes. Turn the dough out onto a lightly floured work surface. Use a chef's knife or dough scraper to divide the dough into three pieces. Form each piece of dough into a smooth, round ball and cover it with a damp cloth. Let the dough relax for at least 10 minutes but no more than 30 minutes.

2. While preparing the dough, heat the oil in a Dutch oven set over medium heat. Add the garlic and hot red pepper flakes and cook until fragrant, about 1 minute. Add the damp

spinach, cover, and cook, stirring occasionally, until just wilted, about 3 minutes. Season with salt and pepper to taste. Transfer the spinach to a medium bowl, squeezing out any liquid with the back of a spoon and leaving the liquid behind in the pot. Set the spinach aside; discard the excess liquid.

3. Working with one piece of dough at a time and keeping the others covered, shape the dough as directed in illustrations 1 through 4 on page 368, then transfer it to a pizza peel that has been lightly dusted with semolina or cornmeal (see illustrations 5 and 6 on page 368).

4. Lightly brush the dough round with olive oil. Arrange one-third of the spinach mixture over the dough round, leaving a ½-inch border uncovered (see illustration 7 on page 368). Dot with ⅔ cup ricotta cheese.

5. Slide the dough onto the heated stone or tiles (see illustration 8 on page 368). Bake until the crust edges brown in spots, 8 to 12 minutes. Remove the pizza from the oven, sprinkle with 2 tablespoons Parmesan, cut into wedges, and serve immediately. Repeat steps 3, 4, and 5 with the remaining two pieces of dough and the remaining toppings.

Three-Cheese Pizza

MAKES 3 MEDIUM PIZZAS, SERVING 6

This classic combination of mozzarella, Parmesan, and Gorgonzola is not a study in excess, as the name might imply. A little of each cheese contributes to a rich, complex flavor. We also recommend adding garlic and olives, although these ingredients are optional.

I	recipe Pizza Dough (page 369)
	Semolina or cornmeal for dusting on the pizza peel
	Extra-virgin olive oil for brushing on the stretched dough

4　ounces mozzarella cheese, shredded
(about 1 cup)

8　ounces Gorgonzola cheese, crumbled
(about 2 cups)

3　medium cloves garlic, sliced thin
(optional)

6　tablespoons pitted and quartered
oil-cured black olives (optional)

6　tablespoons grated Parmesan cheese

1. Prepare the dough as directed in the dough recipe. Place a pizza stone on a rack in the lower third of the oven if oven is not lined with tiles. Preheat the oven to 500 degrees for at least 30 minutes. Turn the dough out onto a lightly floured work surface. Use a chef's knife or dough scraper to divide the dough into three pieces. Form each piece of dough into a smooth, round ball and cover it with a damp cloth. Let the dough relax for at least 10 minutes but no more than 30 minutes.

2. Working with one piece of dough at a time and keeping the others covered, shape the dough as directed in illustrations 1 through 4 on page 368, then transfer it to a pizza peel that has been lightly dusted with semolina or cornmeal (see illustrations 5 and 6 on page 368).

3. Lightly brush the dough round with olive oil. Sprinkle evenly with ⅓ cup mozzarella, leaving a ½-inch border uncovered (see

---

INGREDIENTS: Mozzarella Cheese

If you're going to the trouble of making your own pizza, you certainly don't want to wreck it by using inferior mozzarella. We wondered if you could use preshredded cheese or whether premium buffalo mozzarella (made from water buffalo milk and imported from Italy) was worth the added expense. Could we even compare these cheeses?

To find out which kinds of mozzarella work best in pizza, 16 tasters sampled six brands, including three shrink-wrapped low-moisture cheeses from the supermarket (two made from whole milk, one from part skim milk), a preshredded part-skim cheese also from the supermarket, one salted fresh mozzarella made at a local cheese shop, and one salted fresh buffalo mozzarella imported from Italy. We sampled each cheese both raw and cooked on a pizza. Tasters were asked to rate each cheese on overall flavor (raw and melted), texture, and melting properties.

When tasted raw, the results were quite clear. Tasters liked the gamey, barnyard flavor of the buffalo mozzarella. The fresh cow's-milk mozzarella also performed quite well. Among the supermarket cheeses, there was a clear preference for the whole-milk cheeses over those made with part skim milk. The preshredded cheese had a dry, rubbery texture and grainy mouthfeel. (Even when cooked, most tasters noted that it was chalky or grainy.) Preshredded cheese is coated with powdered cellulose to prevent clumping. Some tasters also felt that the preshredded cheese was drier, attributable to the cellulose or just being shredded months ago.

On pizzas, the results were the same (at least in terms of flavor), but moisture was now a factor. The fresh cheeses exuded a lot of liquid that flooded the surface of the pizza. Unless fresh mozzarella is pressed of excess liquid before cooking (we had success weighting the shredded cheese in a strainer set in a bowl for an hour prior to cooking), it is unsuitable for pizza.

Because most cooks (ourselves included) don't want to weight cheese, we think the shrink-wrapped supermarket cheeses make more sense for sprinkling on pizzas. Stick with a whole-milk cheese and try to choose a brand with a bit more moisture than the rest of the pack. Our favorite supermarket cheese was Calabro whole-milk mozzarella (from Connecticut), which was softer and moister than the other supermarket offerings. Certainly don't use preshredded cheese. The convenience is simply not worth the sacrifice in taste and texture.

illustration 7 on page 368). Dot with ⅔ cup Gorgonzola cheese and sprinkle with one-third of the garlic and olives, if using.

4. Slide the dough onto the heated stone or tiles (see illustration 8 on page 368). Bake until the crust edges brown and the cheeses are golden and bubbling, 8 to 12 minutes. Remove the pizza from the oven, sprinkle with 2 tablespoons Parmesan, cut into wedges, and serve immediately. Repeat steps 2, 3, and 4 with the remaining two pieces of dough and the remaining toppings.

Classic Tomato Pizza with Mozzarella and Basil

MAKES 3 MEDIUM PIZZAS, SERVING 6

Known as pizza Margherita, *this Neapolitan specialty is Italian cooking at its simplest and best.*

I	recipe Pizza Dough (page 369)
	Semolina or cornmeal for dusting on the pizza peel
	Extra-virgin olive oil for brushing on the stretched dough
3	cups Quick Tomato Sauce for Pizza (recipe follows)
12	ounces mozzarella cheese, shredded (about 3 cups)
3	tablespoons grated Parmesan cheese
½	cup packed fresh basil leaves

1. Prepare the dough as directed in the dough recipe. Place a pizza stone on a rack in the lower third of the oven if oven is not lined with tiles. Preheat the oven to 500 degrees for at least 30 minutes. Turn the dough out onto a lightly floured work surface. Use a chef's knife or dough scraper to divide the dough into three pieces. Form each piece of dough into a smooth, round ball and cover it with a damp cloth. Let the dough relax for at least 10 minutes but no more than 30 minutes.

2. Working with one piece of dough at a time and keeping the others covered, shape the dough as directed in illustrations 1 through 4 on page 368, then transfer it to a pizza peel that has been lightly dusted with semolina or cornmeal (see illustrations 5 and 6 on page 368).

3. Lightly brush the dough round with olive oil. Spread 1 cup tomato sauce evenly over the dough round, leaving a ½-inch border uncovered (see illustration 7 on page 368). Sprinkle with 1 cup mozzarella.

4. Slide the dough onto the heated stone or tiles (see illustration 8 on page 368). Bake until the crust edges brown and the cheese is golden brown in spots, 8 to 12 minutes. Remove the pizza from the oven and sprinkle with 1 tablespoon Parmesan. Tear one-third of the basil leaves and scatter them over the pizza. Cut the pizza into wedges and serve immediately. Repeat steps 2, 3, and 4 with the remaining two pieces of dough and the remaining toppings.

Quick Tomato Sauce for Pizza

MAKES ABOUT 3 CUPS

For pizza, you want the smoothest possible sauce. Start with canned crushed tomatoes and puree them in a food processor before cooking them with garlic and oil.

I	(28-ounce) can crushed tomatoes
2	tablespoons extra-virgin olive oil
2	large cloves garlic, minced or pressed through a garlic press
	Salt and ground black pepper

1. Process the tomatoes in the workbowl of a food processor fitted with a steel blade until smooth, about five 1-second pulses.

2. Heat the oil and garlic in a medium

saucepan over medium heat until the garlic is sizzling, about 40 seconds. Stir in the tomatoes. Bring to a simmer and cook, uncovered, until the sauce thickens enough to coat a wooden spoon, about 15 minutes. Season with salt and pepper to taste.

Fresh Tomato Pizza with Arugula and Prosciutto

MAKES 3 MEDIUM PIZZAS, SERVING 6

The arugula for this pizza is tossed with a little oil to keep it moist then sprinkled over the baked pizza as soon as it comes out of the oven. The heat from the pizza wilts the arugula without causing it to dry out.

I recipe Pizza Dough (page 369)
   Semolina or cornmeal for dusting on the pizza peel
2 tablespoons extra-virgin olive oil, plus more for brushing on the stretched dough
3 medium ripe tomatoes (about I pound), cored and sliced crosswise into thin rounds
   Salt and ground black pepper
4 ounces thin-sliced prosciutto
6 ounces mozzarella cheese, shredded (about I ½ cups)
3 cups stemmed arugula leaves, washed and thoroughly dried

1. Prepare the dough as directed in the dough recipe. Place a pizza stone on a rack in the lower third of the oven if oven is not lined with tiles. Preheat the oven to 500 degrees for at least 30 minutes. Turn the dough out onto a lightly floured work surface. Use a chef's knife or dough scraper to divide the dough into three pieces. Form each piece of dough into a smooth, round ball and cover it with a damp cloth. Let the dough relax for at least 10 minutes but no more than 30 minutes.

2. Working with one piece of dough at a time and keeping the others covered, shape the dough as directed in illustrations 1 through 4 on page 368, then transfer it to a pizza peel that has been lightly dusted with semolina or cornmeal (see illustrations 5 and 6 on page 368).

3. Lightly brush the dough round with olive oil. Arrange one-third of the tomato slices in concentric circles over the dough round, leaving a ½-inch border uncovered (see illustration 7 on page 368). Season with salt and pepper to

GRATING MOZZARELLA

Mozzarella and other semisoft cheeses can stick to a box grater and cause a real mess. Here's how to keep the holes on the grater from becoming clogged.

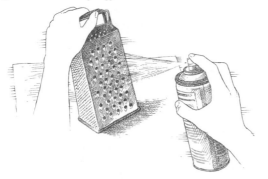

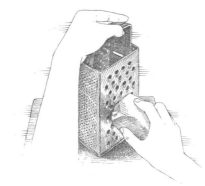

1. Use nonstick cooking spray to lightly coat the side of the box grater that has large holes.

2. Shred the cheese as usual. The cooking spray will keep the cheese from sticking to the surface of the grater.

EQUIPMENT: Box Graters

A box grater is one of those unfortunate kitchen tools that occupies significant cabinet or counter space and is used infrequently, yet is absolutely essential. While food processors come with a grater attachment, not everyone has one, and it's doubtful that those who do would dirty the entire contraption to grate a handful of mozzarella. A number of graters are on the market, from nonstick to heavy-grade stainless steel. We wanted to find out if there was a significant difference between these models—did we need to spend $20 on a grater, or would a $6 grater do the job?

We tested eight box graters ranging in price from $6.48 to $19.99. We grated items of varying texture and firmness, all of which we grate frequently in the test kitchen—mozzarella cheese, celeriac, carrots, and ginger.

The winning box grater would need to rate well in all categories—it would be fast (efficient and sharp, requiring little effort and pressure), stable (no rocking or sliding), comfortable (a good grip on the handle), and easy to clean (a single trip through the dishwasher or a quick scrub with soapy water—all models were dishwasher-safe). With those standards in mind, we grated and rated.

We soon found that most graters had little problem with speed and sharpness—from carrots to cheese, the shreds were clean and uniform, falling quickly from the grater. Ginger proved a problem for two models that sported only the punched, raised-spike holes for grating smaller items. Those spiked teeth grabbed the ginger fibers, leaving juice on the counter and negligible scrapings of actual ginger meat. Graters with miniature versions of the large-holed side were much more successful with ginger.

Stability proved an essential component of a quality box grater. While many models slid a bit if set atop a smooth countertop, testers found sliding the least among evils. Grated knuckles, the unwelcome result of tipping and rocking, were a common (and unacceptable) occurrence with poorly balanced, flimsy graters. The graters with the largest bases sat firmly on the countertop, allowing fast, safe grating.

Several graters boasted "slipfree" rubber bases, which we found both a help and a hindrance. When grating soft items that required little pressure (such as cheese), the bases indeed kept the grater firmly in place. But when grating firmer items (such as carrots) requiring more pressure, the slipfree graters tipped, endangering fingers. Additionally, testers preferred a smooth surface for making uninterrupted passes with the cheese or vegetable. The models with rubber or plastic bases and tops were not composed of a single piece of metal, so the grated item had to pass over or be halted by the attached base or top. The attached base also acted as a trap for juices or tiny bits of grated material.

Comfort was similarly affected by the size of the grater's base; there was no need for a tight grip as long as the grater was well balanced. The most stable graters required merely a hand resting on the top. As a bonus, larger bases offered wider openings at the top, enabling a clear view of progress.

Most of the graters were easy to clean. A simple scrub by hand or a single run through the dishwasher removed all traces of cheese or vegetables. However, the two models that trapped the ginger fibers had significant problems. The fibers were thoroughly enmeshed in the teeth, proving a true challenge for washing by hand, and they remained firmly in place after a heavy-duty dishwasher run, quickly drying into an intractable mess. The fibers had to be delicately plucked by hand from the sharp teeth.

On your next trip to the kitchen store, look for box graters with extra-wide bases, preferably composed of a single piece of high-grade metal, with one side offering tiny raised holes for smaller items. We found the more expensive graters tended to be better. The top-rated graters were the Küchenprofi 6-Sided ($15), the Amco Professional Performance ($19.99), and the Progressive International Perfect Prep ($16.99). You can justify the extra expense and cabinet space with the savings you'll reap in unused Band-Aids.

taste and drizzle with 1 teaspoon oil.

4. Slide the dough onto the heated stone or tiles (see illustration 8 on page 368). Bake until the crust edges start to brown, 6 to 10 minutes. Lay one-third of the prosciutto slices over the tomatoes and sprinkle with ½ cup mozzarella. Continue baking until the cheese melts, 2 to 3 minutes more. Toss 1 cup arugula with 1 teaspoon oil in a small bowl. Remove the pizza from the oven and top with the arugula. Cut the pizza into wedges and serve immediately. Repeat steps 2, 3, and 4 with the remaining two pieces of dough and the remaining toppings.

Mushroom Pizza with Sage, Fontina, and Parmesan

MAKES 3 MEDIUM PIZZAS, SERVING 6

Any fresh mushrooms will work in this recipe, but cremini are especially good.

I	recipe Pizza Dough (page 369)
2	large cloves garlic, minced or pressed through a garlic press
2	tablespoons extra-virgin olive oil, plus extra for brushing on the stretched dough
I	pound fresh mushrooms, stem ends trimmed, remainder sliced thin
I	teaspoon minced fresh sage leaves
	Salt and ground black pepper
	Semolina or cornmeal for dusting on the pizza peel
3	cups Quick Tomato Sauce for Pizza (page 374)
6	ounces fontina cheese, shredded (about 1 ½ cups)
6	tablespoons grated Parmesan cheese

1. Prepare the dough as directed in the dough recipe. Place a pizza stone on a rack in the lower third of the oven if oven is not lined with tiles. Preheat the oven to 500 degrees for at least 30 minutes. Turn the dough out onto a lightly floured work surface. Use a chef's knife or dough scraper to divide the dough into three pieces. Form each piece of dough into a smooth, round ball and cover it with a damp cloth. Let the dough relax for at least 10 minutes but no more than 30 minutes.

2. While preparing the dough, heat the garlic and 2 tablespoons oil in a large skillet set over medium-high heat. When the garlic begins to sizzle, add the mushrooms and sauté until they are golden brown and the juices they release have evaporated, about 7 minutes. Stir in the sage and salt and pepper to taste. Set the mushrooms aside.

3. Working with one piece of dough at a time and keeping the others covered, shape the dough as directed in illustrations 1 through 4 on page 368, then transfer it to a pizza peel that has been lightly dusted with semolina or cornmeal (see illustrations 5 and 6 on page 368).

4. Lightly brush the dough round with olive oil. Spread 1 cup tomato sauce over the dough round, leaving a ½-inch border uncovered (see illustration 7 on page 368). Scatter one-third of the mushrooms and then ½ cup fontina cheese over the sauce.

5. Slide the dough onto the heated stone or tiles (see illustration 8 on page 368). Bake until the crust edges brown and the cheese is golden brown in spots, 8 to 12 minutes. Remove the pizza from the oven, sprinkle with 2 tablespoons Parmesan, cut into wedges, and serve immediately. Repeat steps 3, 4, and 5 with the remaining two pieces of dough and the remaining toppings.

CALZONES

LITTLE MORE THAN A PIZZA FOLDED in half, calzones are savory turnovers originally from southern Italy but now popular around the globe. The name is derived from its shape; calzone translates as "trouser leg." While closely related to pizza, calzones have their own distinct set of problems to overcome, including lackluster flavor, watery fillings, and seams that open and cause fillings to spill out in the oven. Luckily, we found that these were easy issues to overcome and that perfect calzones take only a bit more effort than pizza.

The filling proved the biggest hurdle. Because there is twice as much crust in each bite of calzone than there is in pizza, the filling must be richer and more assertively seasoned than a pizza topping. We favored fillings based on ricotta cheese because the dense, creamy cheese proved a perfect complement to the chewy, crisp crust. We found that high-quality whole-milk ricotta is the best choice, as it does not leach as much water when cooked as low-fat ricotta does. For additional protection against the cheese shedding liquid, we included an egg yolk in the mixture, which helped stabilize it. We also added a small amount of mozzarella to improve the cheese's creaminess and a dusting of Parmesan to round out the sweet dairy flavor.

SHAPING CALZONES

1. Using a rubber spatula, spread the filling in an even layer across the bottom half of the dough round, leaving a ¹/₂-inch border uncovered.

2. Brush the uncovered edge with water and fold over the top half of the dough to form a half-moon.

3. Press the edge shut with your fingers, then crimp it firmly with a fork.

4. Brush the calzone lightly with olive oil. With a very sharp paring knife or razor blade, cut 5 slits, evenly spaced, across the top.

To deepen the flavor of the cheese mixture, we turned to sausage. A variety of cured meats are traditionally used in calzones, including prosciutto and salami, but tasters felt that sausage's rich, meaty flavor permeated the ricotta and added a pleasing texture. While a variety of fresh Italian sausages worked, tasters favored hot Italian links for their spicy flavor and slight pepper burn. Browning the sausage before adding it to the ricotta was essential. The filling did not get hot enough to cook the meat through in the short time that the calzone is baked.

To shape the calzone, we gave up on stretching the dough (our method for pizza) in favor of using a rolling pin. Roundness is not essential to a pizza—eccentric shapes exude a certain rustic charm—but it is key to a calzone. Hand-pulled dough resulted in ungainly calzones with fat, bulbous seams. With the aid of parchment paper and the judicious use of additional flour (tricks we use when rolling tart dough), rolling our pizza dough proved surprisingly easy.

With the dough rolled and the filling assembled, we needed to figure out the best method for stuffing and shaping the calzone. The main issue here is getting a proper seal with the folded dough edges. In early tests, many calzones opened in the oven and spilled their contents. We tried a variety of methods to seal the edges and found that a fork makes the tightest seam. We moistened the edges with water so that the dough adhered to itself, then firmly crimped the now-joined edges with the tines of a fork. While the fork marks became faint during cooking, the edges stayed tightly sealed and did not leak.

As pizza does, calzones need a lot of heat. We had the best results baking them on a pizza stone in a 500-degree oven. Our smooth tomato sauce for pizza is the perfect complement.

Ricotta and Sausage Calzones

MAKES 4 LARGE CALZONES, SERVING 4 TO 6

These are not the overstuffed, gargantuan calzones that most American pizza joints serve. Instead, these calzones offer a relatively thin layer of well-seasoned filling surrounded by a crisp, flavorful crust. While ideally eaten hot, they are also delicious at room temperature, as they are often consumed in Italy. Cutting slits into the top of the calzone prevents the dough from becoming gummy. If you do not have an exceedingly sharp paring knife, you may want to use a razor blade. Part-skim ricotta is too watery to use in this recipe.

FILLING

1/2	pound hot Italian sausage
1	pound whole-milk ricotta cheese
5	ounces mozzarella cheese, shredded (about 1 1/4 cups)
3/4	cup finely grated Parmesan cheese
1	large egg yolk
1	large clove garlic, minced or pressed through a garlic press
1	tablespoon minced fresh parsley leaves
1/8	teaspoon hot red pepper flakes (optional)
	Salt and ground black pepper

1	recipe Pizza Dough (page 369)
	Unbleached all-purpose flour for dusting on work surface
	Extra-virgin olive oil for brushing on the dough
3	cups Quick Tomato Sauce for Pizza (page 374), heated

1. FOR THE FILLING: Remove the sausage from its casing and put it in a medium skillet over medium-high heat. Using a wooden spoon, break the pieces of sausage into small

bits as they cook. Cook the sausage, stirring occasionally, until no longer pink, about 7 minutes. Transfer the sausage to a plate and place it in the refrigerator to cool quickly. Meanwhile, combine the cheeses, egg yolk, garlic, parsley, and hot red pepper flakes (if using) in a medium bowl. Once the sausage is completely cooled, stir it in and season the filling with salt and pepper to taste.

2. Prepare the dough as directed in the dough recipe. Place a pizza stone on a rack in the lower third of the oven if oven is not lined with tiles. Preheat the oven to 500 degrees for at least 30 minutes. Turn the dough out onto a lightly floured work surface. Use a chef's knife or dough scraper to divide the dough into four pieces. Form each piece of dough into a smooth, round ball and cover it with a damp cloth. Let the dough relax for at least 10 minutes but no more than 30 minutes.

3. Roll one piece of dough between two sheets of lightly floured parchment paper to an 11-inch circle, adding more flour as necessary to keep the dough from sticking. Roll a second piece of dough to an 11-inch circle between two more sheets of parchment. (Keep the other two pieces of dough covered

with a damp cloth.) Peel off the top sheets of parchment and place 1 cup filling in the center of the bottom half of each dough round. Using a rubber spatula, spread the filling in an even layer across the bottom half of the dough round, leaving a ½-inch border uncovered (see illustration 1 on page 378). Brush the uncovered edge with water and fold over the top half of the dough to form a half-moon (see illustration 2 on page 378). Press the edge shut with your fingers, then crimp it firmly with a fork (see illustration 3 on page 378). Brush the calzones lightly with olive oil and, with a very sharp paring knife or razor blade, cut 5 slits, evenly spaced, across the top of each (see illustration 4 on page 378). Trim off the excess parchment paper.

4. Place the calzones, still on the trimmed pieces of parchment, on the heated stone or tiles. Bake until golden brown, about 12 minutes. Cool on a wire rack at least 5 minutes before serving. While the first calzones are in the oven, roll, fill, and shape the second batch according to step 3. Bake the second batch and cool as directed. Serve the calzones hot, warm, or at room temperature, passing the tomato sauce at the table.

11

EGGS AND SAVORY TARTS

EGGS ARE AN INTEGRAL PART OF THE Italian diet, used in everything from fresh pasta to tiramisù. Eggs are also served on their own (most commonly in frittatas) and used in savory tarts (the Italian equivalent of quiche).

Depending on the breed of the hen and her size, an egg can weigh as much as 3 ounces or as little as 1 ounce. Size is not necessarily a reflection of quality, nor is the color of the shell. The average weight of one egg for each of the common sizes is as follows: jumbo (2½ ounces), extra-large (2¼ ounces), large (2 ounces), and medium (1¾ ounces). We generally use large eggs in our recipes, but you can use other sizes if you approximate the total weight by relying on the preceding figures. For instance, you would replace four large eggs (which weigh 8 ounces), with three jumbo eggs (7½ ounces) rather than four jumbo eggs (10 ounces).

No matter the size, the egg consists of two parts that can function quite differently in recipes. The white consists primarily of water (about 90 percent) and layers of protein (albumin). The white begins to coagulate at 144 degrees, ahead of the yolk, which begins to coagulate at 149 degrees. The yolk is where most of the fat and cholesterol in the egg are located. The yolk also contains most of the vitamins and nutrients, as well as lecithin, the emulsifier that gives sauces with eggs their smooth texture.

In recent years, numerous outbreaks of intestinal illness have been traced to eggs contaminated with salmonella. Although the odds of getting a bad egg are quite low (some experts estimate that 1 in 10,000 eggs is contaminated with the bacteria), it makes sense to take precautions. This is especially true if you are cooking for the young, the elderly, women who are pregnant, or for people with compromised immune systems.

Thorough cooking of eggs to at least 160 degrees will kill any salmonella that may be present. Given the thickening temperatures mentioned above, if you are concerned about salmonella, you should cook all eggs until fully set; for fried eggs, that means avoiding runny yolks.

Eggs should always be refrigerated to prolong their shelf life. Because the door is actually the warmest spot in most refrigerators, you should keep eggs in their container and store them on one of the shelves. The shelves are likely to be colder, and the box acts as a layer of insulation around the eggs.

EGGS WITH ASPARAGUS AND PARMESAN

IN ITALY, ASPARAGUS TURNS UP IN many guises. One well-known dish is eggs with asparagus and Parmesan. Served as a light main course, this dish combines the freshness of asparagus, the richness of eggs, and the earthy flavor of Parmesan cheese. The ingredient list for this recipe is nearly as straightforward as its name implies, and one would think it is as simple to create.

Unfortunately, we found that this was not the case. The first batch of recipes that we tested yielded overcooked or bland asparagus topped with rubbery, hard-cooked eggs. We wanted to create a dish that showcased each ingredient: fresh but full-flavored asparagus, tender yet properly cooked eggs, all topped with the pleasant nuttiness of Parmigiano-Reggiano.

Working from the bottom up, we started with the asparagus. First, we tested steaming the asparagus over a couple of inches of boiling water, then immersing them in ice water to halt the cooking process. This asparagus was bland in flavor and appearance. Next, we tried blanching the asparagus, a method that entails dropping the spears in salted boiling water for a few minutes, then quickly stopping the cooking process by removing the asparagus from the boiling water and immersing them in an ice water bath. This method produced beautiful emerald-green stalks, pleasing to the eye, and the salted cooking water enhanced the flavor of the asparagus. But tasters felt that the asparagus remained a bit bland.

Finally, we tried broiling the asparagus. We tossed the asparagus in olive oil, sprinkled the stalks with salt and pepper, and placed them under the broiler element of the oven. These spears were amazing. Although the asparagus took on an army-issue green color, the flavor was rich and complex. The broiling brought out a nutty flavor in the asparagus and gave the exterior of the spears a crackling, almost crisp texture.

On to the eggs. There appears to be no traditional method of cooking the eggs for this dish; we found recipes that called for scrambling, hard-boiling, poaching, and frying. We tried all four possibilities, and the methods that yielded soft yolks—poaching and frying—were the favorites. Tasters liked how the soft yolk blended with the cheese and made a velvety sauce that clung to the asparagus, while the firm whites added textural interest. Of these methods, frying was chosen because of its inherent simplicity. But we still needed to find a way to produce fried eggs with firm whites and thick, creamy yolks every time.

For starters, we thought it made sense to investigate the hardware. After testing skillets made from aluminum, hard-anodized aluminum, stainless steel, and well-seasoned cast iron in addition to one with a nonstick

coating, our initial feeling was confirmed: There is no point in frying eggs in anything but a nonstick pan.

Next, we examined the degree to which the pan should be heated before the eggs are added. We learned that there is a pan temperature that causes eggs to behave just as we want them to. When an egg lands in a pan that's at the correct temperature, it neither runs all over the place nor sputters or bubbles; instead, it just sizzles and sets up into a thick, restrained oval. Getting the taste and texture of the white just right depends on achieving this correct set point. A white that's too spread out becomes overcooked, rubbery, and tough, while a white that browns at the edges as soon as it hits the pan ends up tasting metallic—at least to us.

We needed to devise a plan that would incorporate this crucial setting temperature, no matter what type of pan or what cooktop a cook was using. To begin, we placed the pan on a low setting and let it heat for a full five minutes. We had discovered that while eggs might set up well initially if a pan is not completely heated, they then tend to overcook at the finish; five minutes ensures a thorough preheating of the pan. Next, we added the butter, which we allowed to melt and foam. We waited for the foaming to subside before adding the egg. We knew immediately that the pan was too hot; the white sputtered into huge bubbles, and the butter had even started to brown. Fast-forward to the next egg. This time, we again put the pan on the burner for five minutes but set the heat below the low setting. This hit the mark. We added the egg just as the butter foam subsided, and it set up perfectly. On this perfect setting, the butter took exactly one minute to melt, foam, and subside. In an effort to minimize ingredients, we tried frying the eggs in olive oil, as we had used olive oil to cook the asparagus, but the eggs were lacking in flavor. Further, we missed the key visual to determine proper pan pre-heating, so we went back to butter.

Now that the egg was sitting pretty, we moved on to the next part of the cooking process. Thumbing through cookbooks, we found directions for basting with butter, adjusting the temperature, and covering as techniques to get the desired thick and runny yolk. Eggs basted with butter were too rich, and the process was fussy. Adjusting the heat to get both white and yolk to cook properly was actually pretty difficult. In all cases, we ended up with the bottom too browned and the yolk too runny.

We moved on to using a cover during the cooking process. After putting two eggs in the skillet, we put on the lid and allowed the eggs to cook for two minutes. One of the eggs was cooked perfectly, but the other was slightly undercooked. We realized that with such a short cooking time, we had to get the eggs into the pan at the same time. We tried the covered skillet method one more time, but in this case broke each of the eggs into a cup before starting the process. This allowed us to

empty the eggs into the skillet simultaneously. This method worked beautifully. The steam created when the pan was covered produced whites that were firm but not at all rubbery and yolks that were thick yet still runny. A little seasoning with salt and pepper before the eggs had cooked was all that was needed for flavor.

Armed with the perfectly cooked asparagus and eggs, we assembled the dish. We placed the asparagus in four distinct bunches (to facilitate easier serving) on a large platter, topped each bunch with one fried egg, then sprinkled Parmesan cheese over the top. Tasters, however, were not happy that the dish was lukewarm at best, so we popped the dish under the broiler for about 30 seconds, just enough to give it a blast of heat and start melting the cheese but not enough heat to ruin our perfectly cooked eggs.

SLIDING THE EGGS INTO THE PAN

Crack the eggs into two small bowls or cups, then let the eggs slide into the hot skillet simultaneously from opposite sides of the pan.

Fried Eggs with Asparagus and Parmesan
SERVES 4

Because burners vary, it may be necessary to cook an egg or two before you find the ideal stove setting for frying the eggs. Look for the visual cue of the butter foaming, then subsiding, to determine when the pan is hot enough. Timing for this recipe is important. As soon as the asparagus go under the broiler, start heating the pan for cooking the eggs. Be sure to use a heatproof platter to finish the dish under the broiler.

2   pounds thin asparagus spears, tough ends snapped off (see illustration on page 59)
1   tablespoon extra-virgin olive oil
    Salt and ground black pepper
4   large eggs
1   tablespoon unsalted butter
½   cup finely grated Parmesan cheese

1. Adjust the oven rack to the highest position (about 4 inches below the heating element) and heat the broiler. Lay the asparagus in a single layer on a rimmed baking sheet and drizzle with the oil and sprinkle with salt and pepper to taste. Roll the asparagus back and forth to coat them evenly. Broil the asparagus until they are beginning to brown lightly and a knife easily punctures the stalk, 8 to 10 minutes. Remove the pan from the oven and set the asparagus aside. (Do not turn off the broiler.)

2. Meanwhile, heat a heavy-bottomed nonstick 10-inch skillet over the lowest possible heat for 5 minutes. Crack open 2 eggs into a small bowl or cup; crack the remaining 2 eggs into a second small bowl or cup. Add the butter to the skillet and let it melt and foam. When the foam subsides (this process should take about 1 minute; if the butter browns in 1 minute, the pan is too hot), swirl to coat the pan.

3. Working quickly, pour 2 eggs on one side of the pan and the other two on the other side (see the illustration on page 384). Season the eggs with salt and pepper. Cover and cook for 2½ minutes. (The yolks will still be runny.)

4. Place the broiled asparagus spears on a heatproof platter and separate them into 4 even piles. Place 1 egg on top of each pile. Sprinkle the Parmesan cheese evenly over the eggs and place the platter under the broiler to melt the cheese slightly, about 30 seconds. Serve immediately.

FRITTATAS

FOR THOSE WHO LOVE THE IDEA OF omelets but can't handle the execution, there is *frittata,* an Italian dish that consists of eggs and a filling but requires no fancy pan work.

To make an omelet, you must place a filling on top of partially set eggs, wait a second for the eggs to set further, then turn the contents out onto a serving plate in one graceful swoop. This technique is not hard, but it does take practice. For a frittata, you simply prepare the filling in a pan, pour the eggs on top, and cook until the eggs are set. The difference in preparation yields different results. While an omelet is soft, delicate, and slightly runny, a frittata is tender but firm. An omelet encases its filling, while a frittata incorporates it evenly throughout. Aside from simplicity, frittatas have another advantage—they're delicious hot, cold, or at room temperature, so you don't have to sweat the timing as you do with most omelets, which must be served hot.

As few cookbooks agree on a method for making a frittata, we tested a number of techniques to determine which would consistently yield a frittata that was moist but not runny, firm but not tough, and light but substantial. The filling would need to meld with the eggs, not overwhelm them. To get the results we desired, we had to find the optimal ratio of eggs to cooking fat to pan size as well as the best proportion of filling to eggs. But we also had to avoid getting too fussy or precise; the whole point is to make a dish that takes little thought and even less technique. In fact, in Italian, the expression "to make a frittata" (*fare una frittata*) literally means "to make a mess."

To discover the best proportion of eggs to pan size to filling to cooking fat, we began with the recipes in Italian cookbooks, most of which called for six eggs and roughly two tablespoons of oil for a frittata for four. None of the recipes specified pan size, but having eaten very thin frittatas in Italy, we guessed the pan was at least 12 inches in diameter.

Two tablespoons of oil proved too much in the first version we tested. The frittata tasted of oil, when the oil should have mainly just facilitated the cooking, lending only a faint flavor to the dish. Also, the frittata was very thin, almost crêpelike, which we liked but which didn't seem substantial enough for a lunch or supper dish. To retest, we cut the oil in half, to one tablespoon, and used a 10-inch skillet. This turned out to be the right proportion for a firm, flavorful frittata when the filling had few ingredients. However, when the filling had more substantial ingredients, such as mushrooms, potatoes, or asparagus, we found that it was better to return to the original two tablespoons of oil.

To determine the ideal amount of filling, we decided to judge it by sight, adding only enough to cover the bottom of the pan. We didn't want to risk having the filling overwhelm the eggs, and it just seemed sensible that a layer spread across the pan would be adequate for flavor and substance. This approach turned out to be correct, amounting to about ⅔ cup of filling for a 10-inch skillet.

To keep the preparation as simple as possible, we began each test by sautéing the ingredients for the filling in the same nonstick pan in which we would cook the frittata. Then we beat the eggs lightly and poured them over the filling, stirring with a fork to distribute the white and yolk evenly, then proceeded with one of four test cooking methods—stovetop, oven, stovetop plus broiler, and stovetop plus oven.

Stovetop: Judging from the old cookbooks we have from Italy, this is the original method. Once we'd poured the eggs into the pan, we cooked them over medium-low heat until all but the top was set. To set the top, we flipped the frittata with a large spatula, a move that called for great dexterity and involved the risk of tearing. In another test we covered the pan with a heat-resistant plate. This caused the underside to overcook and turn tough.

Oven: Once we'd poured the eggs into the pan, we placed the pan in the center of a 375-degree oven for 30 minutes. The frittata cooked evenly and looked impressive, puffing up a bit and turning golden brown, but it was on the dry side. Hoping to keep it moist, we tinkered with oven temperature (lowering it to 350 degrees), placement of the pan (putting it on a lower rack), and timing (baking it for 20 to 25 minutes). Cooked at the lower temperature, the frittata was still dry. Cooked at the lower temperature in the lower part of the oven, it set unevenly, with parts still runny while others were dry. Cooking it for a shorter period left part of it uncooked.

Starting on the stovetop and finishing under the broiler: We cooked the frittata on the stove until all but the top was set. Then we placed the pan under a preheated broiler 3 inches from the heat for about 40 seconds. Provided you work swiftly to keep the frittata from overcooking, this method ties for the best, making a slightly crispy outer layer but leaving the inside creamy and moist. The only reason we don't rate this method absolute tops is because of the care you have to take not to burn the top; broiling adds an element of stress to what's meant to be an entirely casual process.

Starting on the stovetop and finishing in the oven: We found this method best overall. Instead of going under the broiler as above, the nearly set frittata is placed in the upper third of a 350-degree oven for two to four minutes. While the top won't turn crispy as it would under the broiler, it sets evenly. Moreover, there's more leeway before the frittata burns or dries out.

We also found during these tests that nonstick skillets with ovenproof handles are best for frittatas. Conventional skillets require so much oil to prevent sticking that frittatas cooked in them are likely to be greasy. Eggs often cook more evenly in a nonstick pan because they don't cling to the surface in spots.

Master Recipe for Frittata

SERVES 2 TO 4

Cheese and herbs are the simplest additions to a frittata. This recipe (as well as the variations) can be served for breakfast, brunch, or supper. Chilled or room-temperature frittatas can also be cut into thin wedges or squares and served as an antipasto.

1	tablespoon extra-virgin olive oil
½	small onion, chopped fine
2	tablespoons minced fresh herb leaves, such as parsley, basil, dill, tarragon, or mint
⅓	cup grated Parmesan cheese
¼	teaspoon salt
¼	teaspoon ground black pepper
6	large eggs, lightly beaten

1. Adjust an oven rack to the upper-middle position and heat the oven to 350 degrees.

2. Heat the oil in a 10-inch ovenproof non-stick skillet over medium heat. Swirl the skillet to distribute the oil evenly over the bottom and sides. Add the onion and sauté until softened, 3 to 4 minutes. Stir in the herbs.

3. Meanwhile, beat the Parmesan cheese, salt, and pepper into the eggs with a fork in a medium bowl.

4. Pour the egg mixture into the skillet and stir lightly with a fork until the eggs start to set. Once the bottom is firm, use a thin plastic spatula to lift the frittata edge closest to you. Tilt the skillet slightly toward you so that the uncooked egg runs underneath (see the illustration on page 388). Return the skillet to a level position and swirl gently to evenly distribute the egg. Continue cooking about 40 seconds, then lift

the edge again, repeating the process until the egg on top is no longer runny.

5. Transfer the skillet to the oven and bake until the frittata top is set and dry to the touch, 2 to 4 minutes, removing it as soon as the top is just set.

6. Run a spatula around the skillet edge to loosen the frittata. Invert the frittata onto a serving plate. Serve warm, at room temperature, or chilled.

➤ VARIATIONS

Asparagus Frittata with Mint and Parmesan

Blanch the asparagus pieces in salted boiling water until crisp-tender, 1½ to 2 minutes, then drain and set aside.

2	tablespoons extra-virgin olive oil
1	medium shallot, minced
1	tablespoon minced fresh mint leaves
2	tablespoons minced fresh parsley leaves
⅓	pound asparagus, tough ends snapped off (see the illustration on page 59), spears cut into 1-inch pieces and blanched until crisp-tender
5	tablespoons grated Parmesan cheese
¼	teaspoon salt
¼	teaspoon ground black pepper
6	large eggs, lightly beaten

1. Adjust an oven rack to the upper-middle position and heat the oven to 350 degrees.

2. Heat the oil in a 10-inch ovenproof non-stick skillet over medium heat. Swirl the skillet to distribute the oil evenly over the bottom and sides. Add the shallot and sauté until softened, 3 to 4 minutes. Add the mint, parsley, and asparagus and toss to coat with oil. Spread the asparagus in a single layer in the pan.

3. Meanwhile, beat 3 tablespoons Parmesan

cheese, salt, and pepper into the eggs with a fork in a medium bowl.

4. Pour the egg mixture into the skillet and stir lightly with a fork until the eggs start to set. Once the bottom is firm, use a thin plastic spatula to lift the frittata edge closest to you. Tilt the skillet slightly toward you so that the uncooked egg runs underneath. Return the skillet to a level position and swirl gently to evenly distribute the egg (see the illustration below). Continue cooking about 40 seconds, then lift the edge again, repeating the process until the egg on top is no longer runny. Sprinkle the remaining 2 tablespoons cheese over the top of the frittata.

5. Transfer the skillet to the oven and bake until the frittata top is set and dry to the touch, 2 to 4 minutes, making sure to remove it as soon as the top is just set.

6. Run a spatula around the skillet edge to loosen the frittata. Invert the frittata onto a serving plate. Serve warm, at room temperature, or chilled.

Ricotta Salata Frittata with Olives and Sun-Dried Tomatoes

If you can't find ricotta salata (see page 24), use feta cheese. Because of the cheese and olives, there's no need to add salt to the eggs.

1	tablespoon extra-virgin olive oil
1	small clove garlic, peeled and crushed
1	tablespoon minced fresh basil leaves
1	tablespoon minced fresh oregano leaves
1/4	cup sun-dried tomatoes packed in oil, chopped coarse
1/4	cup oil-cured olives, pitted and minced
1/3	cup crumbled ricotta salata cheese
1/4	teaspoon ground black pepper
6	large eggs, lightly beaten

1. Adjust an oven rack to the upper-middle position and heat the oven to 350 degrees.

2. Heat the oil and garlic in a 10-inch ovenproof nonstick skillet over medium heat. Remove and discard the garlic from the skillet when it begins to color, about 5 minutes. Swirl the skillet to distribute the oil evenly over the bottom and sides. Add the basil, oregano, sun-dried tomatoes, and olives and stir to coat with the oil. Spread the ingredients in a single layer in the pan.

3. Meanwhile, beat the ricotta salata cheese and pepper into the eggs with a fork in a medium bowl.

4. Pour the egg mixture into the skillet and stir lightly with a fork until the eggs start to set. Once the bottom is firm, use a thin plastic spatula to lift the frittata edge closest to you. Tilt the skillet slightly toward you so that the uncooked egg runs underneath. Return the skillet to a level position and swirl gently to evenly distribute the egg (see the illustration below). Continue cooking about 40 seconds, then lift the edge again, repeating the process until the egg on top is no longer runny.

5. Transfer the skillet to the oven and bake

MAKING A FRITTATA

Once the bottom of the frittata is firm, use a thin spatula to lift the edge closest to you. Tilt the skillet slightly toward you so that the uncooked egg runs underneath. Return the skillet to a level position and swirl gently to distribute the uncooked egg.

until the frittata top is set and dry to the touch, 2 to 4 minutes, making sure to remove it as soon as the top is just set.

6. Run a spatula around the skillet edge to loosen the frittata. Invert the frittata onto a serving plate. Serve warm, at room temperature, or chilled.

Frittata with Leek and Potatoes

Boil the potatoes in salted water until tender, 15 to 20 minutes, then drain, cool, and dice.

2   tablespoons extra-virgin olive oil

1   large leek, white part only, sliced thin

2   medium red potatoes (8 ounces), boiled until tender, drained, and cut into medium dice

2   tablespoons minced fresh parsley leaves

1/3   cup shredded provolone cheese

1/4   teaspoon salt

1/4   teaspoon ground black pepper

6   large eggs, lightly beaten

1. Adjust an oven rack to the upper-middle position and heat the oven to 350 degrees.

2. Heat the oil in a 10-inch ovenproof nonstick skillet over medium heat. Swirl the skillet to distribute the oil evenly over the bottom and sides. Add the leek and sauté until softened, 5 to 6 minutes. Add the potatoes and parsley and toss to coat with oil. Spread the ingredients in a single layer in the pan.

3. Meanwhile, beat the provolone cheese, salt, and pepper into the eggs with a fork in a medium bowl.

4. Pour the egg mixture into the skillet and stir lightly with a fork until the eggs start to set. Once the bottom is firm, use a thin plastic spatula to lift the frittata edge closest to you. Tilt the skillet slightly toward you so that the uncooked egg runs underneath. Return the skillet to a level position and swirl gently to evenly distribute the egg (see the illustration on page 388). Continue cooking about 40 seconds, then lift the edge again, repeating the process until the egg on top is no longer runny.

5. Transfer the skillet to the oven and bake until the frittata top is set and dry to the touch, 2 to 4 minutes, making sure to remove it as soon as the top is just set.

6. Run a spatula around the skillet edge to loosen the frittata. Invert the frittata onto a serving plate. Serve warm, at room temperature, or chilled.

SAVORY TART DOUGH

WHEN IT COMES TO TART DOUGH, WE think French in the test kitchen, even when the fillings will be Italian. Pâte brisée is French pie dough, and it is the basis for almost every pie and savory tart recipe made here and in Europe. More substantial than the flakiest pie crust and less crisp than sweet tart dough, savory tart dough should be pleasantly tender, yet strong enough to stand up to the moist fillings that it contains. We also wanted a dough that would be easy to handle and foolproof to make. With an ingredient list so simple, successful tart dough is a matter of proportion, both in texture and in flavor.

We started out with the fat. While a typical pie dough recipe may use butter, shortening, lard, or vegetable oil, tart dough is traditionally made with all butter. It is the richness of the butter that gives the tart dough its great flavor. Although we loved the flavor of the all-butter crust, we felt that it was too dense and heavy. We longed for the flakiness found in an American pie dough with shortening, so we made a crust using all vegetable shortening.

This crust was extremely flaky—a little too flaky for a tart—and, without the butter, lacking in flavor. We started testing combinations of the two fats in hopes of bringing forward their best traits. Several tart doughs later, we arrived at a proportion of 2½ parts flour to 1 part fat—a relatively high-fat crust—made with 6 tablespoons butter and 2 tablespoons vegetable shortening to 1¼ cups of flour. This dough was easy to roll out and shape and, when baked, it was pleasantly flaky and full of great flavor. Although this tart dough is decidedly not Italian (butter or olive oil would be more authentic choices), it was our favorite among the nearly 20 combinations we tested.

Next, we tested flour. High-protein bread flour produced tough dough. Low-protein pastry flour turned out a dough that was not substantial enough for a tart. We found that we liked the texture of the crusts made with all-purpose flour. They were tender yet still strong enough to hold a wet filling. We also found a difference in flavor between bleached and unbleached flour. The bleached flour gave the crust a faint chemical flavor that quite a few tasters could detect. We then tried adding a small amount of baking powder to the flour, a method found in several recipes that reportedly helps give additional lift to the crust. We found this not to be the case, so we stuck with unbleached all-purpose flour.

A food processor is the best tool for making foolproof tart dough. The dry ingredients are combined with a few pulses, then chilled cubed butter is cut in. The shortening is then cut in until the mixture takes on a pale yellow color. The mixture is then turned into a bowl and ice water is added tablespoon by tablespoon, using a rubber spatula and a folding motion. The folding-in of the water allows much of the mixture to be exposed to the moisture without the danger of overprocessing the dough, which can happen easily if using a food processor for this step.

It is also important to allow the dough to rest for at least 30 minutes (longer is better) before rolling it out. This allows time for any gluten that may have developed to relax and makes rolling out the dough easier. We also found that by rolling the dough out between sheets of parchment paper we could minimize the amount of flour added when rolling out. Because of its high amount of fat, it is also important to set the dough at a high oven temperature (425 degrees). This bakes the dough rapidly, before the fat has time to melt, and the tart shell keeps its shape better.

Savory Tart Dough

MAKES ENOUGH DOUGH FOR
ONE 9- TO 9½-INCH TART SHELL

If the dough feels too firm when you're ready to roll it out, let it stand at room temperature for a few minutes. If, on the other hand, the dough becomes soft and sticky while rolling, don't hesitate to rechill it until it becomes easier to work with. Bake the tart shell in a 9- to 9½-inch tart pan with a removable bottom and fluted sides about 1 to 1⅛ inches high. See the illustrations on page 391 for tips on fitting the dough into a tart pan.

1¼	cups (6¼ ounces) unbleached all-purpose flour, plus more for dusting on work surfaces and hands
½	teaspoon salt
6	tablespoons chilled unsalted butter, cut into ¼-inch pieces
2	tablespoons chilled all-vegetable shortening
4–5	tablespoons ice water

1. Pulse the flour and salt in the workbowl of a food processor fitted with a steel blade. Add the butter and pulse to mix in

five 1-second bursts. Add the shortening and continue pulsing until the flour is pale yellow and resembles coarse cornmeal, four or five more 1-second pulses. Turn the mixture into a medium bowl. Sprinkle 3 tablespoons ice water over the mixture. Press the mixture together with the broad side of a rubber spatula, adding more ice water (up to 2 tablespoons) if the dough will not hold together. Squeeze the dough gently until cohesive. Flatten into a 4-inch-wide disk.

Dust lightly with flour, wrap in plastic, and refrigerate at least 30 minutes or up to 2 days before rolling.

2. Adjust an oven rack to the middle position and heat the oven to 425 degrees. Remove the dough from the refrigerator (if refrigerated longer than 1 hour, let stand at room temperature until malleable). Roll the dough between 2 large sheets of lightly floured parchment paper to a 13-inch disk about ⅛ inch thick. Peel off the top sheet,

FITTING DOUGH INTO A TART PAN

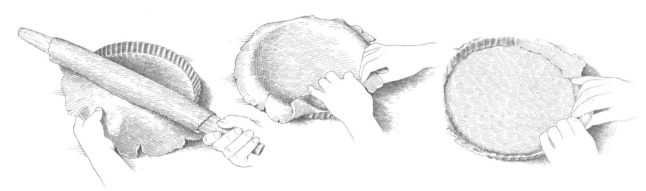

1. Ease the dough over the rolling pin and roll it up loosely. Unroll the dough on top of the tart pan.

2. Lift the edge of the dough with one hand and ease it into the corners of the pan with the other.

3. Press the dough into the fluted sides of the pan, forming a distinct seam along the pan circumference.

4. If some edges are too thin, reinforce the sides by folding the dough back on itself.

5. Run the rolling pin over the top of the tart pan to remove any excess dough.

6. The finished edge should be ¼ inch thick. If it is not, press the dough up over the edge and pinch.

loosely roll the dough around the rolling pin, then unroll it over a 9- or 9½-inch tart pan with a removable bottom. Lift the edge of the dough with one hand and ease it into the corners of the pan with the other hand. Press the dough into the fluted sides of the pan, forming a distinct seam along the pan circumference. If some edges are too thin, reinforce the sides by folding the dough back on itself. Run the rolling pin over the top of the tart pan to remove any excess dough. The finished edge should be ¼ inch thick. If it is not, press the dough up over the edge of the pan and pinch. (See illustrations 1 through 6 on page 391.)

3. Place the tart pan on a rimmed baking sheet. Press a 12-inch square of foil inside the tart shell and fill it with metal or ceramic pie weights. Bake for 30 minutes, rotating the pan halfway through the baking time. Carefully remove the foil and weights by gathering the edges of the foil and pulling it up and out. Reduce the oven temperature to 375 degrees and continue baking until the crust is golden brown, 8 to 10 minutes longer. Transfer the tart pan to a wire rack and cool to room temperature.

Tomato, Mozzarella, and Basil Tart

RIPE TOMATOES, FRESH MOZZARELLA, and aromatic basil are a classic trinity in Italian cooking. As a first course, this combination is known as *insalata caprese*. Placed on a pizza dough, it becomes *pizza Margherita*. A lesser-known manifestation of the trio appears in the form of a tart. This simple preparation is nothing more than these three ingredients layered in a tart shell, suspended in an eggy custard, and baked. But bake up one of these tarts and the problems become obvious—water, water everywhere, not a good thing for keeping a tart shell crisp. It was clear that getting rid of excess moisture would be the key to the success of this tart. But the task was not easy, given plump, juicy tomatoes and fresh, milky mozzarella.

Starting with the tomatoes, we tested beefsteak and Roma (or plum) tomatoes. As we suspected, the beefsteaks contained much more water than the Romas, and the resulting tart suffered. Still, under the duress of heat, even the Roma tomatoes gave up too much liquid and produced a tart with a soggy crust bottom. Next, we sliced the Roma tomatoes and salted them, allowing them to drain on paper towels for 30 minutes. While this did rid the tomatoes of some moisture, it wasn't enough. We tried pressing the tomato slices between sheets of paper towels, and while this method was not completely efficient on its own, the pressing worked wonders in tandem with the salting.

Now that we had the tomatoes in order, it was time to deal with the cheese. First, we tried grating the cheese before topping the tomatoes and baking the tart. On pulling it from the oven, we found that a pool of milky liquid covered the top of the tart. We tried shrink-wrapped mozzarella from the supermarket and, although it shed less liquid, the flavor of the tart was compromised. We needed to figure out how to use fresh mozzarella packed in water in this dish.

Next, we tried grating and squeezing the cheese in a clean kitchen towel. This time the cheese was much drier, but tasters wanted a prettier appearance. We then sliced the cheese, pressed the slices firmly between layers of paper towels, and layered the cheese slices with the tomatoes. This time we had some, but very little, excess moisture, plus the contrasting layers of red and white were beguiling.

Moving on to the custard base, we tried custards made with heavy cream, half-and-half, whole milk, and a combination of these dairy items. We also tried using eggs only, without liquid dairy, as the custard base. Of these, we found that a small amount of heavy cream—about ¼ cup—blended with two large eggs created a custard that was sturdy enough to absorb the liquids that remained in the tomatoes and mozzarella.

Finally, we found that no matter how we sliced it, the beautiful green basil turned an ugly shade of army brown and lost much of its verdant aroma and fresh flavor when introduced to the rigors of a hot oven. Instead, we topped the tart with the shredded basil after it had been removed from the oven, which allowed the basil to retain its fresh flavor and color. A little drizzle of fruity extra-virgin olive oil, and the tart was complete.

Tomato, Mozzarella and Basil Tart

SERVES 4 AS A FIRST COURSE

Use Roma (also called plum) tomatoes in this recipe—they are far less watery than round beefsteak tomatoes.

I	recipe Savory Tart Dough (page 390), baked and cooled as directed
I¼	pounds Roma tomatoes (about 5 medium), cored
	Salt
I0	ounces fresh mozzarella packed in water (about three 2-inch balls), drained
¼	cup heavy cream
2	large eggs, beaten

Ground black pepper

¼ cup shredded fresh basil leaves

Extra-virgin olive oil, for drizzling

1. Place the baked tart shell on a rimmed baking sheet. Adjust an oven rack to the upper-middle position and heat the oven to 400 degrees.

2. Cut the tomatoes crosswise into ¼-inch slices (you should have about 22 slices). Place the slices on a double layer of paper towels. Sprinkle the tomato slices with ½ teaspoon salt; set aside for about 30 minutes. Place another double layer of paper towels on top of the tomatoes. Press firmly, being careful not to smash the tomatoes, until the paper towels have absorbed most of their moisture. Remove the tomato slices from the paper towels and remove any seeds that are still attached to the tomatoes (the majority of the seeds should stick to the paper towels).

3. Cut the mozzarella into ¼-inch slices (you should have about 22 slices). Place the cheese slices on a double layer of paper towels. Place another double layer of paper towels on top. Press firmly on the cheese slices until the paper towels have absorbed most of their moisture.

4. Starting at the outside, begin lining the tart shell with tomato and cheese slices, alternating between the two and leaving ½ inch of each slice exposed. Continue layering the alternating slices toward the center of the tart until the entire shell is filled.

5. Beat the cream and eggs together in a small bowl. Pour the egg mixture over the filling in the tart shell and season with salt and pepper to taste.

6. Place the tart (still on the baking sheet) in the oven and bake 12 to 15 minutes, rotating the pan halfway through baking, until the cheese is melted and the top is just starting to

turn golden. Remove the tart from the oven and sprinkle the basil over the top. Drizzle with olive oil, cut into slices, and serve immediately.

WILD MUSHROOM TART

SAUTÉED WILD MUSHROOMS CAN BE enriched with custard (cream and eggs) and baked in a savory tart shell. Porcini, portobellos, and cremini as well as more exotic mushrooms are all traditionally used in this recipe. We wanted a tart that would bring out the best in the mushrooms. It would be earthy in flavor, but not overwhelmingly so. We also didn't want a custard base with a gelatinous mouthfeel. It should be set enough to slice neatly, but the texture should be soft and silky.

Porcini are the epitome of wild Italian mushrooms, but fresh ones are nearly impossible to find in the United States. Dried porcini are more readily available but still expensive. Even if the price were not a barrier, our tasters ruled out an all-porcini tart; the flavor was overwhelming. It was clear that we would need to cut the porcini with other mushrooms. We tried three fresh mushrooms—portobellos, cremini, and white buttons. The portobellos proved too strong; the tart tasted too earthy and almost muddy. The cremini and the white button mushrooms fared better, with the cremini edging out the button mushrooms for their more robust flavor.

EQUIPMENT: Tart Pans

Tart pans with removable bottoms are available in three types of finishes. The traditional tinned steel tart pan is silver and reflective. The nonstick version is coated with a brown finish inside and out. The third type, a black steel tart pan (also sometimes called blue steel), is quite difficult to find, at least in the United States.

We used a tinned steel pan throughout recipe development of the tarts in this book—without incident. So we wondered what a nonstick tart pan—at 2½ times the cost of a tinned steel pan—could possibly improve upon. The answer is nothing, really. Tart pastry is brimming with butter and is not likely to stick to flypaper, so a nonstick tart pan is superfluous. Despite its darker finish, the nonstick tart pan browned the pastry at the same rate as the tinned steel pan.

The black steel pan was another matter. Colored to absorb heat and encourage browning, it did just that, actually taking the pastry a bit past even our preference for very deeply browned. This pan would be fine for baking a filled tart (the filling slows down the baking), but for unfilled pastry—like the savory tarts in this chapter—it was a bit impetuous. If you own one and are using it to prebake tart pastry, try lowering your oven temperature by about 25 degrees.

TINNED STEEL

NONSTICK

BLACK STEEL

Now that we had the proper mushrooms, we finely chopped them and sautéed them with butter and shallots. Tasters found little to complain about, but the presentation was somewhat lacking. Floating in the custard, the tiny bits of mushroom muddied the appearance of the tart. Tasters wanted to be able to identify what they were eating, so we sliced the mushrooms. This felt more rustic and more Italian. We also found that a mushroom tart should not be anemic when it comes to the main ingredient. It took 12 ounces of cremini mushrooms to fill the tart sufficiently, with just enough custard to hold the mixture together. This yielded a more aesthetically pleasing tart, and each forkful provided a bounty of mushrooms. More, however, was not necessarily better when it came to the porcini. Tasters set their limit at ½ ounce of porcini mushrooms. Any more, and the tart was overwhelmingly strong.

Next, we worked on the alliums. Tasters felt that delicately flavored shallots were too meek to stand up to the potent flavor of the porcini, and we had much better success with their more pungent cousin, onions. We wanted to brighten the mixture, so we tested adding dry vermouth or dry white wine to the mushrooms and found that the latter added the punch of acidity that the mixture needed. Finally, we pulled the pan off the heat and added a touch of garlic and a couple of teaspoons of thyme. Just enough heat was left in the pan to allow the flavors of the garlic and herb to bloom.

On to the custard. We wanted to develop a custard that was sturdy enough to hold its integrity when sliced yet soft enough to give the tart a pleasing texture. Starting with the dairy, we tested tarts made with heavy cream, half-and-half, whole milk, and combinations of these ingredients. In the end, tasters enjoyed the silky richness of the custard made with heavy cream. Next, we tested the amount of eggs needed to set up the custard properly. We found that two large eggs plus one large egg yolk provided the tart with both strength and a pleasant rich texture. To add another texture and flavor, we sprinkled grated Parmesan cheese over the top. In the oven, the cheese became a bit crisp and added nuttiness to the filling.

When it came to baking the tart, we found that a moderate oven worked best. Sitting on the middle rack of our 375-degree oven, the custard baked all the way to the center without becoming hard and overcooked at the edges. In less than 20 minutes, the custard had set up, and the top was browned.

Wild Mushroom Tart
SERVES 4 TO 6
See the illustrations on page 5 for tips on rehydrating dried porcini mushrooms.

- 1   recipe Savory Tart Dough (page 390), baked and cooled as directed
- ½   ounce dried porcini mushrooms
- 3   tablespoons unsalted butter
- 1   large onion, minced
- ¾   pound cremini mushrooms, stems trimmed, remainder sliced ¼-inch thick
- ¼   cup dry white wine
- ¾   teaspoon salt
- ½   teaspoon ground black pepper
- 2   teaspoons minced fresh thyme leaves
- 1   small clove garlic, minced or pressed through a garlic press
- ¾   cup heavy cream
- 2   large eggs
- 1   large egg yolk
- ½   cup finely grated Parmesan cheese

1. Adjust an oven rack to the middle position and heat the oven to 375 degrees. Place the tart pan with the baked tart shell on a rimmed baking sheet.

2. Mix the dried porcini mushrooms with ½ cup hot tap water in a small microwave-safe bowl. Cover with plastic wrap, cut several steam vents in the plastic wrap with a paring knife, and microwave on high power for 30 seconds. Let stand until the mushrooms soften, about 5 minutes. Lift the mushrooms from the liquid with a fork and chop coarsely. Set the mushrooms aside. Discard the soaking liquid.

3. Heat the butter in a large nonstick skillet over medium-low heat until foaming. Add the onion and cook, stirring frequently, until softened, 3 to 5 minutes. Stir in the cremini and porcini mushrooms, increase the heat to medium-high, and cook, stirring frequently, until most of the liquid given off by the mushrooms has evaporated, 6 to 8 minutes. Add the wine, salt, and pepper and cook until the mixture is dry, 2 to 3 minutes longer. Off the heat, stir in the thyme and garlic.

4. In a medium bowl, whisk together the heavy cream, eggs, and egg yolk. Spoon the mushroom mixture evenly into the bottom of the tart shell. Pour the cream mixture over the mushrooms and sprinkle with the Parmesan cheese.

5. Place the tart (still on the baking sheet) in the oven and bake, rotating the pan halfway through baking, until the custard is set and the top is golden brown, 15 to 20 minutes. Remove the tart from the oven and cool on a wire rack for at least 15 minutes or up to 1 hour. Serve warm or at room temperature.

12

FRUIT DESSERTS

ITALIAN BAKERIES IN NEW YORK'S Little Italy, Boston's North End, and other Italian-American neighborhoods around the country are filled with mile-high cakes covered with achingly sweet frostings and lots of brightly colored candied fruits. Based on visits to these kinds of bakeries in the United States, you might conclude that this is how Italians end most meals. However, there's a huge disconnect between the showy, sweet desserts presented in these bakeries and the simple desserts served and eaten in Italian homes.

Most Italian meals at home (as well as in restaurants) end with fruit. Dessert can be as simple as a bowl of perfectly ripe grapes, peaches, figs, and berries. In many cases, Italians gently enhance fruits with a lightly sweetened red wine syrup, caramel sauce, aged balsamic vinegar, bubbly sparkling wine, or maybe a cookie filling. Unlike American fruit desserts (such as cobblers and crisps), the emphasis remains clearly on the fruit, and the sweetness level is quite low.

The recipes that follow represent our favorite Italian fruit desserts. All are simple to prepare, and all start with high-quality, in-season fruit. You might add biscotti (see page 446), espresso (see the discussion at the end of this chapter), or an Italian dessert wine, but keep it simple, just like the Italians do.

Peaches in Red Wine

ITALIANS USUALLY RESERVE ELABORATE desserts for holidays and special celebrations. Everyday Italian meals are often concluded with a simple fruit dessert; quite frequently, the fruits are paired with a wine. Peaches and red wine—sliced peaches combined with a chilled spicy red wine syrup and served, perhaps, with biscotti—is the quintessential way to end a summer Italian meal.

We started our testing with the peaches. Ideally, they should be at the height of their season, aromatic, sweet, and tender, not mealy or bland. However, a less-than-perfect peach can be improved with this preparation. Our tasters preferred peaches peeled rather than unpeeled. The peeled peaches provide maximum exposure to the wine.

If a peach is very ripe, the skin can be pulled off with the edge of a sharp knife. However, more often, the skin resists removal, and chunks of flesh come off with it. A more consistent way of removing the skin is to blanch the peaches in boiling water. It can take anywhere from 30 seconds to 2 minutes to loosen the skin. (Firm peaches need more time, ripe peaches need less.) A quick dunk in an ice bath after blanching stabilizes the temperature of the fruit. The peaches can go back in the boiling water if the skins have not loosened sufficiently. We found that it is better to pull out the peaches too early (and then put them back into the boiling water) than to let them stay in the water too long and become soft and mushy.

Our testing then focused on the choice of wine. With the addition of sugar and spice, the flavor of the wine is considerably altered, and thus the subtleties and refinements of a fine wine are lost. That said, we found that a cheap $4 or $5 wine was too harsh and abrasive for our tasters, even with the addition of sugar. We found that wines in the $8 to $12 range were ideal. At this price, the wine is decent but rarely great, making it perfectly suited to this recipe.

Among the wines we sampled, we preferred the robust, full-bodied, and earthy qualities of the Cabernet. It had a meatiness that worked well with the peaches and black pepper. The Merlot, a close second, had some of the same characteristics as the Cabernet, but it was a bit tamer. At the other end of the spectrum was Beaujolais-Villages, which was very thin, light, and fruity—not bad, but not as rich as either

Merlot or Cabernet. We also sampled a Chianti, which tasted mildly astringent. The bottom line: We preferred the Cabernet, although the other wines worked just fine.

We found that how the wine was treated was more important than the type of wine used. Some recipes called for using the wine straight from the bottle, while other recipes suggested cooking the wine with the sugar and other flavoring ingredients. We found the uncooked version, in which the peaches are combined with wine and sugar and left to marinate in the refrigerator, tasted a bit raw and harsh, and the consistency of the liquid was watery and very thin, something like sangría. The wines that were cooked had a mellower flavor and a thicker, saucelike consistency that we preferred.

We tinkered with the sugar-to-wine ratio

and reduction times to find just the right balance. Too much sugar and/or too much cooking time and the wine became too sweet and thick. We settled on simmering 2½ cups wine and ½ cup sugar for about 15 minutes, with the sauce reducing to about 2 cups. The wine had just the right amount of sweetness and viscosity, not watery and thin, yet not too thick and syrupy. We next sampled the wine mixture with various flavorings. We settled on cloves and a dash of freshly ground pepper. We found that these two spices accentuated the natural flavors in the wine and paired beautifully with the peaches.

Now that we had settled on our wine mixture, we had to find the best method for combining the wine syrup and the peaches. Some recipes call for poaching the peaches in the syrup. This method produced something like

PEELING PEACHES

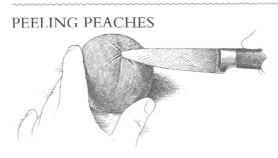

1. With a paring knife, score a small x at the base of each peach.

2. Lower the peaches into a pan of boiling water with a slotted skimmer. Cover and blanch until their skins loosen, 30 seconds to 2 minutes. (Firmer peaches need more time than softer fruit.)

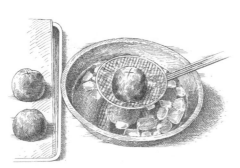

3. Use a slotted skimmer to transfer the peaches to a bowl of ice water. Let stand to stop cooking, about 1 minute.

4. Cool the peaches; then, starting from the scored x, peel each peach, using a sharp knife and/or your fingers.

fruit compote—not quite what we wanted. The texture of the peaches was similar to that of canned peaches, and their aromatic, fresh flavors were completely lost to the wine. We also tested pouring the hot wine mixture over the sliced peaches and letting the two cool together. This process softened the peaches somewhat, making it an acceptable option if your peaches are not perfectly ripe.

However, for a perfectly ripe peach, the best approach is to combine the peaches with the wine after the wine has cooled. At this point, you can cover and refrigerate the mixture and let the peaches marinate in the wine for 2 to 24 hours. We found that two hours was the minimum time necessary for the fruit to absorb enough flavors from the wine syrup. The longer the peaches stay in the refrigerator, the thicker the syrup gets and the fruitier the wine becomes.

No matter how long the peaches and wine are in the refrigerator, they should be brought back to a cool room temperature before serving. Depending on the temperature in your kitchen, this will take from 30 to 45 minutes.

Peaches in Red Wine

SERVES 6

If your peaches are slightly hard and underripe, pour the warm wine mixture over them, which will soften them slightly. Cover and refrigerate the peaches and wine for at least 2 and up to 24 hours. Be sure to allow the fruit to come to a cool room temperature before serving. Serve the peaches and wine on their own or, better still, with biscotti or a small scoop vanilla ice cream, gelato (see page 430), or whipped cream.

I   whole clove
     Pinch coarsely ground black pepper
     (2 or 3 turns of a pepper mill)
2½ cups Cabernet Sauvignon or other
     full-bodied red wine

½ cup (3½ ounces) sugar
6 ripe, fragrant medium peaches

1. Combine the clove, pepper, wine, and sugar in a medium saucepan. Simmer over medium heat until the mixture thickens slightly, about 15 minutes. (The mixture should reduce to about 2 cups.) Remove the pan from the heat. Pour the syrup into a container large enough to hold the peaches, cover, and refrigerate until the syrup is well chilled, at least 1 hour.

2. Bring about 2 quarts water to a boil in a medium saucepan. Fill a large bowl with ice water. Blanch, shock, and peel the peaches according to the illustrations on page 399. Halve, pit, and cut the peaches into ¼-inch-thick slices.

3. Add the sliced peaches to the container with the wine syrup. Cover and refrigerate for at least 2 hours and up to 24 hours. Remove the peaches and wine from the refrigerator 30 to 45 minutes before serving to allow the fruit and wine to come to cool room temperature. Ladle the peaches and wine into individual goblets or bowls and serve immediately.

FRUIT AND PROSECCO WINE

PROSECCO WINE IS A YOUNG, DRY, mildly fruity sparking white wine from the Veneto region. It is sweeter than most Champagne and other sparkling wines, yet drier than many white wines. It is not pretentious or expensive; if anything, it has a reputation for being something of a poor man's champagne. However, mixed with a bit of sugar, some fruit, and liqueur, this humble wine is dramatically transformed into something special—a champagne cocktail and dessert rolled into one. Fruit and Prosecco is a summer fruit salad with fizz.

The first step in preparing this fruit salad is to sweeten the fruit and refrigerate it for at least one hour. We were curious to see if this step could be eliminated. Why not just add sugar, other flavoring ingredients, pour in the wine, and call it a day? As it turns out, the refrigeration is a very important step. The fruits that were allowed to sit in the sugar and macerate produced a fruit salad with a delicate infusion of flavors. The sugar permeates the fruits and concentrates their flavors while drawing out their juices, turning them into a slightly viscous syrup. When mixed with the wine, the flavors intermingle; the fruity syrup brings out the fruity flavors of the wine, while the fruit in the wine accentuates the natural flavors of the fruit.

The next issue was how much sugar to add. Certainly, the amount of sugar required would depend on the natural sweetness of the fruits. However, tasting the fruits before adding the wine is not enough. The wine is somewhat fruity but not really sweet. In addition, several popular brands are on the market, each with its own distinctive characteristics. Therefore, we discovered it was best to make sweetness adjustments after the wine is added. We found that ½ cup of sugar added to the fruit was a safe amount for moderately ripe fruit and moderately sweet wine. The salad should not be too sweet; however, if any hints of bitterness remain, add another tablespoon or two more sugar just before serving.

The final round of testing involved the addition of other flavoring ingredients. The most common ingredient we found in our research was orange liqueur. We tasted batches made with and without liqueur and found that a small amount (2 tablespoons) was a nice inclusion. The liqueur adds another dimension to the salad and enhances the flavor of the wine. Too much, though, and the liqueur was overpowering and harsh. Other ingredients we tested included orange and lemon zest and mint. Of these, lemon zest was the only keeper. Mint tasted a bit medicinal, and the orange was nice but not all that rousing. The lemon zest, on the other hand, added a fresh, bright note to the salad.

As for the fruit, we liked the combination of nectarines and berries best. However, most summer fruits work beautifully in this preparation. Peaches, kiwis, plums, and melons are great substitutions or additions. About 2½ pounds of fruit is sufficient for six to eight people. The fruit salad can be served in individual goblets or in an attractive serving bowl. This is a great idea for brunch. It's best to serve the salad immediately to get the full bubbly effect of the wine.

Nectarines and Berries in Prosecco Wine

SERVES 6 TO 8

Sliced peaches, sliced plums, peeled and sliced kiwi, and melon cut in bite-sized chunks can also be used in this recipe. Just make sure you have about 2½ pounds of fruit in total.

I   pound nectarines, pitted and cut into ¼-inch-thick slices

I   quart strawberries, hulled and cut lengthwise into ¼-inch-thick slices (small strawberries can be halved or quartered)

½   pint raspberries

½   pint blackberries

½   cup (3½ ounces) sugar, or more as needed

2   tablespoons orange liqueur, such as Grand Marnier or Triple Sec

     Grated zest from I lemon

1½   cups chilled Prosecco or other young, fruity sparkling white wine

1. Place the nectarines, berries, ½ cup sugar, orange liqueur, and lemon zest in a large

serving bowl. Toss well and refrigerate for at least 1 hour and up to 8 hours.

2. Just before serving, pour the wine over the fruit. Taste for sweetness and adjust if necessary, adding 1 tablespoon sugar at a time. Serve immediately.

STRAWBERRIES AND BALSAMIC VINEGAR

STRAWBERRIES WITH BALSAMIC VINEGAR may sound like an odd combination, or even a bit trendy. It is neither. At its best, balsamic vinegar is akin to fine port—something to sip in a glass rather than toss in a salad. A few drops of the slightly sweet vinegar enhances the sweetness and fragrant qualities of fresh fruit. As for trendiness, artisan-made balsamic vinegar has been produced in parts of northern Italy for hundreds of years (see page 36 for information about balsamic vinegar) and served over berries for nearly as long.

True balsamic vinegars have brilliantly complex flavors with hints of spice, honey, and caramel. They are soft, mellow, and not at all acidic, and are primarily used as a condiment or liqueur. Artisan-made balsamic vinegars, otherwise referred to as *tradizionale* or *extra-vecchio tradizionale aceto balsamico,* can fetch up to $300 for a 3½-ounce bottle. Of course, most Americans are familiar with industrial balsamic vinegars that cost just a few dollars a bottle. These vinegars are thinner, more acidic, and less complex than traditional vinegars. Such commercial vinegars are perfectly suited for salads and pan sauces, but would they work in this recipe?

Strawberries with balsamic vinegar is a very simple dish to prepare: Cut the strawberries, add a bit of sugar, wait a few minutes for the juices to exude and the sugar to dissolve, then add a pinch of freshly ground black pepper and a drizzle of balsamic vinegar. There is no way to camouflage a muddy, thin, or astringent vinegar.

We were curious to see how the best supermarket balsamic vinegar would fare in this simple preparation. We started with 365 Every Day Value balsamic vinegar, which won our tasting of leading commercial vinegars (see page 36). The result was not totally surprising. The vinegar was somewhat mellow and had a hint of vanilla flavor, but it lacked body and, frankly, just tasted like vinegar. As most Americans are not willing to lay down a couple hundred dollars for the real McCoy, we wanted to find some way to use commercial vinegar so that it would approximate the syrupy texture and complex but mellow flavor of aged traditional vinegar.

The obvious solution was to simmer the vinegar to improve its texture and to add sugar and perhaps seasonings to improve its flavor. Reducing the supermarket vinegar by almost half improved its texture and created a syrupy sauce—a major improvement over the straight vinegar. A tiny bit of sugar tempered its acidity. We also tried reducing the vinegar with vanilla and honey, hoping to create a sauce with more personality. The vanilla was overpowering, and the honey was not noticeably different from the sugar. Finally, we tried a squirt of lemon juice to brighten the flavors; this was well received by tasters.

Now that we had found a viable solution to the vinegar problem, we focused our attention on the strawberries. The strawberries must be sweetened; sugar accentuates the flavors of the berries and balances the balsamic syrup. We found that ⅓ cup was ideal for 3 pints of strawberries. Traditionally, strawberries and balsamic vinegar are sweetened with white granulated sugar. We tested different sweeteners, hoping to find a sweetener that might enhance the flavors of the vinegar. Honey produced a funny aftertaste and was distracting. Dark brown sugar was too strong and distracting. We tried a coarse natural sugar but found no appreciable difference in flavor over white sugar. However, light brown sugar added gentle hints of molasses without being overpowering. Though the difference was subtle, tasters felt that light brown sugar was slightly preferably to granulated white sugar.

Once the sliced berries and sugar are mixed, we found that it took 10 to 15 minutes for the sugar to dissolve and the berries to release some juice. Don't let the berries macerate for much longer. We found that they will continue to soften and become mushy rather quickly.

Strawberries with Balsamic Vinegar

SERVES 6

If you don't have light brown sugar on hand, sprinkle the berries with an equal amount of granulated white sugar. Serve the berries and syrup as is or with a scoop of vanilla ice cream or a dollop of lightly sweetened mascarpone cheese.

1/3	cup balsamic vinegar
2	teaspoons granulated sugar
1/2	teaspoon lemon juice
3	pints strawberries, hulled and cut lengthwise into 1/4-inch-thick slices (small strawberries can be halved or quartered)
1/4	cup packed light brown sugar
	Ground black pepper

1. Bring the vinegar, granulated sugar, and lemon juice to a simmer in a small heavy-bottomed saucepan over medium heat. Simmer until the syrup is reduced by half (to approximately 3 tablespoons), about 3 minutes. Transfer the vinegar syrup to a small bowl and cool completely.

2. With a spoon, lightly toss the berries and brown sugar in a large bowl. Let stand until the sugar dissolves and the berries exude some juice, 10 to 15 minutes. Pour the vinegar syrup over the berries, add pepper to taste, and toss to combine. Divide the berries among individual bowls or goblets and serve immediately.

BAKED PEACHES STUFFED WITH AMARETTI

ITALIANS MAKE GOOD USE OF SUMMER peaches. When they are soft and ripe, peaches are best eaten out of hand or perhaps sliced and served with spiced red wine syrup (see page 400). Ripe peaches that are still a bit firm are better suited to baking; one of the most popular Italian summer desserts is halved peaches stuffed with a cookie crumb filling and baked until the fruit is tender and cookie filling is crisp. Amaretti (store-bought almond macaroons) are the classic choice for this recipe.

The recipe starts by halving and pitting the peaches. The cookie mixture is then stuffed into each half, and the peaches are baked. Right from the start, our tasters said they wanted more cookie filling in each peach. Mounding the filling up over the peach was not successful. Rather quickly, the filling spread over the surface and down the sides of the peaches. A test cook had the bright idea of enlarging the indentation in each peach half made by removing the pit. We scooped out the soft, red-tinged flesh left in each cavity, which could now hold several tablespoons of filling.

Most recipes add sugar and eggs to the cookie crumbs to make a moist, sticky filling. We found that 1/2 cup of cookie crumbs mixed with 3 tablespoons of sugar delivered just the right level of sweetness. A whole egg made the filling too soft. A single yolk was sufficient to bind the ingredients. A little vanilla brightened the other flavors and added complexity.

Some recipes suggest adding butter to the filling, but our tasters preferred using the butter to grease the baking dish and to dot the peaches. The filling had plenty of flavor, but the peaches benefited from the richness of the butter, which also helped glaze the peaches nicely and promoted browning. As a final refinement,

we sprinkled some more cookie crumbs over the stuffed peaches for added crunch.

Our final experiments focused on the issue of oven temperature. At 350 degrees, the filling was a bit pale, but when we raised the temperature to 400 degrees, the filling burned before the peaches softened thoroughly. An oven temperature of 375 degrees proved ideal; the peaches had time to soften, and the filling browned and became firm. With a scoop of vanilla ice cream or cinnamon gelato, these peaches are perfect.

PREPARING THE PEACHES

Here's an easy way to remove the pit from a peach and enlarge the cavity so it can accommodate a cookie filling.

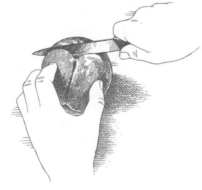

1. Locate the crease that marks the pointed edge of the pit.

2. Position the knife perpendicular to the crease and cut the fruit in half, from pole to pole.

3. Grasp both halves of the fruit and twist apart. The halves will come cleanly apart, without splitting. Remove the pit, which should come out easily.

4. Use a small spoon to scoop out some pulp from each peach half and enlarge the cavity left by the pit. Work over a bowl to catch juices and add the pulp to the bowl.

Baked Peaches Stuffed with Amaretti

SERVES 4

Amaretti can be purchased in many supermarkets and gourmet stores as well as any Italian market. These crisp cookies come in a variety of sizes. Because the cookies are crushed for this recipe, use any size you like. Serve with vanilla ice cream, cinnamon gelato (page 437), or whipped cream.

4	ripe but firm medium peaches
¾	cup crushed amaretti cookies
3	tablespoons sugar
I	large egg yolk
I	teaspoon vanilla extract
2	tablespoons unsalted butter,
	I tablespoon softened

1. Heat the oven to 375 degrees. Working over a bowl to catch the juices, halve and pit the peaches. Use a small spoon to scoop out some pulp from each half to enlarge the cavity left by the pit (see the illustrations on page 404). Add the pulp to the bowl with the peach juices.

2. Add ½ cup amaretti crumbs to the bowl along with the sugar, egg yolk, and vanilla. Mix well to form a wet paste. Mound the filling into the cavity of each peach half and compact the filling with your fingers until smooth.

3. Grease a shallow baking dish large enough to hold the peaches in a single layer with the softened butter. Arrange the peach halves, filling side up, in the dish. Cut the remaining butter into 8 pieces and dot each peach with 1 piece. Sprinkle the remaining ¼ cup cookie crumbs over the fruit.

4. Bake until the peaches are soft and the filling begins to brown, about 40 minutes. Remove and cool slightly. (The peaches can be kept at room temperature for a few hours and reheated just before serving.) Serve warm.

BERRIES WITH ZABAGLIONE

WITH A ZABAGLIONE SAUCE ALREADY developed (see page 424), we thought that the testing for this recipe was going to be quick— just make a few measurements, note some times, and call it a wrap. We knew what we were looking for: soft, sweet, juicy berries topped with a creamy, boozy zabaglione, cooked under the broiler until the berries are just warmed and beginning to exude their juices and the custard sauce is golden brown. This classic dessert is decadently satisfying yet not overly sweet or rich. Sound straight-forward? As it turns out, there was much more to this recipe than we originally thought.

For the first round of testing, we used the zabaglione recipe that we had developed pre-viously. Unfortunately, the top of the broiled zabaglione looked leathery and a bit like blackened marshmallows. The flavor was equally disappointing; the berries were still cold, and the zabaglione was not sweet enough for this application and tasted rather bitter from overbrowning. Before adjusting the amount of sugar in the zabaglione, we decided to try sprinkling sugar on top of the sauce before broiling to create a crunchy caramelized topping, similar to a crème brûlée. We hit the jackpot with this one. Instead of the leathery, blackened look of our first attempt, the sugar-coated gratin was golden and caramelized. As a bonus, the sugar added just enough sweetness, and the crunchy bits on top were a great counterpoint to the creamy sauce and juicy fruits.

In our research, we came upon several recipes that called for adding whipped cream to the zabaglione. We thought this would be worth trying to see if we could enhance our sauce in any way. A few recipes called for using up to 2 cups heavy cream. We could tell just by looking at that whipped cream (it had whipped up to a whopping 4 cups) that it was going to be way too much. Scaling down, we tried the recipe using 1 cup cream. This was also too much; the sauce was too creamy, and the characteristic zabaglione flavor was muted. Scaling even further back, we settled on a mere ⅓ cup cream, which whipped to ⅔ cup. This was just enough to lighten and enrich the sauce without diminishing its flavor.

We next focused our attention on the berry component. We didn't want the fruits to be overly sweet, but even at the height of berry season, a little sugar is often needed to boost their sweetness and heighten their natural flavors. We found that anywhere from two to three tablespoons was needed to sweeten already ripe fruit. We started with 2 tablespoons and adjusted from there to taste.

At this point, we still had consistency problems with the cooking of the gratins. We had established that the best position for the gratins was about seven inches from the broiler element, the second position from the top in our ovens. Our cooking times ranged from two to four minutes. Four minutes was just enough time to warm the berries and brown the tops. However, depending on which oven we used and how long the broiler had been on, the cooking time could be as little as two minutes. This was not really enough time to warm the berries in the center of the gratins, especially a large single gratin.

We tried warming the gratins in a hot oven for five minutes, then turning on the broiler and browning the tops. By the time the tops browned, the sauce was a bit too soupy (from the cream melting), and the berries were too hot. We didn't want the berries so hot that we would have to wait for the gratins to cool; this dessert is best served as soon as it comes out of the oven. To eliminate having to change the setting on the oven and wait for the elements

to adjust, we tried placing the berries in the oven with the broiler on without the zabaglione. Once the berries were barely warm, we removed the gratins from the oven, spread on the zabaglione, sprinkled the top with sugar, and returned the gratins to the broiler for browning. This worked beautifully, with all components cooked to perfection.

Berries with Zabaglione
SERVES 6

This recipe is best prepared in individual gratin dishes, but it can also be made in a single 2-quart gratin dish. For the caramelized sugar crust, we recommend coarse turbinado or Demerara sugar. Regular granulated sugar is a bit too fine and won't caramelize quite as well. Don't use regular brown sugar, which is too moist and lumpy for this purpose.

⅓	cup heavy cream, chilled
1	recipe Chilled Zabaglione (page 425)
1	quart strawberries, hulled and cut lengthwise into ¼-inch-thick slices (small strawberries can be halved or quartered)
½	pint raspberries or blackberries
½	pint blueberries
2–3	tablespoons granulated sugar
2	tablespoons turbinado or Demerara sugar

1. Position an oven rack at the second position from the top, about 7 inches below the broiler. Heat the broiler.

2. Beat the cream in the bowl of standing mixer fitted with a whisk attachment and on low speed until small bubbles form, about 30 seconds. Increase the speed to medium; continue beating until the beaters leave a trail, about 30 seconds more. Increase the speed to high; continue beating until the cream is smooth, thick, nearly doubled in volume, and forms soft peaks, about 20 seconds. With a

spatula, fold the cream into the zabaglione.

3. Combine all of the berries in a large bowl. Toss with 2 tablespoons granulated sugar. Taste the berries for sweetness and add more sugar if necessary. Place 6 shallow individual ceramic gratin dishes (1-cup capacity) on a baking sheet for easy handling. (Alternatively, use a single shallow 2-quart gratin dish.)

4. Divide the berries among the gratin dishes, about ¾ cup per dish. Place the baking sheet with the gratin dishes under the broiler just until the berries are warmed, 2 to 3 minutes. Remove the baking sheet with the gratin dishes from the oven.

5. Spread ⅓ heaping cup of the zabaglione over the berries in each gratin dish. Sprinkle 1 teaspoon turbinado or Demerara sugar on top of each gratin dish. (If using a single large gratin dish, spread all of the zabaglione evenly over the berries, then sprinkle the sugar evenly over the top.) Return the baking sheet with the gratin dishes to the oven and broil until the tops are bubbly and lightly brown, 2 to 4 minutes. Be sure to keep an eye on the gratins because they can easily burn. Remove the baking sheet from the oven.

6. Carefully transfer the hot gratin dishes to individual plates. (If making a single large gratin, spoon the berries and zabaglione into individual bowls.) Serve immediately.

GLAZED ORANGES

FINISHING OFF A LARGE MEAL WITH cool sliced oranges bathed in a fragrant sweet syrup can make even the most self-indulgent eater feel almost virtuous. Recipes for glazed or macerated oranges can be found in many Italian cookbooks. Like most things Italian, there are no hard and fast rules. We found a wide range of recipes in our research called "glazed oranges."

We started our testing by sampling a few of these recipes. The simplest approach—marinating oranges with sugar and orange juice—had a clean and fresh taste, but the juice alone could not create a sauce with sufficient body. On the other end of the spectrum was a recipe that combined thick, sweet sugar syrup (sugar cooked in water until the granules dissolved) with sliced oranges. This was over-the-top sweet, and the syrup obliterated the fresh, tart flavors of the oranges. Other recipes flavored the syrup with warm spices (cloves, allspice, cinnamon) and vanilla. We liked a bit of spice in our syrup but found that the vanilla accentuated the sweetness of the sauce rather than bringing out the flavors of the fruit.

We knew that we needed a syrup that was not too sweet but still had plenty of flavor and body. The plain, unadulterated sugar syrup was bland and uninspiring. Cinnamon and cloves were a good addition, but there was still room for improvement. We had seen a couple of recipes that called for glazing or macerating the oranges in caramel (caramel is sugar that is melted and then cooked until it browns). We made a caramel, adding cinnamon and cloves to the mixture, just as we had with the syrups. The caramel flavor paired beautifully with the oranges and spices and offered a complexity of flavors; sweet, bitter, tangy, and spicy all wrapped into one. We were quite pleased with our progress, although we still had not fully addressed the sweetness issue. We needed to dilute the caramel with more liquid. Rather than use water, which would thin the sauce but offer no additional flavor, we opted to add orange juice. This hit the mark. The sweetness was reduced while the flavor enhanced, and the consistency of the sauce was perfect.

Next, we considered whether or not to poach the oranges. One recipe called for poaching the oranges whole in the sauce. This method had two problems. First, there wasn't enough sauce in which to submerge the oranges completely, and increasing the volume would provide a disproportionate amount of sauce to oranges for serving. Second, the oranges didn't cook evenly. The outside of the oranges overcooked and became mushy and frayed while the flavors of the caramel sauce never actually penetrated the center.

We tried poaching sliced oranges in a saucepan, but we found this even more problematic. The oranges began to fall apart within minutes, even with the temperature kept at a gentle simmer. Next, we simply poured the hot sauce over the orange slices and allowed the two to cool together; then we compared them to oranges that were combined with cold sauce. The oranges that were combined with the hot sauce softened slightly and absorbed some of the flavor from the caramel—a definite improvement over the cold sauce version.

We decided to make one last attempt to devise a method for gentle poaching that would get more caramel flavor into the oranges without ruining their texture. This time we headed for the oven. We placed the orange slices in a baking pan, covered them with the hot caramel, covered the baking dish with foil (to prevent evaporation), and placed the dish in a 325-degree oven for 20 minutes. This proved just enough time for the oranges to steep in the hot mixture without becoming too soft. The oranges had a silky tender texture but were not mushy. But the decisive factor in favor of this method was flavor. The orange and caramel flavors intermingled, making the sauce taste less sweet and more fruity. This method also gave the cinnamon stick and cloves more time to flavor the sauce.

Once the oranges are removed from the oven, they can be transferred to a serving dish, covered with plastic wrap, refrigerated, and chilled. This dessert can be made up to two days in advance and will only benefit from the additional time. We also like using blood oranges, either substituting them for the navels or, even better, using them in combination. Their tart, musky flavor works perfectly with caramel, and their reddish-orange color makes them especially attractive.

Glazed Oranges in Caramel-Orange Sauce

SERVES 6

You can serve these oranges on their own or with a pound cake. See illustrations 1 and 2 on page 35 for tips on removing the peel and pith from the oranges. Wear long sleeves when working with caramel to keep any splatters from causing burns. Although you can easily make this recipe without a candy thermometer, if you own one, you might want to clip it to the side of the saucepan when removing the cover in step 2. When the caramel is thick and straw-colored, the temperature should register 300 degrees. The caramel is done when the color is deep amber and the temperature reaches 350 degrees.

9	medium navel oranges, blood oranges, or a combination (about 4½ pounds)
½	cup water
¾	cup (5¼ ounces) sugar
2	whole cloves
1	cinnamon stick

1. Squeeze enough juice from 3 oranges to measure 1 cup; discard the spent oranges. Remove the peel and pith from the remaining 6 oranges. Start by trimming a thin slice from each end so that the fruit will sit flat on a cutting board. Using a small paring knife, cut down around the orange to remove the peel and pith in long slices. Try to follow the outline of the fruit as closely as possible. Cut the peeled oranges crosswise into slices about

½ inch thick. Place the orange slices in a 9 by 13-inch glass or ceramic baking dish. Preheat the oven to 325 degrees.

2. Pour the water into a heavy-bottomed 2-quart saucepan. Add the sugar, cloves, and cinnamon stick to the center of the pot to keep the granules from adhering to the sides. Cover and bring to a boil over high heat. Uncover the pot and continue to boil until the syrup is thick and straw-colored, 2 to 3 minutes. Reduce the heat to medium and continue to cook until the sugar is deep amber and begins to smoke, 1 to 2 minutes.

3. Remove the saucepan from the heat. Carefully pour in the orange juice (the caramel will harden and splatter). Return the pan to medium heat and cook, stirring constantly, until the caramel is completely dissolved, about 2 minutes.

4. Pour the caramel mixture over the orange slices. Cover the baking dish with foil and bake for 10 minutes. Remove the foil and gently toss the orange slices so that any slices that were not completely submerged will have a chance to sit in the liquid. Cover and bake for 10 minutes longer. Transfer the baking dish to a wire rack and cool to room temperature. Transfer the oranges and the sauce to a serving bowl, cover with plastic wrap, and refrigerate until chilled, at least 2 hours and up to 2 days. To serve, spoon the oranges and syrup into individual bowls.

ESPRESSO

ITALIAN MEALS ALMOST ALWAYS END with espresso. Italians also drink espresso at breakfast and throughout the day, often standing up at *cafés* and downing a shot in a matter of seconds. Thanks to Starbucks and other coffee companies, Americans have discovered the joys of coffee Italian-style. In many American cities, a cappuccino is as easy to buy as a cup of regular joe, and even esoteric drinks, such as macchiato (see page 411), are now widely available.

Because one doesn't always want to go out for coffee—especially with cafés and restaurants charging as much as $4 for a cappuccino—more Americans are trying to make high-quality espresso at home. In our test kitchen, we tested several espresso machines and have perfected a method for making espresso and espresso drinks (such as cappuccino). Here's what we have learned.

Espresso professionals compare their brew to wine. In many respects, they are right: Espresso is an extremely complex beverage with more than 600 individual flavor components, and there are tremendous differences among beans grown in different areas. But there is one clear difference between espresso and wine: Wine is ready to drink when you buy it, whereas making good espresso requires a good machine and proper technique. The type of beans, the roasting method, and the grinding process all make a difference, and even the best coffee can be easily ruined by bad form at home.

Most coffee is brewed by letting water drip or percolate slowly through the ground beans. Espresso, on the other hand, is a relatively new creation, dependent on high-tech devices that generate enough pressure to force hot water through finely ground coffee, quickly extracting the flavor. The first modern espresso machine, which used a manually operated piston, was invented at the end of World War II; electric pump machines date to the 1950s.

Only these two types of machines can create a true cup of espresso. The best of them heat the water to between 192 and 198 degrees (hotter water scalds the coffee and imparts bitterness; cooler water does not extract as much flavor). The typical pull—the term describes forcing heated water through compacted grounds—lasts about 20 seconds. When done properly, the result is a thick, rich brew that captures the essence of the coffee bean. Good espresso never tastes burnt, harsh, or bitter; it is somewhat buttery, with a pleasing level of acidity and a bittersweet flavor that is rich with subtle undertones.

A properly made espresso also features the characteristic light brown topping called *crema*. This foamy extraction adds a smoothness and creaminess not found in other coffee drinks. The presence of a well-defined crema (there should be enough crema to briefly trap sugar crystals sprinkled over the espresso) is a sign that the right coffee has been paired with the right extraction technique.

High-quality espresso starts with high-quality arabica beans. Most experts recommend buying a good espresso blend rather than varietals. Knowledgeable roasters create blends that accentuate the positive attributes of each bean. Few varietals are suited for the quick extraction process of espresso. Even top varietals such as Kenya AA and Costa Rican Tres Rios are usually more one-dimensional than a well-crafted blend.

While there is some agreement among experts about blends, there is little consensus about roasting. On the West Coast (and particularly in Seattle), beans are generally roasted until very dark. East Coast roasters—as well as many Italians—think their western counterparts go too far and actually scorch the beans. Of course, as most espresso in Seattle is consumed with plenty of milk, the bitter taste is less noticeable than it would be in a straight cup.

The key to buying beans for espresso at home is to find a store that sells good beans and then experiment to find a roast that suits your palate. Look for dark brown but not black beans that have an oily sheen; dry, cracked beans are well past their prime.

A large measure of coffee's quality is freshness, so make sure to buy from a store with high turnover, or buy by mail. When properly stored, coffee beans are at their peak of flavor for only two weeks after roasting. The best strategy, then, is to ask the retailer when the beans were roasted; if he or she doesn't know (or if it has been more than a few days), shop elsewhere.

Ideally, you should buy a small quantity of fresh whole beans and grind them yourself as needed. Some experts prefer expensive burr grinders, but we've had decent luck with inexpensive blade grinders. For the best results, grind only small quantities (fill the grinder halfway) and wipe the container clean after each use to prevent a buildup of oils. To promote an even grind, hold the grinder securely and shake it as you grind, much as you might shake a martini. Beans for espresso should be ground quite fine.

Ground or not, coffee should be stored in an airtight container, away from sunlight. Trained palates may pick up a decrease in flavor after just a day or two, but in our tests, we found that this method preserved flavor for a week, even with ground coffee. Freezing causes the natural oils to congeal and, in our tests, produced coffee with less crema. But if you plan to keep coffee for more than a week or two, it's best to store it in the freezer to protect flavor, even at the risk of reducing crema slightly.

A final note about grinding and storing: Coffee inspires a fair amount of zealotry. Many devotees go through the same rituals day in and day out. (One told us he packs beans, a small blade grinder, and a drip coffee maker when he goes on the road.) Your passion for coffee, coupled with your ability to distinguish differently handled beans, should determine how much fuss you are willing to endure.

Properly blending, roasting, and grinding coffee is half the battle; technique is equally important. Because lukewarm espresso is unappealing and will not hold crema, begin by preheating the filter holder, basket, and coffee cup—just run the machine without coffee, letting the water drip into the cup.

Then fill the filter basket (the correct amount, technically, is 7 grams of coffee for each cup) and lightly tamp the grounds. Some machines come with a special tool, and others have a built-in tamper; you can also use the back of a small measuring cup. Tamping is important because, if the grounds are loose, the water will run through them too quickly and the espresso will be watery. However, avoid overtamping, which can completely prevent the water from seeping through the grounds. The correct amount of tamping depends, to some extent, on the grind. Coffee that is slightly coarse should be firmly packed; coffee that is a tad too fine should be lightly tamped.

ESPRESSO DRINKS

Although Americans tend to think more is better, a single portion of espresso contains just 1 1/2 ounces of liquid and should be served in a warmed 2- to 3-ounce demitasse. Espresso can be sipped slowly or quaffed, Italian-style, in one or two gulps. If you want more coffee, make a lungo or doppio (see below).

ESPRESSO RISTRETTO A short or "restricted" espresso of about 1 ounce. To make this, simply cut short the flow of water when brewing this intense espresso.

ESPRESSO LUNGO The opposite of a ristretto, this is made by adding an ounce or two of hot water (not from the brew head) to make a milder or "long" cup. When diluted with more hot water (at least 3 or 4 ounces), this drink is sometimes called an Americano.

ESPRESSO DOPPIO A "double"—3 ounces of espresso made by filling the two-cup basket and letting the contents drip into one 4- or 5-ounce cup.

ESPRESSO MACCHIATO A single espresso "marked" with a tablespoon of frothed milk.

ESPRESSO CON PANNA A single shot of espresso with a small dollop of whipped cream.

ESPRESSO ROMANO Espresso served with lemon peel. Italians turn up their noses at this American invention, and for good reason; the acidity in the lemon peel does not enhance the flavor of the espresso.

ESPRESSO CORRETTO A single espresso that has been "corrected" with a splash of brandy or other spirits.

CAPPUCCINO A single espresso topped with equal amounts of steamed milk and frothed milk and served in a 5- to 6-ounce cup. Europeans usually add plain or vanilla-scented sugar, but many Americans dust the top of the foam with cocoa powder, cinnamon, or nutmeg as well.

CAFFÉ LATTE "Coffee with milk" (known as café au lait in French and café con leche in Spanish), made with a double shot of espresso, 5 or 6 ounces of steamed milk, and very little or no froth. Add more espresso or milk to strengthen or weaken the mix and serve in large bowl-shaped cups (about 9 or 10 ounces) or tall, wide-mouthed glasses.

LATTE MACCHIATO A tall glass of steamed milk (sometimes with froth) into which a single espresso is slowly poured to "mark" the milk with coffee.

CAFFÉ MOCHA A single espresso flavored with 1/2 ounce of chocolate syrup and topped with 4 to 5 ounces of steamed milk and whipped cream. Dust with cocoa or shaved chocolate, if desired.

MOCHA LATTE Latte with chocolate syrup added to the espresso, but no whipped cream or grated chocolate. Other syrups, especially almond, hazelnut, and orange, can be used in the same way to create exotic lattes.

Wipe the excess coffee from the rim of the basket to ensure a firm seal between the holder and the brew head, then slide the filter holder tightly into place. You are now ready to brew.

Turn on the pump and allow espresso to slowly flow out of the machine for about 20 seconds or until the coffee stream has turned light brown. Shut off the pump and allow the stream to finish dripping for several seconds. If the brew head continues to leak, remove the filter holder. (In any case, do not leave the filter holder in the machine when it's not in use, as this may weaken the brew head seal.)

Frothing milk is even more challenging than brewing espresso. With most of the machines we have tested over the years, we were able to make an excellent cup of espresso on the first try, but our initial attempts at frothing milk have been erratic. Although each machine has its own peculiarities, these general guidelines will help.

First, place fresh, cold milk in a narrow container; the most common vessel is made of stainless steel, but you can use a ceramic mug. Make sure the container is not more than one-third full. When the steam light goes on, open the steam valve into an empty cup to let out any accumulated water. Place the steam valve into the milk, just below the surface, open the valve, and gently move the container in a circular fashion to steam and froth the milk. After about 20 seconds, there should be a nice head of froth on top of the steamed milk.

When you're done, open the steam valve into an empty container to remove clogged milk, then wipe the wand to remove any milk particles before they harden.

Most people wonder which milk is best for frothing; some have had luck with low-fat milk, while others insist only full-fat does the job. But our tests showed that temperature and age are much more important than fat content. Skim, low-fat, and whole milk can all be steamed successfully, although skim milk produces drier foam and whole milk yields creamier foam. Because we prefer creamier froth, we use either 2 percent or whole milk. Half-and-half and light cream contain too much fat to froth.

Regardless of the type of milk, we found that milk below 40 degrees froths much better than that which is warmer. Avoid pouring cold milk into a warm frothing container; you might even chill the container in the freezer for several minutes before frothing.

Milk foam is created when the proteins trap the air emitted by the steaming wand. Garth Rand, professor of food science at the University of Rhode Island, says these proteins are more stable and thus better able to trap air at colder temperatures.

Still more noticeable is the effect time has on milk's ability to froth. Milk that has been opened and left in the refrigerator for a week—even if it is still technically fresh—may be impossible to froth. Milk sugars (lactose) are constantly breaking down into lactic acid (which causes the sour taste in old milk), so milk begins to spoil from the moment it is produced, long before we can taste the difference. This increased acidity compromises the ability of the proteins to trap air.

In sum, the freshest, coldest milk produces the most foam when steamed.

13

CHILLED AND FROZEN DESSERTS

MANY OF OUR SOURCES INDICATE THAT Italians (or, more precisely, Sicilians) invented frozen desserts. These sources suggest that snows from Mt. Etna were flavored with fruit syrups and served as icy treats—a sort of prototype for the modern snow cone. Other sources suggest that ice cream originated in China or the Middle East.

The first European record of frozen desserts is from an Italian source dated 1530. At this time, several Italian scientists wrote about the discovery of the endothermic effect—the ability of salt to lower the freezing point of a liquid. Water ices became commonplace in wealthy homes in the 17th century, but dairy-based frozen desserts were not widely made for at least another hundred years.

Perhaps because of their long history of making frozen desserts, Italians are passionate about them. Walk down the main thoroughfare in any Italian city, town, or village, and you are likely to find several shops selling gelato (a dairy-based frozen dessert roughly equivalent to American ice cream) and sorbet (a fruit-based frozen dessert usually made without dairy). At home, Italians make granitas (granular ices not unlike American snow cones).

Italians also make a wide array of half-frozen desserts (called *semifreddo,* which literally translates as "half cold") and chilled desserts, including the increasingly popular tiramisù and panna cotta. These desserts are puddings, although they are quite different from American puddings and French mousses. Tiramisù contains eggs, a lightly sweetened Italian cheese called *mascarpone,* and cookies that have been soaked in coffee. Panna cotta is sweetened and flavored cream that has been thickened with gelatin.

We have included two other pudding-like desserts in this chapter that technically are not chilled (refrigerated before serving). Monte Bianco is a billowy mound of chestnut puree covered with whipped cream (this dessert is cold but not chilled), and zabaglione is a frothy, eggy sauce made with Marsala, which is eaten both warm and chilled.

TIRAMISÙ

TIRAMISÙ LITERALLY TRANSLATES AS "pick me up," and this coffee-laced sweet is generally served in the afternoon in Italy. We've read many stories about its origins. According to our favorite tiramisù story, this dessert was a favorite of Venetian courtesans who needed the caffeine jolt to complete the day's work. No matter its origins, tiramisù has become extremely popular in the United States in the last two decades. It has made its way onto many restaurant menus and can be found in just about every Italian cookbook written in English.

The original recipe is quite simple; a mound of whipped egg yolks and sugar is blended with mascarpone cheese (an Italian equivalent to our cream cheese) and layered between store-bought ladyfinger cookies that have been soaked in espresso. The dessert is refrigerated for several hours or until the cookies break down slightly and form a soft, cakelike layer surrounded by rich, creamy pudding. Most versions are also dusted with cocoa or grated chocolate.

One of our concerns regarding the classic tiramisù recipe is that the filling is made with raw eggs. Some recipes complete the filling by folding in raw whipped egg whites. Given our concerns about salmonella, we wanted a recipe in which the eggs were cooked.

We found several recipes using a zabaglione (see page 424) enriched with the mascarpone. This intrigued us because in a zabaglione, the eggs are actually cooked. Egg yolks, sugar, and Marsala wine are whipped together over a double boiler until the mixture has tripled in volume and is very frothy. However, even with the addition of mascarpone, we found the filling too light and airy and lacking the thick, cheesy density we were looking for. We also sampled a recipe with no eggs at all—just whipped cream, sugar, mascarpone, and liqueur for flavoring. We liked the dense consistency of this recipe but found the flavor a bit bland and one-dimensional.

Going back to the double boiler approach, we eliminated the wine and all of the extra whisking at the stove. Instead we ribboned the egg yolks and sugar with an electric mixer, placed the mixture in a double boiler, and stirred it with a rubber spatula (to keep it from sticking) until the mixture reached 160 degrees—hot enough to kill salmonella. We then let the mixture cool to room temperature and beat in the mascarpone and flavorings. This was quite successful; the filling had great flavor and texture, and it was safe to eat! The only minor problem we had was that, even with the constant stirring during cooking, some of the egg yolk mixture overcooked and caked onto the sides of the pan. Simply by adding ¼ cup heavy cream to our ribboned eggs, we eliminated this problem. The extra liquid loosened the egg mixture and made it less sticky and thick.

Next, we needed to address the issue of the egg whites. We were curious to see whether the addition of whipped egg whites would enhance our filling. However, the whites would also need to be cooked. To do this, we poured 238-degree sugar syrup over the egg whites while they were being whipped to soft peaks. The whites were then folded into the filling, making it slightly lighter and mousse-like. We liked the texture but found that the improvement was slight and not worth the extra effort. We decided to eliminate the egg whites and save much time and effort.

Now that we had our filling, we addressed the cake/cookie layer. We quickly dismissed making a cake from scratch. The cake was too light and spongy and certainly more labor-intensive. Most recipes called for using a large, dry, ladyfinger-type cookie called *savoiardi*. These cookies were ideal. They moistened beautifully, absorbing all of the coffee without becoming soggy. The hard cookie was transformed magnificently into a soft, cakelike layer after several hours in the refrigerator.

ASSEMBLING TIRAMISÙ

 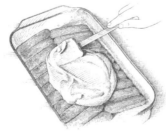 

1. Dip the cookies, one at a time, in the coffee mixture. Arrange the soaked cookies in the bottom of the baking dish.

2. Once the bottom of the baking dish is covered with cookies, spread half of the mascarpone mixture evenly over the cookies.

3. Sprinkle half the chocolate over the mascarpone. Repeat the layering of the cookies, mascarpone, and chocolate, then wrap and refrigerate until well chilled.

415

A few recipes called for using much smaller Italian cookies called *pavesini*. The pavesini cookies disintegrated on contact with the coffee. This round of testing showed that a few too many seconds in the coffee mixture made the cookies—even the savoiardi type—overmoistened and mushy. The cookies should be dunked, turned once, then quickly placed in the serving dish.

Finally, we needed to settle on the makeup and amount of our coffee mixture. First of all, we decided to use strongly brewed coffee in lieu of espresso, which was a bit overpowering and not usually on hand. We liked the addition of alcohol to the coffee, rum and brandy being our favorite types. We also tried coffee and orange liqueurs. The coffee liqueur was a bit cloying and the orange liqueur too subtle. One cup of coffee with two tablespoons liquor provided just the right balance of coffee and alcohol and a suitable volume of liquid (there should be just a small amount of liquid remaining after all the cookies are moistened).

Most recipes call for two layers of soaked cookies and mascarpone mixture, and we found this preferable to the single layer recommended in a few sources. Many recipes add a dusting of cocoa or sprinkling of grated chocolate. Our testers preferred bittersweet chocolate (cocoa was too bitter) at a modest amount of just 2 ounces. We found recipes with three times as much chocolate, but tasters agreed that chocolate should be an accent rather than a dominant flavor in tiramisù.

Although our version requires slightly more effort than the traditional recipe (in order to cook the eggs), this dessert can be assembled in less than half an hour and requires no last-minute effort. Simply scoop portions from the baking dish into small bowls. Tiramisù isn't the best-looking Italian dessert, but its flavors are memorable.

Tiramisù

SERVES 10 TO 12

Mascarpone is a creamy Italian cheese now made on both sides of the Atlantic. It is generally sold in tubs and has a consistency similar to cream cheese beaten with a little heavy cream. Unlike American cream cheese, mascarpone is not tangy and, in fact, it has a buttery, creamy flavor. Although there is no substitute for mascarpone, we find that American versions of this cheese are admirable and work in tiramisù. Don't use regular American cream cheese in this recipe—the flavor is too tart and the texture too grainy. See the illustrations on page 415 for tips on assembling this layered dessert.

1½	cups strong brewed coffee
6	tablespoons rum or brandy
6	large egg yolks
¾	cup (5¼ ounces) sugar
	Pinch salt
½	cup heavy cream
1	pound mascarpone cheese
36	(1½ packages) savoiardi ladyfingers
2	ounces bittersweet chocolate, grated fine

1. Combine the coffee and 2 tablespoons rum in a shallow dish or glass pie plate.

2. Place the egg yolks, sugar, and salt in a stainless-steel mixing bowl. Using an electric mixer at medium-high speed, beat the egg yolk mixture until it is thick and creamy and pale yellow, about 4 minutes. (You can also do this by hand with a whisk; increase beating time to about 8 minutes). Stir in the cream.

3. Place the bowl over a pan of simmering water. Reduce the heat to low and stir constantly until the mixture registers 160 degrees on an instant-read thermometer, about 5 minutes.

4. Remove the bowl from the heat, transfer the mixture to another large bowl, and cool to room temperature.

5. Using an electric mixer, add the mas-

carpone and remaining ¼ cup rum to the egg mixture and beat at medium speed. The mixture will thin and look curdled. Raise the speed to medium-high and continue to beat until smooth and very thick, about 3 minutes.

6. One at a time, dip the savoiardi cookies into the coffee mixture, turning just once to lightly moisten. Cover the bottom of a 9 by 13-inch glass or ceramic baking dish with moistened cookies. With a rubber spatula, spread half of the mascarpone mixture over the cookies. Sprinkle with half of the grated chocolate. Repeat the layers with the remaining cookies, cream, and chocolate. Cover tightly with plastic wrap and refrigerate until thoroughly chilled and cookies are tender and soft, at least 4 hours or up to 24 hours. To serve, scoop the tiramisù into individual bowls.

PANNA COTTA

PANNA COTTA SEEMS TO HAVE ARRIVED on tiptoe—or on wings. It is included in neither Waverley Root's book *The Food of Italy* (1971) nor in Marcella Hazan's *Classic Italian Cook Book* (1973). In fact, no one seems to know much about it. Yet from virtual anonymity 25 years ago, panna cotta has achieved star status in restaurants around the United States, becoming the popular successor to tiramisù.

Though its name is lyrical, the literal translation of *panna cotta*—"cooked cream"—does nothing to suggest its ethereal qualities. In fact, panna cotta is not cooked at all. Neither is it complicated with eggs, as is a custard. Instead, sugar and gelatin are melted in cream and milk, and the whole is then turned into individual ramekins and chilled. It is a virginal dessert, a jellied alabaster cream. It forms a richly neutral backdrop for everything it touches: strawberry coulis, fresh raspberries,

light caramel, chocolate sauce.

That, we should say, describes the ideal panna cotta. There are others. Panna cotta is about nothing if not texture. The cream must be robust enough to unmold but delicate enough to shiver on the plate. Our mission, therefore, was to find correct proportions for four simple ingredients and the most effective way to deal with the gelatin.

We began by preparing five recipes from well-known Italian cookbooks. Each of them used like ingredients in varying proportions and dealt with the ingredients similarly. Two called for powdered sugar (favored in Italian confections). Two simmered the cream; the others merely warmed it. One recipe whipped half the cream and folded it into the base. Procedurally, the recipes were extremely straightforward.

On tasting the recipes, it was clear they fell into two groups. Those with higher proportions of milk were slippery and translucent, their flavor elusive and flat. Those with more cream had a rich mouthfeel and a creamier, more rounded flavor. What united these recipes most noticeably, however, was a slightly rubbery chew, the result of too much gelatin.

It would be practical, we decided, to design the recipe around a single packet of gelatin. Given this amount, we knew we would need to establish the volume of liquid required to set up the cream. Before that, we had to determine the best proportion of cream to milk, critical in terms of mouthfeel. Preliminary tastings put us on the side of a 3 to 1 ratio of cream to milk.

Over the next week, we made dozens of panna cotte in the test kitchen. We were surprised to find textural inconsistencies between batches that should have been identical. Some were flabby, others stalwart. Serendipity saved the day when we realized that the amount of gelatin in a packet is not consistent but in fact varies widely from one packet to another. Using a gram scale, we weighed more than 50 individual gelatin packets and found weight discrepancies as great as 20 percent. In fact, in two packages of four packets each, we found eight different weights. As soon as we began measuring gelatin by the teaspoonful, things began looking up.

In addition to proportions, there was chilling time to consider. Preparation and chilling times should be brief and the dessert quick to the table. Our first priority, therefore, was to create the best dessert to emerge within the shortest chilling time, a panna cotta that would be firm, say, in the space of a few hours. By increasing the amount of gelatin in increments of ⅛ teaspoon, from 2 to 3 teaspoons, we found that 2¾ teaspoons produced a firm enough yet still fragile finished texture after four hours.

INGREDIENTS: Vanilla Beans and Extracts

Almost two-thirds of the world's supply of vanilla beans comes from Madagascar, an island off the eastern coast of Africa. Significant amounts of vanilla beans are also grown in Mexico and Tahiti. Tahitian beans are a hybrid that originated spontaneously on several islands in the South Pacific. Vanilla beans grown everywhere else in the world, including Mexico and Madagascar, are from the same species, and are botanically the same.

Although vanilla beans are convenient to use in custards (the pods are split lengthwise, the seeds scraped into the liquid, and the pods usually added to infuse more flavor), extracts make the most sense for baking jobs, including cakes and cookies. (You could make vanilla sugar by nestling a split bean in some sugar, but this process takes about a week.)

When shopping for extracts, you have two basic choices: pure extract and imitation. Pure vanilla extract is made by steeping chopped vanilla beans in an alcohol and water solution. Imitation vanilla extract is made from vanillin, a product extracted from conifer wood pulp that has been chemically rinsed.

When developing our panna cotta recipe, we tried several kinds of beans and extracts. Tasters preferred the flowery flavor of the Tahitian vanilla beans to other vanilla beans. Most experts believe that Tahitian vanilla beans have a more intoxicating aroma, which we found really shines in an eggless custard. That said, tasters preferred panna cotta made with any kind of vanilla bean to those made with extract, so feel free to use other beans. We should note that the presence of black specks is a visual clue that may have influenced tasters when comparing panna cotti made with beans versus those made with extracts. However, everyone in the test kitchen strongly felt that beans offered more to this simple recipe than extract did.

We wondered if the brand matters when using extract, or if you can tell the difference between real and imitation extract. We made panna cotti with nine extracts (seven real, two imitation) and gathered 18 tasters. We also followed a standard tasting protocol in the vanilla business and mixed each extract with milk at a ratio of 1 part extract to 8 parts milk. Although you would never use so much extract in a real application, this high concentration makes it easier to detect specific characteristics in extracts.

The results of this tasting were so shocking that we repeated it, only to come up with similarly surprising findings. Tasters couldn't tell the difference between real and imitation vanilla. In fact, in the panna cotta tasting, the imitation extracts took first and third place, with Nielsen-Massey and Penzeys leading the pack among real extracts. In the milk tasting, the imitation extracts took the top two spots, followed by real extracts from Nielsen-Massey and Penzeys. Further tests in shortbread confirmed these results. Although we are loath to recommend an imitation product, it seems that most people don't mind imitation extract and, in fact, many tasters actually like its flavor.

Yet we wanted the option of an overnight version as well. Knowing that gelatin grows more tenacious over time—transforming what was a lilting mousse one evening into a bouncing sponge the next—we figured there must also be a statute of limitations on its grip. At what point would the gelatin stop advancing? Research indicated maximum rigidity was reached after about 18 hours. (See page 420 for more information on how gelatin works.) At this point, we recorded the textural changes occasioned by incremental decreases in gelatin and discovered that an implausibly small decrease (⅛ teaspoon) put the overnight version on a par with the texture of the four-hour version.

With flexible time options in place, we moved on to technique. Because gelatin's response is hastened by cold temperatures, it seemed reasonable to keep most of the liquid

REMOVING SEEDS FROM A VANILLA BEAN

1. Use a small, sharp knife to cut the vanilla bean in half lengthwise.

2. Place the knife at one end of one bean half and press down to flatten the bean as you move the knife away from you, catching the seeds on the edge of the blade.

cold. Why heat all the milk and cream when we needed hot liquid just to melt the gelatin and sugar? We gave the milk this assignment, pouring it into a saucepan, sprinkling the gelatin over it, then giving the gelatin five minutes to swell and absorb liquid. Knowing that gelatin sustains damage at high temperatures, we heated the milk only enough to melt the gelatin—a couple of minutes, stirring constantly—then added the sugar off the heat to dissolve. The gelatin did not melt perfectly, and we thought we might have to increase the milk's temperature. Instead, we doubled the softening time to 10 minutes, and the problem was solved.

To do its job of firming the liquid to a gel, melted gelatin must be mixed with other recipe ingredients while its molecules have enough heat energy to move through the mixture. By combining ingredients hastily in the past, we had often precipitated gelatin seizures, causing the melted gelatin to harden into chewy strings, which ruined the texture of the dessert rather than enhancing it. So we stirred the cold cream slowly into the milk to temper it.

Several test cooks in the kitchen had learned in cooking school to stir gelatin-based desserts over an ice bath—allowing the gelatin to thicken somewhat under gentle agitation—before refrigerating them to set. Besides supporting nuts, fruit, or vanilla seeds throughout, this process was said to produce a finer finished texture. Hoping to avoid this step in a recipe that was otherwise so easy, we presented tasters with side-by-side creams, one stirred first over ice, one simply refrigerated. They unanimously preferred the texture of the panna cotta chilled over ice, describing it as "lighter, creamier, and smoother." Given the results, the extra 10 minutes required did not seem unreasonable.

Now it was fine-tuning time. First place for

flavor accents went to vanilla, particularly in the company of fruit sauces. We preferred whole bean to extract and Tahitian to Madagascar (see page 418).

This is a gorgeous anytime, anywhere dessert, proving that you don't have to be flocked, layered, filigreed, or studded—you don't even have to be chocolate—to win.

Panna Cotta

SERVES 8

Serve panna cotta very cold with strawberry or raspberry sauce or lightly sweetened berries. Though traditionally unmolded, panna cotta may be chilled and served in wineglasses and sauced on top. If you would like to make the panna cotta a day ahead, decrease the gelatin to 2⅝ teaspoons (2½ teaspoons plus ⅛ teaspoon) and chill the filled wineglasses or ramekins for 18 to 24 hours. For more information about how gelatin works, see right.

I	cup whole milk
2¾	teaspoons gelatin
3	cups heavy cream
I	piece vanilla bean, 2 inches long, or 2 teaspoons extract
6	tablespoons (2½ ounces) sugar
	Pinch salt
	Raspberry or Strawberry Coulis (recipes follow)

1. Pour the milk into a medium saucepan; sprinkle the surface evenly with the gelatin and let stand 10 minutes to hydrate the gelatin. Meanwhile, turn the contents of two ice cube trays (about 32 cubes) into a large bowl; add 4 cups cold water. Measure the cream into a large measuring cup or pitcher. With a paring knife, slit the vanilla bean lengthwise and scrape the vanilla seeds (see illustrations on page 419) into the cream;

place the pod in the cream along with the seeds and set the mixture aside. Set eight 4-ounce ramekins on a baking sheet.

2. Heat the milk and gelatin mixture over high heat, stirring constantly, until the gelatin is dissolved and the mixture registers 135 degrees on an instant-read thermometer, about 1½ minutes. Off the heat, add the sugar and salt; stir until dissolved, about 1 minute.

3. Stirring constantly, slowly pour the cream with vanilla into the saucepan containing the milk, then transfer the mixture to a medium bowl and set the bowl over the ice water bath. Stir frequently until the mixture thickens to the consistency of eggnog and registers 50 degrees on an instant-read thermometer, about 10 minutes. Strain the mixture into a large measuring cup or pitcher, then distribute it evenly among the ramekins. Cover the baking sheet with plastic wrap,

---

SCIENCE: How Gelatin Works

Gelatin is a flavorless, nearly colorless substance derived from the collagen in animals' connective tissue and bones; it is extracted commercially and dehydrated. Most culinary uses for gelatin rely on a two-step process: soaking and then dissolving. Gelatin is usually soaked in some cool or cold liquid so it can swell and expand. It is then dissolved in a hot liquid and finally chilled to set.

This dual process results from the fact that when unsoaked gelatin is added directly to hot liquid, the outside of each granule expands instantly and forms a gel coating, preventing the inside from becoming hydrated. The center of each gelatin particle then remains hard and undissolved. The resulting gelatin mixture doesn't set properly and is full of hard, granular bits.

In contrast, soaking gelatin in cold or cool liquid allows the particles to expand slowly so that they can tie up the maximum amount of liquid (up to three times their weight). Maximum rigidity in gelatin is reached after 18 hours. After that time, desserts begin to soften again.

---

making sure that the plastic does not mar the surface of the cream; refrigerate until just set (the mixture should wobble when shaken gently), about 4 hours.

4. To serve, spoon some raspberry or strawberry coulis onto each individual serving plate. Pour 1 cup boiling water into a small, wide-mouthed bowl, dip the ramekin filled with panna cotta into the water, count to three, and lift the ramekin out of the water. With a moistened finger, lightly press the periphery of the panna cotta to loosen the edges. Dip the ramekin back into the hot water for another three-count. Invert the ramekin over your palm and loosen the panna cotta by cupping your fingers between the panna cotta and the edges of the ramekin. Gently lower the panna cotta onto the small serving plate with the coulis. Repeat the process with the remaining ramekins of panna cotta. Serve immediately.

Raspberry Coulis

MAKES ABOUT 1 1/2 CUPS

We find that frozen berries are just fine for this sauce, and they are far cheaper than fresh.

24	ounces frozen raspberries (6 cups)
1/3	cup (2 1/4 ounces) sugar
1/4	teaspoon lemon juice
	Pinch salt

1. Place the frozen raspberries in a 4-quart nonreactive saucepan. Cover, turn the heat to medium-high, and bring to a simmer, stirring occasionally, for 10 to 12 minutes. Add the sugar and raise the heat to high. Boil for 2 minutes.

2. Strain the berries through a fine-mesh strainer into a bowl, using a rubber spatula to push the berries through the strainer; discard the seeds. Stir in the lemon juice and salt.

Cover and refrigerate until chilled, at least 2 hours and up to 3 days.

➤ VARIATION

Strawberry Coulis

Follow the recipe for Raspberry Coulis, replacing the raspberries with an equal amount of frozen strawberries and increasing the sugar to 1/2 cup (3 1/2 ounces). Increase the simmering time in step 1 to 12 to 14 minutes.

MONTE BIANCO

ONE OF THE TALLEST PEAKS IN THE Alps that border both France and Italy, Monte Bianco, also known as Mont Blanc, is one of Italy's most loved mountains; it shares its name with a chestnut dessert. In the United States, Monte Bianco the dessert is an undiscovered treasure. With mounds of grated chestnuts draped with whipped cream, Monte Bianco is actually fashioned to look like a craggy white-capped mountain peak. Unfortunately, when we tried making a few versions of this dessert, they tasted far from peak greatness. We noticed two general problem areas: The chestnuts were too bland, and the texture was too coarse. In addition, traditional recipes required far more work than seemed justified for such a simple dessert (we spent a good hour peeling chestnuts).

The first step to making this dessert is to simmer chestnuts with milk to make them soft and tender enough for a dessert. The milk is usually sweetened with sugar and sometimes flavored with spices. Our first problem, then, was of course with the chestnuts. If we used fresh chestnuts, they required much handiwork and patience to boil and peel away the tough outer shell and bitter inner jacket. This issue was easy enough to solve by using precooked chestnuts (available as canned and water-packed or presteamed and jarred) to avoid the unnecessary hassle of fresh ones. We tested both kinds of prepared chestnuts and found no major differences in taste or texture, although the jarred chestnuts did take a bit longer to cook.

We moved on to flavoring the chestnuts. Chestnuts simmered in milk and sugar were a bit bland. We decided to add a cheesecloth pouch filled with cinnamon sticks, bay leaves, black peppercorns, and whole cloves to the milk. The end result was lovely, as the chest-

nuts were not only tenderized but also infused with the delicate essence of the added herbs and spices.

After the chestnuts cooled, it was time to manipulate them into the desired mountain shape. We found three ways to do this: put the chestnuts through a ricer, process them through a food mill, or puree them in a food processor. We tested these three methods and discovered faults with each. Both the ricer and the food mill required a lot of muscle work and were time-consuming. The pureed batch was quick

KEY STEPS TO MAKING MONTE BIANCO

1. Making the herb packet: Lay a 6 by 4-inch piece of cheesecloth flat on a work surface. Place the bay leaves and cinnamon sticks in the center. Add the cloves and black peppercorns.

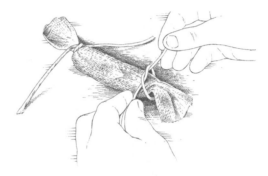

2. Roll the cheesecloth and tie it at both ends with short pieces of twine to seal.

3. Layering the chestnuts and whipped cream: On a large plate, place 1 cup whipped cream. Sprinkle with half of the grated chestnuts and, with your hands, gently press the nuts into the cream, making the mound more compact. Repeat with another cup of whipped cream and the remaining chestnuts.

4. Making the peaks: With an offset metal spatula, spread the remaining 2 cups whipped cream over the top of the mound, using the spatula to create divots in the cream. The cream should generously cover the top of the mountain, leaving the bottom third exposed.

to prepare, but it looked like refried beans and was pasty and thick. We then came up with the idea of forcing the chestnuts through the feed tube of our food processor and onto the grater attachment. This was quick, clean, and required only the press of a button, but the texture of the chestnuts was rough. Adding a couple of tablespoons of unsalted butter to the warm chestnuts as they cooled transformed their texture from rough to silky.

Usually, Monte Bianco is topped only with sweetened whipped cream, but we liked it more when the whipped cream and chestnuts were layered and then the top of the mountain was covered with more whipped cream. This way, the chestnut portion never seemed too mealy, as with each bite the whipped cream was included to cushion the nuts. We topped the layered mound with the remaining whipped cream, manipulating it to look like mountain peaks and crevasses. Although some recipes instruct the cook to fashion figures out of paper to look like skiers descending a snowy slope, we like this mountain better with a light dusting of grated chocolate.

Monte Bianco

SERVES 8 TO 12

We recommend using either canned precooked water-packed chestnuts or presteamed jarred chestnuts. If using water-packed chestnuts, you will need to rinse them before using. Confectioners' sugar sifted over the whipped cream just before serving (otherwise it will dissolve into the whipped cream) and candied fruit make nice finishing touches to this special holiday dessert.

CHESTNUT FILLING

2   bay leaves
2   cinnamon sticks
½   teaspoon whole cloves
½   teaspoon cracked black peppercorns

4   cups (about 2 pounds) cooked chestnuts
2   cups whole milk
1   cup (7 ounces) sugar
2   tablespoons unsalted butter

WHIPPED CREAM TOPPING

2   cups heavy cream, chilled
¼   cup (1¾ ounces) sugar
1   ounce semisweet chocolate

1. FOR THE FILLING: Wrap the bay leaves, cinnamon sticks, cloves, and peppercorns in a 6 by 4-inch piece of cheesecloth (see illustrations 1 and 2 on page 422). Place the chestnuts, cheesecloth pouch, milk, and sugar in a large Dutch oven. Bring to a boil over high heat, reduce the heat to low, cover, and simmer until the chestnuts are tender but not falling apart, about 15 minutes if using water-packed chestnuts and 25 minutes if using jarred chestnuts.

2. Drain the chestnuts in a colander and discard the herb pouch. Transfer the chestnuts to a medium bowl, add the butter, and toss to coat the warm chestnuts. Set aside until the chestnuts have cooled completely, about 30 minutes.

3. FOR THE TOPPING: While the chestnuts are cooling, beat the cream and sugar in the bowl of a standing mixer fitted with the whisk attachment and on low speed until small bubbles form, about 30 seconds. Increase the speed to medium; continue beating until the beaters leave a trail, about 30 seconds more. Increase the speed to high; continue beating until the cream is smooth, thick, nearly doubled in volume, and forms stiff peaks, about 30 seconds.

4. TO ASSEMBLE: Using the grater attachment of a food processor, grate the chestnuts by forcing them through the feed tube and into the blade. Layer the whipped cream and grated chestnuts according to illustration 3 on page 422. Finish the assembly with the remaining portion of whipped cream; using

an offset spatula, form peaks in the cream (see illustration 4 on page 422). Using a microplane or other fine grater, grate the chocolate over the top of the mountain. Serve immediately.

see illustration 4 on page 422

➤ VARIATION

Chocolate Monte Bianco

Follow the recipe for Monte Bianco, increasing the grated chocolate to 5 ounces. Sprinkle 2 ounces of the grated chocolate over the first layer of grated chestnuts and 2 ounces of grated chocolate over the second layer of grated chestnuts. Decorate the top of the Monte Bianco with the remaining grated chocolate.

ZABAGLIONE

ZABAGLIONE, ALSO CALLED ZABAIONE, is a thick, slightly frothy, creamy Italian dessert sauce made of nothing but whipped egg yolks, sugar, and Marsala wine. Italians like to cover fruit with it, use it as a base for chantilly cream or cake fillings, and even like to eat it on its own. Many Italians offer zabaglione to invalids and tout its curative properties.

Like many classic recipes, zabaglione's creation is shrouded in lore. Some experts believe that it originated in the city of Turin during the 17th century. Others argue it was invented farther south, in Florence, and some even insist it was created by accident when a chef accidentally spilled some fortified wine into a batch of custard. What we do know is that today, no one has the time or physical endurance that chefs in the 17th century must have had to whip up a zabaglione dessert sauce. Classic recipes require the cook to whip the egg yolks, sugar, and Marsala wine over a *bain marie* (double boiler) for 15 minutes or until the mixture doubles in volume. Our aim was to create a modern version of this Italian classic that tastes just as

good (if not better) but requires far less beating by hand.

We began by testing the amount of eggs and the amount of Marsala to include in the sauce. We began with three egg yolks and ½ cup of Marsala wine, but tasters complained that the sauce was too light and not rich enough. However, when we increased the amount of egg yolks to four, the sauce was too heavy and custardlike. We found the answer in diluting the four egg yolks with one tablespoon of water. Now the sauce had the rich flavor and creamy texture brought forth by four yolks, but it was a bit lighter due to the water.

Next, we examined the amount of sugar to include. We began with ½ cup but quickly found that when this much sugar was paired with a sweet, fortified wine the sauce was way too sweet. (A fortified wine is created when brandy is added to wine to stop the fermentation process; stopping fermentation results in an increased amount of sugar and alcohol content in the wine.) We reduced the sugar tablespoon by tablespoon, deciding that a mere two tablespoons was enough to sweeten the sauce without overwhelming it.

Now that we had our ratios set, we looked for ways to simplify the process of making the zabaglione. We started by whipping the sauce ingredients over the double boiler with a hand mixer but found a couple of problems with this method. First, the mixer made a mess, spraying the sauce all over the stovetop. Second, because the sauce needs to be whisked constantly (otherwise the egg yolks will curdle from the heat), we had no way to prevent a good portion of it from caking together and sticking to the sides of the bowl. With a whisk, it's easy to scrape away the bits of liquid that occasionally creep up the edges, but with an electric hand mixer, the beaters banged against the pan so hard that we were afraid of toppling our bain marie. In addition, the mixer's beaters aren't as flexible as a hand whisk's wires; with the whisk, one can gently scrape the sides clean, whereas with the electric mixer (even when the machine was stopped for a moment), all attempts at scraping the sides were unsuccessful.

We decided to try whipping the yolks with the hand mixer for half the time (until the yolks were thick and pale yellow), then transferring the mixture to the double boiler to finish whipping (and to bring the sauce to 160 degrees, the temperature at which the risk of food-borne illness is eliminated). This worked out great; although we hadn't completely eliminated whisking by hand, the amount of physical activity was decreased greatly. Instead of 15 grueling minutes over a double boiler, our recipe required only 5 minutes.

The last remaining problem was the sauce caking onto the upper reaches of the bowl. Even when we tried using a rubber spatula to ensure no buildup of cooked sauce, inevitably, bits of cooked egg yolk would find their way into the finished sauce. We decided to push the sauce through a fine-mesh sieve to remove any small lumps. The result was a tiny bit less fluffy, but the texture was now flawlessly smooth, and the flavor was excellent.

Zabaglione

MAKES ABOUT 2 CUPS,
ENOUGH SAUCE FOR 6 SERVINGS
OF FRUIT OR CAKE

If you don't have a hand mixer, you may use either a standing mixer or a whisk in step 1. Zabaglione is great served over fresh berries, peaches, or poached pears. It's also nice served with angel food or chiffon cake. If you don't care for the sherrylike flavor of Marsala wine, you may substitute Muscat (fortified or still), Vin

Santo, Sauternes, or even Champagne; versions made with these wines will be lighter and fruitier than a traditional zabaglione.

½	cup sweet Marsala
1	tablespoon water
4	large egg yolks
2	tablespoons sugar
	Pinch salt

1. Combine the Marsala and water in a liquid measuring cup; set aside. Bring about 2 inches water to a boil in a Dutch oven or other large pot.

2. Place the egg yolks, sugar, and salt in a large stainless-steel mixing bowl. Using an electric hand mixer (or standing mixer or whisk), whip the egg yolk mixture until it is thick, creamy, and pale yellow, about 4 minutes (or 8 minutes by hand).

3. Place the bowl over the pan of simmering water. Reduce the heat to low and gradually whisk in the Marsala mixture by hand. Continue cooking, whisking constantly, until the mixture is thick, pale yellow, has doubled in volume, and registers 160 degrees on an instant-read thermometer, about 5 minutes.

4. Remove the bowl from the heat. Using a rubber spatula, force the zabaglione through a fine-mesh sieve to remove any bits of cooked egg that stuck the sides of the bowl during cooking. Either use immediately or follow the instructions below for chilled zabaglione.

➤ VARIATIONS
Chilled Zabaglione
If you prefer, zabaglione can be chilled before being spooned over fruit or cake. You can also fold chilled zabaglione into 2 cups of whipped cream and use this flavored whipped cream to garnish cakes, pies, or fruit desserts.

Follow the recipe for Zabaglione through step 3. After the zabaglione has reached a temperature of 160 degrees, place the mixing bowl in a larger bowl of ice water and whisk until the sauce has cooled to room temperature, 3 to 5 minutes. The cooled zabaglione can be served immediately or refrigerated for up to 6 hours.

Zabaglione with Vanilla Bean

Follow the recipe for Zabaglione through step 1. Whisk the seeds from 1 vanilla bean (see illustrations on page 419) together with the sugar and salt in a mixing bowl. Add the egg yolks and proceed as directed with step 2, then finish the recipe.

Cinnamon-Orange-Infused Zabaglione

Because zabaglione is so light and frothy, it is best to use a fine microplane grater to zest the orange for this application.

Follow the recipe for Zabaglione through step 1. Whisk the grated zest from 1 orange and ¼ teaspoon ground cinnamon together with the sugar and salt in a mixing bowl. Add the egg yolks and proceed as directed in step 2, then finish the recipe.

SEMIFREDDO

WHEN YOU ORDER SEMIFREDDO FOR dessert in a restaurant in Italy, brace yourself for a surprise. Because all kinds of chilled and frozen desserts come under this heading, which translates as "half cold," you might get anything from tiramisù to ice cream cake. Some Italian cooks consider all chilled desserts semifreddi. Italian cookbooks, however, generally exclude desserts like tiramisù and Bavarian creams from the category, restricting it to dishes that resemble ice cream, such as frozen mousses, zabagliones, or custards, all of which share certain ingredients such as eggs, sugar, and cream.

Despite their great variety, we did eventually manage to sort out three distinct categories of semifreddi: those that use uncooked egg yolks and large quantities of whipped cream; custardlike versions that use cooked egg yolks and a smaller amount of whipped cream; and those that use egg whites cooked by a hot sugar syrup. To determine the characteristics of each type, we made several versions of each—because within these categories there was still a wide variation in proportions, flavorings, and techniques—and held a tasting.

The recipes that used relatively large quantities of whipped cream folded into small amounts of uncooked, ribboned yolks mixed with sugar tended to be hard and icy, somewhat like unchurned ice cream. We tasted two recipes of this variety, one with and one without egg whites. Both had a predominantly milky flavor, a hard consistency, and a lackluster taste for which additional flavorings could not compensate. Between the two, we preferred the one with the whites because, unlike cream, egg whites do not freeze and remelt and therefore do not become icy. We thought this style had potential but would need much work.

On the other side of the spectrum are custard semifreddi made with cooked egg yolks and smaller amounts of whipped cream. This gives them a rich and luxurious texture, similar to soft-serve ice cream. The ratio of egg yolks to cream and flavorings can run the gamut, and alcohol often plays an important role. A typical variation of such a semifreddo is a frozen zabaglione. For a semifreddo, whipped cream is folded into the zabaglione, which is then frozen. Our custard semifreddo had a delicate, silky texture. Although this version was delicious, it was too much like ice cream (and gelato) and so was eliminated.

Finally, a semifreddo can be made with egg whites that are cooked by adding a hot sugar syrup. In this particular method, which contains no yolks, a cup of cream is usually folded into the cooked egg whites. The lack of yolks gives this kind of semifreddo a delicate and light but not overwhelmingly rich consistency. When tasting all the variations side by side, we noted that this recipe had a decidedly pleasant unfrozen feel, almost as if it were not frozen at all. It refreshed the palate without the chilly harshness of some of the other versions.

This last semifreddo was the clear favorite. However, as most Italian recipes rely on an uncooked meringue (rather than a cooked meringue), we figured we should test that style further. We began by whipping egg whites with sugar until they formed soft peaks. Next, we whipped heavy cream and flavored it with dissolved instant espresso (a favorite semifreddo flavor). We folded the beaten whites and cream together along with biscotti crumbs (many semifreddo recipes call for bits of nuts, cookies, or chocolate) and froze the mixture in a chilled loaf pan.

MAKING ITALIAN MERINGUE

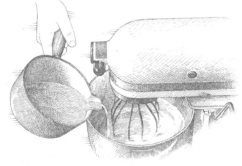

When pouring the hot sugar syrup into the egg whites, make sure the syrup does not touch the beater or the sides of the bowl. Contact with the metal might cause the syrup to solidify into small, hard pieces that won't mix with the whites.

The resulting dessert was not bad; its flavor was good, but the volume was too low. The egg whites had collapsed somewhat from the weight of the biscotti, reducing their volume. The frozen semifreddo was too soft and barely held its shape, while the biscotti crumbs absorbed the moisture from the coffee and sank to the bottom of the mold, where they formed an icy crust. To remove the dessert from the mold, we had to dip the pan in warm water, which melted the surface and made it look messy.

The next time around, we lined the empty loaf pan with plastic wrap and put it in the freezer while we prepared the semifreddo. We reasoned that lining the pan would make it easier to remove the semifreddo and that chilling the pan would jump-start the freezing and thus help prevent the egg whites from losing volume. We also reduced the amount of cookie crumbs so they would be less weighty.

All of our adjustments worked—but too well. This time, the mixture was too airy and the volume too great for the pan. The flavor was still good, though, and the plastic wrap lining made removal much easier.

The time had come to reconsider our working recipe. Because the biggest problem was the egg whites, which were either too airy or not airy enough, we decided to try a different method of making the meringue. In a standard uncooked, or Swiss, meringue such as we had been making, egg whites are beaten just until frothy, and sugar is then gradually added until the egg whites form soft peaks. The meringue is delicate. Care must be taken not to overbeat the whites, or the cell structure of the foam will break down, and the meringue will collapse.

A cooked meringue, which is sometimes called an Italian meringue, seemed the better alternative. Our initial testing of the three main semifreddo styles had shown this to be

427

the case. With this method, a hot sugar syrup is poured onto the egg whites as they are beaten. Because the syrup cooks the whites, this is a more stable and sturdy meringue, which we thought might better support the whipped cream and bits of cookies in our semifreddo. Another advantage is that any concerns about eating uncooked whites are eliminated. We finally decided that a semifreddo should be made with a cooked meringue—a decision that conflicts with most Italian sources.

When our Italian meringue was done, it looked promising; it had a high volume and a thick, glossy, marshmallow-like texture. Folding in the whipped cream was a bit difficult because the meringue was so stiff, but we succeeded with little loss of volume by first adding about one-third of the whipped cream to the meringue, then folding in the rest.

We added the coffee flavoring and biscotti as before and spread the mixture in the prepared pan. The volume was just right for a standard six-cup loaf pan and, after freezing, the semifreddo was perfect. The texture was smooth and creamy, and the biscotti crumbs remained suspended in the thick foam. What's more, the semifreddo held its shape well when unmolded. Even though this method required an extra step in making the syrup, it was not at all difficult and was well worth the extra effort it required.

Satisfied that we had found the best method, we tried a number of flavor variations next. To keep the technique as similar as possible throughout, we avoided watery fruits like fresh berries, which we suspected would become icy if frozen this way. On several occasions, we experimented with adding liqueurs and spirits to the mixtures but decided to eliminate them because the flavor was fresher and clearer without them.

Semifreddo can be frozen in individual molds or cups—a boon whenever the dessert's appearance is particularly important. It is equally good served plain or with a hot or cold fruit or chocolate sauce.

Cappuccino Semifreddo with Almond Biscotti
SERVES 8

When whipping cream during warm weather, you'll get the best results if you chill the bowl and beaters in the freezer for at least 20 minutes first. In this recipe, try to coordinate the sugar syrup reaching 238 degrees and the egg whites reaching soft peaks stage. But don't despair if they are out of sync. Beating the whites can be interrupted just before they reach soft peaks and resumed at any point. If the syrup heats beyond 238 degrees, you can cool it by adding a small amount of cold water; one tablespoon should cool the syrup about 7 degrees, and you can add as much as four tablespoons if need be.

1	cup heavy cream, chilled
3	large egg whites, at room temperature
½	cup plus 2 tablespoons (4½ ounces) sugar
2	tablespoons instant espresso dissolved in 1 tablespoon warm water
1	teaspoon vanilla extract
½	cup almond or hazelnut biscotti, crushed into split pea–sized bits

1. Line a 6-cup loaf pan with plastic wrap, leaving a 3-inch overhang all around. Place the pan in the freezer.

2. Beat the cream in the bowl of a standing mixer fitted with the whisk attachment and on low speed until small bubbles form, about 30 seconds. Increase the speed to medium; continue beating until the beaters leave a trail, about 30 seconds more. Increase the speed to high; continue beating until the cream is smooth, thick, nearly doubled in volume, and forms soft peaks, about 15 seconds. Transfer the cream to another bowl, cover, and refrigerate.

3. Clean the standing mixer bowl and the whisk attachment. Place the egg whites in the bowl of the standing mixer fitted with the whisk attachment; set aside.

4. Mix ¼ cup water and ½ cup sugar in a 1-quart saucepan. Warm the mixture over low heat without stirring until the sugar dissolves, about 4 minutes. Increase the heat to medium-high and continue to simmer the mixture toward its final temperature of 238 degrees. When the sugar syrup reaches 210 degrees, begin beating the egg whites on medium speed until frothy, about 40 seconds. Add 1 teaspoon sugar to the egg whites and increase the speed to high; beat until soft peaks form, about 2 minutes. Gradually beat in the remaining 5 teaspoons sugar. Decrease the speed to medium-high; pour the 238-degree syrup into the whites in a thin, steady stream (avoid hitting the rotating beater and sides of bowl; see illustration on page 427). Continue beating

until the mixture is glossy, doubled in volume, and cooled to room temperature, 4 to 5 minutes. Beat in the coffee mixture and vanilla.

5. Gently stir one-third of the whipped cream into the egg white mixture with a rubber spatula; fold in the remaining whipped cream and 6 tablespoons biscotti bits. Scrape the mixture into the prepared pan, spreading evenly with a rubber spatula. Fold the overhanging plastic wrap over the mixture and press it gently onto the surface. Freeze until firm, at least 8 hours. (Can be frozen for up to 1 month.)

6. To unmold, remove the plastic wrap from the surface and invert the loaf pan onto a serving plate, then remove the plastic wrap; smooth the surface with a spatula if desired. Sprinkle with the remaining biscotti bits; slice and serve immediately, either plain or with Warm Bittersweet Chocolate Sauce (page 430).

➤ VARIATIONS

Vanilla Semifreddo with Almonds and Amaretti

Follow the recipe for Cappuccino Semifreddo with Almond Biscotti, omitting coffee mixture and substituting 6 tablespoons toasted, chopped almonds and ⅓ cup amaretti cookie crumbs (about 6 cookies, crushed) for biscotti. Fold 4 tablespoons almonds and all crumbs into mixture in step 4; sprinkle remaining almonds on unmolded semifreddo before serving. Serve plain or with Warm Bittersweet Chocolate Sauce (page 430).

Chocolate Orange Semifreddo

Follow the recipe for Cappuccino Semifreddo with Almond Biscotti, substituting 1 tablespoon grated orange zest for the coffee mixture and ½ cup crushed chocolate wafer cookies (about 15 cookies) for the biscotti. Fold 6 tablespoons cookie crumbs into the mixture in step 4; sprinkle the

Semifreddo is a cross between frozen mousse and ice cream. It can be sliced and served plain or with chocolate sauce.

remaining crumbs on the unmolded semi-freddo before serving.

Warm Bittersweet Chocolate Sauce

SERVES 8

The warm sauce is the perfect counterpoint to the chilled semifreddo.

  6   ounces bittersweet or semisweet
      chocolate, chopped
  ¾   cup heavy cream

Melt the chocolate and cream together, stirring occasionally, in small heatproof bowl set over a pan of almost-simmering water. Serve immediately.

GELATO

GELATO IS BASICALLY ITALIAN ICE cream. Although the ingredients are similar to American ice cream, the results are surprisingly different. First of all, gelato is often made with flavors we rarely see in America. Hazelnut and the combination of hazelnuts and chocolate, called *gianduja,* are as common in Italian ice cream shops as vanilla or strawberry. Italians make coffee gelato, but because coffee ice cream is a common American flavor, we have not included this recipe. In addition to hazelnut and gianduja, we've developed recipes for fig, amaretti, and cinnamon gelato—all Italian flavors the American palate will find exotic but delicious.

Besides unusual flavors, many American visitors to Italy are struck by the intensity of the flavors in gelato. Gelato should not contain a hint of hazelnuts or cinnamon but rather a strong jolt. Many gelato recipes use large amounts of flavoring ingredients, and some

add liqueurs for a further boost. While American ice cream is often about the cream, gelato is about the flavorings.

There are several reasons for this difference. In general, American ice cream contains more butterfat. The additional fat coats the tongue and dulls the perception of flavors. While we find that American ice cream is best made with equal parts heavy cream and whole milk, we figured that gelato would require a lighter hand. The texture might be less indulgent and rich, but the flavors would be more intense.

Another important difference is temperature. Gelaterias in Italy generally serve their product at a higher temperature than do American ice cream shops. Because cold dulls flavors, a higher serving temperature heightens the intensity of gelato. It also makes gelato less icy, and the creamy texture helps counteract the lower butterfat content. We find that gelato tastes best served at 15 degrees, about five degrees warmer than American ice cream. At this temperature, gelato is not as firm as ice cream, and it should be eaten with a spoon (as it is in Italy) rather than licked from a cone.

The ingredients for gelato could not be simpler: cream, milk, sugar, flavorings, and sometimes egg yolks. The results, however, vary greatly depending on the quantities of each ingredient and the techniques used.

We uncovered recipes both with and without eggs and figured that was a good place to begin testing. Every single taster preferred the custard-type base with egg yolks. Gelato made this way was rich and creamy. Without eggs, the gelato was icy and not creamy enough. Egg yolks are about 10 percent lecithin, an emulsifier that helps maintain an even dispersal of fat droplets in ice cream and also helps keep ice crystals small. The overall effect is of richness and smoothness.

Once we decided that a custard base was the way to go, many other issues arose. How many egg yolks are needed for a 1-quart batch of gelato? What kind of dairy should be used: cream, half-and-half, milk, or some combination? Also, what's the best way to prepare a custard without curdling the eggs?

We tested as many as eight and as few as three egg yolks. Although five or six eggs delivered an excellent texture, we found that the egg flavor was too pronounced. Four egg yolks gave the gelato the appropriate silkiness without overpowering the other flavors.

The question of which dairy products to use proved more complicated. Gelato made with all cream is too buttery. The fat content is so high that churning causes tiny particles of butter to form. Gelato made with all milk or even half-and-half is too lean. These dairy products contain more water than heavy cream, and the result is an ice cream with tiny ice crystals. After extensive testing, we came to prefer about 2 parts whole milk to 1 part heavy cream. The texture of our gelato was rich, but there was no butteriness. Also, there wasn't so much fat that you couldn't taste the

MAKING THE CUSTARD FOR GELATO

Like ice cream, gelato starts with a custard base. Here are the key steps.

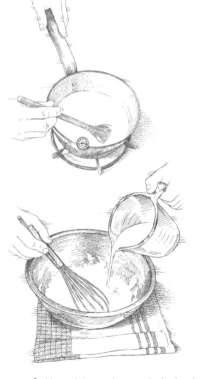

1. Combine the milk, cream, and part of the sugar in a medium saucepan (left). Heat to 175 degrees, stirring often to dissolve the sugar.

2. While the milk mixture is heating, beat the remaining sugar and egg yolks until pale yellow and thick enough to fall in ribbons from the beaters (right).

3. Use a dish towel to steady the bowl with the beaten yolks. Slowly whisk about ½ cup of the hot milk mixture into the yolks to thin them and to raise their temperature gradually. Then whisk the thinned yolks into the saucepan.

4. Stirring constantly, heat the custard over low heat until a temperature of 180 degrees is reached. The custard will be thick enough so that a line drawn through it on the back of a spoon holds for several seconds.

5. Pour the custard through a fine-mesh strainer to remove any bits of curdled egg. The custard is ready to be chilled, then churned in an ice cream machine.

flavorings. Most important, there was enough fat to prevent the formation of large ice crystals, which may occur when a lower-fat dairy combination is used.

Besides adding sweetness, sugar also promotes a smoother, softer, more scoopable end product. This is because sugar reduces the number and size of ice crystals and lowers the freezing temperature of the custard. The latter effect allows you to churn the custard longer before it freezes firm, thus incorporating more air.

In our testing, the texture of a quart of gelato made with one cup of sugar was excellent, but the sweetness competed with other flavors. We tried ½ cup of sugar per quart of gelato and found that the gelato was too firm to scoop right from the freezer. The texture was marred by iciness as well. We found that ¾ cup

of sugar was enough to keep the gelato soft and smooth without making it cloying.

With the ingredient issues settled, we turned our focus to questions of technique. We soon discovered that subtle changes in the custard-making process can have a profound effect on texture. Our goal was absolute smoothness and creaminess. Of course, the danger of applying too much heat to the eggs and causing the custard to curdle (the eggs literally clump together, as in scrambled eggs, and cause the custard to break and become lumpy) always lurks in the background.

We found it best to heat the milk, cream, and part of the sugar to 175 degrees. If brought to a higher temperature, there is a risk that the eggs will curdle when the mixture is added to them. Lower temperatures, however,

---

EQUIPMENT: Two Thermometers for Gelato Making

The precise measurement of temperature is essential in the preparation of gelato (as well as sorbets). Custards should be cooked to 180 degrees for optimum thickening, but no higher, because curdling becomes a danger. Likewise, custards should be fully cooled below 40 degrees to promote quick churning and freezing without the formation of butter flecks.

For these reasons, we recommend the use of an instant-read thermometer when making gelato. Because it is also helpful to measure the temperature of gelato at serving time (we find gelato tastes best around 15 degrees, well above freezer temperature), choose an instant-read thermometer that goes down to 0 degrees.

You may also want to check the temperature of your freezer, especially if using an ice cream machine with a canister that must be frozen overnight. A freezer/refrigerator thermometer that registers temperatures below 0 can be purchased for several dollars at any housewares store. Cold freezer temperatures (below 0) are required for optimum performance of frozen canister-type ice

cream machines. Note that removing frost and excess food can lower the freezer temperature by several degrees. However, if your freezer continues to run well above 0 (say, 5 degrees or higher), you will be better off using an ice cream machine that does not require pre-freezing of any parts.

INSTANT-READ
THERMOMETER

FREEZER/REFRIGERATOR
THERMOMETER

A freezer/refrigerator thermometer keeps tracks of the temperature inside your freezer. An instant-read thermometer lets you know when the custard has chilled sufficiently and you can start churning the gelato base.

fail to dissolve the sugar. While the milk, cream, and part of the sugar are heating, the yolks are beaten with the remaining sugar. We found that adding unbeaten or lightly beaten yolks to the custard results in a gelato with a shocking yellow color.

Because sudden exposure to high heat (even 175 degrees) can curdle eggs, it's important to temper them—or increase the temperature slowly by adding a small portion of the hot milk-cream mixture. Tempering also thins the thick yolk-sugar mixture so that it can be more easily incorporated into the hot milk and cream.

We found that various tricks for determining when a custard is fully cooked were only minimally helpful. Yes, a custard does thicken enough to coat the back of a spoon. Yes, a custard should hold its shape when a line is drawn through it on the back of a spoon. But these things may happen before the custard has reached 180 degrees, the temperature we found ideal for gelato making. Because egg yolks start to curdle between 185 and 190 degrees, our recommended final temperature of 180 degrees provides some room for error but allows the eggs to provide a maximum amount of thickening. A custard cooked to only 160 or 170 degrees will make a slightly less rich, less silky gelato. For this reason, we advocate the use of an instant-read thermometer when making custard for gelato.

No matter how careful you are, tiny bits of egg may overcook and form thin particles or strands, especially around the edges and bottom of the pan. We recommend pouring the cooked custard through a fine-mesh strainer to eliminate these solid egg pieces. However, a curdled custard with large clumps of egg cannot be rescued and should be discarded.

Hazelnut Gelato

MAKES ABOUT 1 QUART

We found that toasting the hazelnuts twice, once before skinning and once after, yields an incredibly delicious and intense nut flavor.

2	cups shelled hazelnuts, toasted, skinned, and toasted again (see illustrations on page 434)
2¼	cups whole milk
1¼	cups heavy cream
¾	cup (5¼ ounces) sugar
4	large egg yolks
1	tablespoon Frangelico or other hazelnut liqueur (optional)
½	teaspoon vanilla extract

1. Process the nuts in a food processor fitted with a steel blade until finely ground. Combine the milk, cream, and ground nuts in a heavy medium saucepan set over medium heat. Bring the mixture almost to a simmer. Remove the pan from the heat and steep for 30 minutes. Pour the mixture through a fine-mesh strainer and into a clean saucepan, pressing down on the nuts to extract as much liquid as possible. Discard the nuts.

2. Add ½ cup sugar to the milk mixture, turn the heat to medium, and heat the mixture until it registers 175 degrees on an instant-read thermometer, stirring occasionally to dissolve the sugar.

3. Meanwhile, beat the remaining ¼ cup sugar and the egg yolks in a medium bowl, scraping down the sides as needed, until the mixture turns pale yellow and thickens so that it falls in ribbons, about 2 minutes with an electric mixer on medium-high or 4 minutes with a whisk.

4. Remove about ½ cup hot milk-cream mixture from the pan and slowly whisk it into the beaten yolk mixture. Gradually whisk the

thinned yolk mixture into the saucepan. Reduce the heat to low and bring the mixture to 180 degrees, stirring constantly, about 5 minutes. The custard should be thick but not curdled or boiled.

5. Remove the saucepan from the heat; pour the custard through a fine-mesh strainer into a nonreactive bowl or container. Place the bowl in a larger bowl of ice water to bring the custard to room temperature.

6. Cover the bowl and refrigerate until the custard registers 40 degrees or lower, 4 to 8 hours. (Custard may be refrigerated overnight.) Stir in the liqueur, if using, and the vanilla extract and pour the custard into an ice cream machine. Churn until frozen but still a bit soft. (Do not overprocess, or the gelato may become icy, with flecks of butter.) Transfer the gelato to a nonreactive container, seal, and freeze until firm. (Gelato will keep up to 2 days.)

➤ VARIATION

Gianduja Gelato

The combination of chocolate and hazelnuts, called gianduja, is a classic in Italian cakes, candies, and ice creams.

Follow the recipe for Hazelnut Gelato, using a rubber spatula to stir ¼ cup Dutch-processed cocoa into the thickened egg yolk–sugar mixture in step 3. Proceed as directed.

TOASTING HAZELNUTS

1. Start by toasting the nuts in a 350-degree oven until they are fragrant and their skins are starting to blister and crack, about 15 minutes. Transfer the nuts to the center of a clean kitchen towel.

2. Bring up the sides of the towel and twist it closed to seal in the nuts.

3. Rub the nuts together through the towel to scrape off as much of the brown skin as possible. It's fine if patches of skin remain.

4. Carefully open the towel on a flat work surface. Gently roll the nuts away from the skins. Return the nuts to the oven and toast them until they have a rich golden color, about 15 minutes.

Fig Gelato

MAKES ABOUT 1 QUART

In season, many Italian gelaterias use fresh figs. Dried figs are more reliable and give gelato an even more intense flavor. Light brown Calimyrna figs work especially well in this recipe.

1	cup dried figs (about 4 ounces), minced
¾	cup (5¼ ounces) sugar
2	cups whole milk
1	cup heavy cream
4	large egg yolks
1	teaspoon vanilla extract

1. Place the figs and ¾ cup water in heavy medium saucepan. Bring to a simmer over medium heat and cook until the figs are tender and the liquid is nearly evaporated, about 10 minutes. Stir in ½ cup sugar and cook, stirring often, until it dissolves. Add the milk and cream and heat until the mixture registers 175 degrees on an instant-read thermometer.

2. Meanwhile, beat the remaining ¼ cup sugar and the egg yolks in a medium bowl, scraping down the sides as needed, until the mixture turns pale yellow and thickens so that it falls in ribbons, about 2 minutes with an electric mixer on medium-high or 4 minutes with a whisk.

3. Remove about ½ cup hot milk-cream mixture from the pan and slowly whisk it into the beaten yolk mixture. Gradually whisk the thinned yolk mixture into the saucepan. Reduce the heat to low and bring the mixture to 180 degrees, stirring constantly, about 5 minutes. The custard should be thick but not curdled or boiled.

4. Remove the saucepan from the heat; pour the custard through a fine-mesh strainer into a nonreactive bowl or container; discard the figs. Place the bowl in a larger bowl of ice water to bring the custard to room temperature.

5. Cover the bowl and refrigerate until the custard registers 40 degrees or lower, 4 to 8 hours. (Custard may be refrigerated overnight.) Stir in the vanilla extract and pour the custard into an ice cream machine. Churn until frozen but still a bit soft. (Do not overprocess, or the gelato may become icy, with flecks of butter.) Transfer the gelato to a nonreactive container, seal, and freeze until firm. (Gelato will keep for up to 2 days.)

Amaretti Gelato

MAKES ABOUT 1 QUART

Crisp almond macaroons, known in Italian as amaretti, are sold in better supermarkets and Italian food shops. Because the cookies are crumbled, either large or small amaretti will work in this recipe. We find it easiest to place the cookies in a zipper-lock bag and crush them lightly with the bottom of a heavy glass. Do not crush the cookies into fine crumbs.

2	cups whole milk
1	cup heavy cream
¾	cup (5¼ ounces) sugar
4	large egg yolks
3	tablespoons Amaretto or almond-flavored liqueur
1	cup crumbled amaretti cookies

1. Combine the milk, cream, and ½ cup sugar in a heavy medium saucepan set over medium heat. Heat until the mixture registers 175 degrees on an instant-read thermometer, stirring occasionally to dissolve the sugar.

2. Meanwhile, beat the remaining ¼ cup sugar and the egg yolks in a medium bowl, scraping down the sides as needed, until the mixture turns pale yellow and thickens so that it falls in ribbons, about 2 minutes with an electric mixer on medium-high or 4 minutes with a whisk.

3. Remove about ½ cup hot milk-cream mixture from the pan and slowly whisk it into the beaten yolk mixture. Gradually whisk the thinned yolk mixture into the saucepan. Reduce the heat to low and bring the mixture to 180 degrees, stirring constantly, about 5 minutes. The custard should be thick but not curdled or boiled.

4. Remove the saucepan from heat; pour the custard through a fine-mesh strainer into a nonreactive bowl or container. Place the bowl in a larger bowl of ice water to bring the custard to room temperature.

5. Cover the bowl and refrigerate until the custard registers 40 degrees or lower, 4 to 8 hours. (Custard may be refrigerated overnight.) Stir in the liqueur and the vanilla extract and pour the custard into an ice cream machine. Churn until frozen but still a bit soft. (Do not overprocess, or the gelato

GELATO AND SORBET BASICS

When we finished developing our recipes for gelato and sorbet, we realized that they all had a few similarities. Once the base for a gelato or sorbet has been prepared, it is handled in pretty much the same manner, no matter the flavor. The pros and cons of various ice cream machines (see page 438 for specific information) are the same whether you are making chocolate gelato or mango sorbet. Here are some general points to keep in mind when making these desserts.

It's imperative to chill the gelato or sorbet base fully before placing it in an ice cream machine. We found that chilling the base to 40 degrees or lower is ideal. We like to start by placing the gelato or sorbet base in an ice water bath to bring down its temperature quickly.

The next step is to pour the base into an airtight container and let the refrigerator do the rest of the work. An instant-read thermometer is essential here. We found that if the base is too warm when it is placed in the ice cream machine, it will need to be churned for much longer (up to an hour) until frozen to a semisolid state. Ice cream machines with canisters that require freezing before churning lose their cooling ability before this stage is reached. Ice cream machines with self-contained freezers can bring a warm base down to the correct temperature, but the extra churning causes the formation of butter flecks in gelato and iciness in sorbets.

Frozen desserts will not emerge from any ice cream maker (including those that cost $500) with a firm, hard texture. Once the gelato or sorbet is well chilled (about 25 degrees), fluffy, and frozen to the texture of soft-serve ice cream, remove it from the ice cream maker. It takes about 30 minutes of churning to reach this stage in most ice cream machines. If you churn any longer, you may promote the development of butter flecks or iciness. In any case, further churning will not freeze the dessert any harder. Several hours in the freezer, where temperatures are much lower, will complete the freezing process.

If you store gelato or sorbet for more than a few hours, the texture will become firm, like that of the ice cream sold in supermarket freezer cases. If you prefer a softer texture, transfer the container with the frozen dessert to the refrigerator 30 minutes to an hour before serving. We find that gelato and sorbet taste best around 15 degrees, well above the temperature maintained by most home freezers.

Unlike commercial products, which are often made with stabilizers and/or preservatives, homemade frozen deserts have a short shelf life. Temperature fluctuations in home freezers promote iciness in all frozen desserts, with melting and freezing taking their toll fairly quickly on homemade frozen desserts. After several days, homemade gelato and sorbet become quite icy. They are best eaten the day they are made but can be held up to two days.

may become icy, with flecks of butter.) About 30 seconds before the churning is completed, add the crumbled amaretti cookies. Transfer the gelato to a nonreactive container, seal, and freeze until firm. (Gelato will keep for up to 2 days.)

Cinnamon Gelato

MAKES ABOUT 1 QUART

Ground cinnamon gives this gelato a warm, rich flavor that is distinctively Italian. Make sure your cinnamon is fresh. To prevent the cinnamon from clumping when added to the liquid, mix it first with sugar, then add the cinnamon sugar to the milk and cream.

¾	cup (5¼ ounces) sugar
2	teaspoons ground cinnamon
2	cups whole milk
1	cup heavy cream
4	large egg yolks
1	teaspoon vanilla extract

1. With a spoon, combine ½ cup sugar and the cinnamon in a small bowl. Combine the milk, cream, and cinnamon sugar in a heavy medium saucepan set over medium heat. Heat until the mixture registers 175 degrees on an instant-read thermometer, stirring occasionally to dissolve the sugar.

2. Meanwhile, beat the remaining ¼ cup sugar and the egg yolks in a medium bowl, scraping down the sides as needed, until the mixture turns pale yellow and thickens so that it falls in ribbons, about 2 minutes with an electric mixer on medium-high or 4 minutes with a whisk.

3. Remove about ½ cup hot milk-cream mixture from the pan and slowly whisk it into the beaten yolk mixture. Gradually whisk the thinned yolk mixture into the saucepan. Reduce the heat to low and bring the mix-

ture to 180 degrees, stirring constantly, about 5 minutes. The custard should be thick but not curdled or boiled.

4. Remove the saucepan from heat; pour the custard through a fine-mesh strainer into a nonreactive bowl or container. Place the bowl in a larger bowl of ice water to bring the custard to room temperature.

5. Cover the bowl and refrigerate until the custard registers 40 degrees or lower, 4 to 8 hours. (Custard may be refrigerated overnight.) Stir in the vanilla extract and pour the custard into an ice cream machine. Churn until frozen but still a bit soft. (Do not overprocess, or the gelato may become icy, with flecks of butter.) Transfer the gelato to a nonreactive container, seal, and freeze until firm. (Gelato will keep for up to 2 days.)

FRUIT SORBETS

MOST GELATO SHOPS IN ITALY ALSO sell exotically flavored fruit sorbets, called *sorbetti* in Italian, such as pineapple, watermelon, and mango. These sorbets are invariably creamy and silky. They literally melt in your mouth, almost like ice cream. Unfortunately, many sorbets made at home taste fine, but their texture is overly icy. We wanted to figure out why.

We began by talking to chefs and reading through dozens of Italian cookbooks for recipe ideas. Most sources reserve the term sorbetti for frozen desserts without cream or milk. Sorbets are basically fruit and sugar, and that was the definition we decided to adopt.

We found a surprising number of possible solutions to the icy sorbet problem. They involved the use of the following ingredients, either singly or in combination: gelatin, egg whites, jam, corn syrup, confectioners' sugar, superfine sugar, and alcohol. So we plotted out

EQUIPMENT: Ice Cream Makers

There are four general types of ice cream machine, each with pros and cons for the home cook. Your choice will be determined by how much you want to spend and how frequently you want to make gelato and sorbet.

All ice cream machines are able to sustain temperatures below 32 degrees; however, each type does this differently. Subfreezing temperatures are needed because sugar lowers the freezing temperature of ice cream to around 27 or 28 degrees. More sugar or the presence of alcohol lowers the freezing temperature even more.

Old-fashioned ice cream makers, which rely on ice and rock salt and come with either a manual or electric churning mechanism, were the standard until the late 1970s. The chilled base is placed in a central container that is surrounded by ice and salt. Like sugar, salt lowers the freezing temperature of liquids. By adding a lot of rock salt (which melts more slowly than table salt), the temperature of the brine falls well below 32 degrees. This in turn lowers the temperature of the base and allows it to freeze into ice cream as it is churned.

We find that these traditional models in wooden buckets are messy to use. They are also less reliable than more modern ice cream machines because they can be affected by ambient conditions. Hot weather makes it difficult to keep the brine below 32 degrees, so the ratio of salt to ice may need to be altered. In general, we find that using these ice cream makers requires practice and patience and that the results are not guaranteed.

However, many of these bucket-type machines have a two-quart capacity, double that of all other ice cream machines designed for home use. Also, there are no parts to prefreeze, so this type of ice cream maker may be appropriate if your freezer is very crowded or runs well above 0 degrees. You can also make successive batches in this type of ice cream maker.

Expect to spend $100 for a traditional bucket-style ice cream machine with a hand crank. Models with electric churning mechanisms generally cost about $150. These machines are increasingly hard to find.

Old-fashioned hardware stores are the best bet.

The making of frozen desserts at home changed with the invention of the Donvier in the late 1970s. Its French-sounding pedigree notwithstanding, the name actually comes from the Japanese term for "very cold." This ingenious invention was created by a Japanese engineer who got the idea after one of his children accidentally spilled milk on an aluminum cooling tray for sushi. He redesigned the tray, which housed a powerful coolant, into a canister shape more appropriate for ice cream making.

To use this type of ice cream machine, you must first place the aluminum canister filled with the patented supercoolant in the freezer overnight. The metal canister is about an inch thick and hollow. The coolant, which is akin to antifreeze, is contained within the hollow walls of the canister and is capable of reaching very low temperatures.

To make ice cream, the chilled base is poured into the very cold canister, which fits into a plastic shell, and a plastic hand crank is attached for churning. The home cook must turn the crank every few minutes to scrape away the portion of the custard that has frozen to the inside of the canister. The crank should not be turned too often, though, or the custard will not get a chance to freeze. Eventually, all of the unfrozen base rests against the supercold metal and freezes.

Although inexpensive (about $50), these ice cream machines do have drawbacks. They do not freeze gelato as solid as some other machines do. You will definitely need to transfer the semifrozen dessert to the freezer for several hours before serving. In addition, these machines require space in a very cold freezer to work. If your freezer is very crowded and/or too warm (temperatures significantly above 0 degrees will not work), the coolant will not get cold enough, and the ice cream will not freeze properly. Last, because so little churning is involved, these machines do not beat much air into frozen desserts. The texture of the ice cream is not as smooth or fluffy as that of desserts made in more expensive machines.

One last drawback is that this machine can make only one quart of ice cream a day, as the canister must be frozen for at least 12 hours before each use. If you buy or own this type of ice cream maker, we suggest that you leave it in the freezer all the time so you can make ice cream without advance planning.

A relatively new variation on this type of ice cream machine adds an electric churning mechanism. An electric motor rests on top of the lid and powers the churning blade. The benefits are obvious. Constant churning beats in more air and results in a smoother texture and less iciness. These models generally cost around $75 (sometimes less) and are a good value. We prefer them to the standard Donvier. We have had good success with the Krups La Glacière in our test kitchen. An additional canister can be purchased so that two batches of frozen dessert can be prepared on the same day.

Without a doubt, ice cream machines with self-contained electric freezers are the best choice for home use. Modeled on commercial machines, these units are twice the size of a standard food processor and weigh 30 pounds or more. The chilled base is poured into a metal bowl that sits in the large countertop unit, which also houses a small freezer. Two switches activate the freezer and a powerful churning blade.

We love our Simac machine from Italy, but the $500 price tag will be an impediment to all but the most dedicated. This Rolls Royce of ice cream makers turns out frozen desserts with perfect smoothness and no iciness. There is no down time between batches, and frozen desserts emerge at a significantly lower temperature and hence with a firmer texture than from other ice cream machines. Ice cream can be served right from this machine without further hardening in the freezer.

| TRADITIONAL WOODEN BUCKET | MANUAL WITH PORTABLE FREEZER UNIT | ELECTRIC WITH PORTABLE FREEZER UNIT | ELECTRIC WITH SELF-CONTAINED FREEZER UNIT |

These machines can be affected by ambient conditions. However, many models have a large capacity, and this type of ice cream maker does not require prefreezing of any parts. As long as you have a steady supply of ice and rock salt, successive batches of ice cream may be made in this machine. We prefer models, like this one, with electric churning mechanisms.

The Donvier revolutionized ice cream making at home. A supercoolant inside the central metal canister lowers the temperature of the custard as you churn with the plastic hand crank. This model is a good choice if your freezer maintains a temperature at or below 0. Note that the metal canister must be refrozen overnight before making a second batch of ice cream.

Similar to the Donvier, this Krups ice cream machine has an electric motor in the base that rotates the metal canister while a stationary blade churns. The constant motion beats more air into the ice cream and results in a better texture. For this reason, we prefer an electric churning mechanism.

This Simac unit contains its own freezer. The texture of ice cream made in this machine is superb, and the ice cream may be eaten right after churning without further freezing. This machine can be used to make successive batches of ice cream on the same day. If money is no object, this kind of ice cream machine is the best choice.

a methodical course for testing each of these variables using a simple sorbet recipe with fresh orange juice.

Gelatin originally seemed to be the most promising of the possible additions. We tried soaking gelatin in cold water, then adding that mixture to hot sugar syrup and fruit juice. As this mixture cooled, it started to gel and become gloppy-looking. We were not optimistic. To our surprise, the sorbet emerged from the ice cream machine as a firm mass that scooped beautifully and had almost no iciness. Unfortunately, it did have an unmistakable gumminess. No matter how we used gelatin (we tried several more approaches, including heating the gelatin and beating it in a food processor to break it up), it gave the sorbet an unpleasant, rubbery quality.

Several Italian cookbooks we consulted suggested folding egg whites into the mix. Some authors folded lightly beaten whites into the sorbet mixture just before churning; others made an Italian meringue by slowly incorporating hot sugar syrup into egg whites beaten to soft peaks. After seven attempts at adding egg whites in various forms, we concluded they do nothing to prevent iciness. Egg whites beaten to soft peaks will make the ice crystals a bit smaller and give the sorbet a texture akin to newly fallen snow. However, the texture will never be creamy or smooth.

A few odd recipes suggested using jam to improve the texture. The logic proved correct, but the implementation was not practical. The cellular material from fruit pulp, especially the pectin, can act as a lubricant. (In this respect, we found that berry sorbets are softer and creamier than citrus sorbets because the whole fruit, which includes a fair amount of pectin, is used.) When we tried adding marmalade to orange sorbet, the texture improved a bit, but after more tests, we realized that it

was really the extra sugar in the jam that was responsible for 90 percent of the improvement in texture. Because adding plain sugar is much easier than calculating how much sugar is in a given jar of jam, we gave up on jam.

Our last major area of concentration was the sweetener. We saw a number of recipes that used corn syrup. Could its thick, viscous quality carry over to the sorbet? The answer was no, and we found that, when used in large amounts, corn syrup masks the fruit flavor. Next, we tried confectioners' sugar and were surprised to detect graininess in the sorbet. We attributed this to the cornstarch that is added to confectioners' sugar to keep it from clumping. We found superfine sugar to perform the same as regular sugar; it is not worth using unless you have some on hand.

Things really started to change when we turned to a recipe in a 20-year-old book by Julia Child. (The French love sorbets almost as much as the Italians do, and most French cookbooks have sorbet recipes that are similar to those found in Italian sources.) Child advocates the use of egg whites in some recipes in *The Way to Cook* (Knopf, 1989), but we liked the "more concentrated sherbet" recipe published in *From Julia Child's Kitchen* (Knopf, 1975). Although this sorbet was too sweet and runny for our taste, it was smooth and creamy. While most of the previous recipes we had consulted used ¼ cup of sugar per cup of fruit, in this recipe, Child used ⅔ cup of sugar per cup of fruit.

This high sugar concentration, simple as it is, turned out to be the key to creamy sorbets. Sugar controls the texture (see page 443 for details). Add more sugar, and the texture improves. Everything else is just a smoke screen. Once we figured this out, the rest of our work was simple. We found that by using ½ cup of sugar per cup of fruit (give or take a few tablespoons, depending on the fruit), we were able to achieve the desired result: a smooth, creamy texture without cloying sweetness.

Even with reducing the sugar in Child's recipe, the sweetness proved pretty intense, but we discovered that adding up to two tablespoons of lemon juice to nonacid fruits helps balance the sweetness. At this level, the lemon flavor is not detectable. Mildly acidic fruits need a smaller boost, a tablespoon or so of lemon juice. Lemons and limes do not require additional acid.

We also found that adding a tablespoon of high-proof alcohol improves the texture of the sorbets and permits a slight reduction in the amount of sugar. Tasteless vodka is our first choice, although any complementary brandy or eau de vie can be used. We tried white wine but found that because of its lower alcohol content, we had to use several tablespoons to achieve much of an effect on texture. At that concentration, the flavor of the wine became noticeable. This is fine in some sorbets—for instance, lemon sorbet with two or three tablespoons of white wine is lovely—but not appropriate in every case.

In the course of our research, we were also able to eliminate the hot sugar syrup step advocated by most cookbooks. Instead of heating sugar and water until the sugar dissolves, we simply mix the sugar right into the fruit juice or puree. Mixing on and off for several minutes is enough to dissolve the sugar; thus we avoided raising the temperature of the mix well above 100 degrees (as happens when a hot sugar syrup is combined with the fruit) and incurring hours of cooling time before processing the sorbet. In fact, if you stir the sugar and fruit mixture over a bowl of ice water, sorbets can be ready to freeze about 10 minutes after you walk into the kitchen.

Master Recipe for Fruit Sorbet
SERVES 4

This recipe can be used to make any fruit sorbet. The proper amount of sugar and lemon juice varies for each fruit. Because vodka is tasteless, it can be used with any fruit, but other suggestions appear in the variations. For fruits not listed, follow directions for a similar fruit. For example, follow the lemon recipe to make lime sorbet.

2	cups fruit puree or juice
¾–1¼	cups sugar
up to 2	tablespoons lemon juice
1	tablespoon vodka or other alcohol

1. Prepare the fruit puree or juice as directed in the variations that follow.

2. Combine the fruit puree or juice, sugar, lemon juice, and alcohol in a large bowl. Stir on and off for several minutes until the sugar has dissolved. (To speed the chilling process in step 3, combine the ingredients in a metal bowl set over a larger bowl filled with ice water.) Rub a finger along the bottom of the bowl to see if the sugar has dissolved.

3. Pour the mixture into a small container. Seal and refrigerate until the mixture registers 40 degrees or lower on an instant-read thermometer. (If the mixture has been stirred over a bowl of ice water, it may already be cold enough, and this step can be omitted.)

4. Pour the chilled mixture into the container of an ice cream machine and churn until frozen. Transfer the sorbet to a nonreactive container, seal, and freeze until firm, at least several hours. (Sorbet can be kept frozen for up to 2 days.)

441

➤ VARIATIONS

Apple Sorbet

Follow the Master Recipe for Fruit Sorbet, using 2 cups apple cider and ¾ cup plus 1 tablespoon sugar, 2 tablespoons lemon juice, and 1 tablespoon vodka, rum, or apple brandy.

Blackberry, Raspberry, or Strawberry Sorbet

Puree 3 cups berries with ½ cup cold water until smooth. Strain through a sieve to remove the seeds. You should have 2 cups smooth puree. Follow the Master Recipe for Fruit Sorbet, using 2 cups berry puree, 1 cup sugar, 1 tablespoon lemon juice, and 1 tablespoon vodka or berry liqueur

Blueberry Sorbet

Puree 2½ cups berries with ½ cup cold water until smooth. Strain through a sieve to remove the skins. You should have 2 cups smooth puree. Follow the Master Recipe for Fruit Sorbet, using 2 cups blueberry puree, 1 cup sugar, 2 tablespoons lemon juice, and 1 tablespoon vodka.

Grapefruit Sorbet

Grate 2 teaspoons zest from 2 large red grapefruits; combine with 1½ cups fresh-squeezed juice and ½ cup cold water to yield 2 cups diluted juice. Follow the Master Recipe for Fruit Sorbet, using 2 cups diluted grapefruit juice with zest, 1 cup plus 1 tablespoon sugar, and 1 tablespoon vodka or Campari.

Lemon Sorbet

Grate 2 teaspoons zest from 3 large lemons; combine with ½ cup fresh-squeezed juice and 1½ cups cold water to yield 2 cups diluted lemon juice. Follow the Master Recipe for Fruit Sorbet, using 2 cups diluted lemon juice with zest, 1¼ cups sugar, and 1 tablespoon vodka.

Mango Sorbet

Peel and pit 3 medium mangoes. Puree the flesh with ½ cup cold water until smooth. You should have 2 cups smooth puree. Follow the Master Recipe for Fruit Sorbet, using 2 cups mango puree, ¾ cup plus 1 tablespoon sugar, 2 tablespoons lemon juice, and 1 tablespoon vodka.

Orange Sorbet

Grate 2 teaspoons zest from 5 large oranges; combine with 2 cups fresh-squeezed juice. Follow the Master Recipe for Fruit Sorbet, using 2 cups orange juice with zest, 1 cup minus 1 tablespoon sugar, 1 tablespoon lemon juice, and 1 tablespoon vodka or orange brandy.

Peach Sorbet

Peel and pit 6 medium peaches. Puree the flesh with ½ cup cold water until smooth. You should have 2 cups smooth puree. Follow the Master Recipe for Fruit Sorbet, using 2 cups peach puree, 1 cup minus 1 tablespoon sugar, 2 tablespoons lemon juice, and 1 tablespoon vodka or peach brandy.

Pineapple Sorbet

Stem, peel, quarter, and core 1 small pineapple. Puree the flesh until smooth. Strain through a sieve to remove the stringy fibers. You should have 2 cups smooth puree. Follow the Master Recipe for Fruit Sorbet, using 2 cups pineapple puree, ¾ cup sugar, 1 tablespoon lemon juice, and 1 tablespoon vodka or rum.

Watermelon Sorbet

Peel and seed 2½ pounds watermelon. Puree the flesh until smooth. You should have 2 cups smooth puree. Follow the Master Recipe for Fruit Sorbet, using 2 cups watermelon puree, 1 cup minus 1 tablespoon sugar, 2 tablespoons lemon juice, and 1 tablespoon vodka or Campari.

GRANITAS

GRANITA, THE ICY ITALIAN DESSERT, is simple stuff: A flavorful fruit puree or juice, espresso, or tea is combined with sugar and flavorings and then frozen. Traditionally, the liquid is frozen in a bowl and scraped every 30 minutes for several hours to produce a shimmering, granular dessert made up of individual ice crystals.

This traditional scraping technique, which has been used in Italy for centuries, poses two problems for today's cooks: It requires hours of off-and-on attention, and it cannot be prepared in advance because it must be served just as the crystals of freezing liquid harden to the proper consistency. After much trial and error, we found that an excellent version of granita can be made using the most modern of tools, the food processor.

To make a granita in a food processor, simply pour the flavored liquid into ice cube trays. A few hours later, when they have hardened, you can store them in a zipper-lock bag (to prevent freezer burn) for up to a week, or transfer them immediately to the workbowl of a food processor and pulse them into tiny ice shavings. The texture, a bit creamier than that of traditional granitas, is often preferred by people accustomed to the texture of sorbets and ice creams.

The biggest challenge in making granitas with this method is obtaining the right texture. Granitas can become slushy when pureed too long or contain hidden mini-icebergs if the processing is too quick. The trick is to chop the ice cubes evenly and finely without making an icy shake. We have found through testing that limiting the number of cubes processed at one time is the best solution. As a rule, do not process more cubes than can fit comfortably in a single layer in the food processor. Use the pulse button, turning the machine on and off 10 to 12 times to ensure even grinding. Generally, bursts of two or three seconds are most effective.

Most granita recipes call for hot sugar

SCIENCE: How to Retard Freezing

Water freezes at 32 degrees. Add sugar (or any substance that dissolves in water), and the freezing point is lowered. As more sugar is added, the lower the freezing point becomes. Why does a lower freezing point make the sorbet taste less icy?

As a sorbet freezes, the water in the mixture forms ice crystals, and the sugar syrup that is left behind gradually becomes more concentrated. These sugar molecules make it harder for the remaining water molecules to bond, thus lowering the freezing point. At some point, the remaining sugar syrup becomes so concentrated that it just won't freeze at the temperatures found in an ice cream machine or home freezer.

Unfrozen syrup keeps the sorbet soft and scoopable. In effect, the syrup lubricates the ice crystals and makes them less icy on the tongue. In addition, water in a high-sugar solution tends to form smaller crystals than water in a plain solution. These smaller crystals translate into a smoother feeling on the tongue. Alcohol works in the same way by lowering the freezing point of the sorbet mixture.

What does this mean in the kitchen? Depending on how much sugar and alcohol are added to a sorbet, it can freeze as hard as ice cubes or remain slushy. The trick to making a creamy sorbet is to add enough sugar to keep it scoopable right from the freezer but not so much sugar that the sorbet is syrupy. Of course, the amount of sugar in the fruit itself has an effect on this process, which means that lemon sorbet needs more added sugar than pineapple sorbet. As for alcohol, we add a little to help keep the sorbet soft but not so much that you can taste it.

syrup to be added to fruit juice. We have found, however, that this slows the freezing process and unnecessarily complicates the recipe. In most cases, brisk stirring suffices to dissolve the sugar used in granitas. The amount of sugar and other flavorings in each recipe varies with the sugar and acid content of the puree; strawberries obviously need less sugar than lemons, for example. You can, of course, alter recipes to suit your taste and the sweetness level of the fruit you are using.

Master Recipe for Granita

SERVES 4

The sugar varies based on the sweetness of the fruit or the desired effect. See variations for specific quantities.

| 2 | cups fruit juice or puree, espresso, or tea |
| ¼–⅓ | cup sugar |

1. Whisk the fruit juice or puree, espresso, or tea and sugar in a large bowl until the sugar dissolves.

2. Pour the mixture into 2 ice cube trays. Freeze until firm, at least 2 hours. (The frozen cubes can be transferred to a zipper-lock plastic bag and frozen for up to 1 week.)

3. Just before serving, place a single layer of frozen cubes in the workbowl of a food processor fitted with a steel blade. Pulse 10 to 12 times or until no large chunks of ice remain. Scoop the crystals into individual bowls. Repeat with the remaining ice cubes and serve immediately.

➤ VARIATIONS

Apple Granita

Follow the Master Recipe for Granita, using 2 cups apple cider and ¼ cup sugar. Add 1 tablespoon apple brandy if desired.

Berry Granita

Puree 2½ cups berries with ¾ cup water. Strain through a sieve to remove the seeds (or skins, if using blueberries). You should have 2 cups smooth puree. Follow the Master Recipe for Granita, using 2 cups berry puree and ⅓ cup sugar.

Caffè Latte Granita

Follow the Master Recipe for Granita, using 1 cup espresso, 1 cup milk, and ¼ cup sugar.

Espresso Granita

Follow the Master Recipe for Granita, using 2 cups espresso and ¼ cup sugar. Add 1 tablespoon amaretto, Frangelico, or sambuca, if desired.

Grapefruit Granita

Follow the Master Recipe for Granita, using 1½ cups fresh-squeezed pink grapefruit juice, ½ cup cold water, and ⅓ cup sugar. Add 1 tablespoon Campari to boost flavor and color, if desired.

Lemon or Lime Granita

Follow the Master Recipe for Granita, using ½ cup fresh-squeezed lemon or lime juice, 1½ cups cold water, and ⅓ cup sugar.

Orange Granita

Follow the Master Recipe for Granita, using 2 cups fresh-squeezed orange juice and ¼ cup sugar. Add 1 tablespoon orange-flavored liqueur, if desired.

Watermelon Granita

Peel and seed 3 pounds fruit. Puree the flesh and strain through a sieve to remove the pulp. You should have 2 cups juice. Follow the Master Recipe for Granita, using 2 cups watermelon juice and ¼ cup sugar. Add 1 tablespoon Campari, if desired.

14

BISCOTTI, CROSTATE, AND CAKES

WHEN IT COMES TO SWEET BAKED goods, Italian home cooks keep things simple. *Biscotti* (twice-baked cookies with a distinctive crunch and long, elegant appearance), simple *crostate* (rustic tarts, many of which are baked free-form), and homey cakes made with ricotta cheese or chocolate and hazelnut are good examples of this restrained style of baking. There are few rich cream fillings or shiny frostings. A chocolate cake might be dusted with confectioners' sugar, a tart filled with jam or perhaps sliced and sugared apples.

This chapter contains some of our favorite Italian cookies, tarts, and cakes. The recipes showcase uniquely Italian flavors and are surprisingly easy to prepare.

BISCOTTI

DESPITE THEIR ELEGANT APPEARANCE, the twice-baked Italian cookies known as biscotti are easy to make. A longer-than-average baking time yields a uniquely crunchy texture and also gives them an unusually long shelf life. Together, these factors make biscotti an excellent choice for home bakers. To find out how to make the very best biscotti, we decided to test and compare dozens of traditional recipes. The results were surprising.

Most recipes had a fairly constant ratio of sugar to flour to flavorings. The major differences in the recipes were the type and quantity of fat used, which varied dramatically. This fat factor, we discovered, has the most dramatic effect on the taste, texture, and shelf life of the resulting biscotti.

Biscotti can be divided into three styles based on the fat content. The richest variety contains butter and eggs. Traditional recipes contain whole eggs, sometimes supplemented by additional yolks, but no butter. The leanest biscotti contain just egg whites—no yolks or butter. We tested all three varieties and found differences in texture and taste.

In the matter of texture, we found that recipes containing butter produced satisfyingly crunchy biscuits that were nonetheless somewhat softer and richer—more cookielike—than those not containing butter. We also discovered that recipes using whole eggs only, without additional yolks, were noticeably less cakelike, with a more straightforward crunch. (Biscotti with whole eggs and additional yolks were more like those with butter.) On the other end of the scale, the biscotti made with egg whites only—no butter or yolks—produced the driest and crispiest cookies, reminiscent of hard candy. In fact, these cookies were so hard that they might present the risk of cracking a tooth if eaten without dunking in milk or coffee first. We liked biscotti made with butter and with whole eggs but rejected those made with just whites.

In the matter of taste, the fresh-baked biscotti containing butter provided a superior and irresistibly rich flavor. On the other hand, the biscotti made with whole eggs but no additional yolks or butter resulted in the truest delivery—lean and direct—of the flavorings in these cookies. Because both styles had their merits, we decided to include recipes for both.

We found that storage and shelf life were also directly affected by fat content. As we experimented with different doughs, we noticed that recipes using butter initially had the best taste and texture but lost their full flavor and satisfying crunch after only one day, as the butter in the cookies began to go stale. Recipes with eggs but no butter held up better in both categories as the days went by. They seemed to get even better with time; they tasted great and remained crisp after a week and, if stored properly, kept for several weeks.

Whatever the amount and type of fat they contain, all biscotti recipes share the characteristics of short preparation time and a relatively long baking time. For most recipes, preparation involves simply mixing the wet ingredients with a whisk in one bowl, whisking the dry ingredients together in another bowl, then folding the dry into the wet and adding flavorings. Because they are baked twice, however, the total baking time for biscotti is longer than for regular cookies. First they are baked in flat loaves for 30 to 40 minutes; then the loaves are sliced and the slices baked again for an additional 10 to 15 minutes. This double baking technique ensures a very low moisture content, contributing enormously to biscotti's great potential for storage—the primary reason bakers go to all this trouble in the first place.

As for flavorings, literally dozens of combinations are used in biscotti, as the plain dough adapts beautifully to various pairings. Some of the best flavor combinations date from the late Middle Ages, when sea trade was active and many new ingredients became available to cooks and bakers. Medieval sailors and explorers such as Columbus and Marco Polo relied on these biscuits for energy and nourishment. Zests of citrus fruits, native to southern Italy, were combined with exotic dry spices such as cinnamon, cloves, and ginger. Dried and candied fruits were used, as were local and foreign varieties of nuts such as walnuts, hazelnuts, almonds, pistachios, and sesame seeds.

The batter may at first appear rather sticky, but resist the urge to dust with flour; too much will make the biscotti heavy and dense. It is preferable to use a rubber spatula, waxed paper, or plastic wrap if you have trouble handling the dough. One final note: Biscotti must be completely cooled before storage to ensure that all the moisture has escaped.

Lemon-Anise Biscotti

MAKES 3 TO 4 DOZEN COOKIES

A Sicilian specialty, this recipe (without butter) produces a relatively hard biscuit—perfect with an afternoon cup of coffee. The cookies are also delicious dunked in a glass of sherry, Marsala, or Vin Santo. See the illustrations on page 449 for tips on shaping and cutting biscotti dough.

2	cups (10 ounces) unbleached all-purpose flour
1	teaspoon baking powder
¼	teaspoon salt
1	cup (7 ounces) sugar
2	large eggs
¼	teaspoon vanilla extract
1	tablespoon minced zest from 1 lemon
1	tablespoon anise seed

1. Adjust an oven rack to the middle position and heat the oven to 350 degrees. Whisk the flour, baking powder, and salt in a medium bowl; set aside.

2. Whisk the sugar and eggs in a large bowl to a light lemon color; stir in the vanilla, lemon zest, and anise seed. Sprinkle the dry ingredients over the egg mixture, then fold in until the dough is just combined.

3. Halve the dough and turn each portion onto a large baking sheet lined with a piece of parchment paper. Using floured hands, quickly stretch each portion of dough into a rough 13 by 2-inch loaf. Place the loaves about 3 inches apart on the baking sheet; pat each one smooth. Bake, turning the pan once, until the loaves are golden and just beginning to crack on top, about 35 minutes. Remove the baking sheet from the oven and place it on a rack.

4. Cool the loaves for 10 minutes; lower the oven temperature to 325 degrees. With a serrated knife, cut each loaf diagonally into

⅜-inch-thick slices. Lay the slices about ½ inch apart on the baking sheet, cut side up, and return them to the oven. Bake, turning over each cookie halfway through baking, until crisp and golden brown on both sides, about 15 minutes. Transfer the biscotti to a wire rack and cool completely. (Biscotti can be stored in an airtight container for up to 1 month.)

Honey-Lavender Biscotti

MAKES 4 TO 5 DOZEN COOKIES

These biscotti are best made with an assertive honey, such as spicy clover. Dried lavender blossoms can be found in spice shops and natural foods stores. The biscotti are delicious even without the lavender. See the illustrations on page 449 for tips on shaping and cutting biscotti dough.

2¼	cups (11¼ ounces) unbleached all-purpose flour
1	teaspoon baking powder
½	teaspoon baking soda
¼	teaspoon salt
⅔	cup (4¾ ounces) sugar
3	large eggs
3	tablespoons honey
½	teaspoon vanilla extract
2	tablespoons minced zest from 1 orange
1	tablespoon dried lavender blossoms (optional)

1. Adjust an oven rack to the middle position and heat the oven to 350 degrees. Whisk the flour, baking powder, baking soda, and salt in a medium bowl; set aside.

2. Whisk the sugar and eggs in a large bowl to a light lemon color; stir in the honey, vanilla, orange zest, and lavender, if using. Sprinkle the dry ingredients over the egg mixture, then fold in until the dough is just combined.

3. Halve the dough and turn each portion onto a large baking sheet lined with a piece of parchment paper. Using floured hands, quickly stretch each portion of dough into a rough 13 by 2-inch loaf. Place the loaves about 3 inches apart on the baking sheet; pat each one smooth. Bake, turning the pan once, until the loaves are golden and just beginning to crack on top, about 35 minutes. Remove the baking sheet from the oven and place it on a rack.

4. Cool the loaves for 10 minutes; lower the oven temperature to 325 degrees. With a serrated knife, cut each loaf diagonally into ⅜-inch-thick slices. Lay the slices about ½ inch apart on the baking sheet, cut side up, and return them to the oven. Bake, turning over each cookie halfway through baking, until crisp and golden brown on both sides, about 15 minutes. Transfer the biscotti to a wire rack and cool completely. (Biscotti can be stored in an airtight container for up to 1 month.)

Spiced Biscotti

MAKES 4 TO 5 DOZEN COOKIES

If you like, macerate ¾ cup currants, chopped raisins, or dates in ¼ cup brandy or Marsala for about 1 hour. Drain and fold into the dough in step 2, adding a teaspoon or so of the macerating liquid. This recipe contains additional yolks and is a bit richer than the preceding biscotti. See the illustrations on page 449 for tips on shaping and cutting biscotti dough.

2¼	cups (11¼ ounces) unbleached all-purpose flour
1	teaspoon baking powder
½	teaspoon baking soda
¼	teaspoon salt
¼	teaspoon ground white pepper
½	teaspoon ground cloves
½	teaspoon ground cinnamon
¼	teaspoon ground ginger
1	cup (7 ounces) sugar

2   large eggs plus 2 yolks

½   teaspoon vanilla extract

1. Adjust an oven rack to the middle position and heat the oven to 350 degrees. Whisk the flour, baking powder, baking soda, salt, and spices in a medium bowl; set aside.

2. Whisk the sugar and eggs in a large bowl to a light lemon color; stir in the vanilla extract. Sprinkle the dry ingredients over the egg mixture, then fold in until the dough is just combined.

3. Halve the dough and turn each portion onto a large baking sheet lined with a piece of parchment paper. Using floured hands, quickly stretch each portion of dough into a rough 13 by 2-inch loaf. Place the loaves about 3 inches apart on the baking sheet; pat each one smooth. Bake, turning the pan once, until the loaves are golden and just beginning to crack on top, about 35 minutes. Remove the baking sheet from the oven and place it on a rack.

4. Cool the loaves for 10 minutes; lower the oven temperature to 325 degrees. With a serrated knife, cut each loaf diagonally into ⅜-inch-thick slices. Lay the slices about ½ inch apart on the baking sheet, cut side up, and return them to the oven. Bake, turning over each cookie halfway through baking, until crisp and golden brown on both sides, about 15 minutes. Transfer the biscotti to a wire rack and cool completely. (Biscotti can be stored in an airtight container for up to 1 month.)

Orange-Almond Biscotti

MAKES 3 TO 4 DOZEN

The addition of a small amount of butter produces a richer, more cookielike texture. Although they will keep for 2 weeks in an airtight container, these biscotti are best eaten the same day they are baked. You can substitute toasted hazelnuts for the almonds in this recipe. A combination of hazelnuts and almonds also works well. See the illustrations below for tips on shaping and cutting biscotti dough.

2   cups (10 ounces) unbleached all-purpose flour

1   teaspoon baking powder

¼   teaspoon salt

4   tablespoons unsalted butter, softened but still firm

1   cup (7 ounces) sugar

2   large eggs

½   teaspoon vanilla extract

¼   teaspoon almond extract

MAKING BISCOTTI

1. Divide the dough in half. Using floured hands, quickly stretch each portion of dough into a rough 13 by 2-inch loaf. Place the loaves about 3 inches apart on the baking sheet; pat each one smooth.

2. Bake the dough loaves for 35 minutes at 350 degrees, remove them from the oven, and cool for 10 minutes. With a serrated knife, cut each loaf on the diagonal into ⅜-inch-thick slices.

3. Lay the slices about ½ inch apart on the baking sheet, cut side up, and return them to a 325-degree oven. Bake, turning once, until crisp, about 15 minutes.

¾ cup whole almonds with skins, toasted, cooled, and chopped coarse

2 tablespoons minced zest from 1 orange

1. Adjust an oven rack to the middle position and heat the oven to 350 degrees. Whisk the flour, baking powder, and salt in a medium bowl; set aside.

2. Using an electric mixer set at medium speed, cream the butter and sugar until light and smooth, about 2 minutes. Beat in the eggs one at a time, then the extracts. Stir in the almonds and zest. Sprinkle the dry ingredients over the egg mixture, then fold in until the dough is just mixed.

3. Halve the dough and turn each portion onto a large baking sheet lined with a piece of parchment paper. Using floured hands, quickly stretch each portion of dough into a rough 13 by 2-inch loaf. Place the loaves about 3 inches apart on the baking sheet; pat each one smooth. Bake, turning the pan once, until the loaves are golden and just beginning to crack on top, about 35 minutes. Remove the baking sheet from the oven and place it on a rack.

4. Cool the loaves for 10 minutes; lower the oven temperature to 325 degrees. With a serrated knife, cut each loaf diagonally into ⅜-inch-thick slices. Lay the slices about ½ inch apart on the baking sheet, cut side up, and return them to the oven. Bake, turning over each cookie halfway through baking, until crisp and golden brown on both sides, about 15 minutes. Transfer the biscotti to a wire rack and cool completely. (Biscotti can be stored in an airtight container for up to 2 weeks.)

EQUIPMENT: Baking Sheets

Most baking sheets (also called cookie sheets) have the same basic design. They are a piece of metal that is usually slightly longer than it is wide. (A standard size is 16 inches long and 14 inches across.) Some are dark, some are light. Some have rims on all four sides. Others have rims on one or two sides but otherwise have flat edges. We tested 11 sheets in a variety of materials and came to some surprising conclusions.

First of all, shiny light-colored sheets do a better job of evenly browning the bottoms of cookies than dark sheets. Most of the dark sheets are nonstick, and we found that these pans tend to overbrown cookies. Shiny silver sheets heat much more evenly, and if sticking is a concern, we simply use parchment paper. Parchment paper also keeps the bottom of the cookies from overbrowning.

In our testing, we also came to prefer sheets with at least one rimless edge, which allowed us to slide a whole sheet of parchment paper onto a cooling rack without touching the hot paper. (When cool, the cookies can be peeled from the paper.) The open edge also makes it possible to slide cookies onto a rack rather than lifting and possibly dropping them.

A final note about lining baking sheets with parchment. Even when sticking is not an issue, we like to use parchment paper. It makes cleanup a snap, and we can reuse baking sheets for subsequent batches without having to wash them first. When parchment is essential, the recipes in this chapter call for it. Otherwise, use parchment at your discretion.

THE BEST BAKING SHEET
Our favorite cookie sheet is made of tinned steel and is manufactured by Kaiser. At just $7, it was also the least expensive sheet we tested.

PASTA FROLLA

PASTA FROLLA, THE BASIC PASTRY dough of Italian baking, is quite different from American pie dough. American pie dough is typically flaky, with minimal sweetness and flavorings. It is a modest means of showcasing fillings. In contrast, pasta frolla is sweet and flavorful—good enough to eat on its own. Just as important, it is tender. In fact, the name *pasta frolla* literally translates as "tender dough."

Many pasta frolla recipes have a small amount of butter and are heavy-handed with the sugar. The advantage of a low butter-to-sugar ratio is that the pastry is easy to manage; it rolls out beautifully and doesn't fall apart. In addition, a lean dough holds its shape better when cooked, making for a more attractive final product.

However, after sampling a couple of lean, sweet doughs, we concluded that even with the large amounts of sugar, they lacked flavor and tenderness. We added more and more butter until we finally settled on 7 tablespoons of butter to 1⅓ cups of flour for a single-crust batch of pasta frolla. This was the maximum amount of butter that could be worked in without compromising the manageability of the dough. With respect to the sugar, we found that ⅓ cup was just the right amount. The dough was tender and sweet, but not so sweet that it competed with the filling.

Whole eggs and/or egg yolks are almost always found in pasta frolla recipes. Whole eggs provide structure, while egg yolks provide tenderness. In a single batch of pasta frolla, one yolk did not provide enough moisture, and two yolks made the crumb too fine. A single whole egg was just right. In the double pasta frolla recipe, two whole eggs produced a crust that was too airy and cakelike. Egg yolks only produced a crust with a very fine crumb. We wanted a bit of both of these qualities, so we settled on one whole egg plus one yolk for the double crust recipe.

The last few ingredients that we needed to consider were vanilla extract, lemon zest, and baking powder. The first two are standard ingredients in pasta frolla recipes; they provide that fundamental cookie flavor. Baking powder, on the other hand, was not used in all of the recipes we uncovered in our research. We tested a version of our final pasta frolla recipe with baking powder and liked the lightness it gave to the crust. We had noticed that our free-form crostate tended to spread out when baked. The crostate made with baking powder puffed up rather than out—a definite improvement.

For all the pastry doughs we developed over the years in the test kitchen, we found that a food processor was the simplest and most consistent means of mixing the dough. Pasta frolla was no exception. In our standard pie dough recipe, we incorporate the fat into the flour with the processor. To avoid reducing the size of the fat particles (large fat particles create larger flakes), the mixture is transferred to a bowl and the liquid added judiciously with a rubber spatula. In our short-crust pastry (pâte sucrée), the mixture is made from start to finish in the food processor. The mixture is homogenous, with few or no distinguishing fat particles, creating a crisp pastry.

With the pasta frolla recipe, we were aiming for somewhere between flaky pie dough and crisp pâte sucrée. To achieve this texture, we found that the liquid ingredients could be added to the butter-flour mixture in the food processor. However, once all of the liquid is incorporated, the mixture should be transferred to a large bowl and gently kneaded until it comes together.

Pasta Frolla

MAKES ENOUGH FOR ONE
SINGLE-CRUST CROSTATA

Don't add too much water to this dough. Add a tablespoon, process the dough, test it (by squeezing a handful to see it comes together), then add more liquid if necessary. To keep from overworking the dough, finish kneading it by hand. If you process the dough in a food processor until it comes together in a ball, the baked crust will be tough and overly crisp, not flaky and biscuitlike, which is the desired texture.

1	large egg
1	teaspoon vanilla extract
1–2	tablespoons water
1⅓	cups (6¾ ounces) unbleached all-purpose flour
⅓	cup (2¼ ounces) sugar
¼	teaspoon salt
1¼	teaspoons baking powder
	Grated zest of 1 lemon
7	tablespoons unsalted butter, chilled and cut into ¼-inch pieces

1. Whisk the egg, vanilla, and 1 tablespoon water in a small bowl and set aside.

2. Place the flour, sugar, salt, baking powder, and lemon zest in the workbowl of a food processor fitted with a steel blade. Pulse to combine. Scatter the butter pieces over the flour mixture and pulse to cut the butter into the flour until the mixture resembles coarse meal, about seven 1-second pulses. With the machine running, add the egg mixture and process until all the liquid ingredients are incorporated. Squeeze a handful of the dough; if it forms a moist ball, no more water is necessary. If the mixture is crumbly and dry, add 1 more tablespoon water and process just until incorporated.

3. Remove the dough from the food processor and transfer it to a large bowl. Gently knead until cohesive, about 30 seconds. Shape the dough into a 5-inch disk. Cover with plastic wrap and refrigerate for at least 2 hours or up to 2 days.

➤ VARIATION

Pasta Frolla for a Double-Crust Tart
Follow the recipe for Pasta Frolla, whisking a large egg yolk with the whole egg, vanilla, and 2 tablespoons water in step 1. In step 2, increase the flour to 2⅓ cups, the sugar to ½ cup, the salt to ½ teaspoon, the baking powder to 2 teaspoons, and the butter to 12 tablespoons. Proceed as directed, kneading the dough until cohesive in step 3. Divide the dough into two equal pieces. Shape one piece into a 5-inch disk and the other into a 5-inch square. Cover both with plastic wrap and refrigerate for at least 2 hours or up to 2 days.

JAM CROSTATA

CROSTATA DI MARMELLATA (JAM TART) IS the quintessential Italian home dessert. This lattice-topped tart, made with sweet, tender pastry and filled with fruit jam, is found throughout Italy. It is a cross between a fruit tart and a jam-filled cookie. The beauty of this dessert is its simplicity; the ingredients are usually on hand, and the recipe doesn't even require a pie or tart pan. The technique for assembling the tart is likewise quite simple. One piece of dough is rolled out to a disk, the jam is spread over the disk, a lattice of dough strips is placed on top, and the edges of the bottom dough and the lattice top are pressed together.

Having developed our pasta frolla recipe, we focused our attention on the filling and assembly procedures. Some recipes call for tart pans. While they may look attractive, they posed one major problem for us: They required too much jam to fill them. Once you press the crust into a tart pan, you need to add enough jam to come at least halfway up the sides of the crust. Use less jam and the tart just looks wrong. But imagine eating a piece of toast with ¾ inch of jam on it. It's just too sweet and intense.

A free-form crostata seemed a better alternative, and this was the route chosen in the majority of our research recipes. With the free-form method, the amount of filling isn't dictated by the size of the pan. One cup of jam translated to an ample filling about ¼ inch thick. (With a tart pan, we needed more than two cups of jam.) The pasta frolla dough was so tender and flavorful that we thought it was good enough to command a larger role in this dessert.

Although we had reduced the amount of jam filling, we still found commercial jams a bit on the sweet side. A tablespoon of lemon juice mixed into the jam balanced the sweetness and brightened the flavors of the fruit.

MAKING A JAM CROSTATA

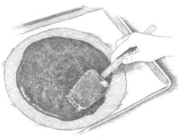

1. Using an 11-inch pot lid or cardboard round as a guide, trim the first piece of dough to a perfect 11-inch circle using a pizza wheel or paring knife.

2. Spread the jam on the dough, leaving a 1-inch border around the edge.

3. With a pizza wheel or paring knife, trim the edges of the second piece of dough to make them even and then cut into ten 1-inch wide strips.

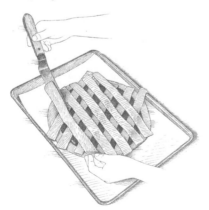

4. Brush the strips with the egg wash and place them over the filling, 5 in each direction in a diagonal lattice. Use a spatula to help move and position the strips.

5. Roll the scraps into a ¾-inch-thick rope about 30 inches long. Brush the rim of the pastry with the egg wash, then press the dough rope into the rim.

We experimented with several techniques for assembling the lattice-top crostata. The main issue we had to contend with was the method of incorporating the edges of the lattice with the border around the bottom piece of dough. We tried several techniques, but they all seemed a bit haphazard and sloppy. Rolling out the bottom dough, smearing it with jam, adding the lattice top, and crimping the bottom dough and lattice ends together worked, but the finished tart was unattractive. Tasters want a proper border, not just some puffed crust around the edge that looked like a pizza. Next, we tried folding the edge of the bottom dough over the lattice strips and fluting the dough by hand, but the crust did not hold its shape in the oven.

The best technique we found was in Nick Malgieri's *Great Italian Desserts* (Little, Brown, 1990). The tart dough is rolled out and the edges are trimmed to make a perfect circle. The jam is spread in a thin layer, and the lattice strips of dough are laid on top. A strip of dough is rolled to form a long rope, draped around the perimeter (so it covers the ends of the lattice strips), and pressed down to form a slightly raised border. This method is easy, and the finished tart is still homey but much more attractive.

One final note. When the assembled crostata was baked right away, the dough spread and lost its neat appearance. We discovered that refrigerating the assembled tart for an hour prevented the dough from spreading and losing its shape. (Refrigerating the dough chills the butter and prevents it from melting too quickly in the oven.) You could never refrigerate a tart filled with fresh fruit, which would exude its juices and create a soggy pastry. However, because the jam is relatively dry, we didn't have to worry about the dough getting soggy.

INGREDIENTS: Raspberry Preserves

Jelly, jam, preserve, fruit spread—what's the difference, and is any of these products better than the others for baking or spreading on toast? We put eight leading brands to a taste test to find out—but before we give you the results, some definitions are in order.

A jelly is a clear, bright mixture made from fruit juice, sugar, and often pectin or acid. No less than 45 pounds of fruit must be used for each 55 pounds of sugar.

A jam is a thick mixture of fruit and sugar (and often pectin) that is cooked until the pieces of fruit are very soft and almost formless—the texture of a thick puree. It is also made with 45 pounds of fruit solids combined with 55 pounds of sugar. Preserves are almost identical to jams, but preserves may contain large chunks of fruit or whole fruit.

Fruit spreads, which have become common grocery store stock over the last 10 years, do not fall under the labeling standards applied to jellies and jams, hence the generic term fruit spreads. These products are usually made with concentrated grape and/or pear juice or low-calorie sweeteners, which replace all or part of the sugar.

In our taste test, we tried all of these products in our recipe for Raspberry Squares and sampled each on toast. Brands that tasted good on toast also worked well in raspberry squares, so there's no need to buy special jam for baking. Although tasters preferred preserves and jams to jellies (they liked bits of fruit), they were most concerned with flavor. Too many brands were overly sweet—so sweet it was hard to taste the raspberries. The top two brands were Trappist Jam and Smucker's Preserves. Interestingly, both of these are made with corn syrup, yet tasters felt they had the strongest raspberry flavor.

Although fruit spreads are less sweet than traditional jams and jellies, tasters felt that the concentrated fruit juices obscured the flavor of the raspberries. The result was a generic "fruit roll-up flavor."

Jam Crostata

SERVES 8

Crostata di marmellata can be made with any smooth jam, including blackberry and cherry, although our tasters particularly liked raspberry jam. (If you want to use a jam with chunks of fruit, puree it in the food processor to achieve a smooth texture.)

- I cup raspberry jam or other smooth-textured jam
- I tablespoon lemon juice
- I recipe Pasta Frolla for a Double-Crust Tart (page 452), chilled
  Flour for rolling out dough
- I large egg white, beaten with 2 tablespoons water

1. Mix the jam and lemon juice in a small bowl.

2. Remove the dough pieces from the refrigerator (if refrigerated longer than 1 hour, let stand at room temperature until malleable). Roll the round dough disk between two large sheets of lightly floured parchment paper to an 11-inch disk about ¼ inch thick. Peel off the top sheet of parchment and discard. Using an 11-inch pot lid or cardboard round as a guide, trim the dough to a perfect 11-inch circle (see illustration 1 on page 453). Reserve the scraps. Slide the dough (still on the parchment) onto a baking sheet. Spread the jam on the dough, leaving a 1-inch border (see illustration 2).

3. Roll the square piece of dough between two large sheets of lightly floured parchment paper to an 11-inch square about ⅛ inch thick. Peel off the top sheet of parchment and discard. With a pizza wheel or paring knife, trim the edges to make them even (reserve the scraps), then cut the dough into ten 1-inch-wide strips (see illustration 3). Brush the strips with the egg wash and place them over the filling, 5 in each direction, in a diagonal lattice (see illustration 4).

4. Combine the scraps and knead them together slightly. Roll this dough into a ¾-inch-thick rope about 30 inches long. Brush the rim of the pastry with the egg wash, then press the rope of dough into the rim. Press the dough rope to flatten it slightly (see illustration 5). (For a decorative finish, press the tines of a fork against the dough.) Brush the border with the remaining egg wash. Refrigerate the crostata on the baking sheet for 1 hour.

5. Adjust an oven rack to the middle position and heat the oven to 375 degrees. Bake until golden brown, 25 to 30 minutes. Slide the crostata (still on the parchment paper) onto a wire rack and cool to room temperature, about 3 hours. Cut into slices and serve.

APPLE CROSTATA

A FREE-FORM APPLE TART (CALLED *crostata* in Italian and *galette* in French) is made in a thin, flat round. The dough is rolled to a circle, the apples are piled in the center, and the dough is gathered along the edges to form a border around the filling. Because a free-form apple tart has only a single crust, and even that does not have to be fitted into a pie plate, it's easier to make a tart than a pie. Even so, a number of things can go wrong, so we wanted to take a close look at how to make this simple, satisfying dessert.

With our pasta frolla recipe already on hand, we figured that developing an apple crostata recipe would be simple. However, we were aware of one potential pitfall. Because a crostata has no top crust, the apple filling can dry out during baking. Obviously, the variety of apple used would be key. Further, the method used to prepare and cook the apples would affect their taste and texture. Should they be sliced thick or thin when placed in the tart? Should they be cooked or raw?

To answer these questions, we gathered some of the most commonly available apple varieties: Granny Smith, Gala, McIntosh, Braeburn, Fuji, and Red and Yellow Delicious. We tested each type in a tart. In every case but one, the apples cooked up tough, dry, and leathery. The exception was the McIntosh, which baked to the other extreme—so moist that the apples turned to mush.

Of the varieties tested, we found that Granny Smiths, Galas, and McIntoshes had the most distinct flavor after being baked. We tested Macs with both Granny Smiths and Galas, and tasters preferred the Granny-Mac combo. The apple filling had good apple flavor and a decent texture, but it was still a bit dry.

Next, we attempted to cook the apples before placing them in the tart, hoping this would make the filling more moist. We sautéed the apples, reduced their cooking juices, and added the liquid to the tart. This was not a success; the apples turned mushy, and the pure apple flavor we had wanted to preserve was lost.

We returned to our original method—layering raw apple slices into the tart—but this time sliced them thinner and increased the oven temperature. These thinner slices were more moist but still not perfect. A colleague suggested that we sprinkle the apples with sugar as they cooked. This turned out to be a great idea; the sugar prevented the apples from drying out in the oven.

We asked several food scientists for an explanation. It seems that when sugar is sprinkled on top of fruit during baking, it combines with some of the moisture the fruit has released and forms a syrup. This syrup doesn't give up water easily, so the syrup doesn't evaporate and thus keeps the filling moist.

Our apple crostata was perfect, but several test cooks wanted individual crostate. With a few minor modifications, we were able to turn produce six small crostate with minimal extra effort. As individual crostate are much easier to serve than a single crostata (no cutting or messy slices), we made them the master recipe. The single tart is offered as a variation.

Individual Apple Crostate
SERVES 6

When all of the apples have been sliced, you should have about 6 cups. Serve the warm tarts with a scoop of vanilla ice cream or cinnamon gelato (page 437) or a dollop of whipped cream.

1	recipe Pasta Frolla (page 452), chilled Flour for rolling out dough
1¼	pounds Granny Smith apples (3 small)
1¼	pounds McIntosh apples (3 medium)
2	tablespoons lemon juice
¼	cup (1¾ ounces) plus 2 tablespoons sugar
¼	teaspoon ground cinnamon
2	large egg whites, beaten lightly

1. Remove the dough from the refrigerator (if refrigerated longer than 1 hour, let stand at room temperature until malleable). Cut the dough into 6 equal pieces and flatten them to 3-inch disks (see illustration 1 on page 457). Working with one at a time, roll the disks between two sheets of lightly floured parchment paper into circles about 6 inches in diameter (see illustration 2). Peel off the top sheets of parchment and discard; trim the bottom sheets of parchment to rectangles about 2 inches larger than the dough. Stack the rectangles with parchment on a plate. Cover the plate with plastic wrap and refrigerate while preparing the fruit.

2. Peel, core, and cut the apples into ¼-inch-thick slices. Toss the apple slices, lemon juice, ¼ cup sugar, and cinnamon in a large bowl.

3. Remove the dough from the refrigerator and arrange the parchment-lined dough rounds in a single layer on a work surface. Following illustrations 3 and 4, arrange about 1 cup apple slices, thick edges out, in a circular mound on each dough round, leaving a 1-inch border. Fold the dough border up and over the filling, pleating it to fit snugly around the apples. With cupped hands, gently press the dough toward the filling, reinforcing the shape and compacting the apples (see illustration 5). Using the parchment lining for support, slide 3 crostate onto each of two rimmed baking sheets (see illustration 6). Chill the formed crostate on the pans for 30 minutes.

4. Adjust one oven rack to the highest position and the other rack to the lowest position; heat the oven to 400 degrees. Slide the pans with the crostate into the oven and bake until pale golden brown, about 15 minutes. Brush the crusts with the beaten egg whites and sprinkle the apples with the remaining 2 tablespoons sugar. Return the pans with the crostate to the oven, switching positions, and bake until the crusts are deep golden brown and the apples are tender, about 15 minutes.

5. Remove the pans from the oven and cool the crostate on the pans for 5 minutes. Using a wide metal spatula, transfer the crostate from the parchment to a wire rack. Serve warm.

➤ VARIATION

Large Apple Crostata

This crostata is formed in the same way as the individual crostate (see illustrations below), but on a larger scale.

MAKING INDIVIDUAL CROSTATE

1. Cut the dough into 6 equal pieces, then round and flatten each slightly to form small disks about 3 inches in diameter.

2. Place the individual disks between squares of lightly floured parchment paper and roll out to 6-inch circles.

3. Arrange the apple slices in an even circle over the dough, leaving free a 1-inch perimeter of dough for the fluted edge.

4. Fill in the center with additional slices, lending support to the circular wall of apples.

5. Fold the outer lip of dough snugly inward over the apples and cup with your hands to compress and shape.

6. Grasping the edges of the parchment, transfer each crostata to a rimmed baking sheet.

EQUIPMENT: Paring Knives

As we sliced our way through pounds of apples en route to developing our recipe for apple crostata, the easiest way to peel, core, and slice apples became a hotly debated subject. We began to wonder about all those kitchen gadgets designed to help with some or all phases of apple preparation. Glancing through catalogs, we came across apple corers, corer/slicers, and a fancy crank-operated gizmo that peels, cores, and slices in a single motion. In addition, we found small paring knives with special curved blades, called bird's-beak knives, specifically designed for peeling round fruits. We decided to give them all a try.

Most corers have a diameter between ¾ and ⅞ inch (ours was ¾), which is too small to consistently remove all of the seeds and the seed cavity. We had the same problem with the corer/slicers, plus the slices were thicker than we wanted.

Crank-operated apple-paring machines were something of an improvement, but they didn't wow us. This tool works best with very hard, fresh fruit. Some of our Macs were less than perfectly firm, and the peeling blade slid right over the skin, failing to do its job. When the peeling blade did work well on a firm Granny Smith, it showered us with apple juice as it peeled.

We then went back to the tried-and-true method, using a paring knife. We tested the straight-edged paring knife against the curved-blade bird's-beak model, but none of the testers found the bird's beak significantly easier to use or more effective.

But which paring knife is best? Prices range from a modest $5 plus change to a grand $50, which invites the obvious question for a home cook: Is the most expensive knife really 10 times better than the cheapest model? To find out, we put seven all-purpose paring knives through a series of kitchen tests, including peeling and slicing shallots, peeling and slicing apples and turnips, coring tomatoes, peeling and mincing fresh ginger, and slicing lemons and limes.

The way the knives were made (by forging or stamping) wasn't much of a factor in our ratings of paring knives. By definition, a paring knife is used for light tasks where weight and balance are not terribly important (it doesn't take huge effort to peel an apple). The way the handle felt in testers' hands was much more important. Most testers preferred medium-sized, ergonomically designed plastic handles. Slim wooden handles were harder to grasp.

Testers also preferred paring knives with flexible blades, which make it easier to work in tight spots. Peeling turnips or sectioning oranges is much easier with a flexible than a stiff blade. Stiffer blades are slightly better at mincing and slicing, but these are secondary tasks for paring knives. Among the knives tested, expensive forged knives from Wüsthof and Henckels performed well, as did an inexpensive stamped knife made by Forschner.

THE BEST PARING KNIVES

The Wüsthof-Trident Grand Prix (left) is extremely agile and was the clear favorite of our testers. The Forschner (Victorinox) Fibrox (center) is quite light, and the blade is very flexible. The Henckels Four Star (right) has an especially comfortable handle, but the blade is a bit less flexible and somewhat less sharp than the blades on our other top picks. Note that the Forschner knife costs just $6, while you should expect to spend about $20 for the Henckels and about $28 for the Wüsthof.

1. Remove the dough from the refrigerator (if refrigerated longer than 1 hour, let stand at room temperature until malleable). Roll the dough between two large sheets of lightly floured parchment paper to a 15-inch disk. Peel off the top sheet and, using the parchment lining for support, slide the dough onto a rimmed baking sheet; cover with plastic wrap and refrigerate while preparing the fruit.

2. Peel, core, and cut the apples into ¼-inch-thick slices. Toss the apple slices, lemon juice, ¼ cup sugar, and cinnamon in a large bowl.

3. Remove the dough from the refrigerator and arrange the apple slices, thick edges out, in a circular mound, leaving a 3-inch border of dough. Fold the dough border up and over the filling, pleating it to fit snugly around the apples. With cupped hands, gently press the dough toward the filling, reinforcing the shape and compacting the apples. Chill the formed crostata on the pan for 30 minutes.

4. Adjust an oven rack to the lower-middle position and heat the oven to 375 degrees. Slide the pan with the crostata into the oven and bake until pale golden brown, about 30 minutes. Brush the crust with the beaten egg whites and sprinkle the apples with the remaining 2 tablespoons sugar. Return the pan with the crostata to the oven and bake until the crust is deep golden brown and the apples are tender, about 30 minutes.

5. Remove the pan from the oven and cool the crostata on the pan for 10 minutes. Loosen the parchment where it may have stuck to the pan; then, using the parchment lining, slide the crostata onto a wire rack. Place a large round plate on top of the crostata, invert the crostata, peel off the parchment, and reinvert the crostata onto a serving platter. Serve warm.

Fig-Walnut Tart

FIGS HAVE A PROMINENT PLACE IN Italian cooking. Fresh figs are served with prosciutto as an antipasto or with sweetened mascarpone cheese and honey for dessert. Fresh figs are also baked into simple tarts. Unfortunately, fresh figs are not readily available in the United States. In this recipe, we tried to capture the essence of the Italian fig experience using dried figs.

While fresh figs are moist, succulent, and not overly sweet, dried figs are leathery, tough, and chewy, with a concentrated sweetness. The first thing we needed to do was to restore moisture and softness. We diced the figs, placed them in a small saucepan, covered them with liquid, and simmered until they were soft and plump.

We tried rehydrating the figs in orange juice, which gave them a fresh fruity flavor. Rehydrating the figs with brandy gave them additional richness and complexity of flavor. We also tried a dry white wine, which produced figs that tasted somewhat sour. We tried adding anise seeds (something we'd seen in several recipes) to the mixture. While some tasters thought the mild fennel flavor added a nice exotic tone, others found it overpowering, even in small doses. We settled on a mixture of brandy and water, adding orange zest at the end. The brandy added the depth we wanted, while the zest gave the mixture some bright notes.

Pleased with the flavors in our fig mixture, we nevertheless felt we needed to provide a textural balance to its sticky, jammy consistency. Enter walnuts. The fig-walnut combination is classic Italian. We found that the walnuts were best stirred into the fig mixture after it came off the stove.

We tested our tart using the three most common varieties of dried figs. We preferred the Turkish and Calimyrna figs to the Mission figs. Calimyrna figs are a variety of the Turkish Smyrna fig tree grown in California. Like Turkish figs, they became softer and silkier than the Mission figs (also from California) when cooked.

In our experience, pastry dough generally tastes better when the crust is deeply browned rather than lightly browned. We assumed that to avoid overbaking the filling and drying it out, prebaking the tart shell before adding the filling was going to be the order of the day. We prebaked the tart shell until lightly browned, filled it with the fig and nut mixture, and placed it back in the oven for 15 minutes—just enough time for the filling to set into the crust. We were surprised that the pastry tasted dry and overcooked, even though it didn't look too brown. We then baked the tart without prebaking the crust. While the edges of the crust were lightly browned, the bottom and sides (where the filling covered the pastry) looked pale and undercooked. To our surprise, the pastry was fully cooked and had a wonderful moist, biscuitlike texture.

So why did our pasta frolla taste done when it didn't look done? The dough contains baking powder, which accelerates baking by lightening the dough. As the pasta frolla bakes, it puffs in the oven and the texture becomes almost biscuitlike. Because the dough is not dense (most sweet tart doughs are more like shortbread), it cooks quickly. Unlike other pastry doughs, we learned, pasta frolla can cook through before it fully browns. In fact, if pasta frolla browns too much, it will dry out.

Now that we were not prebaking the tart shell before filling it, we had the option of making a free-form tart. However, tasters preferred the elegant appearance of the tart made in a pan. Fitting the dough into a pan requires a couple of minutes of effort, but we think this is time well spent.

Fig-Walnut Tart

SERVES 8 TO 10

See page 394 for information on types of tart pans, and refer to the illustrations on page 391 for tips on fitting the dough into the pan. Serve this tart with a dollop of unsweetened crème fraîche or mascarpone cheese.

1	recipe Pasta Frolla (page 452), chilled Flour for dusting and rolling out dough
1	pound dried Calimyrna or Turkish figs, stems removed, fruit chopped coarse
¼	cup sugar
½	cup brandy
1	cup water
	Grated zest from 1 medium orange
1	cup walnuts, coarsely chopped Confectioners' sugar for dusting

1. Remove the dough from the refrigerator (if refrigerated longer than 1 hour, let stand at room temperature until malleable). Roll the dough between two large sheets of lightly floured parchment paper to a 13-inch disk about ¼ inch thick. Peel off the top sheet, loosely roll the dough around the rolling pin, then unroll it over a 10-inch tart pan with a removable bottom. Lift the edge of the dough with one hand and ease it into the corners of the pan with the other. Press the dough into the fluted sides of the pan, forming a distinct seam along the pan circumference. If some edges are too thin, reinforce the side by folding it back on itself. Run the rolling pin over the top of the tart pan to remove any excess dough. The finished edge should be ¼ inch thick. If it is not, press the dough up over the edge of the pan and pinch. Freeze the dough for 30 minutes.

2. Meanwhile, bring the figs, sugar, brandy, and water to a simmer in a medium saucepan over medium heat. Simmer, stirring

occasionally, until the liquid evaporates and the figs are very soft, about 10 minutes. Stir in the orange zest and walnuts and cool to room temperature.

3. Adjust an oven rack to the middle position and heat the oven to 325 degrees.

4. Spread the cooled fig and nut mixture evenly into the tart shell. Use your fingers, the back of a spoon, or an offset spatula to work the filling into the edges of the tart shell. Bake until the edges of the tart are lightly browned, 25 to 30 minutes. Transfer the tart pan to a wire rack, cool for 5 minutes, then remove the outside rim of the pan. Cool the tart to room temperature, about 3 hours. (The cooled tart can be refrigerated for up to several days.) Just before serving, dust with confectioners' sugar and cut into slices.

RICOTTA CHEESECAKE

RECIPES FOR RICOTTA CHEESECAKE appear in most Italian cookbooks. Our research identified three styles. The standard ricotta cheesecake is made in a springform pan, typically dusted with bread crumbs. Skillet cheesecake usually has no crust and is cooked on the stovetop until the bottom begins to set, then is finished in the oven. A third option is to bake the ricotta cheesecake in a pastry crust.

We didn't want to be fussing with pastry dough or negotiating between the stovetop and oven and trying to extract a cheesecake from a skillet. Therefore, we focused our attention on the standard ricotta cheesecake and began our work by sampling a half dozen recipes made in springform pans. The recipes that were most appealing to us were pared down to the basics: ricotta cheese, eggs, and sugar, with minimal additional flavoring.

Excessive spices (such as cinnamon and nutmeg) sullied the sweet, dairy-rich taste of the ricotta, while nuts and dried fruits conflicted with the light and creamy texture of the cake.

Because a basic ricotta cheesecake can be made with either whole eggs or separated eggs, we had to narrow the playing field even further. In our testing, we much preferred the cheesecakes made with separated eggs. Mixing the yolks with the cheese and sugar and folding in the beaten whites at the end produced a light and airy cake that was still beautifully rich and creamy. Whole eggs produced a heavy cheesecake that was more custardlike and that tasters found less appealing.

We next varied the number of eggs in our recipe, using 2 pounds of ricotta cheese (the right amount for a 9-inch springform pan) in each test. Six eggs produced a cheesecake that was very light and airy, but more like a soufflé than a cheesecake. Moreover, the flavor of the eggs overpowered the mild cheese. (We learned that ricotta has a lot less personality than American cream cheese and must be seasoned lightly.) Three eggs produced a cheesecake with a prominent cheesy flavor and a dense creamy texture, but the cake seemed a bit flat and lacked stature. We settled on four eggs, which delivered a slightly more substantial cheesecake with just the right balance of creamy richness and lightness. The resulting cheesecake was a little mousse, a little cake, and a little soufflé all in one.

Fresh ricotta cheese, made in Italian markets, is creamier and less watery than the commercial ricotta cheese found in supermarkets. This explains why many recipes we tried tasted grainy and wet. Obviously, these recipe writers were using this higher-quality cheese. However, we wanted to develop a recipe that would work with either creamy fresh ricotta from an Italian market or cheese shop or the lumpy, grainy ricotta sold in plastic containers in supermarkets. We solved the graininess problem by pureeing supermarket ricotta cheese in a food processor until it was smooth and creamy.

Some recipes use flour to make the cheesecake firmer and thicker and, possibly, to compensate for excess liquid in the ricotta cheese. We found that anything more than a tablespoon or two of flour made the cheesecakes taste slightly gummy. A better solution to the water problem was to drain the ricotta cheese in a paper towel–lined strainer overnight. About ¼ cup of water drained from the cheese during this time. The cakes made with the drained cheese were less wet, a bit creamier, and had a more pronounced cheese flavor. We tried eliminating the flour altogether from our recipe. However, even with drained cheese, we found that 1 tablespoon of flour helped bind the mixture and produced a creamier cake without imparting a starchy flavor.

Orange zest, lemon zest, vanilla, and alcohol (rum, brandy, or Marsala wine) are typical flavorings for ricotta cheesecakes. Our tasters preferred lemon to orange zest. Vanilla was essential; 2 teaspoons enhanced the dairy flavor of the cheese. Rum was our booze of choice. We liked its clean but strong flavor.

Most Italian recipes call for sprinkling bread crumbs in the pan before adding the cheese filling. Our tasters strongly felt that the bread crumbs didn't enhance the cheesecake in any way. They became soggy and marred the surface of the cheesecake with unattractive brown spots. While it is not traditional, we thought that a baked cookie crust (such as you might find in an American cheesecake) might add a nice texture and flavor contrast to the cheesecake. Not wanting to stray too far from the recipe's Italian roots, we used amaretti cookies instead of the classic graham crackers with great success. The almond flavor of the amaretti cookies complemented the flavors of

the cheesecake and offered a crunchy counterpoint to the creamy cheese filling.

Ricotta Cheesecake
SERVES 8 TO 10

The ricotta cheese must be drained in the refrigerator for at least 8 hours (or overnight). To drain the cheese, line a fine-mesh sieve with two layers of paper towels, place the cheese in the sieve, place the sieve over a bowl, and refrigerate.

AMARETTI COOKIE CRUST

2	heaping cups (4 ounces) amaretti cookies, processed in a food processor until uniformly fine
5	tablespoons unsalted butter, melted, plus 1 tablespoon melted butter for greasing the pan

RICOTTA FILLING

2	pounds ricotta cheese, drained
4	large eggs, separated
¾	cup (5¼ ounces) sugar
¼	cup rum
1	tablespoon unbleached all-purpose flour
	Grated zest of 1 medium lemon
2	teaspoons vanilla extract
⅛	teaspoon salt

1. Adjust an oven rack to the lower-middle position and heat the oven to 325 degrees. In a small bowl, combine the amaretti crumbs and 5 tablespoons melted butter and toss with a fork until evenly moistened. Brush the bottom and sides of a 9-inch springform pan with most of the remaining 1 tablespoon melted butter, making sure to leave enough to brush the sides of the pan after the crust cools. Empty the crumbs into the springform pan and press them evenly into the pan bottom. Bake until fragrant and beginning to brown around the edges, about 13 minutes. Cool the pan on a wire rack

while making the filling. (Do not turn off the oven.) Brush the sides of the springform pan with the remaining melted butter.

2. Place the drained ricotta in the workbowl of a food processor fitted with a metal blade. Process until very smooth, about 1 minute. Add the egg yolks, sugar, rum, flour, lemon zest, vanilla, and salt and process until blended, about 1 more minute. Scrape the mixture into a large bowl.

3. Beat the egg whites in a clean bowl on high speed with a handheld or standing mixer until they hold stiff peaks. Fold the whites into the ricotta mixture and pour the mixture evenly into the cooled crust.

4. Bake the cheesecake until the top is lightly browned and an instant-read thermometer inserted into the center registers about 150 degrees, about 1 hour and 15 minutes. (The perimeter of the cake should be firm, but the center will jiggle slightly. It will solidify further as the cake cools.) Transfer the pan to a wire rack and cool for 5 minutes. Run a paring knife between the cake and the side of the springform pan. Cool until barely warm, 2½ to 3 hours. Wrap the pan tightly in plastic wrap and refrigerate until the cheesecake is cold and set, at least 5 hours or up to 2 days.

5. To unmold the cheesecake, remove the sides of the pan. Let the cheesecake stand at room temperature for about 30 minutes, then cut it into wedges and serve.

CHOCOLATE-HAZELNUT CAKE

GIANDUJA IS THE FLAVOR COMBINATION of chocolate and hazelnuts. Just about any cake from the region of Piedmont in northern Italy with these two ingredients might be called a *torta gianduja*. For this recipe, we focused on a classic cake that forms a crackly, crisp,

meringuelike top when baked; the inside is dense and slightly coarse, yet very moist. This cake is rich enough that it does not need a glaze or frosting, just a light dusting of confectioners' sugar to dress up its appearance.

The taste and texture of the cake are based on a delicate balance of eggs, butter, sugar, bittersweet chocolate, ground nuts, and, possibly, a small amount of flour. The eggs are separated; the yolks are added to the batter, and the whites are whipped to stiff peaks and folded in at the end. There is no chemical leavening; the whipped whites are the sole means of leavening the cake.

Because eggs are crucial to this recipe, we decided to begin our tests with this ingredient. We first tried the cake with six eggs. The inside of the cake was very dense, moist, and cakey. However, the top expanded a bit too much and formed a gap between the surface and rest of the cake. Five eggs produced good results, but we found that using six yolks and five whites produced a cake with a slightly firmer and denser center. The surface of the cake was crisp and crackly but did not expand too much.

The texture and crumb of this cake is established largely by the quantity and texture of the nuts. Some recipes call for finely chopped hazelnuts. The coarser the nuts, the coarser the crumb. We found that grinding the nuts in the food processor was much easier and produced a finer consistency than hand chopping. In addition, we found that grinding the nuts with a portion of sugar helps prevent them from clumping in the batter. The quantity of nuts affects the flavor as well as the texture. The flavor of the hazelnuts is quite mild compared with the bold, assertive flavor of chocolate. We tested 6 ounces of chocolate with 1 cup of nuts and found the chocolate overpowering and the texture extremely moist and fudgy—overly so, in our opinion. One and a half cups of nuts was better, but we still felt the cake could be lighter. We tried replacing a bit of the nuts with 2 tablespoons of flour. This hit the mark; the cake retained a moist, rich, melt-in-the-mouth quality but was less dense, with a lighter, cakier texture.

We began our testing using a standard 9-inch cake pan, as most recipes suggest. It became apparent that due to the fragile nature of the cake's surface, removing the cake from the pan was problematic, and we often shattered the crisp crust in the process. We switched to a 9-inch springform pan, which eliminated the need to invert the cake in order to remove it from the pan.

Some recipes suggest finishing this cake with a chocolate glaze or ganache to dress it up and cover the imperfections of the crackle surface. We preferred the cake simply sprinkled with powdered sugar, as it gave the cake a certain rustic charm. Furthermore, the cake is super-rich and intensely chocolate as is, and tasters felt that the extra chocolate was overkill.

Chocolate-Hazelnut Cake
SERVES 8
See page 434 for information about handling the hazelnuts for this recipe.

8	tablespoons unsalted butter, softened, plus additional butter for the pan
6	ounces semisweet or bittersweet chocolate
1⅓	cups hazelnuts, toasted, skinned, and toasted again
1	cup (7 ounces) sugar
2	tablespoons unbleached all-purpose flour
5	large eggs, separated
1	large egg yolk
¼	teaspoon salt
	Confectioners' sugar

Lightly sweetened whipped cream (optional)

1. Adjust an oven rack to the middle position and heat the oven to 350 degrees. Generously butter a 9-inch springform pan.

2. Place the chocolate in a medium heat-proof bowl set over a pan of simmering water. Melt the chocolate, stirring occasionally to speed the process. Remove the bowl from the heat and cool to room temperature.

3. Place the hazelnuts, ¼ cup sugar, and the flour in the workbowl of a food processor fitted with a steel blade. Pulse repeatedly until the nuts are finely ground.

4. Beat the 8 tablespoons butter with a handheld mixer or standing mixer at medium speed until fluffy, about 2 minutes. Gradually add the remaining ¾ cup sugar, beating until creamy, 2 to 3 minutes. Add the 6 egg yolks one at time, beating well after each addition. Add the cooled chocolate and beat just until blended in. Stir in the ground hazelnuts.

5. Put the 5 egg whites and the salt in a large, clean bowl and beat with an electric mixer until they form stiff peaks. With a rubber spatula, fold in one-third of the whites to the chocolate-nut mixture. Carefully fold in the remaining whites in two batches, taking care not to deflate the batter. Pour the batter into prepared pan.

6. Bake until a skewer inserted halfway between the center and the outer rim of the cake comes out clean, 45 to 50 minutes. (The center of the cake will still be moist.) Remove the pan from the oven and cool completely on a wire rack, about 3 hours. (The cake can be wrapped in plastic and refrigerated for several days.) Just before serving, dust with confectioners' sugar. Cut the cake into wedges and serve with whipped cream, if desired.

INDEX